1973

STUDIES IN CULTURE
& COMMUNICATION

Martin S. Dworkin, General Editor

The series is devoted to education in its most comprehensive meaning, embracing the activities of formal instruction and learning carried on in schools, and all the forces of social influence upon the development and behavior of individuals and groups. Drawing upon a broad range of literatures, in many languages, the series presents new and rediscovered works, focusing closely on critical studies of the arts, educational implications of courses of thought and behavior, and tactics and instruments of profession and persuasion. No partiality of doctrine or expression is intended or imposed, the selections following a sovereign purpose to stimulate and inform the continuing critique of ideas, values, and modes of communication that is the growing tissue of education, and perennial flowering of culture.

MODERN AESTHETICS: AN HISTORICAL INTRODUCTION
The Earl of Listowel

JEFFERSONIANISM AND THE AMERICAN NOVEL
Howard Mumford Jones

THE RISE OF THE AMERICAN FILM: A CRITICAL HISTORY
With An Essay:
EXPERIMENTAL CINEMA IN AMERICA 1921–1947
Lewis Jacobs

THE FUNCTION OF TEACHING
Edited by A. V. Judges

MAN AND HIS CIRCUMSTANCES: ORTEGA AS EDUCATOR
Robert McClintock

STUDIES IN CULTURE
& COMMUNICATION

MAN AND HIS CIRCUMSTANCES

ORTEGA AS EDUCATOR

ROBERT McCLINTOCK

TEACHERS COLLEGE PRESS
TEACHERS COLLEGE, COLUMBIA UNIVERSITY
NEW YORK

Typographical Design by Barbara Schneider
Jacket Art by Margrit Tydings; Photograph: Dworkin
Manufactured in the United States of America
Library of Congress Catalog Card Number: 76-149404

for

My Teachers

MARTIN S. DWORKIN
LAWRENCE A. CREMIN
JACQUES BARZUN

Praeceptor Hispaniae

ORTEGA SAID, MANY times and in many ways, that the true hero is the man with the will to be himself. In himself, such a man negates all values and associations he does not choose; that he chooses so much of what he has been given is to define the authenticity of his belonging—and his inevitable alienation. That he repudiates so much else, naming the dead gods and dying rituals of his epoch, is to assert his own being. Such a man stands out, inevitably, even if not purposively, in any crowd or collectivity—the while he maintains his consciousness, his critical self-awareness, at a deliberated distance from the elemental drives, instincts, and preconscious processes of his integral selfhood.

In this view, to think for oneself becomes an act of essential courage, a fateful heroism in a titanic enterprise, the creation of reality as it may be known: ordained as preëxistent, yet always coming-to-be; inescapably contingent and dimensional, yet ever potential and perilously unformed. To think—if we would understand so bold a purpose—is to accept responsibility for oneself, despite one's circumstances but not entirely at war with them; it is, with all critical awareness of history—but no deference to what is merely past—a commitment to beginning anew, to the invention of desirable alternatives, to the creation of "a new revelation" out of a belief in reason and its powers to define and direct the destinies of men.

—A post-Nietzschean conception, to be sure, along the way of so much of modern thought, seeking to find the essential individual in the mass of men, to assert a meaningful selfhood amid the enveloping forces of history and community. But it is as punctually and profoundly counter-Nietzschean, in its affirmation of rational self-governance and redefined moral responsibility. Even more is it counter Marx-Engels and other post-Hegelian ideologies of individual sublimation in fictions of collective rationality. In this sense, for all his profound awareness of the darker tendencies of man's nature, primordial or infinitely civilized, Ortega stands against the fashionable denigrations of human capacity that make abstract forces into idols of new superstitions.

In despair of reason, men turn easily to ideas of thinking as somehow determined, beyond governance of will and measurement of virtue and responsibility. That such anti-reasoning is thinking, too, offers small reassurance—except, perhaps, to the cynically inclined, or those so self-indulgent as to pretend that any reasoning is irrelevant to behavior. To despair of reason is all too simple, and all-too-simply corroborated in the outcomes of uncritical action. But much worse may be to proclaim as rational the mystification of reason as mechanical or foreordained, and notions of human action as ultimately senseless manifestations of uncontrollable processes—call them destiny, or history, or transcendent purpose, or nature, or biological causality, or any other names for what are finally generalizations of individual livelihood. For Ortega, "vital reason," recognizing that reason is inherent in human living, repudiates not only the cult of rationalism, with its myth of pure, disembodied intellect, but also a romanticism that invokes the passions as autonomous forces in the organismic whole, raising them to be mindless judges of the mind.

The argument for the integration of reasoning and responsibility is made with topical specificity, to deliberately oppose the rising unreason of the age. But, on a longer scale of timeliness, Ortega is clearly in the line of humanistic teachers since the Greeks. Further, he is surely recalling his own native preceptors of virtue, reaching as far back as the Iberian Seneca, but most vividly Gracián, demanding *Hombre de Entereza*,[1] the man of integrity, holding to reason in the face of the mob and its fickle

---

[1] Baltasar ("Lorenzo") Gracián, *Oráculo Manual y Arte de Prudencia* (c. 1647), No. 29. A charming, modern bi-lingual edition is by L. B. Walton, *Baltasar Gracián, The Oracle: A Manual of the Art of Discretion* (London: J. M. Dent & Sons, 1953).

passions, and despite the tyrant and his witless force. The spirit, the sense, and even the sound of it are so much like the insistence on being nothing less than a whole man, *Nada menos que todo un hombre*, of Unamuno,[2] who is so often hailed as the defender of a purified Hispanic self-identification, against an imputed denial by Ortega. Ortega the Spaniard is not so well-known, curiously enough, as is Ortega the Spanish European.

That the oversight has often implied political, as well as philo-sophical, misunderstandings may be perfectly exemplified by Jean Cassou, who managed to give the lecture on "Spanish Culture" at the opening session of UNESCO in Paris in 1946, without once mentioning Ortega—not even in disparagement.[3] So soon after the Civil War, the fratricides among the anti-Fascists still went on, and Ortega's vehement enmity to totalitarianism was still not sufficiently orthodox, it may be surmised, to give him status better than that of a literary "non-person." A mere decade later, the sociologist Enrique Gomez Arboleya, following less invidious stan-dards of cultural importance, would bluntly call Ortega, "one of the greatest Spaniards of all time," adding, quite pertinently here, that "He merits the rare title of *Magister hispaniae*."[4] Now, for Robert McClintock, in *Man and His Circumstances: Ortega As Educator*, he is *Praeceptor hispaniae*—but in the many meanings that make him a teacher for all men, the more he is the Spaniard *and* the European.

The Spaniard, however, is also the proto-European, perhaps uniquely so among the peoples of the Continent. And the strands of Ortega's thought run as straightly back to the pre-classical heroes of the awakening of critical intellect in the West, most notably Xenophanes, Heraclitus, and Democritus, as they weave inextricably through the fabric of philosophies and counter-philos-

---

[2] The title of one of his most famous stories, included in Miguel de Unamuno *Three Exemplary Novels*, Angel Flores, trans. (New York: Albert & Charles Boni, 1930; Grove Press, 1956).

[3] Published in *Reflections On Our Age*, Lectures Delivered at the Opening Session of UNESCO At the Sorbonne University, Paris, Introduction by David Hardman, Foreword by Stephen Spender (New York: Columbia University Press, 1949), pp. 151–164.

[4] In the article, "Spain," in Joseph Roucek, Editor, *Contemporary Sociology* (New York: Philosophical Library, 1958), p. 832.

ophies following Plato, Aristotle, and the ensuing schools. But Ortega is heritor of past formulations of thought primarily as rediscoverer of rational beginnings, and only thereafter as reinterpreter—and not at all as epigone or publicist. Indeed, Ortega's relationship to the thinkers and ideas of his own epoch is even more clearly signal of his commitment to criticism as the essence of understanding.

Characteristically, he could be the enthusiastic student of the Neo-Kantians Hermann Cohen and Paul Natorp, later praising them as his *maestros*,[5] while hardly becoming a votary of their school. Again, he could avow strong admiration for Max Scheler, whom he called "my great friend," as well as "the first man of genius in the new land of phenomenology," and, later, a "thinker par excellence, whose death in 1928 has deprived Europe of its best mind,"[6] while subjecting his work to searching, often sharply censorious judgment. It was wholly consistent for Ortega to be at once an immensely influential expositor, and a profoundly dubious critic, of the several strategies of analysis and speculation, in philosophy proper and the social sciences, that came to be generalized as "phenomenology." Similarly, his rôle in the related surge of systematic self-consciousness taking all the varied forms of "existentialism" is not easily assessed according to formulas of doctrinal association and determined influence. Not only his ideas, but his activities as editor and publisher, as well as teacher, reverberate powerfully in its development. Thus, there need not be wonderment at parallels and resemblances between Ortega's historical vitalism and the existentialism of, say, Jean-Paul Sartre— to choose the most widely-publicized exemplar of the school— prompting David Bidney, for only one, to remark that, "Contemporary existentialism . . . is not quite as novel as it has been made to appear."[7] In a way, it may be propriety, as well as respect, that

---

[5] *Obras completas*, VI, p. 383, note; cited in H. Spiegelberg, *The Phenomenological Movement: A Historical Introduction*, Second edition, Volume Two (The Hague: Martinus Nijhoff, 1965), p. 612.

[6] Spiegelberg, *Ibid.*, p. 614.

[7] In "On the Philosophical Anthropology of Ernst Cassirer and its Relation to the History of Anthropological Thought," included in Paul Arthur Schilpp, Editor, *The Philosophy of Ernst Cassirer* (Evanston, Ill.: The Library of Living Philosophers, 1949), p. 492.

has F. H. Heinemann, who created the name *Existenzphilosophie* in 1929, dedicating "To the Memory of José Ortega y Gasset" his authoritative *Existentialism and the Modern Predicament*,[8] which does not treat Ortega in the text.

Such difficulties in fitting Ortega within schools of thought are quite in accordance, it may be said, with his own insistence that man's nature and his situation may not be comprehended in the formulas of doctrinaires, the party men he despised as "walking suicides." It is this spirit that, after all, may be the essence of Ortega's thought, evoking an ideal of man reasoning-in-living, that, of all ideals, is most surely integral in such definitions of individual personhood as do not dissolve uniqueness, privacy, and potential freedom of thinking and choice in abstractions of collective identity. And it is in this spirit that one may read his famous indictment of mass*ness* as personal attack, if one is himself only ensorcelled or cajoled by the grandeur, verve, and rhetorical fluency of Ortega's writing. There is much to be questioned and disagreed with in Ortega's philosophy, as interpreted in the relatively few works of sustained systematic articulation, or in the immense body of variegated writings he produced originally for periodicals. But of his philosophizing, there need only be recognition of the sovereign commitment to thinking for oneself, for there to be vindication of Ortega's essential enterprise. There are thinkers with whom one must disagree on behalf of thinking, of philosophy as the method and measure of thinking. Ortega, a true philosopher, one questions rightly in order to understand, reënacting the prototypal encounter with the teacher we must always seek, as Socrates taught, in order to become the proper teacher of ourselves.

Thus, it is not mere academic presumption to perceive Ortega's intention as firstly and finally pedagogical, as does Dr. McClintock —provided that "pedagogy" is understood in its full, implicit meaning, conveyed in the felicitous translation of "*la pedagogía social*" as "civic pedagogy," and not as only the tutorial and invigilative functioning of schoolmasters. A true sense of pedagogy involves the discovery, definition, and critical measurement of the aspirations of civilization, and takes fully into account the multi-

---

[8] New York: Harper & Bros., 1958.

various ways of teaching and occasions of learning of all the agencies, media, and practices of a living society. Such a conception antedates Plato, yet its recognition now is a signal of a renewed vigor of educational philosophy since mid-century, after years, even generations, of academic disparagement, too often self-corroborated by educationists, as somehow second-rate philosophizing.

At stake is no less than man's meaning to himself, and hence, his meaning in the only universe he can know. In this age of tragic actuality and more horrendous possibilities, a call for pedagogy takes on unprecedented urgency, and the teacher from whom we can learn to think for ourselves is more than ever a preceptor for the very survival of reason. And the spirit of urgency of Dr. McClintock's study of Ortega is plain. This is a young man's book, directed hopefully, but insistently, to the young. It is grounded firmly on history, but as criticized memory, eternally relevant. Above all, it is devoted to reconstituting the destiny of a civilization in fatal crisis, one that, without such effort, must surely be, as Ortega denounced it, bankrupt and devitalized.

There are serious questions to put to the work, but they themselves become part of its own questioning of the future. Ortega had called upon the young to invent, to criticize and originate, to invigorate the forms of living, creating worthy alternatives and acting to realize them. Such teaching risks infinities of danger, but also bears all the hope there is of humane learning, that may advance the growing edge of mankind only in each man's striving beyond fixities of dogma, ignorance, and circumstance; beyond the self defined as somehow less than its aspirations, and their responsibilities. For the teachers, there are agonies and disappointments, needless yet inevitable; but there are special rewards, too, as the young renew the perdurable wonder of education, learning to teach themselves.

MARTIN S. DWORKIN

New York City
July 1971.

Preface

I see in criticism a vigorous effort to give power to a chosen work. . . .
Criticism is not biography, nor is it legitimate as an independent activity
unless it aims at perfecting the work. To begin with, this means that the
critic has to introduce in his essay all the emotional and intellectual
devices thanks to which the average reader will receive the most intense
and clear impression of the work possible. The critic proceeds by pointing
his effort towards the affirmative, and by directing it, not to correcting
the author, but to giving the reader a more perfect visual organ. One
perfects the work by perfecting the reading of it.

ORTEGA[1]

OVER TEN YEARS AGO, while browsing in the Princeton University
Bookstore, my eye was caught by *What Is Philosophy?* Good question!, I thought. I had entered my undergraduate studies with an
instinctive reverence for philosophy as the first among disciplines;
but the philosophy courses I then took were all disappointing: invariably they concerned philosophies, not philosophy. The author of
the book that chance had brought me to, José Ortega y Gasset, was
unknown to me, but on quick perusal he seemed worth reading.
Read him I did, and I have been doing so since.

What Is Philosophy?—with its concern for the *ego* living in
the world, for the person thinking, choosing, doing—is a work well
calculated to move a young man in his last year of college as he
begins to face seriously the question of what he would do with his
life. Ortega offered no substantive answers to this perplexity, for
answers depend on the unique actualities of each separate self and

---

[1] *Meditaciones del Quijote*, 1914, *Obras* I, p. 325.

its particular circumstances, but he greatly reinforced my developing sense of the importance, the continual importance, of deciding on one's future. We live, not for a final answer, but by endlessly asking the question, what am I going to make of the coming instant? By constantly asking this question, one shapes a continual present according to the vision of the future and the comprehension of the past that one commands at each successive instant. Such thoughts, which had already been germinating in me, were brought to life by Ortega's prose; hence from the very start, he convinced me that he was part of the past that I should seek to comprehend should I want to shape my present according to a vision of a future.

In quick order, thereafter, I read *Man and People, The Modern Theme*, and *The Revolt of the Masses*. Here I encountered Ortega's public relevance, a relevance that has grown as the prospect of public affairs has become monotonously more bleak. At the time of first encounter, the Kennedy-Nixon campaign was moving towards its denouement, and the contrast between the noble man and the mass man that Ortega so sharply drew seemed to resonate perfectly with the contrast between Kennedy's apparent style of aspiration and Nixon's self-satisfaction. Thus, despite his own pessimism about the politics of any nation, Ortega at first seemed to explain the why and the wherefore of the political hope dawning within me. After all I had learned from others to think that America was special, exempt from the foibles of the European nations.

Events soon shattered these first hopes and relentless retrospect has made me doubt their reality. Being American for me has ceased to be sufficient, no more significant in itself than my being from New York and you perhaps from Milan or somewhere else. During the last decade, events and Ortega have made me into a European: I pledge my allegiance to that chancy, uncertain, but constructive process of transcending the nation, transcending the state, and transcending coercion in the conduct of public affairs in the post-industrial West. And much of what I have to say about Ortega is intended—in keeping with his own example—as a small but serious contribution to the creative effort of devising a future for the West.

I have shaped this book, however, not only in response to my general circumstances, but to my more immediate ones as well.

I went to graduate school with strong intellectual interests and weak disciplinary commitments. David Steward and I recurringly argued over whether one could follow one's interests within the academic grind. With some luck, some faith, and lots of friendly help, one can. Help first came to me from Lawrence A. Cremin, whose colloquium in the history of American educational thought redeemed an otherwise desolate Spring term in 1962. He convinced me not to drop out of graduate school and to take up the history of education, pointing out that it was a field undergoing thorough revision with plenty of room within it for the pursuit of my interests. His advice was excellent, and his teaching has been central to my development into a professional scholar.

In the Department of Philosophy and the Social Sciences at Teachers College, I studied with George Z. F. Bereday, Philip H. Phenix, R. Freeman Butts, and, most importantly, Martin S. Dworkin. Dworkin is a committed educator; he pours his energy into teaching, into imparting his engagement with the life of reason, into opening access to all he knows. In his seminar on "Education, Ideology, and Mass Communications" I encountered Ortega in a course for the first time, and my work in this seminar was the beginning of the long process by which Ortega became the topic of my dissertation. But Dworkin's teaching has been invaluable to me in other respects. I had studied Ortega on my own, and also knew the work of Camus and Jaspers fairly well. But through a torrent of references to all sorts of thinkers, Dworkin opened to me the diverse elements of nineteenth- and twentieth-century thought. And equally important, he drove me to the Greeks, especially to the pre-Socratics and Plato, not to decide that they held this or that, but to contend on my own with the questions they raised.

During the academic year of 1963–64, I participated in the doctoral seminar on European intellectual history jointly given by Jacques Barzun and Lionel Trilling. Together, they elicit what the aspiring graduate student thinks is his best effort, and each then subjects that effort to thorough constructive criticism. With the criticism I began the unfinished task of learning how written language works. In my seminar paper, which was on Ortega, I contended that a commitment to educate informed all his activities. Professor Barzun encouraged me in this view—one would not be far off applying the same thesis to his own varied accomplishments —and he became co-sponsor with Professor Cremin of my dissertation. Professors James F. Shearer and Francisco García-Lorca commented on the prospectus of the dissertation and the former agreed to oversee the Hispanic side of my studies. Thereafter, my work was cut out for me, and my main intellectual interest was, at last, the center of my academic endeavors.

I spent the summer of 1965 in Madrid working in the archives of the Hermeroteca Municipal and of *Revista de Occidente*. In particular, José Ortega Spottorno and Paulino Garagorri helped make my research in Madrid fruitful and have encouraged me considerably through their continued interest in my work. Garagorri has directed me to much material that I would not have known to look for without his help.

A number of continuing conversations with friends have also deeply influenced this work. In one sense, the book is an attempt at an operational answer to a problem Philip Weinstein and I have repeatedly discussed: how can the critic avoid being a mere parasite living off the work he criticizes? A number of ideas in the book have been sharpened through conversations with Francis Schrag about freedom and the responsibilities of the intellectual who is at once committed to pursuing truth and to acting in an imperfect world. My conception of Rousseau and of the state owes much to discussions with Dan Brock about the limits of authority and abstractions such as the general will.

In producing the book itself numerous persons have helped, particularly Janet M. Simons and Robert Bletter. Here I again especially thank Martin S. Dworkin, this time not as teacher, but as editor. He has had the fortitude to keep me from deciding prematurely that the work was finished. It now embodies my best effort, one which I hope will be found worthy of its subject.

ROBERT McCLINTOCK

Contents

The lord whose oracle is at Delphi neither speaks nor conceals, but indicates.

HERACLITUS, FRAGMENT 93 (DK)

Let my words appear to you as they may. They ought only to lead you to produce in your mind the same thought that I have produced in mine.

FICHTE, THE VOCATION OF MAN

I judge a philosopher by whether he is able to serve as an example.

NIETZSCHE, SCHOPENHAUER AS EDUCATOR

He who would teach us a truth should situate us so that we will discover it ourselves.

ORTEGA, MEDITATIONS ON QUIXOTE

¡Salud!

He who would teach us a truth should situate us so that
we will discover it ourselves.

ORTEGA[1]

WHO WAS ORTEGA? Where did he stand? What did he accomplish?
How should one judge the worth of his work?

Spokesmen for both the right and the left opine that he was a
conservative elitist, a gifted, arrogant exponent of aristocratic prerogatives. More moderately, many scholars locate him in the tradition of liberal elitism, contending that he continued the work of
men like John Stuart Mill and Alexis de Tocqueville. Those familiar
with Spanish history appreciate his effort to reform society and
politics, an effort that made him one of the moving forces in creating
the Second Spanish Republic. In recent years, his stature among
professional philosophers has been rising, for his posthumous tomes
back up his living pretense to have made a significant contribution
to Western thought, especially to ontology. His books, always well
phrased, have won diverse readers, who may value him for his
contribution to social theory, to esthetics, to the philosophy of
history, to literary criticism, to Spanish literature. Other persons,
fortunate to have met the man, not just his work, remember him
as a great teacher, an absorbing lecturer, an engaging conversation-
alist, a professor who helped, for a time, to reform Spanish higher
education. A growing number agree with Denis de Rougemont,
seeing behind Ortega's work a visionary pan-Europeanist, one of
the spiritual founders of a Western future.

During his span of seventy-two years, from 1883 to 1955,
Ortega was intensely active, a fact that complicates the effort to
characterize his life and work. Ortega did many things. He taught
philosophy for twenty-five years; founded several magazines and
an important newspaper; campaigned against corruption, dictators,

---

[1]*Meditaciones del Quijote*, 1914, *Obras* I, p. 336. (Unless otherwise indicated, all translations are by the author.)

and the King. For these efforts he later endured a decade of wandering exile. He wrote voluminously: hundreds of commentaries for the daily press, numerous articles for diverse journals, and books and more books. Ortega talked: he toured the world giving lectures, he stumped Spain making speeches; with everyone he loved to converse in the animated Spanish manner. He took part in politics, in both the politics of Spanish reform and the politics of European union. In short, Ortega met life with chest out, without stopping to bemoan lost opportunities and without bothering to correct misimpressions.

In the United States, special difficulties complicate understanding Ortega's integral character. To begin with, important information about him is hard to come by. The best introduction to his thought in English is José Ferrater Mora's *Ortega y Gasset*, but this work gives few biographical details, even though Ortega insisted that his personal experience was integral to his thought. Almost invariably, American translations of Ortega's works have lacked adequate introductions. For instance, readers of *The Revolt of the Masses* have had no way to know that they were reading a series of newspaper articles that had first appeared in a particular paper, *El Sol*, in a particular place, Madrid, at a particular time, during the decline and fall of the dictatorship of General Primo de Rivera. These circumstances help clarify the argument of the book, yet knowledge of them is not generally available. When readers do not know the real context of a work, they supply whatever context close at hand seems most useful. This practice has led to misinterpretations.

Another complication for Americans seeking to understand Ortega's character is that people are more likely to have read Ortega than to have studied him. This condition has arisen because the works available in English do not fit within a single discipline; instead, each has independently gained a modicum of currency in separate disciplines. Estheticians are likely to have read *The Dehumanization of Art*; philosophers know *What Is Philosophy?*, and perhaps *The Origin of Philosophy* and *The Modern Theme*; sociologists are acquainted with *The Revolt of the Masses* and, if interested in sociological theory, *Man and People*; political theorists will also have studied *The Revolt of the Masses*, as well as *Concord and*

Liberty; persons interested in historical synthesis will most probably have read *History as a System* and *Man and Crisis;* literary critics will have consulted *Notes on the Novel* and *Meditations on Quixote;* educators will have reflected on *The Mission of the University;* and romantics in each discipline may well have mused *On Love.* Owing to this variegation of his work, one encounters one, two, . . . many Ortegas in casual references.

But difficulties in stating precisely who Ortega was do not, by any means, arise solely from problems of translation. The most ambitious biography, to date, *Ortega—I: circunstancia y vocación* by his disciple, Julián Marías, loses the vocation in the complexity of the circumstances. In a bewildering manner, Ortega seemed to combine a number of different careers, simultaneously pursuing a separate course in each, yet remaining faithful to none. From the time that Ortega finished his schooling up to the Spanish Civil War, he pursued at least four concurrent careers: he was a professor of philosophy, a politician, a journalist, and a literary artist. His pursuit of these professions was not always steady, and unsympathetic critics have called him a dilettante, a gifted, erratic, vacillating personality.

The man's protean life, the changing complexity of his activities, presents interpreters with a serious challenge. Ortega insisted over and over again that each man has a destiny, an integral mission, a single task in life that lays down before him his personal path to self-fulfillment. Dabblers were damnable. "We are our Destiny; we are the irremediable project for a particular existence. In each instant of life we note if its reality coincides or not with our project, and everything that we do, we do in order to bring it to fulfillment. . . . All iniquity comes from one source: not driving oneself to one's proper destiny."[2] It will be a significant criticism of Ortega himself, if biographers prove unable to define his mission. Difficulties in doing so point straight to the central issue of his biography. Was he able to live by the very standard of human life that he upheld?

*　　*　　*

Character for man is destiny

HERACLITUS, 119

---

[2]"No ser hombre de partido," 1930, *Obras* IV, pp. 77 and 79.

PART ONE

A Spaniard and His Circumstances

I Am I and my circumstances, and if I do not save my circumstances, I cannot save myself. *Benefac loco illi quo natus es,* we read in the Bible. And in the Platonic school we are given this as the task of all culture: "save the appearances," the phenomena; that is to say, search for the sense of that which surrounds us.

ORTEGA[1]

[1] *Meditaciones del Quijote,* 1914, *Obras* I, p. 322

*T*HE CHRONOLOGY OF LIFE *is very rigorous. . . . With the most substantial, most human themes, it is during the twenty-sixth year that the life-span is lighted by its first* extasis *in which the great eagles that are our future ideas sink their talons in our brains and carry us towards the heights, as if we were innocent lambs. Great ideas are not ours; instead, we are their prey. They will not let us alone for the rest of our lives: ferociously, tenaciously, ceaselessly, they tear at the viscera of Prometheus. . . . There is nothing mysterious about this date in life. It is the year, generally, when we cease to be mainly receptive, and hoisting our bag of learning onto our back, we turn our clear eyes upon the universe.*

ORTEGA[1]

---

[1] "El intellectual y el otro," 1940, *Obras* V, p. 510. Cf. *Prólogo para alemanes*, 1933, 1958, *Obras* VIII, p. 32, 34–5.

I
Aspirations

Bᴵᴸᴮᴬᴼ, ᴍᴀʀᴄʜ 12, 1910. Members and friends of the Society "El Sitio" were seated in their accustomed corner, awaiting their speaker with curiosity. They were confident that of all audiences in Spain, they most appreciated cultural attainments. Tonight they would prove their prowess; tonight they would take a chance and identify youthful talent, rather than savor mature repute. Usually they invited only the better speakers, men of established reputation. But almost twelve years had passed since national disaster had awakened the power of self-criticism in Spain. During those years many established reputations had fallen before the acerbity of critics who realized that, indeed, the given Spain was not the best of all possible ones. The time had come to hear what the young activists had to say for themselves.

Humiliating defeat by the *yanquis* in 1898 had destroyed Spain's pretension to inclusion among world powers. Suddenly doubts had been loosed. And the effects of these doubts on the nation were proving complicated. Members of "El Sitio" were well acquainted with "the generation of '98," as it was beginning to be called, for it comprised well-known critics who throughout the 1890's had been condemning the complacency of Spain's political and cultural leaders. The complete, rapid, seemingly effortless victory of the Americans had given the views of these critics an instantaneous authority; thereafter, they had to be reckoned with as seers. But by 1910 yet other groups were coming to the fore.

Spain fermented with irreverent discontent. If 1898 had provoked many Spaniards to question the established authorities, 1909 had goaded the doubters to combine into powerful forces for reform

7

and revolution.[a]* The immediate cause of the turmoil was the inability of the government to win its costly, frustrating military campaign against Moslem guerrillas in Spanish North Africa. It was a classic case of imperialist paralysis. Enthusiasm for the war came from the established classes—the great landowners, the Church, the Army. Those who derived a mystical allegiance to Cross and Crown from the *Reconquista* could not conceive of forgoing battle with the Infidel. Yet the soldiers sent to wage the battle were from a different class; their allegiance was secular and republican. Military mobilizations called up the poor, and the cost of war most burdened those who lived on modest salaries and meager wages. Little wonder the Moroccan campaign induced serious domestic dissension.

Agitation against the government mounted to a peak in 1909. The sources of protest were diverse. Basques and Catalans had been asserting their autonomy; they had resurrected ancient rights, their unique linguistic heritages, and their memories of a once independent existence; they disliked sending their sons to fight a Castilian war. The traditional backbone of the Spanish opposition, the anti-monarchists and anti-clericals, saw the war as further evidence that neither Altar nor Throne could emerge from the Middle Ages. And in addition to these familiar forces of opposition, new, more ominous, more disturbing ones appeared. Socialism, syndicalism, and anarchism were spreading among workers and even among the rural peasants. Subversive doctrines threatened, or so the secure feared, to sanction the bloody expression of pent-up hate that the multitudes in poverty had for the few who were very rich. As illiterate workers had acquired a taste for European ideologies, they had founded study groups, learned to read, published papers, organized unions, forged political alliances, and even won a seat in the Cortes for Pablo Iglesias, founder of the Spanish Socialist Party. In July 1909 the workers of Barcelona staged a general strike, which became ineffective through gratuitous violence, the "tragic week." Like-to-like, the government panicked; decrying the threat of revolution, it unleashed a heavy-handed repression, which greatly

---

Bibliographical annotations to the points marked by a raised letter will be found in the bibliographical section, beginning p. 487.

widened the breach between those who accepted and those who rejected the established authorities.

In the midst of these events, a new group of critics became publicly visible, much to the malaise of those who were comfortable with commonplace certitudes. These young intellectuals, malcontents still in their twenties, were aggressively stirring the Spanish ferment. They aped the French avant-garde; they made propaganda for radical causes, passionately defended the rights of accused assassins, taught the workers to read and eagerly filled them with thoughts of equality and revolution. These irreverent critics were articulate, well educated, and deeply disillusioned with the recent Spanish past. More often than not they were children of prominent persons in the discredited establishment. In the midst of their education, 1898 had suddenly shocked them into a precocious critical awareness. They grew up feeling that they were the rightful heirs of an unrighteous patrimony. They would redeem their fathers' follies. They would use their talents and position not merely to criticize Spain. They would remake the nation. Or so they seemed to say. They would remake the nation, not by taking over the established positions of power, but by by-passing them, by building up a new system of power in cooperation with those who were excluded from participation in the old. To their elders, these activists seemed dangerously open to controversial ideas and overly eager to confront the difficult problems that the mature were prudently avoiding. They sought the future. They were the future. Yet despite their professed activism, the protesters were adamantly unwilling to work within a political framework that they considered discredited; and many of their elders were quite confused when the young malcontents spoke hopefully of a "new politics."

Traditionally, "El Sitio" gave an enlightened hearing to unorthodox thinkers.b It was natural therefore to provide a forum for these intellectuals, especially so since most members were well disposed towards the humanitarian causes and the democratic, socialist, European outlook vehemently espoused by the malcontents. Many in "El Sitio" would even agree when the dissenters demanded that entrenched interests stand aside or be pushed aside to let new men promote the thorough, rapid social change that had been revolutionizing life in the more exciting parts of Europe. But despite such commonality of commitment, "El Sitio" was proceeding on hope and faith in inviting Don José Ortega y Gasset to address them. He was only twenty-six.

Despite his age, a small reputation had preceded Ortega to Bilbao. The young professor was known to speak with wit and learning about Spain's need to remaster European culture. More importantly, he was showing a talent for holding the reins of journalism, politics, and philosophy at once. He was already working to organize a coalition of intellectuals, workers, and the young, for this coalition was the one most likely to become the backbone of a reformed Spain. In his view, the intellectuals' duty was to help workers master the cultural skills with which they could turn their movements into effective forces of national leadership. Towards this end, he had given lectures at the *Casa del Partido* of the Madrid socialists, and he took active part in agitations among proletarians, such as the recent protests against the trial and execution of the purported terrorist, Francisco Ferrer.[2] Ortega had written eloquently opposing governmental efforts to repress popular movements, even the separatist movements in the Catalan provinces, for he believed repression would simply strengthen both terrorist sentiment and reaction among the established. Moreover, in addition to speaking out on the issues of the day, Ortega had indicated a larger vision. For instance, in *Faro,* a political magazine for intellectuals, he had contended that the nineteenth-century tradition of Spanish liberalism should properly give way to a twentieth-century vision of Spanish socialism.[3]

Unlike a number of young men with similar views, Ortega was clearly marked, from the beginning, as someone to be taken seriously by those in power. Ortega was not caught in the underground. Much of his controversial writing was appearing in *El Imparcial,* a powerful, eminently middle-of-the-road paper, which happened to belong to his family.[c] His maternal grandfather had founded *El*

---

[2] See J. Alvarez del Vayo, *The Last Optimist,* pp. 35–6, for a first-hand account of Ortega speaking against Ferrer's trial and execution. See "Sencillas reflexiones," *El Imparcial,* September 6, 1910. *Obras* X, p. 169, for Ortega's view, at the time, of the significance of these events.

[3] "La reforma liberal," *Faro,* February 23, 1908, *Obras* X, pp. 31–8.

Imparcial and made it one of the better Madrid newspapers. A quasi-official organ of the Liberal party, the paper had become a leading journal of the Restoration—the Spanish equivalent of late-Victorian complacency. But despite its conservative tone, *El Imparcial* had opened its columns in the 1890's to some of the better critics of Spain's recent past. This policy had been the work of Ortega's father, José Ortega Munilla, who had achieved note as the able editor of *Los Lunes del Imparcial*, the paper's prestigious literary supplement. In this way *Los Lunes* had become a major outlet for the writers who gained great authority from the defeat of 1898; thus Ortega Munilla had made their prose, their ideas, and their personalities a part of the family influences under which his son, José, grew up.

Ortega quipped: "I was born on a rotary press."[4] He did not mean merely that he grew up accustomed to the smell of printer's ink and the late hours kept in getting out the city edition. He grew up at home with important writers and publishers and in a family through which the best of Spanish journalism became second nature to him. In the long run this background was important because it armed Ortega with a profound, instinctive understanding of public opinion and how to affect it. For instance, Unamuno wrote more frequently for popular papers and magazines than did Ortega, yet Ortega is remembered as the better philosophical journalist, for his contributions had a special compactness and continuity of thought that gave them a cumulative effect. But in the short run, Ortega's connections to *El Imparcial* were important because they insured his immediate access to an audience, and he quickly indicated that he would use it to propound views his readers were not accustomed to hearing. For instance, in Ortega's first contribution to the political columns of *El Imparcial*, he began to develop one of the fundamental themes of his journalism: "I believe that contemporary liberalism must be socialism."[5]

In addition to his family background, Ortega's education was such that, from an early age, he had to be taken seriously by older

4"El Señor Dato responsable de un atropello a la constitución," *El Sol*, June 17, 1920, *Obras* X, p. 654.

5"Reforma del carácter, no reforma de costumbres," *El Imparcial*, October 5, 1907, *Obras* X, p. 21.

men. Wise elders easily dismiss their young critics as ignorant, for it takes time to establish a reputation for substantial learning. But Ortega's education gave him a strong claim on intellectual respect.[d] Like many sons of the upper middle class, he had been sent away to a Jesuit boarding school. Thus he had missed the enlightened instruction that he might have received at the famous *Institución Libre de Enseñanza*, the Free Educational Institute, which in 1876 had been founded by Francisco Giner de los Ríos and other dissident intellectuals. Instead, Ortega had received the thorough, painful drill in classical languages that his friend, Ramón Pérez de Ayala, tellingly satirized in *A. M. D. G.: Life in a Jesuit College*.[6] From 1898 to 1902, Ortega had studied at the *Universidad Central* in Madrid, receiving his *licenciado* in philosophy and letters; he did well, impressing his masters as being competent and independent, but not extraordinary. Two years later, he received his doctorate at the age of twenty-one, which was not uncommon in his time; among his examiners was Unamuno, who soon thereafter wrote about Ortega in "Almas de jovenes," "Youthful Spirits."[7] Ortega's education, however, did not stop.

Rather than begin his career after receiving his doctorate, Ortega decided to go to Germany for further studies. The decision was a turning point in his life. At the beginning of the century, Spanish intellectuals were not well versed in German thought. In fact, Karl Christian Friedrich Krause, a humane but unexceptional follower of Hegel, was the only German thinker with whom most Spanish intellectuals were well acquainted.

Krausismo is a curious phenomenon that had a complicated influence on Spanish thought. It had started in 1857 when Julián Sanz del Río finished several years of meditating in solitude on philosophical studies he had pursued in Germany. Coming out of seclusion, Sanz del Río began to teach Krause's system, which held that all existence was within God, that a moral law pervaded human life and provided for the organic unity of mankind, and that all

---

[6] Pérez de Ayala, *A.M.D.G.*, in *Obras completas de Ramón Pérez de Ayala*, Vol. IV. Ortega wrote a favorable review of this notorious book, which has become quite scarce, and he said that it rang true to his own experience. See "Al margen del libro *A.M.D.G.*," 1910, *Obras* I, pp. 532–5.

[7] See Unamuno, "Almas de jovenes," May, 1904, in Unamuno's *Obras* I, pp. 1148–1159.

would be well if each person conducted himself in rigorous fidelity to the dictates of the moral law within him. To be sure, in 1857 this introduction of German philosophy into Spain had been a progressive influence, one that engendered persecution from both Church and State. Yet with time, contexts change. Sanz del Río's dedicated, intimate teaching had been effective, and late nineteenth-century reformers in the schools and universities were deeply influenced by his version of Krause's humanitarian optimism. But twentieth-century reformers learned to look on the Krausist system with much skepticism. The vital elements of *Krausismo* were not the ideas peculiar to Krause, but the principles that he shared with other, more important thinkers: with Kant, Fichte, and Hegel. Spanish intellectuals, in spite of themselves, preserved the habits of scholasticism; they adopted *Krausismo* as a self-contained system and absolved themselves of the chore of further philosophical studies. Hence, in retrospect, *Krausismo* seemed to have served as an intellectual buffer between Spanish thinkers and the main line of European speculation. By attracting those who were receptive to change to a closed system, *Krausismo* subtly impeded the development of philosophy in Spain.e

Instead of studying his system, Ortega did as Sanz del Río himself had done and travelled to the German universities. These travels freed Ortega from the sterile controversies of Spanish speculation and his post-doctoral work put him far ahead of his former teachers. Ortega spent almost two years studying German philosophy at Leipzig, Berlin, and Marburg. During 1907, his most productive year in Germany, he worked with Hermann Cohen and Paul Natorp, the leaders of Marburg neo-Kantianism. There he began long acquaintances with Nicolai Hartmann, Ernst Cassirer, and other German contemporaries.

On his return, Ortega's competence was quickly recognized. His writing showed that unlike others, whether they were so-called Europeanizers or Hispanicizers, Ortega had a clear conception of European culture and of its importance to Spain. Consequently, his writing on the subject was surprisingly pointed and precise. His elders did not always understand him easily, for his texts included many not-so-familiar figures: references to Descartes, Leibniz, Spinoza, Kant, Fichte, Hegel, Schopenhauer, Renan, and Nietzsche. But his dexterous use of learning impressed readers even when they did not wholly understand. This mark of erudition served to counter the charge of ignorance with which the well-established might have dismissed a young critic.

Finally, Ortega was to be listened to, even at twenty-six, not only because he had good connections and a good education, but because he was rapidly gaining position in his own right. His *Wanderjahre* through the German universities had already become a pattern being successfully promoted by the *Junta para Ampliación de Estudios,* a group initiated by Giner de los Ríos and directed by Ramón y Cajal to improve the universities of Spain. In 1909, Ortega had become professor of philosophy at the *Escuela de Estudios Superiores del Magisterio,* the leading normal school of Madrid. Here prospective teachers studied and here many youths who lacked the social advantages that gave access to the university still could get an excellent higher education.

Ortega's position was a good one from which he could pursue his desire to improve Spanish education and to stimulate Spain's intellectual elite. Yet in academic circles he was expected to try for the vacant Chair of Metaphysics at the University of Madrid, which was perhaps the most prestigious position open to a philosopher in Spain. Spanish professors win their posts by competing before a panel of judges; and despite his youth, Ortega was given a good chance of outshining his elder competitors, for only Unamuno could match the philosophic background that Ortega gained in Germany, and Unamuno, then at home at Salamanca, had already declined the opportunity to compete for a Madrid post. In Ortega's year of teaching, he had proved effective. Erudition had not overwhelmed his knack for dramatic presentation, and he was known to be quick and telling in the give and take of oral examination.[f] "El Sitio" was anxious to take their own measure of the man to see whether he lived up to his promise.

When the audience had gathered, it was clear that at least word of Ortega's personal appearance had preceded him to "El Sitio," for as a reporter observed in a pleasant Spanish idiom, "not a few" *señoritas* graced his audience.[8] And when Ortega arrived, they were not disappointed. A Spaniard: he was short, but strong and agile. The sense of movement characteristic of his thought

---

[8]"Una conferencia en 'El Sitio': La pedagogía social," *El Imparcial,* March 13, 1910.

actively emanated from his physique: he would soon develop a taste
for driving fast touring cars, and a photograph shows him in a
graceful *suerte de capa* before a real, albeit small, bull. Even when
young, Ortega disdained the flashy garb of *Modernismo* and dressed
in the accepted fashion of the time. Effortlessly, he had a certain
flair, a prepossessing air, which made it unnecessary to advertise
himself with eccentricities. His face was sharply featured and
expressive. The animation of his eyes impressed those with whom
he conversed, and caricaturists enjoyed exaggerating the large fore-
head that rose above his brows. His strong, active hands were almost always in motion, and when he spoke, they complemented his
words with an elegant commentary of gestures.[8] At twenty-six
Ortega was a master of oratory.

*   *   *

Ortega took his invitation to speak to "El Sitio" seriously. The
request came as the first sign that he was winning a well-placed
following for his views; and he realized that his speech would
receive wide attention, for the serious papers usually reported on
"El Sitio's" proceedings. Since returning from Germany, Ortega had
been pre-occupied with a mission, the Europeanization of Spain.
In addition to giving him personal satisfaction, the invitation itself
struck him as a sign of the need for Spanish regeneration, for a
society of "El Sitio's" stature ought not to be inviting novices to
address its meetings. This symptom of the need for Europeanization
he would make an occasion for the pursuit of Europeanization; he
would explain his theory of civic reform in the hope of enlisting his
listeners in his cause. He took care in composing his address, "Civic
Pedagogy as a Political Program";[9] much seemed to ride on it.

In preparation, Ortega might have considered beginning with
a humorous introduction as counseled by classical rhetoric. But no.
He was in no mood for levity. And besides, he had a better way to
engage the attention of his audience. To do so, he would bluntly
point out the significance of his presence at "El Sitio," a mere youth
lecturing his elders. The thought of it angered him; his speech, by
its mere existence, would demonstrate the depressed condition of

---

[9]The text of "La pedagogía social como programa político" is in *Obras* I, pp.
503–521. I have translated "La pedagogía social" as civic pedagogy.

Spain. How galling that the Society had to invite someone so young, someone "who *was* nothing because he had *done* nothing," someone who was signficant merely for his promise! Dwelling on this situation, he would irritate his audience—and rightly so—for the situation should irritate Spaniards. If things went well, he would transform this irritation into a motive force for efforts to change Spanish life. Sorrow and shame, he thought, were the great sources of constructive effort; he would make his speech follow the moral itinerary that Beethoven had identified with one of his symphonies, "to joy by way of sorrow."[10]

Yes, such a dark, aggressive beginning would be appropriate. He wanted to draw his listeners into recognizing the great void in their common lives, the great absence of a future, the terrible inability to conceive of what Nietzsche called a *Kinderland*, the land of one's children, a Spain that might be achieved if men's hopes came to pass. That oppressive cloud, a present without a future: men had to become angry at this miasma; then they might make a morrow. What words would impart this mood? Did they ring true to him?

There are two types of patriotism. One sees the country as the heritage of the past and as a set of pleasing things that we presently are offered by the land in which we were born. The rather legendary glories of our forefathers, the beauty of the sky, the garb of the women, the dash of the men around us, the transparent density of the *jerez* wines, the luxuriant flowering of the Levantine gardens, the capacity for producing miracles that persists in the pedestal of the Aragonese Virgin, and so on—these compose a mass of realities, more or less presumed, that are for many their country. Because they begin with the supposition that all these things are real, that these are here, they need only to open their eyes to see their country; as a result of this notion of the nation, there remains nothing for the patriot to do but to settle down comfortably and to occupy himself with tasting the delectable array. This is the inactive, spectacular, ecstatic patriotism in which the spirit dedicates itself to the fruition of an existing, prosperous destiny that has been fortuitously pushed before it.

There is, however, another notion of the nation. It is not the land of our fathers, Nietzsche said, but the land of our children. The country is not the past and the present, nor is it anything that a providential hand extends to us so that we may have possession of it; the country is, on the

---

[10]*Ibid.*, pp. 503–4.

contrary, something that yet does not exist, that, even more, cannot exist unless we struggle energetically to fulfill it by ourselves. The country is, in this sense, precisely the conjunction of virtues that were and are lacking in our historic home. The nation is what we have not been and what we must be under penalty of feeling ourselves erased from the map.

However perfect may be the life of a people, it is not too great to be improved. Our children expect from us this improvement of the country so that their existence will be less sorrowful and richer in possibilities than our own. The improved country, the perfected nation, is the land of our children. Therefore, it is the real nation for those who are fathers—either by flesh or by spirit and obligation.

By so understanding the country, patriotism becomes for us an incessant activity, a firm and arduous desire to fulfill the idea of improvement suggested to us by the teachings of the national conscience. Our country becomes a task to complete, a problem to solve, a duty.

Thus, this dynamic and . . . futurist patriotism finds itself constantly obliged to combat the other, the voluptuous and quietist patriotism. To know what our country should be tomorrow, we have to weigh what it has been and accentuate primarily the defects of its past. True patriotism is criticizing the land of our fathers and constructing the land of our children.[11]

Yes! Here was the problem: it was not that the old order had collapsed—far from it; it was that the sense of a *Kinderland*, the hope for a future, had been lost. The patriotic task was to rebuild these hopes, to rediscover a stirring possibility, one that might move men to a common future. The patriotic duty was to speak out, to condemn, to suggest, to propose, to activate; an allegiance to the future entailed a willingness to criticize the past and to negate the present.

Might some think that such activities on the part of private citizens were improper, a spontaneous meddling in the work of the King and his governors? Spain, after all did have its official leaders. To be sure, they were not chosen by a particularly representative process, nor were they highly effective governors. Yet, were they not responsible for defining the national purpose? Was it not the citizen's duty to defer to their authority? The Spaniard, at least had to respond with an adamant NO! Perhaps the Germans, English, or French could leave politics to the politicians; the Spaniard could not. Ortega understood that a people were prior to their politics; that

---

[11]*Ibid.*, pp. 505–6.

they were responsible for the failures of their officials; that, rather than the government reform the nation, the nation had to reform the government. Constructing a *Kinderland* had little to do with official politics; the people themselves had to confront their governors with a vision of the future.

"El Sitio" would have no trouble with this point; it was a premise common to the numerous visions of Spanish regeneration. Making the point explicit, however, would prepare the way for his main concern: the people's means for making politics. Politics had two meanings, he would remind his listeners: "the art of governing or the art of obtaining the government and keeping it. Put another way: there is an art of legislating and an art of imposing certain legislative acts. To think that law is for every case the most circumspect and to think that sufficient means are possessed to pretend that this law succeeds at converting itself into written and ruling law, are very distinct matters. . . ."[12]

This distinction had been the tacit basis of his political criticism, especially of his contempt for the Machiavellian practices of Spain's official politicians. In his speech, he would make it explicit. With the art of obtaining the government, a few men work within a given system to conserve their conventional affairs, jockeying incessantly to aggrandize their personal positions. With the art of governing, all men interact in every walk of life to transform, slowly but ineluctably, the given system of authority, and its concomitant conventional affairs, inspiring each other to reject the old and to pursue new aspirations. At its best, the art of obtaining the government would result in prudent lawmaking, provided the government was already a well-made machine. The art of governing would, in contrast, give rise to lawgiving, the only process that could transform a decrepit government into a renewed system for making law.

Spain was deficient in the art of governing. For that reason there was no *Kinderland*. The official politicians were adept only at obtaining the government; they were facile at making and unmaking legislation, but they lacked a vision, a purpose, a goal, a conception of law. He was bitter, like many Spaniards, at the way Spain's governor's used the government in patent contempt for the ideals

---

[12]*Ibid.*, p. 507.

—justice, liberty, legality—on which all government was founded. On another occasion, dwelling on the official abuse of government, he had proclaimed that "revolutions are just."[13] Yet, here was the real problem: like most men, he was not a violent revolutionary. Revolutions were just, but not desirable if they could be avoided: the costs of revolutions, the human costs, the moral costs, the political costs, were much too high. Was there an alternative? He believed there was. He would try to explain the alternative to "El Sitio."

Revolutions aimed at depriving those who had obtained the government of this holding. Revolutions wrested possession of the state apparatus from the established groups. Real improvement, he thought, did not come from this act alone. Real improvement came from exercising the art of governing, which was quite different from holding possession of the state. Yet, in the past, revolutionary movements had concentrated on taking the state away from the old order. Obsessed with the art of obtaining the government, revolutionary movements had had great difficulty with the art of governing. Only at tremendous cost could they manage to build a new state. There was a better way. He believed negative revolution to be unnecessary. When exhausted, self-serving groups occupied the government without assuming responsibility to govern, in its deepest sense, they had effectively abdicated; they reigned without scepter. Obtaining the government was a waste. In an exhausted order, the art of governing could be exercised by whoever could find ways to do so. He would suggest some. He would suggest how concerned citizens might govern spontaneously, how they might indirectly yet ineluctably reform the nation in spite of the government.

"To be sure," Ortega would say, "politics is action; but, all the same, action is movement: it is to go from one place to another, it is to take a step and a step requires a direction that points straight out to the infinite. Among us there has been an improper separation of the politics of action from the political ideal, as if the former could have meaning orphaned from the latter. Our recent history makes patent the point of misery to which an active politics free of political ideals leads." He would call on his audience to turn away

---

[13]"Los problemas nacionales y la juventud," Lecture at the Madrid Ateneo, October 15, 1909, *Obras* X, p. 117.

from official politics, not in overt rebellion, but in a spontaneous creation, one in which private citizens accepted responsibility for the art of governing and spread ideals of public life that would transform the country despite the moral inertia ensconced in the government. "What should it be?" Ortega would put to them. "What is the ideal Spain towards which we can orient our hearts . . . ?"[14]

Here, he might have considered launching into a description of a Spanish *Kinderland*. Spain possessed many deficiencies; hence Spaniards have long excelled in proposing splendid programs of reform. An ideal Spain—the topic would call forth glorious proposals: a democratic, republican government, industrialization, land reform and the mechanization of agriculture, improvements in public transportation, reforestation, reduction of military expenditures, the expansion and improvement of popular education, and so on endlessly. But in view of the demoralization of official Spain, these would be futile proposals. They would all depend on governmental action. They were not ideals by which private citizens could orient their hearts. To promote a spontaneous, popular politics, a vital attempt at the art of governing, the critic could do better than dwell on the promised land. Instead, he would analyze the people's means: civic pedagogy, the education of the public.

Thus he would arrive at the subject he really wanted to put before "El Sitio." Men had other means, besides politics, "to transform the given reality in the pattern of the ideal": education.[15] This means could be used by every man at every moment, for education did not take place solely in the school; civic pedagogy was an omnipresent aspect of life in a community. From his familial background among journalists, from his own experience of having been stirred, not by teachers, but by events, and from his philosophic studies in Germany, he had developed a profound, open sense of the educator's mission. His main task was to explain this mission to "El Sitio."

Civic pedagogy!? The educator's mission!? Why weight the excitement of politics with such dull concerns? In present-day America we know the expectations the young orator had to combat.

---

[14]"La pedagogía social como programa político," 1910, *Obras* I, p. 507.
[15]*Ibid.*, p. 508.

People perceived education to be on the periphery of public affairs. In training up this or that individual, even were he to become a powerful personage, men of affairs would be wasting their time; too many believe Shaw: those who can, do; those who can't, teach. Nonsense! Education was more than tutoring individuals. Everyone, everywhere, all the time—each taught; each learned; life was a great cycle of pedagogic influence. Doers teach; teachers do: education, properly perceived, *was* the art of governing.

Since Machiavelli, men have confused the relationship between politics and pedagogy. Where Plato aspired to put philosophy in equal cooperation with kings, Machiavelli was content to put it in the subordinate service of princes. Machiavelli taught the prince to use reason, not in the pursuit of wisdom, but in a pursuit of power.[h] Since then the possessors of power have exploited the control of education as a means of preserving their position. These practices make for good politics and bad government. They subject solutions to pedagogical problems, problems in the art of governing, to the expedient criteria of practical politics, the art of obtaining and holding the government. As we know, these practices turn educators away from their proper business. They transform the pedagogue in every sphere of activity into a salesman preserving the American way of life, a general planning the national defense, a policeman guarding the sidewalks and patrolling the highways, an economist allocating national labor skills, a technician underwriting future material progress, or a doctor raising standards of public health. All these functions may be necessary and desirable, but they are peripheral to education, to the continuous acquisition of culture, skills, and tastes, a continuous acquisition through which each person forms his character and capabilities and through which each generation assumes its historic qualities. Instead of facilitating education, the school, church, family, marketplace, entertainment, and opinion provide whatever the powerful practical leaders believe will enhance and preserve their position. In both Ortega's Spain and the present-day West, pedagogy, which traditionally concerned lawgiving, has been made a mere handmaiden of the lawmaker.

He would take the argument against this perversion of the civic order beyond justice and back to expedience on a higher level. He would speak of civic pedagogy as a *political program*. He would suggest that if practical men had the courage not to interfere in the people's efforts to educate themselves, the ancillary benefits from expedient programs for training the people would accrue twice over. But he would not take his stand only on the grounds of a higher expedience. He had been schooled in the classical tradition of political philosophy. In this tradition, the problem of pedagogy was the foundation. Pedagogy was not didactics.[i] Far from it! Pedagogy was the basic component of political philosophy.

Classical political theory had explained how a community formed and persisted. Pedagogy was the branch of classical theory that explained, not how a teacher might conduct a school, but how ideals, spirit, mind, might function in the formation of a community. In the absence of a spiritual discipline, each man was the prey of his passions. These would beguile him into foolish deeds. These would destroy any nascent community. Thus Cain killed Abel. To moderate the power of passion, men created ideals of conduct. Ideals described not how men in fact behaved, but how they could and should behave. By reference to ideals men gave themselves a particular character. Doing so, they gained a certain dependability that under trying circumstances they would act in accordance with their self-imposed obligations. To the degree that men shared ideals, creating a common character, they formed communities. Ideals of conduct, taste, and thought enabled men to moderate their divisive passions and to live in harmony, in a common harmony attained without brute subservience of the multitude to a single member.[j]

If the political theorist would seek, like Plato, to engender an authentic community, he would find that his task is not only philosophical, devising the ideals by which men can discipline their character; his task is also pedagogical, leading each man towards the personal formation of the common, rational ideals that the philosopher has discovered. Intellectually, pedagogy would aid men in selecting their common ideals and in communicating these to their peers; it would explain to them how character was created, and through character, community. Practically, pedagogy would help spread common standards among a people; in doing so it would serve in forming a community of men. Pedagogy would be a foundation of public affairs: men can live in common and in freedom only by reference to rational, consistent conceptions of truth, beauty, and goodness, and the acquisition of these conceptions is education, the continual process through which men are entering into their social compacts, forming and re-forming their communities.

In real life, however, the pedagogue's effort to extend the reach of reason, to found community, often would give way to the politician's obsession with obtaining power, with preserving position. Hence, education has frequently been treated as a subsidiary of practical politics, and pedagogy, a concern for the standards that men might cultivate in themselves, has been dismissed as irrelevant to *Realpolitik*. Practical leaders, at heart nihilists, recognized the expediency of appearing to be principled: they gave lip service to generally accepted ideals, which educators, in turn, have been expected to perpetuate without questioning. Convention, false certainty, and hypocrisy thus become the basis for educating the public. Instruction becomes a process of transmitting ignorance, dissimulation, and moral vacuity from one generation to another.

An unbuttressed facade would stand steady, provided the winds were gentle and the earth did not quake. So too, a community might persist for years in an unrecognized disillusionment, provided it encountered no internal or external crises. But, under the logic of expediency, a domestic minority would be exploited, seemingly safely, until it rebels, demanding justice or perhaps repayment in kind. Under the logic of expediency, a nation would be tempted to commit mounting force in protecting its foreign interests, until it consumes its vitality defending bad investments. During the twentieth century, citizens of nearly every Western nation have faced a crisis of common purpose; and in Spain, following 1898, prolonged colonial difficulties and violent domestic separatism combined to nurture a generation of civic pedagogues, men reacting to the lack of significant ideals, men searching for new, common standards, men seeking a spontaneous reform of their nation.

With a reawakening of an interest in human ideals, men would cease to perceive pedagogy as a mere instrument of policy; they would again recognize it as a rudiment of polity. Important matters, therefore, were at stake for Ortega as he planned to affirm that pedagogy was the science of human ideals. He would reassert historical initiative for the intellectual and the teacher. The *clerc* had no reason to betray his office, to defer to the Worldly Wiseman; nay, the *clerc* had good reason to remain true to his duties. To the man of the world, voluntary, rational standards had become irrelevant. *Eppur si muove! Eppure egli vuòle!* Men continued to respond to aspirations. They led themselves out of themselves in an effort to realize their ideals, to remain true to their standards.

Ideas girded any public order. Men who changed ideas would change all else. He would contend, at "El Sitio" and throughout his life, that practical affairs were secondary features of the community; they were dependent on a particular system of aspirations, the formation of which was the primary level of public affairs. Both the means and the ends of political, economic, and social activities followed, for the most part, from the spiritual activities through which persons constituted their polity. Ideals were evoked by teachers, preachers, writers, and thinkers, by men who cultivated ideals according to a pedagogy. Because a group of men received its character in response to the educators within it, he would assert at Bilbao that "pedagogy is the science of transforming communities."[16]

Who made history? That was the question he would seek to raise. Practical men believed that they—the politicians, businessmen, and soldiers—made history. He would disagree. These men simply played out the script that had been composed, for better or for worse, by thinkers and teachers. He might have toyed with quoting Heinrich Heine's wise warning: "mark this, ye proud men of action: ye are nothing but unconscious hodmen of the men of thought who, often in humblest stillness, have appointed you your inevitable work."[17]

Pedagogy is prior to politics. For each pedagogy that men master, they must create a corresponding politics. In his speech and throughout his career, he entertained the possibility that intellectuals could introduce into Spain and Europe a set of ideals, standards, and aspirations that differed from those in force and that would make a different kind of practical life possible, desirable, and finally ineluctable. Thus, he did not perceive the imminence of a

---

[16]*Ibid.*, p. 515.

[17]Heine, *Religion and Philosophy in Germany*, John Snodgrass, trans., p. 106.

post-historic era; on the contrary, it was potentially a *most* historic era!**k** He perceived a complicated, provisional, and open future; one that depended on our personally mastering the many modes of ‚pedagogical power.

Thus, civic pedagogy was no dull weight crushing the excitement of politics, burdening it with didactic do-gooders. Civic pedagogy would be a great leaven, a vital yeast that would set the populace in ferment and make the community rise. The science of human ideals, pedagogy was the science of transforming communities; and it wrought change, not by imposing a Jacobin blueprint on the whole, but by effectively helping to raise the personal aspirations of each member. No worry: his listeners would realize that in turning to education he would not be addressing himself to the special concerns of harried parents and distraught teachers, but to the fundamental sources of further development in the history of Spain and, we might add, of the West.

Through education we obtain from an imperfect person a man whose breast glows with iridescent virtues. Innately, no one is excellent, knowing, or energetic. But a vigorous image of a superior human creature floats before the eyes of his teacher, who, using the skills of pedagogy, injects this ideal man into the nervous apparatus of the carnal creature. This is the admirable, educative operation through which the Idea, the Word, gives itself flesh! . . .

Insofar as it is a science, pedagogy concerns transforming man's integral character, and it encounters two problems: the first is to determine what future form, what human standard, is to point the direction in which the pedagogue should push his pupil. This is the problem of the educative ideal. Should the teacher carelessly arrogate to himself the right to impose a capricious form on the human material that someone has submitted to his nurture? It would be perversely frivolous to define the ideal type through any means except rigorous and careful labor. The pedagogue shares responsibility for the present with other men; but precisely because he prepares the future, the future also weighs upon his responsibility. We are that which moved obscurely in the dreams of our fathers and masters, for fathers' dreams are their sons and the century that will follow. . . .

The science of pedagogy must begin with the rigorous determination of the pedagogical ideal, of the educative ends. The other problem that is essential is finding the intellectual, moral, and esthetic means by which one can succeed in launching the pupil in the direction of the ideal. Just as physics establishes the laws of nature and then, in particular technologies, these laws are applied to industry, pedagogy anticipates what man must be and then finds the instruments for helping man succeed at becoming what he must be.[18]

But wait. Here was another problem. Liberal Spaniards would not like talk about "what man must be"; they had learned to chafe at the divine rights of didacticism that the Church long ago arrogated to itself. Could he use the rhetoric of critical philosophy he had learned in Germany? He would try. The rational necessity explicated by critical philosophy differed from both the moral necessity upheld by scholastic ethics and the political necessity imposed by authoritarian government.[1] He would make it clear. By the human ideal, by "what man must be," one did not mean some sterile image of the perfect person to which all must conform. Instead, the human ideal denoted the common principles that, when used in diverse ways by diverse persons in diverse situations, marked each as a human being. One should base pedagogy on a cogent conception of the humanity of man, of what made the animal, man, into a human. With this contention, he would put his educational theory squarely in the liberal tradition. With Socrates, he would insist that teachers, all teachers regardless of their métier, were responsible for the quality of the nourishment they offered to the human spirit.[19] With Kant, he would base his pedagogy on a philosophical anthropology, on the study, as the great idealist said, not of what nature makes of man, but of what man can and should make of himself.[20] With Wilhelm Dilthey, he would hold that the human ideal was not revealed or imposed; it was the *telos* of all inquiry, or as Dilthey put it, "the blossom and goal of all true philosophy is pedagogy in its widest sense—the formative theory of man."[21]

"Man! Man!" he would exclaim to his audience. "Who is man?"

Here was the question. Answers had ranged from the cynical saying that man was the only creature that drank without thirst and made love in every season to Leibniz's belief that man was a

[18]"La pedagogía social como programa político," 1910, *Obras* I, pp. 508–9.

[19]See especially Plato, *Protagoras*, 313A–314C.

[20]See especially Kant, *Anthropologie in pragmatischer Hinsicht*, in *Werke in sechs Bänden*, VI, p. 399.

[21]Dilthey, *Pädagogik: Geschichte und Grundlinien des Systems*, 3rd, ed., *Gesammelte Schriften*, IX, p. 7.

petit Dieu. "Be careful that interpretations of man fall between one and the other definition," he would caution.[22]

Man was a problem for man: that was his most human feature. Man's unique, human characteristic was that he had to decide what to make of himself. Here was the germ of Ortega's philosophy of life—his idea of "vital reason." Human character could oscillate between the beast who drinks without thirst and a small God; whether men traveled towards the former or the latter depended on their will: they were compelled towards neither. The variability of human character intensified the responsibilities of the pedagogue. Man's problem was that he made of himself whatever he would become, "and once we have let ourselves engage this problem without reservation, I believe that we will approach pedagogy with a religious dread. . . ." Again, he would repeat the fundamental question: "What idea of man should be held by the man who is going to humanize your sons? Whatever it is, the cast that he gives them will be ineffaceable."[23]

Humanization was not a mechanical, strictly causal process, however. Man was not wholly a biological creature. Educating a man was not, like breeding a horse, a matter of bringing the exterior qualities of a species to perfection in a single member. The goals of education would not be found in biology or any of its derivative sciences.m In keeping with the idealistic tradition, especially with the critical philosophy of Kant, he would warn against confusing our knowledge of phenomena with reality itself. "We must ask ourselves: is man a biological individual, a mere organism? The answer is unequivocal: No. Man is not merely a biological case, for he is biology itself; he is not only a grade on the zoological scale, for it is he who constructed the entire scale."[24]

Man was more than a spatial and temporal creature because he carried within himself the idea of space and time. Certainly the human body was a physical body, "but I ask you: physics itself, what is it? Physics does not respond to its own laws; it has no mass, it does not obey the law of universal gravitation. Hence, gentlemen,

---

[22]"La pedagogía social como programa político," 1910, *Obras* I, pp. 509–510.
[23]*Ibid.*, p. 510.
[24]*Ibid.*, p. 511.

physics goes beyond physical facts; physics is a metaphysical fact." Physics was part of a great range of creations—science, art, morality—that were metaphysical entities. These were not natural; they were not, in essence, physical objects. Metaphysical entities were ideals and standards that had been created by man, and through these man gave himself his own specific character. "Science, morality, and art are specifically human facts: and vice versa, to be human is to participate in science, morality, and art."[25]

With this proposition, he would give a general answer to his question, Who is man? The goals of education would be found in the realm of science, morality, and art. All of man's mental creations were human ideals, which latently were common universals that would enable different men at once to particularize and to humanize their personal development. These metaphysical facts were neither natural nor necessary; their continual existence depended on the human will. He would mark off a great realm, which was filled with human ideals, as the special purview and responsibility of the educator. He would secure this realm against those who wished to deny its existence by reiterating the traditional duality between the physical and the ideal, between the rule of necessity and the rule of freedom. Along with certain other twentieth-century thinkers, he would escape the mind-body problem, not by reducing one to the other, but by showing that both existed *in the lives* of actual men, body as their physical life, mind as their spiritual life.

Referring to the idealism of Plato, Hegel, Pestalozzi, and Paul Natorp, he would characterize the rule of freedom as a communal rather than an idiosyncratic rule. Science, morality, and art were not an "individual inheritance." They were a discipline to which one freely submitted in order to partake in common truth, general good, and universal beauty. Considered as a subject of natural forces, each man was unique and meaningless; but as a free being each man could sacrifice a bit of his uniqueness to gain meaning by participating in cultural endeavors. "Inside each of us, two men live in a perpetual struggle: a savage man who is willful, irreducible to a rule or to a pattern, a species of gorilla; and a stern man who is

---

[25]*Ibid.*, p. 512.

found to be thinking exact ideas, performing legal acts, feeling emotions of transcendent value. The wild instincts exist only for the former man, the man of nature; the latter, the man of culture, alone participates in science, law, and beauty." This participation distinguished the human from the animal man.[26]

Thus, to his question, Who is man?, he would answer that man is the embodiment of his common ideals: The metaphysical principles of science, morality and art were the common characteristics that made men human, that permitted community in diversity. Each child was shaped by the standards of his family, his city, his nation, and his heritage; and conversely, a man's family, city, nation, and heritage were particular ideals that oriented each man's personal aspirations. "Concretely, the human individual is human only insofar as he contributes to the civic reality and is tempered by it."[27]

Ortega planned to expound two theses to "El Sitio." First, to determine what pedagogical ideals were most suitable for human aspiration, he would ask who man was and answer that man was human insofar as he fulfilled one or another metaphysical ideal. Second, he would begin contending that pedagogy was the fundamental, formative power of any community, but he would conclude that the given characteristics of a community, its established ideals and standards, were the most powerful pedagogical influences on its members. Were these theses circular? By all means, and that would be the source of their real import.

If men could examine human matters with the rigorous detachment that natural scientists pretend to possess, his circular reasoning would be a mark against his ideas. But, men think because they find themselves shipwrecked in a sea of things and they must think in order to learn to keep themselves afloat. In human matters rigorous detachment was not possible, for the human sciences arose from man thinking about himself: they were inherently circular. Expunging the circularity of our thoughts would do violence to the objects of our intellection, in this case to ourselves. The actual significance of his ideas about pedagogy would be found first by recognizing that pedagogical phenomena required a circular description, and

[26]*Ibid.*, p. 512.
[27]*Ibid.*, p. 514.

second by examining the consequences that followed from this situation.[n]

His first proposition led to a liberal conception of authority, one holding that authority over each person's activities ultimately resides in the person. Teachers needed to know the nature of a man in order to select the ideals that they should develop in their pupils, but the nature of the man was itself determined by the ideals that he adopted. The result was that pedagogical authority ultimately resided in the pupil, not the teacher; each person defined the place in the common, human world he would assume; enlightened ignorance of the pupil limited the teacher to provoking, criticizing, and generally enhancing the pupil's aspirations. No teacher had a basis for imposing his own goals upon another. In civic pedagogy, no part of the polity had the authority to define and impose its particular program on all.

Like most idealisms, his conception of communal authority was subtle, and hence easily misunderstood. Authority resided in each person, but it concerned common problems and potentials. He would reject a complete individualism; for if men renounced their common, intellectual resources in favor of idiosyncratic modes of thought, they would soon plunge themselves back into a state of nature. At the same time, he would not accept a radical socialization of the person. To be sure, he would observe that "the individual divinizes himself in the collectivity."[28] But the collectivity, the community, did not exist apart from and above the person: no man could make an authoritative statement in the name of "society." Civic ideals did not exist independent of the persons who pursued them; and to compel adherence to one or another ideal was impossible, for an ideal, by definition, was the object of a man's *aspiration*. Instead, community depended on the free adherence by many persons to common standards and their voluntary pursuit of common goals. "We have seen how the civic fact appears to us as we search for the reality of the individual because in reality we find every individual always enlaced with others and because we find that, taking each one separately, his interior is prepared from materials common to other men. In essence, gentlemen, the communal is a

---

[28]*Ibid.*, p. 520.

combination of individual efforts to realize a common work."[29] The collectivity through which the individual would divinize himself would not be a supra-personal, organic entity, but a metaphysical ideal that a person shared with other persons.

As the impossibility of objectively defining the nature of man restricted authority to the person's power over himself, the fact that the community was at once the result and the agent of education was the basis of democratic, egalitarian relations between men. If this circle accurately described human reality, if shared ideals were both source and result of education, man's civic relations were intrinsically open; they were continually subject to change and adaptation, yet their change and adaptation would always proceed through evolution, not revolution. A particular citizen or group had no way to fix once and forever the pattern of influence that formed and perpetuated the community, for the pattern was the coöperative work of all, each influencing the others. To introduce a completely novel pattern of influence and produce a revolution, not merely in word, but in deeds as well, was likewise impossible. A community developed as each man defined his vision of the future from the common heritage. To deny certain members of a group the opportunity to define their own place in its future was unjust. Listen now to what the youth would say; later, the mature man would speak again about the matter.

If community is coöperation, members of the community must, before anything else, be workers. One who does not work cannot participate in the community. With this affirmation democracy is impelled towards socialism. To socialize a man is to make him a worker in the magnificent human undertaking, culture, where culture means everything from digging a ditch to composing verses.

It is today a scientific truth, acquired once and for all, that the only morally admissible social system is the socialist system; but I do not affirm either that true socialism follows Karl Marx or that the workers' parties are the only ethically elevated parties. Regardless of what version you take, next to socialism all political theory is anarchic because it denies the supposition of coöperation, which is the substance of society and the regimen of community.

Passive cooperation characterized the slave who built the pyramids; the worker, if he is not be a slave, needs to have a living comprehension

---

[29]*Ibid.*, p. 515.

of the meaning of his work. To me it seems inhuman to keep a man in the corner of a factory unless he is given a vision of the whole so that he can gain a noble sense of his task. . . . Here is the ethical value of civic pedagogy: if each civic person has to be a worker in the culture, each worker has a right to endow himself with a cultural understanding.

Public instruction throughout Europe—not only in Spain—perpetuates through its organization a crime of *lèse-humanité:* the school is two schools—a school for the rich and one for the poor. The poor are poor not only in material matters; they are also poor in spirit. A time will come —disgracefully it is not yet here—when students of man will not need to classify him as rich or poor, as one classifies animals as vertebrate or invertebrate. But even worse, today men divide themselves into cultured and uncultured; that is, into men and submen.[30]

Here he would take the part of the teacher, the political teacher, the civic pedagogue. Here he would criticize current standards; he would propose alternatives; he would invite each listener to seek to define for himself a more perfect Spain, to try to live according to this better vision. He and his audience would be plunged into the cycles of pedagogic influence that he would have pointed out. Spaniards could not, by means of programmatic proposals, impose a different form upon these cycles. Spaniards could, however, question their own civic ideals, provoking others to do the same; and with enough effort, they might bend the course of development, spontaneously making it point in a different, more hopeful direction.

This effort, exerted by each, to learn to live by more taxing, more liberating civic ideals, would be civic pedagogy as a political program. This program would by-pass official Spain. It would be a new politics. It would result in the Europeanization of Spain. As soon as Spaniards would begin to search for the ideals of their *Kinderland,* they would discover Europe. Spaniards could most improve themselves, and through themselves, their nation, by pursuing the standards of European culture; and as proof of this contention he would offer both Miguel de Unamuno and Joaquín Costa. Despite the differences of their doctrines, both men exemplified the potential power of those who would master European intellectual standards. He would leave "El Sitio" with a simple thought: "Spain is the problem and Europe the solution."[31]

[30]*Ibid.,* pp. 517–8.
[31]*Ibid.,* pp. 519–520.

Such were the intentions behind Ortega's words. The address itself went well enough; it was neither disastrous nor epochal. His speech was reported in Madrid, at least by *El Imparcial*. His ideas won favor with those seeking to create a radical "new politics"; they, at least, found inspiration in what he said. Thus, *Europa*, a short-lived magazine of the young regenerationists, introduced excerpts from his speech with the observation that "it contains a virtual program. It gives specific recommendations with which we concur, for we have united the two words Politics-Pedagogy into a single word, the Future."[32]

But the speech itself was not as important as the aspirations it embodied. With respect to these, the speech could not help but fail, for the aspirations were enough to fill a lifetime. The great eagles had sunk their talons. Thereafter, came the ascent towards the heights.

*　　　*　　　*

What mental grasp, what sense have they? They believe the tales of the poets and follow the crowd as their teachers, ignoring the adage that the many are bad, the good are few.

HERACLITUS, 112º

---

[32]Editorial introduction to Ortega's "La pedagogía social como programa político," *Europa*, March 20, 1910.

The precipitate that the years of study in Germany left in me was the decision to accept, integrally and without reserve, my Spanish destiny. It was not a comfortable destiny.

ORTEGA[1]

[1] *Prólogo para alemanes,* 1933, 1958, *Obras* VIII, p. 55.

II
Preparations

Recourse to love, rather than to her antagonist, conditioning theory, is needed to explain two features of learning.[a] The young do not truly know what it is that they want to learn, and most of them dutifully attend to whatever their elders choose to offer. Insofar as this unquestioning acceptance is the case, educational systems ironically perpetuate a radical ignorance. Each generation grows up without knowing why it learned what it learned. There are usually a few, however, who resist the given. In the manner that Socrates explained to Hippocrates, they avidly examine every teacher, testing whatever he proposes to teach to see whether it is really worth learning.[2] They seek to make their education all their own, that is, as Montaigne said, a part of their judgment.[3] When a teacher reveals his lack of judgment by being unable to account for why he teaches what he tries to teach, the young in search of true learning must borrow a fragment here and there and then move on, sadder but wiser men. Theirs is a task fraught with failure, and hence learning has usually been accompanied by a faith that every disappointment simply brings the would-be learner closer to his goal: lovers of wisdom have long known that to define great things it is often best to begin by identifying that which the thing is not. Thus, the first feature of learning that conditioning theory

---

[2]See Plato, *Protagoras*, 310D–314C.

[3]See Montaigne, "Of the Education of Children," in Blanchard Bates, ed., *Montaigne, Selected Essays*, esp. p. 22.

cannot explain is the sustained, skeptical search for the unknown teacher who can set forth that which one intuits to be possible, but which one has yet to encounter.

Then, neither too soon nor too late, the searcher must reverse his nomadic inquiry at the moment that he meets the proper teacher. Many youths, tired of their quest, stop looking too soon and accept as a prize that which happens to be at hand; and others, hardened to skeptical scoffing, pass by their true goal without responding. A few recognize their teacher. Without giving up their powers of criticism, they let their teacher immerse them in influence, for they know that the influence is wholesome and that in time they can organize, edit, and perfect their acquirements. Thus, learning begins in a restless search and culminates in a decisive commitment. What but love could direct such delicate maneuvers?

In Plato's *Symposium* the eulogists who preceded Socrates in speaking in honor of love praised Eros for her genetic prowess. Agathon, the foil for Socrates, concluded his discourse by saying, "Thus I conceive, Phaedrus, that Love was originally of surpassing beauty and goodness, and is latterly the cause of similar excellences in others."[4] Socrates began his questioning of Agathon by asking whether or not there was an object of love, whether there were qualities or objects that love urged us to attain. With the admission that love is a desire for something, genetic theories of the erotic drive cease to make sense: the excellence of beauty and goodness was not in Love itself, but in the absent objects that Love urged us to attain. With this observation Socrates introduced Diotima's erotic teleology, in which love was a desire for the qualities one lacked, not the cause of the qualities one possessed. This desire was directed towards ever more elevating qualities, and hence love was a great educating force.[5] It could sustain a student's search for teachers, men who can help him master his deficiencies, and it could prompt him, whenever he met such men, to open himself to influence.

Thus love directs the student not by its causal power to determine his character, but by its teleological power to attract him onwards, drawing him out and leading him continually to surpass

---

[4] Plato, *Symposium*, 197C, W. R. M., Lamb, trans.
[5] *Ibid.*, 199C–212C.

himself. Ortega explained this power of love as follows: "in the Platonic vocabulary, 'beauty' is the concrete name for what we generally, generically call 'perfection.' Formulated with a certain circumspection, but with rigorous attention to Plato's thought, his idea is this: in all love there resides in the lover a desire to unite himself with another who appears gifted with some perfection. Love is, then, a movement in our spirit towards something that is in a sense excellent, better, superior."[6] For Ortega, as for Diotima, love began with another and spread until it yearned for union with beauty, truth, and goodness.[b] The great diversity of love enabled Ortega to make it a complicated, varied force for the perfection of himself and his people.

We need to start with reflections on love in order to comprehend the tremendous educability that was Ortega's personal genius. Like Wilhelm Meister, Ortega began as a rather ordinary youth. But something drew him on through several *Wanderjahre* that were marked by many twists and turns and a serious lack of an explicit, apparent rationale. Yet in these wanderings, Ortega discovered his destiny; from disparate travels, he developed his sense of mission. A love for Spain drew Ortega onwards, a love for a perfected Spain, his *Kinderland.* In the Platonic conception of love, the excellence towards which our spirit moves is not always an already actual excellence; on the contrary, it is usually a potential excellence, one that must be brought into being if it is to exist among the concrete realities of our lives. Thus, our love at once draws us towards the better and is the agent for bringing that possibility into existence. Ortega understood this point. "In everything there is a suggestion of a potential plenitude. An open and noble spirit will have the ambition to perfect it, to aid it, so that it will achieve this plenitude. This is love—the love for the perfection of the beloved."[7] Ortega's *Wanderjahre* exemplify how the love for the perfection of the beloved guides the lover to the perfecting of himself.

*　　　*　　　*

[6]"Amor en Stendhal," 1926, *Obras* V, p. 571.

[7]*Meditaciones del Quijote*, 1914, *Obras* I, p. 311. Cf. Leibniz, "Discourse on Metaphysics," (1686), "he who loves seeks his satisfaction in the felicity or perfection of the subject loved and in the perfection of his actions." Chandler and Montgomery trans., in Philip Weiner, ed., *Leibniz Selections*, p. 294.

To say that Ortega spent two years studying idealism in the German universities would be true but deceptive, for it might suggest that he went to Germany specifically to learn the doctrines of idealism. We can make an all-too-common error by treating the history of philosophy as a series of systems, each sufficient unto itself, a body of doctrine to be learned as one learns to decline Latin nouns. But philosophy is not a fixed system that can be learned. As a human enterprise, philosophy is a tradition of speculation in which each succeeding effort preserves its predecessors by partially perfecting and perverting them.c By a conjunction of inclination and circumstances, certain men are called to philosophize. Responding to the call, they discover that the tradition of their peers can influence; it is too vast to be learned. Ortega was among the men called forth by a love of wisdom; hence, from 1905 to 1907 he subjected himself to the intense influence of the idealistic tradition. Although he did not become a rigorous idealist, ever afterwards this tradition was an essential, positive element of his thought.

Ortega's studies were not directed by convention; they were wonder-filled years of wandering. His apprenticeship at Marburg culminated an erratic search for an obscure object. This search was sustained by the faith that Spain needed science and that somewhere in the halls of the German universities there were men who could reveal the genius of science to a curious, young Spaniard. Let us not be like those who never wonder at the marvelous mystery that Plato was, out of all the chances, the disciple of Socrates, and that Aristotle was the pupil of Plato. Thus, we should take some care to follow Ortega's studies in a way that will do justice to their great significance, but that will not convert them into an obvious fact to be taken for granted.

In an important essay on Goethe, Ortega suggested that the biographer should learn to comprehend a man "from the inside." This mode of understanding was not that of absolute acquaintance in which the biographer can reconstruct the entirety of a person's thoughts and surroundings at any particular moment. Understanding a man from the inside meant comprehending the powers of the man and the potentials of his surroundings, and perceiving how he meshed these together into a unique accomplishment. "The true inside from which I want you to see Goethe is not the inside of

Goethe, but the inside of his life, of the drama of Goethe. It is not a question of seeing the life of Goethe as Goethe saw it with his subjective vision, but of entering as a biographer into the magic circle of his existence in order to witness the tremendous objective event that was this life and of which Goethe was only an ingredient."[8] In this way, we should try to understand, from the inside, the drama of Ortega's encounter with idealism, an encounter that easily might have led to nothing.

Drama need not be marred by one's knowing the plot before witnessing the spectacle. At the end of 1904 Ortega decided to go to Germany, having become discontented with the intellectual life of his native land. He went to Germany with a vague intuition that the situation of Spain could be improved only through education, but he lacked the intellectual principles for transforming this intuition into a personal program of life. Consequently, when he went to Germany he did not know what to study, where to study it, or with whom; he was a potential student in search of a teacher. First he tried the University of Leipzig for the spring of 1905, and in the fall he switched to the University of Berlin. He found both universities to be impressive, but neither had a fundamental influence on him. Hence, at the end of his first year he was still uncertain about the nature of his quest, and he had yet to find the proper teacher. He then tried the University of Marburg, the center of neo-Kantianism. Ortega stayed there a year, and in 1911 he returned for another. At Marburg he found a true teacher and a significant idea: Hermann Cohen, the teacher, initiated him into the rigorous discipline of philosophic speculation, and Paul Natorp introduced him to a version of idealism that enabled Ortega to envisage a career as the educator of a more perfect Spain.

To appreciate the objective event that Ortega's studies were, it is important to note on the one hand how easily the study of philosophy can be sidetracked into fruitless byways and on the other how utterly devoid of external guidance Ortega's studies were. No subject is more vulnerable to bad teaching or studying than philosophy; and of the schools of philosophy, none is more easily rendered meaningless than idealism. The study of speculative phi-

---

[8]"Pidiendo un Goethe desde dentro," 1932, *Obras* IV, pp. 400-1.

losophy is itself a speculation; its goal is great and delicate, and all but strong spirits are easily diverted from its pursuit. In Germany, there were many times when Ortega's effort might have been shunted along unproductive paths, but Ortega was one of the strong spirits who could recognize when his current opportunities did not pertain to his real goal: thus he was willing to launch himself repeatedly into the unknown, rather than inure himself to inadequate familiarities. He had the courage, the inward faith in himself, not to insist that his studies advance step by step. Instead, as he tried this and that, he built up a tremendous tension between significant but unconnected inquiries; and when this tension reached the proper level, he was ready to master the principles, the ideas, by which these disparate elements could be combined to form a unity, a self, a heroic character.

"Plato saw in 'Eros,' " Ortega observed, "an impetus that succeeded in joining all things to each other; it is, he said, a connective force and a passion for synthesis. Therefore, in his opinion, philosophy, which finds the sense of things, is induced by 'Eros.' "[9] Unrequited love guided Ortega's incessant search. His trip to Germany was an affirmation of his country's potential; his discontent with its performance goaded him through his *Wanderjahre*. A positive act based on a negative judgment: he left, he later wrote, to escape "the stupidity of my country."[10] Seeking an alternative to stupidity, he naturally began with the University of Leipzig since its faculty had a prestigious reputation for erudition. Once there he was dismayed by the impersonality of the institution and by his complete lack of friends and connections. He resolved to master German; he struggled alone with Kant's *Critique of Pure Reason*; and he tried with little success to engage himself in a worthwhile course of philosophic studies.

Ortega's difficulties might have been foreseen. In 1905 Leipzig was not a center of philosophic speculation. The great psychologist, Wilhelm Wundt, was its best known professor, and in general the positivistic, empirical sciences were its forte. Before he was there long, the lonely young Spaniard began to doubt whether a

---

[9]*Meditaciones del Quijote*, 1914, *Obras* I, p. 351.
[10]"Una primera vista sobre Baroja," 1910, *Obras* II, p. 118.

strictly metaphysical career was still possible. After several months Ortega wrote in a most uncharacteristic vein to his friend Francisco Navarro Ledesma, an important literary critic. "Philosophy is nothing in itself . . . ," he confided, "it is only a chemical process for treating a primary material extraneous to it and giving this material an essence. Thus, philosophy must find its subject matter in a special science."[11] In this way, self-doubt threatened to overcome the speculative spirit as philosophers faced the achievements of empirical science, making them suspect that their art would have to become either a positive science or a logical analysis. In this way, even Ortega was moved by the doubt that gave rise to the *Wiener Kreis,* and the whole movement towards a strictly analytic philosophy.d Ortega toyed with the idea of taking up an empirical specialty, and he even enrolled in courses in histology and anatomy, perhaps to prepare himself to study with Wundt.e But his heart was not in such work. For a time he studied philosophy at Leipzig with some concentration, but he found the subject uncongenial and his effort spilled over into a voracious program of reading. Nietzsche and Renan were his favorites, but he also read Ranke and other historians, the Humboldt brothers, Pestalozzi, Herbart, Schopenhauer, Descartes, Kant, and Goethe. His discovery of a collection on the history of Spain convinced him that the standard Spanish histories needed revision from beginning to end.[12] All this reading was stimulating and his letters were packed with various thoughts and insights, but it lacked discipline.

In the fall of 1905 Ortega went to Berlin in search of a better library. Reminiscing about this time, he wrote that often he was too poor to feed his body in the automat, and to make up for it he overfed his head in the library. Still his work lacked discipline and he failed to find a teacher who could give him decisive direction. In retrospect, this failure seems surprising. He heard about Wilhelm Dilthey, whom years later he would call the most important thinker of the last half of the nineteenth century.[13] But by then Dilthey only taught a select inner circle, and thus failed to meet one of his more

---

[11]"Cartas inéditas a Navarro Ledesma," Leipzig, May 16, 1905, *Cuadernos,* November 1961, pp. 6–7.

[12]Leipzig, May 16 and August 8, 1905, *Ibid.,* pp. 7–9, 16, 18.

[13]"Historia como sistema," 1936, *Obras* VI, p. 41.

imaginative disciples. Ortega did, however, attend the lectures of Georg Simmel, who had just published his work on Schopenhauer and Nietzsche. Later Ortega would appreciate Simmel as a significant thinker; but in 1905 Simmel was not a fundamental influence on Ortega, who was already an enthusiast of "my Nietzsche." Simmel probably sharpened this particular interest, without deepening and unifying Ortega's general comprehension of German thought.[14]

If Ortega had had to stop after his first year in Germany, his studies probably would not have been a major influence on his life and thought. His work lacked unifying principles. Consequently, his various inquiries did not cohere and contribute each to the other. They were a multitude of fragments that were not yet cumulative because they were not informed by common ideas. Furthermore, he still lacked significant personal involvement with professors. Without it, he remained a mere observer of German intellectual life; all youths, no matter how brilliant, need a mentor to show them how to take part in any serious intellectual undertaking.

*   *   *

It is not best, however, that students learn without making mistakes and incurring waste effort. By the spring of 1906 Ortega *understood* the difference between two kinds of German universities: those like Leipzig and Berlin, at which diverse specialists conglomerated, and those like the University of Marburg, at which a few men joined to form a "school."f The difference was pedagogical, for the scholarship of the men at both types was equally competent. At the conglomerate institutions, the faculty members agreed on few fundamentals and they made little effort to concert their influence on their students. At Marburg professors and students shared certain basic ideas and dedicated themselves to the investigation and elaboration of certain premises. There Ortega entered a true school of philosophy. His disagreement with its doctrines notwithstanding, his comprehension of what such an institution was had a lasting effect on his work as an educator.

---

[14]The phrase "my Nietzsche" is from "Cartas inéditas a Navarro Ledesma," Leipzig, May 16, 1905 (before Ortega studied with Simmel), *op. cit.*, p. 9. In "El sobre hombre," 1908, *Obras* I, pp. 91–5, Ortega relied on Simmel's interpretation of Nietzsche.

"From the inside," Ortega's encounter with idealism reflects the effects that two teachers had on the ripe student. One must do more than merely learn philosophy; one must undergo conversion to a philosophic way of life. This conversion took place for Ortega at Marburg. It was not a conversion to Marburg neo-Kantianism; it was a conversion occasioned by the Marburg neo-Kantians, and through this conversion Ortega found the intellectual integrity to accept without reserve his Spanish destiny. Until then Ortega was simply amassing more and more knowledge about philosophy; after this time Ortega was a man converted to the vocation of living by his philosophic knowledge.

Discipline and hope were the essential qualities that, as a teacher, Ortega tried to develop in his students; and it was these qualities that his teachers at Marburg inspired in him. In retrospect, he wrote of Marburg that "to it I owe a half, at least, of my hopes and almost all of my discipline."[15] Hermann Cohen, the senior figure among neo-Kantians, was the source of Ortega's discipline, and Paul Natorp, the second great teacher in the school, helped arouse many of Ortega's hopes. They helped Ortega form his mission.

When Ortega met him, Hermann Cohen was an elderly, convivial philosopher, then at the height of his fame.ᵍ Cohen had been nurtured in the Jewish tradition; he was appreciative of the classical Greeks and convinced that the philosopher's task was to carry on systematically, and in spirit, if not in letter, the critical philosophizing initiated by Kant. The relationship that developed between Cohen and Ortega does not fit the stereotype of the aloof German professor. Ortega frequently went to Cohen's house for long conversations in the course of which there was a mutual give and take between the slim student and his portly master.[16] Cohen became Ortega's guide and counselor, the teacher that the youth was seeking; and on returning from Germany Ortega would tell Spaniards that Cohen was "perhaps the greatest contemporary philosopher." Cohen had established his reputation with his *System der Philoso-*

---

[15]"Meditación del Escorial," 1915, *Obras* II, p. 558.

[16]Ortega described these conversations in "Estética en la tranvía," 1916, "Para la cultura del amor," 1917, and "Meditación del Escorial," 1915, *Obras* II, pp. 33, 142, and 559.

phie, a multi-volume work on logic, ethics, and esthetics; and it is tempting to try to use these volumes as a basis for explaining what Ortega might have found in his mentor's teaching that would eventually contribute to the development of his own views. But that undertaking would be an unproductive distraction, for teachers, especially teachers of philosophy, properly influence their students by putting questions, rather than by providing doctrines. We should, therefore leave to another occasion the interesting task of tracing the great web of doctrinal influences that make up post-Kantian humanism; here let us concentrate on the questions and problems that Cohen put to Ortega.

Cohen made Ortega contend with the problem of competence in philosophy. By what standard should a philosopher measure the adequacy of his work? Is a philosopher competent when he proves to be unassailable, having rid his work of every possible ambiguity, perhaps at the price of removing its human significance as well? Or, in contrast, is he competent when he provides a complete, perhaps flawed, system that will attempt to establish intellectual standards applicable to all possiblle human problems? In short, is philosophy a disinterested analysis or a normative system? Should the philosopher know, or should he educate? To see how these questions were put, and to understand the kind of answers Cohen suggested, it is best to study the man—Cohen, the philosopher—not his philosophy.

Germany had attracted Ortega because of its reputation for erudition; he wanted an intellectual life that was more substantial than the one Spain offered. It was this substantiality that Cohen incarnated and communicated. He was a true scholar: man thinking. He could pose a basic question, propose a thesis resolving it, and develop that thesis through its implications by systematically and carefully contending with the ideas of those who had previously thought about the problem. Here is the first point that Cohen put across: competence is achieved not in preparing to be measured by one's peers, but in taking the measure of one's predecessors. This obligation to respect past achievements, to find them worthy of being dealt with seriously, was brought home to Ortega by an incident with Cohen that Ortega never forgot. When Cohen was midway through the composition of his two volume treatise on esthetics, he stopped work for several weeks in order to study *Don Quixote* simply because a conversational remark Ortega had made about Cervantes suggested to Cohen that one of his esthetic propositions was not adequate to deal with such a work.h Here was a teacher who embodied the ideal of thoroughness; and Cohen managed to convey his scholarly standards to his students without turning them into pedants.

Eventually, Ortega criticized neo-Kantianism for having too narrow interests, but it was fortunate that in his youth he had to contend with a man such as Cohen.[17] Cohen imparted to his students the realization that the intricacies of Plato and Kant were important for contemporary European thought—and by "thought" one means not only technical philosophy, but the cultural life of Europe. It was no accident that three of Cohen's students—Nicolai Hartmann, Ernst Cassirer, and Ortega—were among the more competent, systematic thinkers of their time: they had been forced to grapple with their predecessors. In appreciation, Ortega recorded that Cohen "obliged us to make intimate contact with difficult philosophy and, above all, renovated the impulse towards system, which is the essence of philosophic inspiration."[18] Cohen's real achievement was to make the impulse towards system into a deep, personal concern for Ortega.

We touch here on an essential feature of Ortega's philosophic conversion. It was not, to repeat, a conversion to a particular dogma or principle, but to philosophy as a human enterprise. What was the vital significance of a cherubic professor who spent his life composing multi-volume treatises on reason? Why would a youth be inspired by a man who was willing to stop work to check his whole argument because of a chance remark? What was Cohen doing that began to seem profoundly important to Ortega? What was this "impulse towards system" that Ortega began to recognize as "the essence of philosophic inspiration"?

Those who "do philosophy," as some laboriously say, have difficulty appreciating the power and significance of the impulse

[17]See esp. *Prólogo para alemanes*, 1933, 1958, *Obras* VIII, pp. 26–42.
[18]*Ibid.*, p. 27.

towards system. As philosophy turned analytic, it turned in upon itself and became obsessed with the so-called problems of philosophy.i The history of philosophy ceased to have any interest except insofar as it could be pillaged for interesting problems. The most discussed problems concerned whether any possible proposition could actually meet the standards established by the ideal of truth and thus could merit the encomium "knowledge." Men *do* philosophy by analyzing such problems, hoping to win recognition from others who are also content to live by *doing* philosophy. The favored analysis is to show that the so-called problem is simply a question badly put that resulted from a failure to understand the limits of language. Presumably, the impulse towards analysis will terminate when all the problems of philosophy have been solved: on that millennial date philosophers will have nothing more to do and the activity initiated by Thales will become an historical relic, a monument to primitive man's propensity to make life hard for himself. But until that silent hour when, following what Wittgenstein advised, but did not practice, men say only what can be said clearly and pass over in silence all the rest, the problems of philosophy will be a great sport.[19] Although useless to the many who are caught in the affairs of the world and must therefore stand off as spectators, the impulse towards analysis is, as Bertrand Russell eloquently explained, a glorious recreation, the highest good for those who have the time and taste to do it.[20]

Rather than turn philosophy in upon itself, the impulse towards system turns philosophy outward into the community. Systematic philosophers are concerned less with the problems *of* philosophy than they are with those of reason and of man. The problem *for* philosophy has been to help man do what he truly intends, and the philosopher's contribution has been to create reason, to discover mind. We are still burdened with the incubus of faculty psychology and insist on thinking of reason as a mental faculty which is either inborn or non-existent, and which through discipline can be strengthened and exercised. In the systematic tradition, how-

[19]See Ludwig Wittgenstein, *Tractatus Logico-Philosophicus*, esp. p. 3 and the sections on language.

[20]See Bertrand Russell, *The Problems of Philosophy*, pp. 153–161.

ever, reason is recognized as a cultural creation, at first a mere seed that needs to be implanted and then carefully nurtured. The thinking faculty, if we must use the term, has to be shaped into some particular form before it is of any use in living life, and it can be shaped into several types of reason—pure, practical, esthetic, historical, dialectical, mythical,—by systematizing the ways men can effectively reflect on various types of problems that arise in their lives. Epistemology, understood as the critique of reason, is fundamental to all ensuing enquiries, including the more restricted, analytic epistemology that consists in the critique of knowledge. Thus, when Bertrand Russell began to survey the problems of philosophy by asking "Is there any knowledge in the world which is so certain that no *reasonable* man could doubt it?", he unwittingly attested to the prior need to make a critique of reason; for without a standard by which one can determine who is and is not a reasonable man, there will be no way to evaluate answers to the problems of philosophy or, for that matter, to any other set of difficulties.[21]

Reason is the cultural artifact that men have created to answer the myriad of questions that occur to them; and the philosophers' first duty has been to maintain and perfect this supremely productive tool that originates in wonder, in the recognition that on certain occasions men could neither speak clearly nor tolerate silence.[j] Make no mistake, it was not a problem of philosophy, but the fear that Hume's skepticism would render reason useless to men, that roused Kant from his dogmatic slumber.[22] A desire to live by reason motivates the impulse towards system, which is, in essence, an impulse towards making reason a more effective implement for the conduct of those activities that thought must guide. The fantastic superstructure of human activities has come into being only as men have, through fantasy and speculation, developed the intellectual powers that direct these endeavors; and through philosophy men have laid down for themselves the marvelous variety of imperfect rational rules by which they live. The impulse towards analysis draws its strength from the realization that philosophy is the ulti-

---

[21]*Ibid.*, p. 7.

[22]See Kant, *Critique of Pure Reason*, Part II, Chapter 1, Section 2, p. A745; and *Prolegomena to Any Future Metaphysics*, "Introduction," esp. p. 260.

mate adjudicator in human life; but the impulse towards system gets its vigor from the recognition that philosophy is even more fundamentally the ultimate legislator in any human community. Hence, a systematic philosophy is an imperfect, normative theory of how reason should be used to deal with various human problems; epistemology, in its proper sense, is not only a science, but the basis of one or another way of life. By means of systematic philosophy, men create a mental framework within which they can pursue their sundry activities and harmonize their divergent efforts by seeking in them a common purpose.

Many persons, however, distrust systematic philosophy. Ours is not the best of all possible worlds, and systematic philosophy has caused, as well as solved, human problems. Hermann Cohen himself discussed, not without some sympathy, the supposed relation between Kantian thought and German militarism.[23] But, goaded by wartime Germanophobia, American and English critics of systematic philosophy have ignored the real alternatives.[k] To be sure, the preceptive philosophies that helped generate the Renaissance and Reformation, industrialism, the American and French revolutions, and the German state did not function perfectly; they sanctioned intemperate and unjust deeds. But one cannot avoid these imperfections by ignoring normative reason altogether. Whether it is admitted or not, all policies will be based on value judgments and standards of rationality, for one cannot act without existentially affirming the worth of one's ends and the principles that legitimate one's means. Men are free to make these judgements on the basis of either principle or interest; but without a normative theory of reason, there will be no principles for men to affirm freely, and by default justice will quickly become the interest of the strongest party. This reign of interest is precisely the nihilism predicted by those who foresaw that in the twentieth century systematic philosophy would cease to influence men, and the scepter of force has not stood for a particularly stable, humane reign.[l] Thus, so far the critics of systematic philosophy have yet to take into account the consequences of going without systematic philosophy, and recent history does not help their argument. Since normative philosophizing

---

[23]Cohen, "Kantische Gedanken in deutschen Militarismus," in Hermann Cohen, *Schriften zur Philosophie und Zeitgeschichte*, Vol. II, pp. 347–354.

has ceased to be the ground for evaluation of public policy, unprecedented injustices have been sanctioned by the ideologies that replaced systematic philosophy as the standard of practical reason.

As Ortega so often said, the only real way to correct the abuse of an idea or institution is to see to its proper use. This stricture holds true for the impulse towards system. The real causes of the events that the critics of systematic philosophy hoped to avoid were not the rational standards that had been established, but the imperfections in the way men use these standards. By deprivng the true, the beautful, and good of philosophic authority, we make it easier to accord a bogus, scientific authority to less elevating ideals such as the nation, the race, and the class. Furthermore, the seemingly scientific sanction renders these lesser ideals impervious to reason, for men cannot discuss, they can only fight, over judgments disguised as facts. The situation is serious. Ever since World War I, diplomats and publicists have been droning on about the need to find a basis for an enduring peace; but it is simple realism, not pessimism, to point out that it will all be wasted rhetoric unless a single power achieves world hegemony or unless men recreate a philosophic system that has enough prestige to function as a useful, albeit imperfect, implement for the principled harmonization of conflicting aims and interests. Of these two improbable alternatives, the latter seems preferable and more possible.

Cohen awakened in Ortega an impulse towards system, an impulse towards uncovering the principles by which men can live well. Such philosophic systematization is not to be scorned; it may be drudgery, but it is also the precondition of intelligent public leadership. Within the unity of an ideal, conceptual system, men have developed the concord that enables them to tolerate diversity in their practical activities. In effect, then, the discipline that Cohen imparted to Ortega was based on an appreciation of the proper place of principle in public affairs. For Cohen, a philosophic system was a powerful discipline, a willingness to proceed in various matters in accord with fundamental principles. He began with the rich complexity of activities that men perform, and from those facts he tried to go back to the basic principles that were implicit in the activities and that enabled men to create and shape these activities consciously. These principles were to be systematized in a coherent, rational order; and this rigor in the world of speculative thinking was sought, not to confine the world of living actuality in ever-narrowing bonds, but to sustain without self-destructive conflict an ever-growing complexity of vital experience. As men learned to use the principles of systematic philosophy more and more effectively to make their deeds fulfill their intentions, the practical activities that were informed by the principles would be better consummated: more men could do more things without working at cross purposes. In this way speculative philosophy can accomplish a worldly mission. The basis for both Ortega's conception of Europeanization and the importance accorded in it to the mastery of conceptual rigor, of disciplined intellection, is in this impulse towards system.

Note, however, that a teacher who awakens an impulse must forgo the pleasure of satisfying it as well. It was discipline, not discipleship, that Ortega received from Cohen; hence, rather than adopting the latter's system, Ortega learned the importance of developing one himself. Many thinkers, including Cohen, influenced the development of Ortega's principles, but one man did much to give these their characteristic spirit. As Hermann Cohen was responsible for most of Ortega's discipline, Paul Natorp was the source of many of Ortega's hopes. Natorp taught a version of idealism that Ortega transformed into his personal pedagogical commitment.

In the drama of Ortega's life, it was fortunate that he encountered Paul Natorp. To be sure, when mature, Ortega would find Dilthey far more significant than Natorp. But a teacher usually does not influence students in the same way that a philosophic writer does. A writer influences slowly as his works sit close at hand on the shelves of students; and as students continually refer to these, the works become more and more intimately mastered. A teacher, in contrast, influences more rapidly as students accord him a serious authority for a limited time. In any particular encounter, it is a matter of readiness whether the teacher influences at all: in 1905 Ortega probably would not have benefited greatly from Dilthey's teaching had the two met in Berlin; but in 1906 Ortega was ready for Natorp's influence, which acted as an intellectual catalyst.

For over a year Ortega had been reading voraciously whatever struck his interest, but he had not given much thought to the principles that might unify this rapidly accumulating erudition. Cohen pointed out the necessity of such principles. Natorp did too; and in addition, he taught a version of idealism that provoked the young Spaniard to create a philosophic system although Natorp's idealism did not, itself, become a part of Ortega's system.m Certain elements of Natorp's doctrine repelled Ortega;[24] but Natorp nevertheless helped Ortega discover an organizing idea in his varied reading and showed him how he might use this idea to improve Spanish culture. In no sense did Ortega become a disciple of Natorp; at the most, the latter briefly fulfilled Ortega's ideal of a good teacher, and as such a teacher Natorp exerted an essential influence on Ortega's life.

In a letter to Navarro Ledesma, Ortega described the true teacher, whom he had failed to find in Spain and whom he hoped to meet in Germany. Ortega thought that young men matured best by pressing against well-formed ideas. He likened a teacher to the wall of a dam against which the powers of a student accumulated until they finally crested it and issued in a controlled overflow. Without such resistance, the young would exhaust themselves with "infertile license." A teacher had to confront his students with developed ideas and challenge the young to improve on these. "The formation of the intellect requires a period of cultivation in which artificial means are used: hence, morality and discipline. Those who did not, at twenty, believe in a moral system, and who did not stretch and compress themselves into a hierarchy, will be for the rest of their days vague and fumbling creatures who will be incapable of putting three ideas in order." True education, Ortega continued, was like a chemical crystallization in which a bit of crystal had to be introduced into a solution and around this seed a much larger crystal would grow.[25]

A year after writing this description, Ortega found such a teacher when he took Paul Natorp's course on psychology and pedagogy. The neo-Kantian confronted Ortega with a moral system of which education was the fundamental feature. Moreover, Natorp

---

[24]Ortega particularly criticized Natorp's treatment of Plato: see "Prólogo a *Historia de la filosofía* de Emile Bréhier," 1942, *Obras* VI, p. 383, n. 2; and *Prólogo para alemanes*, 1933, 1958, *Obras* VIII, pp. 35–6.

[25]"Cartas inéditas a Navarro Ledesma," Leipzig, May 28, 1905, *Cuadernos*, November 1961, pp. 12–4.

confronted Ortega with a powerful, pedagogical presence; and before describing the remarkable features of psychology and pedagogy as they were understood by Natorp, it is important to reconstruct his probable character as a teacher.

Natorp was a serious soul. He had carefully worked out his theories, and on the grounds that he chose, his presentment was powerful and persuasive. Furthermore, Natorp had sufficient self-confidence to make his students contend with his ideas. Despite this confidence, however, he lacked the pretense that emasculates many educational theorists: Natorp knew Plato, Kant, and Pestalozzi and he spoke about them with authority; but he did not pretend, in addition, to be able to place all other philosophical writers in appropriate cubbyholes. In his teaching, Natorp combined solidity and sincerity; what he spoke and wrote had a definiteness that bordered on dogmatism and a humility that exposed the limits of his knowledge. This combination of qualities enabled him to have a catalytic effect on Ortega. What Natorp proclaimed about Plato, Kant, and Pestalozzi, Ortega immediately recognized to be true of the writers that he knew best: Fichte, Renan, and Nietzsche.[n] Hence, Natorp's virtue as a teacher was courage; he knew there was nothing to fear in exposing his deepest thoughts to critical students. Thus, he explained his thought rigorously and made no effort to hide the fact that his ideas were based on a limited examination of an inexhaustible tradition. By revealing his imperfections without apology, Natorp forced his students to look to the problem at issue, rather than to his answer to it, and he made them rely on themselves for authority, rather than on their teacher. The effect of this teaching on Ortega's life was fundamental, even though, in his subjective vision, Ortega may not have fully realized it.

One of the worst acts of cultural hubris is to forget men of merit. Forgetfulness is tantamount to the inability to keep a matter in mind, and when the matter had merit, it means that the forgetful have lost their sensibility for that particular human strength. American educational theorists have forgotten—more exactly, they never really discovered—Paul Natorp.[o] Our ignorance of Natorp is symptomatic of our inability to appreciate sound philosophic speculation about the problems of education. For Natorp, education did not merely deserve the second effort of philosophers; it was not to be taken up only after thinkers had exhausted themselves in ontology and epistemology. On the contrary, education was the heart of the matter.

Natorp's main interest was the crux of any theory of reason: the relation of the fictional world of thought to the factual world of things. The Parmenidean would deny the latter in order to secure the former: there is nothing but the One—eternal, unchanging, perfect. The materialist, in contrast, would reduce the former to the latter, making thought a function of its material basis and thus gaining a solid footing by renouncing his freedom of mind. Neither extreme attracted Natorp. He accepted both thought and things, and contended that any relation between the two depended on the will of man. His was the simple, fundamental, and humanistic solution to the mind-body problem.

For all their praise of analytic powers, contemporary critics of the concept of mind have made a serious analytic error. The relation of thought and things is an insoluble paradox only for those who try to give referents of one or both of the terms a status independent of man.[26] According to a neo-Kantian like Natorp, there was no way to know things-in-themselves, and consequently there could be no relation between thought and things in this sense. What other point was there to Kant's *Critique of Pure Reason?* For man, material reality was the phenomenal world with which he interacted, and conceptual reality was the ideal, hypothetical, conventional world that man created by means of his intellect. Any relation between these two worlds depends on man's will; and

---

[26]Following his arch-opponent, Descartes, Gilbert Ryle committed this mistake in *The Concept of Mind.* Few besides Descartes—and one may doubt whether in fact Descartes did—maintained what Ryle called "The Official Doctrine" of Mind, that somehow an ideal system of thoughts, a mind, is contained in a real, physical mechanism, a body. Ryle attributes a different mode of being to mind and to body and then asks how these different things can possibly be joined. Most other thinkers have escaped the absurdity of this question by either an idealistic or a materialistic reduction in which mind and body are first shown to have the same mode of being, whereupon a connection between them becomes possible. Natorp began from the idealistic position: all bodies of which there is any empirical evidence are phenomenal.

most of our words denoting character—courageous, just, rational, provincial, liberal, opportunistic, matter-of-fact, dogmatic, hypocritical, capricious, fanciful, hedonistic, imaginative, and so on—denote various ways in which men willfully relate their thought to their phenomenal existence. The mind-body problem was significant, therefore, not so much as a question of epistemology, but as an opportunity for the education of character.

Reflection should show that this statement is not as outrageous as it may at first appear. Remember that we are dealing with systematic philosophies. Natorp, like Cohen, believed that the philosopher was responsible for creating, preserving, and perfecting rational standards that would make the solution of human problems more effective. Reason is not the same as technical knowledge. The various sciences create means for solving this or that particular problem, whereas philosophy establishes ways for dealing with various types of problems—scientific, ethical, esthetic, and so on. To have the greatest human use, the special knowledge of the various sciences should be stored until the particular situation to which it pertains arises. But, in contrast, if the general rational capacities developed by systematic philosophy are to have much benefit for man, they need to become common skills by means of which diverse persons react to the daily situations of life. Hence, besides creating a cogent system of thought, the systematic philosopher had, in one way or another, to disseminate the powers he had thus created.

This insistence on the educational responsibilities of the philosopher, which goes back to Plato, may seem inconsistent with the tendency of systematic philosophers to produce impossibly difficult tomes. Certain systematic philosophers have been seriously amiss in not providing means for making their teachings accessible. But it would be silly to think that the philosopher's duty to educate people in the use of reason is tantamount to the demand that *The Critique of Pure Reason* should be rewritten so as to be suitable for use as an elementary school text. Men develop their rational powers by practicing with many different procedures and problems; reason is not a neat and narrow system. The philosopher's goal—and it is this goal that makes difficult tomes often necessary—is to establish principles that approximate the first principle, the principle that is common to all human endeavors; and the philosopher seeks this first principle, not to reduce all variety to its single mold, but because by means of it the sum total of educating influences might be so concerted that these influences would less frequently cancel themselves out in random conflict and would continually conduce to the fuller, more effective use of reason on the part of all. To carry through this aspiration, the philosopher must devote himself to a great many concerns, fully as many as Plato integrated into his seminal treatise, the *Republic*, in which he first set forth both the epistemological and the educational missions of systematic philosophy.[27] We shall have to leave for another occasion the further examination of the educational responsibilities of the philosopher. Here let us simply recognize that they exist and examine the consequences of their existence that interested Paul Natorp, and after him, Ortega.

In the *Republic*, Socrates observed that "it would be silly, I think, to make laws [concerning behavior]; such habits cannot be established or kept up by written legislation. It is probable, at any rate, that the bent given by education will determine the quality of later life, by that sort of attraction which like things always have for one another, till they finally mount up to one imposing result, whether for good or ill."[28] From this conviction, which Natorp fully shared with Plato, the theory of civic pedagogy followed. As a determinant of the quality of life, legislation was secondary in comparison to education. Natorp produced a series of books and essays on civic pedagogy. According to Natorp, the way in which men applied their intelligence to their experience was shaped by the fundamental ideas, conceived in a rather Platonic way, that defined men's aspirations. The quality of a man's life depended on his character, and the quality of life in a community depended on the civic character of its members. The important reforms that could be made in a community were improvements in the prevalent patterns of character education.[29] These reforms would start with the final stage of such education, that of the "free self," with the

---

[27]See Plato, *Republic*, esp. 472A–541B.
[28]*Ibid.*, 425C, Cornford, trans.
[29]Natorp, *Sozialpädagogik*, pp. 99–389.

personal formation to which men continually subject themselves. As men changed themselves, reform would work back through the school and into the home, for changed teachers and parents would display stronger character to their pupils and children. Natorp was radical and thorough. He used many branches of systematic philosophy to elucidate such reforms: logic, epistemology, ethics, and esthetics were the basis of his civic pedagogy; and the philosophies of religion, history, law, and science filled it out with humanitarian content.[30] His vision of pedagogical reform was a major contribution to the most curious of the Marburg movements, neo-Kantian Marxism.[31]

Ortega followed Natorp's arguments in his speech to "El Sitio" in 1910. Ortega's idealistic socialism, his belief in the political significance of pedagogy, and his conviction that systematic philosophy was the backbone of any enduring reform all took shape at Marburg. In retrospect, Natorp's teaching affected Ortega in two ways.

First, as has been suggested, Natorp's system helped Ortega find an organizing idea in his varied studies. Even in his most systematic writings, Natorp claimed little originality: his theory of civic pedagogy was neither more nor less than the essence of idealism rightly understood. Ortega perceived the significance of such teaching; writing to Unamuno, Ortega conceded a slight disappointment: Natorp had been heralded as a great, original thinker, but was really an original interpreter and critic. "It is clear that this is no mean achievement."[32] Natorp would have agreed. In a major book and several essays he painstakingly showed how the bases of his theories were to be found in Plato.[33] His historical studies of Pestalozzi showed that the Swiss reformer was not to be thought of primarily as a sentimental humanizer of instructional methods; Pestalozzi was a radical who thought that the only way to attain

---

[30]*Ibid., passim,* and *Sozialidealismus,* pp. 167–199.

[31]*Ibid.,* and Karl Vorländer, *Kant und Marx,* esp. pp. 122-140.

[32]Marburg, January 27, 1907, *Revista de Occidente,* October 1964, p. 12.

[33]Natorp, *Platos Ideenlehre, passim,* and *Gesammelte Abhandlungen,* pp. 7–42.

the ideals of the French Revolution was through the education of character.[34] Although Ortega read Plato with care, he never took to Pestalozzi. But what was important was not Ortega's chance to adopt Natorp's valuations. Natorp's studies, historical and philosophical, did not provide Ortega with ready-made interpretations of significant thinkers; they suggested to him an interpretative principle, namely that the whole philosophical tradition could be used to illuminate civic pedagogy. Thereafter, we find Ortega using, in his own, more subtle, more profound way, the idea of civic pedagogy as a principle for criticizing diverse men, ideas, and institutions. Thus, in response to Natorp, Ortega became aware of the hidden unity in his varied interests.

Second, this interpretative principle helped Ortega understand his personal aspirations so well that he developed a deep sense of mission, which was the secret of his genius. A young Spaniard who went to Germany in disgust over the cultural decadence of his nation, who hoped vaguely to find a means for improving the intellect of his people, suddenly found a vocation in the idea of civic pedagogy. The Spanish problem was one of character: a lack of intellectual discipline, an insensitivity to the usefulness of ideas for life, and a failure to appreciate the value of modulating the swings of passion with stable principles. Sustained by hope, Ortega had read and wandered, amassing much learning, but not enough understanding. Thus, he had been, in the fullest sense, ready to hear Paul Natorp explain an educational theory for the deliberate transformation of social characteristics, and on hearing such a theory, a catalytic reaction had occurred in Ortega. When he said that he owed almost half his hopes to Marburg, Ortega paid tribute to the theory that so naturally mediated between himself and his circumstances. It enabled him to clarify the vague, educational aspirations with which he had gone to Germany.

*   *   *

Discipline and hope—systematic philosophy and civic pedagogy— these were the concerns through which Ortega prepared himself to become the *Praeceptor Hispania*. In his German studies, Ortega

---

[34]*Ibid.*, pp. 91–236, and *Der Idealismus Pestalozzis*.

realized that he had to return to Spain and use every means he could to rebuild the intellectual life of his country. He had opened himself to the influence of a tradition that, from beginning to end, commended the life of a philosopher-king, a civic pedagogue, a lawgiver, as the way of duty. Ortega was already disposed to such a life, and in Germany he was unreservedly converted to seeking to live it.

Thus, after a long, erratic search, having finally found his teachers, Ortega realized that he could commit himself neither to them nor to their lessons. He could commit himself only to his idea of what Spain could and should become, for the stimulus of his studies enabled him finally to formulate this idea effectively. In the end, this vision of Spain proved to have been the beloved object that had drawn him on his quest. "To love a thing is to be determined that it should exist. It is to deny, insofar as it depends on oneself, the possibility of a universe in which the object is absent. Note that this argument amounts to giving life, continually and intentionally, to the thing insofar as it depends on oneself. To love is the perennial vivification of the loved one."[35]

Ortega loved "vital Spain," and in Germany he resolved to use whatever means he could to vivify this object of his love. This single mission led him into many activities, into teaching, writing, publishing, and politics. With respect to each of these professions, let us examine his hopes and achievements, his methods and disappointments.

*　　*　　*

It is wise to listen, not to me, but to the Word, and to confess that all things are one.

HERACLITUS, 50

---

[35]"Facciones del amor," 1926, *Obras* V, p. 559.

*F*OR US, THEREFORE, *our first duty is to foment the organization of a minority charged with the political education of the masses. It is of no use to push Spain towards any appreciable improvement unless the workers in the city, the peasants in the fields, and the middle class in the county seat and the capital have not learned on the one hand how to impose the rough will of their genuine desires upon authority, and on the other how to desire a clear, concrete, and dignified future. The true national education is this political education that simultaneously cultivates the impulse and the intellect.*

ORTEGA[1]

---

[1]"Prospecto de la 'Liga de Educación Política Española'," 1914, *Obras* I, p. 302. Ortega's italics in the first sentence have been omitted.

III
Programs

ERRANT MAN has repeatedly realized that he has been distracted
from his purpose because formalized thoughts and ritualized
acts conspire with his natural torpor to betray his aspirations. Early
in the twentieth century, Spanish intellectuals realized that this was
Spain's condition. They knew—just as following the Great War
their counterparts throughout Europe would know—that the shib-
boleths of the nineteenth century stood for nothing. A call for
renovation disrupted Restoration complacency; the critics believed
that a renovated national life had to be achieved without recourse
to the corrupt practices of traditional politics. In discussing the
possible sources of renovation, Unamuno stated the outlook of the
major reformers: "From politics no one expects anything. . . ."[2]
Reform without reliance on practical politics was the goal of the
Generation of '98.

Consequently, although they did not say so, the basic activity
of Ortega's models and teachers was civic pedagogy as a political
program.[3] The reformers were men in search of a vision of what
Spain could and should become and of the means suitable for
launching themselves in the direction of that ideal. Thus, Pedro

---

[2]Miguel de Unamuno, "Renovación," 1898, *Obras* III, p. 687.

[3]Ortega (b. 1883), Eugenio D'Ors (b. 1882) and Gregario Marañón (b. 1887)
are generally not classed in the Generation of '98, for they were still in their
fromative years when Spain lost its empire. Members of the Generation of '98
were educated during the Restoration but achieved their first major public
success after 1898 and as critics of the Restoration. Among them were Ganivet
(b. 1865), Unamuno (b. 1864), Baroja (b. 1872), Azorín (b. 1874), Antonio
Machado (b. 1875), Manuel Machado (b. 1874), Maetzu (b. 1875), Menéndez
Pidal (b. 1869), and Valle-Inclán (b. 1866).

Laín Entralgo opened his history of the Generation of '98 with a chapter on "a country and its inventors."[4] Ortega's precocity was to seize early and explicitly on the fact that Spanish renovation was an educational problem.[a] In 1905 Ortega went to Germany with this conviction dimly formed and he returned two years later with it considerably matured, for he had studied similar theories in Plato, Rousseau, Fichte, Pestalozzi, and Nietzsche, and he had listened closely to explanations of civic pedagogy by his teacher, Paul Natorp. Ortega's prominence within the movement for Spanish reform resulted from his pedagogical awareness. He drew out the positive consequences that followed from the rejection of practical politics, and he became the first of the bourgeois gentlemen to realize that pedagogy was his profession.

*　　*　　*

No historian has shown more effectively than Salvador de Madariaga how the reform movement split into two tendencies, one which proclaimed that salvation would be achieved by the cultivation of the essential Spanish character and another which contended that renovation would require the mastery of European science and philosophy. Angel Ganivet and Joaquín Costa initiated this split between Hispanicization and Europeanization, and, as Madariaga says, Unamuno and Ortega "were destined to take over the dialogue . . . and drive it into the Spanish conscience."[5] Care is necessary, however, not to overdo the superficial contrasts between the two outlooks, for in doing so their essential differences are obscured. When set in opposition, the two views appear to be conflicting ideologies; and, by virtue of a common willingness to sacrifice the person to the cause, there are few things that are more fundamentally alike than conflicting ideologies.

Neither Unamuno nor Ortega would accept the implication that often results from comparisons of Hispanicization and Europeanization, namely that two different visions of Spain's destiny were at stake. For example, as Madariaga wrote: "the first mood of the generation is . . . fiercely negative and critical. Nothing. There is

---

[4]Laín Entralgo, *España como problema*, pp. 353–367.
[5]Madariaga, *Spain*, pp. 88–96; the quotation is from p. 90.

nothing but sham and hollowness. We must begin afresh. And then, as soon as the new men turn their faces toward the morrow, the split occurs. . . . Spaniards broke asunder as to their estimate of what New Spain was to be. Some of them, with Costa and with Ortega, carried forward their European position; we must, they said, make Spain a European people; others, with Ganivet and Unamuno, hesitated to accept all that Europe means. . . ."[6] But Spain's potential future was not that well defined. Unlike European revolutionaries, Spanish reformers were not persuaded that they knew what path history would inevitably take; they simply agreed that Spanish history ought not to continue on the path it had followed for the past century. In the early 1900's few had given a detailed description of the characteristics that would mark a renovated Spain. Joaquín Costa was the reformer who came the closest to having a program, but Ortega thought that this program was too superficial, for it ignored certain difficult fundamentals.

Hispanicizers and Europeanizers did not diverge over their vision of the good life. Allowing for differences of temperament and for occasional clashes of rhetoric, there was a remarkable similarity between the reformed Spain depicted by Unamuno and by Ortega. Neither was extremely precise; and since both dealt with the Spanish future while writing for the daily press, their views were at times parochial. Moreover, in writing about the substance of desirable reforms, they showed many points in common. In politics and economics the two were receptive to socialist and federalist ideas; both favored a more effective political system that would be responsive to the popular will without necessarily following the familiar forms of parliamentarianism, and both desired a much stronger economy with a more egalitarian distribution of the national product. Furthermore, they shared many cultural goals: better and wider popular education, especially on the primary level, and a university system that avoided the twin pitfalls of pedantry and dilettantism; the preservation of traditional Spanish virtues and the avoidance of materialism; the establishment of a cultural commonwealth with other Spanish speaking countries, especially Argentina; and dominion over separatism by making Castile again

---

[6]*Ibid.*, p. 95.

worthy of its pre-eminence and again secure enough to grant sensible autonomy to restive regions. Unamuno, unlike Ortega, seriously considered the place of the church in the past, present, and future of Spain; but this point notwithstanding, the essential differences in their theories of reform were of another order.[b]

Change requires a stable element; for without a principle of order, change degenerates into chaos, a mere random flux. This matter of ordering principles is at once the most demanding, fragile creation of culture and the very motive force of history. The significant differences between Hispanicization and Europeanization will be found by reflecting on the historic function of such principles.

Principles, of course, are not real in a physical sense; they are ideals that men postulate in the realm of freedom. These ideals are not necessary causes of what in fact happens; they do not, like the force of gravity, act on all bodies endowed with physical mass in a fixed, predictable manner. Nevertheless, principles can be, and often are, contingent causes of human action. They can be causes because they can be the conceptual determinants of what men believe they ought to do; they are contingent because men are not mechanically compelled to act as they believe they ought. To what extent this contingent cause operates in history is the subject of long and lively discussion. Ortega was of that group that held principles to be decisive; he even held that the so-called material determinants of history are in fact contingent, working only as a result of the valuation by men reasonably assured of subsistence that material well-being was preferable to spiritual salvation, psychological peace, or rational contemplation.

Debate over the extent to which principles are operative in history need not be settled here. Prescience has been the gift of the great humanistic historians, particularly Tocqueville, Burckhardt, and Dilthey, because they attended to the principles that men professed in both word and deed.[c] They assumed that the character of reform, of both historical change and continuity, depended on the principles with which men informed their acts, on the aspirations by which men channeled their efforts. The achievements of these historians redeem Ortega's belief that principles are historically significant, for they show that his convictions can lead to worthy historical insight.

Recognition that principles are the basis of historic change and continuity also illuminates the problem of nihilism in modern experience. When men recognize that their opponents have principles, albeit ones that are different from their own, they recognize something independent of themselves and their opponents that can be reasonably discussed. A very different situation arises when men deny that their opponents have principles or assert that all principles are mere rationalizations for mechanically determined positions.d Reflecting on this situation, Nietzsche warned that "secret societies for the extermination of non-members and similar utilitarian creations will appear on the theater of the future"; for he understood that the European nihilist, shorn of the old ethic of good and evil and unable to create a new ethic of good and bad, would act on the sophistry that all is permitted, on the principle of unprincipledness.[7] Dostoevsky exposed similar contradictions among the Russian nihilists, who simultaneously denied all principles and still piously hoped to move men to reform by conjecturing a materialistic utopia for future generations. The completely unprincipled man denied himself the means with which he might have been able to convince doubters of the value of his goal, and consequently he could only use force to answer the childish, but profound, question "Why?"

In his *Reflections on Violence*, Georges Sorel showed how, without principles of order, all innovations depend on self-confirming myths with which form can be forcefully imposed upon change. Both revolutionary and reactionary nihilists arbitrarily depict a golden age and use it to batter reality into its shape, gaining for themselves the aura of world-historical men.[8] As soon as principles of order have been denied, there can be no discussion. The myth must reign over all, or all will collapse in anarchy. Hence, as Hannah Arendt has shown, ideologists have a penchant for terror, for they have no other means for resolving basic disagreements.[9] When unprincipled movements clash, each must try to suppress the myth

---

[7]The quotation is from Nietzsche, *The Use and Abuse of History*, Adrian Collins, trans., p. 61.

[8]See Georges Sorel, *Reflections on Violence*, T. E. Hulme and J. Roth, trans., esp. pp. 119–150.

[9]Hannah Arendt, "Ideology and Terror: A Novel Form of Government," reprinted in *The Origins of Totalitarianism*, 2nd. ed., pp. 460–479.

that supports the other; and to do so, terror is used to eradicate alien leaders and to intimidate their followers. Among other tragedies of our time, the Spanish Civil War exemplifies the cost of these clashes.

Hispanicization and Europeanization were not, however, conflicting ideologies, each guided by a myth of Spain's future and each forced to wage war on the other. On the contrary, both were principled theories of reform. Hence, the leaders of both groups could amiably and reasonably discuss their differences, and they slowly merged their theories through a rational synthesis of apparently conflicting principles. The differences between Hispanicization and Europeanization did not result from the destiny that each envisaged, but from the stable element that each chose from the present possibilities for use as a principle of order in the midst of change.

When men are moved by a desire for improvement, they may seek strength from two sources that are often called the romantic and the classic. A troubled man may look inward and ponder his personal self in a search for his proper destiny, or he may gaze outward and examine his surroundings in a quest there for a beneficent order. Contrary to unexamined opinion, these concerns are not exclusive of one another: they are Heraclitean opposites that together form the self and its circumstances.

Spanish complacency had been cracked during the War of 1898, and intellectual leaders who sought national improvement disagreed whether the best source for these improvements would be the Spanish literary and linguistic heritage or the European scientific and philosophic tradition. Certain leaders gave priority to contemplating the Spanish soul and others to emulating the European surroundings. Teachers are familiar with this divergence: should one teach children or subjects? Just as true teachers do both, just as great men are born from a tension between the romantic and the classic, the more effective reformers were at once Hispanicizers and Europeanizers. But they had to learn through mutual criticism— and here is their exemplary value for American educators—that the two sources of national reform were equally necessary, each for the other.

This is not the place to trace fully the dialectic of Spanish reform.e It will have to suffice to describe briefly the preliminary thesis of Europeanization and the antithesis of Hispanicization in order to show how, in 1914, Ortega promoted a Europeanizing synthesis of the two efforts through the League for Spanish Political Education.

Early proponents of Europeanization rejected the external characteristics of Spanish national life and tried to import the economic, social, political, and physical forms of contemporary Europe. The principle of Europeanization was not complicated: what was good for England, France, and Germany would be good for Spain. The hope that Spain's arid lands could be forested illustrates this principle: the effort to reclaim wasteland by planting trees reflected a desire to make Spain's climate and topography more like that of Northern Europe. The contemporary example of nations with temperate climates, rather than the historical example of the Western Caliphate, enabled the proponents of forestation to claim that trees would help to hold the soil and moisture and to temper the extremes of weather, that they would be a source of food and raw materials, and that they would even be a moderating influence on Spanish character.[10] Forestation promised a visible Europeanization.

But early Europeanizers knew Spain far better than they knew Europe. They were men with strong attachments to the Spanish tradition and with great hopes for the Spanish future. National defeat hurt them deeply and they turned, almost desperately, to what seemed an obvious alternative. They assumed, perhaps because they never thought it through, that the products of another civilization could be reproduced in Spain without the prior mastery of the culture that had made those products possible. Furthermore, they did not fully realize that if successful, the physical Europeanization of Spain might entail the radical transformation of Spanish traditions. Hence, like many current theories of modernization, Europeanization was materialistic and simplistic; it held that the one thing needful was to live according to the external, materialistic standard of more powerful civilizations.f Although Joaquín Costa was one of the great historians of the Spanish character and one of the most able students of Spanish legal traditions, his conception

---

[10]See D. Joaquín Costa Martinez, *El arbolado y la patria*, esp. pp. 1–19.

of Europeanization typically dealt with superficial matters. Hence, his thought presents us with a few particulars. He said that to have power and wealth the European nations had expanded their navies and merchant marine, and therefore Spain should do so. He said that to have a disciplined, competent population the European nations had developed effective, practical school systems, and therefore Spain should do so. He said that to benefit from new possibilities the industrial nations had encouraged productive investment and the rationalization of agriculture, and therefore Spain should do so. He said that to free human energies the democratic nations had revolutionized the monarchic social and administrative structure, and therefore Spain should do so too. He said that throughout Europe disorganized peoples had united under firm governments based on effective communications, and therefore Spain should do so too. But could Spain do so? That was another question.ᵍ

Costa was not sanguine, for a specter was haunting Europeanization—the specter of Spain. Industry, foreign trade, scientific agriculture, forestation, impersonal administration, democracy and socialism: these were not possibilities that could be realized by a sole reliance on human and technical engineering. Developmental economists, who pride themselves on their empirical prowess, should note the fact that almost seventy years after the inception of Spanish forestation, the program is still in an incipient stage, not because of Spain's intemperate climate, but because of the Spaniard's intemperate character. As Ortega observed, "Castile is so terribly arid because the Castilian man is arid."[11] Any program of national reform had to come to terms with the nation to be reformed. Here was the principle of Hispanicization.

An oversimplified conception of Europeanization engendered a sharp, well-grounded reaction. Critics observed that their tradition was not uniformly debilitated and out-moded; there were still valuable qualities in the Spanish character. Through a process of reform,

---

[11]"Temas de viaje," 1922, *Obras* II, p. 373. Raymond Carr, *Spain*, pp. 425–6, makes some interesting observations about the difficulty of forestation that results from the peasants' hatred of trees and indifference to nature.

these values were to be preserved, enhanced, and even projected into Europe.[12]

Traditionally, the Spaniard had excelled in the realm of the spirit. The Spanish ideal was a man of courage, faith, and pride; he could die with dignity, having lived with passion. The Reconquest and the Empire had been won by virtue of spiritual power, and the genius of Spanish literature was its profound appreciation of human character. El Cid and Cervantes, the religious mystics and the Conquistadors were human types that were of enduring value. The renovation of Spain would be destructive if it effaced the traditions of these men.

Hispanicizers were not content, however, simply to reaffirm their faith in the Spanish tradition. They, too, believed that Spain needed renovation. Unamuno and others envisaged improvements in the external characteristics of Spanish life that were not very different from those depicted by Europeanizers; but Unamuno insisted that the traditional virtues must not be sacrificed to make way for materialism. He knew Europe better than the Europeanizers did.[h]

Unamuno said that he had begun to learn Danish in order to read Ibsen and he mastered it in order to read Kierkegaard. Only those who had experienced the spiritual struggles of the latter could appreciate the drama of the former. Nor did he think it imperative that Ibsen be performed, for he doubted that an audience could be found anywhere in Europe that could respond to the work.[13] Such observations raised doubts in Unamuno about the wisdom of Europeanization. However resplendent European civilization might appear, Unamuno believed its culture was not sound. The dominant European nations had allowed their capacity for spiritual transcendence to decline, and in its place they had cultivated a material-

---

[12]Chronologically, both the idea of Europeanization and the theories in opposition to it had been worked out well before 1898. See for instance, Unamuno, *En torno al casticismo*, 1895, *Obras* I, pp. 775–869. The defeat of 1898 did not cause either Europeanization or Hispanicization; it simply gave prominence to the two views, both of which had their origins much earlier in Spanish history.

[13]Unamuno, "Ibsen y Kierkegaard," 1907, *Obras* III, p. 289. In his text Unamuno described Ibsen as a Norwegian, but said that he learned Danish to translate Ibsen. As written languages, Danish and Norwegian are very similar and sometimes even called Norwego-Danish.

istic view of life, vying with each other for the preponderant command of physical force. Unchecked materialism would bring destruction. If Spain followed the rest of Europe along such a course, it would be at a serious disadvantage in a doomed competition. Better alternatives were at hand.

What Unamuno called "Regeneration, in truth" entailed no copying of others. Intrinsically, Spain was healthy. But, for too long the state had repressed the inherent genius of the people by imposing constrictions on the effort, communication, and thought of its citizens. Even before the defeat of 1898, Unamuno had formed the basic distinction between a stagnant and a dynamic confidence in Spanish mores. Restoration leaders had had an unfounded belief in the absolute validity of Spanish customs; they *knew* that the external forms of their life were correct. This belief was a gnostic error that hopelessly tied the leadership to the forms of the past. Unamuno contrasted *pistis* to *gnosis*, and he recommended the former, a flexible confidence in one's inner powers, as the way to renovation. Those who believed unquestioningly in their conventions were static, whereas those who had faith in themselves were able to develop real hope, to see the possibility of their true selves flourishing in the midst of altered circumstances. Pistic confidence rather than gnostic belief was the great liberator and humanizer, the basis for our values. "*Pistis*, not *gnosis*; for in *pistis* one finds faith, hope and charity; for from *pistis* men receive liberty, equality, and fraternity; and out of *pistis* springs the sincerity that always lets one discover the ideal and oppose it to reality, the tolerance that allows diverse beliefs to be contained inside the common hope, and the mercy that helps the victims of the unalterable past and the fatal present. Sincerity, tolerance, and mercy."[14]

Certain definite intellectual consequences followed from this idea of the way to regeneration. The teacher would not use the same means to foster faith as he would to induce industrialization. Unamuno stated these consequences concisely: "Now the duty of the intellectuals and the directing classes lies not so much in the effort to mold the people on the basis of one or another plan—each

---

[14]Unamuno, "¡Pistis y no gnosis!" 1897, *Obras* III, pp. 681–5; quotation, p. 685.

being equally Jacobin—as in studying it from the inside, trying to discover the sources of our spirit."[15] At this point, Hispanicization became vulnerable to a more sophisticated conception of Europeanization.

Romanticism is always embarrassed by the fact that the savage rarely proclaims his own nobility. Unamuno fulfilled his duty; no man of his time came closer to discovering the sources of the Spanish spirit. But Unamuno's powers were not purely Spanish. Unamuno was a Basque whose knowledge of European literature far excelled that of his contemporaries. Many thought that his character belied his doctrine, and although he wrote against Europeanization, his accomplishments and aspirations made him an exemplary model of the goal that younger Europeanizers sought. "A great Bilbaoan has said that Hispanicization would be better [than Europeanization], but this great Bilbaoan, Don Miguel de Unamuno, ignores, as is his custom, the fact that although he presents himself to us as a Hispanicizer, he is, like it or not, by the power of his spirit and his profound cultural religiousness, one of the leaders of our European aspirations."[16]

Ortega accepted the Hispanicizers' critique of Europeanization, and he shared their goal of comprehending the Spanish genius. He asked, however, how they were to discover and manifest the sources of their spirit? Why, if Spaniards were to rely wholly on their own genius for the performance of this task, had it not been done before? Some other ingredient was needed to distinguish the twentieth-century Spaniard from his nineteenth-century predecessor. Ortega contended that this ingredient would be the stimulus of the European literary, scientific, and philosophic tradition, for the power of abstract thought that this tradition had cultivated would aid the Spaniard in understanding and perfecting himself.

Returning from Germany with an intuition of the functions that intellect might perform in Spanish reform, Ortega began his critique of Hispanicization. In *El Imparcial* he reviewed the two discourses by Unamuno at "El Sitio." Ortega was enthusiastic about

---

[15]Unamuno, "De regeneración: en lo justo," 1898, *Obras* III, p. 699.

[16]Ortega, "La pedagogía social como programa político," 1910, *Obras* I, p. 521.

Unamuno's politics, but pointedly critical about his metaphysics, which "amounted to a joke." This failing was unfortunate, Ortega contended, because a better metaphysical foundation would have strengthened Unamuno's political position.[17] At the same time, Ortega criticized Ramiro de Maetzu for not appreciating the importance of ideas in the development of Spanish character.[18] In the discussion that ensued between the two young writers, Ortega was careful to keep the disagreement from becoming fundamental. Thus he wrote of Maetzu that "I am in accord with him on the *quid* of the Spanish problem, and I only disagree on the *quo modo* of the solution."[19] All—Ortega, Maetzu, and Unamuno—agreed that the *quid* was to bring the Spanish character to perfection; they disagreed over the *quo modo* because they thought that different pedagogical principles would best guide them to their common goal. Unamuno and Maetzu contended that reformers should rely on the natural, inner responses of the Spanish genius. Ortega suggested that perhaps the genius, the prodigy, could rely only on inner responses; but, he added, comprehension of Spanish virtues could be communicated to the average, educated Spaniard only through greater use of intellect, conceptual discipline, and clear, rigorous thinking. Here was a new idea of Europeanization. "It is necessary that our spirit go with perfect continuity from 'The Drunkards' of Velázquez, to the infinitesimal calculus, passing by way of the categorical imperative. Only by means of an intellectual system will we give the spirit of our people the proper tension, just as a Bedouin, by means of a frame of cords and stakes, stretches taut the light cloth of his tent."[20]

Ortega won over most reformers to his notion of Europeanization. The dialogue with Unamuno continued; but privately Unamuno admitted what Ortega had contended all along: they were

---

[17] "Glosas a un discurso," *El Imparcial*, September 11, 1908, and "Nuevas Glosas," *El Imparcial*, September 26, 1908, *Obras* X, pp. 82–5, 86–90.

[18] "Algunas notas," 1908, *Obras* I, pp. 111–6.

[19] "Sobre una apología de la inexactitud," 1908, *Obras* I, p. 118.

[20] "Algunas notas," 1908, *Obras* I, p. 115.

talking about the same ideas in different words.[21] In 1914 Ortega emerged as the leader of the younger reformers. His youth had enabled him to be late in formulating his position, and consequently he did so with the benefit of having criticized earlier reformers and of securing himself against the weaknesses that they revealed. With the principles of Europeanization that he advanced, he attended to both external order and inner strength; he tried to use the powers of European thought to clarify the authentic Spanish character. Ortega offered a clearer definition of Europe than did Costa, and the former's conception was not as vulnerable to Unamuno's retort that the European nations were not fit to be emulated.

Eventually, Ortegan Europeanization would involve the adoption of advanced productive and administrative techniques; on this point Ortega agreed with Costa.[22] But he criticized Costa for failing to appreciate the source of European technical competence. "For some, Europe is the railroad and good politics; for others it is the part of the world where the best hotels are found; for a few it is the state that enjoys the most loyal and expert employees; for still others it is the group of countries that export the most and import the least. All these images of Europe coincide in an error of perspective: they confuse what is seen in a rapid journey, what leaps before the eyes, what is, in sum, the external appearance of contemporary Europe, with the true and perennial Europe."[23]

In essence, to Ortega, Europe was science. And, as Aristotle had observed, science resulted from the two talents that Socrates had given the West: the ability to make definitions and to use the inductive method. Europe shared everything else with the rest of the world. Ortega cautioned Europeanizers to avoid inducing a demand in Spain for the *products* of a scientific civilization. Instead, they should restrict their efforts to cultivating the scientific *spirit* in the Spanish elites. "Certainly the Spanish problem is a pedagogical problem," Ortega contended in 1908, "but the essence, the

---

[21]For Ortega's attitude see especially the letter to Unamuno, Marburg, December 30, 1906, in *Revista de Occidente*, October 1964, pp. 8–9. For Unamuno, see the letter to Ortega, Salamanca, December 21, 1912, in *Ibid.*, p. 19.

[22]See for instance, *Vieja y nueva política*, 1914, *Obras* I, pp. 304-8.

[23]"Asamblea para el progreso de las ciencias," 1908, *Obras* I, p. 100.

character of our pedagogical problem is that we need, above all, to educate a few men of science, to develop at least a semblance of scientific preoccupation; for without this prior work, the rest of our pedagogical labor will be vain, impossible, and senseless. I believe that what I have just stated gives the precise formula for Europeanization."[24] Ortega perceived that without the mastery of dynamic science, Spain would succumb to what we have learned to call the revolution of rising expectations, for inflamed appetites would continually exceed the meager increases in the nation's capacity to produce consumer goods achieved through crash programs.

Beware of anachronism: science need not be experimental and operational. By science Ortega meant *Wissenschaft*, the body of disciplined theory concerning both man and nature. When he commended science as the art of definition and the inductive method, he was not propounding a positivistic epistemology. Rather, he took speculative philosophy to be the pinnacle of science. The great philosophical system-builders were the true masters of turning meaningful definitions. In *Meditations on Quixote* Ortega extolled Hegel for this skill. "Philosophy has the ultimate ambition of arriving at a simple proposition in which all truth is stated. Hence, the one-thousand two-hundred pages of Hegel's *Logik* are only a preparation for pronouncing, with all its rich significance, this sentence: 'The idea is the absolute.' Apparently so poor, this sentence really has infinite significance; and thinking it properly, all this treasure of significance is exploited in one stroke and in one stroke we see the enormous perspective of the world clarified."[25]

Likewise, when Ortega commended induction he was not touting the experimental method, for he believed that quantified experiment led to the "terrorism of the laboratories."[26] Many European thinkers, among them Ortega, have insisted with good reasons that induction, in its proper sense, is phenomenology, and "all classic idealists—Plato, Descartes, Leibniz, Kant—began with the phe-

[24]*Ibid.*, p. 103. The characterization of Socrates was first made by Aristotle, *Metaphysics*, XIII, iv, 1078b27–30.

[25]*Meditaciones del Quijote*, 1914, *Obras* I, p. 317.

[26]See ¿*Qué es filosofía?*, 1929, 1957, *Obras* VII, p. 298. Cf. "Sobre la expresión fenómeno cósmico," 1925, *Obras* II, pp. 582–3.

nomenological principle."[27] This principle entailed the recognition that all thought deals only with data of consciousness; given this recognition, induction becomes first the qualitative elucidation of what these data signify to their perceiver, and second the critical elaboration of the characteristics of life and thought that make the experiencing of these significances possible. Without pursuing these difficult subjects further, suffice it to say that Ortega's version of Europeanization, the mastery of science, called on his countrymen to cultivate their ability to define and describe phenomena and to theorize about the problems and possibilities thus revealed. Such science would affect Spanish life not as it gave rise to specialized propositions applicable to particular problems, but as it enabled Spaniards to sharpen and discipline their total view of life.

Europeanization, conceived of as the mastery of science, was not dependent on the current example of Europe, for Ortega was not recommending to Spaniards the European reality as such, but a particular capacity for apprehending reality that happened to have been developed in Europe. Ortega could tell Unamuno that "the cultural decadence of Germany is indubitable" and he could disregard the Basque's attacks on materialistic positivism because the actual decay or perversion of scientific practice did not detract from the potential of the scientific ideal.[28] Science was the means men had created for rationally ordering their circumstances, and Spaniards should aspire to master this capacity.

Ortega also attended to the problem of the Spanish self. Here too his procedure was philosophical. He avoided the historical question whether particular characteristics were consistent with the genius of the Spanish tradition. He went directly to the principle of selfhood, and he best exemplified its use in opposing another superficial attempt at Europeanization: Modernismo.i

At the turn of the century certain Spanish writers and artists took up the avant-garde style of symbolist poetry and art nouveau. According to the Modernistas, Paris was the center of Europe, and Mallarmé, Verlaine, and Baudelaire were its greatest geniuses. The

[27]"Sobre el concepto de sensación," 1913, Obras I, pp. 256–7.
[28]Letter to Unamuno, Marburg, January 27, 1907, in Revista de Occidente, October 1964, p. 11.

Nicaraguan Rubén Darío and the Spaniard Ramón del Valle-Inclán were the leading poets of the modernist movement in Spain, and their style may have contributed to Ortega's occasional excess of metaphor.[29] Ortega liked the poetry of Darío and Valle-Inclán, but he warned that the vogue of their work exerted a destructive influence on the young and that *Modernismo* was, therefore, a danger.j

Young artists and intellectuals should realize, Ortega thought, that there was a difference between being conversant with the latest fashion of the avant-garde and being masters of the tradition that enabled the avant-garde to create the latest fashion. Young Spaniards were dazzled by the genius of Darío and Valle-Inclán. Ortega feared that members of the coming generation would fail to form their *selves*. "If we can write good literature and if we are also capable of science, our commitment must unequivocally incline towards the latter, without dabbling in the former. Señores Valle-Inclán and Rubén Darío have an assured place in heaven, just as do Cajal and Eduardo Hinojosa. Those who will probably go to hell— the hell of frivolity, the only one there is—are the youths who, without being Valle-Inclán and Rubén Darío, imitate them badly instead of plunging into the archives and reconstructing Spanish history or commenting on Aeschylus or Saint Augustine."[30]

Against the cult of *Modernismo*, Ortega proposed to be "nothing modern, but very twentieth century."[31] His whole conception of selfhood was summed up in this quip. Mere modernity was not a desirable characteristic, for the essence of being up-to-date was that one would soon go out-of-date. The person who was merely abreast with current styles of thought and expression had no inner strength and was vulnerable to the whimsical ways of the world.

To be "very twentieth century" was another matter indeed. Certain real problems confronted him as a person at once a Spaniard and a European living in the first half of the twentieth century. To achieve selfhood, a man had to identify these problems correctly, cultivate his capacity to meet them, and discipline his will to do so. The sources of this man's strength would be in himself; his power

---

[29]Ricardo Senabre Sempere, *Lengua y estilo de Ortega y Gasset*, p. 23.
[30]"Algunas notas," 1908, *Obras* I, p. 113.
[31]"Nada 'moderno' y 'muy siglo XX'," 1916, *Obras* II, pp. 22–4, esp. 24.

would be his own; and he would be a knot of resistance to the flux of things. This man would be the hero, perhaps a humble hero, but a hero all the same. Perceiving a problem, he would invent an adventure in which he would overcome the problem; and conceiving of his adventure, he would discover the means of living it. Hence, the heroic self resisted the habitual, the ordinary, the fashionable—everything that was given—and in doing so, he made himself the perennial source of change and progress in human life. "To be a hero consists in being one, one's self."[32]

This conception of selfhood transcended the disagreement between those who wanted to perfect Spanish character by cultivating the traditional mores and those who wanted to adopt foreign, mainly French, manners. The true person resisted the adoption of all "roles," regardless of whether they were offered by tradition or by the avant-garde. No one would find himself by identifying with a historical group, no matter how grand and glorious, for life worked the other way around: history was revealed in the selves of living men.[k] To live was to deal with one's problems; and in this imperative to come to grips with one's real difficulties, Ortega found the explanation of why a sense for Spanish character and tradition seemed to have disappeared: "the terribleness of contemporary Spanish life is that the vital problems do not exist."[33] There could be no character in men who complacently perceived no problems. To achieve an authentic life, to create the contemporary Spanish character, one had to examine one's habitual existence, perceive its deficiencies, invent a better project, and muster the will and means to live it. If the Spanish reformers were such heroes, there would be no theoretical problem about the perpetuation or the transformation of tradition; the tradition would be perpetuated and transformed as Spaniards drew on the full resources of their character in a dedicated effort to recognize and surmount their gravest deficiencies.

In sum, Ortega held two ideals before his peers: the heroic ideal and the scientific ideal. He conceived of Europeanization as a

---

[32]*Meditaciones del Quijote*, 1914, *Obras* I, p. 390.
[33]Letter to Unamuno, Marburg, December 30, 1906, in *Revista de Occidente*, October 1964, p. 9.

great adventure invented by his generation to overcome the palpable problems that sensitive Spaniards perceived. The scientific ideal was losing influence throughout Europe; and by rejuvenating this ideal, Spaniards would not only ameliorate the deficiencies in their national life, but they would also remake a positive place for themselves in the European order. These were the educative ends adopted. They were his answer to the first problem of pedagogy, the *quid*.

Recall that the second problem was the matter of means, *quo modo*. In general, a civic pedagogue had two ways in which to work: he could undertake personal activities and he could stimulate social movements. In the ensuing chapters our main concern will be to scrutinize Ortega's personal efforts at reform. But his personal activities, although significant in their own right, will be best appreciated if we first follow a group effort at renovation that Ortega and his friends organized in 1914: the League for Spanish Political Education. The League was an attempt to organize "a minority charged with the political education of the masses."[34] Through it, its founders hoped, Spain would be Europeanized, and a more humane polity and community would emerge.

*   *   *

When certain phrases are uttered, political commentators often perceive only those meanings that are consistently associated with partisan polemic. Their reflexes have been so conditioned by the reiteration of slogans that the sound of certain words, rather than their meaning, elicits a predictable response. No matter how inapposite this response may seem to the impartial witness, the partisan will persist in construing the terms awry, for by questioning his slogans he would cease to be a partisan. Ortega's political theory bears many loaded phrases: elite, aristocracy, duty, destiny, and the two introduced above—minorities and masses. From the left Ortega's writings seem to abound with terms that will start the flow of bile in readers whose reflexes have been conditioned by democratic dogma, and from the right his works are laden with phrases that raise hopes in American conservatives that Ortega can be enlisted in their cause.[1] In many casual references, scholars call him an "aristocratic" or "conservative" theorist; yet his political practice

---

[34]*Vieja y nueva política*, 1914, *Obras* I, p. 302.

was quite democratic.**m** The only ideological position that Ortega wholeheartedly accepted was *au dessus de la mêlée*, and he contended that the political mission of his generation was to transcend the worn out quarrel between liberalism and conservatism.[35] In view of this situation, it is especially important that we follow the principle of basing our judgments, not on our reflexes, but on our reflection.

Many have had difficulty with Ortega's political thought because they have not looked beyond his phrases to the problems to which he referred. Until recently neither the American left nor right was prepared to appreciate Ortega, for neither entertained the premise of his politics: the illegitimacy of the established institutions. Now that Americans have begun to doubt the perfection of their political practices and now that new elements of the American left have even described themselves as "a prophetic minority," Ortega's pedagogical politics can perhaps find a more suitable audience.

For Ortega, politics was not primarily a system for determining who gets what when; it was first a matter of reconstructing such a system that had ceased to work. Most of Ortega's political writings concern problems of lawgiving, not lawmaking. Ortega's columns in *El Imparcial* and *El Sol* show that, as a lawmaker, he was a liberal democrat who believed that laws should be made in accordance with the popular will. But the Spaniard with such aspirations had to ask two questions: was the given political system capable of responding to the popular will? and was the populace capable of articulating its will? To both queries the answer was no: the given system was a chaotic struggle of factions that could perhaps respond to contending class, economic, and regional interests, but not to the interests of the *pueblo*. The Spanish people—poor, undereducated, and disillusioned by endless political abuses—were thoroughly apolitical. Hence, the would-be democratic lawmaker had first to be the effective lawgiver. He had to create a political system in Spain that would reflect the popular will, rather than a balance of factions, and that would develop among the people the desire and ability to express their will on matters of public policy.

None of the familiar systems for lawmaking—democracy,

---

[35]See esp. *La rebelión de las masas*, 1930, *Obras* IV, p. 205.

oligarchy, monarchy, dictatorship—explain or guide the phenomena of lawgiving. The task of making an established political system function is fundamentally different from that of establishing a new, reformed political system, for the former task entails the effective use of existing forms of power whereas the latter involves the creation of previously nonexistent forms. Because in lawgiving men must act in ways that do not presuppose the possession of power, the activity seems quixotic and incomprehensible to those whose conception of politics has been molded by the conventions of law-making, be these democratic, monarchical, or totalitarian.

Lawgiving is inherently hortatory and moralistic; lawgivers must persuade people to accept inwardly new ideals of authority before institutions based on those ideals can be made to operate. Thus, words are prior to deeds. The opportunity for creating new agencies of community arises precisely because the established, institutionalized offices of leadership have become inadequate. Men find that they cannot act; in the absence of legitimate, effective centers of authority, no person or group can properly initiate policy for the whole polity. In such a situation, some will try desperately to impose their favored policies upon the community, and their efforts will lead to tragic destruction; others will more prudently control their urge to act and will try to conceive of new, possible forms of polity that can be spontaneously elicited from the community. When lawmakers are no longer able to act effectively for the whole community, it is time for lawgivers to stimulate the whole community to act for itself, reforming itself in such a way that lawmakers can once again effectively act for it.

In this enterprise of lawgiving, great restraint is essential. The man who wants to engender fundamental changes in a community cannot impose a predetermined program. Changes, when fundamental, are appropriate precisely because the system of power has become inadequate. The established means for working out and implementing predetermined programs have ceased to function effectively. Owing to this situation, the lawgiver can at most stimulate a commitment by the people to new forms and possibilities. Thus, in his relation to the populace, the fundamental reformer is heuristic and protreptic, not didactic and prescriptive: rather than command the people to acquiesce in his infallible will, he provokes them to the discovery of a better community within themselves.

In this heuristic or pedagogical politics, talented elites have an important place. Sometimes our conception of an elite is that of the officer corps of an army: men of special rank and training whose duty it is to command. Such an elite is a recipient of order, has nothing to do with lawgiving, and was not Ortega's model for the gifted minorities. At other times, our conception of an elite is that of a moral remnant: men scattered through every rank of society who take upon themselves the tasks of being witnesses to the truth and justice. Their duty is not to command, but to inspire. An elite of this character has everything to do with lawgiving and was the type of aristocracy that Ortega thought was essential for Spanish reform.

At the point in his intellectual development that Ortega had reached in 1914, he conceived of gifted minorities as the prime movers of progress towards the reformation of Spanish life; and later in his life he would go so far as to state that all communities, like it or not, were aristocratic.[36] But he meant—and this critics often overlook—that communities were aristocratic not in the way they made law, but in the way they constituted and maintained themselves as communities. And by an aristocracy, Ortega did not mean a corps of commanders, but the leaven of the spiritually committed and intellectually competent citizens diffused throughout the populace. The function of the members of this aristocracy was to conceive of more adequate principles of order, to embody these in their personal activities, and, by example, to inspire other persons to understand and to adopt these principles. Such a minority stood in the same relation to the people as the Socratic citizen stands to his peer; the characteristics to be brought out in the community must pre-exist in the people and the duty of the educative minorities is to put the question and to exemplify the answer in order to help the people perceive and manifest their own immanent characteristics. Without effective elites of this type, a people of magnificent potential might not be able to bring their genius to bear upon their common lives. This was Spain's difficulty.

Hence, Ortega's primary goal was to create a capable minority for Spain, to create a prophetic, not a paternal, minority. In substance, this goal was neither democratic nor anti-democratic, for the

---

[36]*Ibid.*, p. 150.

mission assigned to the elite was to make a Spanish democracy possible. But the goal was quite consistent with both the humanistic educational tradition and the liberal political tradition. It was premised on the proposition that virtue is knowledge, and that therefore the common good, the virtue of all, depends on whether all have access to knowledge. An Enlightenment willingness to put confidence in man's capacity for self-perfection characterized Ortega's theory; yet he was not oblivious to the difficulties of getting men to exercise this capacity. Ortega's aristocracy was an elite of intelligence and talent whose purpose was to extend knowledge and to make it accessible to a greater proportion of the people. Rather than the paternal rule of the elites that came to govern Spain, the goal of Ortega's elite was to show Spaniards that they could rule themselves with more humanity and justice. Ortega's so-called elitism was based on the egalitarianism described by Ralph Waldo Emerson when he said: "Democracy, Freedom, has its roots in the sacred truth that every man hath in him the divine Reason, or that, though few men since the creation of the world live according to the dictates of Reason, yet all men are created capable of doing so. That is the equality and the only equality of all men. To this truth we look when we say, Reverence Thyself; Be true to Thyself. Because every man has within him somewhat really divine, therefore is slavery the impardonable outrage it is."[37]

Ortega's first major public undertaking was the organization of the League for Spanish Political Education.[n] The League comprised ninety-eight young intellectuals; the founding of it was an occasion at which they gathered as a group and gave themselves the task of enlarging and perfecting all the sectors of Spanish life that they could affect. On March 23, 1914, Ortega gave its convocational address, "The Old and the New Politics."[38] In this speech Ortega fully expressed the conception of politics he had been developing and he movingly applied it to the Spanish situation. As the phrase "new politics" suggests, his arguments were not unlike those that many young American radicals have voiced since the 1960's, for

[37]Emerson, *Journal*, December 9, 1834, reprinted in Whicher, ed., *Selections from Ralph Waldo Emerson*, p. 19.

[38]*Vieja y nueva política*, 1914, *Obras* I, pp. 267–308.

civic pedagogy is the form of politics natural to all who find themselves living in the midst of illegitimate institutions.

Ortega began with a premise accepted by most Spaniards
except those who happened to be in power. This premise was that
during crises—and none in his audience doubted that Spain had
been in a prolonged crisis—the will of the people was not found in
the established institutions. A crisis resulted when the institutional
skeleton of the community was no longer able to support efforts to
deal with the community's real problems. During crises, the popular
will was found in the projects and aspirations that defined the
people's potential. "And thus it comes to pass that today we see in
our nation two Spains that live together and that are perfect
strangers: an *official Spain* that insists on prolonging the gestures
of a dead age; and an aspiring, germinal Spain, a *vital Spain*, which
although not very strong is still valid, sincere, and honest, and
which, having been obstructed by the other, has not succeeded in
fully entering into history."[39]

In spite of the obstructive function of official Spain, Ortega
did not succumb to the slavish *ressentiment* that characterizes so
many radical and reactionary movements alike. He held, as a basic
pedagogical principle, that one could grow and develop only by
pushing against resistance; and hence political development did not
require the excision of obstructions, a ruthless surgery on those who
opposed the reformers' hopes, but rather the surmounting of
obstacles as sporting proof of the true superiority of the new.
Consequently, in the politics of crisis, one should ignore the traditional points of power—neither seeking them nor shunning them—
and assiduously attend to one's proper business: bringing the
nation's potentials to fruition. Since the old political structure was
designed to deal with problems that existed no longer, it was a sham
that was not worth serious attention. Instead, members of the
League would attend to the people, their problems, their powers,
and their proposals; the League would help clarify and manifest the
possibilities that were to be found across the entire range of Spanish
life. "We will go to the towns and villages, not only to seek
votes to obtain acts of legislation and powers of government, but

---

[39]*Ibid.*, p. 273.

to make our teaching create organs of community, of culture, of technique, of mutualism, of a life that ultimately is human in all its senses, and of a public energy that will rise without cowering gestures against the fatal tendency in every state to envelop in itself the entire life of the society."[40]

Noblesse oblige! A small handful of men belonged to the League and they did not join it to gain attention for their special interests. They had little doctrine and they followed the slogan "justice and efficacy."[41] The League would function in a simple manner. It would hold before all those who were discontented with Spain, especially before educated young dissidents, the mission of Europeanizing, of educating Spain. The League sought members among doctors, economists, engineers, professors, poets, and industrialists; and to those who had the strength and courage to pursue more than their immediate interests, the League proposed a goal. At the age of thirty, Ortega made his appeal to the idealism of youth, calling the young in body and heart to a great task, not because it was expedient, but because it was good.

We shall saturate the farthest corner of Spain with our enthusiasm and curiosity; we shall scrutinize Spain and spread love and indignation. We shall travel through the fields with our apostolic din; we shall live in the villages to listen to the desperate moans that issue there; we shall first be the friend of whomever we shall presently lead. We shall create among them strong bonds of community—cooperatives, circles for mutual education, centers of information and protest. We shall goad the best men of each capital up a commanding, spiritual elevation, for today they are imprisoned by the terrible burden of official Spain, which encumbers the provinces even more than Madrid. We shall let these spiritual brothers who are lost in provincial inertia know that in us they have allies and defenders. We shall cast a net of vigor across the limits of Spain, a net that will be at once an organ for teaching and an organ for studying the facts of Spain, a net, finally, that will form a nervous system through which vital waves of sensibility and automatic, powerful currents of protest will run.[42]

To proceed in the manner of the League is to ignore the obvious realities of practical power. Was it a plausible, meaningful means of

---

[40]*Ibid.*, p. 277.
[41]*Ibid.*, p. 286.
[42]*Ibid.*, pp. 286–7.

action for ninety-eight talented young men to turn their backs on traditional politics, to ignore the conventional measures of ambition and success, to propose, gratuitously and gamely, certain ideals of conduct and competence, and to suggest, with passion and eloquence, that they and their compatriots would live better by fulfilling these more exigent standards? Those inclined to scoff should note that among the young today rejection of official institutions is a commitment that moves many; and if for no other reason than its power to deprive the established order of needed talent, it should be examined sympathetically in order to comprehend its positive rationale. Yet powerful currents pull in another direction and encourage interpreters to treat the League lightly.

With respect to the established institutions, the League was a negative influence; but then, as now, the established institutions had an inordinate prestige. Ortega's rejection was complete: Spanish institutions were so inconsequential that they did not merit active opposition. Hence, Raymond Carr, in his excellent economic and political history of modern Spain, appropriately discusses Ortega in a chapter on "The Protestors"; but Carr is wrong in implying that Ortega's positive endeavors were inconsequential because these commitments endured "characteristically only for a short period."[43] To be sure, the League did not aim at institutional power and it did not endure. But Carr's judgment of Ortega's commitments, and many of his other judgments concerning Spanish history, reflect the deep contemporary bias in favor of institutional action over spontaneous action.

This bias towards institutionalized power underlies one of the more significant critiques of Ortega's life work.º Exponents of this critique contend that between 1898 and 1936 Spain was a country undergoing political and economic modernization. To sustain its development more trained technicians were needed. But instead of turning towards the technical subtleties of engineering, economics, sociology, political science, and business administration, the intellectuals were led by Ortega and Unamuno into excessively speculative, theoretical concerns. Typically, these critics might suggest, the League for Spanish Political Education lacked institutional strength and its members made no organized effort to solve a single practical

---

[43]Carr, *Spain*, p. 537; cf. pp. 524–63, esp. pp. 530–2.

problem within their competence. The League proposed fine goals, but it never organized to ensure that these would be carried out. In the long run, all it did was briefly assuage the consciences of a few intellectuals who thought that they should do something for the nation but who were unwilling to accept the discipline and self-effacement that institutional effectiveness would entail. In short, if members of the League had been truly serious about reform, they would not have opposed a "vital," spontaneous Spain against official Spain; nor would they have argued for a new politics in place of the old; rather, they would have rolled up their sleeves and become the staff of a more competent, "vital" officialdom.

Today, when economic development has become one of the more fashionable topics of academic inquiry, this criticism seems correct. Ortega was no developmental technocrat.[p] He discouraged corporate action on isolated problems; he opposed the kind of academic specialism that would have helped to increase the power and improve the efficiency of the administrative and technical bureaucracies; he relied on spontaneous, rather than organized, effort to improve the nation. The League was little more than a short-lived declaration of intention. Its program was not practicable; it called for renewed purpose and improved competencies without particularizing proposals. We have been taught to think that these characteristics are weaknesses; and if Spain truly needed only a strong shot of technical modernization, these criticisms would be cogent. But the Spanish problem may have been more complicated; and if this is so, the characteristics that seem to have been demerits may prove on reflection to have been the points that gave Ortega and the League their greatest strength and relevance.

Spontaneous civic action is not something that mysteriously erupts from a people, without rhyme or reason; like any other form of action, it is willed with care, and it becomes effective only with the delicate use of reason. Such action is spontaneous, and it is opposed to the institutional, because its power emanates from the personal activities of a variety of individuals, each of whom acts as an individual, not as a corporate official or follower. Thus, even though our personal activities may have great social consequences and are the result of careful deliberation, they are called spontaneous because, from the point of view of any institutional authority, they are initiated in accord with our own intimate intent rather than the will and convenience of official policy. Independent, spontaneous activities gain a civic significance whenever men separately inform their personal acts with purposes that are widely shared by others. All of Ortega's social theory was premised on the conviction that spontaneous civic action was fundamental and that institutional action was secondary and conditioned by the spontaneous.

Ortega made the opposite assumption from that which seems to have been made by most social scientists. Rather than say that personal choice was possible only within certain interstices of institutions, he said that formal institutions were possible only within certain spontaneous matrices. Institutions were effective only when they were legitimated by a prior spontaneous concord; and in the absence of spontaneous concord, it was futile to try to engineer it by the deft or brutal manipulation of formal programs. Instead, one had to try to concert the spontaneous commitments of capable persons; as these persons independently informed their activities with common goals, a significant public potential would begin to become manifest; and as the prominence of this potential increased, more and more persons would define their aspirations with respect to it. On the basis of this concord, a new, effective set of institutions could be established.

The Prospectus of the League was a declaration of intent, not so much of League policy, but of a direction that each person who subscribed to it would follow in the pursuit of his personal vocation. The League needed to endure only for one meeting, for in that one meeting its participants consecrated their lives to Spanish political education. Salvador de Madariaga, who was one of the League's members and who has shown an inspiring fidelity to its principles, has described this consecration best. "This memorable day was the beginning of real leadership in Spanish politics. The spring tapped by Don Francisco Giner and fed by the devoted efforts of the Junta, or Committee for the Development of Studies, had by now become a strong and clear river of intelligent opinion flowing into the troubled and muddy waters of Spanish politics. Great hopes were raised when this body of new men, uncontaminated by the responsibilities of the past and the intrigues of the present, declared their intention to take part in public life and to raise the tone and substance of Spanish politics."[44]

This evaluation of the League is borne out by the fact that in later life its members independently made important contributions to Spanish politics and culture, contributions that were fully in accord with the intent of the League. Since the League did nothing more than attempt to concert the personal aspirations of its members, to inform their activities with a common goal, no causal significance can be attributed to it; it did not function programmatically. Nevertheless, one could write a good history of the growth of the Republic and the pre-Civil War flowering of Spanish culture by celebrating the careers of the "generation of '14," that is, the ninety-eight members of the League. Among them were Manuel Azaña, prime minister and then president of the Republic; Manuel Abril, poet; Américo Castro, essayist and literary historian; Angel Galarza, minister of the interior in the Largo Caballero government; Manuel García Morente, philosopher and translator; Lorenzo Luzuriaga, educational theorist; Salvador de Madariaga, diplomat and historian; Antonio Machado, poet, educator, and essayist; Ramiro de Maetzu, diplomat and essayist; Federico de Onís, educator, essayist, and literary historian; Ramón Pérez de Ayala, novelist; Fernando de los Ríos, professor of law, politician, and diplomat; and Luis de Santullano, director of the *"misiones pedagógicas"* under the Republic.[45] Many other members achieved distinction in their chosen endeavors; and it must have been a great encouragement to each to know that the purposes he had decided to pursue were shared by colleagues in other fields.

---

[44]Madariaga, *Spain*, p. 310.

[45]The Pedagogical Missions were a project in which university students spent their summers in rural villages, getting to know the problems of the poor and trying to introduce the villagers to contemporary cultural and sanitary achievements. See Gabriel Jackson, *The Spanish Republic and the Civil War*, pp. 108–110, for a good description of the *misiones pedagógicas*. Much like VISTA in many respects, the missions put more emphasis than VISTA does on creating substantive communication between the future leadership elite and the rural Spaniard. There was not the condescension implicit in a "war on poverty"; there was the belief that the rural peasant could learn things of value from the urban student and the urban student could learn equally as much from the rural peasant.

Even though the League had no programmatic policy, its historic significance merits careful consideration. As was noted above, we think of the Spanish problem as one of economic and technical underdevelopment, which in part it was. But in seeing Spain as underdeveloped and in need of modernization, we see it through foreign, uncomprehending eyes. To be sure, Spain is economically backward; but that is a mere symptom. The real problem is more fundamental; and consequently, it is irrelevant to judge the League by latter-day standards of modernization. The League for Spanish Political Education was meant to deal with a different, related, more basic difficulty.

Owing to Spain's limitations, it was the first European nation to encounter the crisis of purpose pandemic throughout this century. In this peculiar sense, Spaniards were among Europe's historically advanced peoples: they first experienced the trauma of losing their colonies. After all, Spaniards had constructed one of the early nation-states of Europe, and their colonial expansion had been second only to that of England. But Spaniards had found it very difficult, with a nation that lacked a rich surplus of either men or materiel, to hold their colonies. Throughout the nineteenth century they invested much energy and hope in the enterprise; nevertheless their overseas holdings set themselves free or were taken over by stronger upstarts. By 1900 Spain was having difficulty keeping its meager holdings in North Africa and the millennial tide of the Reconquista seemed about to be reversed.

Spaniards had to face the demonstrated fact that they had become an insignificant power and a people without purpose. Nations are not natural entities that exist come what may; they are continually created and re-created as men grant allegiance to symbols and offices that define for each person a significant future and purpose. At the turn of the century, Spaniards witnessed the dissolution of their national purpose. Hence the Spanish problem was precisely the problem that has become so familiar in the industrialized countries; the problem was nothing more nor less than a collapse of national cohesion.

If all that Spaniards suffered from was political and economic underdevelopment, then the intellectualism and voluntarism, as well as the confidence in spontaneous action, which characterized the League for Spanish Political Education, would have been inappropriate. But Spaniards had sufficient internal resources to improve significantly their material standard of living, the quality of public administration, and the political status of the people. These improvements, however, were impossible because Spaniards lacked the national will and unity, the sense of common purpose, that would have enabled them to overcome the particular problems that impeded improvement. Whether all strata of the Spanish people had ever assented to a particular idea of the Spanish nation is a moot question. However, since 1898 the idea of Spain as a center of imperial grandeur had clearly become ridiculous to important groups of Spaniards, while for others it became a treasured memory, the remains of which had to be carefully preserved. Hence, public affairs were rent not simply by disagreements about the means of government, but by dissension over the very character of the nation that was to be governed. The intractability of powerful interest groups, the agrarian problem, and the regionalist problem were symptoms of a weakened, shattered national purpose; and until that purpose had been strengthened, there would be no way to elicit the sense of sacrifice and altruistic foresight that were the only means by which those impediments to national improvement could be surmounted. And since the reformation of Spain's national purpose was stopped and negated in the Civil War, these impediments still persist.

How can one strengthen a sense of common purpose? How can one create new civic ideals when the established ones cease to move men or become irrelevant to the true problems of a time? Better technical training, an expanding economy, or a foreign war serve at best to postpone the urgency of these questions; public programs cannot answer them. When we come fully to grips with the difficulty of these questions, we will realize that our faith in the all-embracing efficacy of institutionalized authority is shallow and dangerous. Men are not slaves, and no amount of authority *over* men can create purposes *in* men.

Consequently, the Spanish intellectuals of the League should not be merely dismissed as impractical reformers. They tried to deal subtly and fundamentally with the real problems that lurk everywhere behind the glittering facade of modern civilization. Disillusion with the given community—whether it manifests itself in the apathy of the poverty-stricken, the criminal despair of the drop-out, the drugged fantasy of the escapist, or the terrorism of the revolutionary—is not a problem to be solved simply by a reliance on institutionalized programs in the political and economic sphere of life. In one form or another, these symptoms, which are symptoms of a crisis in spontaneously shared values and purposes, have been apparent in the recent history of every "developed" nation. And there is good reason to suspect that many of the programs designed to deal with these symptoms end ironically in reinforcing them.

Historic forces fail and tear themselves asunder in an act of *hubris* committed when men begin to believe that a hitherto successful system can be relied upon to master every problem. Man is limited. The intellectual procedures that he develops are imperfect; they solve certain problems, but in doing so they create other ones. After a mode of thought has been used effectively for a long time, it becomes habitual. Furthermore, after long use there will be many problems that were caused by the very inadequacies of the established way of thinking. These problems will require attention; and heedless men will try to use the familiar mode of thought to solve the very problems that have been created by its inadequacies. Hence, although the development in the past three hundred years of rational techniques in political and economic life has brought great benefits to most citizens of the modern nation, it would be a mistake to rely solely on these techniques for solutions to twentieth-century problems of value. In large part these problems have arisen from our failure to deal effectively with the vital concerns that lie beyond the limits of our political and economic techniques.

We are indebted to the Spanish reformers for their perception of the desirability, in dealing with a deep crisis of national purpose, for something *in addition to* the materialistic modes of reasoning by which even Spanish national power, backward as it was, had been markedly enhanced. Here we encounter the reason why "official Spain" was rejected by the members of the League. Official Spain was an empty but authentic work of nineteenth-century liberalism. To be sure, its implementation of rational policy in economic, political, and social life left much to be desired. But the limiting factor was not a lack of technical competence, it was a lack of national purpose. A commitment to official Spain would mean, in effect, that one was satisfied with the existing formulation of the national purpose and that one was content simply to rationalize and improve the pursuit of it. On the other hand, a commitment to vital Spain meant that one would try to create a more stirring national purpose. Such a commitment entailed a reliance on speculative intellectualism and spontaneous activity, for one could neither legislate values nor create purposes by materialistic modes of thought.

"There is nothing either good or bad, but thinking makes it so." In view of this truth, the reductionizing materialist is hard put to generate ideals and to avoid nihilism. Believing that he must explain his existence by reference ultimately to material reality, he finds that no *thing* is either good or bad; he feels deceived, not because his thinking puts the wrong values on various acts and objects, but because thinking, by itself, seems to place a value on them. Free valuation contradicts his materialism; and in order to maintain his belief, he must seek to think away thought, to reduce it to a material basis. To the degree that he persuades himself that his reduction is effective, he persuades himself that nothing is either good or bad, that all is permitted. All the same, thought exists, although it is not a thing, and as long as thought exists, valuations will be made, even by materialists who sincerely deny their power to do so. The function of thought is to transform the material world into an environment that man can inhabit. Mind fulfills this function by giving the great chaos of things the essential characteristic that, for *human* beings, the chaos lacks: thought assigns values; it creates order; it discovers what is and is not permitted. Human judgment is fallible: occasionally it assigns things the improper value, postulates a dangerous order, or permits the wrong and prohibits the right. But in the face of its imperfections, men are more likely to improve it through reflection, or thinking about thought, than they are by reduction, or thinking away thought. Repeatedly in history, when men have realized that they are confronted in public life by problems of order and questions of value, they have not turned to material nature, with respect to which these problems do not exist, for they realized that such a turn would be mere escapism. Instead, they began to reflect on thought, on culture, on man thinking.

In keeping with this tradition, the League for Spanish Political *Education* was a cultural, not a technical, group. By joining it, sensitive men agreed to plunge into all aspects of Spanish public life to try to make manifest the highest values in it. They wanted to initiate the general examination of life in the capital, in the provinces, and in the villages; and they had the hope that through such meditations Spaniards would eventually be able to say, "On these grounds we can all meet and share a significant, common destiny." To encourage the development of national purposes they had to rely on spontaneous activity, an intellectual appeal to the young and the speculative criticism of established institutions. They were not out to modernize Spain, but to humanize it, and for this purpose their procedure was appropriate.

In Spain, Europe, and throughout the world, twentieth-century life has been beset by problems of order and value, and because the League for Spanish Political Education put purpose before power, it is historically relevant to these problems. The League stands for an important kind of political action, for its procedures differed radically from the practical, materialistic activities that have been relied on to maximize the economic, administrative, and military strength of nation-states. The new politics aims to improve the spiritual power of various peoples and to bring the crucial but intangible questions of ideals, aspirations, and values out of the realm of chance and into that of choice. It is important to recognize that the method and intent of the League has this historic significance, for historical accident aborted the League's practical development.

*   *   *

Unamuno was right: Europe undid Europeanization. Not long after the League for Spanish Political Education had been convoked, World War I began. Other questions besides those concerning the purposes Spaniards could share began to seem more pressing. Why had order collapsed? How long would the conflagration continue? Which side had the just cause? Should Spain enter the war? It was not a time in which men could concentrate on building a new national purpose.

Thus the League met only once, and then broke apart under the centrifugal force of events. But even if the League had held together its significance would not have been its corporate achievements. Long after the League was forgotten, its members were personally pursuing its policies. In keeping with the idea of a new politics, the institution itself was not important; reform was a personalistic, spontaneous endeavor: many different men would separately make their own contributions to a new Spain. Substantial reform would be achieved only when these individual achievements aggregated into a perfected community.

Our task, then, is not to follow how Ortega fitted himself into the shifting conglomerations of his time. It is men who act, not institutions. Ortega's personal activities should be interpreted as the effort of one man to accomplish tasks similar to those that he had proposed through the League. In the course of his manifold activities, Ortega worked to strengthen the intellectual elite of Spain and to bring it into contact with the people. Whether he acted as a teacher, writer, publisher, or politician, his effort was to make intellect enhance the community by using it to increase the capacities of the people and to perfect their sense of common purpose.

This intellectual task was Ortega's vocation, consciously held and intentionally pursued. He was a civic pedagogue, a political teacher, and educator of the public. This vocation is not an arbitrary unity imposed by a biographer on an apparent chaos of Ortega's activities. He repeatedly professed this commitment, and it endured characteristically for a long period. Soon after he published the prospectus of the League, Ortega described his personal vocation: "these essays—like the lecture room, the newspaper, or politics— are diverse means of exercising the same activity, of giving vent to one desire. . . . The desire that moves me is the most powerful one that I find in my heart, and resurrecting the perfect name that Spinoza used, I will call it *amor intellectualis.*" Ortega's love was for Spain, which he intended to bring to perfection by cultivating its intellectual powers.[46] Eighteen years later, when he perceived that circumstances were forcing him to transform his vocation, to direct his *amor intellectualis* towards Europe rather than Spain, he reiterated the single-mindedness of his efforts. "I had to make my experiment at apprenticing the Spaniard to intellect in whatever

[46]*Meditaciones del Quijote*, 1914, *Obras* I, p. 311.

way he could be reached: in friendly conversations, in the periodicals, and in public lectures. It was necessary to attract him to the precision of ideas with a graceful turn of phrase, for with Spaniards, in order to persuade one must first seduce."[47]

For the quarter century during which he was Professor of Metaphysics at the University of Madrid, Ortega's career was an extraordinary personal effort at educating the Spanish public. Ortega fulfilled his own conception of the hero, he invented and pursued a great adventure in which he tried not to swim mindlessly with the currents of his time, but to channel them in new directions so that they would bring barren soils to life. The youth whom we have met was a man with a mission.

*   *   *

The people should fight for the law as if for their city-wall.

HERACLITUS, 44

---

[47]"El quehacer del hombre," 1932, *Obras* IV, p. 367.

*T*o CONCENTRATE *his forces, a writer needs a public as a liqueur needs the goblet into which it is poured. Hence, in* The Spectator *I appeal . . . to readers who are interested in things apart from their consequences, whatever those may be, the moral included; I appeal to pensive readers who are pleased to trace the outline of a subject through all its delicate, complicated structure; to readers who are not hurried, who have noted that any just opinion requires a copious expression; to readers who on reading rethink for themselves the themes they have read; to readers who do not need to be convinced, but who nevertheless find that they are ready to renew themselves by continually passing from habitual creeds to unaccustomed convictions; to readers who, like the author, have kept in reserve a bit of the antipolitical spirit; in sum, to readers who are unwilling to attend to a mere sermon, to become mindlessly moved at a rally, or to judge persons and things according to cafe gossip.*

ORTEGA[1]

---

[1]"Perspectiva y verdad," 1916, *Obras* II, p. 17.

IV
The Pedagogy of Prose

S PANISH REGENERATION was a matter of political education, not
political policy. As things stood, reforms in the state would
be ephemeral unless they were based on effective reforms of Spanish
character and skills. Without the latter reforms, the human capacities to make new institutions work would not be available and the
new procedures would quickly give way to old habits. Because of a
conviction that regeneration had to be based on a reform of character, not of customs, as he had put it in an early essay, Ortega had a
special conception of action.[2] *Scribere est agere.*

For Ortega, significant action elicited change in the character
of men; for him, speaking and writing were more significant forms
of doing things than were buying and selling, designing and producing, legislating and judging. Thus, when Ortega learned in 1905
that his friend Navarro Ledesma planned to enter the Cortes, he
expressed great disappointment. If one had to enter the established
political system, Ortega granted, there were two positions that
deserved to be vigorously upheld, "that of the promoter of instruction and education and that of the moralizer in international politics." But political office was not, Ortega thought, the best way for
a man with Navarro Ledesma's literary gifts to promote these goals.
"I think you are going to Congress to pass time and to not speak
out, which seems to me very bad."[3] In Ortega's judgment, in com-

---

[2]See "Reforma del carácter, no reforma de costumbres," *El Imparcial*, October
5, 1907, *Obras X*, pp. 17–21.

[3]Letter to Navarro Ledesma, Leipzig, August 8, 1905, in "Cartas inéditas a
Navarro Ledesma," *Cuadernos*, November 1961, pp. 15–6.

parison to the opportunity to speak out vigorously and effectively on the fundamental issues of character, the opportunity to legislate with respect to secondary matters was merely a means of passing time. The way to promote Spanish regeneration was through education.

An educator of the public who aimed to Europeanize Spain had to contend with the perennial difficulties of pedagogical action; in particular, with the difficulty the liberal educator encounters in his search for ways to occasion in others a willingness to master the more difficult potentialities of their inner character. Ortega's goal was to bring Spain more fully into the flow of the European tradition. The way to accomplish this integration, as he saw it, was not to emulate externally the superficial features of European life, but to communicate to diverse individuals in all walks of Spanish life the scientific standards and cultural competencies of the European heritage. By mastering European culture, Spaniards could use it to bring their concrete Spanish circumstances to fruition. It is no easy matter to elicit a true mastery of principles in the inner character of other men. Yet, that is what Ortega's conception of Europeanization entailed. This purpose, and his awareness of the difficulties that accompany it, are well reflected in Ortega's prose style, the technique that informed his effort to act by writing.[a]

*　　*　　*

Certain Catholic critics of Ortega's style claim that it dazzles and deceptively hides his inner, philosophical evasion. They assume that a serious thinker should write in a stolid style, and that Ortega's vivid imagery and sonorous diction signify his lack of serious thoughts. Thus, José Sánchez Villaseñor claimed that "his style has betrayed Ortega," for such elegant, engaging, evasive prose made it difficult to decide exactly what Ortega thought. Father Sánchez sensed that Ortega preached "an incendiary message";[4] and when

---

[4]José Sánchez Villaseñor, S.J., *Ortega y Gasset, Existentialist*, Joseph Small, S.J., trans., pp. 136, 138. An effort has waxed and waned several times to grant Ortega's genius as a writer and to deny his capacity as a philosopher. See besides *Ibid.*, books such as V. Chumillas, *¿Es Don José Ortega y Gasset un filósofo propriamente dicho?*, and P. Ramírez, *La filosofía de Ortega y Gasset*. For a summary of this critique see Jeronimo Mallo, "La discusión entre católicos sobre la filosofía de Ortega," *Cuadernos Americanos*, 1962, No. 2, pp. 157–166.

the grounds for such a message seem uncertain, it is prudent—for the sake of the afterlife and spiritual hegemony of the Church—to assume the worst about anyone who so exalted the present life. Father Sánchez doubted that a man with a definite philosophic vision would choose to express it as unsystematically as did Ortega. For many, the task before philosophy is to add another great synthesis to those of Aristotle and Aquinas. To contribute to this endeavor a thinker must publish his thought in systematic treatises.[5] Hence they conclude that Ortega chose the occasional essay as his major vehicle of expression because he had decided to assert, against the claims of systematic reason, an irrational glorification of life. Ortega's style, his rhetoric, was the weapon that he used against reason, for with his playful parlance he so subtly insinuated his dangerous views that no systematic critic would be able to expose their damning contradictions.[6] Fortunately, these critics proved able to prevent, with the aid of the rhetoric they scorned, this latest episode in the Satanic conspiracy to subvert the true philosophy by means of the persuasive arts.

Such appreciations of Ortega's prose do not stand up to critical examination. Not content to suggest that Ortega's use of the occasional essay to express serious thought was a mistake, these critics conclude that it was a sign of bad faith. Rather than look for the rationale of Ortega's style, they absolve themselves of that task by claiming that his prose was patent proof of his disrespect for reason. With a writer who disdains reason the serious critic rightly seeks, not to explain, but to expose; hence their polemic: "Ortega's is a frightening responsibility before history for having exchanged philosophy's noble mission for acrobatic sport."[7] The irony of the argument that unsystematic, occasional, powerful expression betrays irrationalism is that it could so easily be turned against the namesake of Father Sánchez's society. But to avoid such wrangling let us not lose sight of the great lesson that arose from the Greek confrontation of reason and rhetoric: the effectiveness of style tells us nothing for or against the cogency of thought. Augustine had

---

[5]Sánchez, *Ortega y Gasset*, pp. 195–216.
[6]*Ibid.*, pp. 132–142.
[7]*Ibid.*, pp. 232–3.

learned this lesson well: "in your wonderful, secret way, my God, you had already taught me that a statement is not necessarily true because it is wrapped in fine language or false because it is awkwardly expressed. . . . You had already taught me this lesson and the converse truth, that an assertion is not necessarily true because it is badly expressed or false because it is finely spoken."[8] To decide on the cogency of a man's thought we examine the reasons he gives for it, whereas to judge the effectiveness of a man's style we ascertain whether the effects produced by his presentation are consonant with his intentions.[9]

If Ortega's intention was simply to expound his philosophic system, then his style left much to be desired, for in no single work did he give an explicit, complete statement of his essential doctrine.[b] But on one occasion he did state that it would have been too easy to become a *Gelehrte,* a savant who occupied his life writing exhaustive philosophic treatises; after all, he studied under Hermann Cohen, was a friend of Nicolai Hartmann, and won an important chair of metaphysics at the age of twenty-seven. Only choice, he said, prevented him from comporting himself according to the stereotype of a learned metaphysician.[10] Ortega's literary intention went beyond expounding a system of ideas; he aimed at cultivating the ability of his readers to form coherent abstractions and to use those abstractions as means for improving the actual life they led. These intentions gave rise to the rationale of Ortega's style.

Two characteristics mark Ortega's prose: a notable variety of subject matter and an extraordinary constancy of form. Ortega wrote on quite as many subjects as Bertrand Russell, to choose a philosopher well known for his universal curiosity;[c] but unlike Russell, whose treatment of different subjects often seemed to owe little to his basic philosophic convictions, Ortega made his reflections on politics, art, epistemology, psychology, history, and pedagogy all illuminate the essential premises of his thought. The unity

---

[8]Augustine, *Confessions*, Bk. V, Ch. 6, R. S. Pine-Coffin, trans.

[9]A concise statement of the contemporary relevance of this confrontation is in Martin S. Dworkin's "Fiction and Teaching," *Journal of Aesthetic Education*, Vol. I, No. 2, Autumn, 1966, pp. 71–4.

[10]*Prólogo para alemanes*, 1933, 1958, *Obras* VIII, p. 57.

in Ortega's thought was not achieved, however, by going in the direction of more systematic writers, for instance, Ernst Cassirer. Whereas in *The Myth of the State* Cassirer began with an explicit statement of his philosophy of symbolic forms and throughout applied that conception methodically to the illumination of a persistent political problem, in *The Revolt of the Masses* Ortega did not explicitly mention his doctrine of human existence until the closing pages and then it was to observe that the doctrine had been "entwined, insinuated, and whispered" in the text.[11] By proceeding in this way, readers who disagreed with Ortega's basic convictions might still profit from his analysis of European history, but readers who were not convinced by Cassirer's conception of myth could draw little from his application of it to the political past. Thus, Ortega was particularly capable of treating diverse topics in such a way that his essays could simultaneously stand independent from his other works and contribute to the elucidation of his system for those who wished to follow it.

If Ortega's handling of subject matter was unique, so was his choice of form. Twentieth-century philosophic stylists like Unamuno, Santayana, and Sartre have used a variety of prose, dramatic, and poetic forms to to present their thought to the public. Ortega wrote only essays. Furthermore, all his essays, regardless of length or subject, were constructed in the same way: he would write in compact sections, each of which could stand alone as a short essay; and to form larger works he would string related sections together. His art was that of the aphorist, in which he took great care to fit various short, concise statements of principles together into a larger, unified work.

An instance of this variety and constancy may be found in the first volume of *The Spectator*. Included were essays on epistemology; the philosophy of history; love; World War One; joy; "esthetics on a trolley car"; the Castilian countryside; paintings by Titian, Poussin, and Velázquez; the nature of consciousness; and the writings of Pío Baroja. Throughout, certain convictions about thought, life, and the future of Spain insistently recurred. Yet

---

[11]See Ernst Cassirer, *The Myth of the State*. The words by Ortega are from *La rebelión de las masas*, 1930, *Obras* IV, p. 278.

despite the variety of topics, Ortega composed everything in short sections, in each of which he raised a single thought, explored its significance, and pointed towards the idea that would follow in the next. The longest essay, "Ideas on Pío Baroja," comprised fifteen of these sections, which each averaged two pages in length.[12] Throughout his life Ortega continued to write on a variety of topics; and he was always faithful to his basic prose form, composing passages from fifty to five thousand words in length and including from one to fifty or more of these in an essay or book.

Diversity of subject and invariability of form: these are the striking features of Ortega's prose; the rationale of Ortega's style should clarify why he always relied on one form of the essay to write about a variety of topics. The critic's task is to discover whether these features of Ortega's style could help readers form coherent abstractions and provoke them to use these ideas in living their lives.

A young man in search of an ideal Spain could not be content with the established channels of action. Ortega's prospective patriotism recognized his country's traditional weaknesses, and the goal of the *nueva política,* or civic pedagogy, was to create the conditions for a Spanish renaissance, to establish a *Kinderland* that was free of the vices that vitiated the fatherland. Intellectuals had a duty to use every means they could to strengthen Spanish culture. Thus Ortega's prose exemplifies the stylist as educator.

Certain readers may object, however, that didacticism is an enemy of literary grace, and yet Ortega's writing is a model of grace. To be sure, in an ordinary sense didacticism leads to a disquisitional rhetoric. But Ortega's writing was not didactic in an ordinary sense. He devoted little effort to disseminating information or cultivating convention through his prose. He was strangely incapable of exposition. Even his essays on travel were displays of dialectical, not descriptive, skills;[13] and when, in an essay such as *Mirabeau or the Politician,* facts were necessary, he presented them in a blurb

---

[12]*El Espectador—I,* 1916, *Obras* II, pp. 15–125.

[13]See especially, "Notas de andar y ver," 1915, *Obras* II, pp. 249–265; "Temas de viaje," 1922, *Obras* II, pp. 367-383; and "Notas del vago estío," 1925, *Obras* II, pp. 413–450.

of information that became memorable only in the ensuing analysis of principles.[14] Ortega's writing was informed by pedagogical intentions, but not by the pedagogy that is generally espoused by people who believe they possess superior knowledge and who seek to proclaim it to lesser men. Ortega's commitment to the liberal tradition was present in his prose, and hence he always wrote for an audience of peers.

When peers converse as peers, it is a dialogue. This fact has troubled many writers who think of their readers as peers but have difficulty adapting static pages of print to the open exchange of dialogue.[15] The Plato of the Seventh Letter showed an acute awareness of this problem, and the many forms of dialogue promoted by Plato's work provide a key to the art of Ortega's prose. With respect to the reader, Plato's early, so-called Socratic dialogues give a fixed presentation of definite discourse, one that can be seemingly experienced and enjoyed without the reader's critical engagement; these works may appear aporetic only by virtue of their aporetic endings. In contrast, the middle and late dialogues do not so perfectly dramatize possible conversations. But if each statement in these works, for instance, in the *Republic*, is taken literally, the work yields absurdities. Yet the work functions as a powerful heuristic if the reader continually and actively engages himself in the critical interpretation of the possible meanings of Plato's text. Thus the work proves to be internally aporetic; and as soon as Plato's readers engage themselves in reasoning about the just man who may reside in their own hearts, they find that Plato left many clues with which they can thread their way through his artful contradictions. Let us take, then, as the sign that a work is philosophic dialogue the fact that the writer can elicit, by one means or another, the reader's critical involvement in the questions at hand.

Ortega, by virtue of his ability to engage his readers in reason-

---

[14]*Mirabeau o el político*, 1927, *Obras* III, esp. pp. 612–8 where the facts of Mirabeau's life were given. Cf. "Juan Vives y su mundo," 1940, 1961, *Obras* IX, pp. 507–9 where Ortega prefaced his lecture with a blurb of information on Vives.

[15]There is a good discussion of dialogue in Paul Friedländer, *Plato, An Introduction*, Ralph Manheim, trans., pp. 154–170. The discussion that follows has been influenced by this work, by my own reflections on the style of Plato, Nietzsche, and Ortega, and by discussions with Martin S. Dworkin and others.

ing about particular problems, was a master of philosophic dialogue. He did not state his thoughts so that they could be easily mouthed by others. He rarely gave a systematic, abstract statement of a principle; instead he would treat principles in relation to particular situations, leaving it to the reader to *make,* not repeat, the abstraction. Further, he usually presented incomplete arguments, in which there would be gaps that the reader would have to fill for himself. In writing, Ortega continually complemented the particular with the general, the general with the particular; and he left it to the reader to decide whether to read a work, or even a paragraph, as a theoretical reflection or as a polemical designation. Even the very brilliance of his wording made readers continually ask themselves: is this serious or is it simply a phrase? All these features were among the devices that Ortega used to engage the reader's intellectual powers by not making his primary meaning obvious, by not giving it a final, full, fixed formulation, by helping readers to extract from the text their own formulations of its meaning.

Even the critics of Ortega's style testify unwittingly to his ability to refrain from pronouncing the final word and to force his readers to seek it out for themselves. Thus, Father Sánchez observed that it was not "easy to discover what Ortega really holds. He submits his ideas to a scrupulous analysis before putting them on paper. Whoever tries to penetrate his thought has to launch forth on an arduous ideological hunt through the dense jungle of his extensive work. . . . Behind the scenery of his metaphors he artfully juggles his ideas. He calls this his delight, his irony—to wear that masquerade which permits us only by close scrutiny to glimpse his real characteristics."[16] These words, which were meant to damn, were fine praise to a man who wrote in order to create a philosophic dialogue with his readers, for they testify to the skill with which Ortega made his readers think. Thus Ortega hid his thought from casual curiosities and manifested it to those who were willing to search for it "by close scrutiny."

Ortega's style was dialogically effective. This power, however, might have been the result of his intentional art or of accident. His style might be explained as the fortuitous combination of his gift

---

[16]Sánchez, *Ortega y Gasset,* p. 137.

for phrasing striking metaphors with his incapacity for expounding ideas systematically. However much these qualities explain the origin of his style, Ortega was aware that his writing functioned well as dialogue. He cultivated this quality of his prose. "The involution of the book towards the dialogue: this has been my purpose."[17]

Unlike Martin Buber, who made dialogue one of his principle subjects of reflection, Ortega rarely wrote about dialogue per se.[d] For him, dialogue was reflection, it was thought; although he wrote about it infrequently, he took part in it continually. According to Ortega, dialogue was a problem for a serious writer because in its essence thought was dialogue; and to communicate thought one had to produce a dialogue. In this production the writer needed neither to set forth dramatic conversations nor to ramble on about dialogue; he needed to write in such a way as to provoke the reader into dialogue, or thought, concern over real uncertainties. This task was particularly difficult because the dialogue that Ortega tried to stimulate was not so much a direct one between himself and his reader as it was an indirect one between his reader and the reader's circumstances, of which Ortega's books were only a minor part.

How was thought dialogue? It was an open exchange concerning matters that the participants recognized to be significant difficulties. In its fullest sense this definition suggested that the most incessant, productive dialogue was the continual exchange between a man's self and his circumstances concerning the vital problems of his life. Each man lived in the midst of his personal, particular surroundings, and each man's thought comprised an infinitely complicated interplay between himself and these circumstances. This interplay involved the problems that a man perceived as he tried to live by means of limited capacities in the midst of inhospitable surroundings. This exchange, which was always open and always significant, was the primary dialogue of life: "life is essentially a dialogue with its circumstances"; "to think is to converse [dialogar] with one's circumstances."[18] The basic dialogue between a man and his world was that man's unique concern; other persons might help

---

[17]Prólogo para alemanes, 1933, 1958, Obras VIII, p. 18.
[18]The first phrase is from Las Atlántidas, 1924, Obras III, p. 291. The second

shape the objective features of a person's world, but only each man alone could converse with *his* surroundings.

This primary dialogue of life, however, which constituted each man's unique experience, was not a solipsism in which the only reality was the one that a man intimately experienced. Each man informed his own conversation with his circumstances by taking part with other men in intellectual dialogue. To do so, men identified common problems; they created mutually comprehensible terms with which they could discuss these problems and their possible solutions; they embarked on the disciplined, dialectical examination of every proposed solution to their difficulties. With these common means—observation, conversation, and criticism—each man structured and controlled the primary dialogue between himself and his circumstances. Thus, beginning with the unique hopes and difficulties of each, men joined and created a common, rational world, in which they could theoretically solve their difficulties and imaginatively fulfill their hopes. Hence, "the dialectic is a collaboration" by means of which men joined together to enhance their personal exchange with their unique surroundings by confessing common concerns, concerting their goals, and perfecting their powers.[19]

To begin, then, dialogically effective writing required the collaboration of the reader. An auditor could not collaborate in a monologue, and therefore it provoked no dialectical progression of thought. To be effective, a writer had to project from his personal life a set of problems, goals, and powers that the reader could discover implicated in his own intimate existence. For collaboration to take place, the good writer would neither speak nor conceal, but indicate, and the good reader would neither believe nor deny, but consider. Whoever gave dialogue its due would note that the mark of an effective writer was not that he was admired and generally understood, nor was it that he was notorious; it was that those who read him carefully would genuinely apply in the conduct of their lives the powers that he communicated.

---

is from "Prólogo a *Historia de la filosofía* de Emile Bréhier," 1942, *Obras* VI, p. 391. Cf. "El deber de la nueva generación argentina," 1924, *Obras* III, p. 255: "thought is . . . essentially dialogue."

[19]"El deber de la nueva generación argentina," 1924, *Obras* III, p. 256.

Universal truths were the bane of dialogue, for, as Ortega often observed, they were inherently utopian and difficult to adapt to the dialogue of life. Principles were important to Ortega, but discourse that communicated only the letter of principles was inadequate, for men did not live in the realm of pure Platonic forms. Adequate discourse had to carry one up out of the cave into the light of abstract thought and then back down to the shadowy particulars. Both the writer and the reader could avoid empty universals—principles divorced from particulars—by dealing only with words that they could find pertinent to an actual occasion. "All words are occasional," Ortega observed. "Language is in essence dialogue, and all other forms of speaking enervate its efficacy. For this reason, I believe that a book can be good only to the degree that it brings to us a latent dialogue in which we sense that the author could concretely imagine his reader. And the reader should feel as if, from between the lines, an ectoplasmic hand came out to touch his person, to caress him, or—very politely—to give him a cuffing."[20]

In *Meditations on Quixote*, Ortega said of a literary work that its form is the organ and that its content is the function that teleologically creates the form.[21] We have examined the form that Ortega tried to give his prose, "the latent dialogue," a good name for those dialogues that lack dramatized conversation but that nevertheless engage the reader in the active interpretation of the text. But the way that Ortega implemented this form followed from the content —the *telos* or function—that provided him with the occasion for creating the form. If his writing enlisted the collaboration of the reader, it was important that there be something particular that the reader was to collaborate in.

Serious writers simultaneously perform particular and general functions, but the enduring worth of their work rarely results from their skill with respect to particulars alone; they must further put their craftsmanship in the service of some general, transcendent concern. Thus, both the man of letters and the hack writer work

---

[20]"Prólogo para franceses," 1937, *Obras* IV, pp. 114–5.
[21]*Meditaciones del Quijote*, 1914, *Obras* I, p. 366.

with similar immediate aims, ranging from the salacious to the salvational; but in doing so, the literary genius is acutely aware of serving a universal function, whereas the scribbler is oblivious of this aspect of his office.

Regardless of its immediate tone and subject, Ortega's writing performed the general function of apprenticing his readers to intellect. Thus, like the Platonic dialogues, Ortega's latent dialogues had at least two levels of significance: on one level was the ostensible subject of discussion and on another was the attempt to perfect the discussant's rigorous use of intellect. This second preoccupation was so important to Ortega that one can appropriately identify it as the function, the *telos*, the content of his writing. Hence, throughout his literary work, he tried to cultivate the intellect of his readers, even though in the course of his career he made a significant change in the audience he sought. Up to the early 1930's he was primarily concerned with the Spaniard's intellectual powers, whereas after that time he addressed himself to the abilities of the European. Be that as it may, the two audiences were intimately linked; the European grew out of the Spanish as for writers in other countries it grew out of the French, British, Italian, or German. Ortega discovered his capacity to address Europe in the course of writing for Spaniards, and perhaps the secret of his appeal to both was his *power* to speak, by means of particulars, to an enduring concern of man, that is, to the question of man's intellect and its function in the conduct of his life.

Power, as Ortega conceived it, depended less on position, on office, on one's control of "force," than it did on one's ability to influence the intricate, intimate existence that persons experienced, and to do so without diminishing the intricacy or intimacy of that existence. To have power with respect to the state of intellect, one had to occasion significant alterations in the way men actually used their intelligence and culture in the course of their lives. Hence, Ortega resorted to the daily paper and the personal essay, for by these means he could speak to men about concrete matters as they pursued their personal concerns, having coffee in the morning break or meditating in the quiet of their study. All of Ortega's writing was circumstantial; it was related in one or another way to his immediate world.e Many essays concerned things that Ortega met with in the course of taking part in Spanish public life; and the rest he could write "as a spectator" because he was so deeply involved in the press of events that he found himself forced, from time to time, to suspend participation and to consider disinterestedly the quality of the things about him.[22] Thus, even his impetus to reflection gained its strength from his involvement in his concrete surroundings. Consequently, he never assumed that his audience was some disembodied, universal philosopher. In the world of men there was no unmoved mover whose existence comprised only pure contemplation. Noting this fact, Ortega wrote not only polemic, but even disinterested essays, so that, in the cacophony of competing claims on an active man's attention, these reflections might command quiet consideration. From this circumstantiality the power of Ortega's prose with respect to intellect derived.

For instance, take *Meditations on Quixote*. In this small book, and in *The Spectator,* which was its continuation, Ortega made the intellectual function of his prose explicit. "The reader will discover, . . . even in the remotest musings on these pages, the throbs of a patriotic preoccupation. He who wrote them, and those to whom they are addressed, began spiritually with the negation of a senile Spain. But isolated negation is an impiety. When the pious and honorable man denies something, he contracts the obligation to erect a new affirmation. . . . Having negated one Spain, we find ourselves on the honorable course of discovering another. Only death will free us from this task. Hence, should one penetrate into the most intimate and personal of our meditations, he will catch us conducting, with the most humble powers of our soul, experiments towards a new Spain." The purpose of these experiments, Ortega said, was to infect his readers with a desire to understand their surroundings by "sincerely presenting to them the spectacle of a man agitated by a vivid eagerness to comprehend." If this desire became an operative element of the Spaniard's view of life, the old Spain would be transmuted into the new.

---

[22]See the acknowledgment in *El Espectador—I* and "Verdad y perspectiva," 1916, *Obras* II, pp. 11, 15–21.

For centuries, Ortega suggested, Spaniards had been animated by rancor and hate; they closed themselves and could neither love nor understand. Comprehension was an act of love in which one carried the matter in question to its fullest possible significance by the shortest available route. The most important aspect of intellect was not erudition, but the power to use man's cultural creations to enhance one's comprehension of the concrete, personal world in which one lived. "All that is general, all that has been learned, all that has been achieved in the culture is only the tactical maneuver that we must make in order to accommodate ourselves to the immediate." Spaniards had been unable to cope with their circumstances because they had not learned to love their world, that is, to employ their culture to perfect their surroundings.[23]

In a meditation on his method, Ortega amplified this thesis. He began by musing idyllically on the mysterious profundity of a forest, for he happened to be sitting in one near the Escorial. What is a forest? he asked; and with this question he began to contemplate the nature of thought. The forest became the occasion of his thought, the forest became his teacher. "This beneficent forest, which anoints my body with health, has furnished my spirit with a great lesson. It is a majestic forest; old, as teachers should be, serene and complex. Moreover, it practices the pedagogy of allusion, the sole delicate and profound pedagogy." An appreciation of this pedagogy, which is the most difficult one to practice, pervaded Ortega's writing. One can comprehend this pedagogy only by practicing it, and consequently he wisely refrained from particularizing the methods by which it should be pursued: "whoever wishes to teach us a truth should not tell it to us; he should simply allude to it with a concise gesture, a gesture that suggests in the air an ideal trajectory along which we can glide, arriving by ourselves at the foot of a new truth."

If he contemplated the forest, which—for the trees—he could never directly experience, he discovered the lesson the forest taught. Beneath the surface of things, beneath their sensory appearance, there was the idea of them, which would be revealed when he

---

[23]This and the preceding paragraph summarize *Meditaciones del Quijote*, "Lector . . . ," 1914, *Obras* I, pp. 311–328. The quotations are from pp. 328, 313, and 321 respectively; the definition of comprehension is from p. 311.

fused his superficial perceptions with an act of pure intellection. To experience a forest, he had to combine the mental concept, the forest, with his sensations of being surrounded with dense trees, of walking on a bed of leaves and moss, and of hearing the stillness gently interrupted by the songs of birds and the whispers of the breeze.[24]

Concepts, the basic stuff of intellect, were the general, common ideas and definitions by means of which men converted immediate sensory data into personal conceptions that were stable and communicable to others. Spaniards habitually ignored concepts and exaggerated the importance of immediate, unrefined impressions. Consequently, Spanish civilization was "impressionistic" and lacked continuity, direction, and intelligent leadership. With only a bit of irony, he suggested that to correct this imbalance Spaniards should make it a national goal to master the concept. Instead, many mistakenly justified Spanish impressionism by opposing reason to life. Reason was not a substitute for life; concepts were the work of life, and like digestion or reproduction, reason was a vital function of the human being. As a vital function, reason was a great aid, not a threat, to life. Rightly understood, the concept would be the ally of the Spaniard's traditional impressionism.[25]

Like Seneca, Ortega might have quoted Posidonius: "A single day among the learned lasts longer than the longest life of the ignorant."[26] A man with developed conceptual powers would have a greater capacity for the immediate experience of life than would someone with scant ideational ability. In the course of every moment a man experiences a multitude of fleeting impressions; and without some means of fixing his attention, he could not concentrate on one matter long enough to apprehend masterfully any but its most

---

[24]This and the preceding paragraph summarize *Ibid.*, pp. 329–337. The quotations are both from p. 335.

[25]This and the following two paragraphs summarize *Ibid.*, pp. 337–364. For more technical discussions of Ortega's conception of the concept, see "Conciencia, objecto y las tres distancias de éste," 1915, *Obras* II, pp. 61–6; "Sobre el concepto de sensación," 1913, *Obras* I, pp. 245–261; *El tema de nuestro tiempo*, 1923, *Obras* III, esp. pp. 163–8. Ortega's major work on the subject is *La idea de principio en Leibniz*, 1947, 1958, *Obras* VIII, esp. pp. 66–70, 99–114, and 256–323.

[26]Seneca, *Epistulae Morales*, LXXVIII, 29, Richard M. Gummere, trans.

superficial significances. A man fixed his attention and investigated the ultimate significance of a thing by means of concepts. These intellectual tools were by themselves no substitute for the impressions of real experience, Ortega cautioned; concepts complemented and completed impressions by enabling a man to convert his feelings and sensations into comprehension. And a man expanded his life by achieving such understanding. "Only when something has been thought does it fall within our power. And only when the elemental objects have been subdued, are we able to progress towards the more complex."[27]

Culture was not simply a body of great literature; it was the concepts, principles, and ideas that made the literature—as well as the art, law, and science of a people—useful in the conduct of their lives. Because Spaniards had few concepts at their command, they had little culture; despite the fact that they had a rich tradition, they lacked the means for bringing this tradition to bear upon their lives. Here, then, was the writer's task: to communicate fundamental concepts and to show how they were to be used in life. "On the moral map of Europe we represent the extreme predominance of the impression. Concepts have never been our forte; and there is no doubt that we would be unfaithful to our destiny if we ceased to affirm energetically the impressionism found in our past. I do not propose a secession, but, on the contrary, an integration. . . . Our culture will never give us a firm footing if we do not secure and organize our sensualism by cultivating our meditativeness."[28] To develop his readers' reflectiveness, Ortega wrote primarily about concepts. By an allusive pedagogy, he explained various concepts and showed how they were to be used. Thus, the essay we are analyzing was at once a critique of Spanish culture and an introduction to the concept of the concept. By functioning in this second way, his essay helped overcome the deficiency in Spanish character that had been identified as crucial in his cultural critique. Whatever the ostensible subject of Ortega's prose, there was as well a discourse on one or another concept and its significance for life.

Anyone who wished to make reason serve life could not be

---

[27]*Meditaciones del Quijote*, 1914, *Obras* I, p. 354.
[28]*Ibid.*, p. 359.

content with dwelling on a few specially favored thoughts. Ortega had to concern himself with a multitude of concepts, which would run the gamut of the situations that arise in life. Hence, even if he were naturally inclined to specialize, Ortega's purpose would have led him to speak on many matters. A writer who dwelt on a narrow range of concepts would help merely to cultivate learned ignoramuses who were reasonable in esoteric matters and bumbling fools in the mundane concerns of life. Besides permitting Ortega to introduce a useful range of concepts, variety in subject matter permitted him to shun abstraction and to emphasize the concrete even though he wrote about principles. Thus, he could use the pedagogy of allusion.f For instance, in meditating on the concept, Ortega began, not with the metaphysics of essences, but with the forest glen in which he sat. But note, if he had not continually varied the real situations that he used in explicating his ideas, his readers would soon have found either that he was concerned primarily with the situation itself, he being gifted with a minor talent for describing forests, or that the situations, like the tables and chairs often discussed in introductory epistemology, had been converted into technical conventions that no longer served effectively to bring metaphysics down to earth. The variety of Ortega's subject matter enabled him to avoid these pitfalls; he introduced his readers to a multitude of concepts by presenting well-chosen references to daily life.

Ortega relied on short, personal essays as his favorite prose form because through these he could bring latent dialogues to his readers, and with such dialogues he could practice the pedagogy of allusion. In each fragmentary essay Ortega introduced a concept, he indicated and explored certain things that would engage the reader in using the concept, he scattered clues about how the concept might be mastered, and he then broke off, leaving the reader to proceed alone along the ideal trajectory that had been suggested. There are dangers, however, in such a prose form, and in seeing why Ortega would risk these dangers, we perceive his true mettle as an educator of the public.

Anyone who intends to teach by the pedagogy of allusion must risk being misunderstood and he must have faith in the ultimate competence and good will of others. Ortega took that risk and he had that faith. "There is little probability that a work like mine, which, although of minor value, is very complicated, which is full of secrets, allusions, and elisions, and which is throughout completely intertwined with my vital trajectory, will encounter the generous soul who truly desires to understand it. More abstract works, freed by their intention and style from the personal life out of which they surged, can be more easily assimilated because they require less interpretative effort."[29] Here is the choice of Hercules that any popularizer must make. Does one have confidence in the capacity of the audience to make an interpretative effort, or does one distrust its ability? Ortega believed that a man mastered himself and his world by making an interpretative effort; and he therefore believed that a writer misused his readers when he made their interpretative effort unnecessary, for by doing so the writer encouraged readers to be lax before life and to expect life to reveal itself replete with a ready-made discipline.

Ortega's writing gained its pedagogical power from his determination to respect the intelligence and intellect of his audience. By requiring a great interpretative effort from his readers, Ortega risked on the one hand that they might have difficulty precisely reproducing his personal conception of one or another concept, but he ensured on the other that they would be better able to think by means of that concept. Readers who independently pursued the thoughts that he suggested would train themselves in using concepts to order their experience. To encourage such mastery, it was best to refrain from excessive explicitness and to make the reader think through the lesson for himself. Ortega's style produced effects consonant with his intentions. As the forest had been the occasion, not the subject, of Ortega's meditation on the concept, so his meditation was to be the occasion, not the subject, of his reader's own reflection.

By means of his writing, Ortega tried to disseminate throughout Spain a more adequate repertory of essential concepts that would perfect the Spaniard's impressionistic genius. In his essays Ortega called attention to different concepts in the course of writing about a great variety of topics; and he elicited the reader's involve-

---

[29]"Prólogo a una edición de sus obras," 1932, *Obras* VI, p. 347.

ment with these concepts by not providing an exhaustive, abstract interpretation of his subject, and by giving instead a suggestive yet precise indication that could be completed only by the reader's own efforts. There is no better example of these techniques than the final part of *Meditations on Quixote*. In it Ortega meditated on the concept of the novel, for he held it necessary to master this concept in order to do justice to *Don Quixote* and to the great influence on Spanish character that this book had had. In this meditation Ortega introduced and allusively explicated various other concepts that contributed to an understanding of the novel; he wrote passages of five to ten paragraphs on the idea of the literary genre, the exemplary novel, epic, the bard, myth, books of chivalry, poetry and reality, realism, mime, the hero, lyricism, tragedy, comedy, tragicomedy, and the experimental novel. On each of these topics, Ortega at most was suggestive; and the reader was clearly expected to complete his own conception of these matters and to unify them into a general conception of the novel that might prove adequate for intepreting *Don Quixote* and its effect on the interpreter's life.[30]

Throughout Ortega's work, one will find him in this way introducing, explicating, and commending concepts through short, suggestive essays that implement the pedagogy of allusion. Ortega's prose was dialectically effective because of his ability to record allusive actualities, rather than consummate abstractions; and consequently, even through his style he wielded pedagogical power. The principle that gave his prose its power was the principle of respecting the reader's interpretative abilities.

Here again is the choice that every writer must make. Some choose to make reason regulate life by imparting their conclusions directly to others without transmitting the skills by which the conclusions were drawn; others seek to make reason function in life by awakening with their prose the rational powers of their readers. Each writer must choose whether to communicate primarily the results of reason or the powers of reason. Ortega chose the latter course. He believed that when a mind comes alive and begins to vibrate with the power of reason, its duty is not to think paternally on behalf of those who are still inert. With the ineluctable force of

---

[30]*Meditaciones del Quijote*, 1914, *Obras* I, pp. 365–400.

resonance, it should vibrate in sympathy with other reasoning minds and augment with the increment of each the power of the whole, so that all are awakened and a great work may be wrought.

* * *

To those who are awake there is one ordered universe common to all, whereas in sleep each man turns away to one of his own.

HERACLITUS, 89

*S*TRICTLY, *a man's vocation must be his vocation for a perfectly concrete, individual, and integral life, not for the social schema of a career.*

ORTEGA[1]

---

[1] "Sobre las carreras," 1934, *Obras* V, p. 171.

V
The Partly
Faithful Professor

FOR OVER TWENTY-FIVE YEARS, Ortega's career, in the sense of a social schema, was that of a university professor. As had been anticipated, in 1910 Ortega won appointment to the Chair of Metaphysics at the University of Madrid. His character as a civic pedagogue is exemplified in the way he turned this career into an integral element of his personal vocation.

How Ortega's expectations must have soared when he learned, at twenty-seven, that he had won the Chair! Here was a great opportunity; without having to spend years in academic obscurity, he would be able to use his new position to work systematically at educating the gifted elite that he believed necessary for Spanish reform. As he later put it, an "imperative of intellectuality" was a condition of progress in Spain, and there was no better way to cultivate intellectuality in Spain than as a professor of metaphysics.[a]

For Ortega, any substantial civic grouping such as a nation involved the linking together of diverse peoples in such a way that their diversities were preserved, perfected, and utilized. Nationality was not a common character shared by all. The ability to draw, in pursuit of a *Kinderland*, on the different characteristics of diverse peoples, gave rise to a nation in which men with many special geniuses could give, harmoniously and cooperatively, to the common effort what was unique to each. For this federation of diverse elements to occur, it was important that each be "in form," that each have a sense of his uniqueness, of the way that his special character might help enrich the whole. What Ortega called "particularism" developed within a nation not when its component members possessed an acute sense of their unique character, but when these members complacently confused themselves with the whole. Particularist groups, thinking they were the nation, would seek to make policy serve their interests without taking into account the interests of other members.[2]

Ortega thought that Spain's politics was hopelessly particularistic; this condition gave rise to the imperative of intellectuality. Such an imperative did not call on the intellectuals to take over power; as we have noted, an Ortegan elite was not an authoritarian elite. Instead, the imperative of intellectuality called on men who had carefully disciplined their powers of thought to confront "the masses," the uncritical members of all the particularist groups in Spain, with clear delineations of the actual complexity of the nation, the diversity of its members, and the intricacy of their interdependence. If a minority of gifted, articulate thinkers could confront the Spanish people with a cogent presentation of this diversity and intricacy, then a modicum of realism, humility, and altruism might creep into practical politics. "In the intellectual class there resides vaguely, very vaguely, the lone possibility of constituting a select minority capable of profoundly influencing our ethnic destinies and beginning to initiate the new organization of our country, which now destroys and atomizes itself day by day. I believe, therefore, that the Spanish intellectual is not at the hour of triumph, but at the hour of the greatest effort."[3]

In its full sense, this effort would be two fold. In the end it would entail bringing intellectual clarity to bear on every aspect of Spanish life; but that culmination was possible only after a previous labor had been performed, namely, only after a substantial group of Spaniards had truly mastered intellect. It was this aspect of the imperative of intellectuality that Ortega could pursue as a professor of philosophy.

Recall how Ortega's conception of Europeanization gave priority to intellectual rigor as the European characteristic that Spaniards sorely lacked. In general, Ortega took it as his task to enamour his

---

[2]Ortega's best presentation of these thoughts is *España invertebrada*, 1921, *Obras* III, especially pp. 51-71.

[3]"Imperativo de intelectualidad," *España*, January 14, 1922, *Obras* XI, pp. 11-2.

compatriots with a feeling for science, that great tradition of theorizing about experience. Science was idealism, metaphysics, thought about phenomena, both physical and spiritual. Thus, Ortega's purpose, the imperative controlling his vocation, was to make the Spaniard "react intellectually to reality." To accomplish this goal, Ortega needed, through his prose or through his classroom, to influence the integral character of particular Spaniards, to inspire them with a feeling for speculative thought. This aim led Ortega to take up the career of an educator, of a professor of philosophy; and as an educator, he did not simply savor ideas in limbo in his philosophical reflections. As an educator, he had to see that ideas gave themselves flesh, for man thought various ideas so that he could use them in living his life. Hence, when Ortega spoke, as he often did, of transforming the Spanish spirit, he did not envisage exercising some mysterious power over the *Volksgeist*; he proclaimed his intention to have a real effect on the thought and character of actual men, first on those who would make up an elite diffused throughout the mass, and second on every man as the capacities of the elite began to resonate independently in each member of the mass. "I will achieve all my aspirations," he said, "if I manage to cut on that minimal portion of the Spanish spirit within my reach certain new facets that will reflect the ideal."[4] One place where a bit of the Spanish spirit came within Ortega's reach was the classroom of the university.

We have already seen how Ortega found the active concerns of politics and economics to be secondary, derivative elements in public affairs. In contrast to these, one of the fundamental factors in public life was the higher learning. Systematic philosophy was especially important, not for any direct effects, but for its indirect influence. A strong, continuing philosophic elite was the historical backbone of any European nation; for in times of trouble the members of this elite unobtrusively preserved the conceptual capacities by which public affairs could again be given a humane, progressive order, and in times of hope these men were a source of inspiration, constructive criticism, and informed instruction. On his return from Germany, several years before his university appointment, Ortega

---

[4]*Meditaciones del Quijote*, 1914, *Obras* I, p. 314.

had clearly stated that the first order for educational reform was to bring the study of philosophy up to the level that the leading European nations had attained during the nineteenth century.[5] It was this belief that brought him home from Marburg, and his appointment was a practical step giving him the opportunity to attempt the reform.

To demand radical improvement in one or another university discipline is easy; to implement such reforms is difficult.[b] The university is a conservative institution. Its power to perpetuate learning is bought partly at the price of being doomed to perpetuate incompetence as well. But this fact should not cause despair. The university is particularly open to personal influences. Faculties rarely excel as corporate bodies; great schools of scholarship are the work of particular men. The vitality of an intellectual tradition does not depend on its being continuously represented by popular courses in the curriculum; it is more important that here or there a particular professor in one way or another profoundly moves certain students. Through such relationships Ortega himself had been initiated to systematic philosophy. And since the transmission of learning depended on such personal influences, he could hope that a university, although seriously estranged from the philosophical tradition, could make up its deficiencies and develop a corps of men who were at, or near, the front rank of speculative inquiry.

Only rarely does academic reform require action from administrators and senior professors. The real changes depend on the spirit of younger faculty members, of those who do not believe that the present world is the only possible one and who are therefore unwilling to call it the best. As young men define their style of inquiry, their purposes and powers as teachers and students, they define the future character of the university. If their elders reward the mediocre, preferring the familiar to the excellent, it simply means that institutions with present prestige will decline and others will take their place, for the truth will come to light. Here is the secret source of renewal: among the young there is a gravitation towards difficulty, which is less visible than the gravitation towards novelty, but

---

[5]See especially "Asamblea para el progreso de las ciencias," 1908, *Obras* I, pp. 99-110.

which is in the long run the most powerful of all the forces making for beneficial change.

Ortega's teaching provides an excellent example of the power of spontaneous reform. He simply began to teach in his own way, pursuing his own academic ends; students recognized his personal competence and the legitimacy of his purpose; other professors concurred with his goals; without fanfare, the reform was wrought. In this way, "the school of Madrid" emerged. By 1936 Madrileños took pride in the fact that their city was a flourishing philosophical center, and they gave Ortega much of the credit.[6] The change was remarkable and is the first measure of Ortega's accomplishment as a teacher.

Whereas at the turn of the century the most progressive philosophic movement in Spain was *Krausismo*, by the 1930's Madrid was one of the creative centers of existential thought. To be sure, Unamuno had done the most to bring Spanish thought to the attention of those outside of Spain; but it was Ortega who had done the most to bring Spaniards abreast of European speculation. Prodded by Ortega, Spanish publishers discovered during the twenties and thirties that they could flourish by providing a substantial public with good translations of European thinkers, traditional and contemporary. Brentano, Dilthey, Husserl, Scheler, Simmel, Spengler, Spranger, Heidegger, and Huizinga attracted much interest. Talented young men took to the study of philosophy; and in the early 1920's, Ortega had one of them, Xavier Zubiri, go to Freiburg where Husserl taught. There Zubiri came under the influence of Martin Heidegger; and hence even before the publication of *Sein und Zeit*, a link was established between Ortega's version of existential metaphysics and Heidegger's. Zubiri has gone on to become one of the more able philosophers of Europe as is shown by the appearance in 1962 of his treatise, *Sobre la esencia*.[7] In addition to Zubiri, Ortega's teaching had a significant influence on a number of other excellent philosophers—Pedro Laín Entralgo, Julián Marías, José Ferrater Mora, Paulino Garagorri, Luis Díez del Corral, Manuel Granell, and

---

[6]See the articles by Fernando Vela, Manuel García Morente, Xavier Zubiri, Luis Santullano, Gregorio Marañón, Blas Cabrera, and María Zambrano in the March 8, 1936 issue of *El Sol*.

[7]Xavier Zubiri, *Sobre la escencia*, tercera edición, 1963.

José Luis L. Aranguren, among them—all of whom are in one way or another connected with the school of Madrid. Together, they constitute one of the more solid centers of contemporary thought. As examples: Laín's work on "the self and the other" and his inquiries into the ethics of the clinical relation between doctor and patient, Marías's studies in the history of philosophy, Ferrater's reflections on the nature of death, Garagorri's essays on Unamuno and Ortega and his continuation, in the Ortegan mode, of an active role for the philosopher in contemporary Spanish life, and Díez del Corral's profound reflections on European history are but a few examples of how members of the school of Madrid have brought clarity, profundity, and competence to bear on a wide range of concerns.c

Together with his direct influence on the school of Madrid, there is a second measure of Ortega's teaching, namely his continuing inspirational influence in the Spanish university. After the Civil War, Ortega was barred from teaching, but even so he remained one of the more effective influences in Spanish higher education: insofar as students are free men, they will naturally follow the memory of excellence rather than fawn on imposed mediocrity. This influence became manifest at Ortega's death in 1955. Numerous speakers and essayists commemorated his influence as a teacher, for the fact that he had not been permitted to teach had all along been eloquent witness to his power to teach.d Always a master at creating occasions, Ortega was so in death, for his funeral became one of those great events in which the human spirit affirms itself against those who would suppress it by shouting, as General Millán Astray reputedly did when unable to answer Unamuno's criticism, "Down with intellect! Long live death!" The regime was able to censor the obituaries and made a transparent effort to hail Ortega as one of its supporters; but it could not control the elegies of the inward heart. Through these, truths were spoken that could not be suppressed. In memorial after memorial, thousand of students eloquently payed homage to the men, Ortega and others, who should have been the students' teachers. "This posthumous tribute to Ortega y Gasset, professor of philosophy and letters, is the homage of those who would have been his disciples had he not relinquished, for reasons well known, his chair of metaphysics. It is an homage of a university youth without a university which is compelled to seek knowledge outside of classes, from books which are not textbooks and in languages which are not Spanish."[8]

Thus, what happened through both Ortega's presence and his absence as a teacher attests to his capacity; and when viewed in retrospect, there can be no doubt that Ortega's influence through the university was great. Manuel García Morente, Ortega's friend and colleague, gave unequivocal testimony to this fact: "the philosophic teaching that, during the past twenty-five years, Don José Ortega has given at the University of Madrid has actually created the basis of Spanish philosophic throught."[9] And Xavier Zubiri gave a clue to the genius of Ortega's teaching when he described it as "the intellectual irradiation of a thinker in formation."[10]

A major part of Ortega's commitment to renovate Spanish life through civic pedagogy depended on the fact that this irradiation took effect, that his teaching had power. And let us emphasize the word "power." Teaching is not a neutral act; it is a public commitment of considerable consequence. At his best, a teacher occasions change in those he meets; in doing so, he shapes the future—this is the teacher's power. With respect to this power, a detailed reconstruction of the particular lessons imparted by a pedagogue is less significant than the informing principles that allow the lessons to occasion change in their recipients.

*   *   *

Ortega had left Germany committed to reforming Spain by reforming, among other things, the university. In academe, his mission was to raise intellectual standards, to bring dormant traditions back to life, and to cultivate a love of intellect among those who had little comprehension of the capacities that a thoughtful life entailed. In pursuing such a mission one can easily plunge into pedantry. Ortega realized that intellect could flourish only when enlivened with imagination. Higher standards were useful only to those with higher aspirations, and consequently, while

---

[8]From a memorial read at Ortega's grave when some thousand students brought a wreath to it the day after his funeral; quoted by Richard Mowrer, "Unrest in Spain," *The New Leader*, Vol. XXXIX, No. 7, February 13, 1956, p. 14.

[9]Manuel García Morente, *Ensayos*, p. 205.

[10]Xavier Zubiri, "Ortega, maestro de filosofía," *El Sol*, March 8, 1936.

insisting on competence, Ortega provoked his students to essay the most difficult problems of thought. Here were the principles that gave Ortega's teaching its power: intellect *and* imagination. Thus, Ortega taught with a two-edged tongue: the discipline and hope that he had received as a student he tried to transmit as a teacher by simultaneously cultivating the tools and the *telos* of thinking.

Students aver that as a teacher Ortega had style. Those who spent much time with him report that he would use many means of discourse to teach at any opportunity, that always the expression of his thought was taut, and that each particular statement carried with it an intimation of his entire outlook. Ortega not only presented his philosophy, he exemplified it. Thus, the Puerto Rican educator, Antonio Rodríguez Huéscar, recalled that "in Ortega — in his teaching — we witnessed . . . *living reason* in motion, personalized, making itself; Ortega did not *have* a philosophy, he *was it*."[11] Few students could resist the lyric grace of Ortega's discourse. Manuel Granell, a member of the school of Madrid, has recorded how Ortega "seduced" him to give up plans to study architecture and to switch to philosophy. "Never would I have suspected that concepts could take on such flesh. The dry, cold Kantian expression received palpitating life. And suddenly, in the *Critique of Pure Reason*, he opened a small passage that led to the essence of love."[12]

The essence of love, an erotic theory of education: by the time Ortega had returned from Germany, he not only had one, but, believing that people had to feel attracted to learning in order to seek it out, he was ready to make use of his theory. Before his first class at the normal school of Madrid, there was much curious anticipation among the students, for his writing — as it always would — had stirred youthful spirits. Ortega arrived a moment late. The expectant students watched as he drew, silently, but with a dramatic flair, a copy of Plato's *Theaetetus* from his briefcase. Holding the book before the class, he announced that they were beginning a course in philosophy and

[11]Rodríguez, *Con Ortega*, pp. 24-5, quotation p. 24.
[12]Granell, *Ortega*, p. 30.

that philosophy was the general science of love. As such, philosophy was an aspiration, a desire, not for erudition, but for understanding, for the greatest possible comprehension of the connection of all things to all things.[13]

As Ortega realized, such methods involve serious risks. Without care, the teacher who uses dramatic, poetic methods to arouse the interest of his students, can sacrifice his teaching to his drama and poetry. In his particular case, Granell noted how, when students started to take notes, Ortega stopped and warned them that he was presenting an example chosen to engage their powers of thought, not to present noteworthy doctrine. "I must try to seduce you with lyric means; but you must not forget that they are only this: means—means and not ends. Philosophers should permit no other seduction than that of metaphysical ideas."[14] To carry off such a seduction one needs more than sensuous rhetoric. All love is a discipline; but none is more demanding than *amor intellectualis*. What erogenous zones of the spirit did Ortega arouse? How did he turn these desires towards the true, the good, and the beautiful?

Firstly, Ortega required competence. It may seem strange that the seduction of metaphysical ideas should begin with such a prosaic quality that at the start erected a barrier; but the expectation that seduction should be easy simply shows how far we have come to expect that everyone should win great thoughts with little effort; the cult of easy learning goes hand-in-hand with that of easy virtue. Ortega was not intimidated by the thought that rigor would reduce creativity. The idea of rigor intimidates only those who lack strong creative energy; whereas for anyone with sufficient spirit to command his opportunities, rigor is the quality that enables him to seize a thought and turn it into a work of art, science, or ethics. All love is a discipline, and the very essence of *amor intellectualis* is rigor, competence, and precision.

Science, Ortega once observed, meant to speak precisely; and precision, he told a young Argentine, was the requisite of a

[13]Maetzu, *Antología*, pp. 85-7.
[14]Granell, *Ortega*, p. 30.

good thinker.[15] A teacher who wished to initiate his students into the delights of metaphysics should try to impart the standards of precise thinking. One does not, however, speak precisely by incanting the term "precision" and expecting all to understand. When logical positivists think of precision, they dream of a perfect language in which ambiguity is rendered impossible. Such precision was not Ortega's goal. Whereas the theorists of a perfect language aim at the precision of objective statement, Ortega sought the precision of subjective comprehension. He was not interested in training students to repeat, dumbly but accurately, the characteristic terminologies of various philosophers. The terms themselves were meaningless;[e] and they could have meaning only for those who perceived the human problems that a philosopher tried to solve by recourse to the thoughts denoted imperfectly by his terminology. The attempt to do away with metaphysics by exposing the inadequacies of its language is based on a reverse word magic in which the shaman believes that by annihilating the words he can annihilate the thing. But the problems of metaphysics are not dependent on the words; the meanings of the words are dependent on certain problems of man.

A good example of this reverse word magic is Stuart Chase's chaste rebuke of *The Tyranny of Words*.[16] Chase reproduces isolated sentences and paragraphs from various writers, including Ortega, to show how their willingness to use words imprecisely—meaninglessly, without strict observance of the ordinary definitions—makes them get stirred up about senseless matters. Chase's word magic becomes apparent in his expectation that any paragraph should be lucid even when it stands alone, independent of the context the author gave it. With this expectation, a work of art can be nothing more than the sum of its parts. Each word embodies a conventional significance; and regardless of the spiritual whole into which these discrete elements are woven, we are to judge on the basis of conventional meanings whether an isolated passage expresses something intelligible. If the separate parts

---

[15]"La pedagogía social como programa político," 1910 *Obras* I, p. 509, for the definition of science; "Carta a un joven argentino . . . ," 1924, *Obras* II, pp. 348-9, for the requisites of a good thinker.

[16]Stuart Chase, *The Tyranny of Words*, *passim* and especially pp. 369-370.

prove unintelligible, Chase infers that the context, the inclusive whole the author forged from these parts, must be the figment of an excited imagination.

By this method words certainly will never be tyrannical, for they will never require a person to alter his established convictions about the way things are. But whenever tempted to make such criticisms from the part to the whole, we should remember Coleridge's caution. "Critics, who are most ready to bring this charge of pedantry and unintelligibility, are the most apt to overlook the important fact that besides the language of words there is a language of spirits (*sermo interior*), and that the former is only the vehicle of the latter. Consequently their assurance that they do not understand the philosophic writer, instead of proving anything against the philosophy, may furnish an equal and (*caeteris paribus*) even a stronger presumption against their own philosophic talent."[17]

Coleridge meant by "language of spirits" the inner comprehension that arises in a man as he contemplates the wondrous and awesome aspects of his existence. The life of any man is problematic, and words are merely imperfect means that men use to make manifest to themselves and others what they think about their problems. Words receive their human significance from the context of the human problem that occasions their utterance. No matter how carefully defined, words do not serve to communicate fully unless speaker and listener tacitly share common concerns; these concerns give rise to the *sermo interior*, the realm of interior discourse that the true educator seeks to develop. Hence, Ortega contended, any teaching that did not first impart a personal comprehension of the difficulties that had occasioned a particular thought would merely impart a muddled set of ideas, the significance of which the student had no inkling of.

Instructional reforms followed from this contention. Ortega adapted the age-old *lectio* to a novel purpose. A student would read aloud an important passage from a great work and Ortega would give a commentary to it.[18] In doing so, he avoided simple

---

[17]Coleridge, *Biographia Literaria*, Chapter XII, p. 158.

[18]Rodríguez, *Con Ortega*, pp. 21-3, gives an account of his experience as Ortega's reader.

attempts to explain the argument. Such explanations distracted the student from his proper concern, Ortega suggested, because a program of instruction that was designed simply to transmit subject matter was fundamentally false: it merely thrust upon the student a mass of material that he was not prepared to understand. Because most students sought subject matter alone, they usually falsified the very knowledge they tried to acquire. "The solution to such a tough and bicorn problem . . . does not consist in decreeing that one should not study, but in profoundly reforming the human activity of study and consequently the essence of the student. For this purpose, it is necessary to turn instruction around and say that to teach is primarily and fundamentally to teach the need for a science, and *not to teach* the science the need for which it is impossible to make the student feel."[19] Here was the principle of negative education, first noticed by Rousseau, applied to university pedagogy.

Through historicism Ortega made students perceive the opportunity for metaphysics, the source of it, not in theory, but in man's vital experience. Historicist explanations, as he indicated throughout his essay on "History as a System," took account of the fact that everything human, including the pursuit of truth, beauty, and goodness, had an historical setting that was pertinent to understanding the character of the human effort. "To comprehend anything human, personal or collective, it is indispensable to narrate its history. This man, this nation acts this way and is as it is *because* before it acted in another and was something else. Life only becomes a bit transparent to *historic reason.*"[20] With an historicist presentation, a teacher could convey a precise understanding of the issues that had occasioned man's great philosophical systems. Even when explaining the most abstract issues, Ortega usually resorted to historical expositon, either showing how the issue arose in the history of thought or suggesting how it should arise in a hypothetical personal history.

Ortega's historicism was a mode of explanation, not a set of

---

[19]"Sobre el estudiar y el estudiante," 1933, *Obras* IV, p. 554.
[20]"Historia como sistema," 1935, *Obras* VI, p. 40.

ontological assertions about what had "really" happened in bygone times.f Ortega did not suggest that thought was determined by historically inevitable forces. On the contrary, thought was man's free response to his circumstances; and to understand any particular thought, one needed to be aware of the circumstances to which it pertained. "The understanding," Ortega told his students, "and its radical form—philosophy—, are not definitive attitudes of man, but only historical ones, ones of the human present."[21] Hence, to understand a philosophic system, students needed to comprehend its historical setting, to discover what human problems the system pertained to, and to make that system part of their repertory for dealing with the world when the problems to which the system pertained were also their problems.

Whatever its worth as a philosophy of history, Ortega's historicism was useful as a pedagogical means. A student who did not understand the vital problems that gave rise to an intellectual system had no personal control over the system. To be sure, he might be able to reproduce and analyze various arguments, but he would be unable to use them. To help students assert control over their intellects and to improve their use of thought in living their lives, Ortega tried to recreate through historical exposition the problems that men had sought to solve by creating metaphysics. Competence resulted from understanding, not mere knowing; and to understand a matter one needed, in addition to knowing its formal properties, to comprehend its function. Hence, one did not effectively disseminate the tools of intellect simply by explaining various doctrines; one had to exemplify their humane uses.g

Ortega sought first to stimulate the student's power of thought. He cultivated this power in his students by imparting to them an historical understanding of philosophy. Note that a student who had mastered the power of thought would be free to exert himself on whatever problem engaged his interest. In this way, Ortega's first instructional endeavor contributed to a liberal

---

[21]"Tesis para un sistema de filosofía," *Revista de Occidente*, October 1965, p. 6.

education, to an education worthy of free men, for a young man who understood the historical uses of different doctrines would be free to adapt them to his personal purposes. Here the other concern of Ortega's teaching came to the fore—the *telos* of intellect.

Secondly, then, Ortega aroused a sense of mission in his students. In addition to gaining a clear comprehension of the uses of past doctrines students needed to define the purposes through which they could adapt past doctrines to present uses. Without a personal mission, even the best trained thinkers would be dependent on convention; and a man who was dependent on convention, whether his dependence was positive or negative, was not his own master. A teacher could not provide his students with a mission, but he could continually put the issue before them and suggest various possibilities for their consideration. Students responded to Ortega because he provoked their aspirations. Insistently, he advised youths to contemplate their destiny, to define their proper purposes. Frequently, he confronted students with the idea of a mission and the function that it served in personal life. Imaginatively, he suggested novel aspirations for consideration by the students he addressed.

According to Ortega, a person's mission was an activity that he *had to do* in the double sense that the person had certain things he could do, for they were within his sphere of possibilities, and that he not only had them to do, but he had to do them, he was obliged to do them, on the pain of voluntarily falsifying his best self.[h] Each self, in conjunction with its circumstances, had definite possibilities, which would not become actual without effort, but which were not Utopian, impossible goals to pursue. Only the person himself could will to pursue his mission, for although many components of it were public, or at least publicly apparent, the most important element, his will, was locked in the recesses of his spirit. Ortega's conception of mission democratized and universalized his idea of the hero, the man who resisted the ready-made life that his surroundings offered and who invented his own program of life, an adventure in which he overcame the real problems in his circumstances. Every man had a mission, which each had to find in his circumstances; and, like the hero, every man finds that he can pursue his mission only through authentic, personal commitments, not through impersonal, external conventions. Ultimately, the quality of *life* in any community was a function of the degree to which its members freely aspired to fulfill their missions, their destinies.

A man became free by willing to pursue his mission. Each person's mission originated from his own powers and inspiration, and was always dependent on these; hence one's mission was the basis of one's dignity and strength vis-à-vis the manifold stimuli from the surrounding world. No slave can be made of a man who has a keen sense of his mission; a despotic ruler can only exterminate such a man, or drive him into open or covert rebellion. No inner strength, no independence can develop in a man who lacks a feeling for his mission, for he will have no basis for pursuing a consistent course of action in the face of the vicissitudes of experience. Consequently, a liberal education, an education worthy of free men, must somehow address the problem of mission; and one of the great threats to the liberal tradition is that the growing reliance on stereotypes in education, entertainment, and propaganda destroys the power of young men to formulate inspiring, personal conceptions of their destinies.

How can the teacher take up this question? The very nature of a mission complicates the task, for no man can authoritatively tell another what the latter's mission is. The Greek debate over whether virtue could be taught is essential to answering the educational question posed by Ortega's conception of mission. Socrates and Plato worked out the liberal position: virtue itself cannot be taught, but the intellectual skills by which a person can ascertain the proper virtue in any particular situation can be taught. Such skills the teacher could impart, but beyond those, he had to rely on the natural goodness of man, on the fact that no man would wittingly do wrong. The desire to be virtuous came from within the person, and the teacher had to limit himself to hoping that by judicious criticism he might awaken the unwitting to a sense of their error. The teacher could not exceed that limit and instruct others of their duties. Thus Socrates must let the befuddled Euthyphro continue with his impious plan; and despite all Plato's talk about the idea of the good, he gave no substantive definition of goodness itself.[i]

In a similar way, Ortega did not propose to teach people their mission. As we have seen, he did teach his students to comprehend the use of concepts. This instruction would help to free them to think constructively about their personal destiny. But the teacher could do more; he could try to insure by criticism that the young would not be unaware of the problem of their mission. There was a great difference between a teacher who dogmatically proclaimed to his students that they must do thus and so, and one who told them that they should consider what it was that they must do. Ortega took the latter course. He believed that on examining independently their common problems, men would come up with coherent goals. The difficulty was to get the problems before the people. To accomplish this, Ortega devoted much of his effort in his academic courses, his public lectures, and his protreptic essays to making his listeners consider the question of their destiny.

Throughout his life Ortega exhorted students, professors, and the public at large to examine the mission of the university. Currently, we are becoming fully aware that the university will have a central place in any twentieth-century *Kinderland*, for as the possibilities of politics and economics are more and more nearly exhausted, the task of further humanizing life falls more and more explicitly to the men of culture. Ortega reflected on the mission of the university with a full awareness of the intrinsic power of intellect. He did not acquiesce to the apparent inevitabilities of his given present; he keenly studied the art of the possible.

The issue for the future is this: is the university the client of the state, or is the state the client of the university? This question restates the already familiar question: is practical politics the primary problem of public affairs and pedagogy secondary, or is pedagogy primary and politics secondary? We know in general Ortega's answers to these questions. Pedagogy was the primary force moving the public affairs of a community. The state was becoming a great danger, having become for many an end unto itself; and to provide an alternative center for progressive aspirations, the university should be built up as fulcrum for humane initiative. These convictions, fully developed, lead to a European *Kinderland*.

If education has precedence over politics, then the participants in the university have, despite contrary appearances, initiative with respect to their function in the community. Almost everywhere the formal arrangements appear to contradict this fact: universities are chartered and maintained by the political and economic powers that be. But Ortega believed that official politics, with the formal primacy of the state over the university, was a sham; vital politics coincided with the actual relations in the community, and in early twentieth-century Spain there was much evidence that the university was a major source of enlightened theory and humane practice in public affairs. Whether or not full community leadership would ever be located in the university, there were grounds for calling on students and professors to lead the university in unexpected, independent, controversial directions. Intellectuals could assert initiative if professors and students could spontaneously concert their aspirations towards great, *cultural* goals. All that Ortega said about the mission of the university was intended to produce this coalition.

Ortega's reflections pertain to a situation that has many parallels to current unrest in Western universities. There was a crisis of purpose in Spain as presently there is throughout the post-imperialist world. When people have lost faith in their traditions and expect little from official politics, they turn to alternative institutions. Thus in Spain, many hoped that the university could be a source of great reforms, if . . . . If what? If the university could stop being the meek servitor of the established interests and could begin to act independently. The university, that is, the aggregate of students and professors, would act independently if the cultural activities its members performed reflected their autonomous judgment of what was culturally most fit and proper, not the judgment by practical men of what was politically and economically most expedient. Then, and now, the effort to act autonomously was easily sidetracked in a senseless agitation against external interferences. Interferences would be left behind if—if students and professors could somehow concert their efforts at learning and teaching. In the 1920's in Spain, the students were well organized in their peculiar, anarchic way, and the university faculty was at least in part far more progressive than those in official power. The time was ripe for a university initiative, provided students and professors could combine the authentic pursuit of their proper activities into an effective reforming force.

Ortega's efforts to promote university reform, to make the university a powerful force for Spanish reform, aimed to unite faculty members and students in the cooperative pursuit of common cultural goals. In our day, many managers of the so-called multiversities instinctively misunderstand this possibility, for it contradicts their essential policy—divide and rule. For instance, in *The Uses of the University*, Clark Kerr observed that "although José Ortega y Gasset, in addressing the student federation at the University of Madrid, was willing to turn over the entire 'mission of the university' to the students, he neglected to comment on faculty reaction."[22] This remark reveals an inadequate comprehension of both Ortega and the important educational possibility that was in question. In the realities of life, the mission depended on all who participated in the university, and it could be "turned over" to no particular group, neither to students, nor to professors, nor to administrators. The mission could be perfected, however, if all participating persons considered their destiny in the university and honestly refined their aspirations.

In his quip, Kerr did not dwell long enough on the setting in which Ortega enunciated his vision of the university's mission. The central issue was not whether either the students or the professors should dominate within the university; the central issue was the one that has been central since Plato criticized sophistry, and it will certainly continue to be central to academic development throughout this century. This issue concerned putting the school, the university, on an equal footing with the state. Without such balance, the ruler will not respect the thinker, and will expect the latter to do no more than menially improve the means for achieving politically sanctioned ends, whatever these may be.

The Mission of the University, a manifesto declaring the independence of the university from narrowly defined state ser-

---

[22]Clark Kerr, *The Uses of the University*, p. 21.

vice and control, appeared as a series in a daily newspaper during the fall of 1930. Spain was then in the midst of a revolution: the quasi-Fascist dictator, Primo de Rivera, had lost control of the country and renounced his power; the Monarchy was collapsing; a Republic, which not without reason would be called "the professors' Republic," seemed destined. Ortega had published his articles in fulfillment of a promise he had made while addressing the powerful student federation, the F. U. E. The students sought Ortega's opinions because he had been a leader in the campaign to free the university from state interference. In the agitation preceding the Republic, both students and professors wanted the university freed from the customary political interference; they thought, further, that men of culture should take up leadership and transform the university into a bulwark of a liberal Spain. The Madrid students invited Ortega to speak about these possibilities. There was little need for Ortega to comment on faculty reaction, since he was then recognized as a leading spokesman for the faculty.j The students wanted to know what reforms he, a respected professor, thought should be made in the Spanish university. The position Ortega espoused showed his ability to call simultaneously for both discipline and hope, and his fidelity to his conception of Europeanization, that is, to his belief in the historic importance of fundamental principles.

In his speech on the ninth of October, Ortega did not present his personal conception of desirable academic reforms. Instead, he reflected with the students on the qualities that made reformers effective, for if students were to do their part, they would need to develop these qualities in themselves. Ortega spoke in a large hall, filled with a young audience that buzzed with excitement. He brought this excitement to a peak by reflecting on the historic power of enthusiasm.

"If primitive humanity had not possessed this ability to inflame itself with far off things in order to struggle against the obstacles that it encountered close at hand, humanity would continue to be static." But then Ortega brought the students down to earth: enthusiasm alone produced no reforms; the reformer had to act as well as hope, and to act well a man had to be in form, or "in shape," as athletes put it. To get in shape for university reform, one needed discipline and clarity, an awareness of present problems and possibilities, and a knowledge of the strengths and weaknesses of one's own character. The university and its mission could not be discussed substantively in a loud voice before a huge audience, Ortega told the students. These topics, he promised, would be the subject of a special course, which he characteristically conducted through the columns of the daily press.[23]

Ortega began by observing that if students were to occupy themselves, as they should, with the effective reform of the university, they had to overcome their frivolousness and forthrightly contend with the mission of the university. Ortega commended one principle to students who were concerned with such reform: do not exhaust energy agitating against abuses, but build up force by fostering the proper uses of the institution. "University reform cannot consist wholly or principally in the correction of abuses. Reform is always the creation of new uses." Both the faculty and the students had to ask the "capital question": "What is the mission of the university?" If the members of both groups continually examined this question, and if each person, whether student or professor, was sufficiently in form to pursue his own answer to it, then their concerted actions would slowly create a reformed university.[24] "History proceeds very often by jumps. These jumps, in which tremendous distances may be covered, are called generations. A generation *in form* can accomplish what centuries failed to achieve without form."[25]

At this point Ortega stopped directly addressing students, for he would not paternally tell them what they should find the proper uses of the university to be. But he did continue. The mission of the university lent itself at least to Ortega's personal

---

[23]"Actos de la F.U.E.: Conferencia de Don José Ortega y Gasset," *El Sol*, October 10, 1930. It would be interesting to know why the transcript of this speech, an outspoken call to university students to gird themselves for involvement in academic and national reform, is not included in present Spanish versions of *Misión de la universidad*. The American translation by Howard Lee Nostrand includes the speech to the F.U.E. The translation gives only vague information on the dates of the *Mission:* the F.U.E. speech was given on October 9; the remainder of the book first appeared very quickly thereafter in the *feuilletons* of *El Sol* for October 12, 17, 19, 24, and 26, and November 3 and 9, 1930.

[24]*Misión de la universidad*, 1930, *Obras* IV, especially pp. 314, 316-7.

[25]*The Mission of the University*, Nostrand, trans., p. 23.

formulation. He himself acted on this mission, and he hoped that others connected with the higher learning would, on considering the problems, find that they had a similar mission and that they would also act on it. As students and professors spontaneously shared certain aspirations, a better educational program would authentically develop; to impose a plan by administrative fiat would simply pervert the essential nature of the goal. Patience was the virtue of the true reformer.

According to Ortega, the mission of the university was to overcome the multiplicity of studies and to reachieve a unity of culture. The reunification of culture would make the university, once again, a spiritual power, a power that could harmonize the political, social, and economic sectors of contemporary life by suffusing them with value. "Then the university would again be what it was in its best hour: an uplifting principle in European history."[26]

In Ortega's view, it was entirely possible and thoroughly desirable to make the university a progressive influence on European history. The university would not perform this function by maximizing its production of applicable knowledge and using it more aggressively to promote the political, economic, and military strength of the state. That Waterloo was won on the playing fields of Eton or that the German victory of 1871 was the victory of the Prussian schools and the German professor was a *"fundamental error that it is necessary to root out of our heads,* and it consists in supposing that nations are great *because* their schools —elementary, secondary, or higher—are good. This . . . attributes to the school a creative historic force that it neither has nor can have."[27] This was not the uplifting power that the university could possess; and, if anything, Ortega hoped the university would withdraw from many gratuitous service functions in the community. An historically significant university would be a university that served its own mission, not the interests of the state, and that managed, by virtue of serving its mission, to introduce into public affairs various ideas, aspirations, and abilities that would command historic responses.

---

[26]*Misión de la universidad,* 1930, *Obras* IV, p. 353.
[27]*Ibid.,* p. 315.

An infatuation with practical political power can here pervert an understanding of the pedagogical possibility. Ortega carefully called attention to the error of thinking that the university could promote history directly, and in doing so he allied himself with those in the tradition who have denied that the educator could teach men to be virtuous. Nevertheless, such paternalistic expectations have become deeply ingrained in present-day views of how history is made; hence many think that history is made for men by their institutions and that institutions that cannot act directly cannot act at all. In keeping with these beliefs, many expect that the university will promote history through its instructional programs, which will cast present youth in a mold that has been predetermined to suit the future. Instead, history may still be made by men, and another way that the university may promote history is by being of discreet assistance to men as they seek to realize their unique potentialities. The university becomes a sterile servant of the status quo to the degree that it prostitutes itself to programmatic policies. The university wields the indirect power of culture. It shapes history by helping the young inform their hopes and discipline their powers, and thus spring surprises on their elders. Rather than the university program being the historic agent and the students being the plastic stuff upon which it works, free men may be the historic agents and the university may be a simple but significant occasion for their activity. Liberal education gains historic significance in this second manner, by helping the men who will make history make themselves.

By definition, an education is at once general and particular: it includes all the intellectual attributes that a particular person acquires during his lifetime. Not even the grandest institution *gives* an education, specialized or general; the institution offers instruction, the student acquires his education. It is an axiom of liberal pedagogy that responsibility and initiative reside in the person becoming educated; he is the one who must live with the ideals and skills that he acquires. Since in the end each man is his own teacher and the instructional agent is not the cause of education, educational institutions cannot be the servile agents of the established interests, for those institutions do not in fact have the pedagogical efficacy to mold the young to any externally determined form. To stay within the bounds of human possibility, educational institutions can and should do no more than provide the occasions wherein the young can forge themselves into something substantial.

In the past hundred years, however, educational theorists have plunged into pedagogical paternalism.k What was once the student's responsibility has since become the responsibility of the teacher and the institution. Opportunities to receive instruction have been hypostatized into "an education" that exists independent of the persons who acquire it. This hypostatized education is attributed to teachers and institutions, which are thought to have the power to educate. Thus, one "receives" a college education by virtue of doing satisfactorily what a college faculty tells one to do. The pedagogical consequence of this hypostatization has been to shift nearly the whole burden of responsibility and initiative in formal provisions for education off the student and onto the teacher. This shift has had a grotesque effect on didactics: learning theory has become synonymous with conditioning theory.

Ortega's hopes for the Spanish university will be incomprehensible to the pedagogical paternalist. To be sure, Ortega made efficiency the key to a desirable program of instruction, but it was efficiency defined by the student, not the social powers that expected to be served by the university. As a national system for distributing socially useful skills, Ortega's university would become less efficient and less predictable. But his university was not to serve a paternal state, but to contribute to a republic of free men. By respecting, rather than subverting, each person's intrinsic dignity, the university would again become a constructive force in history, in an open, humane history made by responsible persons. The mission that Ortega envisaged for the university was to renounce the pedagogical paternalism that has been the foundation of the corporate state and to offer again an education worthy of free men.

Presently, many despair of life in industrial societies because they have a diminished sense of responsible freedom and of creative significance. The compulsions that people feel are manifold: libidos excited by the media drive us into promiscuity; organization—political, economic, and soical—forces us into all kinds of established group endeavors, which suck the dignity from our sense of self; a premature taste for abundance lures us into debt and catches us in the endless effort to meet our payments on a mounting material wonderland. A young person who sees his future as a series of compulsions rightly judges that there is no reason to educate himself, to give his character a unique, significant form. Men in power think that they have learned to manipulate the public. Adeptly mobilizing idealistic activism here and the complacency of the silent majority there, they believe that the performance of essential social functions can be assured, regardless of particular persons' sense of non-participation. This political nihilism of the adult rulers simply intensifies the educational nihilism of the young by depriving them of an authentic sense of personal responsibility. Thus we incubate the citizens of an ever less-principled, characterless community.

Juvenile anomie can be overcome by one decisive act; let us suppress the *bêtise* that teachers and institutions are responsible for the success of education, and instead, let us recognize the fact that the one thing in life for which the young are absolutely responsible is their own education. This responsibility is unavoidable because the young have the ultimate power, whatever the system of didactics, to accept or refuse instruction, to seek out, select, tolerate, or ignore any particular preachment. A boy's duty is to make a man of himself; the responsibility of youth is to educate itself. No man or institution can do this for the young; life puts it up to them. In educating themselves, the young make or break themselves, for their ability to acquire that highest of all possessions, self-help, fundamentally determines the quality of their commonwealth. Teachers can only challenge — *Sapere aude!* Dare to discern!

On this point, Ortega was *"muy siglo veinte,"* very twentieth century. He broke decisively with the paternalistic conception of the university for the nation's service. To be sure, out of context certain of his points sounded quite paternalistic. For instance, he contended that the university must "make the average man, *above all,* a cultured man. . . ."[28] But the context of this remark was his

---

[28]*Ibid.*, p. 335.

insistence that the university was based on the students, and hence he was putting the responsibility to make the average man cultured primarily on the average man, that is, the student, rather than on the teacher or the curriculum. Ortega did not intend, as Clark Kerr mistakenly suggested, to hand over the entire mission of the university to the students. Ortega's intention was not so simple; he believed that no component of the university — students, professors, administrators — could authentically contribute their increment to the whole unless they recognized that students were the reason for being of the university. "In the organization of superior instruction, in the construction of the university, one should begin with the student, not with knowledge or the professor. The university should be the institutional projection of the student, whose two essential characteristics are a limited, insufficient power to learn and a need to know in order to live."[29]

By recognizing that the university was the institutional projection of the student, the problem of curriculum was posed in a new manner. The alternative to paternalism by the faculty is not a pure and simple abdication to "student power." *Lernfreiheit* and *Lehrfreiheit*, the freedom to learn and the freedom to teach, go together inseparably; and the worst abuse of academic freedom for the faculties of American colleges and universities is our examination system, which impairs the student's freedom to learn in any particular course, and which thus undercuts the professor's freedom to teach. To be sure, there should be a check on achievement to uphold standards and to certify that competencies have in fact been attained; but that check need not come at the end of each separate course, and it would be closer to its proper place if it came when a student judged that he had mastered a whole subject, not a fragmentary course, and that he had acquired the qualifications for a degree. Reliance on course grades signals our distrust of a student's power to judge his own progress. When students are considered to be incapable of autonomous judgment, the teacher finds ascribed to him manipulatory power over the students; and with that power, the teacher seems to become responsible for the results of its exercise. This apparent responsibility inhibits the

---

[29]*Ibid.*, p. 332, italics omitted.

teacher's activity: if it is the teacher's fault that his students fail an examination, then the teacher will feel impelled to spoon feed his auditors. But the man studying, being capable of autonomous judgment, is responsible for his studies. Confronted with men studying, the man teaching finds that his responsibility is to make the matters that he personally considers important accessible to those who also consider them worthy of study. The essence of such a system is mutual respect between students and professor; the enemy of it is the urge to prescribe.

Ortega believed that the mission of the university could be realized cooperatively and spontaneously because he had the twin conviction that students who were unfettered and aware of their responsibilities to themselves would wisely choose what to study, and that professors who were autonomous and confident in their students would intelligently choose what to teach. The existing system, however, was perverted, in the Spanish case, not by misplaced examinations, but by the simple fact that the most important matters were ignored by both professors and students, for all were preoccupied with other people's business. To reform the university, both professors and students needed to get in shape, in form, and by an act of will attend to their proper business: the acquisition, not of skills, but of culture. Ortega asserted that professors who were in form would try to teach culture; and he was confident that, given the opportunity, students would want to make themselves cultured men. And for Ortega, "culture" had a special meaning.

Culture was not some objective good; it was important because the student was a living, throbbing person who had to act, like it or not, in a myriad of ways. Man was limited, an imperfect being; and yet he had to direct himself in the world, often in situations in which the potential consequences were final. Culture was the set of ideas by which men gave direction to themselves in the world. Culture was another way of talking about an education worthy of free men, for it was an imperfect but provisionally complete scheme of the world and of life by means of which a person could direct himself through his life. Culture included certain vocational skills; but the possession of only a particular set of skills was not sufficient as culture, for the man who possessed only particular skills would be dependent on a world in which those skills were needed. Culture was that comprehension of the way things were that enabled a man to readapt continually to ever changing situations and to maintain through those changes his unique, personal character.[30] Culture was a definite, intellectual structure by means of which particular men oriented themselves in the chaos they found around them. Culture was each man's means for making a cosmos of the surrounding chaos.

Ortega observed that students could not learn everything; they had to choose to learn this and to ignore that, or else they would overload their capacity to acquire knowledge. Students who chose frivolously would be shirking their responsibility to themselves and their future; the matter was too important to the young for them to leave it up to their elders. As far as many specialists were concerned, it would be convenient to ignore culture in the university, to forego a sense of over-all orientation in order to gain omnipotence in a narrow matter. But, Ortega thought, the students would be foolish if they did not seek, above all, for culture in its proper sense. If students carefully nurtured their sense of life, its values, principles, and problems, then they would have the power to give a coherent direction to their more specialized activities; and if, on the other hand, uncultured specialists, who lacked a sense of the whole, continued to dominate the important, particular activities of contemporary life, then the community would remain dangerously directionless, unprincipled, and instable. Culture should not be shirked; anyone who thought he could safely ignore the difficult task of making himself cultured was blindly gambling that other men would be willing and able to provide the community with qualities that he himself believed unworthy of his personal concern. Ortega did not believe that the young really wanted to take this risk, and consequently he asserted that "the *primary and central* function of the university is education in the great cultural disciplines."[31]

As a fact of academic life, the great cultural disciplines were not in the existing curriculum. University disciplines had long been

---

[30]*Ibid.*, pp. 340-8.
[31]*Ibid.*, p. 335.

organized to meet technical, rather than cultural, preoccupations, Ortega observed. This situation was harmful even to the future of the sciences, for it created a bevy of investigators who lacked any orientation to life other than that offered by the present state of their art. To rectify this situation, and more importantly, to reassert the mission of the university, professors should cooperate with the deepest demands of the students, and together they should try to create a new faculty, a faculty of culture. In doing so professors and students could give rebirth to the ideal of a liberal education; and doing that, they would lay the groundwork for a renewal of authentically liberal politics.

Culture had been pushed out of the existing faculties by demands from the surrounding society for more and more practical research. The scholar's strength and freedom, however, has always been his ability to wander, if not physically, at least spiritually; hence there were no compulsions preventing a change of direction. Students could initiate that change by taking responsibility for their own education. Having taken it, they would soon realize their need, to perfect themselves as free beings, for culture. Professors then could make good on the revitalization of liberal education simply by shunning the profits of practice and by seeking the consolations of culture. And in the highest sense there would be a great practical utility in such a course: it would reinvigorate the conscience of the community.

When teachers expected discipline and hope from their students, not simply in this or that special sphere, but in a complete view of life, and when students respected and responded to these expectations on the part of their teachers, then the spontaneous reform that Ortega hoped to achieve would be fulfilled. Then the Spaniard could expect that his community would be continually nourished by an influx of imaginative, competent, independent young men who would penetrate into every sphere of life and bring it closer to perfection. By respect for the autonomy of men and for the capacity of free men to make their history, the university could fulfill its historic mission and again become a powerful, indirect source of progress in European history.

If, by such reforms, Spain could get its educational institutions "in form," an open future, one that would bring significant

change in the direction of Spanish public life, might become possible. A university in form would help develop a select minority
that would work, not from the top by virtue of its special skills, but
from every level by virtue of its sense of mission, intellectual clarity, and capacity to live life intensely.

Ortega's conception of Europeanization called for reform by
resonance. A self-appointed elite diffused throughout the community had to set itself in motion; it had to make itself vibrant. On
the appearance of an elite of vibrant spirits, the nation would turn
towards its members in the same way that the admiring gaze of
passers-by turns towards the vibrant man or woman walking down
the street. "Imagine," Ortega mused, "that the general type of
woman preferred by the males of today was a little, a very little
more dynamic than the one loved by our fathers' generation.
Doubtless the children would be thrust towards an existence that
is a bit more bold and enterprising, more replete with appetites and
efforts. Although the change in vital tendency would be slight, its
amplification of the average life of the whole nation would ineluctably bring about a gigantic transformation of Spain."[32]

Working for twenty-five years as an influential professor of
philosophy, Ortega did much to help such an elite bring itself into
existence. But he made himself only "a partly faithful professor,"
as he put it, for cultured elites have all too easily become mere
ornaments on decadent societies. In order to fulfill the imperative
of intellectuality, in order not to lose the benefits of love's labors,
the intellectual must succeed in making reason resound. In keeping
with this part of the imperative, Ortega complemented his work
towards university reform with significant efforts at popularization
through publishing.

*   *   *

*The thinking faculty is common to all. . . . All men have
the capacity of knowing themselves and acting with mode-
ration.*

HERACLITUS, 113, 116

---

[32]"La elección en amor," 1927, *Obras* V, pp. 620-1.

*T*ODAY THE PERIODICAL *article is an indispensable manifestation of the spirit; and whoever pedantically
denies it, lacks the remotest idea of what is happening
in the womb of history.*

ORTEGA[1]

[1]"Prólogo a una edición de sus obras," 1932, *Obras* VI, p. 354.

VI
The People's
Pedagogue

B Y FAMILY TRADITION and personal vocation, Ortega was drawn
into journalism. The Spanish destiny that Ortega discovered
during his studies in Germany, the idea of organizing a minority
charged with educating the masses, the practice of writing to communicate concepts that Spaniards could use to live a fuller life, and
the labor of reforming the university in order to enlarge the vibrant elite of Spain: these aspects of Ortega's vocation were integral with another, his extensive activities in journalism and
publishing. Through newspapers, magazines, and books, Ortega
tried to bring a cultural elite into contact with the average Spaniard. Through the cultural media, not political agencies, the educating minorities would influence the masses. Ortega's insistence that
a prophetic minority was essential in the reform of Spain may in
the end have been a type of paternal authoritarianism or of democratic liberalism. Whether Ortega was a paternalist or a liberal
depends in part on the relation between the elite and the populace
that he sought to establish through mass media.

In more than one sense, our story begins with the year 1898.
Not only did the shock of defeat awaken the critical intellect of
Spain, but also in America Hearst's campaign of yellow journalism
to exploit the sinking of the *Maine* showed that an aggressive press
could effectively fan a nation's martial passions, a demonstration
that heralded the start of a new historic epoch. With universal
schooling, inexpensive books, significant amounts of "free time,"
high circulation papers, radio, movies, television, rapid transit, and

149

a host of other changes, all men have gained an access to information. As this access is widely utilized, the striving to be represented in public deliberations gives way to an urge for immediate participation. Yet as the sources of information come under ever-narrowing control, the possibility that the participation may not be actual, however apparent, arises, for control of the media invariably tempts those in power to manipulate the public totally.

In recent attempts at understanding media, a fascination with apparent changes in the means of communication has led pundits to miss the truly important issue.[2] Man is still the message; and despite man's startling extensions, his fundamental problems remain the same. Men still love and reproduce, eat and assimilate, entertain hopes and suffer disappointments, band together for the pursuit of common concerns and separate in mutual misunderstanding. Throughout these manifold activities, which are rooted not in man's extensions, but in his innards, the problem of judgment is pervasive. No matter how much the technological milieu may change, the intrinsic quality of the problem of judgment remains the same for those who seek to communicate: should one impose on others the judgments one deems correct or should one stimulate in others their powers to judge as they see fit? The new media of communication do not eliminate this issue, they intensify it, for they simultaneously perfect the power to impose judgments on others and to stimulate others to judge for themselves.[3]

Scant consensus has been achieved about how to deal with the problem of judgment through the mass media. A case can be made that the mass media operate on such a scale that those responsible cannot risk relying on the intelligence and interpretative powers of their audience; instead, they must try to ensure that the audience gets their point. Paradoxically, in the case of selling soap we clearly see the damage wrought by downgrading the intelligence of the audience, for the economic goal does not begin to justify the educationally harmful means. But with respect to great

---

[2]See for instance Marshall McLuhan, *Understanding Media, passim.*

[3]In "Seeing for Ourselves: Notes on the Movie Art and Industry, Critics, and Audiences," *The Journal of Aesthetic Education,* July 1969, pp. 45-55, Martin S. Dworkin examines the problem of locating responsibility for making the film responsive to personal judgment.

public issues, a clear-cut judgment is not so easy. In times of war, how far will the egalitarian democrat maintain his faith in the intelligence and good judgment of the common man by allowing partisans of the enemy to state their case, freely and fully, not only on a soap-box at the edge of a deserted park, but also through the most powerful media available? How will the egalitarian introduce the ordinary person to the work of the physicist, not to speak of the difficult poet? What does it mean to believe in the average man, to put one's faith in him? Does it mean to be satisfied with him exactly as he is, or to be willing to wager the success of one's actions on the expectation that the average man will freely excel what he has so far achieved? On the great issues of public policy, will the democratic communicator be content to inform the deliberations of an unfettered popular opinion, or will he seek by one means or another to manipulate the public into a thoughtless acquiescence?

*   *   *

Henri Bergson once observed that "Ortega thinks of himself as a philosopher, but he is only a journalist of genius."[4] For the moment, we need only consider the French essayist's positive evaluation, that Ortega was a journalist of genius.

To begin, one measure of the considerable energy that Ortega devoted to journalism is the frequency with which he helped organize new publishing ventures.[5] True, the number of his initiatives was in part a function of the number of his failures; but only in part. More importantly, the extent and diversity of these activities reflected his intention to reach the people, not by bringing them all beneath the umbrella of a single formula, but by reaching each through his particular interest. To be sure, the resources that Ortega and his friends could command were insufficient for them to span the full range of special interests. Nevertheless, Ortega was

---

[4]Quoted without source citation by Salvador de Madariaga, *De Galdós a Lorca*, p. 112.

[5]The best survey of Ortega's organizing activities is Lorenzo Luzuriaga's "Las fundaciones de Ortega y Gasset." Copies of most of the periodicals that Ortega helped publish can be found in the Hemeroteca Municipal of Madrid. In the following discussion I have relied mainly on an examination of these.

involved in the founding of a popular weekly magazine, a very successful daily paper, a serious monthly review, and two publishing houses that specialized in providing good literature at inexpensive prices, as well as a number of less successful enterprises.

None of Ortega's ventures into the media achieved a truly mass appeal; here is the problem in judging the pedagogical character of his efforts. One might argue that the publications with which he was connected were "elitist" because they did not reach everyone. But that would be an extreme argument, one that would entail holding, for instance, that the *Masses*, a popular magazine of the American left contemporary with Ortega's publications, was also elitist and anti-egalitarian. Even the *Reader's Digest* reaches only a fraction of its potential audience and by a strict count of numbers it is more nonpopular than popular. Furthermore, a magazine is not always edited out of knowledge of its actual audience; in fact, such packaging of the product has been possible only since the techniques of market surveying have been developed. In the absence of these techniques, a magazine or journal is more likely to be edited for an audience the editors would eventually like to win. Whether Ortega's publications were or were not elitist in character depends on considerations more intangible than a simple count of their readers.

Throughout, Ortega's publications reflected a common editorial principle: commission the best writers one can to say whatever they have to say to an audience that is not pre-selected by a commitment to a particular party, ideology, cultural interest, educational prerequisite. A major impetus in Ortega's publishing activities stemmed from the failure of *El Imparcial's* editors to apply this principle to Ortega himself. His style of speaking his mind was cramped by the party connections of the established press, especially by the partiality of *El Imparcial* as an unofficial organ of the Liberal Party. In April 1913 readers of *El Imparcial* were shocked by the first installment of Ortega's essay "On a National Nuisance," for in it Ortega had the quite impartial gall to condemn the Liberal Party as a retrograde factor thwarting Spanish rejuvenation. Three weeks later, Ortega completed the essay, its point and tone uncompromised, by publishing it in *El País*, a competing paper.[6] To sign on with *El País,* however, would not have been a solution, for Ortega was not anxious to toe its line as a Radical Party organ any more than he was to toe that of *El Imparcial.* Ortega set seriously to work to organize a new type of publication in Spain.[a]

This desire was not entirely new to Ortega, for by 1913 he had already learned by several mistakes. Soon after his return from Germany, Ortega had helped found *Faro,* a short-lived weekly in which he discussed many of his ideas about pedagogical reform.[b] Then in 1910 Ortega had helped Luis Bello, who had succeeded Ortega's father as editor of *Los Lunes del Imparcial,* in starting the unsuccessful "review of popular culture," *Europa.* Both *Faro* and *Europa* had a rather narrow appeal to those who already believed in a sophisticated form of Europeanization. The cover of *Europa's* first issue was a drawing of Oscar Wilde, in an art nouveau frame, sniffing a flower in dandy dress.[7] *Europa* was snapped up by those In The Know, but they were not numerous enough to support the magazine, which failed to encourage those Not In The Know to find out what it was all about. The tone of *Europa* was too negative. Even while trying to gain attention for the magazine by writing about it in *El Imparcial,* Ortega stressed the negative, remarking that *Europa's* title could not be more divisive. "*Europa* is not only a negation: it is a principle of methodical aggression against national bungling."[8] *Europa* was elitist in style if not doctrine. Of course, *Europa* expressed the faith that the Spanish people were ready for it, that they would respond to its snobbish notion of Europe and appreciate its excellence. "Those who publish this review," the manifesto of the first issue confessed, "believe one can now give the Spanish people something more than a stamp

---

[6]"De un estorbo nacional," *El Imparcial,* April 22, 1913; and "De un estorbo nacional, II," *El País,* May 12, 1913. Ortega published nothing more in *El Imparcial* except "Bajo el arco en ruina," June 11, 1917, and "El verano, ¿será tranquilo?," June 22, 1917. For the texts of these articles see *Obras* X, pp. 232-7, 241-5, 352-4, and *Obras* XI, pp. 265-8.

[7]Cover of *Europa,* Año I, Núm. 1, February 20, 1910, in the archives of the Hemeroteca Municipal, Madrid.

[8]Ortega, "Nueva Revista," 1910, *Obras* I, p. 144. Cf. *Europa,* May 1, 1910.

album. The public will decide."[9] The public decided; number 13 of volume 1 was the last issue of *Europa*.

From *Europa's* failure to *España's* success was but the ability to learn from mistakes. The new undertaking began in 1914, soon after Ortega broke with *El Imparcial. España*, despite its title, continued the Europeanizing commitment of the young writers who in *Europa* had showed their dedication to improving popular culture —Pío Baroja, Luis Araquistaín, Corpus Barga, González Blanco, Ramón Pérez de Ayala, Manuel Abril, Ramón del Valle-Inclán, Manuel Machado, Ramiro de Maetzu, Bello, and Ortega, among others. *España* was devoted to cultural and political concerns; and, most importantly, its tone was more open than that of *Europa*. The purpose of *España*, like that of the earlier magazine, was to promote Europeanization, to deflate the authority of official Spain, and to concentrate and amplify the powers of vital Spain. But where *Europa* had stressed negative criticism of national deficiencies, *España* encouraged cooperative effort and the fostering of hope.

Ortega wrote the manifesto for *España's* first issue, which set a warm tone of mutual respect in its very title: "*España* Greets the Reader and Says." In what followed, *España* spoke of the sorry state of official Spain. "But *España* has not been founded with the aim of saying only this, which is a negation. Negation is only useful and noble and pious when it serves as a transition to a new affirmation." The task of the new magazine was to bear witness to this affirmation, to give it a voice, to show it gaining resonance in the capital and the provinces. *España* would be the organ of no existing party; it would speak for the ideal party of those who believed in the Spanish future. "We will work in solidarity with every noble intention, with every worthy person, with every just cause whatever its origin and name may be."[10] Ortega stated clearly in the first issues that its editorial principle was to have the best available writers speak their mind to all who sought to build a Spanish *Kinderland*. "Thus, we solicit—

---

[9] Anonymous, "Al Público," *Europa*, February 20, 1910.

[10]"*España* saluda al lector y dice," *España*, núm. 1, January 29, 1915, *Obras* X, pp. 271-3.

and without it we can accomplish nothing—the collaboration of all who aspire to a better Spain."[11]

When *España* was well on its way to success, Ortega withdrew from active collaboration. This withdrawal has been interpreted by some such as Lorenzo Luzuriaga as a sharp break that resulted in *España* falling into other hands.[12] If it occurred at all, this break would have to have come over World War I. Some people thought that Ortega was pro-German because of his studies there. But Ortega was not a Germanophile. During 1915 he repeatedly wrote in *España's* columns that Spain should back England and he averred that he desired "very deeply the triumph of England."[13] But not only was Ortega sympathetic to *España's* position on the war, the record does not even show a clear break between Ortega and *España*.

If Ortega wrote less for *España* in the Spring of 1916, it was because he was hard at work getting out the first volume of *The Spectator*, a series of his personal essays that he sold by subscription. Ortega found time, however, to publish "Cervantes, plenitud española" in the May 4 issue of *España*, which appeared just prior to his leaving with his father on a joint lecture tour in Argentina. Ortega's relations with *España* were still good enough early in 1917 for it to run an article on "Ortega y Gasset in America."[14] In Argentina, Ortega spent most of his time with newspapermen; and on his return he seemed anxious to re-establish his connections with the daily press. He wrote a few articles for *El Imparcial* and *El Día* while working to start up *El Sol*, a major new paper that was to follow the same publishing principles pioneered by *España*.

Money for *El Sol* was put up by the wealthy engineer, Nicolás María de Urgoiti, who wanted to start a newspaper that would give a voice to spokesmen for reform. At first he had tried to buy *El Imparcial*, for its readership was most like that of the

---

[11]*Ibid.* Cf. Anonymous, "Gratitud de *España*" and "Propósitos" in *España*, núm. 2, February 5, 1915.

[12]Luzuriaga, "Las fundaciones de Ortega y Gasset," pp. 38-9.

[13]"Una manera de pensar, II," *España*, October 14, 1915, *Obras* X, pp. 339-344.

[14]J.M.M.S., "Ortega y Gasset en América," *España*, March 7, 1917, p. 11.

paper he wanted to start. However, the deal did not go through.[15] As a result, the capital that would have gone into the purchase of an established readership and an existing, albeit decrepit plant, was put instead into the purchase of new, efficient presses. Now, at last, a Madrid paper was equipped to print a straight line of type on a clean page! This was a source of economic strength and even of political power, which predictably hurt many journalists and politicians, and caused much resentment. *El Sol* was an immediate success; and Ortega, with Manuel Aznar and others, was responsible for its editorial policies. He made it his major means of addressing the public. Not only did *El Sol* publish the quantitative bulk of Ortega's writings, it first published, in *feuilleton* his qualitatively important works: *Invertebrate Spain*, *The Theme of Our Time*, *The Dehumanization of Art*, *On Love*, and *The Revolt of the Masses*, to name only the better known books. In addition to these contributions, Ortega provided *El Sol* with hundreds of reflective commentaries and editorials on Spanish public affairs.

El Sol had grown out of the earlier publishing projects in which Ortega collaborated. The same writers who had often written for *Europa* and *España* appeared frequently in the pages of *El Sol*. Like these magazines, *El Sol* was self-consciously independent of the established parties; and like *España*, but perhaps unlike *Europa*, *El Sol* was not edited in Madrid solely for Madrileños. Much attention was given to news of the provinces, and the intention was clearly to create a national paper. Furthermore, *El Sol* was not narrowly devoted to politics. Close attention was given to culture, economics, technology, entertainment, sports (notably excepting bullfighting), and education. Recall how the imperative of intellectuality called on Spaniards to clarify the full complexity of their common lives, to make manifest the nature of its many different components, to bring each of these to its perfection so that no single Spaniard could absent-mindedly confuse his interests with those of the whole. Here was *El Sol's* function. "The title of this paper," Ortega wrote in its first issue, "signifies above all a desire to see things clearly."[16]

---

[15]Luzuriaga, "Las fundaciones de Ortega y Gasset," p. 40.

[16]"Hacia una mejor política," *El Sol*, December 7, 1917, *Obras X*, p. 368.

El Sol brought many technical innovations to Spanish journalism, for this time an eager staff was backed by an engineer who appreciated the importance of good technique. The paper became the first in Spain to use the graphic techniques of mass journalism and to print legibly in larger characters on good newsprint with high speed presses. By combining quality with unmatched efficiency, *El Sol* offered readers and advertisers a better paper at competitive prices. As a result, Spaniards almost proved that mass journalism need not be sensational, irresponsible journalism. *El Sol* quickly achieved one of the higher circulations in Madrid, 110,000 after three years, and because of its more readable format, it began to cut severely into the advertising revenues of competing papers.[17] By 1920, it began to appear as if the established papers might be driven either to change their ways or to go out of business. But *"la vieja política"* would not let *"la vieja penza"* collapse.

In the summer of 1920, at the behest of the Conservative paper, *A.B.C.*, Eduardo Dato, the Conservative Prime Minister, promulgated two Royal Orders that counteracted *El Sol's* advantages. Ostensibly, the regulations were to reduce the amount of newsprint consumed in Spain. But only *El Sol* and several other technically advanced papers were affected; and these all happened also to be the politically advanced papers. In effect, the regulations forced *El Sol* to cut down to a format of eight pages, rather than its customary sixteen—unless penalties were paid. Formulas were given fixing the price of classified advertisements, requiring *El Sol* either to double its normal charges or to reduce the width of its advertising columns to that of its competitors. Lastly, regulations prohibiting cooperative sales practices made *El Sol* abandon the circulation campaign that had proved successful in building up a national audience.[18]

In a statement protesting the government's fiat, Ortega

---

[17]This circulation was claimed in "La segunda Real orden contra *El Sol*," *El Sol*, July 20, 1920.

[18]On the Royal Orders and *El Sol*, see especially "La R.O. contra *El Sol*: lo que significa la Real orden," *El Sol*, June 16, 1920. Cf. articles on the matter in *El Sol* for June 15, June 17 (by Ortega), June 19 (by Ortega), July 29 (by Ortega and Manuel Aznar), July 30, July 31, August 3, August 4, August 5, and August 9 (by Ortega).

expressed his poignant disappointment by summing up *El Sol's* accomplishments. "Besides being, neither more nor less, a great paper with a European outlook, it has succeeded in three years in ‚creating a format for a daily that is much superior to those familiar in our country. It has created a new journalistic style, and furthermore—a matter I commend to the attention of my readers—it has considerably improved the administrative and editorial techniques of the Press. . ." Then, with his accustomed scorn for mediocrity, Ortega stated the historic significance of the effort to thwart the paper's power. "It is appropriate, in order to orient future historians, to underscore the fact that in Spain around 1920 the possession of a good printing press was considered to be an intolerable vice that the State needed to castigate vigorously."[19]

El Sol survived this crisis; it continued to flourish; and Ortega devoted much of his effort to it during the 1920's. Throughout, Ortega's aim was not primarily to make the paper succeed, but to deflate official Spain and advance the new politics. Ortega and other gifted writers used *El Sol* in an agile pursuit of these more inclusive goals. They were committed journalists, journalists committed not to mere journalism, but to the humanistic regeneration of their country. He and his friends were not as interested in selling newspapers, magazines, and books as they were in apprenticing the Spaniard to intellect. Ortega used publishing, as he used his writing, to make up for the lack of concepts that had traditionally hampered the Spaniard's attempt to deal with the world. Hence, regardless of how popular his audience was, he scrupulously respected its capacity to make a significant contribution to the matter at hand; and usually this involved a fundamental concept that would increase a man's power to live thoughtfully.

Writers could use *El Sol* to pursue such goals because the paper had a flexible format, which developed from Spanish traditions. In the formation of *El Sol*, two points were of major importance: Spanish papers had always been a significant forum for leading intellectuals and had never followed the Anglo-American distinction between factual reporting and interpretative opinion.

---

[19]"Admirable carta de D. José Ortega y Gasset," *El Sol*, June 29, 1920, *Obras* X, pp. 659-662.

These two characteristics stemmed from the fact that the Spanish press, like that throughout most of Europe, had been a party press in which intellectuals were commissioned to interpret events from the party point of view. Like *Le Monde* in France, *El Sol* took these characteristics of the party press and separated them from subservience to any established group in partisan politics, commissioning intellectuals to interpret events independently in the light, as each saw it, of truth and reason. In a partisan milieu, such a paper could serve as a powerful source of enlightenment. With *El Sol*, these characteristics were intentionally forged into a pedagogical rather than a partisan organ.

To begin, the flexible format of *El Sol* enabled the paper to accept irregular contributions from a variety of serious writers. The paper had no regular columnists, whose predictable views would be found at a predictable spot in the editorial pages according to a regular schedule. *El Sol's* layout changed from day to day, depending on the quantity and quality of copy available. Except for departmental pages that were devoted to particular subjects—economics, pedagogy, the provinces, sport, the cinema—various types of articles had no set location. The front page might be laid out in the familiar vertical columns, or in a mosaic of boxed articles; different articles might be composed in various print sizes and in either roman, boldface or italic type. Each day the front page would feature a different combination of news articles, editorials (both signed and unsigned), essays by prominent writers, reports of cultural events, and photographs. Hence although a person could easily become a regular reader of the paper, he could not read it by habit, for to make his way through its ever changing composition, he was continually forced to use his discrimination.

By not being predictable, *El Sol* elicited its readers' involvement with its content, inviting them to find their way anew, each day, through the paper. Many of the articles, and not simply those by Ortega, emphasized the principles pertinent to interpreting the news rather than a factual chronicle of the news itself. Moreover, headlines frequently called attention to intellectual topics rather than to factual events. In this way the reader was informed that a featured article would lead him into considering the principles of parliamentary deliberation, or the concept of localism, or the dynamics of fascism, or the historical significance of Einstein's physical theories. The reader's interpretative powers were respected by freeing writers to use their own interpretative powers to the hilt. As the freedom to teach is secured by recognizing the student's freedom to learn, so the journalist's freedom to express himself fully is gained by having confidence in the reader's freedom to evaluate what he reads.

In part, *El Sol* resulted from the *tertulia*, the conversation groups that met regularly in local cafes and drawing rooms. Indeed, the paper may have originated in a *tertulia*, for from the time of *Europa* until the Civil War Ortega was at the center of such a group, which included the writers who frequented the pages of *El Sol*. But that is not the point; what is important is not the origin, but the function, of *El Sol*. The *tertulia* was a powerful Spanish institution, which could be either a negative or a positive influence on the nation. Whenever a *tertulia* lost access to dynamic ideas and new information, it enforced intellectual stagnation with terrible effect; but whenever a group became porous to external influence or was dominated by persons of wide curiosity, it became a marvelous center for cultural communion, through which profound changes in character could be quickly transmitted from person to person. In *Invertebrate Spain* Ortega analyzed the educational power of the *tertulia* under the heading of "Exemplarity and Aptness"; the tendency toward conformity that existed in any close social group would become a significant source of general improvement if one could introduce exemplary characteristics into those groups.[20] *El Sol* was to do precisely that. It was to be a great conversation piece, the sun illuminating the sidewalk cafes and streaming through the parlor curtains.

As Nietzsche observed of teachers, no philosopher can be expected to be truly profound week after week at appointed hours. This human limitation holds true for the journalist as well, and the genius of *El Sol* was its willingness to accept irregular contributions from many writers. As a consequence, a reader never

---

[20]See "Ejemplaridad y docilidad," *España invertebrada*, 1921, *Obras* III, pp. 103-8. Ortega did not say that he had a *tertulia* in mind, but that is the institution that most closely approximated the relations he described.

knew who would present views in the morning's paper, and writers were not forced to write their columns mechanically, feigning inspiration to meet a fixed commitment. Thus, writers could preserve their sense of mission and readers their sense of discovery. This practice was possible because *El Sol* was not considered to be a packaged product that had, at least, to meet certain minimum specifications day after day in order not to let its consumers down. Rather than maintain a respectable minimum at all costs, *El Sol* daily reached for a maximum. This reach, which sometimes failed, could be justified only with confidence in the discrimination of the audience. The reader, not the editor, had to make the final judgment about the quality of that day's performance. With *El Sol*, responsibility and initiative for informing oneself were left to the reader, and the journalist was freed to speak, as best he could, to the reader's curiosity and concern.

The way Ortega used his access to *El Sol's* columns shows how flexible these procedures were. Ortega was not a dependable source of copy for *El Sol*, and sometimes his copy was, by the American newsman's standards, plainly inappropriate. One after another, series of his articles would appear, and then there might be nothing for many months. Ortega would write on whatever struck his fancy: for a time he would concentrate on day-to-day critiques of contemporary affairs, then he would publish a series of essays about "Love in Stendhal," and then a profound reflection on political theory, the texts of several lectures on epistemology, or a two-part meditation on the migration of birds! If a journalist is a person who writes *for a paper*, then whatever Ortega was, with all due respect to Bergson, he was not a journalist. For Ortega, the newspaper was simply one of many means he used to write *for his audience*.

With *El Sol* and *España*, Ortega collaborated in creating a first-rate daily paper and weekly magazine, yet these left many other publishing areas to be touched. One of the practices the Royal Orders of 1920 had prohibited was the selling of combined subscriptions to *El Sol*, to a monthly literary magazine, and to a book service. Soon afterwards, Ortega and María de Urgoiti collaborated in starting the publishing house, Espasa Calpe, which put out an extensive collection of serious works, classic and contemporary, in a format that almost anyone could afford. Then, two years later, Ortega independently founded and directed the monthly magazine, *Revista de Occidente*. Within a year the magazine generated sufficient resources, financial and literary, to branch into book publishing, a field in which it quickly gained an important place. Next to *El Sol*, *Revista de Occidente* is the most significant of Ortega's efforts to bring a cultural elite into communication with the average man.

Revista de Occidente was not a light magazine; one could not claim that it was for the average man *qua* average man. As Ortega observed in its prospectus, he hoped people who wanted to follow questions in some detail would find it rewarding. With respect to the imperative of intellectuality, *Revista de Occidente* served neither to create the cultured elite that Spain needed to develop nor to confront the average Spaniard with a compelling clarification of the diverse elements of Spain. It would be left to a university in form to nurture the Spanish elite and to periodicals like *El Sol* and *España* to inform the common reader. The function of *Revista de Occidente* was somewhat different: to encourage curious individuals whose desire to understand their world had been stimulated by *El Sol* and *España* to deepen their command of culture. Hopefully, *Revista de Occidente* would help them master culture to the point at which they ceased to be common readers and became members of the cultured leaven scattered through Spain. Ortega did not believe that difficult matters could be made easy. But like Plato, he held that all men possessed the power of judgment; and the opportunity to perfect and live by that power was not to be confined to a closed elite of those who happened to have the good fortune to earn university degrees.

Of the publishing ventures in which Ortega took part, *Revista de Occidente* most clearly bore his mark. Like his prose, its pages brought readers a great variety of articles, almost all of which dealt with important principles that Spaniards might use in living their lives. The *Revista* published articles by leading writers from almost every Western nation. But this fact, by itself, was not the main support for its claim to be a "review of the West." Its real success was in presenting readers the opportunity to acquaint themselves thoroughly with the ideas that were most productive in twentieth-century culture. "Our Review will reserve its attention to the truly important themes, and it will manage to treat them with the fullness and rigor necessary for their general assimilation."[21]

As writers serve both particular and general functions, so do editors. The editing of *Revista de Occidente* showed a keen sense of the universal purposes that a serious monthly could serve. To be sure, editorial details were not ignored. The magazine was technically excellent. For instance, the format and typography of *Revista de Occidente* were carefully conceived and imaginative. Articles were laid out with the reader, not the cost accountant, in mind; the magazine was generous with paper, providing the thoughtful reader with wide margins in which to record his reactions. In starting the magazine, an exclusive contract was taken on a distinctive typeface, which became an identifying feature of the *Revista*. Consequently, when the organization branched into book publishing, any reasonably well-read Spaniard could tell at a glance a book published by the *Revista*. In addition to technical excellence, the magazine could also reward good writing. The *Revista* could pay significant fees to its contributors, Ortega stated in unsuccessfully soliciting an article from Unamuno.[22] Few other important writers declined opportunities to publish in its pages; and month after month it presented in a distinctive way an interesting selection of significant articles by competent writers.

Without succumbing to didacticism, the dedicated editor can have a clear idea of who his readers are, of what potentials make them worthy of his concern, and of how these potentials can be developed by the readers' involvement with the material he publishes. The readers of *Revista de Occidente* were persons in Spain and Latin America with intellectual pretensions. They had the ability to take part in Western intellectual life, but to do so they needed to overcome an ingrained incapacity for abstract thinking. Traditionally Spanish intellectuals had disguised their conceptual

---

[21]"Propósitos," 1923, *Obras* VI, p. 314.

[22]Letter to Unamuno, Madrid, June 6, 1923, *Revista de Occidente*, October 1964, p. 27. Perhaps Unamuno's reluctance resulted from a feeling that "a review of the West" was insufficiently Hispanic to be a proper forum.

poverty by accepting a provincial isolation from the rest of Europe. As its name proclaimed, *Revista de Occidente* would end this isolation. In its "Prospectus" Ortega announced that the magazine would try to develop the Hispanic cultural community through complementary procedures: encouraging Hispanic writers to deal with European themes and bringing the better European thinkers before the Hispanic audience.

A remarkable group of young Spanish essayists, novelists, and poets published in the *Revista,* and on occasion significant contributions were made by Latin American writers such as Victoria Ocampo. No matter how much influence the *Revista's* cosmopolitanism had on its Spanish readers, the magazine seems not to have imparted very much to Spanish writers. Few became preoccupied, centrally concerned, with European themes. Since many of the contributors—for instance Manuel Abril, Pío Baroja, Américo Castro, Eugenio D'Ors, José Gaos, José Martínez Ruiz (Azorín), Ortega, and Ramón Pérez de Ayala[23]—were mature by the time the *Revista* began, it did not shape their personal interests. Younger writers were also not necessarily influenced by the *Revista's* Europeanism. Two promising young interpreters of Spanish character, Federico García Lorca and Miguel Hernández, contributed to the *Revista* without being noticeably influenced by its European concerns. Pedro Salinas, a young poet of marked cosmopolitan character, published much in the *Revista;* but his European interests were formed by several years of teaching in France and England prior to his connection with the *Revista.* For most Spanish writers, the *Revista* did not occasion their taking up new themes; instead it provided a wide-reaching outlet through which they could voice whatever themes—Spanish or European— to which they felt drawn.

The only young writer who was markedly influenced by a desire to address himself to European themes through *Revista de Occidente* was the prolific novelist, Benjamín Jarnés; and one cannot say that this influence was good for him. Jarnés was a

[23]For the essays published in the *Revista* by these men and by those mentioned below, see E. Segura Covarsi's *Indice de la Revista de Occidente.* I have mentioned only those writers who have been written up in the *Diccionario de literatura española.*

novel-a-year man who, from 1925 through 1936, still found time to contribute over seven articles a year to the *Revista*. Although his work was significant, it was not first-rate; his writing, both critical and creative, lacked depth, and this characteristic can largely be attributed to the desire, inflamed by the *Revista*, to encompass too much within his range of reference. For the Spanish writer, the program of the *Revista* was dangerous to the degree that it forced the intellectual growth of young men: a writer cannot simply will to address himself effectively to cosmopolitan questions; he must slowly, naturally nurture this power, as Ortega did for himself, by pursuing the questions immediately before him to their ultimate significance.

Ortega was more successful with the second policy of the *Revista*, bringing the better European writers to Spanish readers. By publishing many translations of important essays, the *Revista* not only brought Spaniards into contact with European themes, it further built up confidence by showing that Spanish writers would not be overshadowed when their work appeared in juxtaposition to that of leading European writers. The cosmopolitanism of the *Revista* did not consist in slighting Spanish culture, ignoring its traditions, and discussing only European themes. Instead it encouraged the better representatives of Spanish culture to mingle with those of other national traditions. To accomplish this integration, it was important that European writing published in the *Revista* have a transcendent, universal signficance, for otherwise it would not serve to stimulate and strengthen the work of Spaniards. Ortega possessed the intellectual and editorial background to know what Europeans might be pointed out to Spaniards and to understand how the former could best be introduced to the latter.

Rather than tell readers about significant men, Ortega sought out ways through which these men could confront readers. The mechanics of this confrontation were quite simple: to publish translations of substantial works by important European contributors to the arts and sciences. As might be expected, this procedure was premised on confidence in the expressive ability of the writer and the interpretative power of the reader. What were the significant ideas being advanced in various fields at that time? Who created these ideas? Which of their works could best introduce these ideas to a curious, intelligent, educated audience? Such questions informed editorial policy. The *Revista* had no formula for addressing an audience of non-specialists such as the one that has proved so profitable for *Scientific American*. Only James Joyce and Edmund Husserl were presented by means of secondary material; and this was mitigated in the case of Husserl by the publication in the "Biblioteca de la Revista de Occidente" of a complete translation of his *Logische Untersuchungen*, which is yet to be translated into English. As for subjects, the *Revista* covered the gamut from literature through physics. But there was more to this procedure than mere mechanics.

Writers and readers of *Revista de Occidente* met as equals because they shared concern for the contemporary cultural condition of the West. "At the present moment, the desire to know 'what is happening in the world' acquires great urgency, for everywhere symptoms of a profound transformation in ideas, sentiments, manners, and institutions surge up. Many people are getting the distressing impression that chaos is invading their existence. Nevertheless, a little clarity, as well as a bit of order and hierarchy in our information will quickly reveal the plan of the new architecture according to which Western life is being reconstructed. *Revista de Occidente* seeks to serve this characteristic state of the spirit in our time."[24] Here was the secret of the *Revista*: it sold neither its readers nor its writers short, for it assumed that both groups sought to develop an integral conception of Western culture. Rather than cajole name writers to tailor their thought to the supposed capacities of the audience, the *Revista* freed thinkers to write from their strength, to explain as best they could what they had to contribute to Western culture, for persons read the review to learn about these essential contributions. Although each issue contained variegated material, the actual subject in most contributions was the fundamental principles of contemporary culture. In this way the *Revista* made good on its claim to be a review of the West.

Take, for instance, the *Revista's* coverage of contemporary literature. The creative writer did much to define the spiritual

---

[24]"Propósitos," 1923, *Obras* VI, p. 313.

possibilities of a people; consequently to make the spirit of the West manifest to Spaniards it was important to have a good selection of the more sensitive Western writers. The *Revista* gave its readers a remarkable introduction to contemporary Western literature. American writing was represented by works of Sherwood Anderson, William Faulkner, and Eugene O'Neill.[25] British writing was more fully introduced with translations of Joseph Conrad, Lord Dunsany, Aldous Huxley, D. H. Lawrence, Katherine Mansfield, Liam O'Flaherty, George Bernard Shaw, James Stephens, and Virginia Woolf. Plays, stories, and essays were translated from the French of Jean Cocteau, Joseph Delteil, Jean Giraudoux, H. R. Lenormand, Paul Morand, and Paul Valéry. From German there were contributions by Franz Kafka, Georg Kaiser, Thomas Mann, Rainer Maria Rilke, Carl Sternheim, and the Austrians Franz Werfel and Stefan Zweig. Finally, three Russians of note, Ilya Ehrenburg, Vsevolod V. Ivanov, and Alexander I. Kuprin, and the Italian, Luigi Pirandello, were introduced to Spanish readers. A review specializing in literature might have been considered successful for publishing writers such as these, along with leading contemporary Spanish writers. But literature was only one of the many subjects covered by the *Revista de Occidente*.

Among the ten internationally known physicists who published in the *Revista*, six were Nobel Prize winners; furthermore the *Revista* was not simply following the judgment of the Swedish Academy of Science, for two of the six—Max Born and Erwin Schrödinger—were awarded the prize after they had written for the *Revista*. These writings concerned many of the basic conceptual problems of physics and the bearing of these problems on cultural matters. In 1926 Max Born wrote on the relation of scientific laws to matter; in 1929, soon after he delivered his

---

[25]In this and ensuing paragraphs, I have mentioned only those contributors who were of sufficient note to be written up in the third edition of *The Columbia Encyclopedia*. Some arbitrary procedure seems necessary in order to keep the discussion reasonably brief. However, this particular criterion leaves out significant figures such as the biologists F. J. J. Buytendijk and Jacob von Uexküll, the historians E. R. Curtius and Wilhelm Worringer, the mathematicians Hans Thirring and Hermann Weyl (a close friend of Ortega), the psychologist David Katz, and the philosopher Eduard Spranger.

paper on the unified field theory to the Prussian Academy of Science, Einstein explained the need and difficulty of this theory to Spaniards; in 1930 Louis de Broglie discussed the question of continuity and individuality in contemporary physics; in 1932 Erwin Schrödinger reflected on the ways in which natural science was conditioned by its milieu and methods; and in 1934 Werner Heisenberg traced the transformations of fundamental principles that had occurred in twentieth-century physics. Besides these essays the *Revista* published examinations of various aspects of theoretical physics and of its significance for a philosophy of culture by Sir Arthur S. Eddington, Sir James Jeans, Abbé Georges Lemaître, Robert A. Millikan, and Willem de Sitter.

Other fields besides literature and physics were well represented. The *Revista* published Leo Frobenius and Sir Arthur Keith on anthropology, Oswald Spengler and Johan Huizinga on history, Werner Sombart on economics, Georg Simmel and Max Weber on sociology, E. F. Gautier on geography, Igor Stravinsky on music, Amédée Ozenfant on painting, Le Corbusier on architecture, H. S. Jennings and J. B. S. Haldane on biology, and C. G. Jung and Ernst Kretschmer on psychiatry. Contemporary philosophers were well represented by A. N. Whitehead, George Santayana, Count Hermann Keyserling, Bertrand Russell, and Max Scheler. Critics like Lewis Mumford, Lytton Strachey, and Edmund Wilson also contributed essays. Many of the writers were not simply published once and then forgotten. Georg Kaiser and Franz Werfel contributed eight pieces each, and Sir Arthur S. Eddington and Sir James Jeans each published four; there were seven contributions by Jung, four by Strachey, thirteen by Simmel, four by Keyserling, five by Russell, and six by Scheler.

In addition to the monthly magazine, the *Revista de Occidente* quickly became a major publisher of serious literature in Spain. Although it specialized in translations of contemporary European writers, significant Spanish writers were on its lists, among them Ortega, Eugenio D'Ors, Antonio Espina, Benjamín Jarnés, Jorge Guillén, Rafael Alberti, Valentín Andrés Alvarez, Pedro Salinas, and Federico García Lorca. The series "New Facts: New Ideas" was characteristic of the *Revista's* publications. In it, inexpensive translations of important works on theoretical physics, philosophy, psychology, and the social sciences were issued. Hermann Weyl, Jacob von Uexküll, Max Scheler, Kurt Koffka, Franz Brentano, Georg Simmel, Hans Driesch, C. G. Jung, Ernst Kretschmer, Sir Arthur S. Eddington, Werner Sombart, Bertrand Russell, Eduard Spranger, and David Katz were among the authors published in this series. There were also series specializing in history, anthologies of great thinkers, the history of philosophy, anthropology, and contemporary literature.[26] In short, almost any curiosity stimulated by articles in the *Revista de Occidente* could be pursued in greater depth through the books published by the *Revista*.

Let us imagine a community in which all men have the opportunity to educate themselves, to shape their character by means of principles. Let us further imagine that each member of this community can partake in a continuous, profound examination of basic theories and the application of these to life. In addition, each person in this community will have open access to unlimited information that exposes the inner workings of the commonweal to scrutiny. In such a community the privileges of power, which have always been based on the fact that a few have had access to superior intelligence and information, would disappear. The state would wither, and men would begin to realize Rousseau's dream of a perfect democracy in which each person, deliberating for himself on the basis of complete information, would independently decide on his course of conduct with respect to the general will. In such a community, the Platonic desire to infuse politics with ethics can be realized. And such a community would be one in which each member would draw, separately yet fully, on the available means of communication: on the schools, books, magazines, newspapers, radio, television, museums, and cinema. From these different media, each member would extract those cultural elements he found pertinent and concert these into his integral, individual mission.

Ortega perceived that the pedagogical usefulness of different

---

[26]*Revista de Occidente* regularly advertised the books it published. A rather complete list can be found in the advertising pages (unnumbered) of the December 1930 issue.

publishing media could be fulfilled only as people individually coördinated the bits of information and various ideas that they extracted from their newspapers, magazines, and books. No one could perform the acts of coördination for the reader, but men responsible for the forms of communication could take into account the fact that alert readers would be drawing connections between thoughts stimulated by different media. Together, *El Sol* and *Revista de Occidente* were a nascent attempt to recognize that men learned by putting things together from a variety of sources.

Ortega's desire to link the newspaper to the magazine and the book depended on his insight into the character of an intellectually alert audience. Often, communicators described the mental character of a potential audience by establishing what lowest educational attainments all its members might have in common; and for a communication to be addressed to one of these groups successfully, it must be couched so that persons of that educational level can absorb it comfortably. Thus, communicators assume that they must shape their appeal to the supposed characteristics of an audience of children, elementary school graduates, high school graduates, college alumni, professionals, or intellectuals. Many people take for granted the existence of various media such as newspapers, magazines, and books; they are content to match the content of these media to the desires and attainments of one or another audience. All too rarely one thinks to link the media together in such a way that they support a man's effort to transform his personal characteristics. Instead, the newspaper, magazine, and book become packaged products marketed to known, predictable audiences, and if these products became culturally effective, inducing significant changes in their audiences, it would seriously complicate their very marketability. Hence the complacent communicator prefers to compete discreetly for particular parts of the static pie.

This conception of the relation between the media and their audiences creates a static situation for both writer and reader. Authors quickly learn to specialize, writing invariably on a single level of intellectual difficulty; and the reader comfortably habituates himself to accepting only those communications—be they in newspapers, magazines, or books—that his present attainments enable him to read with ease. This situation is fine for the middlemen; the young writer discovers how to give certain editors what they want and the reader picks his product and nestles in with a long-term subscription. The editor is the patriarch who dictates what is good for both writer and reader. But this system is bad for the intellectual development of both the writer and the reader, for it discourages both from the open pursuit of their talent and curiosity. When audiences are marked off so as to separate out isolated cultural strata, which are defined, when all is said and done, by the difficulty of the prose that will be tolerated in each, the system forces the writer to conceive of his readers by means of a stereotype; and if the writer has any talent, he will subtly insinuate that stereotype into the character of his actual readers. In this way, the system impedes the full development of the cultural community and impairs the continuous humanization of its members.

Audiences, however, need not be defined by their common, extrinsic characteristics. In Ortega's publishing enterprises much less attention was paid to the external attainments of the audience than to its internal drive. *El Sol* was not a class or regional newspaper; the intention was that workers, farmers, professionals, and intellectuals, that people in the countryside, the villages, the provincial cities, and the capital, would all read the paper. With *El Sol*, as with all of Ortega's publications, one assumed only that the audience was curious and intellectually alert. To match a set of publications to this audience, one had to observe how a curious, alert person conducted his intellectual life. Daily, such a person would sift, without a systematic effort to preserve his findings, a wealth of various materials, some of which he would note to be important; periodically, he would follow with some care a variety of topics that he had found to be important, but not essential, for his abiding concerns; and continually, he would devote himself to permanently mastering those powers — personal and professional — that he found necessary for the just conduct of his life. Thus, the intellectual functions of the newspaper, the periodical, and the book were defined. By coordinating the way these served their respective functions, a powerful pedagogical system was created.

Then, this system was put in the service of a definite, particular conception of culture and of its potential significance in the life of Spain. The topics treated ephemerally, but compellingly, in *El Sol* were examined from time to time with more care and permanence in *Revista de Occidente,* and they were, furthermore, the subject of substantial books published by the *Revista.*

By linking different media to each other, one not only encouraged readers to pursue a passing curiosity to the point of thorough mastery, one helped writers explore and perfect their powers. Writers used *El Sol* to test themes and initiate the public exploration of potential subjects. *El Sol* was a place in which writers could think in public and readers could get a sense of writers as men thinking, watching their concerns germinate, mature, and ripen. In 1927, in a short essay heralding the appearance of a literary weekly catering to young writers, Ortega explained the different functions that newspapers, magazines, and books could serve in literature. The best use of a newspaper, he suggested, was as a great testing ground and clearing house with easy access for young writers. Through the newspaper there would be a productive, personal, ongoing exchange between writers and their readers. The periodical, in contrast to the newspaper, should be open only to material that had survived a more rigorous selection; its articles should concern matters of recognized importance and be worthy of permanence. Through the magazine a reciprocal relation between writer and readers should be maintained, but at a greater distance than in the newspaper. Finally, the book should be reserved for literature, a work that was of sufficient significance to command enduring interest even though the relation between writer and reader would become indirect.[27] This conception of the literary function of the newspaper explains why preliminary versions of Ortega's most important books first appeared in *El Sol.* For instance, *The Revolt of the Masses* was preceded by a series of experimental essays in *El Sol* in which Ortega worked out his argument and prepared his personal audience for its reception.[28] If due care was

---

[27]"Sobre un periódico de las letras," 1927, *Obras* III, pp. 446-9.

[28]See "La política por excelencia," "Dinámica del tiempo," "Tierras de porvenir," and "El poder social," 1927, *Obras* III, pp. 445-505, which were all preparations for *The Revolt of the Masses.*

taken to use newspapers, magazines, and books with a full sense of their interrelations, all sorts of reciprocal effects between the writer and reader might become possible.

Ortega's publishing activities—each by itself and all in concert—were attempts to educate the public. It would be easy to object that the actual effects achieved were not sufficient to make a decisive difference in Spanish life. However, the education of the public is an indirect mode of influence; it is not dramatically decisive and it requires time to produce results. Art is long and life is short, even in an age of instantaneous communication. In this case, life was too short. *El Sol* began in 1917, to endure for a mere twenty years. *Revista de Occidente* appeared in 1923; and although it kept publishing until 1936, by 1930 events began to lure Ortega and his colleagues into more immediate commitments. These proved to be premature, but there was no turning back; by the early 1930's Ortega no longer believed that he could deeply influence the Spaniard's character. Hence, the vision of a coordinated system of media dedicated to helping the populace improve itself remains only a vision.

Nevertheless, this vision is particularly significant. It clarifies principles of culture that are easily ignored in the high finance and publicity politics of mass communications. It illuminates alternatives to the qualitative stagnation that has characterized most of contemporary culture. During the early twentieth century, writers hopelessly confused the concept of culture by cant about various kinds of culture—aristocratic or democratic; high, low, or middle brow; proletarian, mass, elite, popular, primitive, and so on ad infinitum.c The only distinction that needs to be made is between culture and pseudo-culture, or ornaments, roles, "bags," and other disposables. Here culture means precisely what the etymology of the word suggests, that which promotes the growth and development of man. Pseudo-culture, despite its enticements, is too insipid to conduce to the spiritual development of those who produce and consume it. Whereas with culture, the effects on a man's character are essential and those on his appearance are incidental; with pseudo-culture, the effects on his appearance are essential and those on his character are incidental. Real culture is continuous, cumulative in the character of the person, and difficult; it is the result of a man's efforts to develop his mission, to embody what he stands for with respect to the absolute. The capacity for the participants in a community to cultivate their character is the ultimate foundation of their common life. And cultural democracy is the audacious yet desirable attempt to develop a community whose success, whose very survival, depends on the manner in which each member of the community, not only a privileged few, cultivates his character.

No man, however, can force culture on another. True culture is self-culture. In the light of this proposition, Ortega made the assumption basic to all efforts at cultural democracy: any man who asserts his will has the power to cultivate his character; through self-culture all men can expand their abilities and minimize their deficiencies. The basic threat to cultural democracy is the paternalistic assumption that the average man is incapable of cultivating himself and that he should therefore be provided with a veneer of pseudo-culture, something he can consume without having to change his character. And the worst paternalist of all is the professing democrat whose nerves have failed, for his efforts to encourage the people to rely on his superior wisdom will simply reinforce the popular inadequacies that prompted him to exalt himself in the first place.

In his teaching, writing, and publishing Ortega assumed that his audience was composed of sentient, intelligent persons who were to be addressed as peers. He tried to build up the intellectual elite of Spain, not so that its members could think for the people, but so that they could more effectively provoke the people to think for themselves. El Sol, which was the work of intellectuals, tried to win a provincial, rural audience, not to carry another party line to isolated areas, but to bring to rural life a new set of stimuli and, equally, to experience new stimuli itself. "We wish and believe possible a better Spain—stronger, richer, nobler, more beautiful . . . ," Ortega wrote in the opening issue of El Sol. "In order to achieve it, it is necessary that each of us be a little bit better in everything; that an affinity for the powerful, clean, clear life disperses through the entire race; that each Spaniard resolves to elevate by a few pounds the pressure of his spiritual potencies."[29] Cultural democracy would flourish in Spain only when the inhabitants of the central cities and the rural villages had sufficient respect for one another to attempt to converse as equals.

Ortega understood that mutual respect was the principle of cultural democracy. The alternatives that he perceived to cultural stagnation arose from his willingness to act on the premise of respect, even though, judging from past performance, the meager achievements of many men might suggest that such respect was not merited. But Ortega respected the potential that men possessed, not their past achievements. No culture would be created by those who began with the inductive discovery of what, at the present moment, a given group could comfortably comprehend. The teacher, writer, and publisher had to take human potentiality as his starting point; he also had to be able to do justice to all aspects of human endeavor—to technology, economics, law, sport, science, art, speech, myth, love, and morality. The publisher's genius, like that of the teacher and the writer, was to avoid cutting these endeavors down to the size of the average man, and to manage, instead, to introduce each concern in such a way that the average man could, with earnest effort, develop in himself all the possibilities that each realm of culture offered.

If a few men began to use a liberal pedagogy in their teaching, prose, and publishing, Ortega believed that others would respond and that a nation could spontaneously reform itself. Spain almost did.

*   *   *

Men should speak with rational awareness and thereby hold on strongly to that which is shared in common — as a city holds on to its law, and even more strongly. For all human laws are nourished by the one divine law, which prevails as far as it wishes, suffices for all things, and yet is something more than they.

HERACLITUS, 114

---

[29]"Hacia una mejor política: El hombre de la calle escribe," *El Sol*, December 7, 1917, *Obras* X, p. 368.

I FIRMLY BELIEVE *in the possibility—note, in the possibility—that Spain will now begin a new historic ascent. I firmly believe that in a few years we can make of Spain, not the richest or the most learned country, but the healthiest one, politically and socially, of all Europe.*

ORTEGA[1]

[1]"Selección," *El Sol,* August 20, 1926, *Obras* XI, p. 99.

VII
The Spain That Is

ORTEGA—AN UPPER-CLASS RADICAL, passionately in favor of social change, winning note at the age of thirty with his address "On the Old and the New Politics"—exemplifies an apogee of the post-Marxian left. Abhorring bourgeois complacency, the military mind, and the politics of interest groups, he thought that the populace could be aroused to reform the nation by reasoned recognition of abuses, an appeal to conscience, and the impassioned proposal of plausible alternatives. At heart, but not intellectually, he was an anarchist who insisted that any worthwhile social order could not be imposed upon the people, for it had instead to emanate from their spontaneous concord. In retrospect, Ortega seems to have been ahead of his time, especially for a Spaniard. He was convinced that the democratic revolution could not stop once its original material and civil goals had been approximated: the revolution had to be carried through the cultural sphere as well, so that the community would not remain riven in two parts, the cultured and the uncultured. In Spain, furthermore, the material revolution even seemed likely to follow, not precede, the cultural.

Except for educators, especially John Dewey, American social critics have generally not thought democracy is a cultural problem, as much as one of economics and politics. Hence, in the United States, Ortega's political thought did not lend itself to easy comprehension. And owing to the special importance English-speaking leftists gave the word "Masses," especially during the depression, *The Revolt of the Masses* was absorbed immediately into the debate between liberals and conservatives. The former condemned

Ortega as an anti-democratic elitist who wished to thwart the progress of the poor, and the latter welcomed him for his opposition to the further expansion of the state. Although misdirected, these partisan interpretations have persisted.[2] Yet Ortega's political commitments merit more careful treatment, for the old divisions to which he was assimilated tell us little about the new realities to which he spoke.

Throughout the West, the political divisions characteristic of the industrial nation-state are becoming increasingly irrelevant. The traditional separation between right and left resulted from fundamental disagreements over the proper role of government in regulating economic and social affairs. Other, more subtle problems of regulation are coming to the fore, namely those concerning character, culture, and the spiritual quality of life; with these problems there is a reversal of the field. On the one hand, the right is becoming increasingly willing to use the state to uphold the sanctity of established mores and to preserve a cultural quiet, a bourgeois homogeneity, favored by a "silent majority"; on the other, the left more and more calls for individual autonomy, civil liberties, and cultural laissez-faire. Ortega and this new left have much in common. It was the fascist state, not the socialist, that he condemned; and in spiritual matters he stood for intellectual autonomy, cultural pluralism, and the full, free expression of diverse commitments.

Ortega may help clarify the cultural politics arising in the West. If so, the truly important aspect of his political thought will be found in his sense of a cultural *Kinderland*. But the very people who might learn from these reflections are the ones disposed to distrust his supposed anti-democratic elitism. The supposition of this elitism was formed in misunderstanding of his writings and in ignorance of Ortega's actual political activities, which were substantial. To be sure, for him, practical politics remained secondary to cultural politics; but institutional reform was still important.

---

[2]For instance, as recently as 1965, the liberal publicist, Michael Harrington, devoted considerable space in *The Accidental Century* to debunking a reactionary Ortega. With gusto, Harrington destroyed a burlesque of *The Revolt of the Masses*, exposing its retrograde implications. See *The Accidental Century*, pp. 213–9.

"Culture, education will be everything in Spain because the rest is nothing. Political reform signifies only an orthopedic expedient to make the cripple walk and the handless grasp. . . . The substantial reform of our nation will be that of our society, not of our politics."[3] All the same, the orthopedic expedient deserved serious attention, and much of what Ortega taught, wrote, and published concerned the reorganization of Spanish public institutions. This concern, not partisan reactions to *The Revolt of the Masses*, evidences the character of his hard political commitments.

A prolonged encounter with Ortega's political writings shows that through many changes of subject and situation, his method of political reasoning remained constant. He often repeated Fichte's phrase defining the politician as the man who made manifest "that which is."[4] It would be a mistake, made all too easily, to think that the Fichtean politician, responsible to "that which is," would be an unprincipled opportunist, a man at peace with the powers that be, or an officeholder content to take the easiest, safest, most "realistic" course in any situation. A politician who makes manifest "that which is" would not be a man who was eager to follow public feeling dutifully, to avoid all suspicion of "rocking the boat," to respond in sympathy with every whim of his constituents, or to compromise his goals whenever they clashed with the seeming facts of public opinion. After all, both Fichte and Ortega were philosophers; and the calling of philosophers has always been to get beneath the flux of appearance, to uncover a stable reality, to substitute for that which seems to be that which really is. Hence, we can learn more about "that which is" by examining the epistemology of politics, the critique of how men should reason politically, than we could by surveying the political conditions of Berlin in 1807 or Madrid in 1931.

Ortega had a classical view of political reasoning. For him as for the classical tradition, the fundamental political reality was

---

[3]"Ideas políticas, VI," *El Sol*, July 26, 1924, *Obras* XI, p. 49.

[4]See *Vieja y nueva política*, 1914, *Obras* I, pp. 269-270; "Sobre el fascismo," 1925, *Obras* II, pp. 503–4; and *Del Imperio Romano*, 1914, *Obras* VI, p. 102. Cf. *El tema de nuestro tiempo*, 1923, *Obras* III, p. 156; and "La constitución y la nación, IV," *El Sol*, January 25, 1928, *Obras* XI, pp. 217-8.

found in the aspirations that men pursued, not in the conditions under which they lived. As Plato showed in the way that he had Glaucon and Adeimantus introduce the problem of justice, leadership was possible only with respect to intrinsic values that, even under the most horrible conditions imaginable, would still be deemed the proper goals by men.[5] As with Plato and with Aristotle, so with Ortega: the supreme good was the end of political science and the measure of political reality.[6] Ortega insisted that every person and group had a "destiny," which was its best possible achievement, and life was an effort to fulfill this possibility.[7] "Realistic politics is the politics of realization. Realization is the supreme mandate that defines the arena of politics. It does not conflict with the ideal, but imposes concretion and discipline on it." Here Ortega faced the rigorous demands of a truly practical politics. "Realism is more demanding [than idealism]: it invites us to transform reality according to our ideas and, at the same time, to think our ideas in view of reality, that is, to extract the ideal, not subjectively from our heads, but objectively from things. Every concrete thing—a nation, for example—contains, next to what it is today, the ideal profile of its possible perfection. And this ideal, that of the thing, not of ourselves, is truly respectable."[8]

In "Perpetual Peace" Immanuel Kant reasoned that the ideal implicit in any functioning government, no matter how localized its jurisdiction, was a universal government in which the entire human community, not simply its parts, was ordered by a rule of law.[9] Here Kant exemplified how the critical philosopher could

---

[5]Plato, *Republic*, II, 357-368.

[6]This contention was used with effect by Socrates against Thrasymachus in *Republic*, I, 336B-354C, and against Polus in *Gorgias*, beginning 466D; and is at the heart of the discussion between Socrates and Callicles in *Gorgias* 481B-527E, for Callicles was willing to deny it. For Aristotle, see *Nicomachean Ethics*, I, i-iii.

[7]See especially, "No ser hombre de partido," 1930, *Obras* IV, pp. 75-83.

[8]"Entreacto polémico: II: Del realismo en política," *El Sol*, March 18, 1925, *Obras* XI, pp. 63-4. See also, "Hacia un partido de la nación — Platónica advertencia sobre la respetabilidad del Estado," *Luz*, January 15, 1932, *Obras* XI, pp. 419-422.

[9]"Perpetual Peace," in: Immanuel Kant, *On History*, Lewis White Beck, ed. and trans., pp. 85-135.

develop positions of practical significance: one did it by showing precisely what rational consequences were entailed with the profession of a particular aspiration. Kant's procedure was to show men, who recognized in themselves an aspiration to live under a rule of law within a particular locality, that they could rationally uphold the localized legality only by asserting a rule of universal law. This procedure led to a distinctive conception of statesmanship. The statesman would start with a people's professed ambitions; he would then show the people what aspirations these rationally implied; and he would finally help find the way to fulfilling these real goals. As Ortega suggested, such political reasoning was not merely a heady, illusive idealism. It began from certain hard facts and from them proceeded to some of our most cherished political hopes.

In significant ways, aspirations, if they are authentic aspirations, are more fundamental political facts than are physical conditions. Within limits, any ruler has the power to alter at will the conditions under which a people live. A ruler can change conditions by force; he can change aspirations only by reason.[10] To reason about aspirations a ruler needs to accept them as given facts impervious to his arbitrary will; then he can enter into open communication about the meaning of these aims. In doing so he recognizes, in both word and deed, that the humanity of his subjects is equal to his own: the ruler ceases to be a law unto himself. This aspect of aspirations, that they can only be governed by reason, is the human basis of equality before the law. Further, as diverse aspirations undergo public examination, a multitude of personal commitments will be made by all who partake in the discussion; it is these commitments that aggregate into significant

---

[10]I am, of course, speaking here of the ruler of men, not of crowds. The aspirations of a crowd are notoriously easy to sway. But it is a mistake to call the urges that make and move crowds "aspirations." Crowds come into being only where authentic aspirations are absent or suspended. And even with crowds, it is doubtful that a leader can *willfully* manipulate its urges. Instead, he must take its urges into account and address himself to these with a semblance of consideration. See Gustave Le Bon, *The Crowd*, especially p. 113, n. 1, and generally, pp. 101–140. Crowds exist as the symbiotic correlate to the inner emptiness of their would-be masters; and neither crowds nor their masters are good bases for politics. Both are best avoided; see Seneca, "On Crowds," *Epistulae Morales*, VII.

community decisions. Here, then, in the fact that our personal aspirations pattern our daily acts and that these acts shape the real potential of the community, is the basis of participatory government. When confronted by serious, authentic aspirations, a ruler can only lead, he cannot direct. No formal machinery, no Bill of Rights or Constitution, can sufficiently guarantee our freedom and dignity; the vitality of our personal aspirations is the sole, substantial, ultimate check on arbitrary power.[11]

Because aspirations are primary in public affairs, no man has the right to by-pass the will of his compatriots; and this fact means that politics becomes less a matter of power and more a matter of reason. The politician becomes the man who can understand and make manifest the full implications of what it is that his compatriots profess to will. Hence, for Ortega, the great example of the politician was Mirabeau, not because Mirabeau was effective in the Machiavellian sense of gaining and keeping power, but because he divined the one political system—constitutional monarchy—that was suitable for France after 1789: only this system was rationally consistent with the diverse aspirations released by the Revolution; only it could make effective use of the remaining French traditions and provide a stable, progressive rule.[12] Likewise, for Ortega, Antonio Maura epitomized Spanish politics because among the politicians of official Spain, only Maura was willing to ask what the accepted goal of a stronger national system really entailed, and only Maura was willing to pursue wholeheartedly (albeit imperfectly, as Ortega saw it) the difficult, federalist reforms that this goal logically implied.[13]

Make no mistake: this mode of political reasoning, reasoning from aspirations, is not fool-proof. Its use by shallow men is dangerous, for it can lead (by wrong reasoning, one must interject) to a situation in which a limited goal seems to justify unlimited means. But those who are willing to renounce reasoning from

---

[11]An effective examination of certain aspects of this function that aspirations can perform will be found in *The Political Illusion* by Jacques Ellul, Konrad Kalen, trans.

[12]See "Mirabeau o el político," 1927, *Obras* III, pp. 603-637.

[13]See "Maura o la política," *El Sol*, December 18, 19, 22, and 31, 1925; January 7 and 10, 1926, *Obras* XI, pp. 71-91.

aspirations because it is susceptible to abuse should be ready to renounce all that goes with it, for instance, personal reasonableness in public matters, the dignity of man, equality before the law, and the democratic ideal. Unless we hold men responsible for their aspirations and deal honestly with these, there is no substance to our conceptions of reason, dignity, equality, and democracy, for these great concepts will have become mere euphemisms for the tyranny of a self-subsistent state that reigns over all. Beware those favored phrases—"a free society," "the free world."

A general drift into totalitarianism is slowly laying bare a radical choice: politics can either be the critique of aspirations or the manipulation of objects. For Ortega the choice was clear. He renounced paternalistic manipulation. "There is no other way to educate and chastise the public conscience than to make it responsible for its acts."[14] To be sure, when rational politics failed, manipulation and force were necessary; that it to say, they became unavoidable, for they are the consequence of reason's failure; but this is not to say that they are therefore desirable as some think when pronouncing on the mythical "needs of society." Ortega realized that reliance on power was a symptom not of political supremacy, but of political bankruptcy. The true object of politics was not to maximize power, but to minimize it; and one pursued this object by holding people morally responsible for their acts, by giving up all claims to direct their activities authoritatively, and, in doing so, gaining a basis for criticizing, educating, and chastising their aspirations.

Because two *different* principles can guide public affairs—force or reason—Ortega, and everyman, had an occasion for a commitment. Ortega committed himself to reason, not to force. He recognized, to be sure, that occasionally it was reasonable to give way to force, to defer, when reason would not work, to those committed to the rights of might: "when arms are taken up we should put down our pens . . ."[15] But Ortega did not put down his pen to take up arms; he put it down because there was no use

---

[14]*Ibid.*, p. 90.
[15]"Una manera de pensar," *España*, October 7, 1915, *Obras* X, p. 337.

writing for an audience of armed partisans: they cared for prose only insofar as it served as propaganda. Ortega believed that one's rational authority was higher if one relied on it alone. The apparent man of reason, who, when his reasons were rejected, immediately called in force, had little claim to thoughtful attention. Consequently, Ortega's political judgments rarely concerned manipulatory policy; it was not his office to engineer consent.

If critics work with restraint, maintaining rational pressure perpetually against those who rule by manipuation, they can exert tremendous power solely by means of reason. The critic can make politics without resort to force by subjecting every effort to engineer consent to dispassionate scrutiny. If the claims of the powerful prove deficient, more and more people will withhold assent and refuse to cooperate constructively with the regime. As time goes on, the despotic ruler will have decreasing resources at his command with which to maintain his power over a progressively more restive populace. Ortega's opposition to the dictator Primo de Rivera took this form. When Primo de Rivera came to power, Ortega did not rush into overt, armed opposition. Instead, along with other intellectuals, he critically attacked the veil of legitimacy over the Dictatorship. The Dictatorship claimed justification by asserting that it alone could rid Spain of the *vieja política*. Let Primo de Rivera live up to that purpose, Ortega said; let him rid the nation of the "cynicism, unscrupulousness, incompetence, illegality, and caciquism" of which he, the Dictator, was currently the most prominent example; let him abdicate.[16] Maintaining such attacks on Primo de Rivera's presumption of legitimacy, Ortega and other critics abraded the Dictator's authority until the regime, losing its natural backers in Church and State, starved for talent, unable to solve the nation's problems, beset by numerous challengers, withdrew. Here was critical politics in action. For Ortega, political rationalism did not mean reasoning about the use of force, but making politics solely by the use of reason.

Politics, thus, began with the aspirations that men professed; it functioned by bringing men to examine these aspirations and to become aware of the actions that their goals required. The political

---

[16]"Sobre la vieja política," *El Sol*, November 27, 1923, *Obras* XI, p. 30.

critic proceeded by putting certain basic questions. What were the aspirations that did, that could, and that should move men? Were these aspirations possible ones? That is, were they possible with respect to the rational will; could a person will them without willing contradictory things? Were the aspirations possible with respect to the actualities of the time and place in which they were to be pursued? What were the conditions under which one could fulfill these aspirations? How could such conditions be brought about? What particulars could and should one personally will in order to help attain these general goals? Were these particulars consistent with the supreme good? If the critique of aspirations provoked by these questions worked perfectly, politics would merge with education and ethics, and the state would truly wither away. But in the absence of its perfection, the critique of aspirations was still a useful tool of piecemeal reform; as more persons were led to take responsibility for their own conduct, there would be less occasion for the community to be governed by the rule of force. In this way, the critque of aspirations could work within a political system based on force. Its partial effectiveness was Ortega's practical basis for opposing a vital politics to the official politics of Spain.

Ortega's political writings were a continuous critique of the aspirations manifested by leading Spaniards. Taking up a goal that had been widely professed, he would show by critical analysis what conditions would make the goal possible and what particular activities might bring it to fruition. With such a critique, Ortega confronted his readers with three alternatives: show by more cogent reasoning that the aspiration really entailed different particulars, renounce the aspiration as undesirable, or accept the particulars and seek to realize them. In this way, the critique of aspirations would lead to spontaneous, practical consequences without abusing the dignity of other persons.

Together, Ortega's critiques amounted to a vision of a possible Spain, one in which Spaniards faced their true problems and resolved to surmount them. Indeed, Ortega lacked both the means and the intention to compel the realization of this reform of Spanish life; but part of the reformer's discipline—if he would have his work be the result of reason—is to restrain his eagerness and to rely on the choice of those involved to act on principles, not on interest. Without such restraint, the anxious reformer will merely habituate his wards to respond to compulsion, not to conviction, and the reform will be as insecure as those who forcibly imposed it. The reformer can properly do no more than criticize ambitions and show what the hard choices are. The men who are called in a reform to change their ways have to make certain difficult commitments; that is, to prefer magnanimity to force, justice to riches, temperance to satiety, and culture to acclaim. Since such choices have not yet been made by significant Spaniards, the nation's problems have been perpetuated; consequently, Ortega's vision of the Spanish future is still relevant to the present day.

Ortega began his critique with the aspiration to have a Spanish nation. "Are we able to make a national Spain?" When the question whether Spain should or should not exist was put to Spaniards, all but the most extreme separatists would unequivocally affirm the desirability of a national existence. This affirmation could be the basis of a Spanish future. To clarify it, Ortega critically elucidated the consequences of the commitment: What national ideals could move Spaniards despite their great diversities? What particular institutions should Spaniards accept in order to make good on their basic aspiration to have a Spanish nation? If Spaniards were to make their commitment to Spain's existence more than an empty piety, what did they need to do?

Such questions elicited Ortega's reflections on Spanish politics. His answers were twofold: on the one hand, he identified the historical impediments that hindered the achievement of Spain's national potential, and on the other he showed how these impediments might become irrelevant if Spaniards recognized that their national aspirations entailed commitments to regionalism, industry, competence, and democracy.

Ortega *steadily* upheld both the negative and positive side of his position. The critique of aspirations cannot produce instantaneous results; suasion becomes powerful when pertinacious—like a prevailing wind, which by blowing steadily and firmly bends the growing trunk, the unwavering winds of doctrine enduringly point life towards the better. Month after month, year after year, the critique must go on, converting men of power ever anew to higher ideals. Ortega's aim was to change his nation's character; at best it was slow business. "Those who wish a different, better Spain must resolve to modify the repertory of Spanish life, and to judge as superficial all reforms that are not oriented by this resolve. Precisely for this reason, institutions serve reform not when one takes them by themselves, hoping for their abstract perfection, but when one forges out of them instruments capable of transforming the uses of collective life and the very character of the average Spaniard."[17]

* * *

Lawgivers, as distinct from lawmakers, are particularly interested in the effects of various institutions on the character of the people. The elder Plato thus examined the potential preambles to the *Laws*, testing various regulations to see which could justify themselves by their healthful effects on human character. Thus, the French *philosophes* and the American founding fathers insisted that only a virtuous people could maintain civil freedom and that the only institution worthy of free men was one that conduced to preserving their virtue. Thus, too, Ortega was remarkably sensitive to the effects institutions had on character. He rejected the established institutions of Spain because they perpetuated and intensified Spanish weaknesses and caused Spanish virtues to atrophy. He suggested that the reform of the state be designed to reverse these influences.

In a well-known work, *Invertebrate Spain*, Ortega presented the negative side of his position by exposing the historical traditions that detracted from Spain's national existence. Spanish institutions had been adapted to performing a function that had long since ceased to exist, and no new mission had been developed by Spanish leaders. Such a condition was pure frivolity, and participation in it had bad effects on Spanish character.

A nation existed, Ortega contended, because diverse groups shared a common ideal that enabled them to coöperate and compete in an effort to accomplish a sovereign task without

---

[17]"¿Reforma del Estado o reforma de la sociedad?," *El Sol*, November 22, 1927, *Obras* XI, p. 187.

destroying their diversities. The traditional ruling ideal of Spain, imperial conquest, had lost its force. Hence, each subsidiary group that had been a part of Spain now turned inwards. Lacking an ,inspiration that transcended its immediate concerns and brought it into contact with other elements of the nation, each became obsessed with its parochial aspirations and problems. Soon each inward-looking group began to confuse itself with the whole nation. Particularism resulted. Cohesive regions, narrow interest groups, self-serving professions, and separate classes lost the habit of taking account of others, especially of those who were not closely organized. Particularism led to the imbecilic arrogance that typified Spanish affairs. If the "true" Spain was synonymous with the military, with Barcelona's businesses, with landed wealth, or with Madrid socialism, why should the leaders of these groups bother with the rest? Two years before General Primo de Rivera gave further proof of the point, Ortega described the military, with its penchant for *pronunciamentos*, as the group that best exemplified the Spanish tendency to confuse the interests of region, profession, and class with those of the nation. Until this tendency was overcome and replaced with a capacity for prolonged coöperation in the pursuit of high ideals, the Spanish nation would not rejuvenate.

Despite its fame, this historical critique was not the most important of Ortega's political writings. In it, Ortega was uncharacteristically negative. He condemned the attitudes of the ruling groups without offering a significant alternative. Yet Ortega usually dwelt on the positive side: "the important thing is not to castigate the abuses of the governors, but to substitute for them the uses of the governed."[18] Particularism prevented Spaniards from achieving their national potential, but this abuse resulted nearly automatically from the lack of a powerful national ideal. Consequently, the critic needed to do more than debunk particularism. Spaniards would avoid the destructive consequences the present system had for their character, if they could define the proper uses of their public life: a national ideal that would work in the twentieth century. Only the discovery of such an ideal

---

[18]"Sobre la vieja política," *El Sol*, November 27, 1923; *Obras* XI, p. 30.

could end the political frivolity that encouraged particularism. In one way or another, most of Ortega's political essays concerned this possibility.

In his youth Ortega had liked to tell about a noble, but unintelligent, schoolboy. It was the custom in Spanish schools to seat pupils according to academic rank, and one unfortunate fellow always ended up in the dunce's chair. The boy, however, refused to be daunted; to him the seeming desiderata of formal rank were insignificant, and he reassured himself with the thought that someone had to be last and that what mattered was that he made for himself the best of whatever position he had. This boy knew his dignity.[19] In like manner, the realities of resources meant that Spain could not be an imperial power. But national virtue was not displayed by dominion over others and pre-eminence in military and commercial might. The real measure of worth was dominion over oneself. Here Ortega saw a significant opportunity for Spain to take a leading part in European affairs. Ortega foresaw tremendous transformations in the industrial West and he sensed that in the course of these many nations would succumb to a new barbarism. Spain would achieve greatness by maintaining a humane stability through these transformations. Spain could excel if it would simply attend to its proper business; then it would show to the rest of Europe that a people could quietly and reasonably set its house in order.

In his political writings Ortega frequently used the athletic phrase: Spain's destiny was "to get in shape," "to be in form."[20] Latin America and especially Europe needed the example and leadership of a people who were in shape, for the Latin Americans had a new world to master, and the Europeans had the awesome task of transcending their national existences and creating a new, more inclusive polity. In both cases, the job could not be done by people who were out of form. "In 1812 we made a constitution that was copied by the entire Continent. This does not mean that

---

[19]See *Meditaciones del Quijote*, 1914, *Obras* I, p. 332; and "Moralejas," 1906, *Obras* I, p. 46.

[20]See, for instance: "Actos de la F.U.E.: Conferencia de Don José Ortega y Gasset," *El Sol*, October 10, 1930. Cf. *Obras* XI, pp. 194, 198, 236, 252, 257, and 261; *Obras* II, p. 547; *Obras* IX, p. 266; and so on.

we may not now offer it a different model. To do so, it will suffice that Spaniards resolve to shake off their inertia and their prejudices, and that they be, above all, what they have been at certain times in their history: magnanimous and faithful to great tasks."[21]

Americans are being forced, like it or not, to conceive of their national destiny as a matter of thrusting imperial grandeur, excursions into space, and vast military might. Hence some may find the ideal that Ortega offered to be singularly unmoving. As it was, it failed to move certain Spanish personages. Yet for many others it was a meaningful goal. The ideal of national form was analogous to the ideal of personal composure, being at peace with oneself, accepting one's situation and destiny, and steadfastly attending to the fulfillment of these inwardly determined possibilities. A nation that turned away from world affairs and concentrated on getting in shape, would not be isolationist; on the contrary, Ortega realized that such disciplined restraint was the precondition of transcending the outworn national system of Europe. National composure was the basis of neither isolationism nor internationalism, but of supranationalism. Nor did Ortega's ideal entail a withdrawal from the great challenges of life; on the contrary, it required a commitment to doing something substantial about the mundane, difficult problems that persisted close to home.

There was a certain Stoic greatness in the ideal that Ortega put before Spaniards, and the people of Spain, who long ago contributed so much to Stoicism, came close to fulfilling it. Perhaps this fact in part explains the profound, persisting emotions unleashed by the Civil War. The past achievements of the Republic did not make sensitive men from around the world come to its assistance. Rather, the hope that the Republic symbolized throughout the West drew them there. In the years that Italy sank more and more deeply into fascism, Spain worked itself out of a worse situation towards a humanitarian, liberal government. When all the grand nations were suddenly paralyzed by the great depression, Spain gamely embarked on a peaceful and profound reform. As Germany succumbed to Nazi brutalism, Spain

---

[21]"Un proyecto," *El Sol*, December 6, 1930, *Obras* XI, p. 290.

seemed to show that at least one nation could substantially transform itself without tearing itself apart or imposing its worst
elements upon the whole. The Civil War was such a trauma for
idealistic citizens of the West precisely because Spain had symbolized for a few short years the hope that a nation still could
peacefully change for the better, that without bloodshed it could
freely get itself in shape. The ideal that Ortega put before Spaniards was the conviction that Spain could make itself worthy of
symbolizing such a hope.

To get in shape and to lead other states by example, Spaniards
needed to attend closely to the effects of their institutions on their
character. Ortega's discussions of particular reforms all pertained
to this question; as he said, he tried to forge instruments capable
of transforming the uses of collective life and the very character of
the average Spaniard. Here was his vision of the Spain that is;
it was to be realized by fulfilling the possibilities of regionalism,
industry, competence, and democracy.

From 1914 through 1931, these themes kept recurring in
Ortega's political essays. He did not spin out great schemes for
formal institutions. The solutions of Spain's problems would be
achieved when the people perfected their character. Thus regional
laws were not as important as sincere, intelligent tolerance of
regional customs and aspirations. Ortega was less concerned about
the reorganization of industry than he was about the will to work,
for no amount of reorganization would make the national product
sufficient if it continued to be stunted by under-employment,
inactivity, and laziness on every level. Likewise, schools alone
could not improve a people who were unwilling to recognize and
reward competence. Finally, to make a formal democracy work,
Spaniards needed to develop a spontaneous democracy in which
various sectors of the society took an interest, each in the others,
for only then could the power of the *cacique* and other local
despots be broken. Formal provisions for regionalism, industry,
education, and democracy were not, however, unimportant; Ortega
simply contended that the spiritual commitment was the prior
condition of successful, constructive activities. Because the reform
of character was so important to Ortega, most of his political

writings were attempts at political education. In the course of discussing this or that particular, he was trying to cultivate in the character of his readers the qualities that would put Spain in form. Typically, in closing a long essay on "Political Ideas" Ortega exclaimed, "Education! Culture! Here is everything. This is the substantial reform."[22]

Ortega's regionalism began with a commitment to the Spanish nation. He did not accept the validity of the opposition: either regionalism or nationalism. In one essay he claimed that the solution to the separatist problem was an *elegant* one, for it would be arrived at by turning upon the difficulty itself, regional loyalties, and making that the basis of a stronger Spanish nation. "The future of Spain will be made by managing to change the sign of this unique energy and understanding that beneath the provincial negation of Madrid there beats a more healthy, noble urge: the desire to affirm itself."[23]

National divisiveness had been created in the seventeenth century when the monarchy and church had attempted to protect their interests by instituting a centralized government. Spain, Ortega reminded his readers, had originated from the joining of separate kingdoms, none of which gave up their individuality in the merger. The fiction that Spain was a unified nation-state to be ruled by an administration centralized in Madrid was the cause of Spanish divisiveness, for it capped the nation's true well of talent —the regions—and it forced the various peoples of Spain to look elsewhere for fulfillment. To have an efficient administration and to free the genius of the people, the politics of Spain should be organized regionally. As early as 1908 Ortega had written that it was futile to try to suppress separatist terrorism; repressive laws passed in Madrid would simply intensify the combat.[24] The true solution was to show that Spain could encompass both regionalists and centrists. Madrid, unlike Paris, was too weak to be a dominant capital. "In no sense, not even the intellectual, has Madrid fulfilled

[22]"Ideas políticas, V," *El Sol*, July 26, 1924, *Obras* XI, p. 49.

[23]"Provincianismo y provincialismo," *El Sol*, February 11, 1928, *Obras* XI, p. 237.

[24]"Sobre el processo Rull," *Faro*, April 12, 1908, *Obras* X, pp. 47-50.

its mission of being a capital. Madrid has failed."[25] These were hard words for a Madrileño to write, but Ortega believed that they were the key to the solution of the regional problem: Madrid had had its turn and failed; now it was the time to see what the provinces could do when given thorough regional autonomy.

Early in 1926 Ortega made the first of his several proposals for decentralization; his proposals show well how institutional reforms could be used to change Spanish character. A particular political system rewarded a particular set of character traits, and hence by changing the political structure one could take a significant step towards reforming the national character. Ortega saw regional autonomy as a means for increasing the political, economic, and social maturity of the Spanish people. Without an opportunity to use their abilities in signficant situations, the people could not develop their abilities. If the average Spaniard was to take a constructive part in popular government, it had to be in local and regional government, for in these spheres the issues were concrete and they made a difference to the common man. With respect to these issues the *pueblo* could make good use of its innate virtues without being unduly handicapped by its lack of formal education. But Spanish centralism had made local and regional affairs the purview of civil governors appointed by the Minister of the Interior. Instead of being responsible for their local and regional affairs, the people theoretically participated in resolving the abstract questions of national politics, yet they had little liking, capacity, or concern for these general questions. The civic talents of the Spaniards had not developed because self-government had been withheld where it might have mattered and provided where it was irrelevant. "Up to a few years ago, a very few years, the population of Barcelona and its province, with the million inhabitants of its capital, was governed by precisely the same institutions as were those of Soria and Zamora, two tiny villages. And presently some people wonder at Barcelona's singularly subversive inspiration!"[26]

---

[25]"Maura o la política," *El Sol*, December 22, 1925, *Obras* XI, p. 79.

[26]"El estatuto catalán," May 13, 1932, reprinted in Mori, *Crónica*, Vol. VI, p. 126, and in *Obras* XI, p. 469.

Other proposals followed, some of which slipped past Primo de Rivera's censors, others of which were suppressed until after the Dictator fell. The provinces, with their accidental boundaries, should be consolidated into rational regions that would be workable political and economic units. The members of each region would command resources sufficient to promote their own affairs effectively. Such a political structure would encourage the average citizen to transform his deep local ties into political commitments of regional significance, commitments that were personally meaningful and that transcended his immediate, local realm. With time and effort, these regional involvements might gain true national import. In this way, the nation could turn responsibility for all but the very broadest problems over to those who had an immediate interest in their outcome; power would be wielded by men who were actually concerned with the policies in question. Whereas centralization had inhibited the local development of talent, decentralization would encourage it; thus the political structure would be made into a means for cultivating improvements in the Spanish character. "It is evident that if [the average Spaniard] succeeds in motivating himself by resolutely taking into his own hands the responsibility for his local life, we will have converted an inert, routine, torpid person into an active, ambitious, enterprising, restless creature. The tone of the normal existence will have changed. In each corner of Spain the vital pulse will have quickened; in each day more will happen: there will be more labors, more projects, more loves, more hates."[27]

Regional autonomy would open to Spaniards more significant channels of self-development. But autonomy was not a mysterious mechanism that would perfect men by itself. Its results would be salutary only if Spaniards resolutely willed to make themselves more competent. The basic problem in Spanish public affairs, Ortega contended, was the incompetence of the leaders and the people's extraordinary tolerance of incompetence in their leaders. "The absence of the excellent, or what is nearly the same, their

---

[27]"Provincianismo y provincialismo, II," *El Sol*, February 14, 1928, *Obras* XI, p. 238.

scarcity, has acted on all our history and has stopped us from becoming a reasonably normal nation."[28]

Not infrequently, the inability of countries like Spain to achieve a stable representative government is attributed to the absence of a thriving middle class. Many Spaniards, Ortega included, saw the matter differently. To them, the great enemy of reform was the *petit bourgeois*. "Everywhere in the nation the morality, ideology, and sensibility of the *petit bourgeois* reign, dominate, and triumph. And the *bourgeois* is, by definition, the man who is without curiosity, who is incapable of looking beyond his routine horizon, who feels fear before every change, and who is what he is because he lacks the mental agility to depict for himself, in the face of the ruling reality, another aspiration."[29] No reform was possible until this mentality was changed, and the way to change it was to confront oneself and others with disquieting opinions, for incompetence resulted from a complacent character that needed above all to be disturbed.

But Ortega reserved his most biting scorn for the incompetence of the upper classes. It is remarkable that *The Revolt of the Masses* has been thought to have been an attack on the social advance of the lower classes when the financier, the industrialist, the socialite, and the heir were so explicitly made the prototype of the mass-man. To Ortega the Spanish monarch was a prime example of the tendency to meddle in matters where one was incompetent while ignoring one's real duties.[30] In general Ortega condemned the upper classes for thinking that they could leave leadership to others, that they did not need to hold themselves responsible to *hoi polloi*, and that they could while away the passing days longing idly for the golden years when their self-interests were synonymous with the interests of the state. "But— damn it!—to the banker, to the industrialist, to the magistrate, to the powerful trader, to the 'aristocrat' of the Rolls and the cocktail,

---

[28]*España invertebrada*, 1921, *Obras* III, p. 121.

[29]"Vaguedades: I: Sobre todo, que no se reforma nada," *El Sol*, March 6, 1925, *Obras* XI, pp. 51-2.

[30]See "El error Berenguer," *El Sol*, November 15, 1930, *Obras* XI, pp. 274-9.

to the professor, to the bishop, to the prior of the retreat, to the engineer, to the matron's physician . . . , to all these there pertains an enormous burden of responsibility." Their responsibility was to symbolize and actualize the dynamic competence that superior culture gave. Instead the upper classes complained and carped and did their best to thwart the efforts of other groups to improve their lot.[31] For Ortega, a conservative upper class was a contradiction: if the class was truly pre-eminent, it could not help but exert progressive leadership by virtue of its superior abilities; whereas if it truly inhibited the progressive development of the nation, it could not be composed of the most able men and thus it could not be a class worthy of its pretensions to superiority. In shirking their responsibility to be a positive symbol of excellence to the rest of the nation, the "superior" classes proved themselves to be, in relation to their duties, the most inferior of all classes and the most *petit bourgeois* of all Spaniards.

Besides his many-sided effort to undermine the self-satisfaction of incompetent pretenders to position, Ortega carried the theme of competence to the level where it really counted, that of particular, positive skills. One of the groups to whom Ortega most consistently made this appeal was youth. Youth still had the time to make itself competent, and there was nothing that could so disturb the complacency of the established as competent youths seeking to push their ineffective elders from position. Thus, in 1914 Ortega made collaboration with youth one of the primary features of the League for Spanish Political Education. Thus, in 1929 he advised a group of young intellectuals to enter politics with no connections to the past, but with a steadfast willingness to seek out every possible issue and to subject it to rigorous original analysis. In these, as in several other cases, Ortega advised youths to test the mettle of their elders by confronting those in established positions with competent, original undertakings. If the elders lacked the ability to adapt, so much the worse for them; it would simply prove the incompetence of the established leaders. "Today we have to invent everything: great themes, juridical

---

[31]"Ligero comentario," *El Sol*, January 1, 1930, *Obras* XI, p. 112.

principles, institutional patterns, moving emotions, and even the vocabulary."[32]

In addition to youth, Ortega called on the technician to pride himself in his competence. Thus, in discussing agricultural reform he wrote: "No doubt, God will reward our good will, electing us to salvation in the blue prairies of heaven . . . But the good will that suffices to get us to heaven does not suffice to organize the countryside. In this task economic science is alone useful and indispensable. *Et si non, non.* Numbers, statistics, complicated systems, a bureaucratic corps of great wisdom and solicitude, an enormous quantity of prosaic competencies—without these our agriculture will not ascend to heaven."[33] In discussing whether technicians or politicians should head the major ministries, Ortega suggested that to preserve technical excellence and autonomy, the technician should not be converted into a politician responsible for bartering political priorities.[34] Ortega personally took pride in his own mastery of journalistic and publishing techniques, and his scorn for the Spaniard's tolerance of incompetence was fully revealed in his biting reaction to the government's attempt to impair *El Sol's* competitive position.[35] Finally, Ortega's respect for expertise led him to propose, as a member of the Constituent Cortes that constituted the Second Republic, that a Council on the National Economy be created, that it should have on it Spain's best economists, and that it be given wide powers for drawing up and implementing long-term national economic plans like those used in the U.S.S.R.[36]

A characteristic of Ortega's outlook on the problem of competence was his belief that the way to particular improvements had to be paved by those with general abilities. He was often more eloquent about skill in general than about particular skills, about competence as an abstract ideal than about special competencies.

---

[32]See the letter from Genaro Artiles, *et al.*, and Ortega's reply, printed as a pamphlet, Madrid, April, 1929, *Obras* XI, p. 104.

[33]"Competencia," *El Imparcial*, February 9, 1913, *Obras* X, p. 230.

[34]"El momento española: politícos y técnicos," *El Sol*, February 26, 1920, *Obras* X, pp. 629-632.

[35]"Hoy aparecerá en la 'Gaceta' la Real Orden contra 'El Sol,' Admirable carta de Don José Ortega y Gasset," *El Sol*, July 29, 1920, *Obras* X, pp. 659-662.

[36]"Sobre lo de ahora," *Crisol*, August 6, 1931, *Obras* XI, pp. 364-6.

And he had good reasons for this emphasis. Excessive centralization was just one of many means that the Spanish had for shunting talented, skilled persons into closed, ineffectual avenues of endeavor. On the one hand, the problem of competence was a question of the nation's need for many different, particular siklls, and on the other it was a matter of the more basic need to create a demand for these. To foment a demand for various skills, it was important to promote a general respect for ability and to develop an *esprit de corps* among the competent. The way to do these things was to praise the ideal of competence. Hence, Ortega often spoke of competence apart from particular skills: for instance, "Enthusiasm and competence should be the alpha and omega of the new politics."[37]

What Ortega called "enthusiasm" in this slogan, coined in 1915, he later called "work" or "industry." Under this heading he sought to promote both industriousness and industrialization.

In part, Ortega called for the radical social and economic reorganization of Spain, but he added that the reorganization should be wrought by class coöperation instead of class warfare.

A coöperative revolution was not as impossible as radical and reactionary orthodoxies would have people believe. Since Ortega did not subscribe to a materialistic, deterministic conception of man's intentions and since he thought that men could choose rationally the principles by which they would live, he did not believe that class conflict was inevitable. Conflict or coöperation resulted from the intentions of those involved; it all depended on whether the intentions that different groups chose to pursue conflicted or coincided. Class coöperation, however, was difficult; and in Spain it could be sustained only by a common commitment to an ideal of enthusiasm, of work, of industry. Ortega believed that by absolute, intrinsic measures all classes of Spain would be better off economically and civilly if each would stop trying to aggrandize itself at the expense of others and if all would throw themselves with enthusiasm and determination into getting the job done.

---

[37]"Alma de purgatorio," *España*, March 5, 1915, *Obras X*, p. 287.

Clearly, the job to be done was the renovation of Spain. Leadership in this coöperative effort would come from the strongest group, the workers. "On the day that the Spanish workers abandon abstract words and recognize that they suffer, not only as proletarians, but also as Spaniards, they will make the socialist party the strongest party of Spain. And in doing so, they will make Spain."[38] Ortega maintained this conviction, voiced in 1912; and to understand his political economy we need to grasp the depth of his faith in the potential for leadership in the working classes. Too many liberal reformers have become accustomed to deriding the gospel of work as an opium pushed by complacent capitalists. In doing so, we fail to realize that this gospel, albeit according to certain different saints, is the core of most leftist efforts at national development. Ortega was no doctrinaire, he vigorously defended the liberty of industry vis-à-vis the state when the *vieja política* threatened *El Sol*. But as we shall see, for a Spaniard committed to economic renovation under the leadership of the working classes, the doctrine of free enterprise had implications unfamiliar to those accustomed to seeing it put only to conservative uses. Capital was capital; the important thing for Spain was not whether it was owned privately or publicly but that all the scarce capital be fully employed.

Ortega's commitment to the cause of the working classes did not begin with doctrine, but with a search for a dynamic force that could quicken the pace of Spanish economic activity. Development had to be driven by a dynamic force. The most powerful one in Spain was the working classes; more than any other group, the Spanish workers were willing to exert themselves, and therefore Spain's development, its push to fuller employment of all its resources, should be led by the workers. "Whatever are the political differences that exist, or that can exist tomorrow in our public life, it is necessary that none commit the stupidity of not knowing that, for sixty years, the most energetic force in universal history has been the magnificent upward movement of the working classes."[39] Ortega stayed aloof from the Socialist Party per se, for he thought

---

[38]"Miscelánea socialista," *El Imparcial*, October 6, 1912, *Obras X*, p. 206.
[39]"Rectificación de la República," December 6, 1931, *Obras XI*, p. 405.

it was too much like a party of the *vieja política*. But he stayed close to the Socialists. Thus, in the Constituent Assembly he told his Socialist colleagues that "whatever may be the distances between me and the totality of this theory [Marxism], my agreements with it are much more than enough to enable us to walk together for a long time."[40] In the elections to the Constituent Assembly Ortega's organization, the Group in the Service of the Republic, backed Republican-Socialist candidates and appealed mainly to a constituency of intellectuals, professionals, and workers. And Ortega's economic liberalism was not a mere ploy to win election. Thus, his proposal in the Constituent Assembly for a Council on the National Economy was to institute an agency for national planning with real powers; the Council was to be an independent branch of the state that was charged not only with drawing up developmental plans like the Russian, but also with the power and duty to mandate the allocation of the resources needed to implement the plans it drew up.[41]

Both the Socialists and Anarcho-Syndicalists were powerful agencies of popular education and mobilization, but in different ways both had tendencies towards political particularism, aiming to improve their lot not through national improvement, but through the destruction of wealth; this particularism could prevent workers from being sources of national leadership. Ortega devoted much effort to combating this tendency, and his main argument was the idea of industry, the gospel of work. Owing to chronic underemployment, many Spanish workers and peasants held that with increased production, economic and social justice would leave everybody, both the rich and the poor, better off. Ortega tried to keep this conviction in the foreground, for it was the conviction that could make the working classes the source of national reform. Ortega seriously contended that the class struggle could be ended if there was a general commitment to work; and he used this contention, strange as it may seem, as a successful argument in campaigning for election in a primarily left-of-center, working-class constituency.

In Spain, the gospel of work cut both ways. If the capitalist

---

[40]"En el debate político," July 30, 1931, *Obras* XI, p. 352.

[41]"Sobre lo de ahora," *Crisol*, August 6, 1931, *Obras* XI, pp. 364-6. Cf. "Circular de la Agrupación al Servicio de la República," January 29, 1932, *Obras* XI, pp. 427-8.

could demand a day's work for a day's wage, the worker could demand the full employment of capital. In a country in which considerable idle wealth coexisted with severe underemployment, there was good reason for the poorer classes to rally to the idea of industry and there was good reason for believing that the interests of productive labor and productive capital had much in common. In this context there was more sense than would at first appear in Ortega's statement that his "idea of work should make the abyss that exists between workers and those who are not workers disappear, for as the former work with the hoe on the divine earth, the latter will work by means of their capital."[42] The rights of capital depended on its full employment, not as a source of profit, but as a means of production. At a time when villages were spontaneously expropriating idle land so that they could put the hoe to it, Ortega's conception of industrious coöperation was a constructive, humane basis for reforming the chronic condition of underemployment: those incapable of making their wealth productive would forfeit their claim to ownership.

Ortega's life-long political struggle was against the *vieja política*, that destructive competition between organized interest groups for special benefits to be gained at the expense of the nation. The purpose was to create a national economy, an economy to which all Spaniards contributed and from which all Spaniards benefited. Rather than the current slogan, *toda por la patria*, all for the fatherland, which merely rephrases the organic principle of the old politics, *toda de la patria*, all from the fatherland, Ortega would have said *una patria por toda*, a fatherland for all. Thus, with this demand in his political economy for participation in public life by all members of the community, we arrive at the fourth of Ortega's basic political commitments, that is democracy. It was his genuine democratic feeling that truly set him apart from the sectarians of the old politics and the fundamental law.

Exponents of every form of government currently subscribe to democratic rhetoric. Therefore let us be specific: the democrat

---

[42]"Nación y trabajo: he aquí el lema de la Agrupación al Servicio de la República," *El Sol*, February 5, 1932. Cf. "Discurso en Oviedo," April 12, 1932, *Obras* XI, pp. 440-4.

believes in the dignity of man, seeks to implement the general will, and provides for popular participation in the determination of policy.

Men who believe in human dignity believe that each man, no matter how humble he may be, has qualities of unique and noble worth within his capacity. Further, each man shares equally in a common humanity: all men are brothers because the life of everyman is a continual struggle to realize his unique and noble potentials. The function of democracy is to make the governors respect the dignity, the worth, of each person: to do so, democracy gives each a voice in the affairs of the commonweal, so that the governors will not, in their ignorance, suppress the very virtues of the people. Ortega's democratic commitments were based on a belief in human dignity. Consequently, he was not bent, like so many politicians, on getting people to tell him what he wanted to hear; he was sincerely interested in the way other persons defined life for themselves. With the League for Spanish Political Education, this commitment resulted in a spontaneous effort to create channels of communication between the rustic peasant and the urban professional. In the same spirit, Ortega was a peripatetic philosopher who spent much time wandering about Spain, and his bittersweet essays on Spanish character testify to his concern to understand and celebrate the unique characters of diverse persons.

Respect for the dignity of different individuals logically leads the political thinker to a concern for the general will, a concern that was essential to Ortega's conception of democracy. In part, when Ortega distinguished between the old and the new politics, he distinguished between a political life guided by the will of all and one inspired by the general will. To be sure, Rousseau's presentation of these two political drives was flawed.[a] But the distinction between them, which did not begin with Rousseau, is essential to democratic theory. The will of all is a balance of factions; it is the dominant opinion, the one that comes out on top after all the interests favoring different positions have been mobilized and pitted against each other. Most political acts reflect the will of all; it guides the practical operation of power. But Rousseau was inquiring not into the nature of political power. Instead, he reflected on the nature of political legitimacy. "Man is born free, and everywhere he is in chains. He who believes himself the master of others lets himself be more a slave than they. How is this change made? That I ignore. What can render it legitimate? That question I believe can be solved."[43]

What is the general will? This question, to be answered coherently, should be refined into two. What is the concept of the general will? What, in an actual political situation, is the general will? Rousseau offered no answer to this second question; as Plato never gave a substantive statement of what the Good in actuality is, Rousseau never gave a substantive statement of what the general will is. Instead, Rousseau postulated the concept of the general will. If, he suggested, the substantive actuality of the concept was known, authority could be rendered legitimate; and he laid down very rigorous conditions that would have to be met before knowledge of the general will might be attained. As a concept, the general will postulates the *idea* of a common interest, a common interest that comes into being as men choose to live with other men. In theory, authority based truly on this common interest would be a legitimate authority, for in choosing to live in community with other men, a man rationally committed himself to will to act in ways consistent with the interest of the community in which he has chosen to partake. Or, to put the negative: a man who willed to act contrary to the interest of the community would act contrary to his basic intention of living in community with others. Let us leave to metaphysicians the question whether actual communities have real interests, or whether communities really exist apart from their members; Rousseau did not pronounce upon these points. Likewise, let us leave to the historians of political theory the question whether Rousseau bears responsibility for the crimes later committed by erring men who claimed to know and embody the substantive general will. There is, at least, a *concept* of the general will; we have been reflecting on it.

Throughout Platonism, throughout Stoicism, throughout Rous-

---

[43]J. J. Rousseau, *Du contrat social*, Livre I, Chap. I, *Oeuvres complètes*, III, p. 351.

seau's *Contrat social*, there runs the recognition that wise political deliberation will result from a sober, intelligent, informed, independent search, a search that is always humbled by the *idea* of the general will; that is, the idea that the community has an interest, that only this interest could legitimate authority, and that this interest is never clearly apparent, if it can ever be apparent at all, to any individual or group. The idea of the general will is essential to democratic politics and limited government: it reiterates to rulers the humbling fact that the most they can claim for their policies is prudent expediency, never unrestrained legitimacy; it saddles the would-be leader with continuous self-doubt; it creates a never ending need for the serious, open examination of every policy and piety. As happened in history, by immeasurably raising the criteria for legitimacy, the *idea* of the general will significantly reduced men's deference to arbitrary authority.

Once arbitrary authority gives way to constitutional government and a rule of law, due emphasis on the idea of the general will reinforces the fact that democracy entails a tremendous self-discipline on the part of each citizen. Contrary to stereotype, Rousseau was profoundly prudent when he observed that to arrive at a sound popular decision one should ask the people, not whether they approve or reject a proposition, but whether they believe the proposition to be in accord or not to be in accord with their common interests. To answer this question, each person would have to deliberate seriously and independently about the nature of the community in which he sought to participate.[44] The idea of the general will tells men little about what in any particular case should be done. Instead, the idea sets forth criteria that should influence the way men proceed to deliberate about what they should do. Thus Rousseau, who had nothing to say about which policy goals were in fact consistent with the general will, was explicit and rigorous in discussing how men should deliberate about policy.

Standards of public deliberation are always important in public affairs. As history shows, the results at different times of a particular political system vary tremendously in quality: mon-

---

[44]*Ibid.*, Livre IV, Chap. 2, pp. 440-1.

archy, aristocracy, oligarchy, democracy, and even tyranny have each, on occasion, promoted the good life for all, and at other opportunities they have each sunk all into times of trouble. One of the fundamental sources of these variations may well have been the willingness or unwillingness of those who made decisions to do so, not by asking whether they themselves approved of their particular policies, but by pondering whether their policies accorded with the common interest.

Ortega thought that Spaniards needed to alter their procedures for deliberating about policy. If they kept in mind an *idea* of a general, Spanish will, they would greatly democratize their political procedures. The political inertia of most Spaniards allowed the tradition of particularism to persist. Particularism signified that in thinking about public policy, men were considering only their most immediate interests, not their common interests. The *vieja política* responded not to the common interest of the whole community, but only to that of its dominant parts. If numerous members of the community remained silent, it would be next to impossible to take them into account in deliberating on public policy. Hence political apathy played into the hands of particularist groups. Ortega thought that a democratic regionalism would encourage the political participation of the traditionally inert members of the community. To the degree that such regional participation led to more active national participation, the range of opinions that would be articulated in politics would increase; this increase would enhance the possibility of governing in accord with the interests that every Spaniard, each in his separate uniqueness, had in Spain. To find this Spain in which there was room for everyone, each Spaniard needed to contribute his part. "We aspire to institute a state that will be for all Spaniards. We wish to erect a great, commodious house where there will be room for all."[45] Democracy was important, first, as a means of making the political process take every Spaniard into account.

To suffuse a political system with the spirit derived from the idea of the general will, it is not sufficient merely to ensure that all are taken into account. That is only the first step, which

---

[45]"Un proyecto," *El Sol*, December 6, 1930, *Obras* XI, p. 288.

is consistent with both the idea of the will of all and the idea of the general will. The second step, which follows from the idea of the general will alone, is more intangible; Ortega called it the "dignification" of the political process. For years Ortega tried to convince his compatriots that a national parliament would work only if its function was dignified; that is, if the day-to-day details that the national government traditionally meddled with were turned over to the regions where concern for them was appropriate. The national government should confine its attention to full, imaginative deliberation over major issues concerning the whole nation.[46]

When such deliberations are to be conducted by deputies of the people, there is disagreement about the nature of democratic procedure. Some believe that deputies should be bound to represent the express wishes of the majority of their constituents; others think that the deputies should sift all the opinions of the people and advance the one that they find most reasonable. The idea of the general will suggests that the latter procedure is more proper. The practice of Ortega's Group in the Service of the Republic was an excellent example of a representative deliberation in this second sense. No qualifications of doctrine, class, or region were put on those to whom the Group would listen. Ortega was not a cynical democrat; he believed that politics was a work of reason, that men entered politics to reason in common about common problems, and that it was not reasonable to ignore the sincere opinions of any man. As we shall see, this respect for the opinions of all men, this willingness to assume that all deputies in the Constituent Assembly were sincerely anxious to use reason disinterestedly to discover the best possible constitution for the nation, was at once the strength and the weakness of Ortega's political position.

It is ironic that Ortega should have acquired a reputation for being anti-democratic. As soon as one examines his actual

---

[46]See "Ideas políticas: Ejercicio normal del parlamento," *El Sol*, June 28 and July 1 and 2, 1922; "Ideas políticas," *El Sol*, June 29 and July 3, 12, 13, 19, and 26, 1924; and "La constitución y la nación," *El Sol*, January 11, 14, 18, 25, and 26, 1928; *Obras* XI, pp. 14-25, 32-49, and 201-227.

political commitments, one discovers that they were uncompromisingly democratic. As has been suggested, the misapprehension has resulted largely from the selective concentration on certain works and from the difficulty of access to others. For example, Ortega's statement that a society, to the degree that it is a society, must be aristocratic, has become notorious; and people who habitually think of democracy as being opposed to aristocracy generally misunderstand it.[47] But the corollary to his conviction about the aristocratic nature of society is a less well-known assertion about the democratic nature of government. Ortega made this assertion both before and after making his notorious statement in *The Revolt of the Masses*, so it cannot be explained away as a temporary change of heart. The corollary is this: under modern conditions, a government, to the degree that it is a competent government, must be democratic.

The contemporary state requires a constant and all-embracing collaboration from all its citizens, and it does this not only by reason of political justice, but of ineluctable necessity. The problems of the present state are of such quantity and quality that they require the continuous concern of all its members. By this necessity, which the conditions of modern life inexorably impose, the state and the nation have to be fused into a unity; this fusion is called democracy. This means that democracy has ceased to be a theory and a political credo for which some agitate, and that it has converted itself into the inevitable anatomy of the present epoch; it is not only that in the present there are democrats, but that democracy is the present.[48]

Public affairs have reached such a degree of complexity that democracy is a necessity; since the intricate web of interpersonal relations that constitutes the industrial nation-state is the actual locus of public affairs, policy formation cannot in fact be confined to the exalted few—despite pretension, all are involved. This ineluctable democracy was inescapably implied as each person sought to turn on an electric lamp, to open a newspaper, to don

---

[47]See *La rebelión de las masas*, 1930, *Obras* IV, pp. 150-1; cf. *España invertebrada*, 1921, *Obras* III, pp. 93-100.

[48]"Rectificación de la República," December 6, 1931, *Obras* XI, p. 409. Cf. "Dislocación y resturación de España: II: Condiciones," *El Sol*, July 17, 1926, *Obras* XI, p. 96.

machine-woven cloth, or to board a train or trolley; this democracy was the fundamental feature of the Spain that is. Yet this democracy in which each must take account of all, for he depends on all, is the democracy that has been most easily scorned, not only in Spain, but throughout the contemporary West. Blinded by the illusions of power each pridefully takes account only of his friends, his class, his party, his union, his club, or his group. The fatal contradiction of the nation-state in Spain and elsewhere is a disjunction between the citizens' character and their circumstances. When the nation-state finally achieves a thorough integration of its members, linking them together in a web of mutual dependencies, it loses the spiritual inspiration, the common ideal, that prompted each member to look beyond his immediate self-interest and to subordinate his particular urges to the pursuit of a shared ideal. The nascent nation could tolerate diversity yet it was able to achieve spiritual unity; the mature nation necessitates unity yet it can only occasion dissension. Can the nation-state survive when its democratic reality—the need of each to take account of all—is chronically ignored?

*   *   *

To extinguish hubris is more needful than to extinguish fire.

HERACLITUS, 43

WITH MORE GOOD WILL *than perspicuity, some think Parliament would be better if a few professors and writers of respectable stature took part in its internal life. To be sure, today the only figures anointed with a few drops of prestige belong to the scientific, literary, and artistic fraternities. . . . Nevertheless, I doubt very much whether the direct intervention of the intellectual would improve politics. History more properly suggests that in politics intellectuals have been able to do only one thing: to be in the way.*

ORTEGA[1]

[1] "Ideas políticas, II," *El Sol*, July 1, 1922, *Obras* XI, p. 19.

VIII
Failure

ORTEGA'S PUBLIC POWER was that of a *clerc;* he was a man of the world who continually confronted his people with worthy standards and the woeful gap between these ideals and human achievements.

From 1898 to 1931 Spanish history was a halting, definite movement towards the peaceful, thorough reformation of the body politic. Through ups and downs, through dictatorship and freedom, the impetus that at once sustained and modulated this progress was the vigorous political journalism of Spain's best thinkers. It was as if Madison, Hamilton, and Jay had kept *Publius* at work for over thirty years. Unamuno, Ortega, and many others campaigned continuously to enlighten, provoke, and caution the Spanish people. Their effort succeeded.

Greatness beckons when a nation devolops a powerful corps of teachers and journalists who are neither cynical nor utopian, neither doctrinaire nor decadent. Thanks to such a corps, Spain made extraordinary progress towards the peaceful reconstruction of its politics and society. This progress seems all the more remarkable when compared to the concurrent decline of other European countries. Owing to the horror of the Civil War, we often forget that in 1931 Spain had a peaceful yet popular revolution. Bloodless coups and bloody rebellions are commonplace occurrences; but the thorough, relatively stable transfer of power from an ancient Monarchy to republican Spain is unique in recent history. In 1931 there was no putsch, no coup, no rebellion; there was simply a compelling recognition, created largely by the clerisy, that the reasonable course was the transfer of power to republican leaders. Therefore, one observes with regret how the clerisy convinced itself that in 1931 the millennium had arrived: Ortega and other intellectuals hurried to participate in practical politics. Doing so, they destroyed their claim to stand apart as constructive critics who could modulate the clash of conflicting powers. Doing so, they deprived the new Republic of the intellectual leadership that had made its auspicious advent possible. These were decisive errors.

The force of political criticism depends on the critic's separation from direct involvement in the internal political process. As soon as a critic is implicated with immediate responsibility for practical decisions, his criticism will be dismissed as self-serving. Until the Second Republic, Ortega's power as a political educator arose from his independence, his obvious distance from official Spain.

Throughout most of his career, Ortega understood the source of his power. By contrasting official Spain and vital Spain he ingeniously forced listeners to suspend their interest in the gossip of capital politics and to concentrate on substantive issues. The League for Spanish Political Education had critical authority because its members put themselves above the fray, neither seeking office nor shunning office, believing that these were irrelevant to their tasks.[2] In 1925 Ortega described how a clerisy should influence the practical world. Ideally, he said, an intellectual should ignore politics and concentrate on his strictly intellectual concerns. But troubles rent Spain; crises threatened Europe: intellectuals could not prudently disregard mundane affairs. In lieu of disengagement, Ortega offered this principle: "that in order to make politics, the intellectual must make it as an intellectual and not compromise the virtues and imperatives of his vocation and discipline."[3] Two years later he was even more explicit: "even in exceptional cases, it greatly behooves the writer to separate his intellectual labor from his political anxiety, and when he does not

---

[2]See *Vieja y nueva política*," 1914, *Obras* I, especially 277-9.

[3]"Entreacto polémico: Para el Conde de Romanones," *El Sol*, March 15, 1925, *Obras* XI, p. 59.

do this, to require of his political interventions all the elevated virtues that rule intellectual work"[4]

Ortega failed to maintain this principle. As long as he was in opposition, he preserved his independence and remained true to his intellectual vocation. But in 1931, without the tangential discipline of belonging to a non-participating opposition, he became too deeply implicated in partisan politics; soon he began to seek followers rather than to speak his mind. Consequently, when he became convinced in 1932 that he could no longer partici- pate effectively in the very system he had helped create, he could only withdraw and maintain silence, obviously disturbed, but with no grounds for disinterestedly speaking out: he had ceased to be above the fray. New efforts at his old style of criticism were rebuked as sour grapes; a disgruntled aspirant for office found that his prerogatives as a *clerc* existed no more.[a] Then it was, when his Spanish hopes had run aground, that Ortega announced his second voyage.

Ortega began his drift into active politics in 1929. The pre- vious year he had toured Latin America giving highly acclaimed lectures. The President of Argentina had attended when Ortega presented a preliminary version of *The Revolt of the Masses* to the Society of Lectures in Buenos Aires. These talks and his special course on *What Is Philosophy?*, given at the University of Buenos Aires, were enthusiastically received and prominently reported in the Argentine press, especially in *La Nación*. Madrid papers, in particular *El Sol*, echoed reports of Ortega's reception, enhancing his reputation as the Spaniard who could best create living cultural ties between Spain and its former colonies. This reputation was further increased when Ortega addressed the Chilean parliament, an unusual honor. *El Sol* ran several articles analyzing Ortega's sway over Latin American youth: his accom- plishments, the commentators found, suggested that Spain's strength would depend on the ability of its intellectuals to inspire a trans-Atlantic cultural commonwealth to concerted actions.[b]

Ortega returned to Spain in January 1929 to find that he was

---

[4]"El poder social," 1927, *Obras* III, p. 499.

something of a celebrity and that a major conflict between the Universities and Primo de Rivera was brewing. The Dictator developed the delusion that he could at once improve higher education and decrease political opposition from intellectuals by fixing a faster pace on both the faculty and the students. Orders, especially ones that command a forced march, are never well received in academe; hence, as frequently happened, Primo de Rivera's results did not accord with his intentions. The attempt to subject academic requirements to worldly expediencies, the ill-fated Article 53 of the University Statute, put the University of Madrid out of operation for a year and confirmed the intellectual community as the Dictator's implacable foe. Student strikes and demonstrations against Article 53 in particular and the government in general enlivened February and early March. The government could not control the students, and in desperation the Dictator closed all universities for two weeks and that of Madrid until January 1, 1930.

With the students sent home, the professors took up the cause. Ramón Menéndez Pidal, the great historian and director of the Royal Academy, a man not notorious for dabbling in the politics of protest, announced his sympathy with the students. From his unsilent retirement, having years before renounced his university posts over another clash between state and student, Unamuno called on the mature to take up the battle that the young had bravely waged. Ortega was prominent among the professors who answered Unamuno's call, using their talents to oppose the Dictator. Along with four others, Felipe Sánchez Román, Luis Jiménez de Asúa, Fernando de los Ríos, and Alfonso García-Valdecasas, Ortega resigned his professorship to protest the closing of the university. He did not, however, give up his teaching vocation. He hired the Sala Rex, one of the larger theaters in Madrid, and advertised in the papers that he would continue his university course, charging a small fee to cover expenses. His gesture was a great success. Attendance began high and grew steadily: midway in the series he had to hire a still larger theater. His lectures on *What Is Philosophy?* were popularly known as "The Course" in recognition that through them the University was still in operation.

Ortega and his friends were deceived by "The Course." Couching his thought in clear and elegant prose, he presented an existential ontology that was as advanced as Heidegger's. Many who listened avidly to the lectures, or followed them in the papers, were not university students. Observers took the suprising heterogeneity of his audience as a sign that the Spanish people had finally matured, that all the efforts to create a cultivated elite had succeeded. For this reason, *El Sol* asserted in an editorial that "the course of Sr. Ortega y Gasset, besides having been a philosophic course, can very well qualify as an historic fact."[5] What began as a gesture became a desideratum; here, unexpectedly, was the awaited sign that the moment for Spanish renovation had arrived. If the precondition for Spanish regeneration was the existence of a truly cultured minority, one that could give the country a backbone, in Ortega's phrase, then the hour had come: suddenly, in the audience of "The Course," the renovating elite seemed to present itself to the eyes. In describing the sight, Luis de Zulueta became almost lyric with joy: "the theater was full. A numerous and diverse public. Neither a single group, nor a single color, nor a single sex, nor a single class of the society. It is an intellectual selection, but one made spontaneously, freely. . . . An excellent symptom. A favorable sign of the times. Now in Madrid people fill a theater, day after day, only to learn philosophy."[6c]

After years of work, a new politics seemed imminent. The pace quickened. Ortega honed his political journalism to make it move events. His Argentine lectures on the mass man—how timely!—these he worked into a long series of articles that came out in *El Sol* through the fall of 1929 and the spring of 1930. In this, its proper context, *The Revolt of the Masses* was anything but a conservative tract; it served well in the campaign to bring down the Dictator and then the Monarch. As Ortega defined the mass man, there were no more prominent examples than Primo de Rivera, the King, and those around them. The first installment gave the clue: masses did not mean "either solely or principally" the working masses; masses meant men in every social class who

[5]Anonymous, "El curso de D. José Ortega y Gasset," *El Sol*, May 21, 1929.
[6]Luis de Zulueta, "Lecciones de Ortega y Gasset," *El Sol*, May 21, 1929.

were satisfied with themselves, who were unwilling to discipline themselves. Mass men proliferated among intellectuals and the vestiges of "nobilities," nobodies who claimed special privileges in society. "In contrast, it is not unusual today among the workers, who formerly could be patronizied as the purest example of what we are calling 'mass,' to encounter eminently disciplined characters."[7] In the taxing turn Ortega gave to his conception of the truly noble life, in making it denote rigorous self-discipline in the service of man's highest ideals, he provided the rationale for a profound attack on the Spanish monarchy and the established classes, and for a call to visionary reform.

To suggest that *The Revolt of the Masses* was only, or even primarily, a tract against the complacencies of the Spanish Monarch and his minions would be excessive. But in it Ortega contended, in vivid, compelling prose, that power—political, economic, technical, cultural—was exercised by men of no special competence, men who took more from civilization than they contributed. The *señorito satisfecho*, the sated swinger, was anything but the self-disciplined worker and peasant. Repeatedly Ortega likened the character of the mass man to that of the *fils de famille*, especially to that of the hereditary aristocrat. Who would give flesh to these similes? Who but the established groups around the government and the King? Ortega challenged them on the most fundamental grounds: their moral claim to authority.

In summer 1930 Ortega reiterated this critique with his essay on "The Moral of the Automobile in Spain." Spaniards ranked fourth in the number of cars per capita; their roads were terrible and sparse; Spain produced no cars; automobiles in Spain were always clean and luxurious. The lesson was clear: in Spain, neither the automobile, nor the members of the leisured class who owned them, served any use.[8]

The polemic against the ruling groups culminated in the fall.

---

[7]*La rebelión de las masas*, 1930, *Obras* IV, p. 147. The key to this polemic is the attack on "the happy few," *Ibid.*, p. 151. Also the argument, *Ibid.*, p. 150, that there were no longer any genuine aristocracies would, in the context in which it was published, only undercut the *raison d'être* of the Monarchy.

[8]"La moral del automóvil en España," *El Sol*, August 23, 1930, *Obras* IV, pp. 84-8.

In "The Berenguer Error," Ortega used his knack for coining slogans that crystallized strong feelings to denote the King as the real obstacle to reform. When Primo de Rivera had resigned early in the year, Alfonso XIII had General Berenguer form a government, which was charged with promoting a "return to normalcy." Berenguer's task was to reconstruct a government based on the Constitution of 1876, which Primo de Rivera had suspended in 1923. The King asked an impossible task of his General, Ortega asserted, for the King, not the Dictator, had been the fundamental abnormality in recent years. Monarchy was normal only insofar as the Monarch was the educator and spiritual leader of his people, Ortega contended. At this, the King had proved himself incompetent. Hence the greatest abnormality in Spanish life had become the Monarchy. "Spaniards! Your State does not exist! Reconstruct it!" To close his brief against the King, Ortega adapted a phrase from Cato's implacable cry against Carthage; immediately, it became a bond among republicans— "*Delenda est Monarchia.*"—Monarchy must be destroyed![9]

By the end of 1930, agitation for a republic could not be contained; a revolution was merely a matter of time, and not much time at that. Ortega and the clerisy were but a small, yet significant part of those calling for change. Several workers parties, especially the Socialists, several Republican parties, and several regionalist movements, especially the Catalan left, were coöperating, despite some strains, to bring down the government and to constitute a new system. These organized groups were the practical powers forcing revolution. Yet the intellectuals were also essential: they brought popular opinion to the point of accepting a republican solution to the vacuum of authority. In December 1930 an unsuccessful republican uprising had been easily put down. In the aftermath, the Athenaeum of Madrid was closed because that meeting place for intellectuals had become—nay, it had always been—a center of republican aspirations. Such mea-

---

[9]"El error Berenguer," *El Sol*, November 15, 1930, *Obras* XI, p. 279. The effect of the phrase can be gauged by the attention given to it by the monarchist historian, Melchor Fernández Almago, *Historia del Reinado de Don Alfonso XIII*, p. 562; and by Mori's use of it to identify Ortega in the chronicle of the Constituent Assembly, *Crónica*, Vol. I, p. 95.

sures were of no avail; discussions that previously went on in public, now took place in private. In February 1931, Ortega, the novelist Ramón Pérez de Ayala, and the great doctor Gregorio Marañón, organized the Group in the Service of the Republic, giving intellectuals a national organization through which to express their republican commitments. The Group operated as a correspondence society with local chapters all over Spain. It did a great deal to help republicanism come to power without an outright, violent revolution.

General Berenguer had set a "normal" election to the Cortes for February, but abstentions were so heavy that the election was a farce. In an admission that the "return to normalcy" had failed, Berenguer resigned. The government of Admiral Aznar was no more effective. On April 12, municipal elections were held throughout the nation. Returns showed a landslide for republican candidates. The position of the Monarchy had become untenable. Two days later King Alfonso XIII left Spain, and his ministers negotiated the transfer of power to a provisional republican government, most members of which had lately been in jail for their political dissidence.

The fall of the Monarchy had been like the kill in a *corrida*: with the exhausted government's attention fixed on the *muleta*, the red flag of revolution, the republicans pierced the heart from above and in the open, yet unseen and unexpected, with the thin rapier of electoral victory. But unlike a *corrida*, the political spectacle does not end. With the fall of the Monarchy the direction of republican activities had to shift from the negative tearing down of the old system to the positive building up of a new one. Here certain divisions became apparent.

Two developments in bringing down the Monarchy were particularly significant in constructing a republic: the Pact of San Sebastian and the Group in the Service of the Republic. On August 17, 1930, leading Republicans, Catalan nationalists, and Socialists had agreed in the Pact of San Sebastian to work coöperatively for a republic, by use of force if necessary. Although several of Ortega's intellectual allies, including his brother, Eduardo, took part in the Pact, it was primarily a practical political alliance between the major republican organizations. Hard bargains were struck about the means for bringing down the Monarchy and about the future features of the republic. In April, the Revolutionary Committee created through the Pact became the Provisional Government. The blocs represented by the signatories to the Pact were the practical backbone of the Republic; and despite certain tensions and changes in leadership, this coalition clearly dominated the new government at least to the November 1933 elections.

The Group in the Service of the Republic was a new organization, the purpose of which differed from the Pact. The Group, which was not founded by an alliance between existing organizations, was not intended to be a political party. Members of the Group were committed to political education; they had little practical power; their spokesmen did not represent large blocs of votes. The Group aimed to put the intellect of Spain in the service of a republic, or as its manifesto said, "to mobilize all Spaniards of an intellectual office in order to form a copious contingent of propagators and defenders of the Spanish Republic."[10]d

Together the Pact and the Group served a common purpose. No one had to make an either-or choice between the tendencies represented by the Pact and the Group, for both shared a valid, useful, sincere commitment to creating a new republic. The Pact stood for the practical reality of the republic, the Group for its intellectual ability. Members of the latter, however, had to make a serious decision: how could the Group best serve a republic that would be built upon the practical politics of the Pact? This question was especially important in determining the policy of the Group towards the Constituent Assembly. Ortega miscalculated in answering this question.

On December 6, 1930, as a sign of the weakening Monarchy, Ortega had published an essay requesting that a national convention be convened to draw up a new constitution. This essay, "A Project," reveals Ortega's expectations about the Constituent Assembly. He identified two groups as dangerous to real progress: those who did not want a new state and those who immediately

---

[10]"Agrupación al servicio de la República: Manifiesto," *El Sol*, February 10, 1931, *Obras* XI, p. 127.

wanted a radical social revolution. Essentially, both these groups scorned the Spanish nation and looked at politics as means for advancing their particular interests. The views of these extremes were short-sighted; any state founded on one or the other of them would be doomed to perpetual instability. The alternative would be a great, coöperative effort in which *all* could work to organize a new state, a state designed for all, not for one or another of its principal groups.[11]

Ortega might have taken as a motto for his convention Pascal's statement that "we do not display greatness by going to one extreme, but in touching both at once, and filling all the intervening space."[12] Drawing up a good constitution was more an intellectual than political endeavor, it seemed to Ortega. In order to create a governmental mechanism that would allow all groups to coexist and that would nevertheless be politically effective, the framers would have to account wisely for all aspects of the nation, even those they disliked. Destiny called Spain's intellectuals to the task of discovering a political system that could form and implement significant national policies and that could do so without driving any major group into a desperate resistance for the sake of survival. Clearly, Ortega expected the Constituent Assembly to be composed of patriotic personages who, like the American founding fathers, would draw up with a minimum of partisan self-serving an enlightened, enduring, adaptable basis for government. This task done, the founders would then disband and return to their respective occupations. Perhaps Ortega should have read Beard.

Ortega conceived of the Constituent Assembly in the mold of vital politics. Destiny beckoned and the people would spontaneously push forward those men gifted with genius; or, more precisely, the occasion was such that an unexpected excellence and enlightenment would be engendered in those the people advanced. For Ortega, a political movement that merited being called vital, as opposed to the merely official, was a spontaneous unity in the pursuit of a great task. Now the moment approached

---

[11]"Un proyecto," *El Sol*, December 6, 1930, *Obras* XI, pp. 280-290.
[12]Pascal, *Pensées*, no. 353, W. F. Trotter, trans.

when the vital politics of those who had been pursuing Spanish renovation would merge into a new official politics, that of the Second Republic. Ortega saw the Constituent Assembly as the culmination of the vital politics. The Assembly, he thought would be unified by a desire to provide Spain, and through Spain, Europe, with the key to unlock the constraints of the nineteenth-century state and to point the way for the European peoples to regain their proper form.

On the basis of these assumptions, it made sense for the Group in the Service of the Republic to seek an active part in the Constituent Assembly. The deliberations would call for intellectual vision; as in any intellectual consideration, the opinions backed by the best reasons would carry the greatest weight. The Group comprised many of Spain's most respected thinkers. They would be looked to as the men best able to divine the features of a constiution that would prove, through the experience of future centuries, to be exemplary. In an Assembly vitally committed to producing such a document, the Group would be listened to not in proportion to the power of its constituents, but in proportion to the wisdom of its members. Such expectations lured the clerisy into political activism.

Despite the Assembly's glowing oratory of statesmanship, Ortega's belief that official politics would give way to vital politics in the Assembly was invalid. A Constituent Assembly that would have fulfilled Ortega's expectations would have been an extraordinary assembly indeed. Dominated by a non-ideological bloc, it would have studied the nation disinterestedly to discover the kind of state the nation needed as a whole. Then, it would have tried to design a state to fit these specifications. While campaigning, Ortega described such deliberation: "the state is an immense machine that a national collaboration constitutes in order to serve the public life, and the process for inventing a machine is this: first, one decides what are the objects that one wishes to obtain with it and then one molds the parts and the mechanism into the form that best conduces to these objects."[13] But the actual Constituent Assembly did not proceed in this manner.[e]

---

[13]"Ortega y Gasset habla en Léon," *El Sol*, June 28, 1931, *Obras* XI, p. 303.

To begin, the dominant blocs were not disinterested; they had strong ideological commitments. The larger parties had definite preconceptions about the constitution, they knew what they wanted, and bargains had been made to ensure the realization of these expectations. Hence, the Assembly had strong ties to the *vieja política*. Instead of beginning to deliberate by working out agreement about the functional attributes to be given the new state, the Assembly began with a projected draft of the Constitution, the juridical features of which were then re-examined in debate. Although this procedure was the only workable one in a convention of 470 persons, it encouraged partisan groups to ignore careful consideration of the Constitution as a whole and to concentrate on amending the project with their favorite proposals. Most debates concerned amendments, and in the end the Constitution was more a lawyer's derivative from advanced constitutional theory than an original contribution to the advance of that theory. An Ortegan Assembly would have had to go to the people, the whole people, to help them understand the Constitution, to create a genuine desire to live by its rule, and to overcome the fears of republican government. Spaniards were not politically sophisticated, and only if they fully comprehended the constitution, finding themselves deeply in concord with it, would it become the basis of a truly vital yet official politics. In reality, the members of the Assembly knew that they had drafted a divisive document, for most deputies, Ortega included, opposed a plebiscite to ratify their work for fear of unnecessarily aggravating national divisions.

At the outset, members of the Group might have realized that their assumptions concerning the Assembly were wrong. The Assembly was too large to accomplish much beyond endorsing the preconceived opinions of its majority. Its mandate was too strong, enabling well represented groups to try to build a bias in favor of their interests into the system. The Assembly's strong mandate, however, failed to isolate it from electoral pressure, for there was nothing to prevent it from patterning parliament on itself and transforming itself into the first parliament, as in fact it did. Voting by lists encouraged a convention of parties rather than one of personages. All these facts might have suggested to Ortega that the Assembly would not be a body in which farseeing statesmanship would dominate. The Group erred in trying to shape the Republic by taking an active part in the Assembly. By doing so, they had no real effect on the Constitution, and they dissipated the clerisy's influence. Their prestige, which was great, might have been put to better use as a journalistic, educational force keeping the interests of the nation before the Assembly, and interpreting to the nation the work of the Assembly. In this role the Group could have continued, long after the Constitution had been framed, to act as a moral influence, raising the tone of political practice and modulating the swings of political passion.

In retrospect, one can see a serious ambiguity in Ortega's political criticism. Beginning with his convocation address to the League for Spanish Political Education and continuing up to his participation in the Constituent Assembly, Ortega alternated between making two different contrasts: sometimes he pitted the new politics against the old politics and at others he opposed a vital politics against official politics. As long as the new politics was in opposition, the two contrasts could be used interchangeably; but they were not the same. The antipodes denoted by each contrast were different: a *new* politics suggested that the *old* would in time be replaced, or at least reduced to a mere vestige like the British monarchy; but a *vital* politics might very well exist permanently in a continuous, productive tension with the *official*. As long as the *vieja política* reigned in Spain, Ortega did not need to clarify these distinctions. But failing to do so, he was not prepared for the time when the new politics would become an official politics. Then, by being drawn into the new, official politics of the Second Republic, he gave up his basis for engaging in vital politics. Perhaps American proponents of the new politics should ponder this distinction.

Ortega failed to clarify whether civic pedagogy was a permanent complement to official, practical politics, or whether it was a temporary endeavor that would transform the corrupt old ways into a pristine, new system. By taking the Group in the Service of the Republic into the Constituent Assembly, he acted as if the latter were true, as if vital politics were an historical anomaly to be rendered unnecessary by the new constitution. The fall of the Monarchy, however, did not end the need for Spain's clerisy to crusade with their pens for a more enlightened, humane public life. As it turned out, the results of the Constituent Assembly were far from perfect, but they were good enough; instead of establishing a new politics, they laid the groundwork for the thorough reform of the old. With strong, disinterested leadership of public opinion, the Second Republic might have performed with more stability than it did. Such leadership was lacking, for the *clercs* who had performed this office for more than thirty years and who could have continued to do so, had over-engaged themselves and undercut their intellectual authority. In the Constituent Assembly they fell short and did not write the perfect constitution. Thereafter, their criticism, which might have modulated political practice, was liable to be dismissed as the losers' laments.

In the Constituent Assembly, Ortega's claim to intellectual aloofness was steadily eroded. Through the summer and fall of 1931, the aura of partisanship around the Constitution disturbed him. Particularism became prominent. For instance, the regional groups did not contribute a unique outlook on the whole project; they insisted instead that a particular outlook be reflected in certain parts of the project. Hence, Ortega, a leading proponent of regional autonomy, found himself in opposition to the Catalan Statute and certain language matters: rather than grant autonomy for regional affairs, the Statute seemed to grant to a single region the right to speak authoritatively on certain national matters. Likewise, the Socialists seemed less concerned with perfecting the national economy than they were with inserting into the Constitution advanced welfare provisions that were probably not possible given the exisiting level of production in Spain. Ortega strongly welcomed the welfare provisions as humane, progressive, and just; he worried, however, that those who were primarily responsible for these provisions would think they had completed their task and would not carry through by leading a coöperative effort to expand the economy, an effort that alone could make good on the welfare state that the Assembly had so generously promised on paper. Then, to make matters worse, the old anticlericals reveled in pushing through Article 26, which provided the authority to disband any religious order that threatened the state. By disbanding the Jesuits and stipulating that all education be immediately laicized, thus mandating the discontinuation of many more schools than the new government could create, the Assembly severely complicated the new Republic's excellent efforts to improve public instruction.[f]

Such moves struck Ortega as a sacrifice of the national interest to satisfy the passions of large, doctrinaire groups. The Law of the Defense of the Republic, inserted towards the end of the Assembly's work, signified that the deputies knew they had failed to produce a national constitution: the framers of the new state were already preparing to defend it from powerful enemies within the nation. Finally, the Assembly indulged in the gratuitous trial *in absentia* of the King, which served nothing except to aggravate the monarchists. Such developments did not augur well for proponents of the new politics.

Like several other intellectuals who served in the Assembly, and many who observed from without, Ortega had serious reservations about the Constitution. "An immense number of Spaniards," he wrote towards the end of the Assembly's work, "who collaborated in the birth of the Republic by their actions, by their votes, and, what is most effective of all, by their hopes, are now saying between their worries and discontents: 'This isn't it! This isn't it! The Republic is one thing. 'Radicalism' is another. If not, let it wait."[14] When the moment for ratification came, of course, Ortega voted for the Republic; after all, it was a start and a great improvement over either dictatorship or the Constitution of 1876. But then, like any politician who accepts an imperfect work that he has helped to produce, Ortega set out to make the Constitution better by correcting its deficiencies in the realm of practice. Thus Ortega was drawn deeper and deeper into practical politics. Since partisanship was the major deficiency of the new Constitution, Ortega rather desperately decided that the creation of an inclusive, non-partisan party might best correct the weaknesses of the new system.

Even before the fall of the Monarchy, Ortega had called for a party of national unity; and as the work of the Assembly drew

---

[14]"Un aldabonazo," *Crisol*, September 9, 1931, *Obras* XI, p. 387.

to a close, he renewed this plea. Final ratification of the Constitution was to occur in December 1931, at which time the Assembly would elect a President, who in turn would appoint a Prime Minister. To be effective, this non-partisan party would have to elect its candidate as President, so that he could ask the party to form the government. This condition drew the potential party into competition with others, making it a partisan non-partisan party! In November rumors began to appear in the press that Ortega would found a political party. These rumors were compounded with denials into a considerable publicity campaign, which built up to a speech that Ortega gave on December 6, a few days before the final votes. Before a large audience of notables, Ortega outspokenly analyzed the shortcomings he felt would endanger the soon-to-be-established Republic. He addressed himself before the fact to "The Rectification of the Republic," and he asked that "a party of national amplitude" be created under the leadership of Miguel Maura. Only such a party could offset a drift towards the polarization of the Spanish polity.[g]

At first, the idea of a non-partisan party may seem absurd; under the circumstances, it may well have been impossible. The potential plausibility of this party of national amplitude stemmed from the fact that large, conglomerate parties can form in two different ways. On the one hand, coalitions of interest groups, which believe that to the victors belong the spoils, form when the components agree to divvy up between them the best plums of the political process. The Pact of San Sebastian provided the basis for such a party, and Manuel Azaña led this dominant coalition of left Republicans, Socialists, anti-clericals, and Catalan nationalists. On the other hand, occasionally more idealistic coalitions are built upon hopes for the future nation. These have had strong, intuitive appeal in poor, struggling countries. In difficult situations, diverse groups sometimes realize that by concentrating on national development they will be better off by having a smaller share of a larger nation than by taking the maximum share of the present nation. Such a national government ruled Britain in World War II, and analogous examples of "one party democracies" have become familiar in newly emergent nations. Such non-partisan governments usually come into existence either in response to dire threats to a nation's existence or as the result of a charismatic leader winning control over the nation's means of force. Neither condition held in Republican Spain.

Ortega tried to create a disinterested coalition party solely by suasion. Strong currents of political idealism existed in the Assembly; and in Ortega's speech he tried to capitalize on that idealism, hoping to break Azaña's coalition and to replace it with a more inclusive, idealistic one under Maura's leadership. As usual, Ortega was eloquent. He played on all the statesman-like hopes that had been voiced in the Assembly. He appealed particularly to the Socialists, for they were the next to largest group in Azaña's coalition and the one most susceptible to Ortega's nationalistic humanitarianism. He tried to base the new coalition on the three groups that he thought were the best endowed with inner human strengths. The new party would be "constituted by working men, mental workers and manual workers. . . . These workers are called, before anyone else, to this undertaking, for the life of a nation is in substance two things: manufacturing and mentefacturing. These two potencies—these and a third, youth—have to set the tone of any possible new party."[15]

El Sol sampled reactions to Ortega's speech by leading politicians. Predictably Miguel Maura was enthusiastic. Unamuno was complimentary, but refused to comment on Ortega's political propositions. What mattered, however, was the reaction of the Socialists; they proved to be polite but uninterested. Fernando de los Ríos commended Ortega's patriotism, but added that the existing parties could best accomplish the policies called for. Alvaro de Albornoz and Marcelino Domingo thought that the party Ortega sought would, in effect, weaken the left and strengthen the right; it therefore should be opposed. Others believed that the existing parties were sufficient and that it was improper to criticize the Republic on the eve of its being constituted.[16] The party of national amplitude died aborning. Three days later the Assembly elected Niceto Alacalá Zamora as Presi-

---

[15]"La rectificación de la República," *Obras* XI, p. 416.
[16]"El discurso de Don José Ortega y Gasset," *El Sol*, December 8, 1931.

dent, who soon announced that the Azaña government had been formed.

Ortega did not immediately give up hope for a new party. In the following months he toured the provinces studying the possibilities of converting the Group in the Service of the Republic into a national party.h He spoke in the north at Oviedo and in the south at Granada, both times explaining the rationale for a non-partisan coalition. He published a series of articles on its importance, but by the summer of 1932 the impossibility of making a majority party out of a minority organization of citizens and amateur politicans had discouraged him. Further, his efforts at political criticism were being dismissed as the recriminations of a frustrated politician. Putting up a good face, expressing confidence in the Republic and hope for the future, the Group disbanded. Ortega soon announced his withdrawal from politics: he had tried and failed. "This sonorous and perfect failure gives me the right to silence."[17] He broke his silence briefly after the 1933 elections to write in favor of the turn away from domination by the left, and he again called for enlightened, clear-headed government in the name of the whole nation. But the resentful effort by the right to undo two year's work by the left dashed Ortega's renascent hopes. Except for his grudging declaration of allegiance to the Republic early in the Civil War, he thereafter remained silent about Spanish politics.

Yet silence still resounds as a sonorous symbol. Silence, Ortega wrote, was a great teacher, for a well-placed pause signified as much as many words.[18] In this case silence taught that only under certain conditions could the intellectual take an effective part in politics; when those conditions were absent the intellectual should quietly prepare for the day when they would return. Years before Ortega had written that when men begin to fight with one another they cease to discuss their differences rationally. To stay out of such conflicts, the intellectual should say nothing, for whatever he said would be used as a club, not as a reason. Force was the *ultima ratio;* and when men resorted

---

[17]"Carta," *Luz,* April 1, 1933, *Obras* XI, p. 520.
[18]"El silencio, gran brahmán," 1930, *Obras* II, pp. 625-633.

to it, they were impelled to try to mobilize all available talent and power—right became a mere tool of might.

Ortega quickly realized that he was compromised with respect to Spanish public affairs. His self-imposed silence preceded the Civil War: "since August [1932] I have suspended my political activities, not only the parliamentary ones, but absolutely all of them, so that no one can claim without shame that since then I have made any act of political organization or even of expressing simple opinion, apparent or latent, direct or indirect, on the surface or beneath it."[19] From mid-1932 until his death, Ortega maintained, with minuscule exceptions, an adamant silence on matters of Spanish politics. Instead, he devoted himself to the interests of intellect. By doing so, he ensured that, come what may, he could work towards two goals: he could return to the practice of civic pedagogy with respect to Europe rather than Spain, and he could try to preserve the disciplined intelligence that had been nurtured in Spain and that might someday again pervade the conduct of political life.

By being silent, and by not taking part in the looming fray, the intellectual preserved certain possibilities, namely the possibilities of alternatives to the conflict. During his political activities Ortega contended that a peaceful, progressive Spain would be one that was led by a coalition of labor, intellect, and youth. This coalition failed to form in 1931, and since then certain silences have preserved the possibility that sometime in the future it will manage to come into being. Note that *clercs* like Ortega began their silence about four years before the Civil War; it would be wrong to fill in the silence with the passionate shouts that still echo from the conflict. Most of the intellectuals who had labored for decades to regenerate Spain perceived by 1932 that they had failed. The problem was to find a way by which progressive groups could endure the coming conflict without having their competencies crushed. Ideology was incidental: Spanish progress would come only when hard labor, cogent intellect, and vibrant youth managed to concert their efforts spontaneously.

---

[19]"Carta," *Luz*, April 1, 1933, *Obras* XI, p. 519.

The great danger in the coming reaction was not that a retrograde ideology would push out the nominal liberalism of the Second Republic, but that one or more of the truly progressive groups in Spain would be decimated.

For Ortega, the Civil War and the long period of marking time that followed were a tragic but historically insignificant incident. Reaction, a return to past traditions, was impossible, he believed. History was an ongoing movement, a continuous flow from the past into the future; hence a people could not escape into the safe certitudes of yesterday. Reactionary movements could try to impose myths on reality; but the reality would remain, and eventually when people became bored with stasis, leaders would be forced to begin again to deal honestly with the reality and retrace the steps that had previously been taken. Thus, conservatism could not permanently undo the accomplishments of progressivism; at worst the conservative could force the progressive to retrace his steps and forgo for a time further advance. The major steps taken prior to 1931 towards Spanish progress had built up the components of the coalition of labor, intellect, and youth. Through the reaction the task was to preserve these parts and to prepare for the time when they could again try to come together.

That day may be approaching. The victors in the Civil War face a profound political problem: reactionary regimes rarely prepare adequately for the transfer of power, for their eyes are always on the past and they fail to foresee the morrow. But a transfer of power ineluctably approaches and the faint efforts to prepare for it show, both positively and negatively, that the intrinsic power of Ortega's coalition of labor, intellect, and youth will have to be taken into account. The clearest sign is negative: the major efforts to suppress possible sources of unforeseen change in the established power structure have been aimed directly at workers, writers, and students. The vaunted liberalization of Spanish rights in recent years amounts to the following: there will be general freedom of speech and assembly provided that workers, intellectuals, and students do not give themselves independent organizations and do not concert their social concerns.

More important, however, are the positive signs (in 1970)

that Spain's progressive groups are revitalizing. That all men are mortal is obvious; the recent concern about the transfer of power in Spain is not merely, or even mainly, a function of the *Caudillo's* age. The present situation does not presage a resurfacing of the conflict fought out in the Civil War. The silence that preserved the possibility of a coalition of labor, intellect, and youth, also preserved the possibility of a re-alliance of forces. The present interest in the transfer of power has arisen mainly because members of the present government realize that the community of interest between components of Franco's coalition—the Army, the Church, and wealth—is no longer solid. In the thirties, the progressive, republican advance was broken from within by an inane, gratuitous, excessive anti-clericalism. Since then the Church has changed—and so has the outlook of workers, writers, artists, and students. In the newspapers, interesting signs of the time keep recurring. So-called Communist workers are arrested for holding illegal meetings in their churches; a Bishop argues scathingly for the moral necessity of land reform; Barcelona students and professors are besieged in a Convent and arrested for demanding the right to organize independently; young priests are clubbed in a demonstration in support of students. What all these and many other signs mean for the future of Spain depends entirely on what many particular Spaniards decide to do. Labor, intellect, and youth have come through the reaction largely intact. And if the Church were to liberalize. . . . At the present time one can only say that judicious silence has ensured that all is now possible in Spain, and one suspects that the time is not too distant when, ironically, judicious silence will seem to have been an excessively timid commitment.

Yet silence is not the same as inactivity. Ortega's disappointment with the course of events from 1932 onward must have been profound. Fortunately, however, his work was not inextricably bound to his taking an active part in Spanish public affairs. Ortega was a "good European." One of the inspirations for his effort at the reform of Spain had been to point the way by which the European nations could get in shape and transcend their parochial limitations. This European goal remained alive for Ortega; his

Spanish failure even intensified it, for he saw that the failure was a symptom of Europe's decadence.

To see the Spanish failure as a European symptom, one should look beneath the surface of the Civil War and the events before and after it. For Ortega, the failure of Spain, and his own failure with respect to it, went much deeper than the failure of a particular political program. Anyone with Ortega's knowledge of history is fully aware of how changeable political fashion has always been. One finds no fundamental significance in this sphere. The failure of Spanish reform was more profound. The failure appeared to be nothing less than a failure of culture itself; it seemed to be a terrible confirmation of the thesis advanced in *The Revolt of the Masses* that there was a radical defect in European culture. Spain, like the rest of Europe, was showing that its elites on both the right and the left did not understand the principles of the civilization for which they were responsible.

During his long silence about Spain, Ortega devoted himself to an examination of Europe's cultural principles. This re-examination of Western culture has facilitated a re-alliance of forces within Spain and throughout the West, and in this facilitation we find a worldly justification for the quiet labors of Ortega and other reflective men who chose to be silent in times of passion. It is not an accident that religion, labor, intellect, and youth have changed during the past third of a century. Let us turn to Ortega's small but significant part in this reorientation of Western culture.

*   *   *

Greater dooms win greater destinies.

HERACLITUS, 25

Interlude

It would not be better if things happened to men just as
they wished.

HERACLITUS[1]

AT THE AGE OF FIFTY Ortega faced up to failure: he redefined his
task. Yeats' lines sum up Ortega's plight. "Things fall apart; the
centre cannot hold; Mere anarchy is loosed upon the world. . . ."[2]
Spain again became possessed by factional politics; the *vieja
política* returned with a vengeance. Ortega saw no way to reverse
the tendency towards extremism, the terrible tendency that would
lead to dictatorship by way of anarchy and civil war. Moreover,
at fifty Ortega found that Europe no longer offered hope to the
Spanish reformer. Although valid, the European tradition was
in abeyance. Ortega withheld his "Prologue for the Germans"
from publication as a protest against Hitler's ascension to power.
The extremism of Spain was but an episode in the more general
extremism that dominated Europe. Young men could no longer
proclaim that Spain was the problem and Europe the solution,
for Europe, itself, had become the problem—and there was no
foreseeable solution.

Man, however, has the power of abstraction. No person is
compelled to obsess himself with immediate matters; letting these
take what course they may, he can withdraw into his inner counsel
and work towards the more distant future, laying intellectual
foundations for a new attempt at creating a humane order. Thus,
in 1932, Ortega became a posthumous man: he published his
collected works and announced that henceforth he would devote

---

[1]Heraclitus, Fragment 52, Wheelwright, trans.

[2]W. B. Yeats, "The Second Coming," in *The Collected Poems of W. B. Yeats*,
p. 184.

himself to reflecting on the fundamental problems of Western culture. The great journalist lost his passion to publish and many of his important books remained in his workshop until after he died. He devoted all the leisure he could piece together to reflecting in solitude or in the company of a few intimates on the great questions, answers to which might help men rebuild the foundations of their culture. Only since his death have men been able to appreciate the magnitude of his effort, an effort that he called, after Plato, his "second voyage." Ortega's first voyage, like Plato's, was an excursion into practical reform through pedagogical means; and for both, the second voyage consisted in reflecting on the problems that made the first end unsuccessfully. For both, their reflective effort did not begin abruptly, but developed naturally from their active concerns.

Throughout his life, Ortega maintained a tension between the immediate and the distant; always he was both a participant and a spectator. But in his youth he hoped to witness the results of his thoughts and deeds; his aspirations concerned his immediate circumstances. During his second voyage he did not completely lose this involvement. But his work became more abstract. He aimed not at immediate consequences, but at far off goals that concerned the sense of life held by the people who would live in a fully industrialized world. On the thirtieth of June, 1932, Ortega made two recordings for the Archives of Speech at the Center for Historical Studies. These recordings indicate the change in his interests. In the first he retrospectively described his attempt to transform the Spanish character. In the second he prospectively plumbed the secret of history. The first gave an eloquent apology for the life he had led up to then. He called it "The Work of Man."

Life is labor. And the truth of life, that is, the authentic life of each person, consists in doing what must be done and in not doing anything else. For me a man has merit to the degree that the series of his acts is necessary and not capricious. But the difficulty of it is in properly leading one's target, for the only thing that appears to us to be necessary is a repertory of actions that others have performed. These come to us haloed with one or another consecration. They incite us to be unfaithful to our authentic work, which is always irreducible to that of others. True life is inevitably invention. We must invent our own existence; yet at the same time this invention must not be capricious. Hence, the word "invent" recovers its etymological intention of "find." We must find, we must discover the necessary trajectory of our life, for only then will we be truly ourselves and not just anyone, as the frivolous always are.

How can one resolve so difficult a problem? For me there is no doubt about it. One finds that one is like a poet to whom a rhyme scheme is given. This rhyme scheme is one's circumstances. Each person always lives in the midst of unique and unavoidable circumstances. These tell one in a schematic outline what it is that one must do.

In this way I have directed my labor. I have accepted the circumstances of my nation and my time. Spain suffered and still suffers from a *deficit* of intellect. It had lost its dexterity at handling concepts, which are — neither more nor less — instruments with which we make our way among things. It was necessary to teach Spaniards to face reality and to transmute it into thought with the least possible loss. Thus, I dealt with something more ample than science, for science is only one of the many manifestations of the human capacity to react intellectually before reality.

Well then, I had to make my experiments at apprenticing the Spaniard to intellect in whatever way he could be reached: in friendly conversation, in the periodicals, and in public lectures. It was necessary to attract him to the precision of ideas with a graceful turn of phrase, for in Spain in order to persuade one must first seduce.[3]

In his second recording, Ortega turned his attention from Spain to Europe and from the past to the future. A serious problem troubled him: only the arbitrary, capricious willful men like Mussolini seemed capable of acting with any effect in contemporary Europe. Young men could not plan consistent life-programs for themselves, as Ortega had done, for circumstances had changed and no one understood how to act independently upon the new forces of historical development. He took it as his task to discover how men could reassert their historical initiative; and consequently, in his second recording he directed attention to "The Concept of History."

I am speaking at the Center for Historical Studies and I want to use the time and place that I find myself in to manifest my enthusiasm and faith in history. For contemporary Europe, history is the primary condition of its potential health and resurgence, for each thing can have only its proper virtues and not those of anything else. Europe is old; it

---

[3]"El quehacer del hombre," 1932, *Obras* IV, pp. 366-7.

cannot aspire to have the virtues of youth. Its virtue is that of an old man, that is, of having a large memory, a long history. The problems of its life are found at complicated heights, and therefore they require extremely complicated solutions: only history can provide these. Any other procedure would cause an anachronistic disjunction between the complexity of Europe's problems and the youthful simplicity and absence of memory that it would try to give to their solutions. From history Europe should not abstract a blueprint for what it should do — history does not foresee the future —; from history Europe should learn to avoid doing what it must not do, and thus it will give rebirth to itself by always avoiding its past. In this task history helps us by freeing us from that which was; for the past is a revenant, and if one does not dominate it with memories, thus placating it, it will always turn against us and end by strangling us. This is my faith, this is my enthusiasm in history; and it is a vivid pleasure and it has always been my great Spanish passion to see that in this place we concentrate our attention on the past and that we dig into the past, which is the way to make it fertile, just as by digging into old land with a plow, wounding it with a furrow, we fructify it.[4]

Here, then, was the mission of Ortega's second voyage: to master what Nietzsche called "critical history"; to turn back against the past, to criticize it so that one could avoid reincarnating its mistakes. Ortega spent his later years reflecting on the historic possiblities open to Europeans. In these reflections the past imposed only negative limitations, only actualities to be avoided. Let us leave behind us our sentimental attachments to the given; let us ask with Ortega: what is it that European man can and should become?

*   *   *

> *Beware when the great God lets loose a thinker on this planet. Then all things are at risk.*
>
> EMERSON[5]

---

[4]"Concepto de la historia," 1932, *Obras* IV, pp. 367-8.
[5]Emerson, "Circles," *Works*, Vol. 1, p. 198.

PART TWO

Europe:
The Second Voyage

IT IS PATENTLY EVIDENT that during the last ten years Spain has relapsed into a perfect mental inertia; everywhere indolence and stupidity have triumphed. But this time I know that the defect, however undeniable, did not proceed from our own character. This time its cause was in Europe. Someday we shall understand how the great gust of discouragement that blew across the continent grounded Spain at the very moment that the nation launched itself on its first spiritual flight after centuries of slumber. Now the problem goes beyond our frontiers, and it is necessary to transfer our efforts there. . . . Hence, I begin a new task, To sea once again, tiny ship! I begin what Plato called "The Second Voyage!"

ORTEGA[1]

[1]"Prólogo a una edición de sus obras," *Obras* VI, pp. 353–54.

A S THE PEOPLE OF THE WEST *encounter the terrible public conflicts of the present, one of the great misfortunes is that they find themselves equipped with an archaic and dull set of notions about society, collectivity, the individual, usages, law, justice, revolution, and the like. Much of the present confusion arises from the incongruence between the perfection of our ideas about physical phenomena and the scandalous lag of the "moral sciences." The statesman, the professor, the illustrious physicist, and the novelist are accustomed to entertaining concepts about moral matters worthy of a suburban barber. Is it not, then, perfectly natural that the suburban barber sets the tone of the time?*

ORTEGA[1]

---

[1]"Prólogo para franceses," 1937, *Obras* IV, p. 118.

IX

On the Crisis
of Europe

A s TECHNOLOGICAL ARTIFACTS ostentatiously obtrude upon our lives, we are becoming aware that esoteric scientific reasoning has vast consequences for human life. Those of us who cannot appreciate relativity physics for its pure rational beauty still hold its creators in awe for having made both the martial and the peaceful uses of atomic energy possible; here everyone sees clearly that abstract speculation affects the human world. Although most are willing to grant that natural science is a productive mode of thought, a form of power, many doubt that speculation about man has more than therapeutic significance. In past times, thinkers needed to deal with this doubt less frequently; they perceived that the creation of divergent doctrines deeply influenced religious and political life. Recently, however, men have narrowed their view of how knowledge should be put in action. The technical applications of natural science usually follow a pattern in which knowledge guides the human manipulation of things; by habit, we are coming to expect all knowledge of practical value to be applied in this way. But it is at best difficult and at worst dangerous to follow this pattern of application in intensely human matters; thus many distrust social science because it encourages the few to manipulate the many as if they were soulless substances.

Throughout his life, but especially during the second voyage, Ortega contributed to an alternative, the *Geisteswissenschaften*, which we shall translate as "the human sciences."[a] The human sciences were a system of disciplined theory that was not intended to produce technical applications; instead these theories were to lead to personal, volitional incarnations. Founded not on the assumption of nature's continuity, but on that of man's moral autonomy, the human sciences did not deal with inert objects, but with independent, self-directing persons. Consequently, the practical value of the human sciences was not found in the techniques they provided for manipulating the world, but in the principles they yielded by which the free person could more effectively control his own will and character. Ortega's second voyage was a sustained search for such principles; he sought means for strengthening the capacity of each of us to pursue a healthy self-education in an affluent environment.

Although Ortega's reflections were to be applied as they entered into the self-education of diverse persons, his ideas were not of purely personal interest. Civic pedagogy was based upon the premise that the education of the individual was the foundation of the community. Ortega carried this premise over into his second voyage. An essential point, with reference to which he analyzed the problem of leadership in twentieth-century Europe, was the cycle of influences between each person and his social circumstances.

Society is a concept that has been dangerously hypostatized in modern thought. Too often, men talk not only as if society were a thing-in-itself, but further as if they had ways to acquire exact knowledge of this objective entity. Men easily confuse theory with things; having an idea of society, they assume, after Anselm, that this society of which they have an idea must exist in the absolute. Thus sociology has become a hothouse for dogmatic metaphysics. Professed empiricists are loath to take their empiricism seriously; they do not realize that evidence derived from social *phenomena* is no more sufficient to establish the existence of a society or social structure than is evidence of design in nature sufficient to prove the existence of a divine, designing being. Modern theologians actually respect the limits of knowledge far more than their sociological brethren; since Kant, few theologians would risk voicing dogmatics as naïve as those of the venerable Durkheim, who held that "it is unquestionable that a society has all that is necessary to arouse the sensation of the divine in minds, merely by the power that it has over them. . . ." And he continued: since society "has a nature which is peculiar to itself and different from our individual nature, it pursues ends which are likewise special to it; but as it cannot attain them except through our intermediary, it imperiously demands our aid. . . ."[2] We can know nothing of a nature peculiar to itself and different from our own; hence, we should rigorously avoid hypostatizing our ideas into such transcendent beings.

Properly, society is an abstraction. As with the forest, which we never see for the trees, we never perceive society, for our empirical experience comprises only a complicated mixture of different individual experiences. Confronted by the complexity of their interpersonal experience, men use various hypothetical constructs—society, organization, institution, and so on—to group and to explain to themselves the character of the intricate influences that different persons have upon one another. An abstraction proves valuable to men when it helps them experience and act on a welter of particulars with effect, not when it corresponds to the actualities to which it purportedly applies, for an abstraction cannot take existential predicates and remain an abstraction. The influences of man upon man, not the ideas used to make the influences amenable to rational consideration, are the actual realities of social life. Social theorists should attend to these phenomena, the actual influence of particular men upon particular men, if they are not to plunge us into a world of fantastic entities, of ideas that have been laden with a heavy burden of existential predicates.

Ortega frequently decried the dangers of hypostatizing social theory. A common view of life, he thought, endangered the West; namely, the sense that the state, industry, civilization, could all take care of themselves no matter how much unconcern for them was manifested by individuals. This view developed because men hypostatized abstractions such as the state, industry, and civilization: in doing so, men freed themselves from responsibility for

---

[2]Emile Durkheim, "Society and Individual Consciousness," Joseph Swan, trans., in *Theories of Society: Foundations of Modern Sociological Theory*, Parsons, Shils, Naegele, and Pitts, eds., Vol. II, p. 720.

caring in their personal lives for the experiences to which these abstractions properly apply. Thus the heedless have it: the state exists; it is much greater than I am; let it take care of itself. In *Man and People,* Ortega directly criticized the hypostatizing of social theory; to avoid doing so, he suggested, men should not study society or the social structure; they should look for that aspect of their personal lives that could properly be called social. For him, social theory should clarify the quality of relations between men rather than characterize aggregates of men; hence, he was not interested in some mysterious thing called "mass society." One errs fundamentally by reading into Ortega an "aristocratic theory of mass society" that can then be empirically tested by statistical surveys.[3] Ortega studied men, not societies; he inquired into the public significance of personal character, and as he inquired, it was not the statistical uniformities among men, but their intrinsic qualities that interested him.

In a work essential to Ortega's second voyage, *The Revolt of the Masses,* the phrases "masses" and "minorities" rarely denoted groups whose members shared extrinsic uniformities. Usually Ortega spoke of mass-man and noble man; and even when he used the collective names, the phrases defined the condition of various persons' characters. "The minorities" denoted the sum of the individuals who have something special and extraordinary in their personal character; these men set themselves apart from others, making a minority of themselves, by struggling to realize their special genius. Unlike the "minority groups" of contemporary sociology, with which diverse persons are linked by incidental similarities of color, creed, or national origin, the attributes that signified to Ortega that men were of the minorities were the diverse, unique excellences that these persons individually possessed. Consequently, one could not statistically study such elites because the characteristic that made a man of the minorities was precisely that which made him distinct from the others, including the others of the minorities. The masses, Ortega insisted, were not "the common people," "the working people," or "the

---

[3]For an example of this mistake see William Kornhauser, *The Politics of Mass Society,* especially pp. 2-38.

lower classes."[4] Ortega's choice of words here has unfortunate conflicts with common usage in which the masses is a synonym for the proletariat; but on this matter *les jeux sont fait:* we must recognize Ortega's usage and do our best not to confuse it with other modes of speaking. Ortega generally spoke of mass-man and meant by the term a character type, not a social class. Social status was irrelevant; as the sum of mass-men, the masses included for Ortega all men whose personal character was inert, all who placed no demands upon themselves, all who made no effort to excel, to become special by fulfilling their highest potentialities. If one must, however, make an invidious class distinction, Ortega suggested that the upper classes, in the socio-economic sense, had in them the higher proportion of mass-men, a condition that was to be expected since members of the upper classes most fully enjoyed modern abundance, with all the debilitating effects affluence had on character.

Social phenomena happened as minorities in one way or another imparted their special characteristics to the masses. When Ortega asserted that society, to the degree that it denoted real influences of man upon man, was necessarily aristocratic, he meant that social influence was necessarily the influence of one man of some particular excellence upon many others who had not yet developed that quality: regardless of what ideology prevailed, there was nothing for social theory to describe but such influences. "It is notorious that I hold a radically aristocratic interpretation of history. It is radical because I have never said that society *ought to be* aristocratic, but much more than that. I have said, and I continue to believe it each day with more energetic conviction, that human society is aristocratic always, like it or not, by its very essence, up to the point that it is society insofar as it is aristocratic. . . ."[5] Society denotes the influence of man upon man; and this influence is, by the nature of influence, a relation between superior and inferior.

"Exemplarity and Aptness," a chapter strangely omitted from

---

[4]Ortega made this point explicit in *La rebelión de las masas,* 1930, *Obras* IV, pp. 146-8.

[5]*Ibid.,* p. 150.

the American version of *Invertebrate Spain*, best presents Ortega's conception of influence. In it, Ortega sought "to acquire a clear intuition of the reciprocal action between the masses and select minorities," for in his judgment, that action was "the basic fact of all society and the cause of evolution towards the good and towards the bad."[6] Exemplarity and aptness denoted Ortega's intuition of the reciprocal action that gave rise to civic pedagogy.[b] This action was the creative source of all social influence: "the exemplarity of the few articulates itself in the aptness of many others. The result is that the example increases and the inferior perfect themselves in the image of the better."[7]

The inferior were to perfect themselves; Ortega's minorities were not a paternal elite that would indenture the masses to its view of virtue. Ortega had no such rigid theory; a literal version of Plato's guardians would ultimately depend on the very hypostatizations Ortega sought to avoid. Exemplarity and aptness pertained to the human phenomena, to the way that each of us is freely inspired to new pursuits by the example of our peers. The influence Ortega studied did not produce a sterile conformism; it conduced to the personal differentiation of each for the others.

An example may clarify Ortega's theory. In Albert Camus' description of the dance hall at Padovani Beach, we encounter a beautiful presentation of the way the minorities help the masses individualize themselves and define their character, and we further see Ortega's conception of minorities and masses manifested in a most egalitarian setting. Summer in Algiers brought the young to the beaches where they would celebrate the cooling dusk in dance. Perhaps each of us can remember analogous occasions. Out of the mass of waltzing workers, Camus recalled a magnificent, statuesque girl who would dance silhouetted against sky and sea from late afternoon through evening. Her tight blue dress would darken in the back with perspiration; after she whirled by, she would linger behind in a mixed scent of flesh and flowers; and as the failing light obscured all the others, her swelling breast would still be seen, set off by a garland of white jasmine. For

---

[6]*España invertebrada*, 1921, *Obras* III, p. 103.
[7]*Ibid.*, p. 104.

Camus, as for the other, ordinary participants, the community of dancers was defined by the impressions that such extraordinary persons made upon him. And for Ortega, the task of social theory was to explain how these exemplary persons influenced the others, to discover how participation in a community defined by the excellences of the few affected the character of the many. Again, Camus exemplified the issue, for of the scene just described, he observed that "I owe to such evenings the idea I have of innocence."[8] Camus aptly appreciated the exemplary dancer and thus formed an important conception of character.

Ortega did not need to give his readers such an example, for Spaniards already had a developed idea of exemplarity: they had long enjoyed the "exemplary novels;" but in English the idea has different connotations. We think of the exemplary citizen as the man who does all and only the proper things, and we suspect that he who always sets a good example will prove, under pressure, to be a façade, a regular Babbitt. The Spanish idea of exemplarity is richer and more humane; the Spanish exemplar is not a conventional creature. Whereas the American bent on being a good example is adept at forcing infinitely various situations to fit one of the few, particular forms that convention has deemed proper, in the exemplary novels the author or hero can find in any situation the right word or deed for the right person at the right time. It is indicative of the difference that English idiom depicts a man "setting a good example," whereas Cervantes assured his readers that they could always "extract" ("*sacar*") an advantageous example from the often scandalous escapades of his characters.[9] Unamuno made another point about exemplary novels: their exemplarity was aesthetic rather than moral.[10] Thus, "*ejemplaridad*" pertained not to conventional morality, but to the art of life.

Aptness, the complement of exemplarity, can now be rightly understood. It was not a willingness to do as told. That dullness did not interest Ortega. Instead, aptness was a disposition in life

---

[8]Camus, "Summer in Algiers," in *The Myth of Sisyphus and Other Essays*, Justin O'Brien, trans., p. 108.

[9]Cervantes, "Prólogo al lector," *Novelas ejemplares*, p. 16.

[10]Unamuno, *Tres novelas ejemplares y un prólogo*, 1920, *Obras* II, p. 972.

analogous to aesthetic appreciation; as a personal characteristic it was like the mood requisite for making aesthetic judgments, that is, the state of disinterestedness. Aptness allowed men to suspend their immediate concern and to **understand** sympathetically the art of another's example: this **comprehension** could lead to their own mastery of that art. The phenomenon of exemplarity and aptness was, consequently, a means of spreading publicly significant personal virtues, but "virtue" in the Italian sense of *virtù* or the Greek sense of *areté*. Hence, like Plato, Ortega pondered a politics of the inner man in which art was more important than power.

What part, then, did exemplarity and aptness play in the formation and evolution of human communities? In a group of men someone would use more expressive gestures, speak more significant words, feel more appropriate emotions. If the others had "a normal temperament," they would wish to acquire the capacities of the best man. They would not imitate him; "on the contrary, they would polarize and orient their personality towards his mode of being, and they would try to really reform their essence according to the admired pattern."[11] When made aware of something better, men naturally tried to improve themselves. This assumption made the appearance of an exemplar, a teacher, someone better, the most important contingency determining whether the system would work. The learner could be taken for granted. Thus, Ortega contended that the ability to develop progressively, which distinguished man from the animals, resulted from the capacity "to enthuse oneself with the optimum." Aptness was an element of man's psychological nature; it was "an automatic emotion," "a power of psychic attraction," "a law of spiritual gravitation."[12] In sum, aptness was an aspect of normality whereas exemplarity was a question of genius.

Together, the two were the principle of human co-existence. "We will arrive at a definition of community, in its ultimate sense, as the dynamic spiritual unity formed by an example and its

---

[11]*España invertebrada*, 1921, *Obras* III, pp. 103-4.
[12]*Ibid.*, p. 105.

connoisseurs."[13] For a nation to develop fully it had to be rich in exemplary archetypes: intellectuals, artists, soldiers, industrialists, and "even a delightful man of the world."[14] Excessive excellence in one area, to the neglect of others, would imbalance the community and eventually cause its fall. For any particular way of life there was a minimum of competence that the exemplary must attain; otherwise, they would set too low a tone, and consequently, the community would cease to improve itself and fall into decadence. If improvement ceased, dissociation would begin. Thus, exemplarity and aptness was no automatic source of progress. But if there was to be progress or association, it would come from this pedagogical force; for neither the violence of power nor the interests of utility could engender a society where there was no prior association. "Esthetic, magic, or simply vital exemplarity in a few charms the multitude; all the influence or power of one man over others is ephemeral or secondary unless it is this automatic emotion that the archetype or exemplar raises in his surrounding enthusiasts." In sum, Ortega's search for a clear intuition of the reciprocal action between the masses and the select minorities resulted in his idea of exemplarity and aptness—"this elemental gravitation of the vulgar but healthy spirit towards eminent features."

At first, it may seem novel to explain a community as a spiritual unity formed by an example and his connoisseurs; but on second thought, it will appear that this theory reaffirms the classic conception of community in the Western tradition.c In exemplarity and aptness we meet once again the Homeric conception of *areté* and honor. We easily overlook how important this archaic conception is to our comprehension of how men influence one another. A symptom of this oversight is the way that many react to Homer's archetypal analysis of this influence. Inured to the nation's service, we are wont to perceive Achilles' refusal to fight, after Agamemnon had dishonored him, to have been an antisocial act taken out of personal pique. Whatever part

---

[13]*Ibid.*, p. 106.

[14]This and the two following quotations are from *Ibid.*, pp. 106, 105, 106.

pique played among the motives, Achilles abstained fully aware, as were Agamemnon and others, that the act had fundamental consequences for the character of social relations among the Greeks. These consequences were essential to the development of community in the West. Achilles' sulking withdrawal tipped the balance away from a system of despotic rule based on rank towards a community of equals based on honor.

In appropriating Achilles' prize, Agamemnon infringed not against the order of rank, but against the order of honor: he refused to give Achilles' prowess due respect. In doing so, Agamemnon acted as a despot, not as the first among equals. In response, a number of the Greeks besides Achilles spoke out, asserting that honor, the legitimate principle of their community, had been abused. But right, without might, rarely carries weight, and when the hapless Thersites spoke up in the assembly of the Achaeans, claiming priority for the principle of honor over that of rank, Odysseus easily put him down in the name of Agamemnon. But the rights of rank could not so easily suppress the claim of the excellent to appropriate recognition, provided that the claim was put by a man of pre-eminent excellence: Achilles slowly drove home the point; he was of sufficient ability to prove that, if anything, the Greek community would be one of honored excellence. *Si non, non.* In this sense, Achilles waged a revolutionary battle against the residual monarchies of the Mycenean age; and his success was essential to the development of the Hellenic polis. Achilles spoke as a citizen, an autonomous participant in a community who rebelled at being treated as a subject; thus he later answered Agamemnon's envoy, Odysseus, by reiterating Thersites' thought with greater eloquence and power. "Not me, I ween, shall Atreus' son, Agamemnon, persuade. . . . In one honour are held both the coward and the brave; death cometh alike to the idle man and to him that worketh much."[15] If the brave were not to receive due recognition, they might as well pack their ships and sail homeward; this time Odysseus could not mock the speech.

Achilles won his point. Therafter each polis developed as a

---

[15]*Iliad*, IX, 315-8, A.T. Murray trans.

spiritual unity of various examples and their connoisseurs. For the most part, the Greeks understood this feature of their common character quite well, and they soon used it to distinguish themselves and Europeans in general from the pusillanimous subjects of the Asian despots. For instance, the observant Hippocrates based his contrast of Asian and European character on precisely the matter Achilles had insisted on. "Subjects are likely to be forced to undergo military service, fatigue and death, in order to benefit their masters. . . . All their worthy, brave deeds merely serve to aggrandize and raise up their lords, while the harvest they themselves reap is danger and death. . . . But independent people, taking risks on their own behalf and not on behalf of others, are willing and eager to go into danger, for they themselves enjoy the prize of victory."[16]

Over time the particular examples with respect to which the Greeks developed their spiritual unity changed substantially, but the principles of community remained in force. This fact has been well analyzed in Werner Jaeger's *Paideia*. Through an ongoing critical development a succession of poets and lawgivers continually adapted, as contingencies changed, the repertory of heroic examples to celebrate new forms of worth and to reject outworn images; yet, throughout this history of changing ideals, the polis remained primarily a living community of honored excellence. The degree to which this principle could remain in effect, despite marked changes in the particular excellence that was honored, was nowhere better reflected than in Plato's *Republic;* for in it, at a time when change seemed about to overwhelm the city, Plato abstracted from the particular excellences the Greeks had hitherto honored; he pointed out the principle of justice, the form of the good, which was infinitely adaptable and which was the exemplary element common to all communities. The idea of the good could be used to correct the confusions that had crept into the poetic images of excellence, and its example could inspire any man, for "it is laid up as a pattern in heaven, where those who wish can see it and found it in their own hearts."[17]

---

[16]Hippocrates, *Airs, Waters, Places*, XVI: 21-8, XXIII: 34-9, W. H. S. Jones, trans.

[17]Plato, *Republic*, 592B, Lee, trans.

This theory of exemplarity and aptness is the basis of political and social thought in the West. Beginning with the *Crito* and the *Laws,* the authority of law has been held to be dependent on its power to educate. Almost every claim to legitimate authority has been based on the assertion that the established power in question is more exemplary than any other, and almost every claim to just rebellion has been founded on an assertion that the established rulers have ceased to be worthy models for men. Because Western politics has been based on the phenomena of exemplarity and aptness, the polities thus created have developed a remarkable degree of integration and cohesion. No matter how humble, almost all persons have had a productive place in the community. When working well, European polities have been strengthened by a pervasive concord about what is and is not worthy; likewise, the great historic changes have been directed not by policy in the official sense, but by profound changes in people's beliefs about what is excellent and deserving of respect. This fact, which results from the system of exemplarity and aptness, is essential to understanding the genius of public leadership in the West: this leadership has been at its best when its strength was drawn from the commitment of those led. Here was the crucial factor: those led were without commitment; this spelled the twentieth-century crisis of Europe.

Even in times of absolutism, the politics of European communities has had to be an inherently popular politics, for leadership has been the leadership of integrated communities, ones in which all members have an essential, constructive function to perform. Hence, no matter how restricted Europe's highest offices have been at times, Europe has not had the disjunction between a succession of ruling dynasties and an eternal, unchanging peasantry, such as the Egyptian fellahin. To rule in Europe, one must influence the whole community: the great crises of the West have arisen when those with nominal power proved unable to exert such influence. In these crises, the concord of commitment disappeared, and would-be leaders became unable to produce their intended effects.

Ortega thought that Europe had entered such a crisis. So did many others, for the signs were there for all to see. After World

War I, many contended that the Europeans were beginning a new era. A few expected a period of hope; most envisaged a time of trouble; but all sensed that something had changed. To be sure, there had been great upheavals in recent centuries, but these seemed to have been wrought by the human will. The course of events had never been sufficiently predictable to allow public leadership to become a practical science. Nonetheless, a certain grand correlation between intention and achievement had been managed, and leaders had been able to direct the whole through change. Even Napoleon, despite his *hubris*, accomplished enduring legal and administrative reforms; and his eventual defeat yielded a stable order because both he and his opponents fought for clear goals with controlled means. Napoleon was neither the protégé nor the victim of mere directionless events.[18]

But something had changed. Public leaders had become imbecilic. Since Bismarck, the expectations of statesmen have rarely had much to do with their results. Never had such fine intentions yielded such checkered achievements. Despite great apparent strength, twentieth-century Europe was not functioning well. Provisions for popular education led to the stultification of the people by the popular presses and to the manipulation of their freedoms by self-serving leaders. Treaties delineating spheres of influence speeded the competition for unclaimed regions. Colonial competition prepared the European peoples for a continental war. The war, which came in spite of all the efforts to avoid it, was to be short and glorious, but it proved to be long and torturous. In the fighting, protective trenches became pits of punishment, and the warriors' ethic succumbed to the expediencies of total war. With the peace, no power had achieved its war aims, and the possibility of a repeat performance was preserved. Further, when Europe's troubles had finally seemed to pass, confident prosperity collapsed in a destructive depression. It ushered in the politics of barbarism that produced the encore—another, total, more terrible war, and atrocious genocide. In short, the leaders of Europe had lost their command of events.

---

[18]For an appreciation of these powers, see Emerson's "Napoleon" in *Representative Men, Works*, Vol. 2, pp. 369-393.

Reacting in dismay, intellectuals found these developments symptomatic possibly of the decline of the West, possibly of the enmity of Continental Europeans, especially Germans, for an open society, a civilized political liberalism, or possibly of an open European crisis, a revolt of the masses. Ortega made essential contributions to this third diagnosis; the character of his diagnosis becomes apparent in contrasting it to the other two.

A popular analysis of the changes that were transforming Europe was the literature of decay, epitomized by Spengler's *Decline of the West*.d This book was a work of genius and of danger; but with respect to the problem of European leadership, it gave a mere pseudo-analysis, for in the personal, "Apollonian" sense, Spengler admitted no such thing as leadership. Spengler committed scholarly *hubris*: the historian was too proud to let mere mortal men make their own histories. Instead, the historian sought to assert his own pre-eminence among men by revealing himself as the human voice of omnipotent historical forces, in Spengler's case the forces of historical morphology. He asserted an unreserved hypostatization: societies were morphological structures that passed through necessary stages of maturation. Europe was at a divide: it had completed the stage of money and was about to embark on its period of Caesarism. "For us, however, whom a Destiny has placed in this culture and at this moment of its development—the moment when money is celebrating its last victories, and the Caesarism that is to succeed approaches with quiet, firm step—our direction, willed and obligatory at once, is set for us within narrow limits, and on any other terms life is not worth the living. We have not the freedom to reach to this or to that, but the freedom to do the necessary or to do nothing. And a task that historic necessity has set *will* be accomplished with the individual or against him."[19] How comforting!—for those who sought release from the intimate anxieties of conducting their lives in a world of rapid change.

Ortega also spoke of destiny, but it was a personal, provisional destiny, not a necessary one; there was no such thing as an

---

[19]Spengler, *The Decline of the West*, C. F. Atkinson, trans., p. 415.

"historic necessity" that possessed the power to impose a destiny on men. Ortega conceived of destiny as that which one ought to do; the person had a creative initiative with respect to it: he invented it by intentionally forming his personal capacities and character. Spengler, in contrast, conceived of destiny as a set of inevitable acts, ones that would necessarily come to pass. According to Ortega, a person could refuse to fulfill his destiny, thus inauthenticating himself. Since each person was free to shirk his mission, leadership was an exceedingly difficult matter, one of inspiring a person to do those particular things that on the one hand would lead the person to fulfill his excellence, but that on the other were things he was by no means compelled to do. In contrast, according to Spengler, a person was forced by historic necessity to will an obligatory destiny; if destiny would rule regardless of any person's will, be he leader, follower, exemplary genius, or apt connoisseur, leadership simply disappeared as a problem. The view conduced to spiritual weakness: because historic necessity ruled the world, those who wanted power had best not lead, but ally themselves with the inevitable.

Spengler's was the most convincing representative of a varied literature advancing this point. With the idea of decline, one proceeded by describing various stages of civilization, by connecting these stages by necessary causal relations, by locating one's contemporary nation or civilization in the causal progression that had been established, and by then proclaiming what the future had in store. Such proclamations did not help leaders learn how to act effectively; the theories purported instead to identify the kind of activities that were destined to prevail no matter how inept the actors were.

A few writers have lumped Ortega with Spengler, as Kurt W. Marek did by likening the latter to a leviathan and the former to a porpoise "darting over the surface of the millennia in graceful turns, often tossing up a glittering spray."[20] But the comparison is not apt. For Ortega, the essential point was not to identify with Spengler a pattern of decline, but to explicate a pattern of crisis.

---

[20]Marek, *Yestermorrow: Notes on Man's Progress*, Ralph Manheim, trans., p. 20.

Crisis differs from decline: crisis is a self-contained condition whereas decline requires comparison of one condition to another. Any system that shows the symptoms of severe disequilibrium can be said to be in crisis; but to say that a system is in decline one needs to compare its present state with its condition at two or more previous times and to find a steadily worsening relation between them. A decline portends a fall, whereas a crisis can culminate in ruin or renewal. Decline invites a deterministic explanation, whereas a crisis suggests an open situation, which was brought about, to be sure, by determined causes, but which could be resolved in several different ways, depending on the will and competence of the persons involved. Where more pessimistic writers saw a decline, Ortega, an optimist, saw a crisis. He found the future integrally open: "I am here anxious to note that we have plunged into analyzing a substantively equivocal situation— that of the present. . . . And this equivocation is not in our judgment, but in the reality itself. It is not that the siuation can appear to us on one side good and on the other bad, but that in itself the present situation is a double potential for triumph or for death."[21]

A second popular analysis of the collapse of leadership in Europe differs considerably from Spengler's; it can be found in the Germanophobe-Anglophile literature produced during and between the two world wars, typified by Karl Popper's *The Open Society and Its Enemies*. According to the authors of these critiques, the crisis of Continental leadership arose because European intellectuals and politicians inveterately failed to appreciate the enduring truths of Anglo-American liberalism. If only the Europeans would follow the North Atlantic peoples and develop an effective democracy based on popular consent, toleration, prudent compromise, and the respect for impersonal law, all might be well. Unfortunately, German authoritarian philosophy had instead intimidated the people and confused their potential leaders. Consequently, the people were never able to assert their will over the state. This failure left the political system vulnerable to domination by whatever extremist group might convince itself and others

[21]*La rebelión de las masas*, 1930, *Obras* IV, p. 193.

that it represented the eternal values of the nation. Thus Anglo-American critics blamed European instability on the traditional elites and the heritage of social philosophy: both lacked the cardinal virtue of a capacity for compromise. Continental stability would be attained only when the leaders renounced political metaphysics and let the people really try to direct their affairs in a pragmatic, democratic way.

Anglophile writers thus concluded that the hope for Europe's future lay in a democratic pluralism founded on the principles of consent and toleration. Being committed to this particular blueprint for European stability, they took umbrage at analyses of the situation that cast doubt on the capacity of the contemporary populace to conduct their affairs happily by democratic processes. To them, gratuitous questioning of the people's powers seemed to help produce a lack of confidence at crucial moments. They found such doubts, including "the violent garrulities of Ortega y Gasset," to be examples of antidemocratic thought and a threat to the proper reformation of European politics.[22] The problem with the Anglophile position is that it itself becomes a form of political metaphysics and critical escapism; dismissing things as antidemocratic serves only to ingratiate one with the true believers: there is no way to determine whether the doubts of the questioners are really unreal except to deal substantively with the problems raised.

Before turning to these problems, let it be said that there were elements of truth in the Anglophile case. Political philosophy in Germany and France, not to mention Britain with the work of T. H. Green, had certain ambiguities that made it vulnerable to totalitarian abuse. Liberalism has long been frightened by Rousseau's doctrine that men can be forced to be free. Likewise, Hegel's conviction that "what is rational is actual and what is actual is rational" is a very difficult thought that is liable to disastrous misunderstandings; and both the statist epigones of Hegel and the Marxists crudely hypostatized Hegel's subtle conception of the state.[23] These errors, however, were first and thoroughly criticized

---

[22]Sidney Hook, *Political Power and Personal Freedom*, p. 448.
[23]Hegel, *Philosophy of Right*, Preface, T. M. Knox, trans., p. 10, italics omitted.

by another German philosopher, Arthur Schopenhauer. Nevertheless, despite a strong tradition of humanism, during the past hundred years many European intellectuals scorned the principles of toleration and rejected the system of liberal democracy. From positions as opposed as those of Marx and Nietzsche, both could agree in dismissing English liberalism as a storekeeper's philosophy. In the place of a politics of compromise, the state was threatened with takeover by diverse exponents of puritanically perfect policies. And the sympathy of Gentile and Heidegger for totalitarian fascism and of Sartre and Merleau-Ponty for totalitarian communism suggests to many that Continental philosophy may still have a strong bias toward statist extremism.[e]

Despite these facts, the Germanophobe-Anglophile critique of European politics is deceptive. The substantive difficulties must still be dealt with. On the one hand, the critique exaggerates the competence of the English and American political processes; on the other, it ignores the fundamental historic problems that have bedeviled Western politics throughout the century. All the ills of Europe cannot be blamed on German malevolence and French instability. The English bear a major responsibility for leading and sustaining the imperialistic expansion of the European peoples, with the very dangerous competitions this expansion engendered; after World War I the American people undercut efforts at collective security and opened the way to a future economic collapse by making their government withdraw precipitously from the responsibilities it had assumed in economic and international affairs; British foreign policy was a cowardly failure between the wars; and Anglo-Amercan complicity in creating the Cold War has been much greater than we like to admit. These contributions to the European crisis should not be conveniently ignored. The inter-war paralysis of British power is particularly significant in pricking the pride of the Anglophile, for it demonstrated that British politics, like that of Continental Europe, could be deflected from prudent policies by the power of mass movements, in this case by doctrinaire pacifism. As soon as we recognize that Anglo-American politics has been susceptible to the same instabilities as that of the Continent, we can turn to the real problems, the substantive developments in Western life that leaders, regardless of the form of government, found it difficult to deal with. These problems were the European crisis as it appeared to Ortega, for he believed that because of these difficulties the West had to transcend the outworn quarrel between liberal enthusiasts of democracy and their reactionary opponents.

During the twentieth century, three political phenomena that were unknown to the creators of Anglo-Saxon liberalism have become fundamental influences in public affairs throughout the West: these are ideology, bureaucracy, and mass communications.f These developments do not invalidate the ideals of liberalism; let us remain committed, with Ortega, to these values. But the new situation means that we cannot be complacently content with the established institutions of liberalism. To remain true to the liberal spirit, we should join Ortega in subjecting the familiar forms of democratic practice to a thorough critique, facing the new problems so that we can seek solutions to them.

From Locke through Mill, an essential premise in justifying toleration was that men live by the rule of reason. The practice of ideological criticism has turned many against this premise; instead of reason, many see mere rationalizations that deceptively justify one or another self-serving interest. Beneath every principle men expect to find an unprincipled ulterior motive, and all claims of right are dismissed as the mascara of might. The problem is not that for the first time there are men who live by an irrational ideology, but that the theory of ideology, the theory that the thought of all men is determined by their material interests, has made many men lose confidence in the possibility of a rule by reason. As soon as a significant number of men believe that it is impossible to reason with other men whose interests differ from their own, then force in one or another guise becomes necessary to reconcile their differences. Force is the *ultima ratio*, and to disbelieve in reason is to commit oneself to the rule of force. The liberal theory of tolerance does not deal adequately with this situation. Mill assumed that free discussion could only strengthen truth, as in theory it does if the discussants are committed to reason; but he did not foresee the practical case in which organized falsehoods are unscrupulously manipulated under conditions of free speech to predominate against the truth.

This case is not a hypothesis; it is history. With the doctrine of ideology, discourse has not been used as a means of sifting opinion for truth, but as a way of accusing one's opponents of bad faith. To the ideologist, irrespective of his ideology, only arguments from origins seem to carry weight; every person, every thought, every thing is judged by finding whether it comes from a pure or tainted source; and equally for those of the right, left, and center, this mode of argument ends logically with an attempt to eradicate the tainted origin of offending opinions.

Traditionally, liberalism has held each man responsible for his actions. A familiar example of this conception of responsibility is the care with which the framers of the American Constitution guarded against faction, but the theory was not confined to them: among others, Rousseau asserted it in suggesting that to find the general will each citizen should deliberate *alone* with full information about the question at hand. A sense of responsibility is a personal quality, and the theory has been that a humane sobriety in political matters will have the best chance to develop when men are acting on their own personal initiative and responsibility. In the last century, however, the growth of bureaucracy has completely undermined this premise, for bureaucracy has developed as the person has been absolved of certain responsibilities and as these have been transferred to fictitious corporate persons. Men become anonymous managers and civil servants; and huge, peculiarly cohesive factions composed of these emasculated men have arisen, even within the American government despite its ingenious checks and balances. To make matters worse, such bureaucracies have been most highly developed in the industrial-military establishments in every Western nation. The men who seem most absolved of having to act independently on their own personal initiative and responsibility are precisely the men who design, build, and implement the agencies of force in modern life. Thus, the citizens of every developed nation-state are under the continual threat of being dominated by radically irresponsible organizations; and it would be foolish to think that any political tradition is magically immune from the dangers that arise when it has in its midst powerful factions made up of men who are each insulated from having to feel personally responsible for the deeds of the group.

Finally, liberal democrats presupposed that the people would have time to investigate and deliberate over important issues and that popular opinion would reflect the qualities of considered, personal opinions. Instantaneous, mass communications have, however, imposed a completely different pace on public affairs, and they have greatly complicated personal reflection about political problems. These developments have not invalidated the voice of the people, but they raise severe doubts that the voice of the public is in every instance the voice of the people. We recognize that publicity can undercut the possibility of a fair trial before a jury, but we do not carry this recognition over into wider matters. In traditional democratic thought it was assumed that popular opinion would put a check on political leaders. But with the rapid, graphic reporting of world events and with the demand that everyone immediately have an opinion about everything, the manipulation of opinion has come to serve as an ersatz deliberation over public questions, and inflamed popular passions have aggravated, not modulated, political disagreements. As Ortega pointed out, the universal web of news and information was not in harmony with the polycentric politics of Europe; the whole was easily rent as various groups developed deceptive images of their neighbors.[24] All these developments meant that popular deliberations were not occurring as traditional democratic theory postulated that they should.

Phenomena such as ideological reductionism, bureaucracy, and mass communications were the substantive problems that helped produce the European crisis. Significant solutions to these difficulties were needed more than the emulation of political forms that had worked in the past. Thus, although Ortega's conception of the European crisis was not as pessimistic as Spengler's and other theories of decline, Ortega felt that much deeper questions had to be asked of the whole Western system than were asked by those who saw the crisis as a simple failure to emulate the North Atlantic example.

In reflecting on recent history, Ortega hoped to learn why the great advances in human power, wrought by industrialism and democracy, seemed to turn inexorably to negative uses, to mili-

---

[24]"Epílogo para ingleses," 1937, *Obras* IV, pp. 301-310.

tarism and tyranny. To channel man's new power more constructively, he thought, Europeans should reach beyond liberalism,
seeking to solve the substantive problems of the twentieth century.
In trying to transcend liberalism, Ortega was not being anti-
liberal; he was deeply committed to the human values that had
been served by liberalism in the nineteenth century. But he believed that in the twentieth century a blind reliance on the machinery of liberalism would destroy those very values. The nation-
state, democracy, and industrialism were great achievements of
prudent reason and progressive hope; but their potential had been
exhausted. If reason and hope were to continue to benefit men,
new ideals, novel projects, and untried enterprises would have to
be created. The challenge before Europeans was to find a new way
to fulfill the values that had given rise to liberalism, the values
of reason, human dignity, the rule of law, the pursuit of happiness, liberty.

Throughout his second voyage, Ortega sharply attacked the
notion that historic development could stop with the nation-state
and industrial democracy. This attack was no attempt to go back
to an earlier stage of historic development; it was, as he carefully
stated in *The Theme of Our Time,* an effort to open the way for
a creative, progressive advance in political theory and practice.[25]
As a whole, Ortega's second voyage amounted to a vision of a
Western *Kinderland,* a vision of a community that would lead
beyond the ideals of the nation-state and industrial democracy,
but that would do so without giving up the improvements in life
that had been achieved in the past pursuit of these ideals. Ortega's
analysis of the European crisis, which severely challenges the pieties of Anglo-American liberalism, should be taken as a prelude
to an attempt to revitalize the very tradition it criticizes.

For Ortega, the European crisis was more than an act of *lèse
libéralisme,* yet it was certainly not as much as an irredeemable
decline of the West. Instead, it was an open crisis in the European
community, which, going back to Homer, had been a community
to the degree that the many internalized and surpassed the excel-

---

[25]*El tema de nuestro tiempo,* 1923, *Obras* III, pp. 152, 156, etc.

lences discovered by the few. The crisis was a crisis in the social bonds of the West, in the principles that had historically united Europeans into communities.

Europe had been a complicated web of examples and their connoisseurs; but the system of exemplarity and aptness was not working well in the twentieth century. Men were not apt to the lessons of true excellence, and the European communities, especially the nations, were being wracked by divisive movements. Traditionally, Europeans have lived in integrated communities in which each person has a personal part to which he commits himself. A citizen made his commitment because he was personally moved by a shared ideal, because he was apt to certain heroic examples, examples of service, learning, industry, and general excellence. Here is the substantial significance of the familiar phrase of unity *in* diversity: rather than unity resulting from some extrinsic similarity such as occupation, nationality, creed, or race, it inheres in the fact that diversity is an intrinsic quality shared by each member of the group. The citizen has been a citizen insofar as he brings something unique and necessary to the common enterprise; a good community should let each man develop in himself these personal excellences, and a good citizen should honor his peers not for conformity but for genius. Unity *in* diversity is neither a wise saw nor moral instance; it is a difficult conception because it requires men to abstract and to see that when many men are truly diverse, setting themselves apart from one another, they share something important, the quality of being different from their peers.

In a community based on a common appreciation of differences, neither its strengths nor its weaknesses will be readily apparent in its superstructure of formal politics. When spontaneously united, such a people will prove far stronger than one would expect from observing the ability of their titular leaders: thus the Spanish *pueblo* once drew the shrewd Napoleon into a costly miscalculation. But when unseen discord undermines the community, then even the most brilliant rulers will not prevail. As Ortega showed in his essay on Imperial Rome, the spontaneous integration of a community of free citizens depended on a tacit but deep concord about the principles by which each person will independently evaluate the excellences he encounters.[26] Concord meant agreement about who should rule, about what standards should control the effort to settle differences. To achieve concord, the problem was not to avoid attaching different values to the same thing—such diversities were to be encouraged, for there was no reason why different persons should apply their common principles to their unique circumstances in identical ways—; the problem was, however, to avoid applying divergent, discordant modes of valuation to the same thing—such dichotomies were to be discouraged, for contradictory systems of making valuations would set the parts of the whole working in opposition to one another. When concord is lacking, when there is no agreement about how to arbitrate clashing differences, men cease to be able to tolerate the very existence of those differences. Thus, without concord, there is no unity in diversity.

Concord had disappeared in Europe. Men who should have been able to avoid implacable hostilities were no longer able to agree to disagree. Hence, at bottom the European crisis was neither a morphological decline nor a political error; it was the disorientation that arose when men ceased to share a common system of judging value. In Ortega's view, the crisis was serious, for it meant that, as divergent modes of making valuations clashed, ethical nihilism would spread and all would become permitted. But although serious, the crisis did not portend a necessary collapse, for the previous concord had not been the best one possible; if a new one could be developed, stronger communal bonds might be forged between Europeans. Time would tell. Whether the future would lead to descent or to ascent was an open question, the answer to which depended on the Europeans' ability to redevelop a common measure of value.

In short, Ortega was among those who thought the European crisis was a problem of valuation. Consequently, we should locate Ortega's work, especially that of his second voyage, in the succession of thinkers who sought a revaluation of values in Europe. Appropriately, Camus observed that Ortega was "perhaps the

---

[26]"Del Imperio Romano," 1940, *Obras* VI, especially, pp. 59-63.

greatest of European writers, after Nietzsche;"[27] and the link between these two, really between all three—Nietzsche, Ortega, and
Camus—was their search for a basis of judgment that Europeans
could again hold in common. Without such a basis, Europe would
be rent asunder. For Ortega, the European crisis arose because
men had ceased to share, not a common set of values, but a common mode of making valuations; and the way to turn this crisis
towards a hopeful climax was to see to the reform of the practical
reason by which men lived. This reform was the ultimate destina-
tion of Ortega's second voyage.

*　　*　　*

> The best choose one thing in place of all else, "everlast-
> ing" glory among mortals; but the majority are glutted
> like cattle.
>
> HERACLITUS, 29

---

[27]Camus, "The Wager of Our Generation," in *Resistance, Rebellion, and
Death,* Justin O'Brien, trans., p. 243.

NINETEENTH-CENTURY CIVILIZATION *permitted the average man to settle himself in a wealthy world, of which he perceived only its abundance of resources and none of its afflictions. He encountered about him marvelous implements, beneficial medicines, perspicacious governments, and convenient rights. At the same time he ignored how difficult it was to invent these implements and medicines, and to ensure their production in the future; he did not notice how instable the organization of the state was; and he scarcely felt any obligations in himself. This disequilibrium falsified him and vitiated the sources of his vitality to the extent that he lost contact with the very substance of life; that is, its absolute danger and radical uncertainty.*

ORTEGA[1]

---

[1] *La rebelión de las masas,* 1930, *Obras* IV, p. 210.

X
Scarcity and
Abundance

Europeans had ceased to share a common system of attaching value to the things about them: that was the crisis, the dissolution of concord in the West. Symptoms of the crisis appeared in the way different groups were apt to divergent models; men frequently lionized individuals who were unsuited to integrating a people, and leaders instead divided the community by symbolizing good for some and evil for others. Furthermore, many important excellences were simply scorned, not only by the ignorant, but also by the educated. For this reason, the student of the human sciences could not follow the student of the natural sciences and profess faith in the continuity of nature: during the twentieth century something had gone wrong with "the law of spiritual gravitation," the belief that the average man would necessarily attend disinterestedly to the optimum. One could not assume that man would, like a stone, act in the future as he did in the past. To understand the contemporary anomaly, the prevalence of inaptness throughout Europe, Ortega had to reflect more deeply on the phenomena of exemplarity and aptness.

Humanists of Ortega's type hold that the animal man has made himself human by discovering mind and using it to order the chaos that he finds both within and around him. Hesiod celebrated how "the gods kept hidden from men the means of life." Alone among the animals, man was born with instincts insufficient for life; and hence that ingenious god-man, Prometheus, stole the light of reason, the fire in a fennel-stalk that enabled man to become a thinking reed.[2] Since then great humanists have reiterated how man is the creature that is at once blessed and cursed with the task of self-definition; by our own efforts we can rise among the angels or sink among the brutes. Believing that man must make of himself whatever he will become, humanists consequently attach peculiar importance to problems of pedagogy and politics.

Not all political and pedagogical theorists have been humanists, however. Many revered thinkers have been naturalists with respect to both the physical and the human sciences. Following Aristotle, they have held that social rationality was a natural, inborn attribute of men and that reason was hence a premise, not a problem, for the political philosopher.[3] Thus both Hobbes and Locke postulated that reason was a characteristic of man in the state of nature; consequently reasonableness was a given element of their political philosophy and the problem was simply to devise a system that would allow men to bring this feature of their necessary nature to bear upon their experience.[4] Naturalism in the human sciences leads logically to a primary interest in the particular procedures of various political systems, and from the particulars the theorist will abstract his principles: hence, Aristotle collected constitutions.[5]

Following the practical ethics of Heraclitus, Socrates, and Plato, however, humanistic political theorists have not presumed that man is by nature a political animal. Men make themselves political animals by creating one or another rational system by which they can organize their common experiences. Humanists find that social rationality is a practical problem rather than a philosophical premise; before providing for political procedures, the lawgiver must create, elaborate, and disseminate a particular system of political reasoning. Hence, virtue is *knowledge*, the capacity to take part in a rational community, the willingness to abide by artificial, unnecessary standards of reasoning. Conse-

---

[2]Hesiod, *Works and Days*, lines 42-58, Hugh G. Evelyn-White, trans.

[3]Aristotle, *Politics*, I, ii, 1253a; III, vi, 1278b.

[4]Hobbes, *Leviathan*, Part I, Ch. 13; and Locke, *The Second Treatise of Government*, Ch. II, No. 6.

[5]See Aristotle, *Nichomachean Ethics*, X, ix, 21-3; and *Athenian Constitution*.

quently, as Rousseau noticed, Plato perfected the polis in his *Republic* by attending, not to practical procedures, but to pedagogy. Various laws and customs were not "a number of great principles, but trifles all, if care be taken, as the saying is, of the one great thing,—a thing sufficient for our purpose—education and nurture."[6] For the humanist the basic political problem is the question whether virtue can be taught, whether men can learn to reason in common, whether they can develop the will to accept the discipline of reason. The task of social philosophy is not to apply a given, disembodied power of reason to the theoretical rationalization of the community, but to point the way by which each man can bring to fruition his contingent powers of reason so that he can freely and responsibly direct his actual public acts. Humanism in the sciences of the spirit leads logically to a primary interest in pedagogy; therefore Plato showed how the only constitution that truly concerned a man was that of his own character.[7]

Philosophy began in wonder, Plato mused in *Theaetetus* (155D); yet the beginnings in wonder of social philosophy were neutralized by Aristotle's assumption that man is, by nature, a political animal. Men wonder only infrequently about things that come naturally, for wonder is man's amazement that this or that phenomenon should at once be part of a mysterious world and still be so fraught with human significance. All things are natural; hence ascribing things to nature rarely tells us what differentiates the awesome from the ordinary. We wonder at certain things because it strains our credulity to believe that there could be such virtuosity or such solicitude for man in the works of brute nature. Wonder creates that most marvelous interrogative, the one that calls for reasons rather than for facts. Why? Why is the grass green? Why is man a political animal? How dull to answer "by nature," for this answer, like that of an impatient father plagued by a perplexed child, simply suppressed the wonder without providing an explanation of the fact. Man is a political animal—how extraordinary that man is precisely what he must be in order to thrive in the world! Why is it, then, that man is a political animal?

---

[6]Plato, *Republic*, 423D-E, Jowett, trans. Cf. Rousseau, *Emile*, in *Oeuvres complètes*, IV, p. 250.

[7]See Plato, *Republic*, especially 591-592B.

To ask this question is to go beyond the question of current political science—What leaders, symbols, and powers are actually moving men? It is to ask the Platonic question—Why are these leaders, symbols, and powers able to move men? As we observed, the Platonic tradition does not take political rationality as a given; we wonder how the mastery of certain kinds of reasoning conduces to the creation of human communities. Such curiosity led to Plato's profound analysis of the human psyche, its cardinal excellences, and the power of these abilities to create humane associations. Men made themselves political animals by teaching themselves to think in certain ways. With this recognition one learns to approach politics and pedagogy with reverence and awe: men cannot take political capacities for granted. Yet, for the most part the Aristotelian assumption that man is, by nature, a political animal took the mystery from the matter; it discouraged social philosophers from reflecting on the fundamentals of their subject. Thinkers have wondered only sporadically about the marvelous inspiration that prompts men to invent and maintain the cultural creations, the systems of reasoning that have been responsible for their surprising political capacities.

Ortega's philosophic importance results in part, from his effort to reopen these basic questions. In effect, by asking why the masses, men of ordinary character, responded to leadership by the minorities, men of special character, Ortega asked why man was a political animal. In studying exemplarity and aptness and the way it united the minorities and masses in an open community, Ortega inquired into the human characteristics that made politics—that is, leadership—possible. In seeking to discover reasons for the phenomena of politics, Ortega's goal was not to adopt a single explanation and to use it as a principle for constructing the necessarily perfect society. Ortega had a rich sense of human variety; he was not about to proclaim *the* reason why. He had something more interesting in mind.

Previously, philosophers had postulated that men had entered into a social compact out of desire for either a rule of law or a division of labor. Ortega sought not only to identify such purposes; he wanted to find out why men entertained such purposes, he wanted to understand why ordinary men were apt before the exemplarity of the unknown genius who first conceived of a rule of law or a division of labor. He did not doubt that response to both of these and to many other principles of order had been essential to human communities. He did doubt, however, that the response to these principles always came about for the same reason. Perhaps there were many potential reasons why men might respond to leadership; perhaps historical crises occurred when men ceased to accept one reason for responding and began to accept leadership according to a different rationale. If this hypothesis proved true, the fundamentals of political philosophy would be integral to any analysis of the European crisis.

To begin with, one might ask what it means to call man a political animal. Among others, Rousseau has shown that it does not mean merely that men live in the company of other men. Many animals live in groups; the company of men, however, has a unique effect on those who partake in it: the company of men leads to their perfection, to the transformation of each into a more potent being. Despite Rousseau's deep concern for the natural man, he insisted that the basis of man's social and cultural existence was that association could lead to the perfecting of natural man. The corruption caused by culture-misconceived came about because man was "perfectible," for better or for worse, when in the company of other men. For Rousseau, the tension between man and society resulted from an unnatural view of society, one that made it an end unto itself. This unnatural society encouraged a tragic perversion, the suppression of natural man, whereas the only true reason for social bonds was the effort of natural man to perfect himself. Human perfection was the goal of community and a society that corrupted its members was *ipso facto* illegitimate.[8]

Ortega put himself very much in the grand tradition when he observed that "a community is an apparatus for perfecting its members."[9] This matter of perfectibility was essential to his conception of exemplarity and aptness; it meant that his inquiry into

---

[8]See Rousseau, "Discours sur les sciences et les arts," and "De l'inégalité parmi les hommes," *passim*. For the distinction between animals and men see the last mentioned, *Oeuvres complètes*, III, p. 142.

[9]*España invertebrada*, 1921, *Obras* III, p. 106, italics omitted.

why man was a political animal was the same as the study of why man was educable. The basic problem of social philosophy proved, as Plato knew, to be pedagogical: when there are several men, why do certain ones respond to the leadership of others, or, in Ortega's language, why are some men apt and others exemplary?

Owing to the fact that most educational theorists are teachers, examinations of pedagogical situations are usually made from the teacher's point of view. This characteristic holds true even for so-called learning theory, which gives a behavioral description of what a psychologist perceives when he trains animals and humans to perform various tasks. At first, Ortega also paid greatest heed to the teacher in his theory of exemplarity and aptness; recall how aptness was a normal attribute of the average person, "an automatic emotion," and how exemplarity was a function of genius. Soon, however, Ortega had to change this emphasis, for he realized, as many teachers do, that profound instruction will not affect souls unwilling to learn.

If one contemplates the nature of aptness, one finds that it is not a merely passive characteristic. Each man is surrounded by a multitude of potential exemplars; hence each man must choose to contemplate this one and to ignore that one. For this reason a science of teaching is impossible, for the teacher does not possess pedagogical power and initiative. Power, initiative, and responsibility devolve on the students, on the masses; he who learns does so as he decides to attend to this teacher and to that exemplar. Taking these facts into account, one can no longer see exemplarity and aptness as an automatically effective system. The duty of potential minorities was still to perfect their excellences; but the masses could never be merely receptive, a dumb herd blindly forced to follow their shepherd to the shears: the masses willingly committed social power to a chosen few.

What made a man a leader? The masses did by agreeing to follow. This observation permitted important questions to be refined. In asking why man was a political animal, Ortega asked primarily why the average man agreed to follow a particular leader. And in asking why one man agreed to follow another, Ortega found that he had to inquire into the way the follower perceived himself and his circumstances.

Certain views of life, certain patterns of perceiving one's self and one's circumstances, prompted the masses to be apt and to grant allegiance, social power, to the authentic exemplars of the time, to the men of noble, progressive excellence. Other views of life would lead to inaptness, which encouraged the masses to give social power to men of no special worth. Thus, initiative had been shifted from the teacher to those taught. To find why political leadership—civic pedagogy or the system of exemplarity and aptness—would or would not work, one needed to study the character of the masses, to inspect the system from the point of view of the learners. How did life appear to the masses? In particular, was there anything in this appearance that would make the self-satisfied person apt, that would prompt him to present the authentic exemplars with social power?

Ortega addressed himself to these questions in *The Revolt of the Masses*. Through his answers, he diagnosed the problem of leadership in Europe, which prepared him for his second voyage in which he would seek a cure for the problem of leadership. In a normal community the average person would be the apt student of various excellent types. In a crisis, an abnormal situation, the excellent types were ignored and the community ceased to operate as an apparatus for perfecting its members. Ortega contended that, until recently, European history had described a community that was by and large normal; Western leaders had been effective because men of ordinary character, the masses, attended to the excellent. Something had changed, however. To find what it was, Ortega took the perspective of the average man, "to see the show from the inside."[10] He looked for a view of life that would suggest aptness to the unprepossessing person. He found one, and another view that would give rise to inaptness.

*　　*　　*

"To start with, we are what our world invites us to be." The world that a man perceived ineluctably pressed its features into the character he formed in response. To live was to deal with one's circumstances; and thus the world was the sum of impres-

---

[10]*La rebelión de las masas*, 1930, *Obras* IV, p. 149.

sions that a man received in dealing with the circumstances he found himself in. During the past—for the situation had recently changed—almost everyone had discovered that the world offered them only a narrow range of possibilities. Therefore, the world invited men to become aware of their limitations: "round about him the average man encountered difficulties, dangers, scarcities, limitations of destiny and dependence" that he could neither avoid nor surmount. As a consequence of perceiving scarcity and difficulty in life, the mass man became aware of his dependence on those who were more competent than himself; hence he became apt and was willing to accept authorities external to himself. "Before anything, our life is our continuous consciousness of what is possible for us"; and in the past men were, at every instant, aware that it was possible to encounter some crushing difficulty. Man's perception of life as an arduous undertaking culminated in "the supreme generosity," liberal democracy, in which the masses freely gave their power to the minorities that offered the best "programs."[11]

Ortega found that a deceptively simple stimulus had traditionally prompted the masses to agree to follow the competent minorities. Throughout most of Western history, leadership had normally been possible because the pedagogy of scarcity had made the masses apt. The contemporary crisis, the abnormal situation, had arisen when the pedagogy of scarcity was so successful that men created a stable, abundant environment. Such a world invited the masses to be inapt. In this way, the very success of industrial democracy caused the European crisis.

Scarcity and abundance had decisive effects on a community of exemplars and their connoisseurs. Under any circumstances, exemplarity took care of itself. The special or "noble" man, as Ortega called the exemplar in *The Revolt of the Masses*, naturally sought to serve something greater than himself. The noble life was never easy: the essence of nobility was service to a demanding ideal—be the ideal ethical as with Plato's philosopher-kings, erotic as with the noble knights of chivalric romance, or cultural as with

---

[11]*Ibid.*, pp. 180, 180, 165, 191-2.

the "noble man" of Nietzsche. If a man of noble spirit was not invited by his world to transcendent service, then he would invent a new, more demanding standard to which he would aspire sportfully. "This is life as a discipline—the noble life. Nobility is defined by duty, by obligations, not by rights. *Noblesse oblige.* 'To live as one likes is plebeian; the noble aspires to order and law,' Goethe."[12] In defending the ideal of nobility Ortega did not in the least call for the preservation of privileges; he asked that men preserve their commitment to trying tasks. A remnant always would; and hence in this formulation the exemplar was no longer a problem because he would automatically create himself whenever a man put great demands upon himself.

But noble pedagogues were not alone sufficient; bitter experience had taught Ortega that if exemplars were to have any beneficial influence, they had to be invested with social power by the masses. At this point in a community based on exemplarity and aptness, scarcity became significant. Left to themselves, mass men were inert; "they require nothing special of themselves because they found that to live was to be at each instant what they already were: buoys, which, without effort at perfecting themselves, go wherever they drift." Owing to his inertia, the common man would not present social power to the exemplar unless an external force moved him to do so. The noble was autonomous, the mass conditioned. "Nobility is synonymous with the vigorous life, always set on surpassing itself, on transcending from what presently is towards what is intended as a duty and obligation. In this manner, the noble life stands opposed to the common or inert life, which statically secludes itself within itself, condemned to a perpetual immanence until an exterior force compels it to come out of itself." In past times this superior force had been the rigor of the world; scarcity compelled the common man to confront the danger of life and to heed the example of his betters. Hence, the best situation for perfecting human life was in "struggling with scarcity."[13]

In scarcity Ortega found the explanation why exemplarity

---

[12]*Ibid.*, p. 182.
[13]*Ibid.*, pp. 146, 183, 208.

and aptness had functioned rather effectively throughout most of European history. Without reference to the historical condition of an exacting environment, his conception of community lacked an explanation that could show why the apt had normally accepted leadership by the exemplary. Thus, in *Invertebrate Spain* he had fallen back on the dubious assertion that aptness was a law of spiritual gravitation and a feature of a normal temperament. In *The Revolt of the Masses* he pointed to scarcity as a more palpable, if not palatable, reason for the phenomena of aptness. Men could not escape their fundamental impression of the world: it "converts itself into an interior voice which ceaselessly murmurs certain words in the profundity of the person and tenaciously insinuates a definition of life, which is, at the same time, an imperative . . . 'to live is to feel oneself limited and therefore to take account of that which limits.' " Under conditions of scarcity men perceived their own lives in ways suggesting that aptness was the prudent, productive response. "Common men of the past . . . perceived life, *a nativitate*, as a pile of impediments that they were forced to put up with; and lacking sufficient leeway for any other solution than adapting themselves, they lodged themselves on the ledges that were left."[14]

Observe the revision of value that began here. We have been accustomed by psychologists to dwell on the destructive results of excessive anxiety, and we have built up rather sophisticated techniques, ranging from elaborate therapy to ingenious pills, to avoid or minimize our feelings of dread. In contrast, Ortega was among those who found great value, and even delight, in anxiety; care was one of the positive, definitive qualities of life. To live was to be anxious, to be concerned with vital problems. "The insecurity essential to all forms of life . . ., the anxiety—at once dolorous and delicious— that pervades every moment if we live it to the hilt . . .": this awareness of an uncertain future was the truly healthy outlook towards life; this alertness was the outlook that had enabled civic pedagogy, the system of exemplarity and aptness, to work in European history.[15]

---

[14]*Ibid.*, pp. 180, 176.
[15]*Ibid.*, p. 168.

Traditionally, insecurity in a perilous environment had led to the right ordering of the masses and minorities. Anxiety was the intuition that implacably followed from sensing the hazards with which the world confronted men; anxiety made the system of exemplarity and aptness work. Man was a political animal because he was anxious, he was concerned about the future, he was filled with dread of the unknown; therefore, he cooperated with his fellows. A difficult environment stimulated the strong to aspire to live heroically; knowing danger, they would, in Nietzsche's phrase, live dangerously. An inhospitable world moved the mass man to complement exemplary heroes with social power; from those who transcended the habitual, the ordinary would derive better habits. The intuition that life was dangerous, insecure, and uncertain invited the noble spirit to discover his duty. In a tough environment in which not even the privileged could expect, come what may, to be comfortable, the strong would drive themselves to develop to the maximum their powers of creation and leadership. In the same way, the rudeness of life provoked the mass man to accept the authority of excellence, not by slavishly doing as the nobles bid, but by mastering in himself qualities the excellent exemplified. Tremulous with the realization that error could bring disaster down upon himself, and hopeful with the recognition that luck, effort, and competence could lead to better fortune, the average man learned to pay heed to the exemplary few. In short, in the past civic pedagogy had worked because insecurity had taught men to learn their virtue.

Man is not anxious by nature; this corollary therefore followed: a community that succeeded in making life secure for its citizens negated its source of social discipline. Here, the perennial dilemma of social policy reappeared as the basis of the European crisis. As Bacon wrote, "prosperity doth best discover vice; but adversity doth best discover virtue."[16] Liberal democracy and industrialism had created a world of relative stability and abundance; Europe ceased to invite its citizens to be apt. Contemporary public affairs were therefore characterized by a revolt of the masses. Mass men were no longer filled with the anxieties that

---

[16]Bacon, "Of Adversity," *The Essays, or Counsels, Civil and Moral*, p. 54.

had formerly induced aptness in their spirit, and like truant youths they denigrated every example of excellence. Comfort brought with it the reign of the commonplace, which has come to dominate conversation, culture, and the councils of state. The pedagogy of scarcity had succeeded so well that it produced a society ruled by the pedagogy of abundance; hence, Europe had entered into a crisis, a crisis of the complacent.

Although Ortega's conception of the European crisis was not a theory of necessary decline, it did postulate the possibility, even the likelihood, of real disaster. Ortega based his generalizations about scarcity and abundance on substantive features of European history, and the psychological symptoms of this crisis of complacency correlated well with manifest characteristics of European life in the twentieth century. One can easily miss the intent of these reflections by seeing in them nothing but a prophecy of doom; therefore, it is important to be clear about what they were and what they were not.

At first the interplay of scarcity and abundance may seem to yield a cyclical view of history. The ancients were not the only ones in our tradition to see in history a cycle of advance and regression; no less a figure than the father of modern statecraft found it to be the lesson of the *History of Florence:* ". . . valor produces peace; peace, repose; repose, disorder; disorder, ruin; so from disorder order springs; from order virtue, and from this, glory and good fortune."[17] Ortega certainly considered the possibility of a cycle in the history of Europe similar to that which Machiavelli found in the history of his city. For Ortega, civic pedagogy worked when people perceived the arduousness of life and became anxious about their future; and during the industrial and democratic revolutions, exemplarity and aptness had worked splendidly. Men had been aware that their surroundings, material and civic, were not as congenial as possible; fired by hope for improvement, they disciplined themselves and coöperatively created a more stable, productive, equitable environment. As a

---

[17]Machiavelli, *History of Florence and of the Affairs of Italy*, p. 204.

result, many no longer worried about what the morrow would bring; and experiencing this complacency among his peers, Ortega feared that the morrow would bring disaster. If a sense of foreboding was the engine of civic pedagogy, then it was likely that history would record a rise and fall as a needy people increased their powers to such a degree that they satisfied their wants, became complacent, and met disaster.

Some words of caution should here be intejected. Ortega sought not merely to frighten men with the specter of an imminent, inevitable decline. In the next chapter we shall study how he thought the cycle of influences playing on human character might be broken; here let us simply stress: he believed that it could be broken. History was not inevitable. *But*, an understanding of the undesirable prospects that were harbored in historic trends was the basis of any efforts to avoid the actualization of these calamities. "The revolt of the masses *can* be the transition to a new, unequalled organization of humanity, but as well, it can be a catastrophe in the human destiny. There is no reason to deny the reality of progress, but it is necessary to correct the notion that holds this progress to be secure." Instead, Ortega insisted that the future was open, awaiting determination through the deeds of present man. "There is no sure progress or evolution without the danger of regress and involution. All, all is possible in history— triumphal and indefinite progress as much as periodic regression."[18]

Foresight was the essence of avoidance. With effort and self-discipline, the preceding generations had overcome the more palpable insufficiencies of the world. Happily, for the first time a significant number of Europeans could anticipate a life of material ease. Ortega thought that this "increase of life" was a wonderful phenomenon; he had no desire to return to a straitened state.[19] Ortega was not what C. P. Snow has called a "natural Luddite"; and, what is more important in studying Ortega's second voyage, those Snow condemned for not understanding the industrial revolution and for willingly seeking to destroy it, were

---

[18]*La rebelión de las masas*, 1930, *Obras* IV, pp. 193-4.
[19]*Ibid.*, pp. 163-9, 173-4.

unjustly rebuked.[20] By dismissing men like Emerson, Thoreau, William Morris, Ruskin, and D. H. Lawrence as mere Luddites, men who define their human mission in a mechanical opposition to the machine, Snow displays the narrowness of his own response, blinding himself and his followers to the real problem. In contrast to Snow's undiscriminating enthusiasm, these and similar critics asserted that the industrial revolution was a mixed blessing, and they stressed on the one hand the *mixed* and on the other the *blessing*. Like it or not there are destructive demons in industrial dynamism; and if these are to be held in check and kept from undercutting the constructive good produced by material development, we need to dwell on them, we need to use passionate, outraged intelligence to understand the demons so that we may control them. Far from being Luddites, the negative critics of industrialism are the best friends the machine has had, for they were willing to be honest.

Ortega was among the hard-headed social critics; he had the strength of character to risk being called hard-hearted because he treated industrial democracy as a mixed blessing. He wanted to secure the continuation of an abundant world; but to do so, he had to confront the negative concomitants of the postive development. Ortega had no intention of trying to undo the industrial revolution; he warned that unless its power to satisfy appetitive wants was effectively complemented by the ability to satisfy spiritual and moral longings, the industrial revolution would, in all probability, undo itself. Achievement brought changes that had to be mastered. The success of exemplarity and aptness weakened the very forces that had made it successful. Unless a new pedagogy could be found to take the place of scarcity, the masses would abuse their duties of leadership, cause the cultural foundations of industrial civilization to collapse, and thus return men to a condition in which the pinch of hunger and the pang of fear again administered a moral propaedeutic.

---

[20]Snow, *The Two Cultures: and a Second Look*, pp. 27-32. Snow's second look seems as obtuse as the first, *Ibid.*, pp. 79-89. He insists on a separation in our culture by not granting that the artist can be constructive as a critic. Where would science be, if scientists could only celebrate existing achievements, rather than subject them to unrestrained critical examination?

Hence, in criticizing the revolt of the masses, Ortega was not venting a reactionary spleen; he was seeking to perpetuate and further the progressive advance of Europe. If we keep this intention in mind, we can follow Ortega's critique of the masses in some detail without falling into the trap of seeing pessimism where optimism ruled: Ortega's realism was his recognition that Europe had serious problems and his optimism was his belief that these problems could be solved without regression to more primitive stages of human organization.

Long ago Heraclitus exclaimed at the inaptness of his fellow citizens, "may wealth not fail you, men of Ephesus, so that you may be convicted of your wickedness!"[21] Thus, for ages the wise have known that luxury weakens the will.[a] Less is known, however, about the precise way in which this debilitation occurs; yet any remedial effort would depend on that knowledge. To find it, Ortega studied with some care how the contemporary world invited men to weaken their character.

Remember that mass man was, in Ortega's terminology, a characterological, not a sociological, type. There is potentially a mass man in each of us: that person whom we are when we are complacently content with what we are. This contented person will make no demands upon himself. The increase of life achieved by the industrial revolution did not create the "masses" by causing the complete leveling of social and material distinctions; such leveling was occuring, but it was not decisive, certainly not as a cause producing mass men. Instead, the general enrichment, the stabilization of existence, played upon the ordinary self of each person in every sociological category in a way that made each feel more content with his character as he found it, inert at dead center.

Liberal democracy, science, and industry had not done away with the old social divisions; rather, they had fabulously intensified the scale and diversity of activities open to the members of each division. Recall the chance remark that was a catalyst to Ortega's reflections: a debutante had confided to him that she

---

[21]Heraclitus, Fragment 125a, Freeman, trans., *Ancilla*, p. 33.

simply could not bear a ball to which fewer than eight hundred were invited. In each social class, a greater range of possibilities was now within the economic means of its members. Improvement was fundamental: not only did the common man have more creature comforts available than did the very rich of yesteryear, the very rich of today had more wealth than whole nations of former times. Besides an increase in wealth, men enjoyed improved public order and even enchanced freedom from natural catastrophe. Both moral debasement and physical disease were relatively under control; there were still rakes, but their progress was less gruesome than that seen by Hogarth, and there was still a dance of death in which all were chosen as a partner, but the choice, on the average, was forborne a longer time for each. To be sure, certain qualifications would have to be put on this description of the general condition; but those limitations were offset for most by the expectation that men could count on further improvements as a matter of course: not even the supposedly progressive parties seriously contemplated the possibility of a future that *differed* from a linear projection of the present.[22]

Mass man is that person whom we each are when we make no special demands upon ourselves. When life was comfortable, flourishing, this ordinary self would rest content; no upsetting feature of existence would drive mass man out of his natural complacency. In prosperous periods, mass man accepted himself as he found himself and spent his life doing what came naturally. The problem, of course, was that civilization did not come naturally: it was an artifice created through discipline and effort; and of those who were to partake in it, civilization required that they either be exemplary and create their goals freely or be apt and respond authentically to men who could lead them out of themselves.

But in revolt, mass man was neither exemplary nor apt. He was satisfied with his mediocrity, which made him inapt, for he saw no reason to respond to leadership. "He was content just being whatever he happened to be; and without being vain and as the most natural thing in the world, he tended to believe and affirm

---

[22]*La rebelión de las masas*, 1930, *Obras* IV, pp. 168-9.

that everything he found within himself—opinions, appetites, preferences, or tastes—was good." The net result was that satisfaction diminished the aspiration to improve. Mass man had a reasonable, if not enlightened, view: with no compulsions to doubt himself, the commonplace man in every class thought that it was a virtue to be commonplace. "Why not, if . . . nothing and no one forced him to realize that he was a second-class, extremely limited man who was incapable of creating or conserving the very organization that had given his life the amplitude and contentment on which he based the assertion of his character?"[23]

Again, Ortega was not calling for a rigid system of social classes: in each of us there is a first- and second-class man, first if we realize our potential, and second if we succumb to our inertia. Nothing was perverse about the second-class man within us; he merely followed the way of least resistance and took life the way it came to him. The ordinary self accepted appearances, and thus the pedagogy of abundance insinuated a debilitating definition of life into the depth of the spirit. "To live is to meet no limitations, and therefore to abandon oneself peacefully to oneself. Practically nothing is impossible, nothing is dangerous and, in principle, no one is superior to me."[24]

Essentially Ortega's analysis pointed to the danger of ignoring the old adage, "spare the rod and spoil the child." The rod was not desirable in either child rearing or civic pedagogy; but since it had performed important functions, one could not simply dispense with it without engendering difficulties. The many comforts of an industrial environment brought great benefits; yet they brought dangers as well. Spoiled children and intemperate adults perceived life as a snug abundance, and they never learned to discipline themselves because they were never forced by the world around them to become conscious of their limitations. Those who inherited an easy life received all they desired without having to master the abilities requisite for the production of the things they consumed. One prepared disasters, personal or civic, by combining developed tastes with undisciplined talents.

---

[23]*Ibid.*, p. 181.
[24]*Ibid.*, p. 180.

In his *Nichomachean Ethics*, Aristotle united in a single group the spoiled child and the self-indulgent, intemperate man. Both were profligates, he found, for profligacy, ακολασια, had the root meaning of unpunished, unpruned, unchastened.[25] Ortega carried this grouping one further. Using "class" in its logical, not sociological, sense, he put the spoiled child, the profligate heir, and mass man in the class *señorito satisfecho*, the class of sated swingers. In another essay, objecting to the decadent example set by the rich in Spain, he called it "the most despicable and sterile class of humanity," for this type of man produced nothing but had everything made for it and turned all into mere ornamentation. A soft, luxurious environment easily corrupted men by failing to chasten their spirit or to prune their powers so that they could channel and concentrate their vitality. "A world of superabundant possibilities automatically produces serious deformities and vicious types of humanity; we can unite these in the general class, 'heir-man,' in which the 'aristocrat,' and the spoiled child, and much more fully and radically the mass man of our time are only particular cases."[26]

Indiscipline could easily tear apart a community of heir-men: that was the threat to Europe. Industrialism could induce heedlessness and arrogance to a degree that would jeopardize Europe's future. "The very perfection with which the nineteenth century organized certain orders of life caused the benefited masses to believe that these were natural rather than organized. This explains and defines the absurd state of mind revealed by these masses: nothing preoccupies them like their well-being, yet they are isolated from the cause of that well-being."[27] Confronted by a wealth of sophisticated products and services, the consumer had difficulty appreciating the intricate web of men, ideas, and institutions that provided the "goods." The mass man was the man in each of us who shirked difficult chores; instead, he expected the advantages that others produced as if these boons were his right, yet he was unable and unwilling to provide them for himself.

---

[25] Aristotle, *Nichomachean Ethnics*, III, xii, 5-10.
[26] *La rebelión de las masas*, 1930, *Obras* IV, p. 209.
[27] *Ibid.*, p. 179.

Nothing exemplifies this outlook better than the cowardly exodus from the American cities by members of the middle class. These people are quite ready to commute to the city to earn high salaries and to enjoy the cultural and commercial benefits of concentration; yet they are unwilling to stand by the city, to live in it and cherish it, to pay taxes and give talents to solve its problems. When urban difficulties make themselves felt, the mass man in each of us counsels us to move out rather than to risk defeat in seeking solutions to manifest complexities. But it is doubtful that the city can survive continual exploitation by the prosperous, able middle class. Yet the suburban masses are blind to their heedlessness; they think of the nearby city as a natural organism that will always be there, offering remunerative employment regardless of their personal actions. They feel fully justified in choosing the wealth the city offers on the one hand and the comfort and security the suburb offers on the other; they see the provision of both resulting merely from their requests, and they never trouble themselves to consider precisely how either an economic and cultural center or a periphery of insentience are created and maintained.

In this and numerous other examples, we are familiar with the phenomena Ortega observed: people are happy to enjoy the commodities of contemporary civilization, but they are not so ready to preserve the self-discipline and self-sacrifice that brought into being the powers capable of producing these enjoyable things. "Because they do not see the shop windows of civilization as prodigious inventions and constructions that can be sustained only with great force and foresight, they believe their role comes down to demanding peremptorily what seems to them natural rights."[28]

Heedlessness of this sort made severe political and economic disruptions probable. To take the urban example again: in a concentration of people in which the more stable persons have grouped together and isolated themselves from the less stable, one could not expect the less stable remainder to conduct itself according to the exaggerated standard of "law and order" held by the stable isolate—it was only a matter of time before the vivacious

---

[28]*Ibid.*, p. 179. Cf. "Los escaparates mandan," 1927, *Obras* III, pp. 459-463.

would offend the sensibility of the stolid. As with this case, so with innumerable others, the tendency of the comfortably complacent to ignore their unpleasant responsibilities made it probable that unusual, unexpected problems would arise in public affairs: in these matters, nemesis has long had ultimate sovereignty.

To further worsen the dangers that complacency engendered in a seemingly secure environment, the lack of awareness, the indiscipline that underlay the emergence of new public problems, would be a formidable political and intellectual barrier to sound efforts to solve the disruptions. This barrier was a significant aspect of the European crisis.

Being satisfied with himself, mass man had a closed mind; he was content with whatever mental furniture he happened to possess. Traditionally, the mass mind was closed, but humble. In contrast, contemporary mass man was distracted by wealth, yet he still lacked real leisure, and in this state he had begun to believe that he could have theoretical opinions. The effects on intellect were awesome. As Ortega described it in another essay: mass man "meets a partisan fact that passes him by and he catches it as he would an autobus: he takes it in order to travel without fatiguing his own legs."[29] No longer willing to leave culture to the few who had the time for it, the masses lost their sense of intellectual limitation. Thoughtlessly, they made a marketplace of thought. In result, the ideas held by the mass man were not genuine, for they were not achieved by disciplined intellection based on the principles of reason.

Here we meet the contemporary difficulty in the traditional theory of free speech. Free exchange in a quest for truth is not the same as a free exchange in pursuit of profit and power; and habitual participation in the latter exchange has been having dire effects on the standards of the former. As opinion becomes increasingly exploited by non-rational means for unintellectual ends, the relation of opinion to power has been changing in dangerous ways. "To have an idea is to believe that one possesses the reasons for it, and this is to believe that reason, an orb of intel-

---

[29]"No ser hombre de partido," 1930, *Obras* IV, pp. 75-6.

ligible truths, exists. Thinking, theorizing is the same as appealing to an instance, submitting to it, accepting its laws and its sentence, believing therefore that the superior form of living together is the dialogue in which we discuss our reasons for our ideas. But mass man feels himself lost if he accepts discussion and he instinctively repudiates the obligation to respect this highest argument that he finds outside himself."[30] Thus, Ortega contended, the masses simultaneously asserted their right to hold theoretical opinions and to deny that the principles of reason should be the arbiter of conflicting theories. Ominously, the definition of thinking that was operational in public affairs was changing: to have an idea was to find that one possessed the power to compel, badger, or bribe others to profess it, and this was to believe that force, an orb of implacable compulsions, existed.

"Direct action" was the political result: the followers of a mass idea imposed their will on the community by the most effective means at hand. Direct action is one of the characteristic symptoms of the revolt of the masses; it cuts across ideologies and manifests itself in diverse forms. In the liberal tradition, force had always been the *ultima ratio* to which men resorted when discussion, compromise, and law failed intolerably to resolve differences. In contrast to the *ultima ratio*, civilization was an artificial system of indirect methods for reconciling disagreements while avoiding the conjunction of force with passion and all the havoc this pair could wreak. The *prima ratio*, civilization, presupposed the willingness to submit to dialogue in which the merits of conflicting claims were honestly and openly discussed in a search for truth and justice. But men who held their ideas without reasons, as mass men did, could not take part in such a dialogue. For them, force in one or another guise was the only means that could produce agreement and win a further allegiance. Direct action denoted all the means by which rational discourse could be by-passed, subverted, or overwhelmed. And the more the mass man pretended to have ideas, the more direct action would become the norm in public affairs.

In *Invertebrate Spain* Ortega had already indicated the bane-

---

[30] *La rebelión de las masas*, 1930, *Obras* IV, p. 190.

ful influence of direct action on Spanish politics. But the disease spread further. Throughout Europe a politics of force was dramatically apparent in Fascism, Syndicalism, Communism, and other mass action movements. These partisans were not willing to persuade and to be persuaded in accordance with how the *logos* manifested itself in open discussion; they had many means to discount in advance all the arguments their opponents might propound. For them, violence was admittedly the *prima ratio*.

But a penchant for direct action was not confined to revolutionary groups: the idea of the state had come to be equated with actual, extensive, powerful bureaucracies; it was no longer, as it had been for nineteenth-century political thinkers, a symbol of public rationality. Instead, many were coming to believe that the state was a primary reality: the administrative apparatus was there to be taken over by the most powerful. Politicians ceased to believe the liberal premise that government resided in men—of the people, for the people, and by the people; they held that men existed within the government. Listen to Mussolini chant: "All for the State, nothing outside the State, nothing against the State"; and take heed![31]

In short, the greatest danger with respect to direct action and public affairs was the state. Statism in action—not in doctrine— was the most serious threat in Ortega's view. This distinction needs to be made because the more serious aggrandizements of the state are accomplished in the name of free men by those who loudly decry statism. Ortega's warning was not similar to that habitually voiced by American conservatives; on the contrary, Ortega cautioned against the static statism practiced by the established powers in well developed political and economic systems. Certain particulars from Ortega's discussion of statism and its dangers show his real concern.

First, Ortega did not oppose the state per se, but an imbalance between state power and social power, the power of spontaneous movements within the community. As he saw it, to the degree that the strength of the state overbalanced that of the integral community, social revolutions became impossible and the possi-

---

[31]Quoted without source citation by Ortega in *Ibid.*, p. 226.

bility of internal adaptations and renewals of the community disappeared. Members of established groups would avoid having to change their personal way of life whenever serious issues arose, for instead they would have recourse to the impersonal machinery of the state; at most, social tension would lead to the *coup d'état* in which the state was taken over and used in favor of a previously excluded group. The danger that Ortega warned against was the negative use of the state to break up any social movement that disturbed the comfortable majority. "The result of this tendency will be fatal. Time and again, social spontaneity will be capped violently by the intervention of the state: no new seed will be able to fructify."[32]

Second, the positive uses of the state that Ortega condemned were not those that benefited the unprivileged, but those that served the secure, the complacent, and the well-to-do. By describing the example of the Roman Empire, he called attention to the dangerous relationship between industrial and governmental bureaucracy, the military, and the demand for personal security, "the security that gives birth, remember, to mass man." In order to provide security to the comfortable, bureaucracy is brought into being. With bureaucracy, everything is routinized, and the capacity of a people to provide spontaneously for itself begins to wither from disuse. Still, the unforeseen arises and the bureaucracy must force adaptation, which it does through the militarization of the community. The military and its supporting services become a privileged class that, at all costs, must be placated; the army becomes the highest priority to which the remainder of the community must be sacrificed. "State intervention leads to this: the people are converted into the meat and pasta that feeds the mere artifact and mechanism that is the state."[33]

Third, in his critique of statism Ortega described only one concrete example of how the violence of direct action is being institutionalized in the state. The example he chose was not those favorites of reactionary rhetoricians: it was neither the progressive income tax nor welfare for the poor nor even government regula-

---

[32]*Ibid.*, p. 225.
[33]Both quotations: *Ibid.*, p. 226.

tion of various private industries; the example of statism that Ortega considered most widespread and symptomatic of the revolt of the masses was the marked expansion of police forces at the behest of those who wanted local tranquillity at any price. The price, of course, was liberty, for, as J. R. Carey presciently rendered Ortega's Spanish into English in 1932, "it is foolishness for the party of 'law and order' to imagine that these 'forces of public authority' created to preserve order are always going to be content to preserve the order that that party desires. Inevitably they will end by themselves defining and deciding on the order they are going to impose. . . ."[34] Ortega found the true test of one's attitude towards the state in the issue of controlling crime: the statist looked to the police to repress the criminals whereas the man who truly believed that the state should have limits preferred to take his chances with the criminals in order to keep his civil liberties free from state infringement. The police, who were essential to maintaining a regular flow in the spontaneous activities in cities around the world, were at the same time the major danger to those activities whenever services of facilitation were transformed into powers of enforcement.

Statism seemed dangerous to Ortega because it could so easily become a static barrier to the spontaneous, vital development of the community. The state would enforce a seeming stasis, which would sooner or later end in collapse. Such a result would probably come sooner rather than later, for the positions of power, both within and without the state, stood at the apexes of well-established organizations, and the rather banal qualities that made for progress through these organizations were not the qualities that would enable men to discover effective solutions to the authentic difficulties. Furthermore, stasis would not preclude continued development in technology and other superficial aspects of life, and the underlying problems that made continued progress problematic would continually become more difficult. Thus circumstances were joining in a way that made disaster imminent: the maintenance of civilization was becoming supremely complex and

---

[34]*The Revolt of the Masses,* Authorized translation, Anniversary Edition (1957), p. 123.

the men in positions of power were becoming less capable of dealing with complexities. "It is my hypothesis," Ortega wrote, "that the European who begins to predominate will be, in relation to the complex civilization in which he was born, a primitive man, a barbarian emerging through the scuttle, a 'vertical invader.' "[35]

In sum, traditionally men had made themselves into political animals because they found themselves in an inhospitable environment and realized that to live well they needed to coöperate with one another. Through coöperation, Western man had accomplished a novel stabilization of his surroundings and the usual anxieties were greatly reduced. An increase in security brought a decrease in the civic discipline of the average person, the ordinary self in each person. More and more people were content with themselves as they happened to be; this weakening in man's desire for self-improvement made the collapse of European civilization probable. Mass movements, ideological conflict, institutionalized direct action, and social rigidity followed by upheaval would become characteristics of European public affairs. Increasingly, men would lack the strengths of mind and character that would enable them to solve the complicated problems that advanced civilization created. This, in short, was the European crisis.

But practical men rightly distrust pundits who are content to expose the imminent demise of man and who are yet too uninterested in life to resist the disaster. The activist senses that any doom foreseen by such pallid souls must be a faint danger, indeed; and the workaday world goes on with its business, singing *qué sera, sera!*

Insofar as we stress the spiritual effects of material scarcity and abundance, Ortega's theory seems to be one of these pallid conceptions that counsels a useless despair. But, Ortega repeatedly asserted, the revolt of the masses could lead to either advance or disaster, depending on how men reacted to the possibilities. Man was responsible for his own progress. Improvement was not achieved because conditions made it inevitable; betterment was

---

[35]*La rebelión de las masas*, 1930, *Obras* IV, p. 200, cf. p. 174. The phrase "vertical invader" is from Walter Rathenau.

achieved in spite of conditions. Progress occurred when men overcame the conditions that limited their lives. Hence, in Ortega's view, drama was a constituent of human life because danger, difficulty, and suffering were part of the path to safety, comfort, and joy. The pedagogy of abundance was a dangerous condition; precisely for that reason, the taming of it could lead to a real advance in the quality of human life. "Therefore, it is of great importance to understand *à fond* this mass man who is pure potentiality for the greatest good or the greatest evil."[36] Understand in order to influence: that was the imperative of the philosopher-king.

Yet, it was still not clear that influence was possible. Ortega had studied philosophers of history who thought that scarcity and abundance regulated a close, implacable cycle of rise and fall: thus in the Moslem Middle Ages the great North African, Ibn Khaldûn, perceived how poverty begat virtue, virtue begat well-being, well-being begat weakness, weakness begat poverty, and another round began.b For Ibn Khaldûn, history would be an endless exchange as the virtuous Bedouin took over the decadent cities and held them until luxury so weakened him that he became vulnerable to a new wave of desert dwellers.[37] As Ortega knew, many other thinkers had discovered such cycles; and the interesting problem was not to find the cycle, but to find how the cycle might be broken. Helvétius put the question well: "want and poverty are the only instructors whose lessons are always heard, and whose counsels are always efficacious. But if the national manners will not permit [one] to receive such an education, what other must be substituted for it?"[38] One begins to answer this question by reflecting on the critic's power.

* * *

Every creature is driven to pasture with a blow.
HERACLITUS, 11

---

[36]*Ibid.*, p. 174.

[37]See Ibn Khaldûn, *The Muqaddimah: An Introduction to History*, 3 vols., Franz Rosenthal, trans., especially, Vol. 1, pp. 71-86, 249-310; Vol. 2, pp. 117-137.

[38]Helvétius, *A treatise on Man, His Intellectual Faculties and His Education*, W. Hooper, trans., pp. 77-8.

*A*H! IT IS CLEAR! *To propose that life is "principally" this or that is supremely dangerous, for in an instant it will be "exclusively" either this or that. Then terrible things happen. . . . It would be an easy job to exist if we could do things unilaterally. But—and here is the problem!—to live is to travel at one time in every direction of the horizon; to live is to have to do with both this and that.*

ORTEGA[1]

[1]"Un rasgo de la vida alemana," 1935, *Obras* V, p. 191.

XI
The Critic's
Power

MEN CHOOSE to create communities. The forms of reasoning that made these communities possible were not built into men; on the contrary, the forms of reasoning were acquired, they were learned, they were not necessary, they could be rejected. In the past, by and large, men had not rejected sound means of political calculation because they had direct experience, day-to-day, of the dangers in their environment. As a consequence of their prudence, men entered into relationships of leader and follower, exemplar and connoisseur. With these relationships, there arose the function of ruling and obeying; and "the function of ruling and obeying is decisive in every society."[2] The crisis of Europe brought on by the pedagogy of abundance involved the breakdown of this function; Ortega's second voyage was an attempt to reconstruct it.

As we might expect from Ortega's interest in vital politics, ruling did not mean holding high office. Rather, to rule meant to exercise initiative with respect to man's communal life; to rule meant to have an effect on life, an effect that made it better or worse and that could be attributed to the ruler's actions. Since the breakdown in the function of ruling and obeying in Europe, the result was not decline, but stasis, stasis interrupted by catastrophic attempts at desperate departures from the reigning norm. In the twentieth-century West, the acts that made life better or worse could be attributed to a responsible actor only with diffi-

---

[2]*La rebelión de las masas*, 1930, *Obras* IV, p. 242.

culty, while the acts that could be easily attributed to responsible actors seemed to have little effect on the overall quality of life.

Another way to describe this situation was to observe that the traditional offices of practical command had ceased to be positions from which men could effectively rule or shape the whole. To be sure, the men occupying powerful offices could mobilize fantastic armies, organize extensive systems of men and materiel, and draw up budgets of which Midas could not have dreamed. But these men were unable to act; they were constrained by the vast scale of their power, they were exhausting themselves in the desperate, distracting effort to keep the system going; and they had neither the time, the inclination, nor the energy to introduce unexpected initiatives and to change the course of development. The debasing, crushing powerlessness of the powerful was easily overlooked, however, for within their immediate sphere the established offices were still effective; the financier, for instance, was still capable of productive, profitable finance, but he was no longer the creative ruler that he had been during the dynamic phases of the industrial revolution: rather than underwriting revolutionary change, he now served at most to perpetuate a going pattern of life. Ortega perceived great potential power in certain practical offices such as the engineer and the industrial executive; but even with these, their potential power was not latent in their traditional functions, but in new functions that were being thrust upon these offices by the default of others. One had to begin by recognizing these defaults: throughout the West, men who wielded practical power were no longer able to rule.[3]

As a practical matter, the pedagogy of abundance and the revolt of the masses challenged men to rebuild an effective system of power in post-industrial life, a system of power through which individuals could exert significant initiative affecting the quality of life in the community. The first step in discovering the possibility of such power was in learning how the debilitating effects of the pedagogy of abundance might be counteracted. One might

---

[3]For a more recent version of such thoughts, see Jacques Ellul, *The Political Illusion, passim.*

expect that under conditions of abundance, the critic's function would gain in public significance. The altertness formerly engendered by scarcity had now to be called forth by human activity; and the ability to rule, to direct and channel the effort of the whole, passed largely to critics who could spread concern among their peers for significant matters.

To say that the ability to rule passed to the critics was not to say either that they were necessarily exercising the ability or that, if they did, they would exercise it well. In contrast, it was to say something at once more limited and more significant: the critic now must rise to the responsibilities he formerly foisted on others, to responsibility *for* the course of events. The present danger to humane relations among men is that intellectuals and students are becoming aware of this responsibility and of their present inability to fulfill it; thus frustrated, they resort, in well-meaning desperation, typical of novice rulers who expect great things of themselves, to a cold, sanctimonious extremism. But the errors of the righteous radicals do not change the realities: intelligent criticism has become one of the major forms of power, for good or ill, in our time.

Much of the power left in public life is that of the critic. Members of the "power elite" will find this position quixotic, but the office of critic need not be defended from those who secretly fear its renascent significance. With an instinctive appreciation of the things that matter, let us concentrate on the revival of criticism itself. So far critics have not begun to use their present power fully, let alone to use it well. To do so, for Ortega, the first step would be to rebuild the clerisy's confidence in its office. Ortega had personally felt the irresistible attraction of practical politics; this siren song played upon the suspicion that when all was said and done words were of little significance. But as soon as critics understood the crisis of leadership in Europe, they would not be swayed by this doubt. No one would advise a physical return to poverty and instability as a desirable means of inducing aptness in the masses. But how, without giving up the benefits of abundance, could the populace develop its strength of character? The most promising alternative that might be tried was criticism.

And this alternative was not a mere measure of desperation.

As good teachers know, criticism can give more effective discipline and inspiration than can punishment or failure. When looked at with care, anxiety turns out to be a rather dull goad: it continually prompts men to flee imagined evils. In contrast, criticism inspires men to strive *for* something. Criticism, to Ortega, was more constructive than a carping exposure of disagreeable traits in others; in essence, good criticism was an affirmation of worth, a revelation of potentialities. The critics' task in Europe was to set against achieved realities a great potential project, one so stirring that complacent pride in the actualities would diminish in comparison with the possibilities it revealed; then men would again exert effort. Thus, throughout his second voyage, Ortega's aspiration was to erect a vast critical structure that would inspire the masses with the will to lead themselves out of themselves.

Such a statement, however, can easily be read without experiencing its intended meaning. Criticism, like the words in which it is couched, can often be ineffectual. At its best, the criticism Ortega had in mind was a powerful form of public action. To appreciate what Ortega was aiming at, one should not go to famed critical works, but to deep historic transformations. Thus, the sixteenth-century effect of humanist criticism is not to be found in Erasmus' *Praise of Folly* and other books, but in the historic transformation of standards, which over several generations destroyed the authority of medieval dogmas, opening the way to both the Reformation and Counter-Reformation. In this manner, one will find that most significant developments in Western history occurred when a group of critics truly altered one or another basic element in the view of life that people shared.[a] The Renaissance, the Reformation, the spread of nationalism, the revolutionary affirmation of equality before the law, the steady universalization of material well-being were vast events set in motion largely by the action of critics who, bit by bit, actually changed fundamental ideas about man, God, and nature. Ortega aspired to such criticism, which is criticism that can truly claim to be a mode of action; but, in contrast, most putative criticism usually falls without effect.

To have effect, critics need, among other things, both a cause and a canon. The cause is most important, and the one that moved

Ortega, Europe, will occupy us throughout later chapters. In addition to the cause, however, the canon is also significant, for if the canon is faulty, the cause is likely to die without effect. By a canon, one means a conception of how criticism can and should influence those criticized. Today, critics easily find an audience for their views, for people seem to believe that on listening to exposés of their faults, those faults will disappear effortlessly, as if by magic. This belief creates the paradox that makes a canon important: the more people listen to criticism, the less critical they seem to become.[b] This paradox is a serious phenomenon, for it means that people are building up a strong resistance to one of the more significant forms of power presently available. To counteract this resistance, the competent *clerc* needs a means to make his hearers inwardly critical of themselves and their world, rather than mere consumers of criticism. Ortega sought a canon of criticism that would explain how people become critical of their own situation, for he understood that the signficant achievements of criticism had been wrought when an altered view of the world was internalized by many men: then they began to sing lustily "give me ten stout-hearted men and I'll soon give you ten thousand more."

＊　　　＊　　　＊

Commonly, people think that the object of criticism is to demonstrate the error of a belief or practice. In doing so, the critic is expected to demonstrate the wrongness of one position and the rightness of another; and thus the critic is drawn into absolute judgments that consign some to heaven and others to hell. All this is a misunderstanding that stems, in part, from the ubiquity of bad criticism and, in part, from a misreading of the sting that is properly present in the prose of a good critical stylist. Rightly understood, criticism necessarily ceases to be criticism as soon as it begins to propound imperative judgments, positive or negative; criticism concerns the possible relation between an object outside itself and people other than the critic, and to influence this relation, the critic should respect the autonomy of both the object and the audience of his criticism. In keeping with such restraints,

Ortega's conception of criticism had little to do with passing judgment.

Instead, Ortega's critical canon began with the problem of perception. "Human life has arisen and progressed only when the means that it could count on were in equilibrium with the problems it perceived."[4] At first, this proposition seems to be a dull restatement of the enduring truism that the best environment is a temperate one in which a being's needs and means strike a healthy balance. But that reading misses the significant point. Ortega spoke quite intentionally of human *life*, not of the human *being*, and he said that progress depended on an equilibrium, not between the powers of a being and the absolute problems it encountered, but between the means for living and the problems that were perceived (*sentía*) by "it," by human life. These points are central to contemporary humanism.

In recent times, scientists have disagreed about the place of *life* in the so-called life sciences.[c] A number of twentieth-century philosophers, Ortega among them, have been influenced by the vitalism of certain biologists, particularly the German morphologist Jacob von Uexküll. The issue for the vitalists was whether the biologist should assume, at the outset, that the basic stuff with which he worked was matter, the physical substances studied in physics and chemistry, or life, the mysterious quality that made certain systems self-maintaining. The vitalists predicted precisely what has since happened in the breakup of biology into biophysics and biochemistry: if matter was taken as the basis of biology, scientists would learn a great deal about the physical structure by which various living creatures developed and supported themselves, but little would be learned about life itself. To do so, biologists like Uexküll based their research on assumptions that the creatures they studied were alive, that life was the phenomenon with which biology was concerned, and that, at most, biologists, students of life, could use chemistry and physics as ancillary sciences to help explain how the creature in question lived its life.

A vitalistic view of biology accorded well with several important post-Kantian philosophical developments. Kant's critique

---

[4]*La rebelión de las masas*, 1930, *Obras* IV, p. 210.

of the ontological proof that God exists works equally well with respect to any substance, material or spiritual; as we shall see in more detail later, both inductive and deductive knowledge was transformed by this critique into a phenomenalism. In the late nineteenth century, the ontological curiosity, which Kant had seemed to destroy, began to stir again; but this time, rather than following Aristotle in saying that *being* was the ground of all else and that *being* was a substance, they said that reality was not a being, not a substance: it was life, existing, acting. Since this proposition entails a great departure from ingrained habits of thought, we shall keep returning to the matter. Suffice it to say here that from several sources Ortega had learned to mean exactly what he said when he spoke of human *life;* he had in mind the characteristically human pattern of living, of being concerned consciously and unconsciously with all the judgments, speculations, and actions that comprise a human life. He was not thinking of the physical being, the material body, and the conditions under which it multiplies most rapidly or survives for the longest time; he was thinking of the human life, the ongoing activity, and the situation in which this life can rise to its fullest, most significant potential. This life, Ortega thought, was the ground, the occasion of all possible, phenomenal reality: all phenomena existed, not in a world, but in one or another life.

Human life flourished when the means at hand for acting were in equilibrium with the problems *perceived.* Kant had shown that the mind works with phenomena rather than things-in-themselves. In keeping with his Kantian background, Ortega asserted that optimum *vital* development occurred when the *perceived* problems were in balance with the capacity to act that a man had acquired. Absolute needs were beyond our ken. A person was inert with respect to influences that he could not, in some way, perceive. To be sure, unperceived forces could decisively determine the outcome of activities initiated by living creatures, but there was nothing vital about these influences. A living creature could initiate its activities only with reference to the things it perceived.[d] Improvement in life depended on the quality of the initiative that humans took, and men could take initiative only on matters they perceived; therefore, rather than human problems in the absolute, the problems actually perceived were to be in temperate equilibrium with the means at hand. If the problems of which men were aware were not difficult enough to put their abilities to the test, their abilities would decline from disuse; if the perceived problems were too difficult, their capacities would be overstrained and perhaps destroyed. The contemporary situation was dangerous because comfortable surroundings encouraged Europeans to perceive only easy problems, which would neither challenge the existing means of action nor keep them in good condition.

A man *lived* in the world of which he was aware. He subsisted within an objective reality, but he lived among the things his attention took hold of on one or another level. To live is to be alert, alert to everything, to the viral body entering one's bloodstream, to the person behind one on the street, to economic and military decisions being made in far-off places, to an artistic form shaped by an unknown hand that fell still before there was a history.

One gave a definition of life by saying that it occurred within a sphere of awareness. One cannot read Ortega long without meeting an aphorism beginning "Life is. . . ," or "to live is to. . . ." These aphorisms conveyed the connection of life with awareness. "To live is to deal with the world, to direct ourselves in it, to take a stand in it, to occupy ourselves with it." "There is no life without interpretation of things." "To live is to feel oneself *fatally* forced to exercise liberty, to decide what we are going to be in this world."[5] These were more than fine turns of phrase. Ortega's aphorisms restated an important tradition of philosophic and scientific theory, namely the investigation of life as a teleological phenomenon. "To live is to shoot towards something, to move towards a goal." "Life is constitutionally a drama because it is the frantic struggle with things and even with one's character in order to make actual what we are in potential." "To live is to be outside oneself—to realize oneself." "All life is struggle, the effort

---

[5]Respectively: "El origen deportivo del estado," 1924, *Obras* II, p. 607; "Los 'nuevos' Estados Unidos," 1931, *Obras* IV, p. 358; and *La rebelión de las masas*, 1930, *Obras* IV, p. 171.

to be itself." "Life is essentially a dialogue with its surroundings; it is that as much in its simplest physiological functions as in its most sublime psychic functions. To live is to live with, and the other with which we live is the world around us."[6]

In these thoughts Ortega drew on the biology of Uexküll.[e] In 1922 Ortega closed an introduction to one of Uexküll's books with a warm declaration: "I should explain that since 1913 his biological meditations have exercised great influence on me. This influence has not been merely scientific, but also heartening: I know of no suggestions that are more effective than his at putting order, serenity, and hope into the confusion of the contemporary spirit."[7]

Uexküll gave what amounted to a phenomenology of life, one that showed life to be peculiarly teleological. His experiments and theories were based on careful observation of how various animals actually went about living their lives. On the one hand, he studied what kind of perceptual world an animal's sense organs defined; the vital universes of a mollusk and of a man appeared quite different to each because each had extremely different perceptual capacities. On the other hand, he observed the world of action of different creatures; the organs of some gave rise to an extremely limited repertory of acts, those of others to a fascinating variety. With any living creature, Uexküll found, its perceptual world and its world of action were linked by various internal feedback systems, which he called steering mechanisms. Here his theory anticipated the scientific aspects of cybernetics; but, more important for Ortega, his conception of the steering mechanism was useful in working out a canon of criticism.

In Uexküll's theory the function of a steering mechanism was to allow a living creature to direct its perception so that the information needed for a particular act would actually be gathered. Of course, the precise way in which the steering mechanism worked varied greatly with the characteristic organs of perception

---

[6]Respectively: *La rebelión de las masas*, 1930, *Obras* IV, p. 243; "Pidiendo un Goethe desde dentro," 1937, *Obras* IV, p. 400; *Ibid.*, p. 400; *La rebelión de las masas*, 1930, *Obras* IV, p. 208; *Las Atlántidas*, 1924, *Obras* III, p. 291.

[7]"Prólogo a 'Ideas para una concepción biológica del mundo,' de J. von Uexküll," 1922, *Obras* VI, p. 308.

and action of different species. All the same, selective response always entailed a capacity, in some way or another, to control the pattern of perception *in order to* initiate, sustain, or alter a pattern of, action. In human life, the steering mechanisms that mediated between man's complicated perceptual capacities and his powers of action were extremely complicated, and Uexküll did not try to describe them fully. He did indicate, however, that much in both man's perceptual and active world was of man's own making; the human realm was largely cultural rather than natural. Here, in the cultural sphere, the most important steering mechanisms were public functions, in particular, the critic's function.[8]

Uexküll's theories lent themselves well to describing the function of criticism. As an animal had a natural capacity to perceive and to act and had various steering mechanisms that linked these capacities purposefully, so a people had a cultural capacity to perceive and to act and a variety of steering mechanisms, in the form of teachers and critics who sought to stimulate the people's perception so that they could carry through desirable actions. Men learned particular skills, tastes, and standards from a larger repertory, the whole culture; and each man chose to act in any real situation on the basis of the skills, tastes, and standards he had acquired: thus he participated in the common way of life. No matter how original, a particular man could not stand completely apart from these common characteristics; they were intrinsic elements of moving, eating, dressing, speaking. But within this basic cycle of shared cultural perceptions and actions, critics, writers, teachers, and public leaders could try to interest men in important but ignored possibilities. Purposeful action always takes place within the limits established by the constraints of our capacities and surroundings. Public progress depends not on being free from a constraining cultural heritage, but on being able to act within those constraints by channeling attention and ability towards the pursuit of unfulfilled possibilities. The critics who so directed

---

[8]Uexküll's most important work available in English is his *Theoretical Biology*, D. L. Mackinnon, trans. I have discussed Uexküll's work and its place in current thought at greater length in "Machines and Vitalists: Reflections on the Ideology of Cybernetics," *The American Scholar*, Spring 1966, pp. 249-257.

our attention were the civic pedagogues, the cultural steering mechanisms.

Ortega perceived the function of criticism in this way. A community of men had vital needs and abilities; its members might or might not perceive their common needs; they might or might not use their powers: whether they would do so depended on how the masses perceived life and whom they chose to make their leaders. In one sense, civic pedagogy was the unselfconscious way in which all the people of a community perceived their needs and on the basis of this perception selected their leading minorities. The civic results would be good or bad depending on the accuracy of their perception, depending on the degree to which the problems they perceived were in equilibrium with the means they had at hand. The decisive deeds for the community developed ultimately out of this great aggregation of the perceptions and choices that each man made. Thus, Ortega observed, "the new biology recognizes that in order to study an animal it is first necessary to reconstruct its world, to define what elements of the world exist vitally for it; in sum, to make an inventory of the objects that it perceives. Each species has its natural stage upon which each individual or group cuts out a reduced stage. Thus, the human world is the result of a selection from the infinite realities of the universe, and we understand only a part of these. No man lives the entire panorama of his species. Each people, each epoch makes new selections from the general repertory of 'human' objects, and inside of each epoch and each people, the individual exercises the final modulation."[9] This vast process was the basic cycle of civic pedagogy, the process in which a community acquired its abilities and limitations.

In this fundamental sense, civic pedagogy was beyond the control of particular persons; as Ortega put it, each person exercised a final modulation. His effort, however, was to understand the nature of the critic's power. The critic's power could not be direct, complete, and authoritative; what happened would depend on many wills other than that of the critic. Nevertheless, this limitation did not preclude the critic's significance: the basic cycle

---

[9] *Las Atlántidas*, 1924, *Obras* III, p. 291.

of civic pedagogy provided room for many involutions, many steering mechanisms. No one person, no one group could directly control the whole system, but any person and any group could try to influence it by criticizing prevalent patterns of perception, by trying to help people improve the choices they made, and by stimulating men to modulate their lives more effectively. The man who exercised this real but limited influence would be the critic, the civic pedagogue.

Improve? Modulate effectively? These were fine impulses. But if each person's world was the result of a selection from an infinite variety, how could one person improve and modulate the selection made by another? If a man lived in the world of which he was aware, how could another, who lived in a different world, criticize the first? These questions point to difficulties with the theory of criticism that has so far unfolded: they lead to a study of Ortega's epistemological point of view. To clarify the function of the critic as a steering mechanism in the system of civic pedagogy, Ortega had to avoid the Scylla and Charybdis of absolutism and relativism, for with an absolutist epistemology the critic would begin to seek direct, authoritative power and with a relativistic one he would become either completely powerless or willfully arbitrary. Instead, Ortega searched for a middle ground, for an epistemology that would enable the critic to make significant suggestions without being tempted to assert command.

Epistemological reflection has been greatly stimulated by the desire to define accurately the actual relation between a substance and its symbol. In day-to-day matters, each of us has an adequate, working conception of this relation; it has become hard to sell the Brooklyn Bridge and even children intuitively grasp the difference between the symbol $10 and the greenish bill it stands for. But relations such as this one, which we operationally understand in simple cases, prove very difficult to clarify rigorously. It would not be surprising, for instance, if the next advance in sub-atomic physics comes from an epistemological critique of the seeming relation between the signs of various particles, as these signs appear in the form of decay paths recorded on film, and the actual entities these signs supposedly symbolize. Our lives are filled with cases like this one, albeit simpler, in which we take the sign as evidence of the thing; and the urge of the epistemologist is to criticize this practice, showing us when it is likely to deceive and when it will inform us well.

Epistemologists have arrived at no agreement in their critique of the relation between knowledge and reality. There are advantages and drawbacks to the different positions, and the consensus changes as the optimization of these pluses and minuses is made under shifting circumstances. But despite this lack of agreement, the disagreement itself has a form that has been surprisingly consistent over centuries. At one pole is an absolutist epistemology, which holds that signs are true indicators of an absolute reality, of a system of substances as they exist in themselves. There are obvious difficulties with this position, which were manifest in the beginning with Parmenides: we cannot maintain our image of the absolute and still save the phenomena, the whirl of changing objects all around us. At the other pole is a relativist epistemology that holds with Protagoras that "of all things the measure is Man, of the things that are, that they are, and of the things that are not, that they are not."[10] The problem here, of course, is not to save the phenomena, but to save ourselves from the phenomena. Which man is to be the measure when one finds that certain things are, and another finds that they are not? Most philosophers, Ortega included, have tried to find ways to integrate the best parts of both these basic positions into a single, consistent system.

During 1913, the year that Uexküll's biology began to influence Ortega, the Spaniard first explained his theory of "perspectivism." It was a simple but significant epistemological contention: knowledge was such that it had to include a point of view. The world was real, he held, but it was knowable only through the partial perspective of men: there was no ultimate or absolute perspective from which truth could be seen. This assertion was not meant to make man the measure of the thing; on the contrary, each thing had a real, absolute configuration for each man, and each man had to measure himself against the truth of these things. Ortega's contention was not, however, a traditional absolutism,

---

[10]Protagoras, Fragment 1, Freeman, trans., *Ancilla*, p. 125.

for there was no single, universal truth of things set apart from men; the truth of things was integral to each man's unique relation to the things, and the truth varied with each person.

For each person the world had a particular configuration; each man could know this configuration and it was the absolute for him; this configuration was his absolute, for another person a different configuration was the absolute. Knowledge was man's means for making over the chaos of things-in-themselves into a habitable cosmos, one that possessed form and substance; things became absolute for a man as he became aware that he had a definite, unique relation to everything by virtue of his having a particular location in the world.

This epistemology, which suggested that the absolute was each being's particular relation to everything else, was a thorough humanism in which knowledge was conceived to correspond to a fundamentally anthropomorphic universe. Ortega's was a radical anthropomorphism: he did not think that men should naively depict nature in their own image; he held that no matter what precautions were taken to avoid a human bias, knowledge could only concern things as they existed in a definite, absolute relation to the knowing man. The universe *was* anthropomorphic; and to know was to make manifest the real relations between oneself and the world.

This position was not original. Nietzsche had already exclaimed, "How could we ever explain! We operate only with things which do not exist, with lines, surfaces, bodies, atoms, divisible times, divisible spaces—how can explanation ever be possible when we first make everything a *conception*, our conception! It is sufficient to regard science as the exactest humanising of things that is possible. . . ."[11] Furthermore, the importance of perspective had been dwelt on by several previous philosophers, most notably by Leibniz and, again, Nietzsche. Ortega was careful to deny that his views were similar to theirs, and in the case of Leibniz the difference is rather marked. But for our purposes, it is more important to note the similarities, despite the differences, between the three conceptions.

---

[11]Nietzsche, *The Joyful Wisdom*, No. 112, Thomas Common, trans.

Leibniz presented an absolutist metaphysics in which all was derived from a perfect God. The universe was an absolute spiritual reality made up of innumerable parts, each of which was, in the eyes of God, perfect, fixed, and unchanging. Each one of these parts, however, did not have the eyes of God; each saw the universe from a perspective that made things appear imperfect, transitory, and volatile. All the same, this perspective was the best men could attain; and if properly respected, it would serve men well, for God had, through a pre-established harmony, provided for the reconciliation of every partial perspective with all the rest. "It is God alone (from whom all individuals emanate continually, and who sees the universe not only as they see it, but besides in a very different way from them) who is the cause of this correspondence in their phenomena and who brings it about that that which is particular to one, is also common to all, otherwise there would be no relation."[12]

Nietzsche's conception of perspective was in many ways antithetical to Leibniz', for Nietzsche would accept neither Leibniz' reference to an absolute God nor to autonomous, substantial subjects. The way in which grammar imposed upon our thoughts could perhaps have become clear only to a master stylist like Nietzsche; he realized that reason gave no warrant to believe that either subjects or predicates could be anything more than linguistic conveniences. Phenomenal evidence concerned neither the subject nor the object, it concerned the perspective, a perspective that, for convenience, men described as a subject seeing an object; but in truth, this perspective was simply the perspective, the particular seeing without the inferred subject and object introduced as independent entities.

Nietzsche's theory is difficult and obscure, but in a certain way, it is quite close to Leibniz'. The phenomenal universe for Nietzsche consisted in a heterogeneous mass of particular seeings, feelings, tastings, valuings, wantings, and doings; these perspectives were like Leibniz' monads. For both Neitzsche and Leibniz, all the separate perspectives and all the separate monads existed

---

[12]Leibniz, *Discourse on Metaphysics*, No. 14, George Montgomery and A. R. Chandler, trans.

by themselves intermixed but unrelated. The problem was to find a *tertium quid* through which they could become related. For Leibniz, the monads became related through God and his pre-established harmony. For Nietzsche, such a doctrine was untenable, for it required one to believe that the existing harmony was a perfect harmony. Instead, at this point, Nietzsche discovered a will to power at work among the unrelated perspectives; this will sought to work out and establish a *potential* harmony among the perspectives. In every case, the will to power posited itself as subject and sought to gain power over everything else present in what it now recognized as "its" perspectives. "Perspectivism is only a complex form of specificity. My idea is that every specific body strives to become master over all space and to extend its force (—its will to power): and to thrust back all that resists its extension. But it continually encounters similar efforts on the part of other bodies and ends by coming to an arrangement (union) with those of them that are sufficiently related to it: thus they then conspire together for power. And the process goes on—."[13]

Two problems were of central importance to both Nietzsche and Leibniz: the problem of apparent differences and the problem of harmony. By calling attention to the presence of perspectives in all phenomenal knowledge, both broke apart the homogeneous universe and made it possible for differing views to be equally true. Furthermore, both men, especially Leibniz, felt called upon to reconstruct from the perspectival pieces the homogeneous universe. In doing this, both were providing for common standards by which a person could discriminate between various perspectives, saying that, although the perspectives are, as far as they go, equally true, one has significantly greater value than another and the more valuable should have precedence. God's pre-established harmony and the will to power of the life force were rather different standards for making such discriminations; but with respect to the function each performed in the perspectival systems of Leibniz and Nietzsche, they were almost identical. In like manner, Ortega's theory of perspective differed from those of his prede-

---

[13]Nietzsche, *The Will to Power*, No. 636, Walter Kaufmann, trans. Punctuation is Nietzsche's.

cessors in the way that it dealt with the problem of difference and the problem of harmony; but the function of his theory, like theirs, was to deal with these two problems.

Whereas most theories of perspective postulated that a homogeneous reality seen from different points of view would appear different, Ortega renounced the homogeneous reality: from different points of view, reality *was* different. One erred by thinking that truth should appear the same to different men; "a reality that was always identical from whatever point it is seen is an absurd conception." One equally erred by thinking that because truths varied with different observers truth did not exist; this thought was a consequence of an unfounded belief in a homogeneous reality, but now "the concrete determinations, which before appeared relative in the bad sense of the word, change into the sole expression of reality when they are freed from comparison with the universal absolute." Leibniz' Godly point from which all could be perceived at once did not exist, for if there was a God, His knowledge was nevertheless anthropomorphic: "God is also a point of view. . . . God sees through men: men are the visual organs of the Divine."[14]

By recognizing that reality itself was not simple, that it was an infinitely complicated system of overlapping perspectives between this and that, the twin demands of the one and the many, the subject and the object, the knower and the known could be met. Prior to the twentieth century, philosophers had persistently fallen into the error of absolutism or scepticism by not accounting for perspective as a feature of reality. Both rationalists and relativists erred in thinking that reality ought to be some homogeneous object that would, given true knowledge, look the same to different subjects: because of this belief, the rationalist sought to suppress differences in the name of truth and the relativist tried to dissipate truth for the sake of differences. But reality was not some object out there that various subjects could disinterestedly observe; both object and subject were equally a part of reality and the perspectival relation between them could not be transcended. If one accepted the fact that the point of view of the observer was

---

[14]*El tema de nuestro tiempo*, 1923, *Obras* III, pp. 199, 232, 202-3.

a part of the reality he observed, the differences that men authentically perceived would cease to be difficulties for reason; on the contrary, these differences then become the occasion of reason. From different points of view there were different, real involvements with a single object; it would be futile to insist that only one of these involvements was correct, all the others straying from the path of truth, or that any observer could see just what he wanted to see, there being no real object to correlate with the different reports of the various viewers.

Since reality was heterogeneous, the function of reason was not to suppress differences, but to account for them and thus to preserve them, to make it possible for the different realities to co-exist. This function gave no one unlimited license to think as he pleased; on the contrary, it imposed immense responsibilities on each person to think truthfully. The way of truth still differed from the way of opinion; but reality ceased to be a continuous, homogeneous One: it broke apart into a multitude of real relations between the whole and each of its parts. The perspective of each man was his particular, unique, absolute relation to everything else; to live, each man had to maintain his relation to the world; and to maintain his unique place in the whole, a man was drawn into thinking, into accounting to himself for the differences between himself and others so that together they could preserve themselves by preserving these differences.

With this conception of perspective, Ortega took care of the problem of differences; and he used a correlative conception, that of destiny, to deal with the problem of standards. A man's destiny was his inalienable program of life; it was living the optimum, most human life that was open to him to live. Ortega's conception of destiny was related to the classical conception of fate; it took human effort to fulfill both. But the necessity characteristic of destiny differed from that of fate; destiny was a necessary potential, not a necessary actuality. A person could not change his destiny, but he could easily, all-too-easily, rebel against it and refuse to fulfill it. Thus, the European crisis was a *rebellion* of the masses because part of the destiny of men who put no special demands upon themselves was to be apt before those that did, and mass men were refusing to fulfill this part of their destiny, this condition of achieving their optimum, personal potential. The fact that men could reject their destiny distinguished Ortega's conception from that of Spengler and other potentially authoritarian philosophers. Because every man could inauthenticate himself, each was free and responsible; and because each man was responsible for freely fulfilling his personal destiny, his best possible self, it followed that his contribution to humanity would be, no matter how humble, as much a personal achievement, as vitally dramatic, and as publicly significant as that of the greatest personality.

Potentiality is a function of constraint; freedom is not a mere absence of limitation. A destiny, an optimum potential resulted because reality had a particular configuration for each person; this configuration put definite limits on how a man could perceive his life and how he could act within it. His real options were defined by these limits, and his freedom consisted in the necessity of choosing irrevocably between these particular options. Since the activities that a man could initiate were a correlate of his perception, his ability to perform the optimum activities that were among his real options depended in large part on his perceiving the world as fully and accurately as his perspective allowed. For each man his highest potentiality was fixed; it was a function of his perspective, of his particular relation to everything else: hence—"I am I and my circumstances." But it was not fixed that a man would initiate or fulfill his highest potentiality; to do so, he had to see himself and his world truthfully in all its perspectival uniqueness. By thus perceiving his destiny, each man could measure his deeds against his destiny and give form to his life. "What happens to us, then, depends for its vital effects, which are the decisive ones, on who each one of us is. Our radical being, the project of existence that we constitute, qualifies and gives one or another value to all that surrounds us. The result is that our true Destiny is our very being."[15]

By accepting a multi-faced world, perspectivism provided a place for truth and a place for differences: that was the essential point. "Perspective is one of the components of reality. Far from

---

[15]"No ser hombre de partido," 1930, *Obras* IV, p. 77.

being a deformation, it is reality's organization. . . . The inveterate error is to suppose that reality has, in itself and independent of the point of view from which it is grasped, an inherent physiognomy. . . . For it is the case that, like a countryside, reality has an infinity of perspectives, all of which are equally true and authentic. The one false perspective is the one that pretends to be universal."[16]

Here was a basis for criticism: a critic could not tell men how truth should appear from their points of view, but he could identify and expose falsified perspectives by their pretensions to substantive universality. In this, Ortega's conception of the perspectivist critic was closely paralleled by Karl Mannheim's conception of the sociologist of knowledge. An important difference, however, was in their different modes of exposing falsifications. Mannheim assigned a rather paternalistic, positive power to the sociologist, who in the end would know better than the untutored person what that person's real ideas should be. Thus, in Mannheim's system the sociologist would work out, rather authoritatively, the objective, substantive criteria by which ideological thinking could be unmasked; the upshot would be a contention that such and such a proposition was not what it purported to be because it was, in fact, the rationalization of this or that social interest.[17] In contrast, Ortega held that no such substantive criteria could be propagated; the Ortegan critic could expose illusion and dissimulation only with formal criteria that did not lay down what a person's point of view should be, but pointed out simply that a professed perspective could not be what it was professed to be. According to these formal criteria, there were two important sources of illusion and dissimulation: the absolutism and the nihilism to which traditional thinkers were susceptible.

First, rationalism posed a straightforward problem: rationalists believed they knew universal truths. Ortega inveighed against rationalistic absolutism through most of his writings. Abstractions

---

[16]*El tema de nuestro tiempo*, 1923, *Obras* III, pp. 199-200, italics in parts of the quotation omitted.

[17]See Mannheim, *Ideology and Utopia*, *passim*, and especially pp. 237-280. The paternalistic side of Mannheim's thought comes out most clearly in his *Man and Society in an Age of Reconstruction*.

gave only abstractions; reality could not be grasped in a universal truth. He did not bother with the dogmatic anti-metaphysics so popular among some twentieth-century philosophers; to him the case had long been closed and to pursue it would be to beat a dead horse: there could be no knowledge of universal absolutes. But Ortega went much further than the anti-metaphysicians, who were overly impressed with the achievements of science; Ortega did not accept scientific rationalism. As he saw it, positivists had given up the search for a universal absolute and limited themselves to a search for universal truths in secondary areas. Positivism, the presumption that the facts and laws of nature could be positively established, was another dangerous form of rationalism: it left uncultivated the profound problems of life in order to pursue inauthentic truths about less important questions. Scientists could tell us nothing about the laws of nature; they could only establish the laws of science, which would stand until later scientists inscribed better ones in their books. To be sure, Ortega granted that there was an "instrumental utility" to rationalistic thought, both positivist and absolutist; "but it is necessary not to forget that with it one will not know reality."[18] Revolutionary and utopian demonism arose when men confused their conception of a universal with a potential reality. The critic's task was to indicate the limits of rationalistic knowledge: the universality of rationalism was a fiction that was justified only to the degree that it enabled us to understand particulars more fully.

Second, relativism posed a more subtle problem than rationalism, for at first glance the relativist did not pretend to universal knowledge. His disbelief in truth, however, itself a negative universal, led to a dangerous outlook. The relativist believed that there was no reality beyond appearance and that whatever men believed was true for them. It was a short step from this position to an ominous extension, usually made in the name of the common good; namely, if each man's opinion was as good as another's, why not proclaim the opinion of the strongest (or the neediest or the greatest number) as the universal? Being strongest, we will call our will the truth. Ortega observed that direct action and blind

---

[18]*El tema de nuestro tiempo*, 1923, *Obras* III, p. 199.

partisanship resulted from such relativism. Relativists were the men who asserted the right to have opinions but renounced the duty to have reasons. "Every man would be the member of some party, and his ideas and sentiments would be partisan. No one would reconcile himself to the truth, to good sense, to justice, or to prudence. There would be neither a truth nor a justice; there would be only the party consensus; it would be their truth and justice."[19] To a certain degree, every man had to adopt "partisan facts" and the ideas of others because each person could not think through his own beliefs on every possible subject; but this necessity gave men no warrant to partake in a drive to make their beliefs dominant without more ado. The duty of the critic was to remind men that borrowed facts and theories were not their own; before taking ideas not their own so seriously, seeking to impose them on others, they should make the ideas their own by thinking the matters through and forming intelligible reasons for their views. Then, if still convinced of their rectitude, they might try to persuade others, not compel them, to perceive the truer point of view.

In short, the critic should provoke each person to live his own life, to make his own decisions, to form his own ideas, to recognize his perspective and to accept his destiny; in the Platonic phrase, the critic was to help each man keep to his proper business.[f] The critic could not tell men how to live, choose, or think; but he could note whether men were doing these things for themselves or whether they were relying excessively on the ideas of others. For determining the vital effects, or rather the anti-vital effects, it did not matter whether the ideas men mouthed were rationalistic or relativistic; either way, men would falsify themselves as they attached themselves to an idea without absorbing it and understanding it, without making it part of their view of life. The critic could identify these intellectual perversions, and then he could show how such distorted ideas were put to destructive uses.

When a man adopted counterfeit ideas he falsified himself; he rejected his own perspective and ignored the destiny that was his. He who lost himself in the images that others offered would not come to terms with himself; he would not find his real needs;

---

[19]"No ser hombre de partido," 1930, *Obras* IV, p. 81.

he would remain unaware of things that were essential to his destined life. "Whoever refuses to be what he must be kills himself while living; he is the walking suicide. His existence consists in a perpetual flight from the one authentic reality that he could be. Nothing that he does results directly from the sincere inspiration of his vital program; on the contrary, everything is an effort to compensate, by means of adjectival, purely tactical, mechanical, and vacant acts, for his lack of an authentic destiny."[20]

Self-deception and the resultant self-destruction occurred when men accepted falsely universalized opinions. With these, men could blur their own true perspectives and avoid the perception of the particular problems that their destiny was to surmount. Depersonalized opinion permitted men to embark on an easier but futile course: to occupy themselves by reacting to conventional occasions in the accepted way. Men filled their vacancy with dead dogmas, some absolute and others arbitrary. By criticizing these compensatory universals, the civic pedagogue could propel men towards the examination of their true destiny. In turning men towards their authentic lives, the critic would gain an indirect influence over the education of the public.

Recall: on the basic level, civic pedagogy was the aggregate pattern of spontaneous obedience and considered resistance that a people manifested as they surveyed their circumstances and pursued their possibilities; this system worked best, it allowed life to optimize its possibilities, when the problems that people perceived were those that would extend but not overwhelm their powers. No man could control this system. Yet the critic who followed Ortega's disciplined canon would indirectly improve the whole process, for he would undercut certain compensations by which men avoided confronting their significant, truly taxing difficulties. Ortega did not claim to have a positive knowledge of the destiny of other persons, for his point of view was not theirs; nevertheless, he did claim to be able to indicate when people were substituting ideas that had been mindlessly derived from others, putting these in the place of those that were proper to their destiny: a derivation could be identified because it had lost its integral con-

---

[20]*Ibid.*, pp. 78-9.

nection with any particular man's perspective. If the critic could insure that men were preoccupied with their authentic lives and not with some fake derivative, the dispensation of social power would be in a better balance with the actual problems and potentials of the community. Thus, to begin with, the civic pedagogue exercised his power not by propounding truths, but by criticizing errors in intellectual procedure. But this negative beginning was simply the beginning.

Criticism is the form of indirect action, par excellence; it is indirect because both the object and the audience of criticism have perspectives that differ from that of the critic. The critic respects the autonomy of those he criticizes when he limits himself to exposing false pretensions to generality; the critic cannot categorically proscribe or prescribe anything. Instead, he gains his true power by exposing inauthentic views that he encounters in himself and others. But in doing so, the critic performs only part of his task. The exposure of the inauthentic is a largely negative endeavor, which is significant as it helps men discover their personal destiny; but there is also a positive side to criticism, which is necessary to realize its full, indirect power. Criticism would not yield cumulative civic effects without postive principles that could guide its use. With these principles, the critic becomes able to inspire men to a common hope; and by sharing aspirations men become able to concert their powers spontaneously. Ortega's canon included such positive principles; with these, he made room in it for his cause.

Each man had a unique perspective and destiny; this fact gave rise to the negative power of criticism, for the universal was inauthentic whenever it conflicted with this uniqueness. But if the particularity of perspectival isolation exhausted critical possibilities, if critics confined themselves to insisting that the inner isolation of each should always be respected, then the community would soon be torn asunder by an exaggerated sense of independence in its members. Here is the most paradoxical universal of all: the universal by which one insists that every thing is utterly unique, particular, and dissimilar. To fulfill his canon, Ortega had to subject the canon to its own strictures; with a perfect solipsism one encourages men to inauthenticate themselves, thinking of themselves as isolated absolutes devoid of real bonds to others. The critic could avoid such absurdity by realizing that common, but not identical, features existed in the perspectives and destinies of other men. Because the destinies of different men included elements in common, the civic pedagogue could inform his criticism, his efforts to influence the public's self-education, with positive principles.

Let us not confuse this point, for confusion could lead to the very absolutism Ortega wanted to avoid. A common destiny did not arise because the destinies, the lives, of different men were in part the same, but because, in pursuing their different destinies, each had to deal in his own way with certain common problems. Communities and institutions were possible because analogous difficulties and desires arose in the lives of men; each had to feed himself, not in the same way, nor with the same food, but since each needed nourishment, all shared a problem of nourishment. Thus there were many common, shared problems with respect to which institutions arose; but all the same, each man still had to find his own, authentic relation to each common problem. If many men fulfilled in their personal lives the possibilities they had towards a common problem, then an integral community would form around it, a community that would appear cohesive and unified, and yet voluntary, variegated, and diverse.

As a critic, Ortega frequently wrote about common destinies. In doing so, he did not try to tell others how to live, saying that to be a good patriot one must think this and do that; instead, he observed that in the course of their distinct lives, each member of a group would probably take up, independently and in his own way, a problem common to all. In speaking of a common destiny, Ortega did not seek to impose one view on many men; rather, he hoped to make many men diversely conscious of a particular want, a particular absence in life, so that they could in their different ways shower the problem with a variety of potential solutions. Consequently, when he said that "the destiny of our generation is not to be liberal or reactionary, but precisely to disengage ourselves from this antiquated dilemma," he was not trying to foist a third orthodoxy on his peers, but to suggest that as each lived his life the occasion would probably arise in which the particular destiny of each called him to go beyond the comfortable opposition of the liberal and the reactionary.[21] In his view, members of his generation would each meet separately a common problem of transcending a political distinction that had become sterile; Ortega did not propose to make the leap for each person; he merely observed that the challenge seemed to be common, but each solution to it would have to be personal.

Thus, civic pedagogues could call attention to problems that they thought were of common concern. In doing so, they were not advancing false universals or imposing their view of life on others; they left it up to each man, first, to ratify the critics' concern by finding the problem significant in his own life, and second, to project as a program of personal action his own solution to the difficulty. Hence, the positive element in criticism comprised invitations, not commands. In this way, Ortega's writings frequently allured readers towards an interest in certain difficulties. With his stirring presentment, he invited others to join in considering the problem and their personal possibilities with respect to it. For instance, he wrote about *Spain* as a possibility, *Spain* as a political problem, the mission of the *university*, the idea of the *theater*, the theme of *our time*, the revolt of the *masses*; and in each case Ortega asked his readers to consider how they stood with respect to the problems that he suspected were confronting the groups in question. He invited each reader to help solve the problem by taking it into account in deciding on the way to conduct his life.

There was a solid rationale for this idea of action by invitation. The liberal tradition includes an ongoing skepticism about the power of the teacher to edify the pupil; following Socrates we confine ourselves to helping the pupil edify himself. A modern statement of the maieutic is in a note from Nietzsche's *Will to Power*: "*Not* to make men 'better,' *not* to preach morality to them in any form, as if 'morality in itself,' or any ideal kind of man were given; but to *create conditions* that *require stronger men* who for their part need, and consequently will *have*, a morality (more

---

[21]*El tema de nuestro tiempo*, 1923, *Obras* III, p. 152.

clearly: a physical-spiritual discipline) that makes them strong!"[22]
With Ortega's Uexküllian conception of environment, to create
the conditions that Nietzsche sought one would try to create an
awareness of more demanding challenges, challenges that would
call forth stronger men. Ortega's invitations were intended to
elicit the perception of greater possibilities; he believed that if
men perceived more taxing potentialities, they might give themselves a stronger physical-spiritual discipline and spontaneously
act with greater mastery.

In sum, each man lived in the world of which he was aware.
Far from making criticism impossible, this fact became the
basis of a carefully conceived canon of criticism, a theory of
civic pedagogy.

The education of the public took place on two levels: the
one was fundamental and inexorable, the other was secondary and
voluntary. On the basic level, a community formed and acquired
its characteristic virtues and vices as its members each gave social
power to one or another exemplary person. Civic pedagogy
created a community because innumerable choices, each made by
an individual, aggregated into the selection of the group's leading
traits. The prevailing conditions—scarcity or abundance, for
instance—could influence the aggregate quality of these choices.
But on closer examination, it became apparent that the conditions
themselves were not the actual determinant of the character of
the community. What mattered was the way men perceived their
conditions. In a healthy community people encountered, in the
course of living, problems and possibilities that would require them
to develop their abilities fully; whereas in an unhealthy community
people perceived only deadening difficulties, problems that would
either coddle or overwhelm them. Men who lived in a sparse
environment found serious, demanding efforts thrust upon them;
but men who lived in the midst of luxury had to make a special
effort to become alert to inspiring possibilities, for they could
be comfortable taking things as they were. Therefore, with the

---

[22]Nietzsche, *The Will to Power*, No. 981, Walter Kaufmann, trans.

development of a stable environment throughout the industrial democracies, the basic process of civic pedagogy should be augmented by the purposeful provocation of awareness throughout the community. To provoke the people: that was the task of civic pedagogues, critics, men who cared for the secondary, voluntary education of the public.

A critic could not work directly on a community. The common character formed according to the quality of the choices each person made; there was no choosing for them. Nonetheless, the civic pedagogue was not powerless; he could try to ensure that the members did not falsify their opinions about important questions and that they would have sufficient intellectual resources to form their own opinions. Such criticism would help the community arrive at a better definition of its possibilities, its destiny, by making its members meditate on their destinies. Furthermore, the critic could invite others to examine certain common problems to see if these were significant elements of their personal destinies. Thus, within the basic cycle of civic pedagogy, which occurred when the masses gave social power to particular elites, a civic pedagogue could do important things: explain and interpret a problem that he thought confronted many persons; build up the intellectual capacities that people might use to resolve the common difficulty; criticize seeming universals by means of which men avoided facing their personal destiny directly; and incite men to search themselves so that they would discover how common problems appeared from their particular perspectives.

These critical activities were similar to the procedures followed in Socratic discourse. Socrates began his discussions with a question of significance in the lives of his interlocutors. Through his concern for proper definition he attempted to build up intellectual tools suitable for resolving the problem. With his persistent effort to make others recognize the contradictions in their opinions, while himself claiming not to know, he practiced the kind of criticism Ortega advocated; with it, he provoked men to examine what they intimately, personally believed. Finally, Socrates' effort to secure the assent of his interlocutors had the effect of Ortega's incitement of others to search themselves; in both cases, the critic called on men to take a stand without the comfort of joining a dogmatic movement. Socrates, however, was more of a personal pedagogue than Ortega; but the smaller size of Athens, in comparison to contemporary Europe, lessened the gap between personal and civic pedagogy. Thus Plato observed that Socrates was the only true statesman of Athens, and the Athenians attested to Socrates' public influence when they executed him as an enemy of the city. Whenever the official powers feel compelled to use their command of force to suppress the voices of defenseless individuals they unwillingly exemplify how substantial a public power the lone critic actually wields when he effectively acts on the secondary, voluntary level of civic pedagogy. Efforts at thought control are self-defeating: they are the most conclusive witness to the power of unfettered thought.

Ortega's critical canon provided a humanistic alternative to materialistic theories of change. By giving due weight to the importance of perception, he broke the fatalism that results when the ideologists postulate that thought is a function of man's material conditions. If it was sometimes true that a man's character was a function of his environment, it was also frequently true that a man's environment was a function of his character. All depended on the man's ability to perceive his conditions differently: the same surplus, which, when perceived as comfort, induces complacency, will occasion great cultural striving, if perceived instead as a bracing leisure.

Here, Ortega put himself in the ranks of twentieth-century visionaries who looked beyond a politics of power to one of character; instead of relying on force, education was to be their means to reform.g They did not deny that human life could be ordered by conditions, force, and manipulation; they merely added that it could also be ordered by choice and aspiration. Furthermore, given a choice between the two sources of order, aspiration was more desirable than force. To make that choice, one needed to understand how force might operate so that one could anticipate how to foil it. Thus, Ortega opposed those absurd revolutionaries who breathlessly pride themselves on their ignorance of the past; he knew that in the past Europeans had shown an ingenious ability to alter their established forms of community, and he believed that anyone who understood the history of that ability

would not conclude that the power to change was a dead attribute
of the past. Reader—be prepared: when Ortega spoke of Europe,
the crisis of intellect, and the reform of reason, he was not trying
to cloak old orders in new sets of verbal clothes. He was serious
about the critic's power.

As a young man, Ortega wrote that "there is no theory besides
a theory of practice, a theory that is not practiced is not a theory,
it is merely an ineptitude."[23] Ortega practiced his theory of civic
pedagogy. Through much of his writing he examined the major
problem confronting Europeans in common, namely the possibility
of unifying Europe. He repeatedly proposed changes in the cultural
institutions in order to nurture the capacities that Europeans
would need if a Europe, at once unified and diversified, was ever
to be achieved. Further, by arguing for reforms in our conceptions
of technology and reason, he sought to undermine two powerful
misconceptions about science and history, for these errors eased
the way for men to ignore the problem of European unity.
Finally, by regarding philosophy as a way of life, as the living
of an examined life, Ortega incited men to search within themselves for their European destiny. Throughout all, Ortega's goal
was to unleash the historic power of critical thinking. "At this
height of the times, when we live in old, completed societies, we
cannot make history by mere proposals. We need a technique
of invention; we need to 'cultivate our garden,' the school, the
preparation of the intellect."[24]

Criticism might counter the pedagogy of abundance because
the effects that vital conditions had on human character were
mediated by man's powers of perception. As Wolfgang Köhler
and other gestalt psychologists had shown, particular conditions
could be perceived in various ways depending on the frame of
mind of the perceiver. In particular, the sense of power, security,
and well-being that the pedagogy of abundance insinuated in the
average man might become the basis, not of complacency, but of
a new, unprecedented striving if the expectations of the average

---

[23]*Vieja y nueva política*, 1914, *Obras* I, p. 290.
[24]"El poder social," 1927, *Obras* III, p. 500.

European could be inspired with a great new vision, a vision that would make the achieved actualities look tawdry. A possible vision, Ortega thought, was a vision of a united Europe. Europe was the common problem: if each man could perceive it in his separate way, the masses might again become apt before the exemplar.

During the 1920's, when Ortega was occupied with the renovation of Spain, he nonetheless won widespread repute as one of the better "good Europeans." He achieved this reputation by the impression he made on leading Europeans while introducing them to Spain, for in addition to wide correspondence as editor of *Revista de Occidente*, he was host and sponsor of lecture tours through Spain by men such as Albert Einstein, Paul Valéry, and Count Keyserling. Afterwards, Valéry wrote that Ortega and his friends had made Madrid "one of the most precious spots in my memory."[25] And in his book on Europe, Keyserling wrote that "it is a remarkable effect which . . . Ortega produces against the background of his homeland: he is one of the finest and most universal of Europeans; he will someday be acknowledged as one of the leaders of this age."[26]

*   *   *

> *It is hard to fight against impulse; whatever it wishes, it buys at the expense of the soul.*
>
> HERACLITUS, 85

---

[25]Paul Valéry, letter to Ortega, in *Revista de Occidente*, 1924, No. 11, p. 259.
[26]Count Hermann Keyserling, *Europe*, Maurice Samuel, trans., p. 93.

*T*HE AUTHENTIC SITUATION *of Europe amounts to this: its long, magnificent past has carried it to a new stage of life in which everything has expanded. But, at the same time, the structures that survive from the past are dwarfish, and they impede the present expansion. Europe developed within the form of small nations. In a sense, the national idea and spirit have been its most characteristic invention. And now Europe is obliged to surpass itself. This is the plot of the enormous drama that will be performed in the coming years. Will Europe learn how to free itself from its survivals? Or will it remain a prisoner of what it has always been? Once before it happened in history: a great civilization died because of its inability to surpass its traditional idea of the state.*

ORTEGA[1]

---

[1] *La rebelión de las masas,* 1930, *Obras* IV, p. 249.

XII
Towards an
Exuberant Europe

Count KEYSERLING suggested that some day Ortega would be recognized as a leader of "this age." Clearly, Ortega was not a leader of the age of world wars and the great depression; he appears insignificant compared to Churchill, Stalin, Hitler, Roosevelt, and de Gaulle. But Keyserling wrote about *Europe*, and he punctured the self-importance of official politics, national and international, with a telling irony. Keyserling was interested in spiritual leadership, and he was capable of laughing scornfully at the political pieties of his time. His book, he said, gave him a wonderful sense of inner liberation; he meant to occasion the same sense in his readers.[2] So, too, did Ortega in his search for Europe.

With a happy laugh and a gracious gesture beckoning us to join him, Ortega renounced the fatalism of the sensitive seers who find themselves

> *Wandering between two worlds, one dead*
> *The other powerless to be born. . . .*

The paralysis that Matthew Arnold recorded in his rueful rumination on the Grand Chartreuse seemed too easy a pose.

> *Silent, while years engrave the brow;*
> *Silent — the best are silent now.*
>
> *Achilles ponders in his tent,*
> *The kings of modern thought are dumb;*
> *Silent they are, though not content,*
> *And wait to see the future come.*

---

[2]Count Hermann Keyserling, *Europe*, Maurice Samuel, trans., pp. 8-9.

When men sink into despair, they cannot give birth to a new age; they can only stand mute, watching and waiting. With respect to despair, Ortega offered real leadership. In him the ancient will to believe awakened to a new life; he did not accept the self-pity implied in Arnold's depiction of the future that could not be born.

> Years hence, perhaps, may dawn an age
> More fortunate, alas! than we,
> Which without hardness will be sage,
> And gay without frivolity.
> Sons of world, oh, haste those years;
> But, while we wait, allow our tears![3]

Allow our tears, our dull indulgence? More happy years will not rise, without effort, unaided, from the ways of the world. The belief, the expectation that if we wait, sorrowfully but patiently, the future age will rise ineluctably of its own accord, is the source of our sterility, of our inability to give birth to this age. Ortega devoted himself to destroying this superstition that stood in the way of a new enlightenment.

With a hard gaze at the worst in the world, Ortega found that there were still great reasons for living and that men who had a significant *raison d'être* needed to ask for nothing more from life. From this affirmation there flowed a sense of possibility, a willingness to search out and try new potentialities; his adventurousness is unusual in twentieth-century thought. Ortega's writing resonated with the sounds of an authentic future, one that promised truly novel possibilities. His words resound with the affirmation that alert, thoughtful men can create great new works, a meaningful *Kinderland*, if they will disengage themselves from the obsessions of the moment and look to the past and to the future.

Yet men have difficulty disengaging from the immediate; and those who think about politics by profession, the political scientist and political commentator, have special difficulty standing back from day-to-day developments, for they have become deeply involved in the conduct of politics; their attention is occupied by

---

[3]Matthew Arnold, "Stanzas from the Grande Chartreuse," lines 85-6, 113-8, 157-162, in Arnold, *Lyric and Elegiac Poems*, pp. 214-217.

planning for contingencies, advising on priorities, and mobilizing opinions. With a few exceptions, even the more thoughtful columnists in our daily papers depend for their copy, not on their powers of original reflection, but on their access to men in high places; and political science has gained a quasi-official function, to wit, to rationalize established political practice as best one can. In pursuing this function, political scientists have become amazingly adept at hiding the human reality—the tragic, brutal, comic, joyous, loving, messy flesh and blood with which he ultimately deals—behind sterile ciphers and turgid phrases. Further, both newsmen and political scientists are busy men; they are obsessed with practice and hence they are chained to the endless now. For the most part, students of government lack leisure, the leisure that is the basis for all profound historical and theoretical reflection. As a result, we are rarely confronted by the serious, thoughtful construction of possible futures, by speculative visions like the European future sketched by Ortega. In short, political discussion rarely imparts a sense of liberation.

Keyserling and Ortega experienced a refreshing freedom. In thinking about politics, they ceased to feel limited by the issues their predecessors posed. They perceived the opportunity to ask new questions rather than offer yet another answer to the old. In this ability to pose political problems anew, the few visionaries like Ortega, managing to disengage themselves from obsession with the moment, were similar to the great political thinkers of the Enlightenment. Yet, owing to a deep involvement in practical affairs and lack of leisure most political thinkers now have difficulty perceiving the link between current political speculation and the Enlightenment. For most, the Enlightenment denotes a time of great theoretical innovation during which our current political and economic orthodoxies were worked out. We confuse the intellectual genius that conceived of these theories with the particular theories thus worked out, and in defending the latter we suppress the former. In this way, the very prestige we attach to the Enlightenment blinds us to the ongoing phenomena of enlightenment in European thought.

Take, for instance, the thesis that Judith N. Shklar has advanced in *After Utopia*, namely that "the grand tradition of political theory . . . is in abeyance."[4] For Shklar, the grand tradition was epitomized by the Enlightenment with its two salient characteristics of social optimism and radicalism, "the belief that people can control and improve themselves, and, collectively, their environment."[5] Thus Shklar identified the grand tradition with a substantive task, the effort to control the external environment, the pursuit of an open political and economic future; and the point has seemed to stand, for since the Enlightenment political theory has in fact been concerned primarily with the means for perfecting the social and economic life of the community. But in twentieth-century Europe, the most articulate writers on politics have been, as Shklar described them, either romantics or Christian fatalists, and in both cases they completely rejected the social optimism and radicalism that is supposedly indicative of the grand tradition. Shklar found that the "romantic" theorists, a group that included Sartre, Camus, Malraux, Marcel, Heidegger, Jaspers, Arendt, and Ortega, were in basic opposition to the Enlightenment; since these writers renounced the pursuit of the substantive tasks that Enlightenment thinkers had made the goals of political theory, the current writers must have forsaken political theory itself.

To be sure, twentieth-century romantics in Europe have denied, for the most part, that political reform and institutional innovation can bring much human progress. With the possible exceptions of Merleau-Ponty and Sartre in his later work,[6] the writers Shklar studied have throughly rejected the particular kind of social optimism and radicalism developed in the Enlightenment. Jaspers with *Man in the Modern Age*, Marcel with *Les hommes contre l'humaine*, Ortega with *The Revolt of the Masses*, and

---

[4]Shklar, *After Utopia*, p. 272.

[5]*Ibid.*, p. 219.

[6]For Sartre see *Critique de la raison dialectique, Tome I: Théorie des ensembles pratiques*, in which he tries to work out a conception of practical action that will be at once Marxist and existentialist and thus the basis for unifying the two movements. For Merleau-Ponty, see *Humanisme et terreur*. Shklar attributes to Merleau-Ponty the conviction that one can be neither "pro- or anti-communist" (*After Utopia*, p. 150), whereas Merleau-Ponty said "*On ne peut pas être anticommuniste, on ne peut pas être communiste*" (*Humanisme et terreur*, p. xvii). Surely, Merleau-Ponty's whole argument was pro-communist, affirming that communism was not yet fully developed, that the humanist should protect and encourage its development in the expectation that someday one could be communist.

Camus with *L'homme révolté* all turned their readers away from the tradition of optimistic reform initiated in the Enlightenment; and a book like *The Political Illusion* by Jacques Ellul, which appeared after Shklar's study, seems to confirm her thesis well, for Ellul draws upon the tradition she calls "romantic" and he thoroughly rejects the illusion that further progress can be achieved through political action. All these writers have asserted that the false spontaneity of crowds, which has become the stuff of politics, is not informed by man's better qualities, and that since man in a rigorous sense has no nature, but a character that he gives himself, reliance on politics for human self-definition is likely to impose the stamp of the worse upon the better. They have contended, further, that an outmoded rationalism inherited from the Enlightenment will lead to the reduction of man to an insignificant object, if such rationalism continues to be the epistemology upon which men base their political reasoning. Thus, contemporary "romantic" writers have voiced strong criticism of the Enlightenment.

But a writer who claims, like Shklar, to have studied Hegel should be careful not to confuse a philosopher's criticism of something with his rejection of it. Men who despair of the morrow do not write on *The Future of Mankind, Homo Viator,* or "The Past and Future of Present Man." It was Karl Jaspers who reaffirmed Kant's definition of enlightenment, "*sapere aude!*"; and there is no better advice for those studying contemporary political theory in Europe.[7]

Ortega, and others among the "romantics," attacked the letter of the Enlightenment in order to revive its spirit. The problems of comprehension, in responding to their work, are ones of perspective. One now easily sees Enlightenment thinkers as proponents of an optimistic social and economic radicalism; likewise, one easily perceives the contemporary Europeans as pessimistic proponents of cultural despair: such views come naturally to any-

[7]For "Sapere aude!" see Jaspers' *The Idea of the University*, p. 24. This book and Marcel's *Homo Viator* could have been consulted by Shklar. Ortega's "Past and Future of Present Man," with its very optimistic conclusion was available in the proceedings of the 1951 conference, *La connaissance de l'homme au XXe siècle*, sponsored by Rencontres internationales de Genève. Jasper's *The Future of Mankind*, with its concluding prophecy — a very prescient one — of a new politics, was not published until 1958 in German and 1961 in English.

one who is comfortable with the present order of things. But all the writers in question were acerb critics of the status quo in which they found themselves. From the point of view of the status quo, any critic is liable to be dismissed as a proponent of cultural despair; and the despair over man's foibles expressed by contemporary "romantics" does not go beyond that recorded in Swift's satires, Voltaire's *Candide*, Johnson's *Rasselas*, or Rousseau's *Discours sur les sciences et les arts*. William Burroughs' prose is no more destructive of human pretension than William Hogarth's pictures. Thus, it is by emphasizing one aspect of the Enlightenment and another of the present that a false dichotomy is set up—an age of hopeful theory against an age of sad despair.

In truth, each era was an age of both criticism and theory. The only real opposition is that current theorists are criticizing the substance of earlier theories. Hence Shklar correctly noted that the "romantics" have not been enthusiasts of either the social optimism or the economic and governmental radicalism of their Enlightenment predecessors, for the contemporary critics no longer believed that these particular concerns would produce the good life. But since European theorists like Jaspers and Ortega were not tied to the established system of practice, they did not need to confine their concern to given political, economic, and social practices; their optimism and radicalism, which was no weaker than that of their predecessors, becomes apparent in somewhat different concerns. Instead of social optimism, twentieth-century theorists have advanced an ethical optimism; and in place of governmental and economic radicalism, they have put forward a cultural and spiritual radicalism.

Ortega, in particular, embodied the three cardinal traits by which Shklar defined the Enlightenment—radical optimism, anarchism, and intellectualism; but these traits were to operate through a heirarchy of activities that differed from the hierarchy envisaged by Enlightenment thinkers. Shklar unwittingly recognized the optimistic and radical character of Ortega's aspirations when she said that "in Ortega . . . the ethics of authenticity becomes ridiculous."[8] She failed to notice that this "ridiculousness" under-

---

[8]Shklar, *After Utopia*, p. 139.

mined her whole argument. To prudent Europeans anxious to win favor in the courts of Louis XV and his like, Enlightenment theories of social and political organization were ridiculous because, like Ortega's ethics, they called on men to learn to live according to a better, more difficult rule of life. Louis XV was so oblivious to the changes building up around him that posterity has had to credit him charitably but apocryphally, with at least observing, *"Après moi le déluge"*. The incredulity aroused in the old regime as the rights of man replaced the rights of monarchs can be inferred from the innocence reflected in Marie Antoinette's "let them eat cake." And every implementation of Enlightenment political theory was decried before the event as patently impossible. Any truly optimistic, radical theory cannot help but seem ridiculous to the conventional opinion of the time; for an optimistic, radical theory is one that cannot justify itself on the basis of what is given: instead, it invites men to transform the given to fulfill the possibility that it describes. Thus, Shklar's mystification at the ethics of authenticity should be taken as a sign that the spirit of Enlightenment still thrives.

Rather than being in abeyance, the grand tradition has merely been transformed: the desire for material progress that has animated Western history for the last three hundred years is turning into an equally powerful desire for cultural and spiritual progress. This transformation should come as no surprise. Anyone familiar with the function of theory should expect contemporary political philosophers to have lost interest in the social, economic, and governmental problems of the industrial democracies. Theory concerns ideal entities. The old concerns are *theoretically* relevant only to the developing nations where the rational organization of society, the economy, and the government is still a mere ideal. But in the developed nations, the social, economic, and governmental systems are going concerns; consequently, in these countries, the need is not for theory about these matters, but for competent, dedicated administrators who can preserve and perfect these ongoing, established enterprises. Hence, there is an end of certain sorts of ideology.[a]

But civilization still has its discontents; life is not perfect; we have not been born after utopia. In the West, theorists have the opportunity that arises only infrequently in history; they can turn way from familiar problems and, with a fresh, expectant feeling, they can make love to a new mistress, namely, to the possibilities in human life that have arisen with the pedagogy of abundance. In times of abundance, human shortcomings and human possibilties are most marked in the ethical, spiritual, and cultural realms. Well then, let us turn our perfective powers upon these matters. Hence, social philosophers have tried to conceive of politics anew, this time of a politics of the spirit, for they feel a longing, a need for theory about the intangible work of man.

Ortega was a leader of the cultural optimists and ethical radicals—the contemporary exponents of the grand tradition. He criticized the present in the name of a possible future, a European future. He had none of the solemnity about present practices that we have grown accustomed to encountering in political scientists. His conception of Europe touched but lightly on economics, for in Europe what counted was the politics of the pure spirit, not the politics of the gross national product, with its buoyant ups and depressing downs, which everywhere seem to set the tone of national life. With the question of Europe we meet a youthful mood, a soaring of the spirit, a sense of vast possibilities, an impatience with plain realities, a willingness not only to criticize the given, but to try further to create something new.

Such soaring hopes, however, were a movement towards joy through sorrow: men like Ortega were optimistic about the possibilities for Europe because they were thoroughly pessimistic about the possibilities of the narrow nation-states. In the United States the creative despair that has taken hold in the European nations is only beginning to be felt. Most Americans sense that they have been born into a going enterprise, one that provides a structure within which they can achieve personal fulfillment. The situation was different for Europeans like Ortega; for them, the nations into which they were born came to seem confining. Their outlook reveals much about what is happening in the world around us.

"Nation" was the name for a huge but finite set of possibilities in the lives of particular men; it denoted important, different elements in the destinies of diverse persons. In times of national development, these various possibilities were as yet unfulfilled, but they were apparent as potentials to men. Thus, for one man the nation was a challenge to realize the possibilities of a great public office, for another it was an opportunity to accumulate wealth, for yet another it was a promise of military glory, for a fourth it was a tradition that invited him to literary creation, and for many others it was an occasion for sharing values, hopes, and reminiscences. The nation, which began as a pure form denoting manifold possibilities for diverse persons, was slowly brought into being as men dedicated themselves to realizing the personal possibilities that their ideal nation put before them. During the nineteenth century, Europeans had lived at the height of their times and achieved their destinies by struggling to fulfill the personal possibilities that had become conceivable for each as liberal democracy and industrial technocracy were joined within the national form. But in the twentieth century the national forms within Europe had been filled out; these denoted for men things that they already were, inevitably and without effort, not things that they might become with hard work and imagination "For the first time, the European meets in his economic, political, and intellectual projects with the limits of his nation; he perceives that his possibilities of life, his life style, are incommensurable with the size of the collective body in which he is confined. He then discovers that to be English, German, or French is to be provincial."[9]

Men had fulfilled the most significant possibilities for human life that they could set before themselves through the idea of the nation. This fulfillment encouraged men to perceive the state as an actuality; it no longer seemed to be a potential that by one's personal actions might be given a conditional actuality. The nation-state was a fact, a completed structure. Like the surrounding countryside, the nation-state was a thing that one found oneself in the presence of. Note the consequence. "No human being thanks another for the air he breathes because the air was not manufactured by anyone: it pertains to the class of things that 'are there', of things we call 'natural' because they are never lacking. The

[9]*La rebelión de las masas,* 1930, *Obras* IV, p. 248.

spoiled masses are sufficiently unintelligent to believe that the material and social organization, which is put at their disposal like the air, is of the same origin because it will apparently never fail and is as perfect as nature."[10] That the residents of the world's great cities can no longer take for granted the air they breathe upsets Ortega's imagery, but it even better exemplifies his fundamental point: the complacent confidence that anything of human significance will take care of itself is supremely dangerous, for man has made himself personally responsible for the whole of his existence.

Ortega drew a parallel between the mass man and the "mass nation," the nation that seemed to be there, complete and secure, as natural as the air we breathe. Both the mass man and the mass nation did no more than assert their right to be exactly what they were; the status quo was supreme and "more of the same" was its apotheosis. Both belonged to the class of heirs: they could take what was given and add not a whit, for both lacked a sense of potential, a vision of the future. Within the mass nation no exacting projects could be formed, for all the authentic ones had been finished and those that might be tried would prove to be perversions, as was the case with Fascist nationalism. Without being able to live personally involved in a developing enterprise, the European could not remain true to himself. "Europeans do not know how to live if they are not launched on a great, unifying enterprise. When this is lacking, they debase themselves, they lose courage; their soul goes out of joint. The start of this is today apparent to those who look. A century or so ago the districts that have called themselves nations arrived at their maximum expansion. Now they can do nothing more with themselves unless they transcend themselves."[11] Only mass men could find fulfillment in the mass nation.

Paradoxically, the very limitation of the national form, the fact that it no longer denoted taxing possibilities, enabled the mass man to avoid perceiving his own limitations. Being relatively complete the nation-state did not force upon its citizens many

[10]*Ibid.*, p. 179.
[11]*Ibid.*, pp. 272-3.

great problems against which they could measure their capacities. It provided for a stable existence; and as long as one was content to take whatever it gave, the person had little need to learn to know himself. A larger, less limited, less fulfilled form was needed if men were to be able to test their own mettle; an occasion for finding in oneself the capacity to create more commanding offices, juster laws, more difficult enterprises, more productive theories would help men discover their limits. This occasion was Europe. "Only the decision to establish a great nation from the group of continental peoples will begin the pulsation of Europe again. They then would again believe in themselves, automatically they would require much of themselves, they would discipline themselves."[12]

Europe—the curious maiden riding Westward with uncertain excitement on the back of a divine bull—has always been a shared adventure. With their national adventures completed, the Europeans needed to find a new undertaking. To maintain their vitality, men endowed with great powers had to dedicate themselves to heroic tasks, to the labors of Hercules and the journeys of Jason, all of which are given to strong men simply as significant tests of their strengths. Life was laying down another such challenge. The nineteenth century had taught men to aspire to a destiny defined within a national form; and with that destiny achieved, the European was challenged to the hardest task of all: to renounce the sovereignty of a familiar, established pattern and to accept freely a more demanding ideal.

Europe was the common destiny that would enable Europeans once again to get in shape. Europe was a form, a potentiality, with respect to which diverse persons could define different but convergent aspirations. In the twentieth century, the offices of *national* politics, economics, society, law, art, literature, schooling, and scholarship had been fully developed, and they required of the men who would perform them merely that these persons "take office" as the phrase now goes. In contrast, the offices of European life—of its politics, economics, society, law, art, literature, schooling, and scholarship—were not at all developed; these offices were possibilities, a teeming world of possibilities, each of which chal-

[12]*Ibid.*, p. 273.

lenged a different man to develop them in his day-to-day activities. Creative discipline would again invigorate European life as men independently devoted themselves to the pursuit of these European possibilities.

Europe as a possibility, this Europe gave Ortega's distinction between the complacent mass and the heroic individual a constructive, open, positive quality. He did not seek to contrast the happy few with the vulgar many. For him the heroic ideal had become an open, democratic ideal, a unifying rather than a divisive quality; Europe presented a common challenge and the excellence it could engender was an excellence open to everyman. The essential difference between a man of noble character and one of mass complacency was not in the type of actions that each undertook, but in the spirit with which each pursued outwardly similar acts: the noble man chose to make his deeds serve a demanding ideal, whereas the mass man was content if his acts satisfied his immediate appetites. Beginning with identical endeavors, the noble would find greater possibilities in them because he was continually bent on transcending the given. But to be meaningful, transcending the given always depended on there being a given that could be pursued more easily than various other possibilities. A man could aspire to nobility only if there were possibilities beyond the given to which he could aspire sportfully. Hence, nobility became a meaningful possibility for everyman when, as with the pedagogy of abundance, the inertia of the mass ceased to be something imposed upon men by the paucity of their environment and became merely one of their alternatives in a world of leisure and luxury. In this situation, the self-satisfaction of the mass man became a revolt precisely because the mass man no longer needed to be of the mass, someone who asked nothing special of himself, for he could, if he cared, lead the noble life. Thus, the revolt of the masses was at once a sign of weakness *and* a sign of greatly increased potentiality.

Achilles' nobility lay not only in the deeds he did, but in his choice, in the fact that he chose to do heroic deeds rather than live a long life of comfortable obscurity. Without that latter alternative, his heroic achievements would have lacked an important element of their nobility, namely, that Achilles did them despite the fact that he could easily have done less, much less, and still have been a good and decent man. Here for a single person is exemplified the positive, common potential that Ortega perceived in the revolt of the masses and the decadence of the nation-state: these developments made it possible for everyman to pursue nobility of character. Each European could now renounce the way of inertia and define his own excellence by not being content to pride himself in the superficial, established accomplishments of his national existence, by seeking instead to consecrate his personal activities to realizing the European possibilities that fell within his destiny. In the heart of the danger the courageous man found his greatest opportunities. "Is it as certain as I have claimed that Europe is in decadence and resigns its power and abdicates? Could this apparent decadence be the beneficial crisis that will permit Europe to be literally Europe? The evident decadence of the European *nations* is an *a priori* necessity if a United States of Europe is ever to be possible, if the European plurality is to be sustained by its formal unity."[13]

Many Americans feel that a United States of Europe would be a convenient political development. This attitude was particularly explicit under the Kennedy administration; and in general many hope that a resurgent Europe would be a healthy buffer between Russian and American power, preventing their potential clash. Those who hold this vision usually support the European unionists against the neo-nationalists like de Gaulle. American support was beneficial; but the Europe that Ortega and many others hoped to engender was considerably more dynamic and less predictable than the convenient buffer dreamed of by those responsible for American national interests. The question Ortega asked was "who rules the world?" and he thought that precisely that question was raised with the possibility of European union.

For men like Ortega, de Gaulle's Europe of the fatherlands would never do, for at a minimum Europe was their fatherland. European unity was not to be a way to aggrandize national grandeur. In *The Idea of Europe*, Denis de Rougemont indicated that

---

[13]*Ibid.*, pp. 241-2.

Ortega's importance in the three thousand years of speculation about Europe was his realization that the decadence of the European nations was the basis and precondition for the vital emergence of a unified Europe.[14] The thing that American politicians have not considered is the locus of this unified Europe that may rise like Phoenix from the national ashes. How far East would it range? How far West would it reach? What would be its center? its substance? and its form? Far from a mere buffer, a dynamic Europe might well include both Russia and the United States.

Ortega dreamed of a dynamic Europe. He was not an institutionalist. To be sure, he called on politicians to work out the machinery of European unification; but he seemed to put little store in mere machinery, and spoke much more often of the historical traditions that gave civic substance to the European idea. For Ortega the sense of a European destiny would spread among the people before meaningful institutions could be organized by the people. When you and I, as we are beginning to do, stop thinking of ourselves as Americans first, and Europeans second, if at all, and when we, along with countless Germans, Englishmen, Italians, Spaniards, Frenchmen, Poles, Russians, Swedes, Swiss, Czechs, Argentineans, Australians, and many others, begin to think of ourselves primarily as Europeans, and when these other labels mean no more to us than New Yorker, Burgundian, or Züricher, then Europe will be on its way to dynamic unity. We already speak of ourselves as Westerners; and the dynamic Europe of which Ortega dreamed may well be galvanized when this vague term, which is now so often used without feeling as a euphemism to cloak power politics deployed in the service of national interest, gains a common mystique, the power to stir up a sense of shared adventure and mission.

Starting in his youth, Ortega repeatedly advanced a dual conception of community, for multi-sidedness was a constant characteristic of his thought.[b] One hailed from two countries, he told "El Sitio": there was an official Spain and a vital Spain. Inhabitants of the first country liked to reminisce about past glories; participants in the second aspired to fulfill stirring com-

---

[14]Denis de Rougemont, *The Idea of Europe*, pp. 354-362.

mon projects. The official society was established; its subjects encountered it as a given element of their lives. The vital society was in flux; its citizens made it an ever-changing creation of their effort. In short, a community could be understood as a reality or as a potential. If one were to use the Aristotelian distinction, Ortega wrote, tradition would be the substance of a community and a purposeful enterprise would be its form. More lightly, he observed that "it is a matter, then, of the great difference between what a man is from behind and what he is from the front, or what he is by tradition and what he is by purpose and enterprise."[15]

From behind, there had long been a traditional Europe, which, in fact, had preceded the nations in historical development. As a young Europeanizer, Ortega had maintained that Europe was science: disciplined intellect, taste, and action. He maintained this view: a capacity for spiritual discipline had been the substance of Europe. Thus, Europeans shared a set of common intellectual attitudes, customs, morals, laws, and skills all of which dated back to Greek philosophy and poetry, to Semitic religions, and to the Roman Church and Empire. Consequently, men erred by conceiving of a nation as a self-contained community that could be abstracted away from the cultural ambience in which it subsisted. That ambience was Europe. Europe was an integral element of each developed nation, for the citizens of each nation not only partook daily of the European cultural traditions, but, further, the creators of each nation had proceeded precisely by using European skills and ideas to solve regional problems. For Ortega, recognition of this European precedence was essential to any coherent discussion of European unity, for it showed the inadequacy and nationalist subterfuge in theories of inter-nationalism.[c] "European society is not, then, a society whose members are nations. As in all authentic society, its members are men, individual men, to wit, Europeans who, *besides* being European, are English, German, or Spanish."[16]

Not only had the nations been founded by the aid of customs deeply rooted in the traditions of official Europe; tradition-

---

[15]*Meditación de Europa,* 1949, 1960, *Obras* IX, p. 278.
[16]"En cuanto al pacifismo," 1937, *Obras* IV, p. 296, fn. 2.

ally, Europe had a powerful political means for making itself felt in the affairs of men. This means was the balance of power, the established, official mechanism of European politics. The presence of Europe had been a changing yet stable equilibrium that reflected the unity of diverse components. The balance of the whole was the unity that had maintained the diversity of the different nations. No part, with its economic, linguistic, and political peculiarities, had been able to overwhelm the other parts and impose its peculiarities on all because the same European skills and principles that enabled any particular part to generate expansive power were equally available to the other parts to generate a countervailing defensive power.

Furthermore, not only had the European traditions enabled the various nations to maintain their diversity, many of the specifically European traditions had provided the raw material for creating and intensifying national diversities. Latin was the common basis from which a whole family of different languages had developed, each with its different literature; Christianity was the common religion from which the national churches had developed, with variously interpreted Bibles and liturgies; and the very idea of nationality was a common, European idea by means of which national peculiarities had everywhere been organized, preserved, and perpetuated. Traditionally, Europe had been the concord that, by preventing one part from supplanting the others, had preserved national discord and had made these different parts the creative fount of the European spirit.

This tradition had entered into crisis. The crisis, as we have seen, arose because various nations no longer recognized or utilized the common, spiritual principles of Europe. On the eve of World War II Ortega criticized two countries for most egregiously abdicating their European heritage. On the one hand, in a profound analysis of what was happening in Germany, Ortega controlled his ideological rancor and found the source of Hitler's power in an exaggerated faith in the efficacy of technical solutions. Writing early in 1935, Ortega contended that all checks to the principle of organization had been withdrawn: everything would be treated as a technical question, and the individual, no longer seen to be of intrinsic worth, would be totally subordinated to the collectivity. *L'esprit géométrique* was running wild in Germany and was being applied to everything without the slightest qualification by *l'esprit de finesse*. The absolute collectivization of life was an inhumane denial of Europe; and if carried out, horrible tragedies could be expected, Ortega warned with painful foresight.[17]

On the other hand, British pacifism revealed a dangerous incomprehension of the European political system, Ortega wrote in 1937. War was not an aberration that men could willfully avoid by refusing to fight; war was a political technique that men had invented to resolve complicated problems of life. Peace was not a simple absence of war; and a pacifism that amounted to an arbitrary refusal to commit British power in the defense of its national and European interests was an egregious abuse of responsibility. Peace had to be constructed by inventing new means for resolving the problems that war had traditionally settled. In the absence of such invention, pacifism was false; it was an attempt to think away the realities of the European political system in which the pacifist lived. To create peace, one had to create a system that would take over the functions of the balance of power. For this purpose, all conceptions of *inter*-nationalism were inadequate, for the balance of power stabilized by periodic war was the *inter*-national basis of European politics. The danger to official Europe, especially in light of the reigning absurdities in Germany and Britain, was that Europe was not something sufficiently more than an inter-national system: therefore, misguided national policies could disrupt the relations among European peoples. Official Europe was not adequately developed to resolve the present problems without tragic effort and sacrifice. The Europeans needed to reorganize themselves, creating a stronger Europe; and as a result, rather than an inter-nation, "Europe would be an ultranation."[18]

Here Ortega shifted from the back to the face, from considering the actuality to the potentiality, from the historic substance to the prospective form, from the tradition to the enterprise, from official Europe to vital Europe. Eventually, a European ultranation would have an institutional framework, but these institu-

---

[17]"Un rasgo de la vida alemana," 1935, *Obras* V, especially pp. 203-6.
[18]"En cuanto al pacifismo," 1937, *Obras* IV, p. 309.

tions would be a farce without something more, something vital to animate their official forms. Only a moving enterprise, which each person would find in his own, particular way to be of direct, intimate significance, could make great institutions pertinent to our inter-personal lives. Without such a mystique, the institutions of a unified Europe would be like the League of Nations, a sham for which Ortega reserved some of his most biting scorn, a gigantic association for administering the status quo.[19] Ortega was not a prudential politician; he called on Europeans to aspire to something more. He tolerated the European technocrats, but he was not content with their vision. "The historic genius now has before him this formidable task: to advance the unity of Europe, without losing the vitality of its interior nations, its glorious plurality that has produced the unrivaled richness and vigor of its history."[20]

Again, we touch on a problem of perspective. We Americans, along with many others, are only now beginning to be left unmoved by our national symbols. Few have transcended the liberal-reactionary opposition, an opposition integrally connected to national politics. We still argue about issues that arose in the course of knitting together different parts and strata of the national population, yet the basic commitments to integrating the people have been irrevocably made. Hence, from Ortega's point of view our whole framework of political discourse is anachronistic; this disjunction makes Ortega, especially the Ortega of the second voyage, hard to understand. One easily overlooks the depth of his radicalism, as he himself warned, and one reads what he wrote as if it pertained to the institutional tinkering over which the left, right, and center perpetuate their quarrels.

If one avoids this anachronism, one is then likely to connect Ortega to the destructive resentment that surges through the disengaged youth of our day. To be sure, Ortega's attack on the legitimacy of national sovereignty was as thorough and profound as any yet produced. But he did not make his attack for its own sake; he considered it merely one stage, an intellectual stage, in

---

[19]*Ibid.*, p. 295.
[20]"La sociedad Europa," 1941, 1960, *Obras* IX, p. 326.

his positive effort to promote European unity. Ortega asserted that the nation-state was illegitimate, not to justify acting against the state with a clear conscience, but to provoke the discovery of what authority had now become legitimate, so that one could freely act in accord with it. Ortega remained true to the Cartesian method of doubt, for this method stipulates that until one has developed new principles to replace those that are found wanting, one should continue to live by the old; by preserving the past until the future is generated, this method is a constructive skepticism. Ortega's skepticism about the nation-state was profound; but it was nonetheless constructive: active negation was not necessary; the nation-state would automatically be demoted when it paled into insignificance next to an emerging European ultra-nation.

Significantly, Ortega did not describe the features of the common project that would unify the European people. He pointed out that a unified Europe should provide substantial economies of scale. Further, it should have marked spiritual effects. As Ortega had thought that Spain could draw national strength from cultivating its regional diversities, he believed that Europe would draw strength from its national diversities. At a minimum, Europe should encourage the mutual comprehension of its parts, for the great weakness of the national system was that various European peoples confused the ephemeral images of their neighbors with reality, creating misunderstanding, distrust, and dissension. Also, the European enterprise should help the young find and fulfill their authentic destinies. That, really, was the whole point: the spirit was caged behind national bars and the young lacked the occasion to develop their real capacities. "Today," Ortega asked rhetorically, "can a youth of twenty form for himself a project of life that has an individual shape and that, therefore, can only be realized by his independent initiatives and his peculiar abilities?"[21] Men could not form their character fully, intentionally, within the narrow nation; the European enterprise would be a great new form that would create spiritual space within which the young could grow and test their limits.

---

[21]"Prólogo para franceses," 1937, *Obras* IV, p. 132.

But these functional features did not amount to specifications for the form. Ortega never explicity presented his European ideal. Politically, it might be a federal unity. Reading between the lines in his later writings, however, one senses that he continued to think that Europe was intellect, science, morality, and art, and that cultural institutions would be important in the efforts to realize the possibilities of Europe. One point Ortega did make clear: a unified Europe might be as different from the nation-state as the nation-state was from the feudal system or the Roman Empire had been from the classical city-states.[22] Without going into details, one can observe in the contemporary industrial democracies the beginnings of a cultural community in which the seminal issues will concern intellectual, educational, and cultural policy; in which the great public figures will be philosophers, scientists, artists, teachers, and mass communicators; and in which the decisive events might shift the community's effort from maximizing the material enrichment of its members to helping them achieve spiritual self-mastery or vice versa. These possibilities should be left, however, to later speculations. Ortega remained reticent about the details of his European ideal. He did not try to subject the European future to his favorite blueprint.

And Ortega had good reasons for his reticence. His critical canon made it unlikely that he would advocate a particular set of institutions for Europe, or present his personal conception of a European project as if it were valid for others. As no nation meant exactly the same thing to any two of its citizens, the form of Europe would have a unique physiognomy for each European. Recall that a civic ideal helped men create a community, not because it was identical for every person, but because it was a complicated, yet common, form that could be filled with a functional substance that, in each case, was different yet related. Such a form conduces at one time to both diversity and unity. Since innumerable substantial relations to this form can be established, it helps different persons define unique life programs for themselves; but since each unique life program will have been worked

---

[22]*Ibid.*, p. 119; cf. *Meditación de Europa*, 1949, 1960, *Obras* IX, pp. 277-282.

out with reference to a common form, the form helps diverse people harmonize their aspirations.

What the Europeans should seek, therefore, was not a single vision of a European project that would be forced upon all, but millions of independent visions, each of which would inform the life of a particular European with certain new, more interesting, more taxing possibilities. As these possibilities were fulfilled by each separate person, a single European achievement would aggregate from the myriad of different European projects. Thus, neither Ortega nor anyone else, not even a great group, could define Europe for the Europeans; to present a well-wrought plan would be to build a castle in the air. The real plan would be determined by the independent movement of many persons towards individual goals that they defined with reference to a common form. The men, the forms, and the ideas that would constitute Europe depended on the different determinations made by particular Europeans, each acting for himself. But the way that each would act for himself depended on the way that he perceived the possibility of Europe; and the European pedagogue could try, not to control, but to influence this pattern of perception.

Ortega's critical duty was not to produce a unifying project for all, but to provoke or invite many men to produce personal projects that, among other things, were each premised on a wider, more inclusive unity and harmony than Europeans had ever before taken seriously. To stimulate men in this way, the critic had to help them perceive the possibility, the desirability, of making real commitments to truly problematic matters. Here we meet yet another way of viewing the noble style of life: the adventurous, the heroic, the ethical always involves serious effort on something that offers no assurance of success. The revolt of the masses was a stampede away from such disciplined risks. The problem in creating Europe was one of redeveloping among men a tolerance for the profound anxiety and the keyed up pace, the alertness, that comes with any adventure, any spirited undertaking that carries men into the unknown.

What encourages a man to define his personal hopes and duties by reference to great things, difficult things, ones that do not yet exist? What moves a man to determine his most important aspirations with regard to an indeterminate ideal, one that might lead him to greatness or to abject failure? In the past, what human capacity prompted men to plan their actions *as if* a nation-state or an industrial economy existed, even though there was little industry and no developed national state that could force national characteristics upon "its" citizens or even indicate what those characteristics were to be? What human capacities had been the sources of man's historic creativity? How could these capacities be used to bring forth from the European peoples a great movement towards unification?

To answer such questions, Ortega reflected on the origin of the state. To be sure, he did not plan to reveal man's destiny by projecting into the future the erratic course that man has taken from his primeval past to his immediate present. A modicum of history teaches one to leave room for surprises. Thus Ortega did not study the origin of the state in order to force on the future the attributes of the original, essential state, of the *"Urstaat"*; Ortega was out to promote the *kind* of activity that had once originated the state and that might in the future create new social forms.

These two forms of projection differ in an important way. To project into the future a mode of action is not the same as to project onto the future a pattern of action. For millennia men have walked; they have not always walked to the same places for the same reasons. One can nurture a particular mode of action without predetermining the definite deeds to which it shall give rise; and through the turmoil of history there has been ordered change because men have preserved their basic modes of action and produced with these ever changing actualities. For instance, as men have used, between lapses, a particular combination of deductive and inductive reasoning, they have worked out physical theories as diverse as those of Ptolemy, Newton, and Einstein. In like manner, on various occasions the disciplined use of certain capacities had enabled men to create novel forms of community. Ortega sought in the origin of the state an insight into the kind of activity that had given rise to the state so that alternative means of human organization might be encouraged by encouraging the recrudescence of the originating mode of action.

Two questions can be asked about the origin of society, only one of which Ortega aimed to answer. One can inquire back through the origin in an attempt to understand the nature of its ingredients, or one can study the process of origination in an attempt to comprehend what the originator was doing to the ingredients. Anthropologists assure us that primitive clusters had a social organization even though the members of the cluster were probably unaware of their organization. In one way or another, this unconscious system of organization reflected the familial principle; and in one sense these instinctive divisions were the source, the origin, the ingredients of the first intentional efforts at conscious social organization. But this origin was not what Ortega was after; he wanted to understand the process by which particular members of a cluster first became aware of giving a definite organization to themselves. Ortega recognized that the unconscious organization of the cluster influenced the results of the first efforts at conscious organization. But he wanted to learn what impulse prompted men to become conscious of their organization and to try to shape it towards particular, desired ends. What motivated and empowered primitive men to make their cluster into a tribe with a purpose and mission?

A theory of social contract was more pertinent to this question than was a theory based on the familial principle.[d] By definition, contract theory pertains to the origin of intentional social organization; and Plato, Hobbes, Locke, Rousseau, Kant, and many others used it largely as a philosophical interpretation that did not need to be true to historical fact. Instead, contract theory has been an "as if" construction used to explicate one or another political theory. Ortega's conception of "the sportive origin of the state" included several contracts, and was in the end as much an "as if" construction as the earlier theories; but on one matter Ortega thought his predecessors were far from historical fact and seriously in error.

Previous contract theorists had been primarily interested in the terms of the supposed contract, arguing whether it made the sovereign responsible to the law created or whether it put the sovereign above the law. They all took for granted, following Plato, that either way the reasons men had for entering the contract were basically utilitarian: men made a social compact to overcome the threat of the war of each against all or to avoid starvation by initiating a division of labor. Throughout these conceptions, and throughout familial theories, which based community on the needs of child rearing, theorists assumed that men were motivated by necessity, by utility, by prudence. These theories drew their conception of human motivation from the middle-class anthropology of the Enlightenment, from the bourgeois romances of noble savages and *Robinson Crusoe.*

Ortega, on the other hand, was schooled on the historical anthropology of Greece and Rome, and he was less ready to assume that primitive man would necessarily have acted like English merchants transposed to the wilderness. Ortega admitted that utility could be a common criterion for selecting one from among a variety of present possibilities; but utility did not bring those possibilities into being. Thus, the proverb that makes necessity the *mother* of invention was more carefully composed than one might think, for it leaves unanswered the truly interesting question—who was the father? . . . Ah! Prometheus! Delightful rogue, did you steal the fire to serve your needs? Not at all! You stole it in a sportful play of wits with the great Zeus. Needs did not create the power of invention; it was quite the reverse. You first gave this power to the phratry of virile males who lived before women were created, and with this power they could have lived joyfully and on a par with the gods. But then, in fear and spite— at least as that old misogynist, Hesiod, tells it—Zeus fashioned the seductive Pandora and sent her with her vase of nagging needs to ensure that men would have to use their creative fire in mundane matters. But the fire was still sportful; needs held inventiveness down to earth, but the inventing itself always broke beyond the given, the expected, the habitual. Creation!—creation was the work of exuberance!

Creation always involved something that soared above and beyond the existing necessities. Previously, we noted how Ortega believed that in the balance between needs and abilities the perceived needs were more important than absolute needs. Here he took up the balance between capacities and desires in a slightly different way. Remember: "whoever aspires to understand man—

that eternal tramp, a thing essentially on the road—must throw overboard all immobile concepts and learn to think in ever shifting terms."[23]

Absolute needs, needs-in-themselves, were beyond human ken. Ortega concerned himself only with the palpable desires of men. For healthy development, these palpable desires had to be trying but not overwhelming: otherwise a man would break from the tension or go slack. Further, the needs a man perceived should be various in character; here Ortega departed from utilitarianism. Among the many things that men perceived as desirable, some were thought of as established necessities and others were considered interesting but superfluous. Man's creative capacities, his genius for adaptation, arose in the moments of leisure when a man suspended concern for the established necessities and when he indulged in a playful pursuit of the superfluous. Utilitarianism was useless. A people who settled dutifully to ministering to their established necessities and only to these would be devoid of creative power; they would never originate new, higher necessities of life. Furthermore, such sober people, men who consumed their energies in doing diligently what needed to be done, were likely to be upset by circumstances, for as circumstances changed, the established necessity would easily become a secondary matter and the secondary would become an issue of crucial concern, one whose importance the utilitarian would not recognize until it was too late.

Over and over, Ortega called attention to the productive power of the sportive, the jovial, the playful. The genius of life for adaptation resided in its exuberance, which enabled the living to entertain both the primary and the secondary and to alter, when appropriate, these valuations. Great things are done for the joy of it, and man's many-sidedness is a function of the fact that he is a laughing animal. "Without greater solemnity, I would say that life is a matter of flutes: the most necessary is the superfluous. Whatever is content to respond strictly to the necessity that rules it will soon be swept away; life has triumphed on the planet because, instead of attending to the necessities that inundate it, life

---

[23]Ortega, *Concord and Liberty*, Helen Weyl, trans., p. 75.

has flooded the world with exuberant possibilities, permitting the failure of one to serve as the basis for the victory of another."[24] The origination of the state came, Ortega suggested, in such an exuberant flowing over.

Primitive man first lived in clusters that lacked an intentional social organization. To be sure, there were instinctive divisions: the women, children, and old men; the youthful males; and the mature males. Of these groups, the virile youths were the ones who were exuberant; they had the excess energy and impulse, after they had attended to their established needs, to band together and plan common enterprises. The state, the conscious organization of effort in the pursuit of a common goal, stemmed from their superfluous energies. Ortega hypothesized that the original organization, a phratry of virile males, came into being as the young men of a cluster joined together to steal and carry home the young women of a neighboring cluster.

To be sure, in retrospect the utilitarian will say that these women, who were thus swept off their feet, served the need of preventing inbreeding. But only a Victorian prudery could lead one to believe that, in prospect, the youths initiated their audacious foray with the sober, righteous observation that for the good of the community they *needed* women other than those in their cluster. As the contemporary frat still says, they *wanted* new talent and they had sufficient excess energy to go out and find it. Thus the college fraternity is only a slightly sublimated version of the original phratry; and precisely the very virility of the males who made up this phratry had enabled them, Ortega thought, to originate purposeful social organization. The rapes they planned and performed led to war, and "with the war that love inspired arose authority, law, and a social structure."[25] The male youths banded together to form secret societies for which they created codes, rites, and festivals. In response, to protect their interests, the women of a tribe set up a counter organization; and whether the male or the female organization became dominant was recorded long after the battle by whether rights of succession were

---

[24]"El origen deportivo del estado," 1924, *Obras* II, p. 611.
[25]*Ibid.*, p. 616.

traced through the maternal or paternal lineage. In any case, Ortega thought, the development of exogamy, war, authoritative organization, asceticism, law, and cultural association had been initiated by young men dispelling their excess energies in various unnecessary intrigues.[e]

Free, principled endeavor originated from the exuberant, sportive powers of men, from man's ability to turn away from important matters and to create and play a flute. The double meaning in English of the word "sport" is thus profoundly appropriate to Ortega's thought: the sport, the variation in normal type, occasions human development and at the same time is the creature of sport, of activity that gives enjoyment, recreation, pastime, and diversion. "It suffices for my purpose to present in the origin of the state an example of the creative fecundity that resides in the sportive potency."[26] As Ortega saw it, all of man's great cultural works—law, science, religion, morality, art—were originated in sporting acts. This was the basis of his revaluation of values.

Scant similarity is apparent, however, between the exuberant search for women by a band of primitive youths and the ethical conception of a European ultranation. At our stage of historical development the appearance of willful fraternities would be a regression, a clear case of juvenile delinquency, and the development of an alternative to the nation would be an advance. But from the point of view of the participant in each enterprise—we should practice perspectivism along with Ortega—there was an important similarity. In both, the participant voluntarily took a place in a group, one that was not an established enterprise, joining in order to pursue the goal that the group had set itself. In both, the participant accepted rules, which were external to his whim, as standards that he should willingly attempt to fulfill. The essence of both systems was self-discipline; the source of both was a surplus, a set of possibilities that remained after necessities had been attended to. Ortega perceived, in the sportive origin of the state, that the primitive rules of the band had been the crude basis of law and ethics. He did not mean that primitive rules

---

[26]*Ibid.*, p. 619.

were an adequate substitute for ethics, but that primitive rules and each improvement that had slowly transformed the rules into ethics came from the same vital spring of the human spirit: sport. Any further improvement could also be expected to flow from the same source. Ethics were neither natural nor necessary; they were the self-imposed rules by which men ordered their super-fluous spirit.

Two problems make it difficult to accept this coupling of exuberance with ethics. First, sobered by our Puritan heritage, we fear that exuberance is unethical: Dionysius seems to sponsor sin. For instance, Fascism provides an example of the sinfulness of a state with a sportive origin, for unquestionably both Mussolini and Hitler gained power through their ability to organize and manipulate the excess energies of groups that were unable to find an outlet in the established society. The Brown Shirts were a contemporary example of an association of virile males for the exploitation of those about them. The rules of this band were not a contribution to ethics, although they may be said to have had a sportive origin. Ortega would admit these observations and add that they were too superficial to be conclusive.

Fascism was most significant, Ortega wrote in 1925, for what it revealed about the general condition of contemporary Europe. Fascism was essentially negative. The fact that it could gain power was a sign that European social movements generally lacked a significant, positive content. "Fascism and its imitators capitalize on a negative force, a force that is not their own: the debility of the others."[27] The barbarism of the Fascists was a clear retrogression from the ethical level that Europe had attained, for the Fascists were not at the height of their times and could not improve upon the sophistication that Europe had achieved. But Fascism also clearly indicated that Europe could not simply rest at its established level. This retrogressive system was a palpable demonstration that the ideals of the nineteenth century had ceased to be effective in the twentieth. "If no one believes firmly in any form of legal polity, if there exists no institution that inflames the heart, it is natural that whoever ignores all these and occupies

---

[27]"Sobre el fascismo," 1925, *Obras* II, p. 504.

himself directly with other things will triumph. Hence, it results that the power of the Fascist shirts consists, rather, in the skepticism of the liberals and democrats, in their lack of faith in the ancient ideal, in their political shirtlessness."[28]

According to Ortega the ethical problem conjured up by referring to Fascism was of greater scope than that movement alone. To be sure, Fascism wrought great evil. But one would learn little by failing to take the Fascist seriously and dismissing him as a totally malevolent being. Fascism was a symptom, not a cause, of Europe's troubles; and by being content merely to suppress the Fascist, one simply forced the disease out of sight and gave it more time to incubate its terrors without resistance. The ethical failure of Europe was not caused by the presence of Fascism; rather, Fascism was an indication of the presence in Europe of fundamental ethical difficulties. Hence, it would be to put the cart before the horse to use the example of Fascism to suppress our exuberant sense of spiritual striving. To evaluate the significance of Fascism for ethics, one should use one's critical powers to show that it was a vacuous response to a real difficulty, namely, the filling out of the European nations.[f] As an error, the Brown Shirts did not show that exuberance necessarily led to evil, but that men in search of an ethic could easily deviate and arrive at a bad one. To Ortega, Fascism was yet another demonstration that life "is the one entity in the universe whose substance is danger."[29]

In the second objection, men grant that exuberance does not necessarily lead to evil, yet they doubt that sport can lead to good. For instance, Johan Huizinga separated the sphere of play from the "serious" questions of morality.[30][g] In contrast, Ortega held that moral acts were freely willed; if they were compulsive there was no sense in distinguishing questions of morality from those of natural necessity. From where came voluntary effort? Certainly not from the capacities that allowed for mere subsistence, for these were fully occupied with the effort to provide for the root, physical necessities of life. Therefore, ethics had to come

---

[28]*Ibid.*, p. 503.
[29]*La rebelión de las masas*, 1930, *Obras* IV, p. 194.
[30]Huizinga, *Homo Ludens*, pp. 1-27, 213.

from man's surplus capacities, ones that remained after he had attended to his subsistence. Man had superfluous power, and his energy overflowed the walls of necessity; for this reason, man could invent rules for himself and will to follow them. Without exuberance, man would have no energy for ethics. Hence, the same play-element that Huizinga found to be so productive in culture was equally creative in the supposedly serious sphere of ethics.

In the same way, sport was the source of discipline. The essence of discipline is self-control, the acceptance of a code of conduct, and the voluntary submission to authority. Many confusions in educational theory have resulted from inability to distinguish between discipline and oppression. Although discipline often must be enforced, usually by one's peers rather than superiors, it really comes from within; whereas oppression comes from without. An example: the Spartans developed an extraordinary discipline in order to continue their cruel oppression of the Helots. There can be no discipline when one is compelled to do something. In sport, Ortega observed, men strove hard to accomplish things that they need not have accomplished. To succeed at his frivolous goal, the athlete submitted himself to a rigorous regimen; doing so, the athlete became the first ascetic, as the etymology of "ascetic"—self-denying in the cause of gymnastics—proved.[31] Discipline was the means to "being in shape"; it was the result of the spiritual desire to excell all others, "to be the best man," as Homer put it. Discipline did not come from attending to truly serious matters. Even "solid and stable wealth is, in the end, an emanation of energetic spirits and clear minds; but this energy and this clarity are acquired only in purely sporting exercises that have a superfluous aspect."[32]h

Freedom and duty were a unity. The man who could only respond, who had no power of initiative, had neither freedom nor duties. Freedom arose as a man gained a sense of choice, the power to do more than nature commanded. Duty arose when the man who perceived his freedom thought that he ought, in order

---

[31]For the etymology see "El origen deportivo del estado," 1924, *Obras* II, p. 617. Cf. "Discurso en el parlamento chileno," 1928, 1958, *Obras* VIII, p. 379.

[32]"Carta a un joven argentino que estudio filosofía, 1924, *Obras* II, p. 347.

to pursue a chosen ideal, to affirm one and reject his other alternatives. Only men with agile spirits, a rich sense of the possible, and the courage to choose the more difficult alternative could have duties; *Noblesse oblige!* The free man exercised his freedom by creating duties for himself.

Ethics, discipline, and duty were self-imposed procedures that differed from the way of least resistance. Exuberance, sport, and freedom made such self-imposition possible because they were the overflow of force that gave men the power to pass up the way of least resistance and to take a more arduous route. "Moral perfection, like all perfection, is a sportive quality, something that one adds luxuriously to what is necessary and indispensable."[33]

Europe would be developed through such sportive activity. Communities were the free, unnecessary creations of genius, a genius that might originate with a few but that could be shared by all. Again and again Ortega harped on the point: a society was a desirable project, an enticing task, a stirring hope, an exuberant aspiration that was conceived of by men. Imaginative men, who were strong enough to shake off the yoke of established necessity, were the originative source of vital societies. Caesar was a good example. At a moment of great confusion, Caesar perceived the outline of what was possible and initiated the realization of this order. "Imagination is the liberating power that man possesses. . . . The closed imagination of the Roman, represented by Brutus, advised itself to assassinate Caesar—the greatest visionary of antiquity."[34]

In the creation of new political forms, the men who first did the conceiving might not be paragons of prudence, good sense, or rational calculation. One of Ortega's creative heroes, the Marquis de Mirabeau, showed such imbalance; his youth had been leavened by great excesses and yet his imagination conceived—before it was necessary—that constitutional monarchy was the system that would bring order to Republican France. "Impulsiveness, turbidness, histrionics, imprecision, lack of intimacy, thickness of skin: these are the organic, elemental conditions of the

---

[33]"No ser hombre ejemplar," 1924, *Obras* II, p. 358.
[34]*La rebelión de las masas*, 1930, *Obras* IV, p. 263.

political genius."[35] These characteristics helped suppress the demands of apparent necessity and allowed the exuberance of the spirit to flow forth.

Obviously, this view contained a Nietzschean element. Nietzsche also praised the creative power of Mirabeau;[36] but for both Nietzsche and Ortega, the demonic elements of the creative character, which were clearly present in Mirabeau, were not to be valued for their own sake, but to the degree that they freed a man to create more effective, more demanding values. By this measure, most of the gratuitous demonism of the contemporary *avant-garde* is mere trivia. Yet, even with that said, the dangers in assigning values a sportive origin should be recognized; the objection that making sport of serious matters can lead to abuses is true. The Marquis de Sade, as much as the Marquis de Mirabeau, sportively used his imagination to depict a possible way of life. Neither Ortega nor Nietzsche contended that a world that invited human self-definition was the best of all possible worlds, but that it was the world in which man found himself and that only by accepting this fact could men avoid the nihilism eventually engendered through self-deceiving myths.

Necessity was still the *mother* of invention; hence Ortega insisted that the exuberant creation of values should be followed by the prudent, reasoned examination of those values. Here was the proper function of reason, to evaluate the possibilities when one was perplexed about what one should do. But when one found oneself with insufficient or unsatisfying possibilities, prudent calculation was not the best means for creating new ones. In such straits, one had to be willing to rely on genius, on imagination, on exuberance, with the demonic element that often came with it. The fact that the demonic made abuses possible was the reason why life required men to be alert.

Genius alone was not enough. For a nation and, even more, for something greater, for Europe, many men of genius would have to conceive of great, unnecessary, yet interesting enterprises,

---

[35]"Mirabeau o el político," 1927, *Obras* III, p. 625.
[36]Nietzsche, *The Joyful Wisdom*, No. 95, Thomas Common, trans.

and they would have to succeed in inviting others to join in pursuit of these goals, to join personally, intimately, with something integral to each contributed by each. A community of this kind Ortega described as a "daily plebiscite," a conception he borrowed from Renan.[i] The daily plebiscite was a social contract of sorts, but one that did not bind the future; daily, men continually renewed or slowly eroded the spiritual bonds of a vital community. This daily plebiscite occurred as each member of a group went about his business, either recognizing deep within that he was part of a significant common enterprise or feeling estranged from such an adventure. To Ortega the daily plebiscite maintained a vital society as each member of the group continually reaffirmed its desirability by freely choosing to define his personal aspirations with reference to the common goals, the unnecessary possibilities that the group represented.

With the idea of a continual plebiscite, political philosophy broke away from the conception of a community as a substantive bond, be it of blood, language, or history. A nation, for instance, was no longer viewed as something that was forged in the past and that should necessarily be perpetuated into the future. The official, traditional society had no rights of primogeniture over the prospective, vital community, for a moving project, the national future, was born before the national past and a moving project always preceded and was the condition of legitimate institutions. Men could not make authentic social commitments solely to past accomplishments, for the existent institutions were by themselves an established, developed enterprise, which meant that there would be nothing exurberant, sportive, unnecessary, or moral in a commitment to them alone. Authentic commitments were to a future that was not given, but was to be made. Moreover, the daily plebiscite meant that the vital significance of a group would disappear for any individual as soon as he ceased to define his aspirations with reference to its projects. Hence, in contemporary slang, participants in any group are free to "opt out." But to make good on this option with respect to the nation-state, which has become omnipresent in the world, the person can not merely opt out; he must further manage to define his aspirations with reference to some larger, more inclusive standard that may, some day, subject the nation-states to a higher law, as in the past the nation-states subjected the localities to more inclusive principles.

Human life is a matter of making things, of realizing in the future what was the hope of the present. Whereas the realization is rational, the work of prudential calculation, the hope itself is exuberant, the creation of the sportive overflow. In order for the rational calculations of each person's self-interests to cohere and aggregate into a cooperative community, each man had to be fired by a common hope stirring enough to command mutual allegiance, for men do not work and sacrifice for yesterday's realities, but for the morrow. "The state is always, whatever its form may be— primitive, antique, medieval, or modern—, the invitation that a group of men gives to other human groups to undertake a task together. This task, whatever its intermediate stages may be, consists ultimately in organizing a certain type of common life."[37]

In sum, then, to create Europe would be a labor of love, a lark, an aspiration, a soaring free above the bonds of existing political necessities. The European creators would be masters of potentialities, rather than realities; their very existence was unpredictable: suddenly creative geniuses might appear. Their work would be the work of exuberant imagination; in the symbolical, metaphorical, spiritual realm beyond the existing necessities, they would perceive a possible Europe and challenge their peers to see who, for the fun of it, could most fully realize its possibilities. Thus, Europe would be built by invitation, for in answer to an interesting invitation men would spontaneously discipline themselves in order to join in the pursuit of the proffered goal. The work of making Europe would be free and difficult, for it would mean that the Europeans would do more than they needed to do. Then, European life would be a truly moral life, that is, a life in which one freely sets a taxing standard for oneself and holds oneself to it. To create Europe, men would use their freedom, their sportive powers, their imagination, their capacity for choice and dedication, their moral sensibility. And here the European critic

---

[37]*La rebelión de las masas*, 1930, *Obras* IV, p. 263.

encountered the real problem, for most Europeans had lost faith in these capacities. "Here is the difficulty: Europe has been left without an ethic."[38]

Europe was an ethical problem, for Europe could be created only if men were willing to act exuberantly by conceiving of higher standards and holding themselves to these. At the close of *The Revolt of the Masses* Ortega suggested that Europeans would not create a European ultranation because their willingness to follow an ethic had disappeared. Youth was a *chantage*, an extortion, because adults erroneously believed that youth had no obligations, and in the name of universal youth the adults demanded carefree comfort. Thus men failed to see that precisely because the young were not yet overburdened by mundane cares, they were free to accept obligations in the significant sense. Because he did not confuse obsessive routines with exuberant obligations, Ortega castigated the cult of youth, by which the mature sought to escape the complexities of their lives, and at the same time he appealed to the young themselves to discipline their exuberant energies with a European ethic. Yet, this appeal ran against the temper of the times. "The mass man simply lacks an ethic, which is in essence the feeling of submission to something, a consciousness of service and obligation."[39]

Men felt themselves to be mere foils for many forces. Necessity seemed master over all. Each individual was subservient to "the needs of society," and every rationalization of outrage began with an apologetic, "You must understand, we have no choice but to. . . ." People could not act on principle if they perceived life as a series of compulsions, for acting on principle was choosing to act in accord with a self-imposed standard. Ortega did not believe that a man could rightly say that he had no choice; men always had a choice, for the power and possibility of choice inhered in the will of man, not in the objective situation. Human life was a moral effort; life was a struggle against one's circumstances to affirm one's chosen duty. Yet a radical defect in European culture

---

[38]*Ibid.*, p. 276.
[39]*Ibid.*, p. 277.

blinded men to the openness of their lives. What was it in European culture that made men feel that they were not free to accept moral imperatives or to embark on exuberant adventures?

Unless Europeans rediscovered their ethical sensibility and their sporting spirit, Ortega feared that they would not build a European ultranation, for they would lack the playful character that enables men to undertake desired but unnecessary enterprises. Ortega did not regret the disappearance of a particular moral, a particular ethic, or a particular duty; he was disturbed by the disappearance of the *capacity* for moral activity, the *aptitude* for ethical thought, and the *inclination* to feel duty bound. Expediency seemed the only persuasive ground for action, which greatly diminished the European capacity for development.

Here, then, we have come full circle. The claim that Ortega was a leader of *this age* depends on his having helped set in motion the movement towards European unity. As he saw it, this movement would be a sportive movement, one undertaken in an exuberant spirit, a free acceptance of the rules that would create a more difficult, more interesting game. Without such a movement, the European man who let himself be confined in his nation-state would settle further into insentience and inertia. The problem, however, was that a sportive movement towards unity offered no guarantees to anyone; it would come about only if multitudes of men responded personally to an uncertain invitation. Here was Ortega's optimism and radicalism. Unlike the calculating political scientist, he believed that Europeans had deep within them the capacity for ethical effort; Europeans would respond creatively to the right invitation. If the human soul is inert, recognizing a reason for action only in the calculations of expediency, this ethical radicalism will be ridiculous. Ortega himself observed that it was out of harmony with the times. But Ortega was still willing to put the matter to a test, to a long-term test: he was not about to argue interminably whether the sportive creation of Europe was possible, necessary, and inevitable; he did not care to insist at the start that men have assurance of success. Ortega was engaged in a serious but playful experiment, trying through his sportive effort to help set in motion the process of European unification. One of the first steps of this experiment was a critique of the very attitude that would hold it suspect.

Where the expedient was sovereign, experiment was suspect. To encourage the European to experiment with unity, the critic sought to expose the cultural defect that made the expedient seem sovereign.

*   *   *

If you do not expect the unexpected, you will not find it;
for it is hard to be sought out and difficult.
                                        HERACLITUS, 18

*T*ECHNIQUE IS *the production of the superfluous: it is that today as it was in the paleolithic age. It is, all the same, the means for satisfying human necessities. Now we can accept this formula that yesterday we rejected, for we now know that human necessities are objectively superfluous and that they are only converted into necessities by one who requires well-being and by one for whom living is essentially living well. Here is why the animal is a-technical: it is content with living and with what is objectively necessary for simple existence. From the point of view of simple existence, the animal is insurmountable and in need of no technique. But man is man because for him existing signifies pure and simple well-being; therefore the technician is a nativitate the creator of the superflous. Man, technique, and well-being are, in the last analysis, synonymous.*

ORTEGA[1]

---

[1] *Meditación de la técnica*, 1939, *Obras* V, p. 329.

XIII
The Reform
of Technique

MEN BECAME HISTORICALLY creative when they dedicated their excess energies to the fulfillment of an ideal. Human life, the moral life, was a rich, exuberant overflow of the spirit; men could make Europe into an ultranation if they would spontaneously break their established patterns of living, letting their spirit run in new channels. The Europe of which Ortega dreamed was necessary precisely because it was unnecessary. Europe was the path of opportunity; and by pursuing it, the European could remain true to himself, he could ask much of himself. The European had historically been the man of adventure, the person who voluntarily set himself to the performance of unnecessary tasks. Dauntless, audacious, valiant, gritty, enterprising, self-reliant, stout-hearted, venturous: so men would be as they leaped over their national walls and set out for the fun of it in the pursuit of a more distant ideal.

Ortega was not sanguine, however, about the likelihood that Europeans would gamely devote themselves to realizing an ideal Europe, for the exuberant spirit was depressed and the reigning cults of efficiency taught men to frown on excess energy. Rarely did men now seem to make public commitments for sportive reasons; instead, they justified every kind of public action solely with utilitarian arguments. Thus the paradox: in the so-called free world everything of public significance is described as a pressing necessity. When most men had sufficient energy to respond only to the expedient, then the noble spirit, the great-souled man who could obligate himself to a transcendent adventure, was not given

substantial social power. The spokesmen for compulsion, not creation, seemed to win the allegiance of men; hence, at the close of
The Revolt of the Masses Ortega observed that he had arrived
at the real problem: a radical insufficiency in European culture
allowed men to feel as if life were amoral, as if the pursuit of principles was insignificant in comparison to the push of necessity.[2]

Note that Ortega spoke of an insufficiency in European
culture.[a] To have done otherwise would have been to take the
matter out of the moral realm and to put it in the realm of
necessary, material determinants. As Ortega saw it, the sense
of amorality did not arise because some pernicious element in
"the culture" positively caused men to feel amoral. Historic
creation and the moral life were matters of exuberance and
sport precisely because they came freely from within and were
not fully explained by the causal mechanisms of the external
world. Ortega did not think of culture as a natural, objective
entity, over and above men, an entity that could act mechanically upon them; instead, he conceived of culture as a repertory of
principles that men had created in the fictional world of imagination and that they could use to define their humane possibilities and to direct their real efforts to fulfill these opportunities.

Culture is to character what food is to the body. One continually takes in languages, skills, and ideas, digesting and
absorbing them, extracting energy and substance from them, so
that one can draw on them in order to act more masterfully in
actual situations. Amorality was signified by the behavioral fact
that men were not acting exuberantly, sportively, freely, or
spontaneously, but were instead acting heavily in a dull response
to imagined needs. Hence Ortega inferred that the spiritual diet
of the contemporary European had in it certain deficiencies. The
deficient diet failed to sustain the person's efforts to cultivate
his ethical character; men were unable to nourish their moral
sense and they became accustomed to substituting for it the
plastic convenience of amorality.[b]

Much that is said about amorality does not convey a distinct
conception of what the phrase signifies. Ortega was not concerned

---

[2]*La rebelión de las masas*, 1930, *Obras* IV, pp. 276-8.

about a doctrine of amorality; if the question was merely doctrinal, countering it would involve the relatively simple matter of advancing a better argument. But amorality was not a doctrine; on the contrary, amorality resulted from a general inability to formulate principles and to act freely with or against them. In important activities men were able to respond only to seeming necessities, whereas formerly they had regulated their conduct in these matters by the imaginative creation of standards and by either free acceptance or free rejection of these guides in action. Amorality was not an ethic of neutrality; men were not amoral by virtue of choosing to control their actions by an absurd principle of amorality. Men became amoral when they became convinced that objective necessities really ruled their deeds and that the maxims that ethically legislate personal conduct were therefore irrelevant to any experience controlled by compulsion. So convinced, men would exempt their actions in these areas from moral rules, believing it impossible to feel either moral or immoral with respect to actions taken out of necessity. In this state of mind, men ceased to act exuberantly, for it did not occur to them that they could nevertheless seek to act, over and against the expedient, in accord with self-set standards.

Abstract statements about amorality should be exemplified with particulars, at least to the scant degree particulars can be given. By and large, men exempt their activities from moral judgment because their decisions seem to pertain less and less to particular, personal deeds and more and more to abstract, impersonal processes. Of course, one can still treat all sorts of questions concerning sexual relations, politics, economics, and social mores as moral problems; morality and immorality will always be, if they exist at all, a part of the realm of freedom, for the possibility of morality and immorality comes into being the instant that one recognizes an obligation as obligatory. But people have increasingly found that purported obligations are mere expressions of personal preference, which have nothing at all obligatory about them, and that the real "obligations" are not those by which a particular person freely determines his conduct, but those that determine the objective working of various psychological, political, economic, and social processes. A notorious example of this switch, in which an essential element of life is being withdrawn from the moral realm and is being viewed with a titillating amorality, is apparent daily: fashion, fiction, and the film show how completely the old moral obligation of chastity is being replaced by an amoral, psychological need for sexual adjustment.

Our purpose is not to decide which set of obligations, the moral or the psychological, best conduces to a healthy man's fulfillment of his erotic potentialities, for that question deserves more than passing discussion and is not essential to our present concern. Here we take sexual adjustment simply as an emblem of the spreading sense of amorality that characterizes our views not only of sex, but equally of politics, economics, social relations, and much else. In each of these matters, men are increasingly unconcerned whether their personal actions follow or violate ethical standards, provided that they find their deeds to be in rough harmony with the objective processes they believe to be at work within and around them. As consequence, this view of life makes the realm of freedom contract and the realm of necessity expand.

This contraction and expansion particularly worried Ortega. The amoral outlook should not disturb because it leads people to violate old pieties more often—it is not at all certain that they do. For instance, whether in fact people who accept a theory of sexual adjustment are more or less promiscuous that those who believe in an ideal of chastity is unclear. What disturbed Ortega was that as men continually deliberated over their acts by reference to the amoral necessities of objective processes, they cultivated an inertia in their personal character, an inertia that diminished the likelihood of spontaneous, historic innovation. Thus, the great exemplars of herioic love would have been impossible without some ideal of chastity both to accept *and to deny;* and the political geniuses who gratuitously led man out of his primitive state would have been unimaginable had they always adjusted their vision carefully to the necessities of the moment. Yet, as men experienced important aspects of life as amoral, they abstracted a general proposition from the particulars, and this propostion—that life itself was amoral—dampened their exuberance and suppressed their power to unify Europe spontaneously.

In the conviction that life was amoral, Ortega saw one of the most dangerous misapprehensions of his time. "How have men been able to believe in the amorality of life?" Ortega asked incredulously.[3] By putting this question to people, he hoped to elicit an awareness of how absurd the amoral sense was. Such awareness would help refurbish the European's capacity to envision a significant future, a *Kinderland*.

*   *   *

Life as life is lived, Ortega believed, is a continual moral effort, an attempt to achieve, one after another, various things that the person recognized as "good." A man cannot *act* without being aware of a goal, and when he is in form, the goals of all his acts aggregate into a life project that, he recognizes, is his self-made destiny. This destiny is a demanding regimen. To sustain the great, constant effort that the pursuit of a life project entails, a man needs to believe in its significance; hence, to assure himself of the worth of his work, he resorts to moral reasoning, crude or subtle, naïve or sophisticated, as the case may be. To be sure, he could accept his project as a mere preference, a hobby, an amusement, a pastime; in that case his personal life itself becomes a pastime, and in the inevitable moments of trial he will be unlikely to remain true to such an insignificant project. But the widespread sense that life is amoral does not even allow a man this reduced justification, for it makes the personal preference pale to insignificance in comparison with objective necessities.

When inclinations seem overwhelmed by compulsions, the feeling that the whole life is amoral, that it is a series of experiences that are necessary but not obligatory, begins to extract psychic costs. A man's natural desire to dedicate his efforts to a transcendent principle does not simply disappear when he experiences his life as something subject to the impersonal imperatives of objective processes. A sense of commitment does not develop *ex post facto* as a rational conclusion entertained only after all the objective evidence has been gathered and weighed; on the contrary, a feeling of engagement is the emotional heat generated with every serious action: as such, enthusiasm can be done away

[3]*Ibid.*, p. 278.

with only in the absolute quiescence of death. When the living perceive their lives as amoral, it means that they have repressed their urge for moral commitment; then, like any repressed drive, the ethical sense demands a distorted fulfillment.

In criticizing the absurd sense of amorality, Ortega called into question one of the major distortions by which Europeans clouded their view of their world, shirking their destiny. By merely experiencing life as if it were amoral, men did not succeed in making life amoral; instead, they simply confused their sense of life and introduced into their efforts to shape their character a deceiving distortion for which they would continually attempt to compensate. These compensations were terribly destructive, for they caused neuroses perhaps more serious than those that result from efforts to repress baser drives in the name of false moralisms.

Sophisticated systems of thought seem to sanction the tendency to objectify oneself and one's world and to treat both as factual phenomena that properly have no personal meaning or value. Dostoevsky, for one, was concerned with this problem; and although his ultimate critical intentions were rather different from Ortega's, his analysis of "hyperconsciousness" is pertinent. In *Notes from Underground*, Dostoevsky showed how excessive objective awareness destroyed the personal will by prompting men to repress their sense of involvement in their activities. When Dostoevsky's hero used positive, objective reason to analyze every personal incident and twinge, be it of his conscience or his liver, he dissipated his motive energies, for he convinced himself that even the most humiliating situations were caused neither by himself nor by other men, but by the universe and its implacable ways. Since all persons were impotent in the face of nature's objective processes, the rage of the hyperconscious man became all the more unbearable, for he could not help becoming angry, yet he believed that no action of his own would lessen his ire. "I was always . . . to blame for no fault of my own but, so to say, through the laws of nature. . . . Even if I were magnanimous, I would only have suffered more from the consciousness of all its uselessness. After all, I would probably never have been able to do anything with my magnanimity—neither to forgive, for my assailant may have slapped me because of the laws of nature, and one cannot forgive the laws of nature; nor to forget, for even if it were the laws of nature, it is insulting all the same."[4] In such ways, hyperconsciousness engenders a powerful frustration during the trials of life.

Complicating the matter further is the fact that the underground man was a true hero, for he resisted the ultimate degradation of losing his self-awareness. Most hyperconscious men, whose sense of personal commitment has been destroyed by their awareness of how objective processes function in all their experience, are likely, in compensation, to be possessed by all sorts of collective urges. Listen to zealots speak on burning causes. When convinced of their personal insignificance, men abdicate and passionately acquiesce to the necessary thrust of history. With this personal abdication and impersonal attachment, hyperconciousness leads, like various false moralisms, to neurotic attachments by way of unnatural repressions. Owing to the dynamic of this neurosis, the conviction that life was amoral endangered the European future.

When generalized into a complete view of life, the sense of amorality conflicts with the feeling of commitment that is the natural, healthy concomitant of intense activity. As the price of effort, the psyche demands the gratification of involvement, participation, and conviction; each exertion engenders passionate attachments, which in turn occasion moral reflection, for one wishes to know whether the object of one's passion merits the value one is attaching to it. Yet the belief that life is amoral can only be maintained if each conviction is explained away, reduced to a neutral necessity. Passion becomes a trivial matter that no longer occasions serious reflection, for it has no significance in comparison to the majesty of objective forces. The psyche slowly rebels at the repeated withdrawal of spiritual gratification, and it starts to fight back, insisting by subterfuge on a place for value in a world of facts. With this deception, the danger develops.

Observing that the hyperconsciousness puts store only in facts and objective laws, the psyche becomes ideological and disguises its commitments in the garb of their opposite, in the

---

[4]Dostoevsky, *Notes From Underground*, Ralph E. Matlaw, trans., pp. 8-9.

favored guise of facts and objective laws. Thus, everybody's pet project is described as one of society's needs, as an imperative of the time, or as an historic inevitability. This psychic practice feeds the debunking urge of the hyperconsciousness; and with the added debunking, the psyche develops ever greater cunning, until it manages to pass off an absurd belief or a destructive self-deception as a scientific truth. At that point a great pent-up desire for commitment and participation is permitted an aseptic, amoral satisfaction. Men fail to recognize that the object of their attachment, which purports to be a scientific truth, is a value-laden, spiritual goal that merits careful evaluation; they perceive it instead as a natural necessity that will come to pass regardless of how it is evaluated. This perception exempts the commitment from moral criticism and doubt; then great energies can be unleashed in the performance of terrible deeds, deeds whose terribleness will be recognized only in the pained stillness of the morning after. Hence, amorality is dangerous because it makes ethical goals, which are actually affirmed by man's overflowing, exuberant energies, appear as natural, inevitable necessities, and these are thus never evaluated in a test of their propriety. Then, all is permitted.

For years in the post-industrial world, hyperconsciousness and a general feeling of amorality have encouraged men to repress their desire to make positive, personal commitments for which they can hold themselves responsible in the court of moral discourse. As a result, they have a strong proclivity to clothe diverse value judgments in the garb of necessity. And, to worsen matters, certain characteristics of contemporary culture make it ever easier for men to ignore the fact that their goals are exuberantly chosen and to believe that these are imposed by objective historical forces. In addition to hyperconsiousness, a chronic lack of clarity in political and social theory has obscured the fact that human goals are freely chosen superfluities and that men should always examine the desirability of these.

With the omnipresence of mass communications and universalization of a superficial education, the danger that the psyche can fabricate a pseudo-scientific goal for the suppressed sense of commitment is significantly increased. Both imprecision and pretension abound.

During his second voyage, Ortega was cautious with respect to both imprecision and pretension. Willing to travel through Europe and the Americas in response to invitations to give lectures and to take part in various conferences, Ortega was reluctant to drum up a following. Even though he was speaking, thinking, and writing about some of the great themes of the time, he hesitated to publish, and one finds in many of his posthumous works a serious caution, a marked effort to be precise with concepts such as the state, law, the nation, the very concepts that can easily become the objects of amoral commitments. This caution cannot be attributed to a withdrawal from the great problems of practical concern, for the visionary aspects of Ortega's later thought were extremely far-reaching. His caution was the antithesis of a reluctance to shake the foundations; it emanated rather from a desire not to win a following among those who would misapprehend his thought and, in doing so, emasculate it. Ortega was careful not to propound an ideology; his aim was to shake the foundations by making massed, ideological commitments intellectually more difficult and by increasing the influence of responsible personal choices in public affairs.

In every field, the popular thinkers—the seers and the leaders —are habitually inarticulate; all vernaculars are suffering the degradation manifested in medieval Latin, and with parallel results: there is much ado about nothing. This is the situation that Ortega sought to avoid; he did not want his books to become badges, nor did he want his words to create a spectral world that men would confuse with their realities.

Norms of diction and grammar are neither to be imitated nor rejected, but to be used, and *si non, non.* When men become careless in their expression, they create unnecessary concerns that arise, not from the thought they express, but from the inadequacies in their expression of thought. The results of such carelessness can be deadly. This fact makes the standards of grammar and diction more significant than the mere prescripts of pedantic purists. Men who express fine thoughts carelessly can cause destructive misunderstandings. Unwittingly, in a lapse of grammar or diction, they propagate myths; millions of persons become convinced that the entities populating these myths really exist; and then terrible things happen. Inadequate powers of expression have been a basic cause of superstition; and superstitions have most often occasioned man's inhumanity to man. And beware: in no period of history have men been more superstitious than in the twentieth century.

Hyperconsciousness and amorality are dangerous qualities because we who enjoy an enlightened education rarely realize how thoroughly superstitious we have become in spite of the matter-of-fact awareness our science supposedly inculcates. The naïve sophisticates of our day—who in two centuries of "progress" have not inched beyond Voltaire's scorn for supernatural superstitions—fail to sympathize adequately with those who duped themselves into hunting witches. Men rarely learn from history because they sympathize spontaneously only with the victims and do not realize that in order to learn how not to be a villain, they had best sympathize with the villains of yore. As with witch hunters, well-intentioned men have repeatedly performed terrible deeds because they slipped up in one small matter, committing unawares the fallacy of misplaced concreteness. Thanks to Voltaire and others we can see the error of those who thought that witches were real, and we know the sad costs this error incurred. But let us still be humble; we are as human as our superstitious forebearers: we too are superstitious, for we too are susceptible to misplacing concretions.

Jacques Barzun appropriately called a book in which he warned against the misuse of racial concepts, *Race: A Study in Superstition.* Race is a costly example of an abstraction that can lead to untold suffering when people hypostatize it and attribute to it imaginary substantiality. Race is a theoretical construct devised to interpret various phenomena about man; but no matter how well race works as a theoretical construct, there is no possible warrant for asserting that races exist in the flesh and blood world of man: like all abstractions, race is by definition a conceptual fiction and only superstition can make it seem real. We are beginning to understand our proclivity to be superstitious about the concept of race; but racial concepts simply typify a much larger set of concepts upon which we are still prone to misplace concreteness. And as with race in Nazi Germany, these concepts are peculiarly suited to giving the hyperconsciousness an object of emotional attachment or repulsion that does not call into question the myth of amorality.

Psychological, social, political, and economic theorists have created in their speculations many profound conceptions describing the aggregate phenomena of human life. As theories, these conceptions are ingenious, interesting, and often effective; but they do not always remain ethereal theories. Numerous neophytes at such speculations are prone to misplace concreteness. And, in turn, the empiricist with his cult of facts easily forgets that his empiricism is a phenomenalism, an idealism; in his rhetoric, a conceptually postulated force, process, or entity is hypostatized and spoken of as if it were real, substantial, actual. Such slips are easily made. A harmless example is from Newtonian physics: one naturally shortens the circumspect statement that the theory of universal gravitation provides an apparently adequate explanation for the phenomena of falling bodies into the metaphysically rash assertion that gravity makes bodies fall. In making the same linguistic shortcuts a heedless speaker will forsake the cautious proposition that a theory, for instance about the social determinants of knowledge, gives a tenuous but interesting explanation why certain people often think certain thoughts, and he will instead assert the blatant superstition that a man's social origin determines his thoughts. Here myths are in the making.

Scholars in every social science have properly hypothesized numerous forces, processes, and entities in their efforts to explain human phenomena; but each hypothesis stands, as in this very phrase, waiting to be hypostatized by slack thinkers. Men have difficulty observing Max Weber's caution that "sociology does not recognize a 'behaving' (acting) collective personality."[5] Such cautions have not been sufficient to make us systematically skeptical of the innumerable assertions that are made daily about the behaving collective personalities that supposedly animate the political, economic, and social realm in which we live. Examples

---

[5]Weber, *Basic Concepts in Sociology*, H. P. Secher, trans., p. 43.

374 :: MAN AND HIS CIRCUMSTANCES :: PART II

abound; and perhaps the one fraught with the most obvious dangers shoud be mentioned first. Hitler's *Mein Kampf* was a mad struggle of active collectivities, and the seeming objective requirements of these entities gave the docile person unlimited license in his conduct towards other persons: "The German Reich as a state must embrace all Germans and has the task, not only of assembling and preserving the most valuable stocks of basic racial elements in this people, but slowly and surely raising them to a dominant position."[6]

But this example is not a good one insofar as we think of Hitler as a man beyond the pale; Hitler's doctrines have become anathema, yet his way of thinking has become endemic. For instance, despite a completely different ideological commitment, Herbert Marcuse persistently hypostatizes "society" and other collective creatures and makes them the prime movers in man's fate: "man's struggle with Nature is increasingly a struggle with his society, whose powers over the individual become more 'rational' and therefore more necessary than ever before."[7] And, if one finds Marcuse too far towards an extreme, look instead at the rhetoric of spokesmen for the American consensus, which is itself a false object of many superstitions.

Here, the most costly hypostatizations are those made by the very model of a modern Major-General, the national defense planner. As "the Free World" has defended itself over the years from "Communist threats," men have convinced themselves that there exists a complicated system of communication, not between opposing commanders, who are merely impersonal parts in the mechanism of national defense, but between the military monsters themselves. As in the mating rituals of certain birds, this system of communications is based on the relative "national defense postures" of opposing powers, and the planners hope that as "they" adopt a certain posture, "we" can respond with that perfect stance, which will send "them" into an ecstasy of acquiescence; and short of that elusive perfection, "at the minimum, an adequate deterrent for the United States must provide an objective

---

[6]Hitler, *Mein Kampf*, Ralph Manheim, trans., p. 398, italics dropped.
[7]Marcuse, *One-Dimensional Man*, pp. 240-1.

basis for a Soviet calculation that would persuade them that, no matter how skillful or ingenious they were, an attack on the United States would lead to a very high risk if not certainty of large-scale destruction to Soviet civil society and military forces."[8]

Public leaders base almost all their policies, not only those of the military, on the presumed behavior of collective personalities; and this condition is both reflected and extended by the way daily papers describe the deeds of men as the affairs of organizations. It is now an unusual headline that describes a human action: instead, "U. S. Proposes . . . ," "High Court Hints . . . ," "Assembly Votes . . . ," and so on. All of these constructions, the extreme, the sophisticated, the day-to-day, reflect our civic superstitions, and hypostatized abstractions have become central concerns in the discussion of every public issue and in the formulation of every political persuasion.

Ortega found these abstractions portentous for public life. "Today people constantly talk of laws and law, the state, the nation and internationalism, public opinion and public power, good policy and bad, pacifism and jingoism, 'my country' and humanity, social justice and social injustice, collectivism and capitalism, socialization and liberalism, the individual and the collectivity, and so on and so on. And they not only talk, in the press, at their clubs, cafés, and taverns; they also argue. And they not only argue; they also fight for the things that these words designate. And once started fighting, they kill each other—by hundreds, by thousands, by millions."[9]

When men hypostatize concepts concerning their common lives, they incur greater dangers than they do on becoming superstitious about the rest of nature. It is benign to say that gravity makes bodies fall, for little harm could result if a few eccentric literalists decide to stop the fall of certain bodies by incanting magic formulas against gravity, but it is malignant to believe that certain races are of intrinsic value, others of intrinsic depravity, and that the state can raise up the former and suppress the latter, for wanton fatalities resulted when men decided to

---

[8]Herman Kahn, *On Thermonuclear War*, p. 557, italics dropped.
[9]*Man and People*, 1939, 1957, Willard R. Trask, trans., p. 11.

root out depravity by eliminating its imagined racial cause. We recoil at this particular example, knowing well the horrible costs of Nazi racial superstitions. What we do not appreciate is that this supersition was simply the most dangerous example, to date, of a generic superstition that is still very much with us despite the demise of Nazi ideology. Race typifies an extensive repertory of hypostatized concepts derived from the sciences of man; and the superstitions based on these concepts provide peculiarly effective ruses by which the hyperconciousness can have its passionate commitments without recognizing life as a moral matter. For this reason, Ortega carefully stressed that ferocity in the name of behaving collectivities was not confined to a single nation, but had become a universal phenomenon in the century of total war.[10]

Belief in behaving collective entities confuses a person's conception of action; with such superstitions, the person begins to see himself, not as the responsible actor, but as the agent of a superior force or being. Having hypostatized one or another concept that he frequently uses to interpret the phenomena of civic life, the person begins to think that the active collectivity, of which he is merely a subsidiary part, follows its own course according to its own necessary laws. By reference to this entity—the times, race, class, society, nation, corporation, union, club, party, or what have you—the person can disguise morally dubious goals in the garb of necessity, which makes the moral questioning of his goals seem irrelevant.[11] With the hypostatization of political principles, major activities of life seem to pass from the realm of freedom to the realm of necessity, and in doing so, they cease to be subjects for moral reflection and become objects of scientific investigation.

Here, then, was the great cultural deficiency that sapped the European strength: men were habituating themselves to reasoning from impersonal necessities. A superior power seemed to impose

---

[10]*Ibid.*

[11]Note, for instance, how Henry A. Kissinger dismissed a humanitarian plea by George F. Kennan for increased spending to ameliorate racial tension, to improve urban conditions, to perfect popular education, and to lessen ignorance. "But the times do not permit such an order of priorities. We do not have the choice between improving ourselves and dealing with the menaces to our country." Kissinger, *The Necessity for Choice*, p. 9.

on men their significant purposes. Dignity was dead. Men could only accept as given and unquestionable one or another collective goal that was laid down by historic necessity. Men thought away their initiative; be it the defense of the nation, the superiority of the race, the power of the union, the supremacy of the party, the growth of the economy, or the overthrow of the exploiters, the person could not question the goal that fate imposed upon him: he could only ask how he could best serve as a means to the necessary end.[12] For years men had been hypostatizing collectivities and projecting into the human realm all manner of imagined necessities; as they accustomed themselves to acting only with derivative purposes, with respect to which they felt neither autonomous nor responsible, they degraded their capacity for historic spontaneity and made the exuberant affirmation of an ideal Europe unlikely.

Ortega's rejection of hypostatized social concepts gained much of its cogency from his ontology and his attempt at a reform of reason, matters that will be taken up in the next chapters. But in addition to his critique of the belief that societies were substantial things, he also sought to undercut the prevalent practice of reasoning from necessities. In this effort, he called into question the thought that the needs of society, or of some other abstract entity, gave justification for any definite course of personal action. He found a particular occasion for his general criticism in the implications for personal action that men derived from modern technology.

That Mephistophelean creature, Technology, has been an extraordinary ally of the hyperconsciousness, inducing men to believe that the necessities of mythical collectivities pre-empt personal purpose.[c] Nearly all grant that Technology is a crafty character, one who is capable of wondrous feats whenever he sets his mind to it. But as with almost every superstition about a

---

[12]"There are limits to what we as a union can tolerate. The very last thing any one of us would want is another shutdown. But if that is the only alternative, if necessary, we will have to close the school system down." Albert Shanker, president of the United Federation of Teachers, as quoted in the New York *Times*, March 25, 1969, p. 43.

hypostatized concept, Technology splits men between the pros and the antis, with both sharing a belief in the veritable existence of Technology, only disagreeing adamantly about the nature and intention of the awesome creature. Thus men disagree over the significance of Technology's accomplishments for the quality of life: some greatly appreciate the comforts that Technology brings, while others worry that, like Faust, they may have sold their souls for the bargains of affuence. This disagreement intensifies when Technology is perceived in union with that other popular divinity, Society: many men strive mightily to meet the imagined needs of "our complex technological society," offering huge sacrifices to Its greater glory, while others rebel hopelessly at what they perceive as an exploitative yet omnipotent god.

Two tales recently reported in the news exemplify the tension: on the one hand, an august commission of Harvard professors pronounced that, verily, technology had advanced human individuality, yet on the other, at the acme of a demonstration, raucous radicals in Montreal destroyed the ultimate technological icon, a multi-million-dollar computer. One suspects that as the conflict between these superstitions sharpens, Technological Society will prove to be, like the god of the Deists, a rather remote being; and when the contending parties clash, He will not be there between them keeping them apart, nor will He even be at a proximate distance to pity the victims and succor the wounded.

To make light of the matter is therapeutic; something darkly comic hides even in tragic superstitions. But despite a comic side, the hypostatization of technology is portentous, for the superstition is integral to whether we conceive of ourselves and other men as ends or as means. Both those who believe that technology is a good thing and those who know it is a bad thing find their goals inherent in that *thing:* service on the one hand and opposition on the other. Thus, the imagined entity imposes the human end when men believe the entity exists; then the superstitious person considers himself to be a mere means. Unfortunately, although one easily bemoans this mode of thinking, one has difficulty avoiding it, for technology truly seems to be an independent process that follows laws of its own and that imposes its purposes on innumerable human activities. We are all inured to acting at the convenience of various machines, and even the very young have already found themselves required to adapt their habitual patterns of action to the ever novel artifacts of technology.

Technological superstitions do not emanate from man's natural appreciation of the comforts created by ingenious craftsmen. The superstition is not the spiritual consequence of our materialism: even Plato made ample provision in his ideal state for the material softening of life. The hypostatization of technology is the very opposite of a healthy appreciation of the technician, who becomes incidental in the view of the superstitious. In the believer's mind, technology appears as an objective process at work in history, laying down according to its own inner dynamic various imperatives that men must either fulfill as technology prescribes or reject and thus forever alienate the beneficent god. Like the Calvinist, the worshipper of technology begins to believe that if one postulates an active place in creative work for mortal persons, one blasphemes the might of God, implying that he is not omnipotent and that instead he must rely on the help of men in the great work of salvation.

Damn the divinity!—with technology, as with any other religion, the human effects are neither better nor worse than the humanity of its worldly representatives. The historic failure of humanistic educators is simply that they have sulked as technicians have become more and more important in education; thus, the humanists, too, have been superstitious about technology and have bemoaned its spread while allowing the office of technician to be filled by anonymous persons. But let us not leap ahead. The hypostatization of technology has dangerous effects on the technician; this fact led Ortega to assert that the technician typified the mass mentality.[13] Something in the technician's art made the hypostatization of it possible, at which point the technician could cease to strive, being content to serve. How does the hypostatization work?

Technique is an attribute of every skill, the two are nearly synonymous; and we usually think of technique, not in the abstract as with technology, but in the particular as it is manifested by definite persons. Thus we compare the painterly techni-

---

[13]*La rebelión de las masas*, 1930, *Obras* IV, pp. 193-200.

ques of Michelangelo and Titian, the mathematical techniques of Weyl and Einstein, and the nuts-and-bolts techniques of two master mechanics. In addition to such particulars, during recent centuries a rather different "technique of techniques" has developed; this we identify less frequently with the art of individual technicians. On the contrary, the technique of techniques is what seems to make the individual technician insignificant.

In part, the technique of techniques is derived from that venerable myth, the scientific method, which has not been, as critics are showing, the historic method of scientists. The technique of techniques, however, is not used primarily to increase our knowledge, but to perfect worldly action. In essence, practitioners of it follow these steps: for any given operation, or technique, one can rationalize its performance by breaking the total operation into its component steps, eliminating any that are unnecessary studying each of the remaining ones and carefully bringing to bear on the matter all that is known about the materials involved, devising and testing alternative means to perform each step in order to find which means is most efficient, and finally integrating the most efficient, effective components into a rationalized system. Technology is our name for the widespread application of this technique of techniques to the production of goods and services and to the psychological, economic, and political manipulation of various publics. And because the phenomena that technology denotes seem at once to be omnipresent and independent of particular persons, technology is a concept that is easily hypostatized: "it is a system of ideas, techniques, and machines that puts us, in terms of power, about where God is, or used to be. And this system, evolving steadily, progressively displacing nature, tends increasingly to assert itself as the ultimate reality."[14]

When men hypostatize technology, they begin to think of the technique of techniques as an objective process that, having been set in motion in history, will thereafter follow its own course regardless of what particular technicans do. Bacon had pointed out how the reasonable man should ally himself with the necessities of nature, rather than hopelessly opposing them; and ever afterward, technology has been a great fount of reasoning from

---

[14]Elting E. Morison, "Technological Man," *New York Times Book Review*, March 30, 1969, p. 1.

necessity. Given the goal and the available material, a necessarily "best," most efficient means exists; and when the technique for finding this best means seems itself to have become an established feature of the universe, churning onward in every sphere of endeavor, regardless of our idiosyncratic preferences, then the technician feels himself freed from being responsible for the actual consequences of his art. A necessarily most efficient means for every job seems to exist, and discovery of that most efficient means seems foreordained by the reality of technology, by the universal presence of the process. If one person refuses to apply the technique of techniques to this or that matter, someone else will be found to do it, and perhaps he will make room in the job for even less of a humane residue.

In effect, all is permitted to the technician who finds himself in such an irresponsible subservience to necessity. In recent years, many have decried this irresponsibility. For instance, Herbert Marcuse has suggested that a feeling of subservience to the inevitable makes the technician lose the age-old sense of sin and guilt and develop "the happy consciousness." The technician considers himself to be a part of a dynamic process, larger than himself, that is essentially good and that therefore justifies the performance of certain questionable acts done to preserve it. The happy consciousness allows technicians not only to think about the unthinkable, but to help perform the unthinkable without a twinge of conscience, for it convinces them that the necessity of thinking and performing these deeds is imposed, if not on themselves, then on others, by the inherent dynamics of the technological process.[15] This state of mind is the euphoria, a rather resigned euphoria, in which men who know better allow themselves to commit atrocities. This euphoria is no different from the political and religious superstitions that have repeatedly possessed men, no different except that in its resignation and distance the technological superstition seems cruely cold—when death comes unseen and unheard from above, those executed are not even permitted the dignity of looking their executioner in the eye.

Efforts in recent years to debunk their technological super-

---

[15]Marcuse, *One-Dimensional Man*, pp. 74-83.

stition have been numerous and diverse. It is difficult, by means of a critique of technology, as such, to avoid the hypostatization, as a careful reading of Marcuse's *One-Dimensional Man*, for instance, will show. In it, the myth of technology was left intact and merely given a negative value in place of the normal, positive one. Marcuse believed in the reality of behaving collective personalities; and in the end, he created his own happy consciousness, that of the righteous radical who finds complete justification for every and any deed initiated with the intent of opposing the machinations of that most malevolent reality, Technological Society. Marcuse called in question real abuses with his negations: he and his followers began with a humane intention; but they lack adequate conceptual clarity to break down the widespread hypostatization of technology. It is ironic to seek slavishly a desperate liberation from a non-existent power.

As Jacques Ellul has indicated throughout his work, the *description* of closed technological systems may be helpful if it serves to provoke the individual technician to assert his inward autonomy. Unlike Marcuse, Ellul did not hypostatize the system of techniques he described in *Technique: The Engine of the Century*, for he developed a description of technological society that men could use to better understand aspects of their actual experience. As a result, Ellul concluded not with a plea for negative thinking, but with a call for autonomous thinking. The attempts to negate a material and political system of applied techniques would, Ellul suggested, lead only to the elaboration of a system of counter techniques; and one can see these building up as professional protestors become more experienced. Ellul has shown the near omnipresence of technique rationalized by technique, and all his work ends, in effect, with a *"Hic Rhodus, hic saltus"*: here is the challenge, find your own way to meet it.[16]

Ellul took a calculated risk in choosing his rather Socratic

---

[16]Ellul speaks briefly about his method in his "Foreword to the Revised American Edition" in *The Technological Society*, John Wilkinson, trans., pp. xxvii-xxxiii. His rejection of counter techniques may be found at *Ibid.*, pp. 425-7, and much more fully in *The Political Illusion*, Konrad Kellen, trans., esp. pp. 199-240.

mode of persuasion: he assumed that most men, on seeing the degree to which the technique of techniques was being used in their day-to-day activities, would seek naturally, spontaneously, to resist, to find concrete ways to lessen their own, personal reliance on such procedures. Thus, although he avoided the hypostatization of technology, Ellul did not provide arguments that might bring the superstitious back to their senses. Those who are already uneasy about the function of techniques in their lives will find that Ellul's phenomenology of technique clarifies their situation; but those who are happily conscious of living in a complex technological society will find Ellul's description a further proof of the seeming fact, a proof inexplicably spiced with strangely anguished rhetoric.

In reflecting on technique, Ortega shared with Ellul the virtue of not succumbing to superstition. But Ortega went much further than Ellul to meet the oblivious believer on his own ground. Ortega's conception of technology differed from those that Ellul dealt with in that Ortega's was meant to be philosophically, not historically correct.[d] Thus, Ortega arrived at his idea of technique by means of reasoned speculation rather than through an historical generalization about techniques already in use. This procedure allowed for unforeseen future development in technical activity, for his conception of the possible was not confined to the class of phenomena that were already actual. As a result, Ortega included wider problems and possibilities within the technician's purview than other critics have. Like Ellul, Ortega presented a phenomenology of technique, but Ortega included the problem of value in his conception of technology; and with this inclusion, Ortega put before the technician a depiction of technical activity that undercut the technological superstition.

For better and for worse, contemporary man was epitomized by the technician, Ortega suggested. Engineering, medicine, law, government, business: all were dominated by the technician, and through his character the technician set the tone that typified these and many other activities. The problems of amorality, of hyperconsciousness, and of the deficiencies in European culture resulted from the behavioral fact, observable in recent decades, that the technicians in all fields were, as a group, phlegmatic concerning possible goals and most imaginative about possible means towards actual goals that happened to be at hand. This state of mind made for the dangerous condition manifested during the twentieth century, especially in Europe and the West: rapid growth without development.

Note how Ortega's discussion, thus, was not concerned with an imagined process, technology, as much as with the substantial man, the technician. On the basis of recent conduct, the technician exemplified all the inertias characteristic of mass man; yet at the same time, this technician represented to Ortega the hope for a European future, for nothing but spiritual inertia prevented the technician from overcoming his subservience to necessity and affirming himself as an exuberant, sportive creature. Here was the irony: no group seemed more impressed by expediency than the technicians, yet no man's mission, when faithfully understood, was less limited by the expedient than that of the technician.

Ortega spoke, to be sure, of technology; but what was crucial to Ortega was not the myth of a technology-in-itself, but the definition of technology by which the living technician guided himself. With this idea the technician delimited his concern; and the one-sidedness of the reigning conception was largely responsible for the weakness of the technician's character. In short, the technician had made himself into a mass man to the degree that he reduced his art to one of its components: the methodical search for the most efficient means to a given end. Uninspired men brought modern technicism into being by using this conception as an operational definition; but merely acting as if it were the essence of technique did not mean that in fact it was. Ortega looked to the ancient past and to Asiatic mystics and found quite different techniques. With this perspective he contrasted to the mean conception of the mass technician a more open definition of technique: namely, the invention and selection of purposes and the means suitable for carrying them out. By including the problem of purpose, as well as that of procedure, within his conception of technology, Ortega found the technician responsible for meeting all the questions of ethics, morality, and value that the contemporary mass man suppressed by adopting whatever goals his immediate surroundings put before him. If Ortega's argument was found persuasive, the apparent transfer of major matters from the realm of freedom to the realm of necessity would be reversed, for men would cease to experience life as an amoral matter if they became aware that even all their technical activities were based on exuberant, ethical commitments.

Knowledge had an instrumental function, Ortega contended. He was not a pragmatist if one thinks, as Ortega did, that a pragmatist holds that the truth of a statement depended on its usefulness.e For Ortega the truth of something depended on its correspondence with reality, as it had in classical philosophy, but for Ortega the reality to which the truth corresponded was not that of objective, substantial things, but the reality of life as life was lived. With respect to the realities of life, knowledge had more attributes than truth or falsehood. For an omniscient being, truth might be the sole criterion with respect to knowledge. But men were confronted by an infinity of possible objects of knowledge, not all of which they could master; they had therefore to pay attention only to certain matters, ones they chose to concentrate on. Consequently, it was equally as crucial that what men knew should be useful, important, and valuable, as that it should be true. For example, in *Meditations on Quixote* Ortega contended that concepts are tools that we use for defining and holding things steady while we act on them.[17] Forty years later he still maintained that proposition: "Our life is nothing more than an inexorable activity with things. On account of this there are actually no 'things' in life. Things—that is, realities that have nothing to do with us, but that are there, by themselves, independent of us —exist only in scientific abstractions. For us everything is some thing with which we must have some use or occupation and with which we will find it necessary, sooner or later, to occupy ourselves."[18] Here was a basis for a thorough critique of all hypostatizations.

In addition to being true, all knowledge should further be instrumental; despite its sportive origin, men nurture knowledge

---

[17]*Meditaciones del Quijote*, 1914, *Obras* I, pp. 349-354.
[18]"Campos pragmáticos," 1953, 1962, *Obras* IX, pp. 642-3.

on finding that it has a value for life, on discovering that they can put it to a use.f On this point, Ortega agreed with the practical technician: it was to live a lie to spend one's life occupied with sómething of no vital worth. But if this conviction were taken seriously, the central problem for the technician was to determine which possibilities of inquiry were most significant and richest in vital worth. To estimate the real usefulness of any concern, showing that it served one or another established purpose was not sufficient, for the important question was the comparative value, the significance of a given purpose when weighed against other possible purposes. To make this comparison the technician needed a theory of valuation.g Thus, by beginning with the premise of the practical man and by elaborating it, Ortega showed that questions of value were more important for the technician than were problems of rationalizing procedures. No expenditure of resources is more irrational than one to rationalize the performance of activities that have ceased to have vital significance.

Presently, students of science are arriving at a similar view of the situation: confronted by more possible topics of scientific inquiry than there are scientific inquirers, researchers will have to make value judgments between the topics, and the scientist may have to give up his pretension to disinterestedness. Unfortunately, the pretension to disinterestedness opens the scientist to the most dangerous form of interestedness, namely the naïve. Many laymen and initiates still believe the myth that scientific and technical advance comes from unexpected inspirations, serendipity, and strokes of genius, which occur happily yet mysteriously from the free play of curiosity in every possible corner of inquiry. Insofar as this myth pertains to the psychology of the individual scientist, it may be accurate; but it has long since lost all plausibility as a description of science as a social activity. We have passed the stage in which intellectual resources were spontaneously attracted to channels of inquiry that were unexpectedly opened by strokes of genius; we are instead at a stage in which particular channels of inquiry are opened and made productive by the decision to pump intellectual resources systematically into them. The problem with the pretension to disinterestedness, to value-free inquiry, is that many are loath to admit that value judgments are being used to direct effort into this channel and not into another, and these judgments are instead irresponsibly disguised as social needs, technical imperatives, or historic inevitabilities.

In view of this tendency, what was important to Ortega, and what is still important for the development of a wise system of allocating technical effort, or "human capital" as it is now called, was to make it possible to subject the pertinent values to examination. The way to do this was not to advance, first, a system of values by means of which the decisions might be explicitly made. Rather, what was important at the outset was to drive home the fact that such allocations were problems of value and were not amoral expediencies resulting from the imagined needs of society, technology, or any other hypostatization. A hint of Ortega's reasoning is in the phrase, which we encountered above, "the most necessary is the superfluous." Vital worth had little to do with those mealy-mouthed "necessities" with which weak men are ever wont to hide their value judgments. Necessity did not compel the human will to perform certain acts; on the contrary, the human will selected and defined those supreme values that men called necessities. Hence, necessity being the creature of value judgment, by no appeal to necessity could one exempt oneself from the responsibility to justify one's goals to oneself and others through moral discourse.

Ortega did not mean that responsibility and moral autonomy were inherent in technical activity because it gave rise to an affluence in which numerous choices between alternatives arose. Well-trained consumers are quick to respond diligently to induced needs, as Galbraith and others have shown; but this argument pertains only to certain sectors of certain economies, and does not show that all technical activity involves value-laden superfluities. Ortega based his contentions on fundamentals that would hold even under conditions of subsistence. Nay, his point, in fact, would probably be much more obvious when men were on the brink, for then their will to live, even to live well with regard to seemingly small matters, would be apparent. Thus, what seemed to be the basic necessity, the necessity to live, was not a material requirement that was universally and necessarily sovereign, as laws of gravity seem to be over physical masses. The necessity to live was really a *desire* to live that, as it was felt by man, was not built into the human physiology. To live "is the necessity created by an act of will."[19] The need to live was a subjective desire that was revealed by acts of trying to stay alive—by our nocturnal loneliness and fear of death and by our daytime fancy for doing deeds of greatness.

Echoing Plato and Seneca, Ortega further asserted the recurrent truth that defines the importance of philosophy for life: man does not seek merely to live; he seeks to live well.[20] Once a man had made the value judgment that it was worth the effort to live, he had physiologically to fulfill only a scant minimum of objective requirements in order to preserve his life: numerous examples show that man *can* live in the midst of cold on little food and beneath scant shelter. Hence, the invention of techniques did not serve man's objective requirements; "technique is not what man does in order to satisfy his needs."[21] Man could live by foraging without technique; but in the course of that life, man intuited better, unnecessary possibilities: if he tended this plant, if he sharpened that stick, if he stoked that fire, he could not only survive, he could have the leisure in the evening to enjoy the warm embers and to feast on baked bread and roasted rabbit. "Man has no desire to be in the world. What he wants is to be in it prosperously. Only this appears necessary to him and all the rest is necessary only insofar as it is a means to well-being. Thus, for man only the objectively superfluous is necessary."[22] The function of technique was to produce the superfluous; therefore the goals of the technicians were always determined not by amoral necessities, but by ethical decisions, by judgments of value.

Men erred in thinking that technology was the human analogue to the instincts of animals. Instincts provided for minimum self-preservation; technology provided for the "good life." In-

---

[19]*Meditación de la técnica*, 1939, *Obras* V, p. 321.

[20]See Plato, *Crito*, 48B: "It is not living, but living well which we ought to consider most important," H. N. Fowler, trans.; and Seneca, *Epistolae Morales*, 90:1: "Who can doubt . . . but that life is the gift of the immortal gods, but that living well is the gift of philosophy," R. M. Gummere, trans.

[21]*Meditación de la técnica*, 1939, *Obras* V, p. 324.

[22]*Ibid.*, p. 328.

stincts were fixed because they were tied to the permanent biological needs of a species. Technology changed continually, not
only by progressing towards the more efficient fulfillment of set
goals, but more radically by the periodic transformation of its
basic goals, which occurred because men shaped it in accord with
the conception of the good life that they historically held. "On
the one hand the simple life, life in its biological sense, is a fixed
magnitude that is defined with each species once and for all; and
on the other, the good life, what man calls well-being, is a good
that is always moving and endlessly variable." Since man's conception of the good life varied, technology could not rigidify into
a fixed or independent pattern without becoming a check upon the
further development of human well-being. "Since the repertory
of human necessities is a function of [well-being], these turn out
to be no less variable; and since technique is the repertory of activities provoked *by*, originated *for*, and inspired *in* the system of
these necessities, it is also a protean reality that is in constant
mutation. Hence it is vain to study technique as if it is an independent entity or as if it is propelled in a single direction that can
be known beforehand."[23]

Ortega suggested that technicians reading his "Meditation
on Technique" would become uncomfortable, and well they might,
for the implications of his argument were immense. The clean,
dust-free world of laboratory facts turned into a derivative structure built upon certain historically conditioned values. Technology
ceased to appear as a thing-in-itself dependent on the laws of
nature; it was instead the repertory of means by which man tried
to create a world in which he could lead a good life, and the
particular features of the good life were continually subject to
complete change as men formulated and reformulated various
conceptions of the good. As with Plato, Ortega found the form
of the good to be the determinant principle of every feature of the
human world; and also as with Plato, Ortega found that the form
of the good was never subject to a final, fixed formulation that
would impose upon the human world of flesh and blood, of daily
life in an actual community of men, a determined set of unchang-

---

[23]*Ibid.*, p. 330.

ing features. In short, nothing was given, nothing except a completely indeterminate existence that had to be given shape by a continuous series of value judgments.

Consequently, neither the technician nor anyone else could accept a particular goal as given, for even the concerns that men called their needs depended on how they defined the good towards which they aspired. Although no living man could refrain from aspiring towards one or another conception of the good, the particular formulation of the good to which men aspired was subject to continual change. Here, as in so much of Ortega's thought, the Platonic conception of Eros was important. According to Socrates, the potency of love came from an awareness of not having that which we desired, which meant that technique, man's genius for creation, would not be static. Aspirations were never satisfied, for with every achievement, Eros, man's creative drive, would transfer its effort to some further possibility. Whenever a desired goal was fulfilled, it had to be replaced by another, more excellent object of man's spiritual eroticism. Hence, the happy fulfillment of one's ability to achieve established purposes is never enough; mere fulfillment is rather the mark of decline, for virile man, true man, would want to respond to new and greater purposes. Hence, the technician's satisfied confidence that the familiar needs of industrial democracy could forever provide a clean, amoral guide to European aspirations endangered the European future. Established needs were never secure. Ortega's humanism could not be more complete: "if something in man presents itself as static and immutable, this suffices for us to infer that it pertains to the part of man that is not human."[24]

Nothing "in technology," as the superstitious might say, required human development to continue along the lines charted in the recent past; and whatever direction human development took in the future would depend, as it had in the past, on the weight of the value judgments that diverse people made about the good life. On the basis of these convictions Ortega rebuked the contemporary technician for spiritual inertia. Engineers were content to be engineers; financiers to be financiers; politicians to be politicians; scholars to be scholars and not men thinking. This

---

[24]"Vives," 1940, *Obras* V, p. 495.

inertia would not maintain itself, for the success of European civilization had thrown its traditional categories into crisis; men could not treat unstable vocations as independent entities whose function and direction were already known. No necessary deeds were to be amorally performed by men who have no choice. The materialistic technology, dominant in the recent past, would probably not continue as the most important source of well-being in the near future. Ortega raised the question of the shrinking work-week: "What is the worker going to do with the enormous balance of his time, that empty ambit that remains of his life?"[25] If nothing else, the law of diminishing returns made it imprudent to expect that an ever-increasing power to purchase material goods would continue for long to be *the* standard of living.

With such reasoning Ortega called upon the specialists to open themselves to all sorts of questions about value that they habitually ignored. Technicians should not prepare to serve only the established purposes; they should entertain purpose in general, the form of the good. If the technician would recognize that his arts dealt with the realm of the superfluous, that is, with well-being and the good life, then they would have to admit that their work was based on value judgments and that it entailed moral commitments. In this way, the myth of amorality would loose force and technicians would be ready to respond to questions of value, knowing that they would want, at least to themselves, to stand by the ethical decisions that underlay their choice to work on one particular problem out of the many upon which they could spend their effort. The simplicity of the specialties was apparent rather than real; their seeming freedom from the complexity of moral uncertainty resulted from the failure to perceive the ethical sources of technical activities.

But as matters stood, specialists showed little awareness of the latent profundities in their concerns. Men of intellect rendered themselves neutral. They made technique responsive only to the established goals of material enrichment. The intellectual institutions prepared a man to do a particular job and provided him

---

[25]*Meditación de la técnica*, 1939, *Obras* V, p. 334.

with sufficient diversion to keep him functioning efficiently while he performed his deadening labor. Men of culture failed to move the technologist to ask whether the job was worth doing, and they did not provide the average specialist with the cultural capacities that he would need in order to reason about the relative worth of the various jobs that he might perform. Europe had no future in this course. At best, it would rumble on in an eternal present, forever producing more and more of the same.

In contrast, Ortega had a vision of a world in which intellect did not leave technique tied to a particular way of life, but freed it to adapt to a variety of goals, material and spiritual. By developing greater cultural sensitivity, the technician would learn not only to solve a given problem, but to select with finesse and intelligence the problem that he wanted to solve. With such an openness to potential goals, the growing tension between enthusiasts and opponents of a materialistic technology could be lessened. Ortega did not believe that technology was inherently materialistic, and he envisaged the possibility of a Europe in which technology did not serve the exclusive materialism that has become equally characteristic of both capitalism and socialism. Technique could serve spiritual goals as well as material; and if men recognized that all forms of technique had an ethical basis, they would be less inclined to suppress one form in order to meet the "needs" of another. A more manifold, variegated European way of life would arise if the technicians would free themselves from the shackles of ignorant single-mindedness, mastering the *Geisteswissenschaften* as well as the *Naturwissenschaften*.

Technological superstition was put aside by Ortega. Showing that the problem of value was an integral part of every technique, he linked in the person of the technician the power of both natural knowledge and moral knowledge. This linking opened up all manner of possibilities for the future; but to make good on these possibilities, the technician had to awaken to the fact that in his humanity both powers, the natural and the moral, were combined. Then, the technician could cultivate both sides of his character.

But one can already hear the practical planner exclaiming ironically, "Beautiful! Beautiful! But how will we implement our value judgments? How will we engineer consent to policy if we admit our policy is based merely on the vision of the good and not on some implacable necessity, some imperative expediency?"h

This question has a serious point. Ortega's position, his critique of all hypostatization, is profoundly subversive, in a spontaneous, diffused way, of the established public order. Precious little agreement now exists about what is expedient, let alone about what is good. The practical planner realizes that a minimum of agreement is essential to the implementation of any policy, and he rightly shudders at the thought of having to secure even a modicum of agreement that this or that policy goal is "good." He points out that reason, itself, is not well adapted to securing such agreement: individuals who enter the public forum raising doubts about the good often end as martyrs to a cause, and whole peoples who become obsessed by the matter lose their power to act decisively in concert. Hence, even many intellectuals believe that, owing to the limitations of reason, explicit concern with the good in public questions is unwise. Instead of harping on questions of principle, they suggest, the intellectual will accomplish most by applying his powers to improving the performance of policy with respect to important particulars.

Two caveats can be entered to this outlook. First, the view of the practical planner is not cogent unless the important public issues are ones that can be dealt with only through the implementation of agreed upon policies. Historically, however, the most significant public developments have not been either initiated or directed through explicit policies; but, quite to the contrary, the ultimate safeguard of the rights and liberties of "we, the people" has been our continual ability to maintain initiative, to steal many a march on those responsible for forming and implementing policy: in short, to act spontaneously. The historic leadership that Ortega hoped the technicians would give did not involve the rationalization of formal policy as much as a spontaneous, diverse break with established goals. In place of the obsession with formal policy, Ortega hoped that diverse men would each concentrate on his own personal self-formation, as a result of which the autonomous, informal activities of Europe would be invigorated, broadened, and deepened.

Second, the practical planner displays in his doubts a rather narrow view of reason. He shares with the technologically superstitious the belief that reason should be confined to the rational analysis of means to a given end. He receives this belief, not from the superstition that the end is really given, but from the fear that reason cannot handle the question of purpose rationally. To avoid stirring up an impossible problem, he takes up whatever purpose seems to come to the fore and concentrates on perfecting it, leaving to the mysteries of fate the task of changing purposes over time. Ortega would agree that all elites, no matter how cultured, were inherently unable to use reason to define the good for all; but such a paternal definition appeals only to the planner's mentality. Each, however, independently uses his rational intelligence to evaluate his own purposes; and Ortega saw a function for a cultured elite, not in telling each man what to think, but in stimulating each to think more incisively. The power of command, which presupposes that the few tell the many how to act, was a political power that intellectuals should avoid. The power to stimulate was a cultural power that every man could exercise by accepting moral responsibility for his acts and entering into moral discourse with his fellow men.

By 1900, many men of culture had developed a powerful rationale for not using their cultural power. They abhorred leadership, even of a protreptic sort, and sought only to serve others because they had lost faith in the rational legitimacy of purpose. They learned to conceive of man as a helpless responder to the chance stimuli of the universe. What appeared to be motives and purposes they knowingly explained to be mere rationalizations of manifold behavioral determinants. Science would soon explain these forces; and many even believed that Marx, Freud, Pavlov, and others had already revealed the essential mechanisms. With this knowledge man could merge himself with nature. He could let nature take her course and cease trying to impose his fallible will upon himself. Science would take the place of history; continuity would supplant change; natural cause would redeem the folly of human choice. Selective, cultural formation of the human animal seemed an insolent, overweening effort to resist the implacable forces of nature. Values were dangerous conceits that perverted the natural man by discouraging him from what came naturally. When the last remnant of culture was eradicated, when the last commitment to a value was renounced, then man would be released from this terrible bondage to himself. He would be freed forever to respond docilely to every law of nature. He would dutifully perform his destined part in the mute, meaningless, behavioral spectacle that the scientist so passionately sought to understand.

Here, then, was another version of amorality. This version was not dependent on the hypostatization of collective concepts; it arose instead with the simple conviction that reason could rightly work only on matters of fact and that all values were as much a matter of prejudice as were those based on myths of race, nation, or class. This view rested on the faith that man's natural urges were healthy, if not good, and that the source of human perversion and self-destruction was frustration over his inability to fulfill his natural urges. Reason, therefore, should not be wasted in futile attempts to evaluate operational purposes. It should be be set to work clearing away the frustrating impediments that stand in the way of whatever intention men happen to entertain. Only when all the infringements have been cleared away can man act in an entirely natural way, a full-fledged citizen of the objective universe.

But did such a natural, neutral object so excite the scientist's concern and solicitude? Should man make himself into a natural creature, oblivious to ethical choice, a purely responsive being for whom morality, purpose, and value are meaningless conceptions? Could man make himself into a celestial mechanism that was, itself, its own watchmaker? Ortega thought not, and he contended that the conception of reason that suggested such a possibility was inadequate.

*　　*　　*

And to these images they pray, as if one were to talk to one's house, knowing not the nature of gods and heroes.
HERACLITUS, 5

*P*HYSICO-MATHEMATICAL *reason, in its crass form of naturalism or its beatific form of spiritualism, was unable to confront human problems. By its very constitution, it could do no more than look for the nature of man. And clearly it did not find this nature because man has no nature. Man is not his body, which is a thing; nor is he his soul, psyche, conscience, or spirit, which is also a thing. Man is not a thing, but a drama, that is, his life—a pure and universal happening that happens to each one of us and in which each one, on his part, is always happening. All things, whatever they are, are ultimately mere interpretations that man exerts himself to give to whatever he encounters. Man does not encounter things; he assumes or supposes them. What he encounters are pure difficulties and pure facilities for existing. . . . To speak, then, of man's being, we need to elaborate a non-Eleatic concept of being, just as others have elaborated a non-Euclidian geometry. The time has come for the seed of Heraclitus to yield its mightly harvest.*

ORTEGA[1]

[1]"Historia como sistema," 1936, *Obras* VI, pp. 32 and 34.

XIV
The Reform of
Reason

W E HAVE WITNESSED the fruition of Baconian aspirations. Reason has become the handmaiden of nearly all our acts. We have learned to side with nature, to uncover her laws, and to enlist her power in efforts to wreak our will. The Baconian program has been tried; and in its unquestioned success, it has been found wanting. For over three hundred years reason has been used to plumb the secrets of nature's causal powers. The resultant knowledge has enabled men to manipulate once unimagined forces. The frail, thinking reed has learned to wield the most secret energies of the universe; and the consequent increase of life—and of death, as well—is worthy of awe. Thus man trembles on a precarious balance between omnipotence and extinction.

Yet man is limited. To progress in one direction a limited creature must forgo moving in other directions. Bacon understood this fact. He admonished men to accept their divine duties without insolently demanding reasons for these obligations, and he cautioned men to confine their inquiries to the manifest world of nature. In the paradise of Eden the inquisition of nature had not been forbidden. "It was not that pure and uncorrupted natural knowledge whereby Adam gave names to the creatures according to their propriety, which gave occasion to the fall. It was the ambitious and proud desire of moral knowledge to judge of good and evil, to the end that man may revolt from God and give laws to himself, which was the form and manner of the temptation."[2]

---

[2]Bacon, "The Great Instauration," in *The New Organon and Related Writings*, Fulton H. Anderson, ed., p. 15.

Here, in capsule, is naturalistic amoralism: seek the secrets of nature and let God define duty.

Since the great instauration, we have progressively empowered ourselves with more and more natural knowledge; and, without entirely suppressing the proud desire for moral knowledge, we have markedly curtailed it. Doubtless, the benefits from natural knowledge that Bacon promised have been forthcoming several times over; thus, the problem is not with the positive part of the Baconian program. Yet, the suspicion has spread: having been expelled from Eden, men are forced to judge alone, perhaps of good and evil, and surely of good and bad, of right and wrong. As Bacon said, knowledge is power. Therefore, men cannot make the neat dichotomy between science and duty; moral perplexity is not alone in perverting the paradise, for with our natural knowledge we also blight the garden as our man-made poisons perceptibly pollute both air and water. Thus, the fact is inescapable: natural knowledge has been misused. It has built bombs. It has spread poison gas. It has unleashed fires that have seared cities to ashes. If the world were Eden, we could, *perhaps,* accept the Baconian limitation, but then perhaps, too, we would have no interest in the secrets of nature. But these are idle speculations, for the world is not Eden. Consequently, the negative part of Bacon's vision is dangerous: since reason is the best tool of judgment that men have yet created, they are foolhardy to restrict it to harnessing nature's powers and to refrain from using it to improve the quality of human choice.

On its own ground, the Baconian program has been a marvelous triumph, but its ground is a defile too narrow to traverse with stability. Hence, intellect has entered into crisis, a crisis of imbalance that arose not because we have lost our knack for natural knowledge, but because we have begun to feel a palpable lack of moral knowledge. Many have noticed this imbalance, Ortega included: "a good part of the contemporary confusion stems from the incongruence between the perfection of our ideas about physical phenomena and the scandalous backwardness of the 'moral sciences.' "[3]

---

[3]"Prólogo para franceses," 1937, *Obras* IV, p. 118.

One might like to blame this backwardness on Bacon and launch into an attempt to refute the naturalist's skepticism about moral knowledge. But one should not counter the Baconian amoralist in the same way that one does the hyperconscious man. Skepticism about the capacity of reason to deal with ethical matters will not be refuted any more than Bacon refuted the scholastic's doubts about the power of reason to master natural matters. Skepticism is always irrefutable until one does the impossible, or what seems impossible according to the skeptic's dogmas. Sensing this situation, an increasing number of thinkers have taken up the effort to balance the sciences of nature with equally effective sciences of the spirit.

Die Geisteswissenschaften have consequently preoccupied recent European thinkers. In their critique of historical reason—that is, in their effort to clarify the foundations of the human sciences, the system of reason by which we make practical, vital decisions —the *Geisteswissenschaftlers'* problem was not simply to lay an epistemological foundation for the study and pursuit of the arts; the real problem, as Vico had perceived, was to create a program for *l'esprit de finesse* as powerful as the one Bacon had conceived of for *l'esprit géometrique*. Vico failed.[a] But he did indicate the nature of the task: Bacon's crude conception of scientific methodology had not made his work so influential; rather his inspired understanding of the potential power to be gained through the application of scientific knowledge to the physical problems of man won him his followers. If the human sciences are to balance the natural adequately, the former need to harbor similar power, which will prove equally productive when applied to the spiritual problems of man. This condition is a large order.

Talk of applicable power in the moral sciences conjures up visions of the Inquisition and all sorts of prudish paternalisms. These visions result from our dangerously dull conceptions of application. To be applied productively, knowledge need not be applied programmatically. Serious students of the human sciences have not envisioned discovering the laws of moral behavior, nor have they contemplated promulgating a rule to which all must conform. Such intentions would run counter to the most fundamental element of the scientific view: respect for the phenomena one studies. Moral behavior is inwardly determined behavior, and any undertaking that entails the subjection of moral behavior to outwardly determined, objective rules or norms is unscientific in the most egregious manner possible. Hence, the first step in developing the moral sciences is to break away from the expectation that has seriously vitiated the social sciences, namely, the expectation that discovery of the laws of human behavior should permit the manipulation of men in the same way that the discovery of the laws of natural behavior permits the productive manipulation of natural phenomena.

Powerful application is essential to the human sciences, but slavish emulation of the applications typifying the natural sciences is to be avoided. Recognizing this condition, Wilhelm Dilthey and others of his time attributed the potential power of the human sciences to indirect action, to the fact that by occasioning, not causing, the enrichment of man's cultural, inner life, one indirectly but decisively influenced man's external, public achievements. Natural science gained power when men gave up the hopeless effort to make nature act as one or another man believed it should. The human sciences would likewise gain power when, through a seeming restriction, men gave up the arrogant attempt to make others act according to the rule that one or another man deemed proper. Instead, by means of a yet newer organon, students of the human sciences hoped to make available to each person a system of reasoning by which each could more effectively initiate and carry through significant moral acts in the community of men.

Theorists had thus found that the power inherent in the human sciences differed from that in the natural sciences. From the latter, the scientist learned to manipulate the world around him; from the former, the scientist would learn to control the world within himself. In this sense, the power of the moral sciences was pedagogical, not mechanical. Rather than subject others, treated as objects, to causally necessary manipulations, the human sciences would help a man judge what ideals were worth his personal effort and would help him learn how to bring his actual accomplishments to a more adequate realization of the goals he willed. Count Yorck made the distinction well when he exclaimed to his friend Dilthey: "the reproach is entered against us that we do not make good use of natural science! To be sure, presently the sole justification of all science is that it makes practice possible. But mathematical praxis is not the only one. From our standpoint, the practical aim is pedagogical in its widest and deepest sense. It is the soul of all real philosophy and the truth of Plato and Aristotle."[4]

Ortega was acutely aware that through pedagogical application the human sciences could exert immense power; and this power would be of Platonic, not Machiavellian quality. The point was not to gain and keep office; the point was to clarify the character of reason in such a way that the disciplined rationality of every man would prove more educative in his personal life. Each man lives a life of emotion and thought, wondrous perplexities, stirring aspirations, and heroic actions; every man perceives himself as the central figure in an intense and fascinating drama. Reason does not directly affect this human world by subjecting the diverse, innumerable, integral personalities to a single mold, breaking each man apart and recombining the abstract fragments as norms labeled Economic Man, Political Man, Behavioral Man, and so on. Quite the contrary, reason becomes significant in the human world as each man finds it valuable in living his personal drama; and Ortega believed that certain reforms in reason would make it a more vital tool to each man. If this were so, qualitative improvements in man's powers of self-liberation would be won, and in the aggregate these would amount to a great historic development. "Imagine for a moment that each of us takes care of himself just a little bit more every hour of every day, that he requires of himself a little more presence and intensity; and, multiplying all these minimum perfectionings and invigorations of each life by the others, calculate the gigantic enrichment, the fabulous ennobling that the human community would share."[5]

To have such effects, the reform of reason that Ortega envisaged would have to be more than an academic reform of reason. It was nice, perhaps, to perform before one's colleagues, to spin

---

[4]Count Yorck to Wilhelm Dilthey, June, 1884, in Dilthey, *Briefwechsel*, pp. 41-2.

[5]*¿Qué es filosofía?*, 1929, 1957, *Obras* VII, p. 436.

glorious paradoxes while the world worried and warred. But a real reform of reason had to occur somewhere outside of unread reviews. Here again we meet the impulse that turns systematic philosophy out into the community. Recall Nietzsche's dictum: "I judge a philosopher by whether he is able to serve as an example."[6] Because we judge philosophers by their ability to serve as examples we treat Nietzsche with caution, knowing that for some he served as a bad example. Philosophy does not justify itself by its ability to erect hydroelectric dams or to organize, arm, and deploy grand armies; philosophy proves itself by its ability to educate. For Ortega, the philosopher's function was to exemplify to men how they could gain a better theoretical understanding and surer practical command of the lives they lived. This real reform of reason had to prove itself by helping every man to educate himself with more effect.

An effort to reshape reason by developing the human sciences carried with it certain serious doubts: the conception of reason propagated by the natural sciences was inadequate. We have touched on the character of these doubts, on the concern that progress in naturalistic knowledge needed to be balanced by progress in moral understanding; but we should notice, too, the very fact of the doubts, the fact that men question the established character of reason. To many persons, to question the adequacy of reason and to seek to reform it seems dangerous.

Many who are quick to scorn faculty psychology still think of human rationality as a natural faculty, one that is fixed and unchanging, a part of man's necessary psychological make-up. As a result, they view a criticism of man's rational power as an attack on reason, as a diatribe against this power that is what it is and that cannot be anything else. Hence, they easily misunderstand an attempt to reshape reason; they view the attempt to reform reason as an effort to reject reason. Thus, Nietzsche, a thinker who was profoundly concerned for the future of reason, is still roundly condemned as an irrationalist because he tried to reform the reigning conception of reason.[b] Nietzsche the man was

---

[6]Nietzsche, *Schopenhauer as Educator*, Hillesheim and Simpson, trans., p. 18.

not always rational, but his philosophic undertaking was, both in conception and execution. Yet those who believe that the nature of reason has been fixed forever can find in his efforts only a destructive attack on reason. Likewise, a critic committed to a static conception of reason will find Ortega's reflections on the human sciences, on historic reason, to be an attempt to deny and negate reason. Hence, one of the thought-clichés that has attached itself to Ortega's work is the belief that he was an irrationalist.

Several writers have taken Ortega to task on this point, usually for remarks he made in *The Theme of Our Time,* a book that was so susceptible to accusations of irrationalism that Ortega wrote an article to debunk such interpretations. But the stigma of irrationalism in the work of Ortega and his peers goes deeper than the misinterpretation of a single book. Contemporary European philosophers have indeed mounted a thorough attack on rational-*ism* and its narrow idea of reason derived from the natural sciences. Both friend and foe alike have popularized these criticisms as a defense of the irrational and as an attack on man's aspiration to lead a reasoned life. Such assessments miss the point entirely: by setting up an opposition between the rational and the irrational, one polarizes the problem and diminishes the opportunity to reform reason. The whole purpose of attacking rationalism was to defend reason from its own excesses.

Failure to do justice to this point has been most serious among the friends of the reformers. For instance, in *Irrational Man* William Barrett sympathetically explained existential philosophy, including in it a bit of Ortega's work. But he dramatically overemphasized the discontinuity between contemporary thought and the philosophic heritage; as a result, a great work of reason was degraded, especially for readers not well acquainted with that heritage, into a willful assertion of unreason. The popularizer's purpose should not be to convey the mood, especially the demonic pose of certain existential thinkers; his purpose should be to impart the conceptual powers that will enable men to profit from the reform and to reason more effectively about all aspects of their lives. This purpose is not well served by dwelling on the dramatic achievements of Kierkegaard and Nietzsche and passing lightly over the important but difficult contributions of the pre-Socratics,

Plato, Aristotle, Descartes, Spinoza, Leibniz, and especially Kant, Hegel, Dilthey, and Husserl.[7]

Barrett left an erroneous impression: that contemporary European philosophers had tried to restrict the reign of reason by showing that the irrational is as authentically human as the rational. This interpretation leaves intact the static view of rationality; both the rational and the irrational seem to be primary qualities, twin ghosts locked disharmoniously in a machine. But instead of merely balancing a fixed rationality with an equally fixed irrationality, existential thinkers have subjected reason to a decisive reformation. Viewing reason not as a primary quality, but as a secondary characteristic, and locating it not within the realm of necessity, but within the sphere of freedom, contemporary thinkers have greatly widened the scope of reason. In doing so, they preserved the rationalistic tradition, not as the whole of reason, but still as an essential element; they challenged men, not to give license to irrational impulse, but to live by a far more complete and exacting regimen of disciplined intelligence.

Contemporary thinkers contended that rationalism had created irrationalism by basing reason on a too narrow, yet absolute, foundation. By finding reason to be a freely formed attribute of the human person, rather than a necessary quality of some self-subsistent reality, material or spiritual, contemporary ontologists have freed men to make reason encompass all the phenomena that rationalists had rejected as irrational. As Ortega put it, the reform "will carry us, by a few steps, to dealing face-to-face with a future reason, one that is most distant from the venerable pure reason and that is nevertheless the exact opposite of vagueness, metaphors, utopias, and mysticisms. A reason, therefore, much more reasonable than the old, one from which 'pure reason' appears as an enchanting folly, and in addition, one for which many things will cease to be irrational that formerly suffered this pejorative qualification. . . . Historic reason, disposed to swallow reality without nausea, prudery, or scruples, will regulate it by bringing

---

[7]See William Barrett, *Irrational Man*, pp. 149-205, for the treatment of Kierkegaard and Nietzsche. Compare this with the brief mention of Husserl and no mention of Dilthey.

within the reach of rationality chance itself, that demon of the irrational and the *ci-devant* enemy of history."[8] The upshot of this reform was to encourage standards of character and conduct antithetical to irrationalist license.

The reform of reason wrought in the development of the human sciences was a real re-*forming* of reason. As has been noted, those who still view reason as an inborn, natural faculty recoil at this effort, for if reason is to be re-*formed*, reason must be a cultural artifact developed through certain historic acts. Few have studied reason in this historical manner; and the limits of our historic awareness are indicated by the fact that we have innumerable histories of science, art, literature, and philosophy, but none of reason itself. Yet reason has a history;[c] for the neo-Hegelian, reason even is history. Ortega did not go that far. But, deeply influenced by historicism, especially by the historicism of Dilthey, Ortega inverted the Hegelian position: "far from history being 'rational', it happens that reason itself, authentic reason, is historical."[9] Reason was historically conditioned, not simply in the fact that the problems to which reason was applied at any particular time were historic problems, but more fundamentally in that the character of reason itself was conditioned by its development in history. To reform reason, one first examined its formative history in a search for alternative paths of development that might be pursued. Ortega was not the only twentieth-century ontologist to find that, on going back to the history of reason, Heraclitus offered a different possibility that merited pursuit.

In musing on its history, let us not hypostatize reason: reason is our name for a human activity, for a particular mode of thinking. Reason, consequently, is not a thing, but an action: that old, invidious distinction between action and contemplation does not hold, for contemplation is itself simply a form of action. By reason we mean true thinking, thinking that gives rise to knowledge as distinct from opinion, that puts us in touch with reality rather than mere appearances.

---

[8]*Origen y epílogo de la filosofía*, 1943, 1960, *Obras* IX, p. 392.
[9]*Ibid.*, pp. 366fn.

Metaphor, however, muddies our conception of reason, and it leads to confusion to say that reason "puts us in touch with" reality. This phrase is an untechnical description of the correspondence theory of truth, which is essential to working out the form of thinking called reason. An effort in recent years to do away with this theory has had some success, for there are serious difficulties with the conception that reason gives rise to propositions that correspond to reality: my idea of the mountain obviously does not physically correspond to the mountain itself. But criticism of the correspondence theory has been misdirected, for the most part, because the concept of correspondence has been made to seem far too vulnerable by loose metaphors such as "puts us in touch with." Kant's ontological arguments undercut any such palpable correspondence; but that is not the end of the matter: correspondence is not the definitive term in the whole theory, for what we mean by a proposition corresponding to reality depends entirely on what we take reality to be.

To deny categorically the possibility of correspondence is to deny the possibility of reason, which is thinking disciplined by an ideal of thinking in accord with reality, whatever that may be. Men form reason by aspiring to think according to a definite regimen, a regimen of thinking thoughts that correspond to reality. Unless men aspire to this ideal, the distinction between truth and opinion breaks down by becoming arbitrary. Consequently, before dispensing with the theory of correspondence, men should reflect on what they consider reality to be.

Speculative ontology precedes a critical epistemology. Thus, Kantian epistemology can prove the impossibility of thinking in correspondence with the reality of dogmatic metaphysics, but it cannot preclude the possibility of reasoning in accord with a reality yet to be defined by a different metaphysics. Nicolas Berdyaev put the matter well: through epistemology "one cannot arrive at being—one can only start with it."[10]

By starting with being, men could invent reason. That is, men formed reason, a disciplined mode of thinking, as they asserted the existence of a reality, distinct from appearance, and postulated

---

[10]Berdyaev, *The Destiny of Man*, Natalie Duddington, trans., p. 1.

the possibility of thinking in accord with this reality rather than with the appearances encountered by undisciplined perception. At first this formulation may offend, for it makes man responsible for what many believe is the gift of either God or Nature. The offense might be lessened, however, by observing that many such intellectual inventions are well documented in the history of art and science. Mathematics is an exploration of the operations made possible through the assertion of certain axioms, and it is not offensive to say that men have invented their powers of mathematical reasoning. In the same way, Galileo invented the science of mechanics when he projected freely in the realm of thought certain ideal forms: "imagine any particle projected along a horizontal plane without friction. . . ."[11] So too, someone invented reason when he intuited the possibility of true discourse, of thought that corresponded to a definite, unchanging reality. Imagine, he might have said, a reality that does not change continually as do the appearances we experience through our senses and emotions: seek always to speak in accord with that honest reality. From that time on it was open to men to accept freely the discipline of the rational ideal, using, as with the science of mechanics, a rather implausible set of postulates to anticipate and direct experience.

Ortega contended that in originating philosophy men followed precisely this procedure. "When one says that philosophy is a searching for Being, one understands that it is going to proceed by discovering the constitutive attributes of Being or of the entity. But this implies that one already has Being before one. How did it manage to be before the senses? Would it not seem more credible that men, having lost the fundamental principles of their life, inquired for some X that would have certain *prior* attributes— precisely those that would justify what they were seeking?"[12] In the early moments of philosophy, two sets of attributes for

---

[11]Galileo, *Dialogues Concerning Two New Sciences*, Crew and de Salvo, trans., p. 244.

[12]*Origen y epílogo de la filosofía*, 1943, 1960, *Obras* IX, p. 434. This is the final statement in an unfinished, unpolished work, one that is important yet difficult to use. Its parts were composed over a period of ten years. Although in conception the work is a book, in execution it is, as it stands, a series of fragments.

that mysterious X were put forward, one by Heraclitus and another by Parmenides. Ortega believed that philosophy began with these two men, and in his unfinished work on *The Origin of Philosophy* he treated them together in analyzing the historic situation with which both grappled. But in the parts of the work available, Ortega did not dwell on their respective doctrines, except to connect Parmenides with the doctrine of Being that Ortega wanted to reject.[13] We know from other references that Ortega identified Heraclitus with the doctrine he wanted to develop. "After twenty-five centuries of intellectual experience we find ourselves forced to abandon interpretations of reality as substance, and we are picking our brains to see if we can acknowledge . . . that all reality . . . is the contrary, is the deficient being, the indigent being that does not suffice for itself, that is deficient and that nevertheless is. The matter seems acrobatically paradoxical and ultradifficult to understand, for our mental habits since the birth of the European nations have been formed with the ferule of Greek discipline, and the Greeks, excepting Heraclitus, thought the contrary: they thought, with one or another accent, that reality is the sufficient being, the substantial being."[14]

Heraclitus first stated explicitly the correspondence theory: "although this Logos is eternally valid, yet men are unable to understand it—not only before hearing it, but even after they have heard it for the first time. That is to say, although all things come to pass in accordance with this Logos, men seem to be quite without any experience of it. . . ."[15] Heraclitus here asserted the principle of the principle, of an eternally valid concept in accord with which all came to pass; and this principle, this Word or Logos, was the reality to which reason should correspond. The basic ideal of reason was implicit through all of Heraclitus' fragments. There was in the endless flux of appearances a valid, unchanging coherence, a reality that might be known: "this universe, which is the same for all, has not been made by any god or man, but

---

[13]*Ibid.*, p. 384, for philosophy beginning with Parmenides and Heraclitus. *Ibid.*, pp. 399-412, for his discussion of them. *Ibid.*, pp. 433-4 for his identification of Parmenides with Being.

[14]*Una interpretación de la historia universal*, 1949, 1960, *Obras* IX, p. 212.

[15]Heraclitus, Fragment 1 (DK), Wheelwright, trans., *Heraclitus*, Fr. 1, p. 19.

it always has been, is, and will be—an ever-living fire, kindling itself by regular measures and going out by regular measures."[16] In this fragment, as in many others, Heraclitus made an effort to suggest, with oracular reserve, the nature of the reality that gave reason, the Logos, its cogency; only in correspondence with that reality, which was the same for all, could truth be found by men, for "human nature has no real understanding; only the divine nature has it," and "man is not rational; only what encompasses him is intelligent.[17]

Soon men began to call Heraclitus "the obscure," and for good reason: he was not exactly explicit about what the intelligent encompassing was. This obscurity is not necessarily a sign of weakness: the idea of reality permits the invention of reason not because the reality is perfectly known and absolutely clear, but because the idea allows us to aspire systematically, and perhaps confusingly, to perfect knowledge and absolute clarity. For the sake of the search, Heraclitus seems to have been intentionally obscure about the one, the divine Logos, for "the Sibyl with raving mouth utters solemn, unadorned, unlovely words, but she reaches out over a thousand years with her voice because of the god in her."[18] Almost immediately his raving voice began to show its reach as Parmenides took up the effort to define more clearly the reality that might give rise to right reason.d

"Come," Parmenides invited, "I will tell you—and you must accept my word when you have heard it—the ways of inquiry which alone are to be thought. . . ." Note that Parmenides is here striving for rigorous argumentation, for words that one must accept on having heard them; this cogency is an important feature of the system of thinking, that is reason, or the way of truth as Parmenides called it. Parmenides continued to make the great distinction between the two basic ways of inquiry: "the one that IT IS, and it is not possible for IT NOT TO BE, is the way of credibility, for it follows Truth; the other, that IT IS NOT, and

---

[16]Heraclitus, Fragment 30 (DK), Wheelwright, trans., *Ibid.*, Fr. 29, p. 37.

[17]Heraclitus, Fragments 61 and 62 (W), Wheelwright, trans., *Heraclitus*, p. 68. The authenticity of Fragment 62 is contested by some scholars; Fr. 61 is Fr. 78 (DK); Diels did not include Fr. 62.

[18]Heraclitus, Fragment 92 (DK), Wheelwright, trans., *Heraclitus*, Fr. 79, p. 69.

that IT is bound NOT TO BE: this I tell you is a path that cannot be explored; for you could neither recognise that which IS NOT, nor express it."[19] This passage at first seems far more obscure than any by Heraclitus; but, once one overcomes the archaic stiffness of the formulation, it is a rather rigorous statement of the correspondence theory of truth: true thinking must be in accord with Reality, that which is what it is and which does not change, whereas deceptive thinking is in accord with that which is not what it is, for this appearance yields no measure by which its actuality can be tested or articulated. To put it another way, one can have confidence in the results of thinking only if what one thinks about is a reality that in itself is stable and unchanging, for if what one thinks about is mere, volatile appearance, the most rigorous investigation will yield results that become untrue the instant the appearance changes. And, furthermore, only by postulating the stable, unchanging reality can we even recognize and express definite changes in appearance.

Here Parmenides went a long way towards linking the way of truth to reality and towards making this link differentiate reason from appearance. Parmenides went so far, in fact, that he verged on absolute idealism: "that which it is possible to think is identical with that which can Be."[20] With this conviction, Parmenides proceeded, as philosophers have ever since, to reflect on what it is that has Being, real and absolute existence, and to deduce from the properties of this Being certain standards of cogent reasoning. If it were not for his follower Zeno, these deductions might have prompted men to call Parmenides the paradoxical, for in spite of obvious appearances, he held that reality, Being, was one, an unchanging, homogeneous whole that included everything and that was eternal.

Parmenides seemed to have postulated an impossible conception of reality, for superficially it contradicted the most common phenomena, those of change and differentiation. But, in keeping with Berdyaev's dictum, this conception of reality quickly became

---

[19]Parmenides, Fragment 2, Freeman, trans., *Ancilla*, p. 42.

[20]Parmenides, Fragment 3, Freeman, trans., *Ancilla*, p. 42, fn. 2, variant reading.

immensely fruitful for epistemology, and it is still a vital force in the history of reason. Thinkers soon freed themselves of the particular image of reality that Parmenides depicted, the image of a single, solid, unchanging, eternal sphere; but the criteria that Parmenides set forth as indicative of that-which-is have remained in force with minor adjustments until recent times. These criteria called for a finite, unchanging substance that was unified and universal. Reason was thinking that could claim to give rise to truth, to knowledge, because it told about being, about that which is, was, and ever will be, about that which met the criteria of reality, for only propositions about things that met these criteria would prove dependable: all others might be upset by a capricious change in their referents.

Unless reason corresponded to a finite, unchanging substance that was unified and universal, its results would be undependable: if not finite, it could not be wholly known; if not unchanging, today's opinions would not be dependable tomorrow; if not universal, opinions that are here true might be false there; and if not unified, opinions would concern arbitrary compounds that would hold only for those inclined to make the same grouping. Such criteria are still very much in force, for the contemporary sicentist who might observe with Heraclitus that nature likes to hide, must also agree with Parmenides that nature is not capricious, or else the whole fabric of reason loses its continuity and tears apart.

Reason has developed historically as certain men further elaborated on the reality to which it corresponded and as many others learned to use the mental discipline the few thus created. Parmenides' image of the universe, of absolute reality, was inconsistent, as we noted, with almost all experience; and his immediate followers, especially the atomists in one direction and Plato in another, worked hard to save the phenomena without departing from the way of truth that Parmenides sketched out. The atomists observed that many of Parmenides' difficulties could be avoided if, instead of there being only one One, there were many, each a unified, homogeneous whole, an atom. The dynamic, changing, sensible universe could then be built up as the innumerable atoms cohered according to regular principles. Plato tried to save the phenomena in a different way: he etherealized Parmenides' image of reality, attempting to divest it of any sensible features. The One was a pure principle, a Form, that was universal, eternal, and unchanging; and our dynamic, sensible surroundings were simply imperfect reflections of this perfect Form.

Both elaborations on Parmenides have made fruitful contributions in the history of reason; many of the Platonic ones are essential to this work. For the present argument, however, it is most convenient and sound to concentrate on Aristotle's great synthesis of his predecessor's metaphysical speculations. Heraclitus, Socrates, and Plato (presuming a non-Aristotelian interpretation) may not have thought of reality as something out there in the surrounding universe. The great tradition, however, has only recently come to a realization of this possibility, for Aristotle's synthesis has dominated reflection on the subject. Ortega intended to reform reason first by rejecting Aristotelian metaphysics and the conception of reason founded on its definition of Being and then by basing a new conception of reason on a new specification of reality.

For Aristotle, metaphysics was the study of Being *qua* Being, and it was the highest of all the speculative sciences (*Metaphysics: IV, i; I, i–ii*). Here Aristotle planted himself firmly in the tradition that developed from Parmenides: Knowledge must correspond to reality, to Being, and the study of Being is the study from which all standards of rationality ultimately follow. The Parmenidean conception of reality had already been considerably elaborated by the time Aristotle wrote; and instead of Parmenides' rather stiff IT IS, Aristotle dealt with the same concern under the much more familiar heading of "substance." With this concept Aristotle was able to reunite, by reasoning too involved to trace here, the two basic elaborations of Parmenides: the materialistic and the idealistic. There were two kinds of substance, Aristotle contended, the sensible and the immutable. Sensible substance was subject to change and consisted in matter; immutable substance did not change, for it was the unmoved mover whose necessity we could deduce, whose works we could observe, but whose presence we could not palpably sense. Aristotle's influence has been immense. With varying emphasis, first on immutable substance and then on sensible substance, the discipline of reason recognized in the West from then until recent times largely received its authority by virtue of its claim to yielding propositions that corresponded to substances as set forth by Aristotle.

Throughout our past, both body and spirit have been conceived of as real substances: bodies have been thought of as material things and spirits as immaterial things. In philosophic literature, the term substance was frequently denoted *res*, thing or entity, but in any case this *res* could be either material or spiritual. Thus there was a *res extensa* and a *res cogitans*, and the function of reason with respect to both was to give rise to truths that corresponded to these two forms of reality. Over the centuries, investigations into the *res extensa* produced our vast system of natural science, and inquiry into *res cogitans* led to considerable development of the deductive and theological sciences. Metaphysical controversy remained, until about 1800, within the Aristotelian boundaries with champions of sensible substance on the one hand and immutable substance on the other arguing that their favored reality was the one true one.

About 1800, Kant decisively overturned this tradition by developing a critical epistemology that encompassed dogmatic ontology entirely within a system of ideas. Because Kant worked out his position in reply to professed skeptics and because he had every intention of providing a firm basis for reason, certain consequences of his critique of reason were slow in becoming apparent. Kant severed the relation between reason and reality, an act that at first seemed to be a convenient way of escaping difficulties such as those raised by Hume about causality. In making this break, Kant simply carried to a logical conclusion a trend that had begun with Descartes, which had seemed quite benign because thinkers had lost sight of the primacy of ontology over epistemology. Kant did away with traditional ontology. Reason could, after Kant, claim no link to things-in-themselves; and the category of substance, which for Aristotle was the one category that "*is* primarily, not in a qualified sense but absolutely,"[21] became for Kant a mere conceptual category, one that could be said to exist only by virtue

---

[21]Aristotle, *Metaphysics*, VII, i, 5, Hugh Tredennick, trans.

of our thinking it. He stated the conclusion clearly: "the concepts of reality, substance, causality, even that of necessity in existence, apart from their use in making possible the empirical knowledge of an object, have no meaning whatsoever, such as might serve to determine any object."[22]

In *Leibniz's Idea of the Principle* Ortega showed in some detail the flaw in Aristotle's metaphysical speculations.[23] In Book IV of the *Metaphysics* Aristotle first used the actuality of substance to prove the law of contradiction, that a thing cannot both be and not be at the same time. Then a few chapters later Aristotle used this law to prove the necessary existence of substance. Because of this circular reasoning, Aristotle did not actually offer an ontology; he created instead a speculative rationalism that postulated a reality dependent on the accepted laws of thought. Parmenides' proposition—"that which it is possible to think is identical with that which can Be"—was turned around unwittingly —"that which can Be is identical with that which it is possible to think." Being became more and more dependent on thought and epistemology became more and more prominent in comparison to ontology.

As Ortega observed in his lectures on *What Is Philosophy?*, the transmutation of post-Aristotelian metaphysics into the epistemology of critical idealism began in earnest with Descartes. The legislative reason, which was at work surreptitiously in Aristotle, became explicit with Descartes. Starting with systematic doubt, Descartes used his famous *cogito* to establish, it seemed, an indubitable relationship between his thought and absolute reality. Descartes believed that "I think, therefore I am" assured man of his own existence as a *res cogitans;* and from this unquestionable example of *res,* of a substance, he assured himself of the absolute existence of both the spiritual and material universe. Descartes, like Aristotle, was unaware of the degree to which he had made reality dependent on reason rather than the other way around; or more precisely, as a rationalist convinced that reason

---

[22]Kant, *Critique of Pure Reason*, I, Pt. 2, Div. 2, Appendix, A677:B705; Norman Kemp Smith, trans.

[23]*La idea de principio en Leibniz*, 1947, 1958, *Obras* VIII, pp. 155-213, esp., p. 195.

was a necessary attribute of reality and not the creation of the human mind, Descartes saw no danger in grounding a theory of reality in the laws of thought.

Leibniz, Ortega noted, began to make explicit the idealistic implications of Descartes' theorem by restating it as *sum cogitans*, "I exist as thinking," adding that many things are thought by me. With this statment, what seemed to be an ontological argument was perilously close to an epistemological one. Kant completed the idealization of the *cogito* by showing in the Transcendental Doctrine of Elements in his *Critique of Pure Reason* how we construct a vast phenomenal reality by means of the laws of disciplined thought. Strictly, the Cartesian *cogito* meant, "I think, therefore I perceive myself as existing"; and Kant went on to demonstrate that no proposition could inform us about things-in-themselves, be they material or spiritual. In doing so, Kant created the problem of contemporary ontology, not by his invalidation of traditional ontological arguments, but by his having locked reason in a purely phenomenal realm. Thus Ortega noted that "the tragedy of idealism results from its having alchemically transmuted the world into 'subject,' into the content of a subject, enclosing the world inside of it; and then there was no way left to explain why this [world] appears so completely distinct from me if it is only my image and a fragment of me."[24]

Kant offered a taxing discipline for the three major modes of reason that had been developed, the scientific, moral, and esthetic. This discipline, plus the rigor of his arguments, obscured the fact that Kant withdrew from reason its fundamental claim, namely that its propositions corresponded to reality. Kant showed that all conceptions of a transcendent, substantive reality, of an actuality that existed apart from its manifestations in experience, were in fact transcendental ideals, mere conceptions that told us nothing about reality in itself, but that were used *as if* they did in order to establish intellectual standards.[e] Kant knelled the death of the correspondence theory insofar as it pertained to substances, *res*, *ens*, entities, bodies, to any reality out there somewhere.

Kant's personal discipline was strongly internalized, which

[24]*¿Qué es filosofía?*, 1929, 1957, *Obras* VII, p. 403.

may account for the fact that he made no provision in his system for the external authority of reason. Recall how carefully Parmenides had devised a way of speaking that "you must accept . . . when you have heard it," for he had experienced the same capriciousness that had led Heraclitus to complain that men ignored reason even when they came in contact with its teachings. The whole import of the correspondence theory was to make reason something that men must accept on hearing it because it articulated a truth dependent not on the whims of human imagination but on the rationality of the encompassing, of reality itself. In breaking with this tradition, Kant's transcendental ideal gave rise to a system of reason far more elaborate than that of the ancients, but Kant's pure reason was voluntary. Kant asked how various forms of reason were *possible,* and he brilliantly worked out the conditions of their possibility. But whether these possibilities would ever become actual, he left to the free choice of man. The romantic movement quickly showed that other men might choose to discipline their imaginations in ways that differed from the rationalistic rigor that Kant chose.

Many, however, stayed within the Kantian path, relying on reason, not emotion, to deal with human concerns. In natural science the transcendental ideal worked magnificently, so well in fact that many scientists still believe that empirical methods give them a positive knowledge of objective reality and not of a phenomenal world. For other scientists, the Kantian critical method, not his particular results, proved most liberating, for it opened the way to new forms of geometry, logic, and mathematics. Whole new worlds were brought into existence by postulating categories whose possibility did not occur to Kant.

In these matters, the transcendental ideal worked so well because the scientist, who might be very interested in his findings and their significance for him, was nevertheless disinterested with respect to the phenomena he studied. This disinterestedness was not the case in the other areas of inquiry—politics, economics, ethics, esthetics, value theory, and so on—where the transcendental ideal proved less effective. For this reason, philosophers who are primarily interested in natural science and its limitations are still usually content to live with Kant's ontological skepticism, whereas philosophers working in the human sciences feel that refurbishing the correspondence theory is important.

In intensely human concerns, with respect to which the observer can only feign disinterestedness, the trancendental ideal has been inadequate. A human standard justified by an absolute reality had an authority that seemed ineluctable; and its prestige, its correspondence to actuality, helped in the important but difficult matter of inspiring men to subordinate their interests to their principles. But a standard based simply on a transcendental ideal, and on nothing more substantial, easily seemed, in difficult situations, to be merely optional, depending on the convenience of the moment; and this lack of prestige, this correspondence to a mere concept, made it more easy for men to subordinate their principles to their interests. Marx tried to salvage this situation with a leap of faith. He accepted systematically the subordination of principles to interests and placed all hope in the ultimate benevolence of history: if conflicting interests are allowed ruthlessly to consume one another, a time will arrive when men will no longer need interests, and principles will be free to flourish. But history may not be benevolent, unless in making it men guide themselves by the principle of benevolence.

Schopenhauer soon began to grapple with the practical effects of idealistic subjectivism by going beyond Kant. Schopenhauer saw clearly that men would not resist their egoistic urges unless they belived that morality had an equally palpable foundation. "If, therefore, we take the matter seriously, artificial concept-combinations of [the Kantian] kind can never contain the true incentive to justice and philanthropy. On the contrary, such an incentive must be something that requires little reflection and even less abstraction and combination; something that, independently of the formation of the intellect, speaks to every man, even the coarsest and crudest; something resting merely on intuitive apprehension and forcing itself immediately on us out of the reality of things."[25] This something, Schopenhauer held, was compassion, which was the root feeling from which the two great moral virtues, justice and loving-kindness, were derived.

---

[25]Schopenhauer, *On the Basis of Morality*, III, #12, E.F.J. Payne, trans.

Schopenhauer's treatise was refused the prize for which it was submitted. The Royal Danish Society for Scientific Studies could not "pass over in silence the fact that several distinguished philosophers of recent times are mentioned in a manner so unseemly as to cause just and grave offense."[26] But in addition the judges had a more substantive point. Schopenhauer wrote an erudite philosophical criticism and a profound essay on the psychological basis of moral feeling. But the metaphysical section was relegated to an appendix and was not a good example of Schopenhauer's metaphysical abilities. In effect, he showed that, given compassion, one could derive the moral virtues from it; but he did not show that compassion transcended Arthur Schopenhauer and was an ineluctable feature, not only of his perception of reality, but of an absolute reality confronting all men.

Many other philosophers took up the problem of re-establishing a link between moral reasoning and reality so that principles might maintain their prestige. Any adequate discussion of the recent history of reason would have to follow closely the contributions of Nietzsche, Dilthey, Brentano, Bergson, to mention only a few. None was wholly successful, and the problem is still very much a problem of man, not merely one of philosophy. Ortega put the difficulty well and his theory of historic reason was an attempt to deal with it. To this theory we shall shortly turn.

Ortega joined Nietzsche in attempting a transvaluation of values, for such a transvaluation seemed the most desirable response to the profound nihilism that arose as numerous shocks to the authority of reason, particularly the Kantian criticisms, slowly worked their way into the European's consciousness. We might sum up, in the Aristotelian terminology, which we shall soon try to shed, Ortega's view of twentieth-century life: the formal cause or the ultimate reason why the characteristic problems of the time had arisen was the Kantian critique, the material cause or substrate in which the problems manifested themselves was the revolt of the masses, the efficient cause or the source of shaped change in contemporary affairs was the reform of reason,

---

[26]"Judicium Regiae Danicae Scientiarium Societas," in *Ibid.*, p. 216.

and the final cause or purpose, the goal, of these developments was an exuberant Europe. We have looked at some detail at the material and final causes of the second voyage, at the revolt of the masses and a sportive Europe. The formal and efficient causes were for Ortega closely linked, for the reform of reason followed out of the Kantian critique and its aftermath.

When men were left with a mere ideal and when they ceased to discipline their character by contrasting it to a transcendent actuality, their arbitrary will became the motive force of human affairs. In 1933, in trying to determine "What's Happening in the World," Ortega suggested that the collapse of reason as an effective, legitimate authority was the spiritual source of the major upheavals in twentieth-century life, the source of the new art, the glorification of sport and the body, the cult of youth, and the politics of direct action, especially Fascism. The reasoned traditions of the past were simply being ignored, for, having learned about philosophy without learning to philosophize, youths felt no compunctions making them take reason seriously. Belief in naturalistic reason lost its power when it ceased to be buttressed by a transcendent authority, when it lost its claim to correspond to a substantive reality. In the absence of an alternative, people based their actions on their arbitrary will, for to the untutored the will seemed far more immediate and solid, more real, than did obtuse mental images. "The politics of today means that the new generations do not want to be reasonable, not because they have no reason, but because they do not want to heed their reason even if they have it. They do not want an idea of things, but the things themselves. They do not value those who think, but those who will. In essence, they prefer volition to intellect."[27]

Contemporary Europeans were disillusioned; they lacked a faith; in their hearts they believed all was permitted. Frightened by this situation and the specter of chaos lurking in it, men arbitrarily selected features of their circumstances and exalted these, trying desperately to make absolute realities of them. Thus, the Fascist and the Communist exalted the state and the party so that these could substitute for the principles that had informed the

---

[27]"Qué pasa en el mundo," *El Sol*, June 3, 1933.

politics of liberal democracy. Men who found no authority in thought turned desperately to a myth of an organic state or an organized proletariat; the discipline they could no longer derive freely from their reason, they found in the prosaic facts of state and party, which would at least impose a totalitarian form on life, for slavery was preferable to intolerable chaos.

Ortega did not hanker for such a solution to the situation. Wherever the desperate, arbitrary will ruled over all, there was no check on those who wielded power. As events would show, a willful flight from freedom was the surest route to chaos; and what seems to have been the stability won in blood by certain authoritarians may well prove to be mere interludes of exhaustion. For Ortega, the problem was not one to be solved by the man of dominant volition. The problem had its formal cause in carefully reasoned arguments and the efficient cause, by which men might resolve it, would be of the same nature: a reasoned reform of reason. Hence, in spite of the fighting and the fury, Ortega believed that men of intellect should not exalt the will, but redirect their inquiry back to the foundations of reason.

Men who were dazzled by experimental brilliance had for too long ignored the most important questions about the nature of the universe and of human life. A backlog of fundamental problems had been created by the Kantian revolution; and popular culture was being bedeviled by irresolution about these matters. Contemporary Europe was endangered in part because many of its better thinkers had turned away from the problems of man, ignoring the profound questions that arise as men find themselves alone in a world. "That experimental science cannot resolve these fundamental questions in its own manner gives it no cause for the gratuitous gesture, like the fox before the grapes that were out of reach, of calling them 'myths' and inviting us to abandon them. How can we live unmoved by the final, dramatic questions? From whence comes the world and whither does it go? What is the formative power of the cosmos? What is the essential meaning of life?"[28]

Questions do not disappear by invalidating their traditional

---

[28] ¿Qué es filosofía?, 1929, 1957, Obras VIII, p. 311.

answers. When the old answers dissolve, some men resolve to find new means to make new answers. Thus, in speaking of the diversity of means that exist for arriving at a single goal, Montaigne made an appropriate observation: "Certes, c'est un subject merveilleusement vain, divers et ondoyant, que l'homme. Il est malaisé d'y fonder jugement constant et uniforme."[29]

What follows, then, is an attempt to adumbrate, not Ortega's solution to the ontological problem, but what Ortega envisaged as the desirable, historic solution to the problem. He indicated several lines of endeavor along which diverse men working in different ways in various human concerns could develop a renewed conviction in the authority of reason.

* * *

> Wisdom is one thing — to know the thought whereby all things are steered through all things.
>
> HERACLITUS, 41

---

[29]Montaigne, "Par divers moyens on arrive à pareille fin," *Oeuvres complètes*, p. 13.

*L*OSING HIMSELF *in the jungle of ideas that he himself created, man does not know what to do with intellect.* He continues to believe that it performs an indispensable service, but he knows not what this is. He knows only that its service is not the one attributed to it during the last three centuries. He predicts that reason will have to be given a new place in the system of actions that make up our life. *In short, having been the great solution, intellect has become for us the great problem.*

ORTEGA[1]

---

[1]"Apuntes sobre el pensamiento: su téurgia y su demiurgia," 1941, *Obras* V, p. 524.

XV
The Dawn of
Historic Reason

I N 1951 ORTEGA PAID TRIBUTE to the profundity of Martin Heidegger's philosophic style. Although much of Heidegger's writing
was difficult to read, his prose was marvelously adapted to his
purpose: to reform the vocabulary and syntax in such a way that
men could express new thoughts more effectively.[2]

Ortega spoke from experience, for he had had a new thought,
but he could express it effectively only after he had contended
with Heidegger's prose. This fact has prompted some to suggest
that Ortega was a disciple of Heidegger, a suggestion to which
Ortega did not take kindly.[3] On this matter, only two points
should be made. First, there is a difference between having been
influenced and being derivative. Ortega was no follower; several
years before Heidegger's first publications Ortega had uncovered
and discussed the reality on which he would base a reformed

---

[2]"Entorno al 'Coloquio de Darmstadt,' 1951," 1962, *Obras* IX, p. 634.

[3]In *La idea de principio en Leibniz*, 1947, 1958, *Obras* VIII, pp. 272-3, Ortega
went to some pains to establish the chronology of his intellectual development
vis-à-vis Heidegger's. In *Prólogo para alemanes*, 1933, 1958, *Obras* VIII, esp. pp.
43-54, Ortega explained his relation to phenomenology and Husserl. Ortega's
petulance at being called a litterateur in comparison to thinkers like Heidegger
came out sharply in a note in *The Origin of Philosophy*, Toby Talbot, trans.,
p. 86, fn. 7. "Perhaps it is further noteworthy that there has never been a *genus
dicendi* truly adequate as a vehicle for philosophizing. Aristotle was unable to
resolve this problem that fools ignore. His work has been preserved because he
held onto his own lesson notes. I personally have had to contain myself for
thirty years while fools accuse me of producing only literature, and the worst
part is that even my own students find it necessary to pose the question of
whether I have been writing literature or philosophy, along with other ridiculous
provincial notions of this order!"

reason.[4] All the same, Ortega doubtless found *Being and Time*, which was published in 1927, to be a good heuristic, for starting in 1928 he produced a series of substantial essays about the correspondence of reason to the realities of life, and from the first of these he acknowledged the value of Heidegger's work.[5] Recognition of this influence detracts nothing from Ortega's achievement, which was a personal achievement that followed its own course and that led in a direction rather different from Heidegger's aloof *Gelehrsamkeit*.

Second, properly treated, the doctrinal formulas of both men are irrelevant to the actual concern, for no one can copyright reality. During the early twentieth century, many serious thinkers were reflecting on the problem of reality and its importance for the authority of reason. With respect to fundamentals, one does not devise ingenious formulas, one hopes to *uncover* that which is. What matters is not that one or another person first worked out the correct doctrine, but that as various men point the way—and there were many in addition to Ortega and Heidegger—Europeans manage in the day-to-day complexity of their common lives to reform reason and shore up its authority. Were this a book on the reform of reason we would turn not only to Heidegger, but also to Dilthey, Brentano, Husserl, Scheler, Blondel, Croce, Rickert, Cohen, Vaihinger, Jaspers, and many others.[a] It is, however, a book on Ortega, who would have a prominent place in the larger story and who is the central concern in this preliminary version.

But although Ortega is the occasion of our inquiry, his theories should not be the object of our inquiry. He set forth his own position at length, repeatedly, and with elegance. For a full exposition of Ortega's ontology and his conception of historic reason, the reader should go to Ortega's own works, to *What is Philosophy?*, *Unas lecciones de Metafísica*, "Prólogo a *Veinte años de caza mayor*," *The Origin of Philosophy*, and most importantly, to *La Idea de principio en Leibniz*.[b] The last mentioned is a major philosophic treatise, the richness of which would be impossible

---

[4]*Meditaciones del Quijote*, 1914, *Obras* I, pp. 320-1.

[5]See the extensive reports on Ortega's lectures on "¿Qué es la filosofía?" in *La Nación*, (Buenos Aires), Nov. 10 and 14, and Dec. 25 and 28, 1928; and ¿*Qué es filosofía?*, 1929, 1957, *Obras* VII, pp. 275-438.

to summarize adequately. But to do so is not our purpose. Studying "Ortega as educator," our task is to grasp the gist of his ontology, his conception of historic reason, to see how these pertained to his mission as an educator, one committed to furthering European unity.

For a number of intelligent critics, the problems of European life in the twentieth century seemed to be rooted in the stigma that had become attached to reason, not to Reason disembodied, but to the personal reason according to which each man may choose to live his life. In every class, in every profession, in every nation, too many men seemed willing to pursue their respective activities without thinking seriously and personally about what they were doing. Of course, the causes of this heedlessness were manifold: on the material level there was the pedagogy of abundance; on the political level there was a simultaneous complicating and narrowing of alternatives as the possibilities of the nation-state were realized; on the cultural level there were new market-places for ideas that encouraged men to adopt positions, not to think thoughts.

In addition to these and other fundamental causes of the European crisis, another type of problem complicated the situation. Basic developments such as the pedagogy of abundance were serious but open developments; that is, the cycle of influence involved could lead either to degradation or improvement, depending on whether innumerable, diverse individuals perceived the surrounding abundance as an exuberance of possibilities or a cornucopia of achievements. If men viewed their surroundings as a basis from which to work at unifying Europe, Ortega believed that the concrete achievements of the men who had built the European nation-states would not be perceived as a comfortable, undemanding inheritance; instead, each particular man would find that some definite aspect of his national ambience offered him an exciting, demanding intimation of a supranational destiny, one in the pursuit of which he could nobly discipline his character. Critics were unlikely, however, to stir the technicians working in diverse spheres of activity, the men who might invent powerful supranational offices, because these men did not believe in the task. To them, reason should invent only means, not ends.

Reason thus presented a double problem with respect to the reform of European affairs. First, owing to the traditional conception of reason as thinking in correspondence to *res*, substance, be it physical or spiritual, many were strongly attracted to hypostatizing important ideas like society, to asserting that the idea must correspond to a thing, and to finding their purposes in the needs of these imaginary entities. Second, the better educated, who had followed the philosophical developments since the mid-1700's, no longer had confidence in the rationality of the traditional conception of reason; they could point out the error of hypostatizations by slack thinkers, but they had few alternatives to offer. The most thoughtful had the least conviction, a condition that made them weak in the bedlam of public voices. A new ontology was important for practical affairs because it would help the more serious, careful thinkers speak out with intelligent conviction.

Whether Ortega's philosophical reforms could have the practical implications claimed for them can be best judged after contending thoughtfully with the problem that Ortega contended with himself in working out his theories. The problem, recall, was this: in the past, the reality to which reason was supposed to correspond consisted in things, substances, in bodily things and in spiritual substances; but after Kant's criticisms, faith in the reality of any *res*—of any thing or substance, spiritual or material —would not sustain a system of reason, for the link between reason and *res* could not be made and any attempt to do so would end ultimately in skepticism. There was simply no way to test the actual correspondence between a phenomenal depiction of a thing and the thing-in-itself; and the profound effect of this fact on the traditional distinction between reason and opinion was beginning to be generally felt throughout the public, for it made reasonable men hesitate to speak with conviction and it made impulsive men more ready to act impulsively. Every man thus had before him this question: was a correspondence between the results of reason and an authentic reality still possible?

Ortega thought such correspondence *was* still possible, but not if one simply refurbished the traditional theory. He returned to the human problem that gave rise to philosophy; he did not dwell only on the theories recorded in philosophy. "Without now pretending to express a formal opinion on the point, permit me to insinuate the possibility that what we are now beginning to do under the traditional banner of philosophy is not a new philosophy, but something new and different from all of philosophy."[6] As a result, what is important is not his formulas, his theories, which, stated baldly, and secondhand no less, will seem meaningless; what is important is the problem and the answer to it. If one seriously entertains the problem—Is there a reality to which reason corresponds?—then Ortega's formulas may help suggest a solution to the problem as one perceives it. The basic mistake of academic philosophers has been their expectation that solutions to the problems of philosophy should be encased in the formulas expounded by their peers. But the problems that are worth concern are human problems, your problems and my problems; and the test of a philosopher's formula is not whether it is an eternal truth, but whether or not it serves as an occasion, helping you and me grasp and resolve the problems we perceive. Thus, we shall not bring Ortega's ontology to the bar of analytic judgment; we shall instead try to put his question and suggest the lines along which he thought a man might answer it.

To begin, note that nothing in Ortega's view denied the independent existence of the world out there. Many persons—and not only the naïve—are put off by the apparently infinite arrogance of the idealist who seems to make the entire universe a work of his meager imagination. All Ortega held, following Kant, was that the objective universe, which certainly must exist apart from our ideas of it, could not serve as the foundation of reason, for reason could properly tell us nothing about the universe, material and spiritual, as it existed in and for itself. Our ideas about the universe did not correspond to the universe-in-itself. Still following Kant, Ortega held that *res* was a transcendental ideal, a concept, not a substance, that men postulated in order to map their material and spiritual surroundings. With this position, neither Kant nor Ortega denied an external world, they asserted

---

[6] *Origen y epílogo de la filosofía*, 1943, 1960, *Obras* IX, p. 397.

instead that the foundation of science was not *in* that external world. To encounter the reality to which reason corresponded, one had to look for something other than substance.

Let us pose the question, what is real? On reading this question, one may take it as a mere phrase, three words cast in a particular grammatical construction. In that case, we should call the phrase a mere appearance, for there was no correspondence between the conceptual intention the words carry, namely to put a question about the character of reality, and one's mode of concentration on reading them, which may have been that of daydreaming to pass idle time, speed reading to acquaint oneself with a curious character, or fatigue: in any case the question What is real? did not correspond to what one was actually thinking. On the other hand, the phrase may have been a truth, for on reading it one might not have merely mouthed the words; one might have actually entertained the problem by wondering what it is that is really real. One might have stopped, recalling the profound perplexities that moved one once on looking up at the night-sky, filled with distant stars, on running sea-sand through one's hand while viewing an expanse of beach, or on seeing an ancient fossil exposed when the spring frosts laid bare a new surface of shale. At times, one wonders: is it all as it seems, or is it a vast deception? Who am I, an animate speck, a thinking spark, lost in the midst of immensity? What is real? What is true? What is the basis of this vast spectacle before me and within me? People who are perplexed by such questions philosophize; and with the comparison between reciting by rote the phrase What is real? and the actual feeling of perplexity at the uncertainty the question is meant to denote, we uncover the reality to which, Ortega believed, disciplined intellection could truly correspond.

Before any of us can concern ourselves with the reality of *res*, we are living thinkers who, in the reality of our lives, posed the question of reality. Ortega was not pointing here to our phenomenal lives, which we are aware of retrospectively as the sum of our experience. The reality of our lives is not for each of us phenomenal; the reality is not our report, public or private, that this feels hot and that that tastes sweet, for these reports can easily be falsified, both intentionally and unwittingly. The reality of our lives is instead the succession of instantaneous presences, of active actualities: now feeling the heat, now tasting that which we call sweet, now seeing, hearing, thinking, doing, wanting. Whereas we can falsify the experience in the reporting of it, the experiencing itself was what it was, a dynamic reality that is the absolute, irrevocable ground against which we judge the truth or falsehood of the phenomenal experience reported in hindsight. It will seem paradoxical at first, but it is a fact of life, a simple, inescapable, yet fruitful fact: experiencing is *a priori*. Active experiencing is prior to experience, to our phenomenal awareness of what transpired; experiencing this or that is a definitive actuality, it is the ground, the reality, to which our experience, our phenomenal awareness, can and should correspond.

We find ourselves in a world, doing certain things: I am writing, you are reading; both of us are in definite places, I scratch my eyebrow, toying silently with words, testing their adequacy to my intention. We each stop, wondering what in all of this is real, and following Ortega we decide to put aside, temporarily, millennia of metaphysics; we decide, instead, to look at ourselves and our immediate surroundings, feeling that if we cannot find reality here before us, we will have scant basis for finding it far out there. Thus we note: "the being of the world before me is . . . a functioning upon me and, likewise, my acting on it. But this— a reality that consists in an I seeing a world, thinking it, touching it, loving it or hating it, being enthused or grieved by it, transforming, enduring, or suffering it—is what has always been called 'living,' 'my life,' 'our life,' that of each one of us." Each of us is living his life; that is the occasion of our joining in an effort at communication. This living is the reality that gives rise to all our experience of the world without and the world within. "Hence, let us wring the necks of those venerable and consecrated words, 'to exist,' 'to coexist,' and 'to be,' in order to say in their place that the foundation of the universe is 'my living' and all the rest that is or is not is in my life, inside of it."[7]

---

[7] *¿Qué es filosofía?*, 1929, 1957, *Obras* VII, pp. 410-1.

In due course we will touch on some of the difficulties that arise in this revision of reason, but our purpose here is not to debunk the argument, but to try experiencing the reality that Ortega believed was the basis of reason and of the distinction between truth and appearance. To treat the matter fully would take us far afield, for as Ortega showed in his work on *La idea de principio en Leibniz*, the topic is a substantial problem for philosophers, one to which many of the more technical tomes in the philosophic tradition are centrally important. Furthermore, a full excursion into the subject would not only require a discussion of the philosophic past far more extensive than the one attempted here, it would also entail a much more extensive inquiry into the philosophic present, which includes numerous lines of parallel reflection. This inquiry would carry us not only into the work of such well-known figures as G. H. Mead, Husserl, Heidegger, Merleau-Ponty, and Sartre, but also into the writings of important but less renowned men such as Herbert Spiegelberg and especially Alfred Schütz.[8] Here let us stick to Ortega.

The reality to which reason corresponded, Ortega held, was not being, but living; not substance, but life. If living is actually a reality, it is here for each of us, here as reality, not as doctrine; hence we need not depend on Ortega's doctrine to be free of difficulties; rather we can welcome the difficulties, for once we have called attention to the reality, the difficulties make it possible for each of us to go to the reality, to test it, to investigate it, to become familiar with it, and eventually to use it or reject it as the basis of the rationality by which we discipline our thought.

Our reports of sensations and feelings can be most easily tested against the reality of living rather than being. Thus, what used to be, according to the old ontology, secondary qualities are now primary, for these are, when truly reported, in direct correspondence with our acts of experiencing. Perhaps the following will show how simple and fundamental this correspondence can

---

[8]See for parallel views by Schütz his essay "On Multiple Realities," (1945) in Alfred Schütz, *Collected Papers*, Vol. I, pp. 207-259. Schütz knew of Ortega's work, but primarily of Ortega's sociology as expressed in *Man and People;* see Schütz, *Ibid.*, pp. 142-4.

be. The child of a friend was running along a rocky path intent on his goal when he stubbed his toe on a stone. As he cried, his father tried to distract him from the pain by telling him to think what a beautiful day it was. "But it hurts!" the child replied. "It hurts! It hurts! . . ." And in concentrating on formulating and reiterating this reply so that all would hear, the child distracted himself from the pain and then turned to other concerns. Now we can see that the child's first reply was a truth that corresponded to the actuality of feeling pain, which was then the reality that he was living; but as soon as he started to articulate his feeling of pain, he began to live another competing reality, namely that of articulating his feeling, which soon became his dominant concern, so much so that the refrain, "It hurts!", kept up until after his toe had stopped hurting. Then, suddenly, when the child recognized that his report no longer corresponded to his feeling, he skipped happily off to play.

This example gives a simple instance of the way intellection, the child's throught that it hurts, at first corresponds and then fails to correspond to the reality of his life. This example indicates how such a theory of correspondence can be the basis of a regimen for our thought about our immediate sensations, emotions, and intuitions: our phenomenal reports of these should always correspond as closely as possible to the real sensing, emoting, and intuiting that provides the basis of the report. We see, thus, that basing reason on the reality of living brings into the sphere of reason aspects of life that were formerly "irrational." With respect to the standard of life, neuroses result, for instance, not from an inability to contain one's irrational drives, but from a failure of one's reason, in an expanded sense, for the neurotic person chronically dissimulates his experience and consumes great energies in falsifying his conscious reports of his innermost imaginings.

But let us not lose ourselves in byways. A correspondence between disciplined intellection and the reality of living is rather simple when what we are living are direct sensations and deep emotions. As we noted, these were formerly secondary and now seem primary. What is more difficult is to see how the primary qualities of old correspond to the realities of life. Yet if such correspondence cannot be elucidated, the reform of reason would simply trade a new one-sidedness for the old.

"The truth is not that I exist because I think, but, on the contrary, that I think because I live, because life puts to me basic, inexorable problems."[9] With this reversal of the Cartesian *cogito*, we encounter the vital source of the realm of *res*, or things, of the world out there. In Ortega's view, this world was not the primary reality, the ground of reason, but a derivative reality, a result of reasoning. In the course of living, men gave definite form to their phenomenal surroundings in order to act on them more effectively. Encountering difficulties in life, men sought to think about their surroundings because they wanted to think through these difficulties, which seemed centered out there in their environs. In order to deal with these concerns, men postulated a cosmos, a dual realm of matter and spirit. The sense of substance, therefore, is not in the correspondence of this concept to the things-in-themselves, but in its correspondence to the realities of life, to the fact that by its means men have been able to convert the inhospitable chaos in which they find themselves into a habitable cosmos in which they can anticipate, and even control, what the world will do to them and what they will do to the world.

In the conduct of life, each person had to think, he had to anticipate his performance, he had to *preoccupy* himself with the way he would live in this or that circumstance, because much of living was dealing with particular circumstances that could easily overwhelm him. "Each of us lives surrounded by things, by immediate objects that present themselves and make themselves obvious by themselves. Many of these things are mineral, others are living beings, and others are persons; and furthermore, still others are the intimate objects that we find to be no less immediate than those outside of us—our sadness and sentiment, our appetites, intentions, and ideas. The conjunction of all these things that are immediate entities that present themselves to us we call our circumstances or world."[10] With respect to one's circumstances,

---

[9]"¿Qué es el conocimiento?," *El Sol*, Feb. 23, 1931.
[10]*Ibid.*, *El Sol*, Jan. 18, 1931.

living was more involved than the immediate reflex of feeling pain on kicking a stone; life often involved choosing, deciding, acting, judging. To facilitate these complex activities, men invented, transmitted, and ever expanded the realm of *res*.

Even the most abstract forms of reason had a vital basis, which ultimately was the ground of all rational authority. Ortega elucidated the basis of both moral and natural reasoning in the living of life; men had designed both, through the free play of speculation, to aid man in dealing with particular kinds of difficulties that arose in the course of living in a world.

Moral reasoning corresponded to the realities of living in a world of partly indeterminate circumstances. A man's circumstances included all that the world had been for the person, everything in the sum of his actual life up to his immediate present, the *now* that he was living; and as such, this man's world delimited a definite realm of future possibilities, of potential circumstances that were yet to be determined in their actuality and that the person had *now* to choose between. Living at this instant meant deciding between these possibilities. Man's dignity, anguish, and joy was that the influence of past circumstances in present decisions was not deterministic, for his world included his appetites, intentions, and ideas, which he could use to affect the value and force of his past, external circumstances. Here, in exercising one's freedom, men became aware of a desire for a system of moral reasoning, which would strengthen them in sportively resisting the inertias of their past and empower them to shape their future.

"Deciding between this and that is the part of our life that has an element of liberty. Constantly we are deciding on our future being, and in order to actualize it we have to take account of the past and make use of the present to operate on actuality; and we do all of this inside of 'now', for our future is not any future whatsoever, but a possible 'now', and our past is the past up to now, not that of someone who lived a hundred years ago."[11] One's life is one's *now*, at this instant, one's reading these words. One can comprehend these words first because one makes the

---

[11]*¿Qué es filosofía?*, 1929, 1957, *Obras* VII, p. 435.

commitment to take the effort to understand them and second because a multitude of past actualities has brought one to them and them to one; all of these circumstances contribute to making it possible for one to interpret their significance. Further, a wide range of future possibilities, significant or not as the case may be, depends on precisely how one interprets their meaning and on how one exerts his volition in the light of this comprehension. In short, in reading one is making a series of judgments that have irrevocable consequences for one's life, and these judgments are what one is now living. " 'Now' is our time, our world, our life. . . . Into it, we come encrusted [with particulars]; 'now' impresses on us a repertory of possibilities and impossibilities, of conditions, of dangers, of conveniences, and of means. It limits with these features the liberty of choice that moves our life, and it is, over against our liberty, the cosmic pressure; it is our destiny."[12]

In living life, each man continually encountered a definite set of real choices between which he was compelled to choose. To facilitate this choosing, to make an unexpected wisdom possible, men early invented various systems of moral reasoning, not because absolute moral principles actually ruled over their choices, justifying certain ones and condemning others, but because with each choice a man obligated himself to make future choices from a range of possibilities limited by the past choice. Men quickly learned the desirability of being able to foresee the character of these obligations, to anticipate how present choices shape future options. Men soon discovered that in many situations the immediately easiest course could prejudice their future options: by lying, deceiving, and exploiting others, a man might attain his present ends while making his future choices untenable as others learned to distrust and hate him. Another man, a noble spirit willing to resist necessity, might have presently chosen a more difficult course, foreseeing that the ensuing choices to which it obligated him were more desirable. In the quest of such foresight, men invented the world of spirit in which they postulated the soul, eternal, all-knowing gods, the form of the good, and many other ethical principles.

---

[12]*Ibid.*, p. 435.

We need not here recapitulate the history of ethics, showing how different systems in different ways all serve to forewarn men about the likely character of the future obligations created by present commitments. What matters here is first the recognition that the realities of living have aspects that men can deal with only through some form of moral reasoning, by some means for evaluating the quality of the obligations to which they are now committing themselves, and second the realization that whatever the principle from which particular men deduce their system of practical reason, the authority of that system lies not merely in its internal consistency, but further in its truth to the realities of the lives men live. Living meant choosing continually and thus creating real obligations. Hence, a man's moral reasoning was more than a nice set of edifying preachments, for he was going to live, and even die, dealing with whatever obligations he now took on. A man's moral reasoning was his means, good or bad as the case may be, of *pre*occupying himself with his obligations, trying to make them as sound as possible.

To be effective, then, a system of moral reasoning had to correspond to the realities men were living. To inform a man about future obligations, ethical reflections must not falsify the character of his present mode of living. The quality of hypocrisy is informative only if it corresponds to a mode of living hypocritically. The concept of honesty is meaningless if it is used by a flatterer without attention to the way of living of the man called honest. All our ideals of character, in short, properly correspond to realities of living, and when they are used in such correspondence they can help us foresee what sort of future obligations, limitations, and situations are implicit in various present alternatives. This foresight would enable us to shape our lives according to a pleasing and possible pattern. Intentional self-formation, Ortega held, was the result of "preoccupation," our anticipation and evaluation of various possibilities through sportive, ethical reflections. "Life is preoccupation; and it is so not only in the difficult moments, but it is always so and in essence it is nothing more than this—preoccupying oneself. In each instant we have to decide what we are going to do in the next, what is going to occupy our life. It is, then, occupying oneself by anticipating; it is preoccupying oneself."[13]

Moral reasoning, thus, was man's great means for pre-occupying himself with his life. To live was to find oneself in a definite world endowed with particular powers and a determined past; to live was to find oneself forced to be continually deciding on which of the finite possibilities for the future would be the particular possibility that one would strive to realize. The consequences of these decisions were absolute. These determined one's life; hence in living one became either a *petit Dieu* or a *petit Diable*, for in living each man freely created major features of his inner and outer world, and these features would be either good or bad, beautiful or ugly, true or false, depending on the real character of his choices. Living one's life, bringing a self and a world into existence, endowing these with definite character, was serious sport: sport because one was free to make of oneself whatever was within one's powers and serious because one was responsible for living with the consequences. Thus, men invented concepts of the self, of the soul, and of spiritual qualities, not to describe some intangible substance within or around them, but to analyze the actualities they lived so that with their inalienable freedom they could avoid blind self-destruction and achieve full self-realization.

Whereas moral reasoning corresponded in such ways to the realities of living in a world of partly indeterminate circumstances, of exercising one's freedom of choice, natural reasoning corresponded to the realities of living in a world of partly determinate circumstances, of acting in definite ways. Our phenomenal world, the world as it appeared to us, depended only in part on how we used our liberty, on what we chose to do; in doing what we chose, we had also to contend with a wide panorama of givens, of conditions, of facts that had to be dealt with. These conditions posed threats and offered challenges. Man early sought to devise ways to think about these determinate surroundings, not to understand the personal and social obligation that he took on in the course of choice, but to predict the consequences in the event of action.

---

[13]*Ibid.*, p. 436.

For this purpose men postulated, in addition to a realm of spirit, a realm of matter in which the concept of substance was used to delimit more tangible things. As with moral reasoning, natural reasoning should not correspond to the things-in-themselves, but to the realities of living in a determinate world, a world that might or might not be determinate in itself, but that was clearly determinate with respect to the living, willing, thinking person. "Being, the *essence* of a thing, originally signifies the image of it that gives us vital security with respect to it."[14] This test of scientific reasoning considerably broadened the scientist's purview. The essence of a thing was neither the image of it that put man subjectively at peace with it, nor the idea that let him think that he objectively knew and had control of it; the true, vital essence was the conception that put man as he lived his life in actual control of it. To grasp the practical significance of this distinction, take the case of our knowledge of the atom. For many centuries men were subjectively at peace with respect to the atom, for although a few had postulated its existence, all were ignorant of its nature. During the first half of the twentieth century men seemed to gain objective control of the atom, successfully using it in both war and peace. But whether our disinterested knowledge of atomic energy is adequate to give us *vital* security with respect to the atom is still moot, for although on objective grounds we have rather sophisticated control of atomic fission, on vital grounds we are dangerously uncertain whether we can control our control of the process. And if we do not, we will live the consequences—cataclysmic death.

Many may find it difficult, however, to conceive of scientific reasoning as corresponding to the realities of living. This difficulty may be met head on. We are accustomed to thinking of the scientist as a completely disinterested spectator; even more, many believe that repeatable experiments and standard measures can open a window into nature herself. What one scientist sees can be seen by any man who repeats the experiment and conforms to the standards. Hence, to assert that scientific reasoning should, like emotional and moral reasoning, correspond to lived reality

---

[14] "¿Qué es el conocimiento?," *El Sol*, March 1, 1931.

seems to open a carefully controlled system to the foibles of subjective judgment. But on examination, this danger disappears. The proper insistence on controlled observations, in Ortega's view, stipulates that the phenomena about which the scientist theorizes be *real* phenomena; that is, data about actual occurrences in the lives of certain men. The transformation of magic into science came when men stopped speculating about what they would like to have happen in their lives and when they began to reflect on what actually was happening, there before them. Being scientific about science, we will recognize that what is crucial for scientific observation is providing a systematic point of correspondence for scientific theory, a correspondence not to the objective universe, but to carefully recorded realities in the lives of particular investigators, repeatable experiences described by standard, common measures. The insistence on repeatability in experiments makes sense precisely because scientific theory should correspond not to things-in-themselves, but to the data the investigator actually experiences. Repeatable experiment is not a window into nature, but a means of keeping the scientist honest.

Here is another way of explaining the enlarged responsibilities of the scientist. He is first responsible for thinking in strict correspondence with the results gathered as he observes the particular events he seeks to understand. But this observing is not the whole of his living. From time immemorial, the great source of arbitrary error has been the failure to know oneself, to know what sort of life one was really, irrevocably living. The genius of rationalistic science was to perceive that for certain problems one could best control for lack of self-knowledge by recognizing as pertinent only the results of the scientist's controlled observing, declaring irrelevant all the rest of his living. This procedure worked so long as men could safely separate the domains of moral reasoning and natural reasoning. But the separation depends on a fortuitous condition: namely, that many "things" around us function independently of us and can therefore be isolated for purposes of observation. In observing in our lives things that function independently, we do not need to consider how they act on us or how we might act on them; thus, we can pretend that we, as living persons, are not implicated in these "objective" events beyond our act of observing them.

This pretense breaks down, however, whenever the thing we observe enters into our lives in any capacity other than as the object of disinterested observing, that is, whenever we begin acting on or with what we have been observing, or whenever what we are observing, perhaps a human being, has claims on our benevolent interest. As a result, we find that the methods of "objective" science are mere conveniences, appropriate only under special conditions. Consequently, natural science does not provide a model for all reasoning, especially for reasoning about man. In the human sciences, and even in applying the natural sciences to the pursuit of human purposes, the thinker has to take into account a far wider range of realities than those resulting from his carefully limited observations. As Ortega saw it, natural science was not the great exemplar. If reason should correspond to the realities of living a life, natural science was a special form of reasoning applicable only in unusual circumstances. "After having suffered shame when men of science disdained philosophers, throwing in their face the taunt that philosophy was not a science, today philosophers are . . . pleased by this insult; for, catching the taunt, we return it, saying: philosophy is not a science because it is much more than a science."[15]

Living one's life was a reality to which emotional, moral, and natural reasoning should correspond. If Ortega's vision is valid, then the true test of any system of reasoning is its truth to life; and this test will be performed in the human world as each man finds, examining the matter for himself, either that he can, or that he cannot, live better by thinking in correspondence to the realities of life. This vital test can take place only slowly as diverse persons begin to examine what disciplined thinking entails, what grounds exist for it, and what place such thinking has in their immediate, irrevocable living. This vital test is not yet complete—it has barely begun; and rather than here declare

---

[15] ¿Qué es filosofía?, 1929, 1957, Obras VII, p. 300.

a verdict, one way or another, let us look instead at what Ortega believed would be the signs indicating that men were beginning to live by means of historic reason.

In his essay on "Wilhelm Dilthey and the Idea of Life", Ortega insisted that the biographer had to complete his subject's work in order to do justice to it, for only then could the significance of it be properly appreciated.[16] Ortega's biographers should do something similar, for throughout his old age he contemplated but never wrote a magnum opus. The book was to be *The Dawn of Historic Reason*, which was to contain his invitation to the future. But events were not kind to the aging Ortega. From the outbreak of the Civil War until his death in 1955, his life was one of continual wandering and intermittent sicknesses; of fleeting leisure, fitful work, and interrupted activities. Through these two decades he accomplished much in spite of the distractions, and a draft of *The Dawn* may yet appear from among his unpublished papers. But so far, it remains merely a repeated promise made in various notes from 1936 onwards.

All the same, *The Dawn of Historic Reason* is an essential book for our purposes. In his published works there are several indications of the subjects that Ortega intended to cover in it, and he even put a draft of its opening chapter before the public. But for the most part, we should leave the content of the work for the future, and we should concentrate instead on its *function*. Even if the work was never written, the idea of it served an important function in Ortega's mature thought. If we can grasp this function, we will find that most of his later writing contributed to its fulfillment. Perhaps this "great philosophical memorandum book," as he once called *The Dawn*,[17] was never finished because it was not a book at all, but the sum of his work.

In 1936 Ortega announced the impending publication of this book, calling it *On Living Reason*. It would be, he said, "an essay at a *prima philosophia*."[18] First philosophy is the Aristotelian name for metaphysics, which Aristotle defined as "a science which

---

[16]"Guillermo Dilthey y la idea de la vida," 1933, *Obras* VI, p. 174.

[17]*Ideas y creencias*, 1940, *Obras* V, p. 379.

[18]"Historia como sistema," 1936, *Obras* VI, p. 38.

studies Being *qua* Being, and the properties inherent in it in virtue of its own nature."[19] Since Aristotle held that Being was always a substance, a *res*, we might be surprised to learn that Ortega contemplated a work on first philosophy; and this surprise will be further compounded when we examine his other references to *The Dawn*, for they do not seem to point towards metaphysics in any Aristotelian sense. For instance, in the early 1940's Ortega described his projected work as his "historic catechism," and in 1947 he claimed that in it he would distinguish between "the creators of a land" and "its inhabitants," referring with the phrase "land" to the few great philosophical systems. In 1946 Ortega promised that one of the chapters would present "The Principles of a New Philology," and in 1940 he published a draft of *The Dawn's* opening chapter, which was a preliminary critique of historic reason called "Ideas and Beliefs."[20]

Thinkers working in the post-Aristotelian tradition will be hard put to understand how an essay on first philosophy, the study of Being *qua* Being, could properly include reflections on the philosophy of history, philology, and epistemology. In the Aristotelian hierarchy of studies, these are secondary subjects. Certain readers will have noted a similar reversal when in discussing the correspondence of reason to the realities of living we began with the emotional and moved from it to the moral and then to the natural. These reversals are symptomatic of the fact that with the dawn of historic reason Ortega envisaged a fundamental break with the Aristotelian first philosophy; and a major concern in Ortega's later work was to show that the Aristotelian conception of Being *qua* substance was simply a theory that did not adduce Being *qua* Being at all. Hence, Aristotle's metaphysics was not a first philosophy, but a secondary one that was dependent in actuality on the transcendent reality of certain men, that is, on Aristotle and his readers living their particular lives and thinking in those lives certain metaphyiscal propositions. Conse-

---

[19]Aristotle, *Metaphysics*, IV, i, 1; Hugh Tredennick, trans.

[20]Respectively: *Origen y epílogo de la filosofía*, 1943, 1960, *Obras* IX, p. 385; *La idea de principio en Leibniz*, 1947, 1958, *Obras* VIII, p. 300; *Velázquez*, 1950, 1958, *Obras* VIII, p. 493; and *Ideas y creencias*, 1940, *Obras* V, pp. 379-409.

quently, a part of the reform of reason entailed redefining *prima philosophia*. By virtue of this redefinition, the topics mentioned by Ortega, as well as several others that he discussed from 1936 onwards, found a proper place in a first philosophy.

Aristotle contended that metaphysics should be the study of Being *qua* Being because it seemed to him that only in this way could he find the first principles and ultimate causes that he sought to understand. With Ortega's ontological reforms, substituting for Being the fact of living, first philosophy would tell about the living of living instead of the being of being. In first philosophy one would search for the first principles and ultimate causes not of life as a thing, but of the living of life. Thus, one would need an historic catechism; a distinction between creators and fulfillers; an understanding of the use and disadvantage of words, of ideas, and of beliefs for life. The hierarchy of studies would be turned upside-down. The theoretical sciences and especially the study of Being *qua* Being would become secondary, for these concerned the dependent, hypothetical substances that, in the course of living, men had created by postulating various concepts. In the place of these studies, the practical sciences would become the primary ones, for these had direct reference to the first philosophy, that of living *qua* living.

After an ontology of life has replaced that of *res*, an inquiry similar to the Aristotelian conception of ethics would become the *prima philosophia*; but the similarity would be one of concern, not of doctrine, for the *Nicomachean Ethics* was of a piece with the *Metaphysics*. Aside from their different places in the hierarchy of studies, the major difference between the new and the old ethics would be that, in accordance with an ontology of life, the unmoved mover ceased to be some distant divinity and became the living man who found himself alive and had to live by moving, choosing, acting, and doing. The first cause was my living, your living, your finding yourself shipwrecked in a world and forced to keep yourself afloat or to let all end; the regress of real causes was not infinite: for each person, it had a finite beginning and end in the actualities of the life that he lived. My living is the cause of my thinking, as well as the cause of all that I have to think about; the final cause, the *telos* of it all, is not the quiescent contemplation of a pure and absolute mind, but the fullness of the active instant, here and now. Thus, we do not live to think; we think to live: "life is not fundamentally what it has been believed to be for so many centuries: contemplation, mind, theory. No; it is production, fabrication, and only because of these does life require thought. Therefore, afterwards and not before, life is mind, theory, and science. . . ."[21]

Life began with living, in that act was life's first cause, for by looking outside of life for its being, one could never approximate its realities, even if one perfectly catalogued its ingredients. Life was its own first principle and ultimate cause. Living was always some form of doing, a special type of which was thinking. Hence, the human endeavor was not to proceed towards contemplation by means of action, but to proceed to action by means of contemplation. A man who lived in this manner, by acting in accordance with his thinking, would occupy himself significantly in philosophizing, in thinking particularly about ethics, the practical science par excellence, the purpose of which was to elucidate through contemplation the means for living a good life. In spite of themselves, Ortega suggested, past philosophers had by and large followed this procedure in practice. "Knowledge perfects work, pleasure, and sorrow; and vice versa, these drive and direct [knowledge] Therefore, after its initial stammers and fortuitous discovery, when philosophy formally began its historical passage of millenary continuity, it established itself in the Platonic Academy as an occupation originally with ethics. From this perspective, Plato never ceased to be Socratic. Whether larval or palatine, philosophy always implied the 'primacy of practical reason.' It was, is, and will be, as long as it exists, the *science of doing*."[22]

For Ortega, first philosophy was a study of the way life was lived, a study that was undertaken in order to learn how to live better. First philosophy did not, however, give rise to a corpus for instructing others how to live their lives; the study of how one man could manipulate others was not the study of living *qua* living, for the lives of others could be influenced only by pallid abstrac-

---

[21]*Meditación de la técnica*, 1939, *Obras* V, pp. 341-2.
[22]*La idea de principio en Leibniz*, 1947, 1958, *Obras* VIII, p. 268.

tions about other peoples' business. In contrast, first philosophy dealt with actualities, for it concerned each man's understanding of his life; and hence it amounted to a regimen for self-formation, for living one's life was a matter of giving form to oneself. First philosophy was first in the sense that it concerned a man's shaping of the immediate, irrevocable realities of his life, in that it involved his determining the life he lived and his bringing his self into existence; and all else depended on this first philosophy because everything else that he perceived was a function of the reality he lived. In cultivating his self he laid the foundation of everything else; and the theory that he used consciously or unconsciously to guide his cultivation of his character was the foundation of all his secondary reflections about the things he met with in his life. First philosophy was the personal attempt by a man to give his historic reason, the reason by which he shaped his life, a firm foundation. In this sense, first philosophy was a pedagogy of self-education. Ortega's conception of historic reason was reason viewed as the means, not the end, of self-culture.

Self-education was the concern of first philosophy, for the basic reality was a man's living his life, and the particulars within his life were created through his course of self-formation while living his life. As a man shaped his capacities in this way and not that, as he chose to live here and not there, as he willed to concentrate on this concern and not that, as he cultivated his self in this manner and not that, he determined what phenomenal world he would inhabit. This situation—more precisely, this manner of situating himself in a world—was not solipsistic, for, no matter what, the man's life would involve both his self and a vast, chaotic flux of *actual* circumstances. There would always be real elements in his living that were outside his self, but the particular nature of these elements depended *first*, although not completely, on how he formed his self. This self-centeredness of a man's reality gave him no justification for exploitative, egotistical arrogance towards others. The self brought into being through a man's self-education was not his "self-image," his phenomenal conception of his self as it was touched up by wishful thinking. On the contrary, the self created by first philosophy was the man's real self, which was what he lived immediately and irrevocably, in spite of his pretty self-images. This real self gave no sanction to ego-tism. Although a man's real self was the basis of all else, it did not justify either his insensitive exploitation of others or any other vital shortcut, for in adopting such views, he was not justifying exploitation, but making himself an exploiter; and in this case, his arrogant egotism simply became his means of hiding from his subjective self-image the real character of his actual, trans-cendent life.

Alétheia, uncovering, unmasking, has always been what first philosophers sought to do to reality; and in the twentieth century, when reality has come more and more to mean the actualities of living our lives, the whole urge of European philosophy has been to break the persuasiveness of the elaborate collective abstractions by means of which men can hide from the realities of their lives. Here is the common commitment binding such diverse creations as Heidegger's obscure and difficult efforts to reform philosophical language; as Camus' clear, biting, and pointed outrage in "Pour-quoi l'Espagne?"; as Sartre's infatuation with men beyond the pale in his appreciation of Genet; and as Ortega's plea for clarity about the collective abstractions that cloak senseless passions with empty justifications. The truth thus spreads: to improve the quality of our lives, we should act on the realities, not merely on the fictions. Hence, the great problem for self-fulfillment and common development has been to shear away our paltry means of self-deception and to free men to care for the one reality of which they may be the master, themselves.

Self-education is possible, although it seems paradoxical, it being the art of leading oneself out of oneself. If historic reason, reasoning in correspondence with the realities of life in order to cultivate the possibilities of life, were ever to become a character-istic concern of Western men, it would be through a seemingly paradoxical development in which historic reason would be spread as men lived by means of historic reason. This paradox can be resolved only by reference to—nay! only by the presence of faith. There is no easy escape from this age-old problem.

Those who suddenly feel uneasy by this talk of "faith" need not despair. The paradox that historic reason can come into being only through historic reason calls on men to have faith, to have a living faith that has nothing to do with dogma, official doctrine, or certified confession. Faith should be our willingness to act by means of precisely those powers that we hope to perfect through our actions. Thus, faith should equal self-education; faith enables a man to learn a language by using the language, to create trust by having trust, to develop historic reason by thinking by means of historic reason. Such faith does not result from producing a professed allegiance to one or another doctrine; the attempt to force, manipulate, or cajole men into accepting particular tenets is a sure sign that such faith is absent, for faith should always be a spontaneous commitment to a matter without which the matter would be impossible. Causal necessities do not produce faith; faith is the fount of all possibilities, upon which causes may thereafter play. Men spread faith by having faith, for faith is a vital commitment, a lived decision to recognize and pursue this or that possibility. Faith itself, not the object of the faith, is thus the unmoved mover of all human development.

Faith cannot be produced, and in the absence of it, a man can produce nothing. To plant a seed, the primitive farmer must have had faith in its power to grow: that argricultural science began in religious myth was not irrational. The same would be true of historic reason: to allow it to develop, one would have to have faith that it would develop. Without that faith, the paternal teacher would overstep the bounds, he would try to use abstractions to impart historic reason to his dependents. Such a program would simply spread a dependence on abstract tutelage. Hence, Ortega devised no plan for forcing his view of historic reason on other men, for he had the faith that on encountering historic reason other men would also spontaneously have faith in it. There would be nothing more absurd than paternal instruction in the art of self-culture, in historic reason.

When a man had faith in historic reason, he would live with the personal recognition that reason was not some enormous body of abstract truths, but a means of his self-formation. He would act with the understanding that reason was, like his hands, legs, or eyes, a part of his anatomy that could, when properly disciplined and coordinated, aid greatly in living a good life. Recognizing that reason was a crucial element in living his life, the man would know immediately that right reasoning derived an ineluctable authority from its correspondence to the realities he lived. Thus, when a man had faith in reason, when he went ahead and lived by the aid of reason, he provided reason with a transcendent sanction and overcame the impossibility of providing from within the realm of pure thought alone, an effective justification for the authority of reason. By living reasonably, a man provided a justification from the realm of reality. Men need not live by reason because it has a proven authority; reason could gain a proven authority because men live by its means, and the only way to disprove this authority of reason would be to live *completely* without resort to it.

Historic reason signified the adaptation of all modes of thinking to assisting a living man's effort to shape the realities of his life. Unlike abstract reason, historic reason was not a corpus of timeless truths. Instead it was the continuous recurrence of timely truths; hence the skeptic could not deny historic reason in principle unless he could rigorously avoid in practice his own resort to any form of disciplined intelligence, any thinking that accorded with the occasion he was vitally experiencing. Since historic reason was not the sum of teachable truths, it could not be spread programmatically. For instance one could never officially base a school curriculum on historic reason, for "the curriculum" was a fiction that could not be endowed with vital reality. Any such pretension would miss the living actuality of historic reason, namely that it is the reason that has historic reality because it is my reason, your reason, the reasoning that each of us actually uses in living life. Historic reason could not be an attribute of one or another fictional program; it could only be a an attribute of particular, living persons. Historic reason could at most make itself felt in an educational program when particular persons went beyond the official prescriptions of the program and acted as they saw fit according to the light of their own reasoning. For example, when the Ford Foundation asked Ortega to suggest a program of education for the future, Ortega replied that such a pronouncement, no matter how profound, would saddle educators with an anachronistic view. Educators themselves had to clarify their views of the future continuously.[23]

In keeping with such restrictions, Ortega offered no program for promoting historic reason. He simply *invited* each man to proceed on the faith that he would accomplish something significant for himself and his peers if he successfully perfected his historic reason, that is, the disciplined intellectual powers that he used in living his life. As Ortega saw it, such an effort could authentically arise only from an ethical, sportive commitment; causal force of one sort or another could not produce allegiance to historic reason. Such force would only reduce man to his least common denominator; and our most gratuitous yet important task is to save ourselves from the forceful fools who are at once too solicitous of our future and too suspicious of our power to permit us to save ourselves! "Here is the greatest danger that today threatens civilization: the statalizing of life, the interventionism of the State, the absorption of all social spontaneity by the State; that is to say, the nullification of the historic spontaneity that ultimately sustains, nurtures, and impels the destinies of man."[24] The failure of faith embodied in orthodoxy, the mistrust of man that underlies statist paternalism, leads to the constriction of man.

Instead, when a faith spreads as men find it in themselves, life does not constrict, narrowing into the dull repetition of favored formulas; on the contrary, with a faith life expands, for with a living faith men accept new possibilities and begin to base their efforts on potentials that in the absence of faith would not exist. The spread of historic reason might revitalize the ethical sensibility of Western man, and this revitalization might in turn renew the European's power of historic initiative. But this possibility was not a blueprint for renovation; the future could not be implemented by a mere policy, for the future was that which confronted each and all with a radical contingency: not the *right*

---

[23]"Apuntes sobre una educación para el futuro," 1953, 1962, *Obras* IX, pp. 665-675, esp. pp. 672-5.

[24]*La rebelión de las masas*, 1930, *Obras* IV, p. 225.

of self-determination, but the *inevitability* of self-determination. Hence, historic reason could become a faith only if men freely gave themselves to it, having faith in it, accepting it exuberantly as an unnecessary possibility that they would nevertheless use to guide their lives.

Ultimately, Ortega came back to a reliance on man's exuberance, his aspirations to excellence, his ethical urges, his erotic drives. Historic reason could spread only through the game willingness of men to take a chance, to have faith, to act on something that would exist only if men freely acted on it. The only hope was man's power to hope, for there was no necessary source of the unnecessary. Morality always arose through prophecy, not manipulation. Men have freely acted ethically because the attraction of a possible future drew them forward, not because the causes of a completed past pushed them from behind: punishment might force men to conform to sanctioned practice, but it would never inspire them to act autonomously. Therefore, Ortega did not lay out a program through which a faith in historic reason could be assuredly produced. He was content to prophesy a potential future and to invite others to join in finding diverse paths to its fulfillment.

We arrive at nothing more or less than an invitation to reform—but what an invitation! Recall how Plato said that the only politics one can take part in is the politics of one's own character. To change the community we each must have a change of character. The realities of life are such that any particular person, after he has seen to the conditions of his own character, can only invite others to do the same, for no power in the world can either force another to perfect himself, nor can any power, but death, force another to stop seeking self-improvement. If men could devise a sound understanding of the art of self-formation, they would have a tremendous defense against their paternal, statist peers. Men could turn away from the hopeless inertias of practical politics, and with a great-souled joviality they could leaven public life with diverse personal initiatives. With faith in the dignity of personal existence, the radical concern in living became the effort to realize one's self, the fullest human possibility that one could live.

Self-culture, self-formation, self-education became the basic problem of life. Ortega's second voyage, which death terminated long before the journey was complete, was an invitation to see whether innumerable, small spontaneous reforms in the life each man lived could aggregate into such a transformation of the Europeans' character that an undreamed of political, economic, and social life might become possible.

* * *

I searched into myself.

HERACLITUS, 101

MAN NEEDS A NEW *revelation, for he loses himself in his arbitrary and boundless inner cabalism when he can no longer contrast and discipline himself in the clash with what he knows to be an authentic and inexorable reality. Reality is the only true pedagogue and governor of man. Without its inexorable and pathetic presence, there can be no serious culture, there can be no state, there can not even be—and this is the worst of all—reality in one's personal life. When man remains alone, or thinks he does, without another reality that is distinct from his ideas and that sternly limits them, he loses the sensation of his own reality, he becomes for himself an imaginary, spectral, phantasmagoric entity. Only beneath the formidable pressure of some transcendence can we make our person compact and solid, and produce in ourselves a discrimination between what we are in effect and what we merely imagine ourselves to be.*

ORTEGA[1]

---

[1] "Historia como sistema," 1936, *Obras* VI, p. 48.

XVI
On the Past and Future of Present Man

MAN IS BORN A MAN, but everywhere he is treated as a thing. Each person is registered at birth; and thereafter he is repeatedly counted and classified under a variety of numbers; he is continually mobilized as the nation, economy, or society may demand; and he is finally released when death converts him from the consumer to the consumed. In current mythology, human aggregates have been as thoroughly personified as were the forces of nature in primitive religion. The lawyer's fiction of the corporate person has been confounded with reality; and the men of an era yet to come will find us, insofar as we inveterately describe human events as the work of various loving, hoping, wise, wrathful institutions, as curious as we find the Homeric Greeks when they disguised their heroic deeds as the work of Olympian Gods.

History is no longer the story of heroes; it is not even the story of liberty: history has become the record of nations, classes, parties, groups, and processes as they are raised up by causal forces and ruined by objective determinants. A myriad or myriads are mobilized in war; hundreds of thousands starve in famine; millions are exterminated in bestial acts of genocide. In such a world the person seems implacably ground into an object, as a once vital shell is ground to sand when waves endlessly wash it, back and forth, over the grating surface of the shore.

Yet, the fullness of life is best attained as men try to realize their *selves*, not impersonal abstractions, through the use of principles. To facilitate this endeavor, we might radically humanize our understanding of history, sociology and philosophy. Then, these subjects might pertain to our lives, not to corporate fictions. Then they might illuminate the history that exists as an influence in and upon my life, the community that ought to exist through my life, and the philosophy that can best guide my life.

Intellectual work can be judged against various purposes. Great reforms in the human sciences will follow as new purposes generate new intellectual standards. Building empirically true models in social, political, and historical sudies, as well as making exhaustive analyses of procedural points in philosophy, serve the purpose of establishing the repute of the model-builder and the analyst within academe. But as a prelude to acting in one's life upon one's world—as the work of man thinking, not the scholar —model-building is singularly inadequate. Reliance on induction protects the model-builder from criticisms of his personal judgment. In addition, induction makes his models, even models of revolution, radically reactionary, for the inductive modeler confines himself to simple variations on past accomplishments. Furthermore, most models are not made to human scale: they locate the man in the institution, as it were, rather than the other way around. Such models help officials act on unwary individuals, but they do little to illuminate the all-important problems of our personal conduct of life. To empower the person to affect his vital world—the fascinating web of hopes and fears, of abilities and deficiencies, of intentions and performances that compose each particular life—the human scientist would concentrate on principles, not facts, for principles are timeless universals that are *applicable,* that is, susceptible of being applied by the active individual, to every occasion, whereas facts are unique to each situation and are not a suitable basis of applicable generalizations.

Principles become powerful when particular men use them to make and implement personal valuations. Command of principles is not developed by creating models of what happened in various cases; it arises from reflection on what failed to happen. As the laws of physics explain why interventions in nature did not produce the results that men naively expected, historical principles explain why actions by men of good will incurred consequences that failed to fulfill the actors' intentions. Heraclitus was profound when he observed that war is the father of all and that men know of justice only by the fact of injustice.[2] Reflection on failure is the essence of all critical theory; and the purpose of the resulting principles is not to perpetuate established practices, but to free the future of past errors.

"History," Ortega said, "is not only to recount the past, but to understand it, but I should now add that to understand the past, history must necessarily be to criticize it and, in consequence, to become enthused, afflicted, and irritated with it, to censure, applaud, correct, complete, lament, and mock it. History is not a way of saying things: seriously, history is an integral way of living in which the man, the historian, takes part completely— if he is, in truth, a man—in part with his intellect and in part with the whole pack of his most powerful passions, *cum ira et studio*."[3]

In studying "history as a system," Ortega did not try to create a positive model of what happened in history in the manner of Spengler, Toynbee, and others. The past interested Ortega as a record of definite human mistakes, and rigorous reflection on the erring past was valuable to the degree that it yielded principles by which persons could avoid repeating such mistakes in living their particular lives. History would be useful to a man educating himself insofar as it helped him avoid having to repeat the errors of others. "We need history whole to see if we can escape from it, not to fall back into it."[4]

Ortega was not alone in appreciating the negative importance of historical principles. Professional historians easily overlook the radical revision of historical method arising from the "critical history" that Nietzsche advanced in examining the use and disadvantage of history for *life*. Superficially, critical history seems similar to the practices of academic historians, for Nietzsche agreed with the professional in deprecating two other forms of history: the antiquarian and the monumental. In the former, the historian indiscriminately, minutely, and pedantically reconstituted every detail of the past without making any effort to

---

[2] Fragments 53 and 23, Freeman, *Ancilla*, pp. 28, 26.
[3] *Origen y epílogo de la filosofía*, 1943, 1960, *Obras* IX, pp. 411-2.
[4] *La rebelión de las masas*, 1930, *Obras* IV, p. 206.

explain, whereas in the latter, the historian depicted great, moving examples of human achievement without paying close attention to the constricting facts that might diminish the monument. But Nietzsche envisaged doing more through critical history than the professional did with his sound account of essential events and his judicious estimation of their probable causes and historic significance. Nietzsche wanted more than "an interpretation"; he wanted the past to be rigorously analyzed, judged, and *negated*. "Man must have the strength to break up the past, and to apply it, too, in order to live. He must bring the past to the bar of judgment, interrogate it remorselessly, and finally condemn it."[5]

For Nietzsche, critical history accomplished more than reconstructing the past; it became a chisel with which to shape the present. Here the professional historian may resist, uncomfortably wondering how he can effect normative judgments in the present without molding the past into a tool of propaganda. But history used to shape the present would be the antithesis of a "presentist" history, one that interprets the past anachronistically through the categories of present concern. Rather than recount the past to suit the complacencies of the present, Nietzsche suggested that men could criticize the past in order to worry out principles by which they could lead a life different from the one their immediate past, their habits and assumptions, projected into the present. In this way, men would empower themselves to reject the inertias of their past and to make their present from this negation. Here was history in the service of self-formation; here was history with a maximum use and a minimum disadvantage for life.

For Ortega, "history as a system" would be a Nietzschean critical history. Ortega did not mean that history was a physical system like a system of faults in the crust of the earth, the reproductive system of an animal, or the weapons systems of modern armies. He did not want to subject history to "systems analysis." History, like philosophy, was a great *speculative* system; it was the set of principles by which men could make sense of the phenomena of completed human lives. By working out such a system, a man could use it, not to predict the future, but to make the

---

[5]Nietzsche, *The Use and Abuse of History*, Adrian Collins, trans., pp. 20-1.

future, to make, not an abstract future, but his own actual future. History was *about* the past; but it existed in the living present of particular persons. Such history was an intellectual system that yielded principles that living men could use in the present to define their problems and to direct their effort. A particular man could pursue his destiny when he learned to anticipate how his life would unfold over time and to perceive how to deal with challenges to the growing integrity of his character.

A man learned which of his possibilities merited his personal concern by using historical principles to weigh their potential contribution to the reality he sought to live. For example, Socrates' conduct with respect to his trial and execution showed a keen sense of critical history. Socrates understood what actions were a threat to his character, and he used this understanding effectively to defend his chosen way of living. Men should always study history with the Socratic goal in mind; turning back to the past, they could make history a speculative, theoretical discipline that would prove pedagogically practical as men found its results helpful in their concern for self-culture. Progressively, man can "take fuller possession of his past. When the current struggles cease, it is probable that man will, with a fury and eagerness now unknown, occupy himself in absorbing the past to an unheard of degree and with an unprecedented vigor and precision: this is what I call, and have foretold for a number of years, *the dawn of historic reason.*"[6]

Two concepts by which men might take fuller possession of their past were "the generation" and "beliefs." These ideas were not offered primarily to the historian so that he could organize a better narrative of the past; instead, they were to be used by the philosopher, or better yet, by every man who would live philosophically, to define his situation in life, to describe to himself his duty and destiny, to pre-occupy himself with what it was that he had to do. Although these concepts were not primarily to help us write history—their purpose was to help us make history—we can learn much about them by observing how they served historical explanation. One could not use the generation or beliefs

---

[6]*Origen y epílogo de la filosofía*, 1943, 1960, *Obras* IX, p. 362.

effectively in a retrospective narrative of finished events; but one could use them to sharpen one's understanding of the prospective expectations that the participants in events may have had. Thus, Ortega contended that to reconstruct the hopes and fears that had animated historically creative persons one needed such concepts. Generations and beliefs were particularly helpful in revitalizing the essential phenomena in history, the spontaneous concerting of concern among men who may have had no inkling of each other's existence. Helping to make credible how in the past spontaneous personal initiatives could effectively cohere without being organized by some outside force, they might equally well help living men foment such unorganized cooperation.

To explain the substance of these concepts in detail is unnecessary; Ortega did it at greater length and with greater lucidity than could be managed here. Our purpose is to indicate how these components of historic reason were to be used. Heroic, historic adventures were sketched out with concepts like the generation and beliefs. A generation was a temporal grouping of diverse persons who shared, through their separate perspectives, a concern for common historic problems and who saw their lives animated by similar historic tasks.[7] Beliefs underlay another historic grouping, one that could include parts of several generations but perhaps not all of any. Beliefs were certain basic standards of thinking that shape our preception of our world and of ourselves; beliefs determine what we will and will not find convincing. Beliefs were not thoughts, which occur to us at a particular time and place and which we arrive at through a particular act of intellection. "On the contrary, these ideas that truly are 'beliefs' form the container of our life; and, consequently, they are not so constituted as to be particular contents inside of our life. This means that they are not ideas that we have, but ideas that we are. And even more precisely, because they are fundamental beliefs, they are confused by us with reality itself—they are our world and our being—; and, therefore, they cease to have the character of thoughts that might very well not have occurred to

---

[7] *En torno a Galileo*, 1933, *Obras* V, esp. pp. 21-80.

us."[8] In defining his personal aspirations, any particular man relied on certain beliefs and thought of himself as a participant in a generation that had a definite historic mission. If you and I share beliefs and our personal conceptions of our generational tasks mesh together, we will cooperate in our historic activities even though we may never meet and consciously concert our efforts.

With personal conceptions of our generation and beliefs, with the empty concepts filled with content drawn from our personal lives, we can sharpen our understanding of the relation between our selves and our historic circumstances. In developing such comprehension, we prepare ourselves to act more independently, more precisely, more effectively in our world. Without having to know the official vita of another, we can estimate his generation and beliefs from our personal experience of him. Such estimates can become a secure, tacit basis for spontaneous coöperation. Tremendous historic energy inhered in the bonds of belief and in the succession of generations. History as a system was to help particular men—everyman—learn how to control that energy in his personal life.

If through critical history men developed concepts for explaining how they might shape their actual historic destinies, forming vital alliances with other persons, an important improvement would be made in the means that each person found at hand in his self-education. Likewise, reflection on "the social" could serve a similar purpose. Academic sociology failed this purpose; a model of the social structure, of what society is in itself, was at once intellectually impossible and vitally uninteresting. It would be both possible and interesting, however, to gain a clear comprehension of "the social" as it exists in our actual lives and as it helps and hinders our efforts to act; furthermore, each man could use such understanding to perfect his free pursuit of his authentic purposes. The social theory of historic reason would not make "society" function more efficiently; it would help men function more effectively.

---

[8] *Ideas y creencias*, 1940, *Obras* V, p. 384.

A first step towards developing such a theory would be to cut down to human scale that bane of all clear thought—Society, the Social Structure. Great sociologists like Comte, Spencer, Durkheim, and Bergson had failed to determine rigorously what constituted a social fact, Ortega observed.[9] This vagueness led to numerous hypostatizations in which men groundlessly assumed that one or another social model corresponded to some actual entity, variously called society, the social structure, classes, elites, and so on. No such entities existed; the only real referents of social theory were particular aspects of the actual lives of various men, namely the dehumanized side of their lives. "This idea of the *collective soul*, of a *social consciousness*, is arbitrary mysticism. There is no such collective soul, if by *soul* is meant—and here it can mean nothing else—*something* that is capable of being the responsible subject of its acts, *something* that does what it does because what it does has a clear meaning for it. . . . The collective soul, *Volksgeist* or 'national spirit,' social consciousness, has had the loftiest and most marvelous qualities attributed to it, sometimes even divine qualities. For Durkheim, society is veritably God. In the Catholic DeBonald (the actual inventor of collectivist thought), in the Protestant Hegel, in the materialist Karl Marx, this collective soul appears as something infinitely above, infinitely more human than man. . . . The collectivity is indeed something human, but it is the human without man, the human without spirit, the human without soul, the human dehumanized."[10]

Ortega's sociological treatise, *Man and People*, is incomplete. He had planned a course of twelve lectures, the last six of which were to be on the State; Law; Society and its forms; the Nation, ultra-nation, and internation; "Animal societies" and human societies; and Humanity. Ortega was not one to adhere rigorously to a schedule of topics; and the transcript of his twelfth lecture introduces the topic of the State, as if he planned to continue on, and he proposed eight additional lectures that would have covered the topics listed above. Whether he gave these lectures or whether, if

---

[9]*El hombre y la gente*, 1949, 1957, *Obras* VII, p. 81.
[10]*Man and People*, Willard Trask, trans., pp. 174-5.

he did, the transcripts have been preserved, is not clear.[11] The incompleteness of the public record is not too serious, however, for our present endeavor; sufficient portions of his sociology are available for grasping its character.

In *Man and People* Ortega displayed his mastery of phenomenological description, using it to elucidate the nature of social facts as they appear in lived life. His method differed radically from that identified with sociology, and he explicitly rebuked the use of sampling techniques to make inferences about *public* opinion from evidence about *private* opinions.[12] Public opinion was not the holding of similar private opinions by a large number of individuals. Rather public opinion existed among the opinions of each separate person, as he was taken separately; public opinion comprised that portion of man's mental baggage that he possessed, not by virtue of his own intellection or volition, but because it was pressed upon him by his linguistic, cultural, and communal circumstances. The study of public opinion was not to tell men of affairs which ideas were receiving majority or minority backing at various moments, but to help each person become aware of how his conditioned opinions functioned in his vital experience, so that he might gain greater conscious, independent control over his public opinions and increase his sphere of responsible, volitional activity. To accomplish such purposes, sociology had to help individual men gain command of social usages, the various rote gestures, informal customs, commonplaces, and formal laws that were pressed from without on the members of a community.

Ortega envisaged a mission for the sociology of usages similar to that Mannheim, Scheler, Znaniecki anticipated for the sociology of knowledge, except that Ortega more closely circumscribed his conception of the social. If used rigorously, his conception would exclude knowledge from the social realm, locating it in the more hospitable spheres of the personal and the interpersonal. He

---

[11]*El hombre y la gente, Apéndices,* 1949, 1957, *Obras* VII, pp. 270-2. The compilers suggest that at least the notes to these lectures exist and will eventually be published after all Ortega's more finished posthumous papers have been published; *Ibid.,* p. 72.

[12]*Ibid.,* p. 265.

founded his social theory on careful distinctions between these realms of experience.

In the quest for self-knowledge, clarifying these distinctions was important, for the personal, the interpersonal, and the social were real elements of the life one lived. Thus, in rejecting past conceptions of a self-subsistent society as a form of mysticism, Ortega did not seek to deny the reality in our lives of social constraints, for he knew well from his experience as a Spaniard that a man's social circumstances were a determinant of the possibilities that he could pursue both separately, personally, and in common with other men, interpersonally. The social was not some grand, mysterious entity that existed apart from us and that demanded our worship and sacrifice; it was a set of real constraints that affected, for both good or ill, our immediate, transcendent existence. The reality to which social theory corresponded, therefore, was this operational presence of social constraints in our personal lives.

Ortega's ontology invalidated all social theory that hypostatized society, treating it as a self-subsistent entity, the reality of which did not depend on its existence in the particular lives of actual persons. For this reason, Ortega generally avoided the word "society" and replaced it by "the social," for the only reality of the social was adjectival; the social could only describe elements of our actual lives. "Society," when used at all, clearly referred to certain phenomena in one's life. "The theory of human life is, to begin with, the theory of personal life. But inside of our personal life we encounter not only other persons who are like ourselves and who do not give rise to a discipline unlike the personal, but we also encounter them together in an aggregate, that is distinct from each of them and all of them, taken one by one: we call this aggregate the society or the collectivity."[13]

Ortega phenomenologically described how an awareness of the social developed in the life of a person. On finding himself alive in the world, a child began by living with other persons; and from his direct, interpersonal experience of "we," of living with other persons, he developed conceptions of "I" and "you," of my

---

[13]*Una interpretación de la historia universal,* 1948, 1960, *Obras* IX, pp. 75-6.

living with myself and of your living with yourself. By means of
these conceptions, a person could create a multitude of interpersonal worlds in which many different you's and I's entered into
innumerable definite relations. Most of our real experience of
other people fell into this interpersonal realm; and as complicated
as these relations were, the interpersonal sector of my life was not
the social sector. Social facts should not be confused with interpersonal relations. The social comprised a different set of facts;
namely, the innumerable *usages* that each man found pressed
upon him in the course of living his particular life: innumerable
forms of speech, salutations, customs, traffic regulations, and
so on.

Part of Ortega's contemplated contribution to a first philosophy was to have been a study of the use and disadvantage of
usages for life. Curious readers will find the details in *Man and
People*, and we will not follow his reasoning closely here. Suffice
it to note that usages have an anomalous character; they present
themselves to us in our lives as *faits accomplis*. The observation
of usages is never mandatory or inescapable, but refusal to conform carries an impersonal penalty that is characteristic of usages.
To drive on the "wrong" side of the road is dangerous; and people
who refuse to shake hands, who converse in boorish phrases, or
who flout the law all feel, in different ways, the self-enforcing
power of social usages. Hence, the social is that aspect of our
lives that is predetermined by the usages of the people with
whom we live. But the person was not necessarily the helpless
prey of usages, forced to acquiesce or suffer grievous consequences.
Usages were much like habits, the humane value of which William
James so profoundly explicated. While limiting the possibilities
open at any time, usages greatly facilitated, within the limited possibilities, a man's capacity of effective action. Full understanding
of the definite usages in force in a group would minimize the limitations imposed on one's actions by the usages and would maximize one's power to make the usages facilitate one's efforts to act.
Thus, like a good handbook on linguistic convention, the social
theory of historic reason would put the person in control of the
great power that was locked in usages.

A paradox in Ortega's conception was that the social turned

out to be a dehumanized sector of human life. The impersonality of the law is proverbial, and the policeman who enforces it does not act at least in theory as a man, but as an officer. Usages exist because "one" accepts them, and they are thus devoid of particularized human interest. This dehumanization revealed the social as a completely derivative realm that could not be justified as a goal for personal endeavor; the social gained value only if it served to facilitate the pursuit of definite human purposes. For instance, speech was a social fact consisting of "what people say." Scientific students of language could compile, codify, and comprehend the entirety of speech; but the fulfillment of their inquiry was not in the abstract comprehension of language itself, but in the definite improvement of efforts by particular persons to say what they had to say. While the mechanical act of speaking was social, the intelligent act of saying something was personal, fully human. Social facts were themselves dehumanized, and their justification for existing in our lives was that they help us to realize our possible, personal humanity. Properly understood, usages are an essential aid in our self-formation: they free us to concentrate on more significant matters. As Socrates explained to Crito, despite occasional abuses, the laws educate us by providing a form within which we can determine our personal character. The laws were sovereign indirectly; namely, by serving a man as he sought to be the sovereign of his soul.

Because the human value of usages was indirect, a complicated problem of enforcement arose, a problem that, once understood, showed why it was so important for the quality of common life that people be united by stirring, difficult aspirations. *Man and People* ends just when Ortega arrived at this problem, introducing the paradox that society is as much an occasion for dissension as an opportunity for community. However, in other works he explained the gist of his views, especially in *An Interpretation of Universal History*.[14]

Since usages were justified only to the degree that they helped men pursue their authentic purposes, they were vulnerable to the resentment of those who experienced the established usages as

---

[14]*Ibid.*, pp. 64-119.

destructive impediments blocking self-fulfillment. Repeatedly, situations have arisen in which many have found that the established usages impeded their personal formation; then, the Socratic willingness to cherish the laws, come what may, quickly disappeared. Such situations led to great historic crises similar to the one that Ortega thought the European peoples were experiencing.[15] Now, in our time, the prominence of national usages seems out of proportion to the scant degree that they facilitate the pursuit of interesting personal purposes. Hence, the nations, especially the more grandiose ones, are vulnerable to a seething resentment in the young: they widely perceive national usages as unjustified impediments to the fulfillment of their higher possibilities. The managers of the nation-state can do little to preserve their present prominence; change is under way. But, as Ortega realized, progress or regress in the transformation of national usages depends on whether they are anarchically torn asunder or sportingly transcended, whether we restrain the agents of the nation-state by turning against them in anger or by turning away from them in admiration for something else. Only the latter course can conserve the real accomplishments of our national traditions without making of those traditions an intolerable barrier against man's further self-realization. "The infamy and irresponsibility of politicians has brought Europe to this hour of debasement, in which it feels like Atlantis, for it seems about to submerge itself in the elemental fluid that is history. But thanks to its inexhaustible or almost inexhaustible interior riches, well beneath the skin of this, its debasement, it subterraneously prepares the basis of a new culture . . . , but the surface, the conspicuous part of both the collectivities and the greater number of individuals, is patently miserable."[16]

To revalue national usages constructively, men need a social theory that is antithetical to the ones that make the person more docile before established authorities; men need a social theory, like that of historic reason, that will recreate a personal sense of authority by helping them understand how social usages can be

---

[15]See especially *En torno a Galileo*, 1933, *Obras* V, pp. 81-164; and "Un capítulo sobre la cuestión de como muere una creencia," 1954, 1962, *Obras* IX, pp. 707-725.

[16]*Meditación de Europa*, 1949, 1960, *Obras* IX, p. 268.

harnessed to personal concerns. Few now have the Socratic realization that the established laws are our educators and that these can, when attended to properly, help us form our selves. Instead, we have accustomed ourselves to thinking of usages, especially those of the nation, as objective powers that have their own internal dynamic before which our personal concerns pale into insignificance: some revere, others hate these august powers. But the social forms of the nation merit allegiance only insofar as they serve in our efforts to educate our selves. By this standard, the national idea is on the verge of losing our allegiance. But men will not find real alternatives to the nation by deferring to even more grandiose abstractions; we will find alternatives when we give allegiance to social usages that transcend the claim of any particular nation and that effectively help each live a fuller life. We must find these usages within our lives. As Ortega often reiterated, men are the only agents of historic initiative; they do not exercise that initiative by irritably seeking to suppress established usages, but by adapting existing usages to the service of surprising, new purposes.

In sum, as historic reason replaced abstract reason, marked changes would occur in disciplines pertinent to the conduct of life. Generally, studies would be reoriented so that everyman could use them in his effort to live his life well. Particularly, history would lose its traditional character as a descriptive subject, becoming more theoretical, whereas sociology would cease to be so theoretical, becoming more descriptive. Such reorientation would make these studies more effective in informing the reason by which we shape our personal lives. For instance, Americans have already had a taste of the practical power generated when descriptive sociologies spontaneously inform the historic reasoning of many youths, shaping the beliefs of a generation. Thus, in recent years corporate businesses have had difficulty recruiting talented young men and women, each of whom decides separately against corporate life on the basis of how certain sociologists have trenchantly described the usages governing giant organizations.[17] In this

---

[17] An excellent case study in the processes of civic pedagogy in the United States would be an imaginative inquiry into the influence of descriptive sociologies like William H. Whyte's *The Organization Man* on the expectations of those who acquired their education during the 1960's.

way, historic reason affects the practical world. Spontaneous confrontations between social usages and personal intentions have only begun; a theoretical history and a descriptive sociology may produce many more.

Be that as it may, descriptive history and theoretical sociology still dominate their disciplines, but a basis exists in the realities of life for a reversal, or at least a merger, of their interests. The person learns little about the living of life from a knowledge of historical facts or of social theories, but he might learn much from historical theory and social facts. Living our life is a dynamic, temporal enterprise; to live our life well, we need theories that explain how we can act on relationships that function over time. Furthermore, to act well at any particular time and place, we need to know the established usages that will facilitate or hinder our efforts. Taking history and sociology as coöperative enterprises, which hopefully will function far into the future, one might further contend that the historical theorist will gain more from a mounting heritage of careful sociological descriptions than the social theorist will gain from a continually revised body of historical description. Regardless of how these matters work out, for Ortega *The Dawn of Historic Reason* would herald an effort by both historian and sociologist to inform, expand, and perfect the rational powers diverse persons used in living their lives. The philosopher, too, had a similar task.

Having already surveyed Ortega's philosophical reforms, we need to make only one further point in showing how he invited men to make philosophy, as well as history and sociology, more useful and less disadvantageous for their lives. In basing philosophy on life and in using it to guide living, men should be careful not to narrow undesirably their repertory of truly vital concerns. "Vital concerns" means the actual hopes and fears that beneath all the rationalizations really move men in the course of their living their lives. It means the real motive: the love of the good, pure or perverted; anxiety; joy; exuberance. Ortega's stature vis-à-vis his philosophical peers will be found in the richness of his sense of life, in his surer sympathy for man's vital concerns. Ortega found thinkers like Kierkegaard, Heidegger, and Sartre unable to do justice to the dramatic, joyful side of life; and in comparison to them Ortega excelled by virtue of his ability to draw on a truly catholic sense of life in filling out his reform of reason with concrete concerns.

A guiding philosophy that does not do justice to the actual concerns that move men will automatically become destructive as men impose it upon themselves, for it will prompt them to suppress authentic parts of their lives. Valid parts of their destinies will appear as matters not recognized according to their partial views. Persons seriously involved with the vital issues of experience will be deceived into inauthenticating themselves and trying, even, to impose their imagined limitations on others. Men give inward consent to a system of practical reason only when it makes sense with respect to the realities they are actually living; and standards based on an incomplete sense of life will not gain inward consent and will spread only as the few impose them on others, forcefully cutting life down to fit a narrowed image. Consequently, it was of the utmost importance that any conception of practical reason begin with a full inventory of the moving concerns of life.

On this point, Ortega held a number of influential thinkers to have been too narrow. Like the technicians, important humanists exaggerated the moving power of anxiety while they underestimated that of exuberance. Ortega most seriously opposed writers who condemned an outright determinism by arguing that human freedom was authentically manifest only in anguish. Any conception of practical reason that made anxiety the sole sign of authentic concern would necessarily end, despite the philosopher's intentions, in a deterministic stimulus-response psychology. Man would be seen as free, but biased by a desire to diminish his most palpable uncertainties and to preserve his most cherished certainties, to lessen his anxieties. Ortega acknowledged that anguish was *one* authentic manifestation of human freedom, but not the only one, for through anguish alone men could not sustain freedom. Driven only by anxiety men would seek consistently to escape from freedom.

Man's creative potency, his ability to sustain his freedom, his power to initiate unnecessary acts, sprang from his sporting, joyous exuberance as much as from his anxiousness. "Life is anguish and enthusiasm and sensual pleasure and bitterness and innumerable other things."[18] To avoid distorting practical reason by unjustly narrowing its base, Ortega showed that enthusiasm was equally as authentic a part of life as was anxiety. Our awareness of our freedom, even more, the actuality of our freedom, did not always give rise to anguish: frequently it provoked profound feelings of exhilaration. Joy, hope, and exuberance moved us into the unknown, which in turn produced a sense of anxiety, an alertness towards possible landmarks. The real basis for practical reason was the open interplay of joy and anguish, and only the dialectic of the two could give an adequate alternative to closed stimulus-response theories of behavior. "My idea, then, is that the tone adequate for philosophizing is not the wearisome seriousness of life, but the halcyon joviality of sport, of play."[19]

Historic reason made sense only if men were actually moved by positive, sportive concerns. If men used reason predominantly to minimize their anxieties in the face of their freedom, then they would not take to historic reason, for in effect such reasoning would increase their anxieties by continually expanding their freedom. But if men used reason predominantly to maximize their personal, positive accomplishments, then they would find historic reason to be a great aid. Anxiety and joy were the concomitants of any personal effort, and the philosopher should seek to adapt reason to strengthening the positive effort rather than to drawing attention, one-sidedly, to the anguish.

Ortega could not accept the Sartrean lament that it was futile to speak of the good life with men who were hungry; too often, the hunger has been caused by various conceptions of the good life, for instance, that cattle are sacred or that a man's virility should be tested by the number of children he sires. Even hungry, downtrodden men gamely face life as a sporting matter, proposing goals and accepting certain standards. They have a sense of personal dignity, freedom, and power. The job of philosophy was to build on these positive qualities, to arm them with greater foresight, surer skills, and a sharper sensibility. The good life had not resulted from men banding together in an anguished effort to

---

[18]*La idea de principio en Leibniz,* 1947, 1958, *Obras* VIII, p. 297, n. 1.
[19]*Ibid.,* p. 306.

defend themselves from danger. Well-being resulted from man's sportive exuberance by which millions of independent efforts aggregated into a great qualitative improvement of life. The philosopher would serve human well-being to the degree that he founded a humanistic, practical reason on the full range of man's authentic concerns, on the joyful as well as the anguished. Then everyman had to harness this reason to improving his personal ability to pursue his positive aspirations.

In sum, Ortega invited men to cease making academic specialities of history, sociology, and philosophy and to begin letting these serve more directly in forming the actual rationality that everyman employs in living his life. These subjects would not work magically, providing perfect programs to the abstract difficulties of the time. These subjects were not meant to perfect primarily our civic programs, but to help the civic substance, men, perfect themselves. The education of the public was thus a matter for self-culture, not paternal instruction; and this faith in the public significance of self-education departs sharply from present practice. In effect, historians, sociologists, and philosophers were invited to stop treating their subjects as the vehicles of truth, so to speak, and their students as empty receptacles into which the truths of their subjects are dumped. By basing all forms of reason on the realities of living, the students become the vehicles of truth, the truths of life, and the subjects become receptables into which truths that have been proved in various persons' lives are gathered. "Philosophy is not to demonstrate with life that which is the truth; it is strictly the contrary, to demonstrate the truth by being able, thanks to it, to live authentically."[20]

What might happen if men take up the human sciences in the spirit of Count Yorck and Wilhelm Dilthey, believing that the significance of these studies for human practice is pedagogical? What might result if men responded to Ortega's invitation, making culture serve the fullness of life, of the life that each lives? These questions have no predetermined answers, for the point of the invitation was to bring spontaneity back into public affairs, to call on the men of eminent capacity to follow their own lights.

---

[20]*Ibid.*, p. 316.

Ortega urged men not to be content to impose the abstract plans of today upon the living reality of tomorrow.[21] He did not merely invite historians, sociologists, and philosophers to make their subjects serve the pedagogy of self-formation. He further called on men, on everyman, to make full use of this pedagogy, refurbishing the historic spontaneity that has been characteristic of Western history.

Ortega expended much effort in his later years in addressing diverse groups — librarians, architects, educators, corporate executives, dramatists, lawyers, doctors, scholars, and scientists. With each group, his plea was the same: *"¡Pensar en grande!"* The practitioner of any occupation based on intellect was a man of culture, not a specialist; this man of culture was responsible, not only for performing his limited duties effectively, but further for basing this performance on a definite conception of its implications for the whole of life. All men of culture, especially the young, had a mission to perfect their imagination and intellect, to enter every profession without abdicating their initiative to the formalized rituals of a career, and to inform their performances with a definite conception of what significance their special competencies had for the complete cultural repertory of their time. Let the librarian find ways to make the book, of which he was the custodian, serve as a more effective stimulus to life. Let the men of the theater discover how to transport the audience to an intimation of yet unimagined human possibilities. Let the lawyer not be content to administer existing law but to create desirable, new forms of law. In short, let cultured individuals in every walk of life continually take initiatives that will keep every habit and every institution in permanent disequilibrium, in a perpetual need for adaptation.

As is common these days, Ortega's vision of the future called for marked changes in cultural institutions. Numerous critics have perceived that the great era of organizational reform in politics, economics, and social relations has approached completion in the West. They recognize that the locus of constructive change has shifted from practical organizations to educational, scientific, and

---

[21]"Apuntes sobre una educación para el futuro," 1953, 1962, *Obras* IX, p. 675.

cultural concerns. Thus, many have suggested that these be reorganized to take account of their novel power.[a] But usually the desired reorganization is impossibly unrealistic. The plans are utopian *not* because they fail to take into account the existing circumstances; about the present situation planners are often painstakingly precise. They are utopian *not* because they lack specific prescriptions; with these they abound. They are utopian because the planners do not understand the character of cultural power; they are unaware of its proper source and its peculiar mode of operation. Pedagogical planners confuse cultural power with political power, and out of inertia they treat cultural concerns as if they were practical organizations. Like the politician, businessman, and warrior, they propose a glorious campaign, break it into plausible steps, and expect their underlings to perform as planned. They have read the *Republic* but failed to sense its irony.

Political power is prescriptive; cultural power is protreptic. Politics commands the will; culture persuades the understanding. The two must go together, but they do not mix: the protreptic politician is a demagogue and the prescriptive intellectual is an ideologue. These distinctions help one comprehend the genius of Ortega's hortatory reforms, his invitation to innovation.

Ortega's proposals to the men of culture were protreptic, not prescriptive. He wanted to inspire dramatists, executives, lawyers, librarians, teachers, writers, scholars, even man-thinking with a vision of an intellectual life greater than any now known. The university, its students, its faculty, its libraries, the professions it served, the schools it drew from, writers, publishers, and scientists too: all could rise up, and each, independently, could inform his work with a grander design. What held for the university, held for every aspect of culture: "the origin of university reform is in coming fully to terms with its mission. All change, repair, or refurbishing of our house that does not begin by first revising with energetic clarity, with decision, and with truth the problem of our mission will be a labor of wasted love."[22] The protreptic reformer believes that if free men are in concord about purposes,

---

[22]*Misión de la universidad*, 1930, *Obras* IV, p. 314.

they can work in community even though each attends only to his personal performance.

Not only was Ortega's grand design for intellect protreptic rather than prescriptive, it was extensive rather than intensive. Most pedagogical prescriptions concentrate on one set of institutions. Planners specialize: they cannot lay down the law for all. Hence, in 1945 a Harvard committee on general education thought it had cast its net wide by precribing possible reforms for both the secondary schools and the colleges. But a year later, Howard Mumford Jones showed that such proposals were impossible without reform of the graduate schools.[23] No matter where one begins to plan, soon all is drawn in. Ortega understood this fact: to exhort students to move towards one goal was useless, if the faculty had a different bent, the libraries had another, and the professions yet a fourth. Therefore, Ortega incited many groups that worked with intellect to contemplate their mission. The particular design of each group, of course, would differ, but Ortega hoped that each would inform its mission with a problem common to all: to wit, improving the use of cultural power in contemporary life. By doing so, men of culture would greatly expand their capacity to exercise initiative, a publicly significant private initiative, in the contemporary West.

Readers interested in Ortega's particular ideas about cultural institutions had best go to the sources.[b] Because each had its own mission, the way each might serve historic reason had to be taken up separately. Nevertheless, when Ortega's ideas about the library, writing, the theater, art, the liberal professions, and the university are juxtaposed, his single purpose becomes apparent: to exhort men of culture to use their power independently. A national humanities foundation was not needed for the human sciences to affect public life. At every instant, men of letters influenced the ethical concord within which all public affairs took place. To do so with optimum effect, each needed to contemplate his per-

---

[23]See The Committee on the Objectives of a General Education, *General Education*, esp. pp. 4-5; and Howard Mumford Jones, *Education and World Tragedy*, esp. pp. 109-178.

sonal abilities and intentions, and, with a profound personal commitment, to appoint himself to the task of continually provoking himself, his peers, the people, and their leaders to examine their purposes and powers. Men of culture of every type could each determine what function he could perform in the further liberation of man; and then, if each strove self-consciously to fulfill this mission, all would be pushed beyond their present limits.

Culture was the means men had invented for thinking about their purposes. "Life is a chaos, a savage forest, a confusion. Man is lost in it. But his mind reacts at his sensation of shipwreck and ruin; it works to find in the forest 'paths' or 'ways', that is, clear and firm ideas about the universe and positive convictions about what things and the world are. The conjunction or system of these is the culture in the true sense of the word." In this true sense, he continued, culture was the opposite of ornament. "Culture is that which saves us from vital shipwreck, which permits man to live, and without which his life would be a tragedy lacking sense, and hence, a radical debasement."[24] Culture was a cosmos of conceptions, the tools of historic reason, within which men could define and discuss their purposes; and whoever freely refined these conceptions, sharpening the tools with which men think in the course of living, would spontaneously enlarge and perfect the possibilities open to men. Ortega invited us to have faith in historic reason and to use this power; this was his invitation to autonomy.

His invitation to the men of culture was thoroughly protreptic. Officials cannot keep the initiative in the face of protreptic reforms; they can only try to prevent potential reformers from appealing to their peers. Many people, out of habit, are inclined to belittle protreptic reform, seeing it as a threat to rational organization, which has served so well as a source of progress in past centuries. But Ortega invited us to embark once again on a great departure from past forms. Western communities had rigidified with the actualization of their major political, economic, and social aspirations; therefore the historic responsibility of protreptic reform was great: it alone could turn our effort towards uncharted seas. Ortega's appeal to librarians, playwrights, and

---

[24]*Misión de la universidad*, 1930, *Obras* IV, p. 321.

professionals, to students and professors, to all men of culture, was that they set their own standards, that they define their respective goals, and that they find ways to order their lives on the basis of these integral purposes. In making this appeal, Ortega was not pandering to parochial perversities; he was arguing for the highest historic service. Possibilities for historic initiative had been exhausted in the practical walks of life; nevertheless, men would create new historic enterprises by realizing that the great, unfilled possibility was to uncover and exercise the uses of cultural power.

*　　*　　*

Soul has its own principle of growth.

HERACLITUS, 115

*I*N THIS HALF-LIGHT *in which the very principles of our civilization have disappeared beneath the horizon, we must try to see things clearly. Every crepuscule . . . is a light that can be equally either the last hour of the day or the beginning of the dawn. Therefore it divides us into two groups: on one side there are those whom I call the "vespertine," who believe that all is concluding, and on the other there are those who believe, like myself, that it is necessary to be "matutinal." This is not pessimism, but the contrary. It is the announcement that something great is going to begin: that is to say, it is not yet here, it is not yet known, it is still problematical and difficult; and for persons who accept life only as a convenience, it is still dead. But any man whose veins throb with a bit of blood has a need for the opposite: a perpetual inconvenience and inquietude, and, with an imperative sense of creation, a going towards something new. These new principles are not utopian matters, they have here and now begun to be.*

ORTEGA[1]

[1]Ortega, remarks in the discussion of "Pasado y porvenir para el hombre actual," at the conference "La connaissance de l'homme au XXᵉ siècle," Rencontres internationales de Genève, 1951, as printed in *Hombre y cultura en el siglo XX*, pp. 351-2.

¡Pensar En Grande!

S ENSITIVE, CAPABLE youths are being oppressed by a mood of
déjà vu; we have already seen and rejected the obvious
options before us and our minds are swollen by a plethora of
abstractions that blot from view our authentic, novel possibilities.
As a consequence, those who might be the fount of a significant
future are turning to the bizarre, the extreme, and the frivolous.
Why not? In the absence of stirring aspirations, extravagance is
next best, for at least it permits an exuberant examination of all
modes of modishness. But unstructured experiments at living by
turned-on imaginations have their own discontents; and when the
rock group, the Jefferson Airplane, closed their high-flying
version of Alice in Wonderland with the insistent suggestion—
"FEED YOUR HEAD!"—they may unwittingly have been pushing a stimulant more lasting and humanizing than pot or LSD.

We are starving from mental malnutrition because we have
been fed a steady diet of indigestible abstractions. Most ideas
recommended as very important matters are useless in an individual effort to form one's personal character; yet one's character,
not the ubiquitous abstractions, is what each person is destined
to live with and by. The young are not anti-intellectuals—far from
it! For them, intellect has ceased to be the sum of disembodied
truths about things out there. Intellect is the intellect of each person, the sum of skills and principles that each has mastered and
that each can bring to bear in continually making his encounters
with the world and other people as significant, just, and joyful
as possible. In this sense, intellect thrives on principles, not

abstractions; yet academe has lost itself in abstractions and offers mainly these.

Principles are unapologetically mere conceptions that men are free to use *hic et nunc* to guide their actual acts in the flesh and blood immediacy of life. Abstractions, in contrast, serve to define within the immediacy of particular lives a more inclusive, diffuse sphere of activity in which both natural and civic processes seem to follow courses all their own. Here is the difference: a man may have recourse to principles as he sires and raises a child, whereas officials must rely on abstractions if they are to resolve problems of overpopulation. The malaise is not that we lack abstractions by means of which we can define significant public problems: we have been surfeited as pundits pronounce on the problems of population, peace, poverty, progress, and pollution. But the more immediate problem, which is felt by those who combine a generous impulse with critical awareness, is that these and other serious difficulties are defined in ways that make it almost impossible for any particular person to act on them out of principle with any definite, significant effect.

Abstract generalities about pressing problems of public affairs do not define a *Kinderland*. The constant call to public action does little to help any man define his personal aspirations with respect to the definite realities of his life. In our actual lives, the great, established institutions—the corporation, union, church, school, and state—are all too often experienced as imperious, bumbling intruders. Thus men have ceased to experience the state as a mere *idea*, a hope, that they can freely use in their personal lives to orient their independent activities. Instead, men have grown accustomed to experiencing the state as a deficient monolith, a magisterial entity beset by overriding needs. Hence authority is on the verge of dissolution, for a deficient monolith is absurd. *Delenda est imperium!* Sentient men cannot live as self-respecting human beings by solely aspiring to solve abstract difficulties, those of the public and *its* problems, the one that, as officials might say, "functional analyses and statistical projections reveal as threats to the viability of the complex, dynamic processes that sustain modern societal and economic systems." *Ecce homo!*

Our task is to nurture our spontaneity and to channel it towards a *Kinderland* of common, personal significance.

*　　*　　*

We reach the climax of Ortega's thought. Throughout his later works, he spread prophetic utterances inviting men to turn away from concern for sustaining the established order and to join in founding radically new forms of life. Recently, we have become surfeited by the frivolous use of such phrases by professional puffers and are nearly incapable of seriously contemplating substantial changes in our way of life. We expect the newness of the new to be described in attractive detail and our empirical sensibility rebels at expecting the unexpected. Those modern augurs, the futurologists, assure us that the year 2000 will be much more like 1970 than 1984. Ortega, instead, foresaw aspects of the future, not by projecting present trends ahead, but by anticipating trends that were not now present. He called explicit attention to the radicalism of his views, for his radicalism, which was based on the only real radicalism possible, a philosophical revision of first principles, was easily overlooked.[2] If first principles were transformed, a coherent yet spontaneous transformation of everything else becomes probable especially in the seemingly fundamental realm of politics. This Emerson understood: "the history of the State sketches in coarse outline the progress of thought, and follows at a distance the delicacy of culture and aspiration."[3]

The twentieth century was a time of true transition into a yet unknown, indeterminate way of living, Ortega believed. The external forms of living that would characterize the coming era might be as different from those of the nineteenth century as were the concerns of the nineteenth from those of the thirteenth. Real change was afoot. Anything could happen. Men no longer had faith in the realities in the midst of which their predecessors had for millennia lived. All was possible, even stasis. Faith in a new reality might spontaneously develop, bringing an unexpected

---

[2]See *La idea de principio en Leibniz*, 1948, 1958, *Obras* VIII, pp. 281-5.
[3]Emerson, "Politics," *Works*, Vol. 1, p. 368.

transformation in its train, or one or another relic of the outworn authorities might use the state to impose a sterile, empty order on the world. The state might overwhelm our spirit. Our spirit might rise above the state. There was no assurance of anything, except whatever would happen, be it renewal or collapse, would happen because of what each man did freely, responsibly, and finally in the particular life he lived.

Ortega rejected any claim that the established order deserved positive allegiance. He equally denied any assertion that the established order merited negative opposition. Western man was in the midst of another great, historic transformation; in the face of the impending metamorphosis, the course of events with respect to established institutions paled into insignificance. Involvement in the state, with it or against it, could end only in statism. The significant developments depended on how each cultivated his own character; and to direct attention to this concern, Ortega was quite willing to slight traditional conceptions of public affairs. In his late work, the former political commentator was silent about practical events. He barely mentioned World War II or the Cold War; and despite his strongly voiced interest in a supranational mode of life, he showed no concern for the Marshall Plan, NATO, or the United Nations. A remark from the 1920's perfectly characterizes his later attitude: "I hope that our century will react against the belittling of educative work. There will arrive in Europe an exemplary devaluation of all politics. Having been in the first rank of human preoccupations, it will decline in status and end as the lowliest. And to everyone it will be evident that it is politics that must adapt itself to pedagogy, which will then achieve its sublime and proper goals."[4]

A social order could be legitimate, Ortega contended, only when founded on a living faith, a common belief about the character of reality. Only from a shared belief about reality could a system of reasoned discourse about common problems gain sufficient authority to harmonize—freely, without external compulsion —the conflicting interests of men. In the absence of a common belief, even the best intentioned, most scrupulously legal rule

---

[4]"Pedagogía y anacronismo," 1923, *Obras* III, p. 133.

could do nothing but force its will upon men who did not share the beliefs of those in power. Since men in the industrial world lacked a concord about fundamental realities, no system of rule was legitimate and there was no way to legitimate any system of rule until one or another conception of reality spontaneously became a common belief. The illegitimacy of the present order, however, did not legitimate disobedience, *dis*-obedience, which in a paradoxical way affirmed the established order. "The very first thing that is to be done with illegitimacy is to swallow it."[5] One wastes one's effort warring against a doomed order, for the cause of the doom is not in the strength of those who oppose the order, but in the weaknesses of the order itself: hence many an ancient regime has preserved itself by sucking vigor from its vocal opponents.

For Ortega, all systems of order were radically illegitimate; none had an iota of power to make itself legitimate, for the source of the illegitimacy was not in the government, but in the people, in their lack of common beliefs about fundamental matters. Consequently, the upshot of Ortega's theory of illegitimacy was not an engagé argument, one holding that all governments were illegitimate, but that some were less illegitimate than others and that these might, given support, evolve into legitimate ones. Such reasoning, which persuaded Merleau-Ponty and Sartre to support Soviet communism, carried no weight with Ortega. No government could cause itself or be caused to become legitimate, for legitimacy rested on authentic beliefs of the people, not on attributes of the government. The lack of such beliefs could not be solved by any form of group manipulation, for even though men could be temporarily forced to profess allegiance or momentarily beguiled into believing that they believed, a living, enduring faith existed only as an unmoved mover.

Faith could not be produced in others; each man, on communing with himself, found that deep within him, either he had it or he did not. In a time of disbelief, men could only search within themselves. Thus, the illegitimacy that Ortega found characteristic of our time did not justify aggravating the unscru-

---

[5]*Una interpretación de la historia universal*, 1948, 1960, *Obras* IX, p. 155.

pulous competition between groups for the control of organized force; rather it showed the competition to be null. Contemporary illegitimacy threw each man back upon himself; it drove each man to seek out his beliefs and to manifest these in his personal conduct of life. "I have nothing to do with politics and nothing of what I speak is political, but something enormously more profound and more grave than all politics."[6]

Let us soar free with Ortega. We are in the midst of a radical transvaluation of values. Reality itself is changing. Hence, in the interim, man has no authority outside himself upon which he can rely for justification; each determines what it is that he shall stand for, and that determination is final: for good or ill, it is the ethic he will have lived by in the reality of his life. Life is self-realization, and to realize one's best self one needs to recognize his endeavor as an exuberant, sporting lark. This joviality was the very essence of the transvaluation of values that Ortega foresaw. The serious could not stand against the expedient; values could be upheld only for the joy of it. The established order harbored little joy; if left alone, it would fall into disuse as more and more men found it void. But Ortega did not see the old order tumbling in a dramatic collapse; Rome no more fell in a day than it was built in a day. Although the old would persist, a new order would ineluctably emerge as persons recognized that the demands of the old were illegitimate and turned within themselves, searching for ways to perfect their immediate lives.

Men will develop a new order through self-education. Historic spontaneity is a function of man's capacity for self-culture. The configuration of the future will develop as diverse persons take responsibility for themselves and develop in themselves qualities that, by their exemplarity, will become the basis of a new system. In the end, Europe is not for the Europeans; the Europeans, whomever they may be, will make Europe. To change our world we must discover how to change ourselves; and if we learn to change ourselves, no power on earth or in the heavens can prevent us from changing our world. Here is Ortega's optimism:

------

[6]*Ibid.*, pp. 224-5.

self-education is the most fundamental of all historic determinants. It is a fact of life: each man is individually free to orient all his cultural surroundings to the concern of self-formation. By doing so, Ortega thought, men would break with the familiar line of development. Progress would cease to mean improving the institutionalized performance of economic, social, and political functions. The national histories that stretched from the Renaissance, Reformation, and Enlightenment up to our recent past would close. With this break, men would rediscover that to live was to aspire to an uncertain future.

Needless to say, one could criticize the anticipation of such a crisis as the advocacy of cultural discontinuity. Ortega was not awed by institutions or offices; he was willing to see venerated ones decline, contract, and disappear. In matters of civilization, too, he was venturesome: he foresaw a marked revision in the hierarchy of valuations that underlay contemporary materialism. But even in his most apocalyptic moments, Ortega did not advocate historical discontinuity.

Previously, Western man had experienced historic changes as sharp as those that Ortega envisaged; yet there remained a Western tradition. In precisely that fact one touched on the true genius of the men who had made Western history: they never gave themselves over entirely to a single way of life, to a static set of institutions, or to an unchanging pattern of thought. Historical continuity does not require stasis; the deeper one sinks one's roots the higher one can raise one's character and stand steady in the midst of howling change. Ortega showed no frivolous anti-intellectualism; unlike those who feel that their most banal surroundings are naturally new, he held that the men who could *make* their future were the ones who could master their past. To the degree that in his late writings he ignored the present and prophesized about the future, he studied his past, especially the record of classical politics and philosophy, for continuity would be created in the course of change by men who understood the principles of their predecessors.

In believing that Ortega argued for a break with his tradition, one not only misinterprets Ortega, one more seriously misunderstands the continuity characteristic of our tradition. When Ortega asserted that " 'Western civilization has died! Long live Western civilization!' " he asserted the very opposite of historical discontinuity.[7] There is no continuity in stasis. A tradition, like a bicycle, is stable only when moving. The culture by which men have lived in the West rests on the principle of the infinite profundity of the person. When the chips were down, the human person has alway been considered to be greater than any of his creations. The fixity of external characteristics has continually given way to transformations in internal chraracter. What binds Socrates, Jesus, Abelard, Sir Thomas More, and Albert Schweitzer is not the government they recognized, the ways they earned a living, similarities in their choice of friends, the conventions they heeded, or their style of dress; they are bound together by their willingness to think through their convictions and to live or die in fidelity to their conclusions. Up to now in the West, institutions have remained protean forms, allowing any person who has the will to break loose, not without cost but with effect, to explore the endless possibilities of his character. As a consequence, each man in each successive generation has found himself with a richer heritage to draw from and with greater goals to aspire to, *should he so wish it.*

Institutional discontinuity has been the price of characterological continuity. Should our external way of life become fixed, then we will deprive our progeny, each one in his particularity, of the glorious quest for the whole man, for the fullness of life, that we have inherited from our forebears. The continuity of our culture develops from an eternal recurrence. Our culture continually comes back to life when particular men find themselves unable to rely satisfactorily on the established externals. Our culture will die only when the established externals are exalted mindlessly into rigid molds for human conduct. Hence, to see Ortega's disdain for existent institutions as a desire to renounce the accomplishments of ages is unjust. Quite the contrary. The surest way to renounce our past is to be content with our present, to elevate a passing instant into a timeless standard, and to be so dull as to be unable to imagine a world in which great nations

---

[7]"Pasado y porvenir para el hombre actual," 1951, 1962, *Obras* IX, p. 661.

and immense industries had become minor matters. Continuity is an attribute of change; and to appreciate our fatherland, we need the strength to aspire to our *Kinderland*.

Western history has been dynamic because the men who made it shared a conviction, well expressed by Heraclitus, that the human spirit is infinitely deep and inexhaustible. In the face of each person's profundity, no particular way of life can claim finality. "You could not discover the limits of soul, even if you traveled every road to do so; such is the depth of its meaning."[8] This conviction has been a standing invitation to each man in every age to plumb his spirit ever more deeply. So far, whenever our forefathers seemed to settle onto a static level of life, this invitation has been courageously renewed.

So it was by Ortega. Surveying the existing forms of civilization, he found them exhausted; the going patterns of politics, science, and art offered little hope to any particular person that he could travel further through them towards the limits of soul. As a result, Western man had begun to doubt the forms of his civilization, which was a most healthy sign, for civilization did not die from doubt. Let us free ourselves from servile attendance to sterile forms. Let us return to the Heraclitean spirit. Let us have faith that man is more than his accomplished works. When present forms were exhausted, the past and the future invited men to invent new ones. Facing his audience, as he had done at Bilbao over forty years before, the aged master again invited the young to meet the challenge before which their elders were faltering.

We have arrived at a moment, ladies and gentlemen, in which we have no other solution than to invent, and to invent in every order of life. I could not propose a more delightful task. One must invent! Well then! You the young — lads and lasses — Go to it![9]

---

[8]Heraclitus, Fragment 45 (DK), Wheelwright trans., *Heraclitus*, Fr. 42, p. 58.
[9]"Pasado y porvenir para el hombre actual," 1951, 1962, *Obras* IX, p. 663.

BIBLIOGRAPHICAL ANNOTATIONS

I: ASPIRATIONS

I: a. SPAIN FERMENTED WITH IRREVERENT DISCONTENT (p. 8). Spanish social history is intriguingly complicated. Three good general histories are Raymond Carr's *Spain: 1808–1939,* Salvador de Madariaga's *Spain: A Modern History,* and Rhea Marsh Smith's *Spain: A Modern History.* Gerald Brenan does an excellent job unraveling the different popular movements in early twentieth-century Spain in *The Spanish Labyrinth: An Account of the Social and Political Background of the Spanish Civil War.* Juan Díaz del Moral's *Historia de las agitaciones campesinas andaluzas* is a marvelous book, rich in detail but circumscribed in scope; it is essential for giving a sense of the grass-root reality of the movements. James Joll's *The Anarchists,* an intrinsically less valuable work, nevertheless is useful in locating one of Spain's popular movements in its European context. The ferment was not only socio-political, but cultural as well, and this side of Spanish life was depicted excellently by J. B. Trend for the years immediately following World War I in his *Picture of Modern Spain.* A sense of how the cultural and the political interpenetrated is communicated well in certain memoirs, such as those of J. Alvarez del Vayo in *The Last Optimist.* My sense of this period has been greatly enriched by going through long runs of *El Imparcial, Faro, Europa,* and *España.*

The intellectual history of the time is very important. For the condition of Spanish thought in the first decade of the twentieth century see Julián Marías, *Ortega I: Circunstancia y vocación,* pp. 33–72, 113–173. Perhaps the fullest and best study of the effect of 1898 on Spanish cultural life is *España como problema* by Pedro Laín Entralgo. Another shorter, excellent work, which did much to give a scholarly definition to the "generation of 98," is by Hans Jeschke, *Die Generation von 1898 in Spanien,* in *Beihefte zur Zeitschrift für Romanische Philologie,* 1934.

I: b. TRADITIONALLY "EL SITIO" GAVE A HEARING TO UNORTHODOX THINKERS (p. 9). The best characterization of "El Sitio" that I have been able to find is Ortega's own, which he gave in his introductory remarks to "La pedagogía social como programa político," 1910, *Obras* I, pp. 503–4. Meetings of "El Sitio" were usually covered by *El Imparcial* and other serious Madrid newspapers. Ortega wrote two articles on addresses by Unamuno to "El Sitio," "Glosas a un discurso" and "Nuevas glosas," *El Imparcial*, September 11 and 26, 1908, *Obras* X, pp. 82–5, 86–90. Ten months after Ortega spoke there, "El Sitio" listened to Alejandro Lerroux, who was at that time becoming notorious as an anti-clerical demagogue. See "Lerroux en Bilbao: Conferencia en El Sitio," *El Imparcial*, January 9, 1911. For Lerroux's ideas see Raymond Carr, *Spain: 1808–1939*, pp. 534–5. Ortega addressed "El Sitio" a second time on October 11, 1914, "En defensa de Unamuno," bitterly protesting the dismissal of Unamuno as rector of the University of Salamanca. See *Obras* X, pp. 262–8.

I: c. "EL IMPARCIAL," WHICH HAPPENED TO BELONG TO ORTEGA'S FAMILY (p. 10). For a first-hand account of Ortega's family, see the book by his brother, Manuel Ortega y Gasset, *Niñez y mocedad de Ortega y Gasset*. A shorter account is in Marías, *Ortega*, pp. 113–122. See Manuel Ortega y Gasset, *"El Imparcial": Biografía de un gran periódico español*, for an account of *El Imparcial* and its place in Spanish intellectual life.

I: d. ORTEGA'S EDUCATION (p. 12). Manuel Ortega, *Niñez y mocedad de Ortega*, gives a good account of Ortega's intellectual development prior to his trip to Germany; see especially p. 11. There is a detailed account of Ortega's education in Marías, *Ortega*, pp. 116–122, 165–170. Domingo Marrero, *El Centauro: Persona y pensamiento de Ortega y Gasset*, also has a good discussion of Ortega's education. For Ortega's relation to Unamuno as a student, the best source is Unamuno's "Almas de jovenes," 1904, in his *Obras* I, pp. 1148–1159.

For an excellent history that emphasizes the importance of the Institute, see Yvonne Turin, *L'Education et l'école en espagne de 1874 à 1902: Libéralisme et tradition*, especially pp. 204–267. A short but sound account of the Institute is in *The Origins of Modern Spain* by J. B. Trend, pp. 67–70. For the Institute and related developments, see also Mazzetti's *Società e educazione nella Spagna contemporanea*, which carries the account further into the twentieth century than does Turin, but without the depth and insight Turin gives. A good summary of the work of the *Junta para Ampliación de Estudios* is in Salvador de Madariaga, *Spain: A Modern History*, pp. 81–4.

I: e. KRAUSISMO SUBTLY IMPEDED THE DEVELOPMENT OF PHILOSOPHY IN SPAIN (p. 13). For Krausismo see Juan López-Morillas, *El*

Krausismo español: Perfil de una aventura intelectual; Pierre Jobit, *Les Educateurs de l'Espagne contemporaine,* Vol. 1, "Les Krausistes"; and J. B. Trend, *The Origins of Modern Spain,* pp. 37–49.

I: f. ORTEGA'S CHANCE TO WIN THE CHAIR OF METAPHYSICS AT MADRID (p. 14). In a letter to Unamuno, December 30, 1906, Ortega chided his former teacher for shunning a chair at Madrid; see *Revista de Occidente,* October 1964, p. 9. On Unamuno's professorial career see Yvonne Turin, *Miguel de Unamuno, Universitaire.* María de Maetzu, who was a student in Ortega's first course, described it and his petition for the Chair of Metaphysics in María de Maetzu, ed., *Antología siglo XX: Prosistas españolas,* pp. 79–82.

I: g. WORD OF ORTEGA'S PERSONAL APPEARANCE (p. 15). For this description of Ortega I have relied on impressions gathered from a large picture album kept at the offices of the *Revista de Occidente;* pictures in Manuel Ortega y Gasset, *Niñez y mocedad de Ortega,* and in Guillermo Morón, *Historia política de José Ortega y Gasset;* descriptions of his presence as a speaker as in Madariaga, *Spain,* pp. 309–310; and conversations with persons who knew Ortega.

I: h. EVER SINCE MACHIAVELLI PUT POLITICAL THEORY IN THE SERVICE OF PRINCES (p. 21). The nature of Machiavelli's influence on later political theory is an extremely difficult question for intellectual historians. The point is well taken that Machiavelli was interested in the foundation of an Italian state; see *The Prince,* Chapter XXVI; *The Discourses,* Chapter IX; Hegel, "The German Constitution," in *Political Writings,* T. M. Knox, trans., pp. 210–223; and Leo Strauss, *Natural Right and History,* pp. 177–180. But as Hegel suggested sympathetically, Machiavelli was so convinced of the overriding expediency of unifying Italy, and as Strauss suggested critically, Machiavelli was so desirous of success, he concentrated on the practicalities of getting and preserving power, rather than on the determination of the fit uses of power as classic political theory had done (in addition to the above, see Leo Strauss, *What is Political Philosophy? and Other Studies,* pp. 40–9, 286–290). As a lawgiver, Machiavelli seems to have panicked from the pressure of events. In this context, as Hegel said, he must be read with the history of the Italian principalities clearly in mind. However, Machiavelli has had the most significant influence, not on men such as Hegel or Fichte, but on practical politicians, the lawmakers, and on the political science they utilize. These men were not interested in Machiavelli's lawgiving; they have been struck by his rationalization of political practice and have carried his inquiry much further in this direction, not in order to found better states, but to administer and preserve the given ones. Machiavelli began the confusion between practical and pedagogical politics by introducing the techniques of the former into the pursuit of the latter. Unfortunately, studies such as Friedrich Meinecke's *Machiavellism: The Doctrine of Raison d'Etat and Its Place in Modern History*, Douglas Stark, trans., have preserved and deepened this confusion. The way towards overcoming the difficulties is pointed out by Alberto Moravia in his brilliant characterological critique, "Machiavelli," in *Man as an End: A Defense of Humanism*, Bernard Wall, trans., pp. 89–107.

Obviously, my conception of classical political theory has been deeply influenced by Plato, primarily by the *Republic* and *Gorgias*, and secondarily by *Protagoras, Meno, Apology,* and *Crito*. I have been initiated into a study of Plato by Martin S. Dworkin through many long conversations and through his courses at Teachers College, Columbia University, on "Aesthetics and Education" and "Education, Ideology, and Mass Communication." The conception of Plato he nurtured in me has been reinforced by Eric A. Havelock's *Preface to Plato* and by Werner Jaeger's *Paideia: The Ideals of Greek Culture*, 3 vols., Gilbert Highet, trans.

I: i. PEDAGOGY WAS NOT DIDACTICS (p. 22). This confusion has arisen in most modern languages, but it has been especially serious in English. In the late nineteenth century, the word "pedagogy" was identified with a system of didactics that reformers wanted to destroy. They at least managed to do away with the phrase "pedagogy." For a typical example of the educationist's attitude towards pedagogy see the entry under that heading in Monroe's *Cyclopedia of Education*. The article laconically proclaimed that the term had a dubious past and that wherever possible "education" should instead be used to escape the stigma of pedagogy. At the time the author was right, for "pedagogy" had generally been used as a synonym for "didactics," as "education" is now used carelessly as a synonym on the one hand for "training" and on the other for "propaganda." Perhaps we can steady the pendulum of fashion by insisting that both "pedagogy" and "education" be used rightly and whenever appropriate. Another amusing indication of the educationists' distaste for the word "pedagogy" is the metamorphosis of *The Pedagogical Seminary* into *The Journal of Genetic Psychology, Child Behavior, Animal Behavior, and Comparative Psychology*!

I: j. CIVIC IDEALS GAVE A COMMUNITY ITS CHARACTER (p. 22). Ortega rather fully explained the importance of governing goals in *Vieja y nueva política*, 1914, *Obras* I, pp. 267–308. See also "Asamblea para el progreso de las ciencias," 1908, *Obras* I, pp. 106–110, where Ortega contended that training in particular, practical social skills would not really have an effect unless their underlying cultural principles were previously mastered. The conception of civic ideals introduced in this section was characteristic of Ortega's thought. See, for instance, "La pedagogía social como programa político," 1910, *Obras* I, pp. 507, 514–7; *Vieja y nueva política*, 1914, *Obras* I, especially pp. 271–6, 288–294; and *Mirabeau, o el político*, 1927, *Obras* III, pp. 601–637. The influence of Ernest Renan on Ortega was important concerning the concept of civic ideals; see "La teología de Renan," 1910, *Obras* I, pp. 443–467; and *La rebelión de las masas*, 1930, *Obras* IV, pp. 265–270.

It is worthwhile to note the similarity of Ortega's conception of a civic ideal as something that points to the infinite and Edmund Husserl's conception of the *telos* of European man as an infinite, rather than a finite goal, "Philosophy and the Crisis of European Man," in *Phenomenology and the Crisis of Philosophy*, Quentin Lauer, trans., pp. 157–8.

I: k. RATHER THAN A POST-HISTORIC ERA, IT WOULD BE MOST HISTORIC (p. 25)! The literature that seeks to declare an end to history seeks to do it on several levels; thus there is a literature of cosmic acceptance and a related one of a technocratic millennium in both of which there is manifest the desire to declare the resolution of some long-standing historical conflict. For cosmic acceptance see Pierre Teilhard de Chardin, *The Phenomenon of Man*, Bernard Wall, trans., and *L'Avenir de l'homme*; Roderick Seidenberg, *Post-Historic Man: An Inquiry*; and Kurt W. Marek, *Yestermorrow: Notes on Man's Progress*, Ralph Manheim, trans. For the technocratic millennium, see the last mentioned and Karl Mannheim, *Man and Society in an Age of Reconstruction*. A practical result of the belief that the end of history is nigh is the increasing interest in describing the future, not only the issues that should be dealt with in the future, but the character of the solutions that will be arrived at in the future. An excellent debunking of these efforts is "The Year 2000 and All That" by Robert A. Nisbet, *Commentary*, June 1968, pp. 60–6.

For Ortega's expectation of a most historic era, see especially *En torno a Galileo*, 1933, *Obras* V, pp. 69–80, which gives the fullest development of his contention that Western history was going through a crisis. Ortega's essay "El ocaso de las revoluciones," 1923, *Obras* III, pp. 207–230, in which he argued that violent, rapid social revolutions were no longer possible, should not be taken to mean that historical change would stop.

I: 1. THE RATIONAL NECESSITY EXPLICATED BY CRITICAL PHILOSOPHY (p. 26). This matter is properly the subject of another book, but some remarks may be ventured. Rational necessity leads to the justification or rejection of assertions on educational grounds. In order to develop such educational justifications and critiques, we need to remaster philosophical idealism, for idealism alone yields an educational ethic, and idealism is comprehensible only if reason, thought, intellect, mind, or spirit are understood essentially as educational achievements of man. Men do not think because they are endowed with a physical apparatus capable of gathering and processing information, but because they have learned to think. Thus, as Hegel said, "it is education which vindicates a universal." (*Hegel's Philosophy of Right*, T. M. Knox, trans., Addition to #20, p. 281.) See also on this point the observation by W. H. Auden that ethics are to be implemented through pedagogy in "Die Bombe und das menschliche Bewusstsein," *Merkur*, August 1966, p. 707. The significance of this tradition for American educational theory and practice should be great, but it is a complicated question that can only be outlined here.

American law proceeds on the basis of a practical ethic: One may do more or less as one pleases provided the concrete consequences of an act do not infringe on the rights of others. This procedure is well and good, for positive law must deal with concrete instances, which cannot be ordered on the basis of universal principles. This point is basic in the idealistic tradition, a fact that is often overlooked by critics of idealism. (See Plato, *Statesman*, 294 f., *Republic*, IV, 425 f., and *Laws*, 788, 807.) However, besides positive law, with its courts and police power, there is a moral or spiritual law, which is enforced by criticism, exhortation, self-discipline, and the real, but mysterious, *nemesis*. Whereas the weakness of Continental rationalism has been a tendency to attempt to legislate the moral law into a positive law, the failing of Anglo-American pragmatism has been a tendency to judge the moral law on the basis of its practical, positive ethic, when in fact a spiritual, educational ethic has been in order. Thus many contemporary rhetoricians do not understand criticism of their persuasive practices. The criticism is pitched on the spiritual level and it objects to the rhetoricians' debasement of the standards of truth, beauty, and propriety. The rhetoricians understand the criticism on the practical level and quickly wrap themselves in the Constitutional defenses against those who would deprive them of their freedom of speech. For instance, note how, in Edward G. Bernays, ed., *The Engineering of Consent*, especially p. 8, a problem of educational ethics is reduced to one of practical ethics: surely the critics of public relations would not want to do away with our rights to speak freely? But the objection was not against the practice, but against the principle implicit in practice. The critics are really asking the PR men to decide freely to speak in a different manner. Bernays does not entertain this possibility in his breathless justification of the persuader's rights.

A practical ethic passes on whether a concrete act infringes on the rights of others; an educational ethic examines the general rule implied by a concrete act. To be sure, the categorical imperative cannot replace common sense as the guide to our practical actions, nor one may add, was it meant to do so. The categorical imperative is, however, the formal principle of educational ethics. In our concrete activities we not only accomplish specific acts, but we also make existential affirmations of general principles, even though we may not be aware of it. Now, we should act so that the principles thus affirmed are ones that we would be willing to uphold as general rules of moral conduct, of esthetic creation, and of intellectual activity. Thus, we should conduct our activities on the practical basis of common sense within the spiritual limits of a categorical imperative. Practical matters are not divorced from questions of principle any more than are real questions of principle independent of practice. Thus, in *The Vocation of the Scholar*, Fichte put the matter this way: "I may here . . . express the fundamental principle of morality in the following formula:—'*So act that thou mayest look upon the dictate of thy will as an eternal law to thyself.*'" William Smith, trans., *The Popular* [sic!] *Works of Johann Gottlieb Fichte*, 1889, p. 152.

I: m.   THE GOALS OF EDUCATION COULD NOT BE FOUND IN BIOLOGY (p. 27). In "Biología y pedagogía," 1920, *Obras* II, pp. 273–307, Ortega seemed to renounce this contention that pedagogical goals cannot come from biology. However, in "La pedagogía social como programa político," 1910, *Obras* I, pp. 411–2, Ortega had had in mind traditional, materialistic biology, whereas in "Biología y pedagogía" he was discussing the method of inquiry developed by vitalistic biologists like the German Jacob von Uexküll. The results, when Uexküll's method was used to analyze the child's view of life, Ortega found applicable to pedagogy.

I: n.   HUMAN MATTERS REQUIRED A CIRCULAR DESCRIPTION (p. 30). Martin Heidegger made a similar point in a more difficult but more systematic manner in *Being and Time,* I, 5, 32; and II, 3, 63; John Macquarrie and Edward Robinson, trans., pp. 193–5 and 262–3. The actual issues that are raised with this question are immense. The fundamental issue concerns the type of rigor that the human sciences should pursue. The choice is between the rigor characteristic of abstract and natural science or that of a dialogue between two intelligent, informed men about a problem of common concern. Ortega, Heidegger, and many others were strongly in favor of the latter type of rigor. Any other, less anthropocentric rigor would put too great a strain on the tenuous bonds between principles and practice. At the time of his "El Sitio" speech Ortega would have been influenced by Fichte's *Grundlage der gesamten Wissenschaftslehre,* Hegel's *Wissenschaft der Logik* and *Phänomenologie des Geistes,* as well as by Georg Simmel and the Marburg neo-Kantians. Later he would be, like Heidegger, deeply influenced by Wilhelm Dilthey.

I: o.   HERACLITUS EPIGRAPHS (p. 33). The fragments quoted at the end of Chapters III, IV, V, X, XI, and XV have been translated by Kathleen Freeman in her *Ancilla to the Pre-Socratic Philosophers.* The fragments quoted at the end of Chapters I, VI, VII, VIII, and XVI have been translated by Philip Wheelwright in his *Heraclitus.* By Wheelwright's numbering system the fragments quoted are 10, 83, 88, 70, and 45. The fragment quoted at the end of Chapter IX has been translated by G. S. Kirk and J. E. Raven in *The Pre-Socratic Philosophers* where it is numbered fragment 254. The fragment quoted at the end of Chapter XII has been translated by John Burnet in his *Early Greek Philosophy,* fragment 7. The fragments at the end of Chapters II, XIII, and XIV have been translated by W. H. S. Jones in the Loeb Classical Library edition of *Heraclitus*, fragments I, CXXVI, and XIX.

II: PREPARATIONS

II: a. RECOURSE TO LOVE . . . IS NEEDED TO EXPLAIN TWO FEATURES OF LEARNING (p. 35). In addition to Ortega's writings on the subject discussed below, my views have been influenced by Plato and Goethe. Plato's *Symposium* is, of course, fundamental, but his attitude also is insinuated through most of his works and a familiarity with these is helpful in trying to follow Diotima's teaching as it is recounted by Socrates in the *Symposium*. There are useful discussions of Eros in Plato's philosophy in Paul Friedländer, *Plato: An Introduction*, *passim* and esp. pp. 32–58; F. M. Cornford, *The Unwritten Philosophy and Other Essays*, pp. 68–80; G. M. A. Grube, *Plato's Thought*, pp. 87–119; and Julius Stenzel, *Platon der Erzieher*, pp. 191–248. Goethe's great examination of the relation of love and self-culture is in *Wilhelm Meister, passim*. An excellent study by Ortega's contemporary, Max Scheler, is *Wesen und Formen der Sympathie*, a book that Ortega was quite familiar with. A striking book on *Eros and Education* could be written.

II: b. FOR ORTEGA, LOVE YEARNED FOR UNION WITH BEAUTY, TRUTH, AND GOODNESS (p. 37). Some of the more important essays by Ortega concerning his theory of love were "Psicoanálisis, ciencia problemática," 1911, *Obras* I, pp. 216–238; *Meditaciones del Quijote*, 1914, *Obras* I, pp. 310–4; "Leyendo el Aldolfo, libro de amor," 1916, *Obras* II, pp. 25–8; "Vitalidad, alma, espíritu," 1924, *Obras* II, pp. 451–480; "Para un psicología del hombre interesante," 1925, *Obras* IV, pp. 467–480; and *Estudios sobre el amor*, 1941, *Obras* V, pp. 551–626. In her dissertation, "José Ortega y Gasset: The Creation of a Literary Genre for Philosophy," Sister Mary Terese Avila Duffy includes some interesting observations on Eros in Ortega's style, but for the most part, the importance of Eros for Ortega's thought has been ignored by commentators.

II: c. PHILOSOPHY IS A TRADITION OF SPECULATION (p. 38). See Ortega's "Prólogo a *Historia de la filosofía* de Karl Vorländer," 1922, and "Prólogo a *Historia de la filosofía* de Emile Bréhier," 1942, *Obras* VI, pp. 292–300, 377–418, as well as *Origen y epílogo de la filosofía*, 1943, 1960, *Obras* IX, pp. 349–434, for his views on the history of philosophy, which have influenced my views here. One of the better histories of philosophy for studying Ortega's preparations is *The Spirit of Modern Philosophy* by Josiah Royce, for in it he treats idealism as a living tradition rather than as a series of closed systems.

II: d. THE DOUBT THAT GAVE RISE TO THE WIENER KREIS (p. 41). For the impact of science on late nineteenth-century thought see Jacques Barzun, *Darwin, Marx, Wagner*, esp. pp. 115–126. On the origins and impulse of the *Wiener Kreis* see H. Stuart Hughes, *Consciousness and Society: The Reconstruction of European Social Thought, 1890–1930*, esp. pp. 397–401. The view that Ortega almost took up is clearly expressed by A. J. Ayer in *Language, Truth and Logic*, esp. pp. 57, 151–3.

II: e. AT LEIPZIG ORTEGA TOYED WITH AN EMPIRICAL SPECIALTY (p. 41). Domingo Marrero said that Ortega was enrolled in these courses in *El Centauro*, p. 184. Marrero seems to have checked the registration records at Leipzig and Marburg and on such matters he is good authority. However, writing in 1951, he had access to neither *Prólogo para alemanes* nor the letters. He tried, imaginatively but mistakenly, to reconstruct from Ortega's later work which professors Ortega must have been influenced by in Germany. He imagined an influence by Wundt, whom Ortega did not treat kindly in "Sobre el concepto de sensación," 1913, *Obras* I, pp. 246–8; he exaggerated the influence of Simmel, whose significance Ortega did not seem to appreciate until two decades later; and he underemphasized the influence of Cohen and Natorp. In *Ortega*, pp. 204–220, Julián Marías gives a good secondary account of Ortega's experience in Germany. Marías is better than Marrero on influences and not as good on chronological details, and Marías also wrote his account before Ortega's letters from Germany were available. For Ortega's own views of his experience at Leipzig, see *Prólogo para alemanes*, 1933, 1958, *Obras* VIII, p. 26, and Ortega, "Cartas inéditas a Navarro Ledesma," *Cuadernos*, November 1961, pp. 3–18. For the scientific emphasis at Leipzig, see Ortega's "Una fiesta de paz," 1909, *Obras* I, pp. 124–7, in which he commemorated the 400th anniversary of the University of Leipzig and especially commended its physics and chemistry. For Ortega's views of Berlin, see *Prólogo para alemanes*, 1933, 1958, *Obras* VIII, pp. 26–7, and "En la Institución Cultural Española de Buenos Aires," 1939, *Obras* VI, p. 235.

II: f. AT MARBURG ORTEGA ENTERED A TRUE SCHOOL OF PHILOSOPHY (p. 42). See Henri Dussort, *L'Ecole de Marburg*, which is the best work on the school of Marburg although it is fragmentary and unfinished owing to its author's untimely death. For the place of the school, or at least of Hermann Cohen, in modern thought, see Jules Vuillemin, *L'Héritage Kantien et la revolution Copernicienne*. Ortega's fullest description of his experience at Marburg is in *Prólogo para alemanes*, 1933, 1958, *Obras* VIII, pp. 26–42.

II: g. HERMANN COHEN WAS AN ELDERLY, CONVIVIAL PHILOSOPHER (p. 43). For a good introduction to Cohen's character and thought, see the appreciation of him by Ernst Cassirer, "Hermann Cohen: Wörte gesprochen an seinen Grabe am 7 April 1918," in Cohen, *Schriften zur Philosophie und Zeitgeschichte*, Vol. I, pp. ix–xvi. Cohen's capacity to contend systematically with a subject is well exemplified by his major works, three commentaries to Kant's three critiques and then three critiques of his own, one on pure reason, one on ethics, and one on esthetics. See Hermann Cohen, *Kants Theorie der Erfahrung*, 1871; *Kants Begründung der Ethik*, 1877; *Kants Begründung der Aesthetik*, 1889; *Logik der reinen Erkenntnis*, 1902; *Ethik des reinen Willens*, 1904; and *Aesthetik des reinen Gufühls*, 2 vols., 1912. The last three books make up Cohen's *System der Philosophie*. In addition to discipline, Cohen imparted certain ideas to Ortega, for the latter mentioned that Cohen's logic supported his own idea of life; see "Pidiendo un Goethe desde dentro," 1932, *Obras* IV, p. 403.

II: h. COHEN STOPPED WORK FOR SEVERAL WEEKS IN ORDER TO STUDY DON QUIJOTE (p. 45). The account of this incident is given most fully by Ortega in "Meditación del Escorial," 1915, *Obras* II, p. 559. It is noteworthy that Cohen's discussion of Don Quixote treated it as an *Erziehungsroman* in a class with Goethe's *Wilhelm Meister*; see *Aesthetik*, Vol. 2, pp. 112, 119–123. Historians of education should make a study of the pedagogical ideas imparted through the *Erziehungsroman*. For Cohen's conception of system, see particularly, *Die systematischen Begriff in Kants vorkritischen Schriften*, 1873; *Logik der reinen Erkenntnis*, pp. 601–612; and *Aesthetik des reinen Gefühls*, Vol. 1, pp. 3–67.

II: i. AS PHILOSOPHY TURNED ANALYTIC . . . (p. 46). Basic examples of the impulse towards analysis are A. J. Ayer, *Language, Truth and Logic*, and *The Problem of Knowledge*. The absence of an historical interest on the part of those moved by an analytic impulse can be measured by comparing the last-mentioned work by Ayer with a book on the same subject written by a man moved by the systematic impulse, *The Problem of Knowledge* by Ernst Cassirer, Woglom and Hendel, trans. For an example of how the conception of reason as a mental faculty still persists, see the article "Reason" by G. J. Warnock in *The Encyclopedia of Philosophy*, Vol. 7, pp. 83–5. In contrast to systematic philosophers who seek to discover the proper standards of reason, Warnock contended that it would be better to proceed directly to "the logical and epistemological analysis and classifications." But how, without first at least an implicit critique of reason, can professional philosophers set forth to themselves acceptable logical and epistemological standards of analysis and classification?

II: j. IN THE SYSTEMATIC TRADITION, REASON IS RECOGNIZED AS A CULTURAL CREATION (p. 47). Thus there is an awesome succession of critiques of reason. An excellent history of this elaboration of reason up to the twentieth century is Léon Brunschvicg, *Le progrès de la conscience dans la philosophie occidentale*. Nor is this succession of critiques by any means a dead tradition. For important twentieth-century contributions, see Wilhelm Dilthey, *Gesammelte Schriften*, especially Volumes I, V, and VII; Ernst Cassirer, *The Philosophy of Symbolic Forms*, Ralph Manheim, trans.; Ortega, *La idea de la principio en Leibniz y la evolución de la teoría deductiva*, 1947, 1958, *Obras* VIII, pp. 61–356; and Jean Paul Sartre, *Critique de la raison dialectique*. An example of the analytic bias in favor of the critique of knowledge rather than the critique of reason is to be found in the long article by D. W. Hamlyn on "Epistemology, History of" in *The Encyclopedia of Philosophy*, Vol. 3, pp. 8–38. Hamlyn defined epistemology as the critique of Knowledge; he treated Kant as an epistemologist in this sense, ignoring the whole problem of how reason is possible; and he completely ignored Dilthey, among other systematic epistemologists.

II: k. GOADED BY WARTIME GERMANOPHOBIA, ANGLO-AMERICAN CRITICS ATTACKED SYSTEMATIC PHILOSOPHY (p. 48). During World War I, German philosophy came under severe attack from American and British philosophers who were trying to contribute to the war effort by showing that German philosophy was to blame for the war. *The Oxford Pamphlets* that the Oxford University Press distributed widely were most influential.

Typical examples were "How Can War Ever Be Right?" and "Thoughts on the War" by the classical scholar Gilbert Murray; "Nietzsche and Treitschke: The Worship of Power in Modern Germany" by the student of Greek political theory, Ernest Barker; and "German Philosophy and the War" by the philosopher, J. H. Muirhead. See also, Muirhead's *German Philosophy in Relation to the War*, 1915. American thinkers contributed to the same kind of literature. See John Dewey, *German Philosophy and Politics*, 1915; and George Santayana, *Egotism in German Philosophy*, 1916. Similar works appeared in France; see, for instance, Léon Daudet, *Contre l'esprit allemand: De Kant à Krupp*. The French critics did not have the prestige of the English and American writers, however; and this might help explain why Anglo-American philosophy veered so sharply from the Continental tradition and why British idealism was unable to withstand the postwar attack by analytic writers, several of the more important of whom, ironically, were German. It was in this climate of putting philosophy in the service of the war efforts that Ortega said that in time of war the thinker must be silent, for that is the only way he can maintain his allegiance to the truth. See "Una manera de pensar-I," *España*, October 7, 1915, *Obras* X, p. 337. The most influential Germanophobe work of World War II was *The Open Society and Its Enemies*, by Karl Popper, 1950. Charles Frankel, *The Case for Modern Man*, 1959, contributes to this critique of the continental tradition, but without direct connection to the war. Many other books might be mentioned. My characterization of the position draws from these and others, as well as from conversations with colleagues, but it is not given concisely by any of them.

The effectiveness of this critique of systematic philosophy has permitted some thinkers to ignore the real alternatives. Here let us mention only John Dewey's *The Quest for Certainty*, 1929, for it lacks some of the partisan drawbacks of the wartime books, but is, nevertheless, a systematic critique of the systematic effort to construct a prescriptive conception of reason. Dewey made the same error as Russell did later and as many anti-systematic philosophers do: he imputed a prescriptive theory of knowledge to thinkers in the grand tradition who expounded a prescriptive theory of reason. To prescribe how reasoning should proceed if it is to be cogent is not to prescribe a set of true beliefs that all must mouth. Furthermore, it is one thing to go along with Dewey and to give up prescriptive standards with respect to knowledge, standards that purport to lay down eternal certainties forever valid for all, but it is quite another thing to give up prescriptive standards with respect to reason, standards that describe the mental steps by means of which we can think about the phenomena we perceive with reasonable certitude. The irony of Dewey's critique is that most of his own speculation is a good example of "the quest for certainty," reasonably understood.

II: l.   THE SCEPTER OF FORCE HAS NOT STOOD FOR A STABLE REIGN (p. 48). There is a substantial literature on the relation between philosophical and ethical nihilism and political brutalism. On this matter, of course, Ortega's *La rebelión de las masas*, 1930, *Obras* IV, pp. 113–31, is one of the essential references. The other three are Friedrich Nietzsche, *Aus dem Nachlass der Achtzigerjahre*, in *Werk in Drei Bänden*, Vol. 3, 491ff., 507ff., 530, 533, 546, 548ff., 553ff., 557ff., 567ff., 583, 617–623, 625f., 634f., 638ff., 666, 670, 675, 676ff., 737f., 774f., 792f., 852f., 854ff., 881f., 893f., and 896; Alfred Weber, *Farewell to European History, Or the Conquest of Nihilism*, R. F. C. Hull, trans.; and Rudolf Pannwitz, *Der Nihilismus und die werdende Welt*, especially pp. 104–127. In addition to these works, see Raymond Aron, *The Century of Total War*. On the general problem of maintaining a sense of principle, see Wolfgang Köhler, *The Place of Value in a World of Facts*, and Jacques Barzun, *Darwin, Marx, Wagner*. In *Nihilism: A Philosophical Essay* by Stanley Rosen, there is a spirited critique of contemporary philosophical movements that end in nihilism. Rosen argues that the solution is a return to past modes of thought; I think Nietzsche was more acute when he argued that the only way to solve the problem of nihilism is to pass through and beyond it.

II: m.   NATORP TAUGHT A VERSION OF IDEALISM THAT PROVOKED ORTEGA (p. 51). The best introductory essay on Natorp is by Ernst Cassirer, "Paul Natorp: 24. Januar 1854—17. August 1924," in *Kant-Studien*, Band 30, 1925, pp. 273–298. Natorp's conception of civic pedagogy was developed in his *Sozialpädagogik: Theorie der Willenserziehung auf der Grundlage der Gemeinschaft*, 3rd. ed., 1909; and *Gesammelte Abhandlungen zur Sozialpädagogik*, 2nd. ed., 1922. A closely related work was *Sozialidealismus: Neue Richtlinien sozialer Erziehung*, 2nd. ed., 1918. Natorp's conception of philosophy is presented on a popular level in his *Philosophie: Ihr Problem und ihre Probleme*, 2nd. ed., 1918; and on a more systematic level in *Vorlesungen über praktische Philosophie,* 1925, and the posthumous *Philosophische Systematik,* edited by Hans Natorp, 1958. Perhaps Natorp's best known work, and one that is very important for his theory of civic pedagogy and of philosophy, is *Platos Ideenlehre: Eine Einführung in den Idealismus,* 1903. For a good discussion of Natorp's views, see Heinrich Levy, "Paul Natorps praktische Philosophie," *Kant-Studien,* 31, 1926, pp. 311–329.

II: n. WHAT NATORP PROCLAIMED ABOUT PLATO, KANT, AND PESTALOZZI, ORTEGA RECOGNIZED IN FICHTE, RENAN, AND NIETZSCHE (p. 52). The last three authors were the ones Ortega most frequently referred to in his early writings and his letters of the time. See "Cartas inéditas a Navarro Ledesma," *Cuadernos,* November 1961, pp. 3–18; "El sobre hombre," 1908, *Obras* I, pp. 91–5; "La teología de Renan," 1910, and "Renan," 1909, *Obras* I, pp. 133–6, 443–467; and in "Asamblea para el progreso de las ciencias," 1908, *Obras* I, p. 108, the lament that nowhere in Spain were the works of Fichte available. Natorp made only scattered references to these men, although their work could be viewed as civic pedagogy.

II: o. AMERICAN EDUCATIONAL THEORISTS HAVE FORGOTTEN NATORP (p. 52). In 1900, a short review by Arthur Allin of the first edition of Natorp's *Sozialpädagogik* appeared in the *Educational Review,* Vol. 19, March 1900, pp. 290–295. A more substantial essay, "Paul Natorp's Social Pedagogy," by M. W. Meyerhardt was published in *The Pedagogical Seminary,* Vol. 23, March 1916, pp. 51–62. One of the few other significant pieces on Natorp published in the United States is the short, lucid article by Horace L. Friess, "Paul Natorp," in the *Encyclopedia of the Social Sciences,* Vol. 11, p. 283. Another excellent review of Natorp's accomplishments is the translation of an article, "Paul Natorp," by Mariano Campo in *The Encyclopedia of Philosophy,* Vol. 5, pp. 445–8.

III: PROGRAMS

III: a. ORTEGA'S PRECOCITY WAS TO REALIZE THAT SPANISH RENOVATION WAS AN EDUCATIONAL PROBLEM (p. 62). This conviction was apparent in some of Ortega's earliest essays. See "La pedagogía del paisaje," 1906; "Sobre los estudios clásicos," 1907; "Pidendo una biblioteca," 1908; and "Asamblea para el progreso de las ciencias," 1908; in *Obras* I, pp. 53–7, 63–7,

81–5, and 99–110. See also "Reforma del carácter, no reforma de costumbres," *El Imparcial*, October 5, 1907, *Obras* X, pp. 17–21. In the letter of May 28, 1905, to Navarro Ledesma, Ortega wrote about the educational responsibilities of the Spanish reformers; see "Cartas inéditas a Navarro Ledesma," *Cuadernos*, November 1961, especially p. 12.

III: b. UNAMUNO AND ORTEGA SHOWED MANY POINTS IN COMMON IN WRITING ABOUT SPANISH REFORM (p. 64). There is need for a a study comparing the view of Spanish reform held by the two critics. Paulino Garagorri's excellent work, *Unamuno, Ortega, Zubiri en la filosfía española*, is confined, as the title suggests, to a comparison of philosophical views. A study of their theories of reform should be encouraged by the recent appearance of Ortega's political writings in *Obras* X and XI, and of the definitive edition of Unamuno's works. Such a study would stretch from the 1890's up to 1936 and might point out similarities and dissimilarities between the reactions of the two to events. I have made a much less ambitious comparison, confining myself to the period up to World War I for the most part, comparing views on more general political, economic, and social matters, not particular events. Unamuno seems to me to have dealt with these matters more explicitly, but with less commitment.

Both favored an effective political system responsive to the popular will but not necessarily following familiar parliamentary procedures. Such a position was an integral element in most views of Spanish reform because one very important aspect of Spain's difficulties was that its population had never been integrated into a single body of citizens all of whom had an equal stake in the community. With numerous elements of the people effectively excluded from participation in national life, democratic machinery frequently served very undemocratic ends. In 1898, Unamuno sounded these themes in "Architectura social," *OC* XI, pp. 53–9; "Mas sociabilidad," *OC* XI, pp. 60–7; and "Renovación," *Obras* I, pp. 686–8. (The abbreviation *OC* is used for the 1958 edition of Unamuno's *Obras completas* published by Afrodisio Aguado; the abbreviation *Obras* is used for the Definitive Edition of Unamuno's *Obras completas* published by Escelicer, beginning in 1966. For some essays it has been necessary to use the earlier edition, as the later one is not yet complete.)

Some of Unamuno's clearest statements on the form of politics he would like are in "La civilización es civismo," 1907, *Obras* III, pp. 303–7, and "Glosas a la vida: sobre la opinión pública," 1904, *Obras* III, pp. 308–310. In the latter article Unamuno contended that the great problem in Spanish politics was the difficulty of building up an effective system of public opinion about public affairs in the Spanish populace; and he was not sanguine because with such a large portion of the populace composed of illiterates and semi-literates, the spread of public opinion was greatly impeded. In the former article Unamuno condemned the tendency in Spanish politics to over-represent rural areas because the rural populace could not then hold its representatives accountable; popular government turned into an irresponsible government. Urbanization and the mechanization of farming were conditions of the reform of Spanish politics, he suggested. For somewhat later views along parallel lines, see "Los profesionales de la política," 1914, *OC* IX, pp. 797–801, and "Hacer política," 1915, *OC* IX, pp. 843–7.

Ortega's views of political reform will be treated at some length in the text. His major pre-World War I statement on politics is *Vieja y nueva política*, 1914, *Obras* I, pp. 265–307. Earlier expressions may be found throughout *Obras* X, *passim*; especially in "De *re* política," *El Imparcial*, July 31, 1908, *Obras* X, pp. 62–7; "Pablo Iglesias," *El Imparcial*, May 13, 1910, *Obras* X, pp. 139–142; "Sencillas reflexiones," *El Imparcial*, August 22 and September 6, 1910, *Obras* X, pp. 162–170; "De puerta de tierra: la opinión pública," *El Imparcial*, September 19 and 20, 1912, *Obras* X, pp. 186–194; "Ni legislar ni gobernar," *El Imparcial*, September 25, 1912, *Obras* X, pp. 195–199; and "De un estorbo nacional," *El Imparcial*, April 22, 1913, and *El País*, May 12, 1913, *Obras* X, pp. 232–7, 241–5.

Both Unamuno and Ortega desired a stronger economy and a more egalitarian distribution of the national product. This was a fundamental concern for anyone aiming at Spanish reform. As early as 1896 Unamuno came out strongly in "La dignidad humana," *Obras* I, pp. 971–7, for a more humane, egalitarian use of the economic product. In this essay Unamuno spoke out against nineteenth-century liberalism in both economics and culture, for laissez-faire individualism expended energies destructively in efforts by each to differentiate himself from others. The proper measure of the value of things material and spiritual was not the degree to which they differentiated one man from the others, but the degree to which they facilitated each man's effort to fulfill his human dignity. Such views lead to the twentieth-century liberalism of the welfare state. For other essays by Unamuno explaining his economic views, see "Doctores en industria," 1898, *Obras* III, pp. 692–7; "La conquista de les mesetas," 1899, *Obras* III, pp. 702–711; "Hay que crear necesidades," 1899, *OC* XI, pp. 71–4; "La dehesa española," 1899, *OC* XI, pp. 75–82; "Examen de conciencia," 1900, *OC* XI, pp. 95–101; "Pan y letras: el campo y la ciudad," 1908, *OC* XI, pp. 163–7; and "Campaña agraria," 1914, *OC* XI, pp. 300–313.

In a letter to Ortega, Salamanca, November 21, 1912, in *Revista de Occidente,* October 1964, p. 20, Unamuno contended that for liberalism to be relevant to twentieth-century Spain, it had "to make itself democratic and socialist." This was a position Ortega had himself been developing at some length. Ortega's development of this argument can be followed in the following: "La reforma liberal," *Faro,* February 23, 1908, *Obras* X, pp. 31–8; "El recato socialista," *El Imparcial,* September 2, 1908, *Obras* X, pp. 79–81; "La ciencia y la religión como problemas políticos," lecture in the Madrid Casa del Partido Socialista, December 2, 1909, *Obras* X, pp. 119–125; "Pablo Iglesias," *El Imparcial,* May 13, 1910, *Obras* X, pp. 139–142; "La herencia viva de Costa," *El Imparcial,* February 20, 1911, *Obras* X, pp. 171–5; "Miscelánea socialista," *El Imparcial,* September 30, and October 6, 1912, *Obras* X, pp. 200–206; and so on.

Perhaps the essay that best shows the link between Unamuno's economic and educational views is "La pirámide nacional," 1898, *Obras* III, pp. 689–691. In it Unamuno contended that as the production of goods for popular consumption was the basis of the strength of a national economy, so the creation of culture for popular consumption was the foundation of a nation's intellectual strength. Spain needed a great extension of popular education, but it lacked the teachers, Unamuno observed. In the face of this situation, it was important that many teachers on the higher levels convert themselves into primary school instructors. This emphasis on the broadening of popular education went along with another emphasis, one on the qualitative improvement of higher education, a concern that both Unamuno and Ortega were intimately involved in. At first the stress on wider popular education and more thorough higher education may not seem to go together. Unamuno put the theory well in "Los escritores y el pueblo," 1908, *Obras* III, pp. 294–8. It was not essential that high culture be popular if it was to have a public effect; to do so it needed to be inwardly virile, robust, powerful. A literate populace would not directly consume high culture, but they would contribute to it and be affected by it indirectly if that culture were powerful, not weak and diluted. Thus the best condition of a nation's culture would be achieved with very extensive popular education and very rigorous higher education.

Unamuno produced many essays on education. A good study of his work as a leader in the university is *Miguel de Unamuno, universitaire* by Yvonne Turin. In "La educación, prólogo a la obra de Bunge," 1902, *Obras* I, pp. 1021–2, Unamuno made a distinction, similar to that which was important for Ortega, between the education of the person, *"pedagogía,"* and the education of the community, *"demagogía"* in the Greek sense or *"demopedía."* Because Unamuno used his essays to conduct *demopedía,* a number of those concerning the preservation of Spanish virtues and dealing with the problem of separatism in the provinces were about education. This holds especially for Unamuno's views of the Catalán question, for he primarily feared *linguistic* localism as a threat to the full development of Spanish culture. In addition, however, to his many acts of *demopedía,* Unamuno published much on pedagogy per se. The long essay, "De la enseñanza superior en España," 1899, *Obras* I, pp. 734–772, is an excellent introduction to the problems of higher education in Spain. In "Los cerebrales," 1899, *OC* XI, pp. 89–94, and "Cientificismo," 1907, *Obras* III, pp. 352–7, he raised questions about the unreserved pursuit of pure intellect. In "Recelosidad y pedantaría," 1912, *OC* XI, pp. 197–200; "No hipotequeís el pensamiento," 1913, *OC* XI, pp. 251–3; "Arabesco pedagógico" and "Otro arabesco pedagógico," 1913, *OC* XI, pp. 290–300; and "¿Barbados? ¿Pedantes?", 1914, *OC* XI, pp. 806–810 he entered into polemics of the time for and against trends that were attracting attention.

Ortega also devoted much attention to both popular and higher education, agreeing that the former should be greatly extended and the latter substantially improved. For Ortega the most objectionable feature in popular education was the split between schools for the rich and schools for the poor, a phenomenon that he decried in "Reforma del carácter, no reforma de costumbres," *El Imparcial,* October 5, 1907, *Obras* X, p. 20; "La pedagogía social como programa política," 1910, *Obras* I, p. 518; and elsewhere. Ortega's educational views are discussed throughout the text; representative sources for this period include "Catecismo para la lectura de una carta," *El Imparcial,* February 10, 1910, *Obras* X, pp. 133–8; "Diputado por la cultura," *El Imparcial,* May 28, 1910, *Obras* X, pp. 143–6; "Sobre los estudios clásicos," 1907, "Pidiendo una biblioteca," 1908, and "Asamblea para el progreso de las ciencias," 1908, *Obras* I, pp. 63–7, 81–5, and 99–110.

Both Unamuno and Ortega sought to preserve Spanish virtues and to avoid materialism in Spain. This point is crucial for Unamuno. Well before 1898 he had developed it at length in *En torno al casticismo*, 1895, *Obras* I, pp. 775–869. In 1898, in "De regeneración: en lo justo," *Obras* III, pp. 700–1, Unamuno put very well the task of the enterprise that would occupy Spanish critics for many years: "Today, the first duty of the directing classes in Spain is, more than teaching the *pueblo* physics, chemistry, or English, to study it, *à fond* and with love, drawing from it its unconscious ideal of life, the spirit that moves it through its passage on earth, comprehending its regional differences in order to conserve them by integrating them, and studying the prospects of capital and labor." In "Afrancesamiento," 1899, *OC* XI, pp. 68–70, Unamuno spoke out against the inflated copying of French mores at the sacrifice of the Spanish; in "De patriotismo," 1899, *Obras* III, pp. 712–4; "El pueblo español," 1902, *Obras* III, pp. 715–7; "El individualismo español," 1903, *Obras* I, pp. 1085–1094; and "Sobre la independencia patria," 1908, *Obras* III, pp. 730–2, he analyzed aspects of Spanish character he believed essential to Spain's future; and in "Escepticismo fanático," 1908, *Obras* III, pp. 358–362, and "Materialismo popular," 1909, *Obras* III, pp. 363–7, he warned against intellectual outlooks that were easily adopted yet that were threats to Spanish culture. In "La supesta anormalidad española," 1913, *Obras* III, pp. 733–7, Unamuno criticized Ortega for calling Spain an abnormal nation.

Despite this criticism, Ortega's views were not far from Unamuno's, as I explain in the text. For Ortega's concern for Spanish character, see "Reforma del carácter, no reforma de costumbres," *El Imparcial*, October 5, 1907, *Obras* X, pp. 17–21; "La cuestión moral," *El Imparcial*, August 22, 1908, *Obras* X, pp. 73–8; "El lirismo en Montjuich," *El Imparcial*, August 10, 1910, *Obras* X, pp. 159–161; and "Moralejas," 1906, "La epopeya castellana," 1910, "Nuevo libro de Azorín," 1912, and "Al margen del libro *Los Iberos*," 1909, *Obras* I, pp. 44–57, 146, 239–244, and 494–8.

On the question of separatism, both Unamuno and Ortega saw the source of the problem to be, not in regional malevolence, but in the weakness of the capital. Both would solve the problem by recognizing authentic diversities and making Castile more worthy of pre-eminence. Unamuno was deeply concerned by the problem; unlike for Ortega, it was something that he, a Basque, had to face in his inner character. Unamuno clearly gave his allegiance to Castilian, and owing to this, he was in some ways less sympathetic to linguistic separatism than Ortega. Thus, in "La cuestión del vascuence," 1902, *Obras* I, pp. 1043–1062, Unamuno was not sympathetic with those who wanted to preserve Basque as a living language at any price. Different aspects of Unamuno's view of the whole question can be found in "La crisis del patriotismo," 1896, *Obras* I, pp. 978–984; "Injustia inútil," 1899, *OC* XI, pp. 83–5; "La reforma del castellano," 1901, *OC* III, pp. 273–280; "Contra el purismo," 1903, *Obras* I, pp. 1063–1073; "La crisis actuel del patriotismo español," 1905, *Obras* I, pp. 1286–1298; "Mas sobre la crisis del patriotismo," 1906, *Obras* III, pp. 865–875; "Sobre el problema catalán," 1908, *OC* XI, pp. 147–162; "Sobre el regionalismo español," 1915, *OC* XI, pp. 357–361; "La soledad de la España castellana," 1916, *Obras* III, pp. 763–7; and "Los solidos y los mestureros," 1917, *Obras* III, pp. 768–770; and so on.

Unamuno put great store in the cultural value of Castilian Spanish, which he hoped would become a great inclusive, linguistic tool, binding all of Spain and Spanish America together. Ortega put less store on a language as the foundation of a culture; thus he wrote far less about the genius of languages than did Unamuno and he looked on separatism more as a political problem than did Unamuno. Unamuno's linguistic view of the separatist question came out very clearly in his essay "Política y cultura," 1908, *Obras* III, pp. 299–302. In it Unamuno recognized the political strength and value of Catalán nationalism, but he contended that it was not a strong force culturally, for what little would be gained by resurrecting Catalán would be far outweighed by what would be lost by making Castilian a second language in the Catalán provinces. Since Spanish progress depended primarily on cultural improvement, Unamuno thought that, over all, Catalán nationalism was not a constructive force.

Like Unamuno, Ortega aimed to preserve Castilian pre-eminence in Spain, and he thought that the main source of separatist sentiment was the weakness of the center. However, Ortega did not think that the cultural strength of a nation should be based on linguistic unity; for Ortega, a nation was more properly an articulation of diversities. Consequently, he was a bit more receptive to Catalán nationalism than Unamuno was. Early views of Ortega's appreciation of diversity within a nation may be found in "Sobre el proceso Rull," *Faro*, April 12, 1908, *Obras* X, pp. 47–50; "Diputado

por la cultura," *El Imparcial*, May 28, 1910, *Obras* X, pp.
143–6; and "Ni legislar ni gobernar," *El Imparcial*, September
25, 1912, *Obras* X, pp. 195–9.

That both Unamuno and Ortega envisaged a cultural
commonwealth with Spanish America is clear, not only from
what they wrote, but from what they did. Unamuno published a significant portion of his essays in Argentine newspapers and in them he often responded to queries and criticisms made to him by Spanish American correspondents.
Furthermore, Unamuno wrote voluminously about Spanish
America; see especially *La lengua Española en América, Obras*
IV, pp. 569–703, and *Letras de América y otros lecturas,"
Obras* IV, pp. 709–1084. See also, "Sobre la argentinidad,"
1910, *Obras* III, pp. 543–7, and "Algunas consideraciones
sobre la literatura Hispano-Americana," 1906, *Obras* III, pp.
900–924. Ortega had similar involvements. He started
writing for *La Prensa* at least as early as 1913, as a reference
by Unamuno (*OC,* IV, p. 1099) shows. A thorough examination of that paper and *La Nación* might turn up earlier articles.
In "Nueva España contra vieja España," *España*, February
19, 1915, *Obras* X, pp. 282–3, Ortega noted that Spain was
not respected in Latin America, a sign of the need for Spanish
rejuvenation. Soon afterwards he went on a lecture trip to
Buenos Aires, the success of which was reported with some
pride in *España*. See: J. M. M. S., "Ortega y Gasset en
América," *España*, March 7, 1917, p. 11.

Unamuno was much more explicit than Ortega about the
place of the church in Spain. For Unamuno's views see "Mi
religión," 1907, *Obras* III, pp. 259–263, and "Verdad y vida,"
1908, *Obras* III, pp. 264–8, in which he explained his conception of religion—finding truth in life and life in truth—
using it to criticize both the dogmatic Catholicism and the
dogmatic anticlericalism prevalent in Spain. See also "La
Fe," 1900, *Obras* I, pp. 962–970; "Religión y patria," 1904,
Obras I, pp. 1108–1115; and "El Cristo español," 1909,
Obras III, pp. 273–6. Ortega said very little about the Church
in Spain. In some of his early essays he criticized the Church
for making religion into a divisive, anti-social force; on this
point see especially "La ciencia y la religión como problemas
políticos," 1909, *Obras* X, pp. 119–127. In this lecture, which
Ortega gave in response to an invitation to give an "anti-
clerical" lecture, he observed that people were too frequently
against things and too seldom for things. This feeling probably explains why Ortega said so little about the Church.
Years later Ortega stated his attitude concisely: "Gentlemen,

I am not Catholic, and since my youth I have tried, even in the humblest official duties of my private life, to order my life in a non-Catholic way; but I am not disposed to let myself be inspired by the figurehead of an archaic anticlericalism." *Rectificación de la República*, 1931, *Obras* XI, p. 409.

III: C. PRESCIENCE HAS BEEN THE GIFT OF HUMANISTIC HISTORIANS (p. 64). Much remains to be done by historians in America if the potentialities of idealistic historiography are to be realized. What is needed is not a history of ideas, as such, but a history of character as it is oriented by ideals and limited by particular circumstances. The works of Tocqueville, Burckhardt, and Dilthey provide substantive examples of what can be expected of idealistic historiography. None of the three spent much time examining the material causes of events. Each was interested in the ways that tradition and custom, thought and art influenced history. In *The Old Regime and The French Revolution*, Stuart Gilbert, trans., Tocqueville examined how easy it was to proclaim a change in ideology and how hard it was to transform ingrained patterns of thought and the concomitant patterns of action. The historical consequences of ideas is a constant theme in *The French Revolution and Correspondence with Gobineau*, John Lukacs, ed., especially pp. 33–45, 226–230. Finally, Tocqueville's method in writing *Democracy in America* was to seek the characteristic ways of thinking of Americans and to project the probable historical consequences of these ideas. Needless to say, this is a far more humane version of historicism than are those grounded in materialistic or ethnic theories. Like Tocqueville, Burckhardt based his interpretation of *The Civilization of The Renaissance in Italy* on an examination of the way men thought. He made this method explicit in *Force and Freedom* by making man's three great intellectual creations—the state, religion, and culture—the fundamental determinants of historical change. Dilthey's great historical work is his *Weltanschauung und Analyse des Menschen seit Renaissance und Reformation* in *Gesammelte Schriften*, Vol. 2. His views on history will be dealt with at more length in later chapters. Werner Jaeger's great work, *Paideia: The Ideals of Greek Culture*, 3 vols., Gilbert Highet, trans., points the way for bringing this historiographical tradition to bear on the history of education.

III: d. WITHOUT PRINCIPLES, INNOVATION DEPENDS ON SELF-CONFIRMING MYTHS (p. 65). Ernst Cassirer's *The Myth of the State* is a profound history of the function of myth in Western politics from Plato through Fascism. Cassirer perceived that Plato was the basis of our struggle against political myths, rather than the source of these. His is a far more lucid examination of our tradition, especially with respect to Plato and Hegel, than is that of Sir Karl Popper with its mythical horde of historicist bogeymen who seek to subvert the champions of the open society. See Popper's *The Open Society and Its Enemies* and compare the sections on Plato and Hegel to those by Cassirer. Paul Natorp's *Sozialpädagogik*, for all its rigorous idealism, is a profound and rather hard-headed appreciation of the function principles play in public affairs. Political theory could be greatly improved if, prior to the study of "who-gets-what-when-and-where," there was a study of "who-will-do-what-why"; that is, if a study of possible motivations preceded a study of actual rewards.

III: e. THE DIALECTIC OF SPANISH REFORM . . . (p. 67). It is important that careful consideration be paid to the chronology by which various positions developed. Pedro Laín Entralgo based his examination of Europeanization on the work of Ortega with little reference to earlier theories; see *España como problema*, pp. 648–666. This procedure is convenient but deceptive if it causes Unamuno's writings on Spanish renovation to be read as if directed at Ortega's views. First of all, Unamuno's writing was addressed to Spanish-speaking people, not simply to Spaniards; a major portion of it appeared originally in Argentina: qualifications Unamuno introduced for Latin Americans did not mean that national regeneration was not as central a concern to him as it was to Ortega. Second, the critic should note how Unamuno used other people's opinions in constructing his essays; he very frequently made his essay a critique of someone else's view, not to combat that view, but to develop his own. Unamuno's one essay giving an extended critique of Ortega's view is a good case in point. "La supuesta anormalidad española," was published in *Hispania*, a British magazine, and it criticized a single observation that Ortega made—Spain is an abnormal nation—in an article published in the Buenos Aires newspaper, *La Prensa*. Unamuno was simply using Ortega's remarks to raise questions about what one means by a nation and how these meanings should be applied to Spain; neither agreement nor disagreement with Ortega's view of Spanish reform was really implied. (See *Obras* III, pp. 733–7.) Third, as was suggested in the bibliographical remarks above, Unamuno and Ortega were not that far apart on substantive questions of reform.

Although Unamuno did not direct his essays at Ortega, it does not mean that the nonchalance was reciprocal. Throughout his early essays Ortega appreciatively, yet distinctly, referred to Unamuno as a chief exponent of a view to be combated. Examples of this practice are "Glosas a un discurso," *El Imparcial,* September 11, 1908, *Obras* X, pp. 82–5; "Nuevas glosas," *El Imparcial,* September 26, 1908, *Obras* X, pp. 86–90; and "Unamuno y Europa, fábula," 1909, *Obras* I, pp. 128–132. By 1910 however, Ortega was claiming that whatever Unamuno's doctrine, his example was the inspiration of Europeanization; and in 1914 Ortega vehemently expressed his outrage at the removal of Unamuno as rector of the University of Salamanca. See "La guerra y la destitución de Unamuno," 1914, "La destitución de Unamuno," 1914, and "En defensa de Unamuno," 1914, *Obras* X, pp. 256–7, 258–261, 261–8.

III: f. LIKE MANY CURRENT THEORIES OF MODERNIZATION, EUROPEANIZA-
TION . . . (p. 67). The literature on modernization has gone through something of the same dialectical development that the Spanish Europeanizing literature went through. For many, modernization is seen as a simple transfer of the external characteristics of industrial societies to industrializing ones. Typical of this outlook is *Industrialism and Industrial Man* by Clark Kerr, John T. Dunlop, Frederick H. Harbison, and Charles A. Myers. The authors treat industrialism as a set of attitudes and outlooks that should be substituted through education, training, and manipulation for the sense of life that arises from the traditional mode of living. In real life, change is much more complicated, for the traditional sense of life does not disappear; it cannot be pushed out by a new, industrial view; it must be transformed. The example of Nigeria, which used to be Professor Harbison's favorite example of the power of formal, Western education to induce industrialism, shows well how ineffective this view is in the face of cultural complexity. A more recent school of thought about modernization is well represented by C. E. Black's *The Dynamics of Modernization.* Black does not indulge in the simplicities of cultural transfer. However, there are problems that arise from his attempt to plot several patterns of modernization by abstracting from historical generalizations. This effort purports to define direction in development without making value judgments. But the concept of development, when not based on rationally defended value judgments, be-

comes dangerous: either the future is reduced to the fulfillment of an inevitably as with Marx, or the person is asked
to pattern his actions on the basis of hypostatized theory that
does not really tell the person anything about the real conditions under which he acts.

III: g. COSTA'S CONCEPTION OF EUROPEANIZATION DEALT WITH SUPERFI-
CIAL MATTERS (p. 68). My statements radically condense selections from Costa's works that were themselves a major
reduction and simplification of his thought. Hence, I present
them, not as a characterization of Costa, who was a serious
thinker and complicated man, but as indications of views to
which overly optimistic Europeanizers responded. Although
Costa's views were more complicated than those of popular
Europeanization, he did much to feed that movement. For
sea power, see Costa, *Ideario*, pp. 55–82; for education see
Ibid., pp. 93–106, and Costa, *Maestro, escuela y patria*; for
industrialization and agriculture see *Ideario*, pp. 107–120,
145–172; for the social and administrative revolution see
Ibid., pp. 121–144; and for the policy towards regionalism see
Ibid., pp. 209–245, 274–282. There is a good characterization
of Costa in Trend, *The Origins of Modern Spain*, pp. 153–
168. For Ortega on Costa, see "La herencia viva de Costa,"
El Imparcial, February 20, 1911, *Obras* X, pp. 171–5.

III: h. UNAMUNO KNEW EUROPE BETTER THAN THE EUROPEANIZERS DID
(p. 69). In "La europeización como programa," Pedro Laín
Entralgo pointed out that Unamuno was able to criticize the
more superficial Europeanizers because he understood the
genius of Europe better than they did; see *España como
problema*, p. 649. Unamuno particularly despised French
materialism and he denounced it sharply in "Afrancesamiento," 1899, *OC* XI, pp. 68–70. His general opposition to
materialism is well expressed in "Cientificismo," 1907, "Escepticismo fanático," 1908, and "Materialismo popular,"
1909, in *Obras* III, pp. 352–367. The fear that the importa-
tion of European externals might destroy the traditions of
Spanish character was expressed very early by Unamuno and
Angel Ganivet in their exchange *El provenir de España*, 1898,
Obras III, pp. 637–677. Other essays by Unamuno pertinent
to Europeanization are "Sobre la europeización," 1906, *OC*
III, pp. 783–800; and "Programa," 1906, *OC* XI, pp. 137–
142. The extent of Unamuno's knowledge of Europe can be
estimated from his *Letras italianas*, *Obras* IV, pp. 1087–1131;
Letras inglesas, *Obras* IV, pp. 1135–1203; *Letras francesas*,

Obras IV, pp. 1237–1316; *Letras portugesas, Obras* IV, pp. 1319–1364; *Letras alemanas, Obras* IV, pp. 1367–1394; and *Letras rusas, Obras* IV, pp. 1397–1405. Most of the essays dealt with in these collections date from a period somewhat later than that with which we are here concerned, yet they indicate Unamuno's interests well. His earlier essays show a remarkable knowledge of European literature, as well as several marked preferences that compare interestingly with Ortega's. Of non-Spanish writers Unamuno was clearly most influenced by Carlyle, Kierkegaard, and William James, three men about whom Ortega had very little to say. On the other hand, Nietzsche and Renan, whom the young Ortega referred to frequently, were not central to Unamuno.

III: i. ANOTHER SUPERFICIAL ATTEMPT AT EUROPEANIZATION: MODERNISMO (p. 75). On *Modernismo* in Spain see Guillermo Díaz-Plaja, *Modernismo frente a noventa y ocho.* At the turn of the century there was also a reform movement called *Modernismo* in the Catholic Church. This movement was based in Italy, but it was influential in Spain and it was quite different from the literary and artistic *Modernismo*. For Ortega's approbation of the religious *Modernismo*, see "Sobre 'El Santo'," 1908, *Obras* I, pp. 430–8.

III: j. ORTEGA LIKED THE POETRY OF DARÍO AND VALLE-INCLÁN (p. 76). In a letter to Unamuno, Marburg, December 30, 1906, in *Revista de Occidente*, October 1964, p. 7, Ortega adopted a verse by Rubén Darío as "my verse." For sympathetic critiques of modernist poetry see "La 'Sonata de estío' de Don Ramón del Valle-Inclán," 1904, *Obras* I, pp. 19–27; "Algunas notas," 1908, *Obras* I, pp. 111–123; and "Los versos de Antonio Machado," 1912, *Obras* I, pp. 570–4.

III: k. HISTORY WAS REVEALED IN THE SELVES OF LIVING MEN (p. 77). "No ser hombre de partido," 1930, *Obras* IV, pp. 75–83, was Ortega's most pointed rejection of ideological commitment, but it is characteristic of all his writing. For the period here in question, see *Vieja y nueva política*, 1914, *Obras* I, especially pp. 285–8. In "¿Hombres o ideas?", 1908, *Obras* I, pp. 439–443, Ortega expressed a complicated theory of how history revealed itself in the selves of living men, for he was careful to make thought an important determinant, in some ways a more important one than the act. Nevertheless, the person's self was essential as is perhaps showed best in his analysis of historic individuals: *Mirabeau, o el político*, 1927,

Obras III, pp. 601–637; and "Maura, o la política," *El Sol,* December 18, 19, 22, and 31, 1925, and January 7 and 10, 1926, *Obras* XI, pp. 71–91.

III: 1. ORTEGA'S WRITINGS CONTAIN PHRASES THAT REPEL AMERICAN LIB-ERALS AND ATTRACT REACTIONARIES (p. 78). When *The Revolt of the Masses* was first published, several American conservatives reviewed it, greeting it as a polemic against democratic government. For instance, Ralph Adams Cram, *The Atlantic Monthly,* December 1932, "Bookshelf," found it somewhat perplexing "that one who courageously proclaims himself an aristocrat by conviction and a dissentient from the works of democracy should be a supporter of the present republican regime in Spain and a member of the democratic Cortes. . . ." But this perplexity was not sufficient to make Cram question whether *The Revolt of the Masses* might be something other than a conservative tract. From then on the book has had high standing with right-wing writers.

Thus, conservatives, such as Albert J. Nock in *Our Enemy, the State,* have drawn on Ortega's work for their criticism of the expansion of American government. Ralph Adams Cram relied heavily on Ortega's writings for his critical analysis of *The End of Democracy,* pp. 10–1, 24–5, 66, 86–8, 102–4, 112–9, 249–250. Both Nock and Cram quoted passages from *The Revolt of the Masses* that coincided with their own views without trying to give an analysis of Ortega's complete argument. Francis Stuart Campbell bolstered his very reactionary contentions in *The Menace of the Herd, or Procrustes at Large,* pp. 18, 35, 92, 100, 105, 330, 337, 340, 344, and 356, with references to Ortega, especially the American compilation called *Invertebrate Spain.* Norman L. Stamps referred to Ortega's *Revolt of the Masses* in *Why Democracies Fail: A Critical Evaluation of the Causes for Modern Dictatorships,* but he reduces Ortega's argument to a paraphrase of Gustave Le Bon's *The Crowd.* Representing a younger generation of conservatives, William Buckley, Jr., is reported to be writing a book on Ortega; see Ronald Martinetti, "I've Been Reading: Wild Bill Buckley," *The Columbia University Forum,* Fall 1967, p. 45.

With such friends, it is not surprising that Ortega has made enemies among American enthusiasts of democracy. In *Patterns of Anti-Democratic Thought,* pp. 96, 106–7, and 132, David Spitz identifies Ortega among the enemy, mainly on the basis of Cram's praise of Ortega in *The End of Democracy.* In *The Revival of Democratic Theory,* pp. 41, 85–6, and 144–5, Neal Riemer characterizes Ortega as an opponent of democracy, contending that the doubts Ortega raises about the average man lead logically to an espousal of a paternal, totalitarian dictatorship. In *The New Belief in the Common Man*, p. 246, Carl J. Friedrich includes Ortega among those who impede democracy by casting excessive doubt on the common man. In *The New Democracy and the New Despotism*, p. 75, fn. 2, Charles E. Merriam included Ortega among the anti-democrats, but on pp. 203–5, he used Ortega's ideas as an effective aid in analyzing the totalitarian problem. In *The Accidental Century*, pp. 213–219, 220, 223, 228, 229, Michael Harrington criticizes Ortega as an aristocratic spokesman whose theory of the masses was a reactionary impediment to the development of egalitarian democracy.

The ideological use of Ortega's work is not, by any means, always negative by American liberals and always positive by conservatives. The most critical book in English on Ortega was written by a conservative Catholic priest, José Sánchez Villaseñor, S.J., *Ortega y Gasset, Existentialist: A Critical Study of His Thought and Its Sources*, Joseph Small, trans. Several enthusiasts of democracy have drawn effectively on Ortega's ideas. T. V. Smith, in *The Democratic Way of Life*, quoted Ortega in his explanation of the intellectual responsibilities of the democratic citizen. Sigmund Neumann, in *Permanent Revolution: Totalitarianism in the Age of Civil War*, 2nd. ed., pp. 96–7, 247, sees Ortega as a liberal philosopher who analyzed the spiritual source of totalitarian dynamism Perhaps the most eloquent and profound use of Ortega's thought on the democratic side is by Charles Lam Markmann in his justification of "letting every voice be heard" as the basis of making democracy work; see his excellent book, *The Noblest Cry: A History of the American Civil Liberties Union*, pp. 242–3.

III: m.   SCHOLARS CALL ORTEGA AN "ARISTOCRATIC" OR "CONSERVATIVE" THEORIST (p. 79). Both liberal and conservative social theorists casually refer to Ortega as an "aristocratic" theorist. See Daniel Bell, *The End of Ideology*, p. 23, where Ortega is found to be against modernity; p. 26, where he is against science; and p. 298, where he is an exponent of an aristocratic conception of culture; William Kornhauser, *The Politics of Mass Society*, pp. 22, 26, etc., where Ortega is a major example of the "aristocratic" critics of mass society; Dwight Macdonald, *Against the American Grain*, p. 69, where Ortega is classed as a conservative; and Francis G. Wilson, "The Anatomy of

Conservatives," in W. J. Stankiewicz, ed., *Political Thought Since World War II*, p. 347, where Ortega is offered as a specimen. Sir Herbert Read, himself anything but a reactionary, saw the matter differently: "Ortega was not, in any way, a reactionary figure . . . ;" "Mediodía y noche oscura," *Revista de Occidente*, July 1966, p. 1.

III: n. THE LEAGUE FOR SPANISH POLITICAL EDUCATION (p. 82). Salvador de Madariaga, *Spain*, pp. 309–310, gives an account of the first meeting of the League and Ortega's address to it, and this account is particularly interesting since Madariaga was present at the event. Julián Marías, *Ortega*, pp. 235–244, devotes a section to the League. He rightly states that the League was important because it was the first time Ortega tried to conduct, rather than just think, politics. But he tells us little more about Ortega's conduct and is content to summarize Ortega's thoughts about the League. A very interesting contribution to comparative politics and education might be made through a study of the various organizations for political education that have arisen in the nineteenth and twentieth centuries in the course of national formation and reconstruction.

III: o. THE BIAS TOWARDS INSTITUTIONALIZED ACTION UNDERLIES A SIGNIFICANT CRITIQUE OF ORTEGA (p. 85). Because it would be an exercise in "useless" polemics, this critique is usually not explicitly stated, but one will frequently hear it in the course of discussion, especially among social scientists. The criticism has been put to me vigorously in conversation with Professor Juan Linz. With respect to Ortega, the criticism comes down to a lament that Ortega should have been someone other than the historic Ortega, but the criticism is most interesting not for what it tells us about Ortega, but for what it tells us about ourselves. It would be very illuminating if someone would do an extensive study of the different ways various influential scholars in the diverse disciplines conceive that historically significant actions are brought about, for a good part of our disagreements over the significance of various men and events may well be rooted in our confusions about how history gets made.

III: p. ORTEGA WAS NO TECHNOCRAT (p. 86). In "Competencia," 1913, *Obras X*, pp. 226–231, Ortega showed a keen appreciation for the importance of high technical competence within industry and government ministries. Thus, in saying that he was no technocrat, one is not saying that he scorned technical excellence. The question, rather, concerned the kind of shared aspirations that might bring about and sustain technical excellence. To achieve technical excellence, a people had to aspire to much more than technical excellence, for the truly competent technician was the man who had set out to master the pinnacles of science and who found along the way that his proper contribution was working somewhere short of that goal. This view was fundamental to Ortega's analysis of the dangers to modern civilization inherent in a general lowering of aspirations, and he gave a good early expression of it in "Asamblea para el progreso de las ciencias," 1908, *Obras* I, pp. 99–110. The greatest menace to technology was the technocrat who believed that technology would alone suffice.

IV: THE PEDAGOGY OF PROSE

IV: a. ORTEGA'S PURPOSES ARE REFLECTED IN HIS PROSE STYLE (p. 98). There have been several studies of Ortega as a writer. A rather technical but useful work is *Lengua y estilo de Ortega y Gasset* by Ricardo Senabre Sempere, although Senabre goes too far towards considering Ortega's style independent from his thought. Sister Mary Terese Avila Duffy does not do this in her interesting dissertation, "José Ortega y Gasset: The Creation of a Literary Genre for Philosophy"; but Ortega's style was more than a philosophical genre. Julián Marías has a thoughtful section on Ortega as a writer in *Ortega, I: Circunstancia y vocación*, pp. 259–353. In *Origen y epílogo de la filosofía*, 1943, 1960, *Obras* X, pp. 400–2, Ortega briefly discussed the importance of style for comprehending philosophy, and it is a subject that merits much further study. It is surprising, in view of all the attention that has been paid in recent years to language in philosophy, that the techniques of the literary critic have not been more fruitfully applied to the works of past philosophers. *A Grammar of Motives* and *A Rhetoric of Motives* by Kenneth Burke indicate the possibilities that might arise for systematic philosophy and *Preface to Plato* by Eric A. Havelock the possibilities for historical interpretation.

IV: b. IN NO SINGLE WORK DID ORTEGA GIVE A COMPLETE STATEMENT OF HIS DOCTRINE (p. 100). Ortega's posthumous works, generally not devoted to the task of Europeanization, were more systematic than his earlier writings. But only *La idea de principio en Leibniz y la evolución de la teoría deductiva,* 1947, 1958, *Obras* VIII, pp. 59-356, approaches being a systematic work of philosophy, and even it has many features that suggest a series of occasional essays. Ortega's discussion of the character of books and of reading in the opening part of his "Comentario al *Banquete* de Flatón," 1946, 1962, *Obras* VIII, pp. 751–767, are very important for studying why Ortega chose to present his philosophy in the form that he did.

IV: C. BERTRAND RUSSELL, TO CHOOSE A PHILOSOPHER KNOWN FOR HIS UNIVERSAL CURIOSITY . . . (p. 100). For the range of Russell's interests see Robert E. Egner and Lester E. Denonn, eds., *The Basic Writings of Bertrand Russell.* In many of Russell's excursions into topics outside his central epistemological interests one can sense that his analysis of the topic has benefited from the continual sharpening of his intelligence in his analyses of philosophical problems; but one often finds no direct carry-over from his technical to his general concerns. Thus *Power: A New Social Analysis* and *Education and the Good Life* might have been written by any lucid thinker, not necessarily by a man of Russell's particular philosophic convictions. A complicated problem arises when there is no integral relationship between different aspects of a man's work, for if he achieves greatness in one matter, his reputation will carry over and affect the way all his work is received, even though the ideas responsible for his reputation are irrelevant to his other concerns.

IV: d. UNLIKE BUBER, ORTEGA RARELY WROTE ABOUT DIALOGUE (p. 105). For Buber's conception of dialogue see *I and Thou,* 2nd. ed., R. G. Smith, trans., *passim;* and *Pointing the Way,* Maurice S. Friedman, trans., esp. pp. 63–105, 237–9. Also, unlike Ortega, Buber wrote literary dialogues; see *Daniel: Dialogues on Realization,* Maurice Friedman, trans. The following from Ortega's "La pedagogía social como programa política," 1910, *Obras* I, p. 520, raises the question whether the I-Thou philosophy was not very much "in the air" in early twentieth-century thought in Germany before Buber's fame. "In this way Jesus softly admonishes us: do not content yourself with making your *I* high, wide, and deep; find the fourth dimension of your *I,* which is your neighbor, the *Thou,* the community."

Most of Ortega's explicit statements about dialogue will be quoted below, but these alone do not give a sufficient idea of the importance of dialogue for him. To grasp the full importance of dialogue it is necessary to keep in mind Ortega's perspectivist epistemology as it is explained in *El tema de nuestra tiempo*, 1923, *Obras* III, pp. 145–242; his conception of the history of thought as a creative, dialectical development as he explains in "Prólogo a *Historia de la filosofía* de Emile Bréhier," 1942, *Obras* VI, pp. 377–412, and *Origen y epílogo de la filosofía*, 1943, 1960, *Obras* IX, pp. 349–434; and his sense for the problems of writing and reading as they are explained in "Prólogo a una edición de sus obras," 1932, *Obras* VI, pp. 342–354; "Miseria y esplendor de la traducción," 1937, *Obras* V, pp. 433–452; and "Comentario al *Banquete* de Platón," 1946, 1961, *Obras* IX, pp. 751–767.

IV: e. ORTEGA'S WRITING WAS CIRCUMSTANTIAL (p. 109). This was true not only of the way Ortega's writing was meant to be encountered by his audience, but also of the way it was composed. While I was researching at the offices of *Revista de Occidente*, Ortega's method of composition was explained to me by his daughter. Ortega had special note cards on which he would record a single thought whenever it occurred. He would study these cards, and in the light of his basic convictions, he would arrange various thoughts into an argument on a subject, carefully elaborating this skeleton of thoughts into a developed work, each thought becoming a short essay.

Many scholars consider it a mark against a man's intellect that he should cultivate conversation. This prejudice underlies a criticism of Ortega. Thus, Raymond Carr writes: "This emphasis on conversational exchange and journalism was one of the main weaknesses of Spanish intellectual life: conversation was the essential foundation of Ortega y Gasset's work." (*Spain*, p. 60 n.) This suggestion depends, like Father Sánchez's argument, on an improper inference from style to substance. The two founts of Western intellectual life, Greek philosophy and Judeo-Christian religion, generated from conversational exchange. No form of intellectual exchange is, in itself, good or bad, strong or weak; such qualities depend on how well the form in question serves its intellectual functions. There is more to this matter, moreover, than a mere qualification to a criticism of Ortega. We are too much in the habit of identifying the quality and even the content of thinking with the style of thinking, and in doing so, we greatly confuse the problem of absorbing new aids to thinking. Except for a few studies like *The Art of Memory* by Frances Yates, *Immagine e parola nella formazione dell'uomo* by M. T.

Gentile, and *Preface to Plato* by Eric A. Havelock, educational historians have failed to entertain the possibility that modes of thinking in past times differed from those now dominant. As a result, it has been possible for contemporary critics such as Marshall McLuhan in *Understanding Media* to spread much confusion by not discriminating between changes in modes of thinking and continuity in the basic problems of judgment.

IV: f.   THUS, ORTEGA COULD USE THE PEDAGOGY OF ALLUSION (p. 113). Owing to the narrowness of our present conception of pedagogy, important dimensions of comparison between the work of various thinkers are difficult to perceive. For instance, there are difficulties explaining how the philosophical views of Ortega and Heidegger differed; yet these difficulties would disappear if we could compare the allusive pedagogy Ortega used in explaining his position with Heidegger's pedagogy of specification. Compare how Ortega and Heidegger handled the problem of ensuring that philosophy referred to life as it was lived. Whereas Ortega chose to explicate his ideas by means of references to everyday situations, Heidegger conceptualized the everyday and insisted that the problem for ontology was to understand the Being of *Dasein* "in its average *everydayness.*" (*Being and Time*, Macquarrie and Robinson, trans., pp. 37–8.) Both men began with the same insight into the transcendent primacy of personal existence, and from there one proceeded to convert the technical into the everyday and the other the everyday into the technical. By considering the pedagogical dimension, the way a philosopher chooses to present his views, certain significant questions open up. For instance, what part of the human consequences of a doctrine stems from the doctrine itself and what part from the pedagogy chosen by the philosopher to inform his presentation of his doctrine? This question is significant, for many choose their philosophies according to the human consequences they believe these bear, and it is not always clear whether objectionable consequences derive from the doctrine or the teaching of the doctrine. Thus, in *Nihilism: A Philosophical Essay*, Stanley Rosen severely criticizes Heidegger for nihilism, suggesting that Heidegger equated silence with the source of significance. One comes away, however, from Rosen's critique with an unsatisfied question: do the doctrines themselves lead to silence or the modes of presenting the doctrines chosen by particular adherents to them?

V: THE PARTLY FAITHFUL PROFESSOR

V: a. TO CULTIVATE INTELLECTUALITY IN SPAIN (p. 119). In giving Ortega the Chair of Metaphysics, the university was taking a surprising step, for Ortega had been outspoken about the existing inadequacies of the university and had made known his intention to try to change things. Articles unlikely to endear Ortega to the complacent academic establishment were "Sobre los estudios clásicos," 1907; "Pidiendo una biblioteca," 1908; "Asamblea para el progreso de las ciencias," 1908; and "Una fiesta de paz," 1909, Obras I, pp. 63–7, 81–5, 99–110, 124–7. Other essays that reflect the same views are "La reforma liberal," Faro, February 23, 1908, Obras X, pp. 31–8; "La conservación de la cultura," Faro, March 8, 1908, Obras X, pp. 39–46; "Sobre la pequeña filosofía," El Imparcial, April 13, 1908, Obras X, pp. 51–5; "La cuestión moral," El Imparcial, August 27, 1908, Obras X, pp. 73–8; "Catecismo para la lectura de una carta," El Imparcial, February 10, 1910, Obras X, pp. 133–8; "Pablo Iglesias," El Imparcial, May 13, 1910, Obras X, pp. 139–142; "Diputado por la cultura," El Imparcial, May 28, 1910, Obras X, pp. 143–6; and a lecture given in La Casa de Partido Socialista Madrileño, December 2, 1910, on "La ciencia y la religión como problemas políticos," Obras X, pp. 119–127. It is interesting to compare Ortega's views in this lecture with those of some radical students and professors today who are suggesting with some basis that in times of deep division even the seemingly most disinterested studies are not really apolitical. Somehow we need to learn how to claim protection for the origination and exploring of ideas without asserting the sterile pretension to disinterestedness.

V: b. TO DEMAND RADICAL IMPROVEMENT IN THE SPANISH UNIVERSITIES ... (p. 122). For the condition of the Spanish universities and especially their philosophy instruction at the start of Ortega's career, see Marías, Ortega, especially pp. 125–173; and Manuel García Morente, Ensayos, pp. 201–7. For a more general view of the situation see Yvonne Turin, Miguel de Unamuno, universitaire.

V: c. MEMBERS OF THE SCHOOL OF MADRID HAVE A WIDE RANGE OF CONCERNS (p. 124). For a general discussion of the school, see Julián Marías, La escuela de Madrid in Obras de Julián Marías, V, pp. 207–507. Marías concentrates on Ortega's work in the studies included in this book, and he locates the school more in Ortega and certain of Ortega's contemporaries, whereas I locate it primarily in the students of these men who are now carrying on their work. For representative works by the members of the school see the following. Pedro Laín Entralgo has produced a variety of studies in intellectual history, medical history, and philosophy; Ortega's influence shows clearly in Laín's series of major studies: *La espera y la esperanza: Historia y teoría del esperar humano*, 1957; *Teoría y realidad del otro*, 2 vols., 1961; and *La relación médico-enfermo: Historia y teoría*, 1964. Julián Marías has written extensively on numerous subjects, but his most important work is *Historia de la filosofía*, which gives a good account of the philosophic tradition, showing how Ortega and other twentieth-century thinkers relate to it. José Ferrater Mora is one of the most cosmopolitan of contemporary thinkers. His *El ser y la muerte: bosquejo de filosofía integracionista*, in *Obras selectas*, II, pp. 297–484, draws effectively on both Anglo-American and continental philosophic traditions as well as on both theological and scientific studies of life and death. This ability to draw on all the current schools of thought is also reflected in Ferrater's *La filosofía en el mundo de hoy*, in *Ibid.*, pp. 13–171, which is a very useful study for placing Ortega in twentieth-century philosophy. Finally, his *El hombre en la encrucijada*, *Obras selectas*, I, pp. 369–579, is a substantial essay in the history of philosophy. On the surface of things, Paulino Garagorri's work looks less substantial than that of those already mentioned, but such an appearance is deceiving. His studies of Ortega in *Ortega, una reforma de la filosofía* and *Unamuno, Ortega, Zubiri en la filosofía española* are useful contributions. In addition, the essays gathered in *Ejercicios intelectuales* show a wide range of interests, a lively style, and a capacity for penetrating criticism. These qualities, plus his work as managing editor of *Revista de Occidente* and his involvement in the reform movement in contemporary Spanish public affairs, make him one of the closest followers of Ortega, the only one who preserves the spirit as well as the letter of the master. Simply one work by Luis Díez del Corral need be mentioned, *El Rapto de Europa: una interpretación histórica de nuestro tiempo*, which contributes in important ways to extending Ortega's concern for Europe's future.

v: d. FOLLOWING ORTEGA'S DEATH, NUMEROUS ESSAYS COMMEMORATED HIS POWER AS A TEACHER (p. 124). See, for instance: Julián

Marías, "Ortega: historia de una amistad," *Obras de Marías*, V, pp. 377–381; Antonio Rodríguez Huescar, "Aspectos de magisterio orteguiano," *Con Ortega y otros escritos*, pp. 19–30; Manuel Granell, *Ortega y su filosofía*, pp. 27–35; Paulino Garagorri, *Ortega, una reforma de la filosofía*, pp. 170–181. There were a number of commemorative issues of various journals dedicated to Ortega. Among them see *La Torre* of the University of Puerto Rico, No. 15–16, July and December 1956, and *Homenaje a Ortega y Gasset*, Instituto de Filosofía, Universidad Central de Venezuela, 1958. The controversy over Ortega's allegiances at his death may be sampled even at the distance of *The New York Times*. The obituary in the October 19, 1955, issue stressed Ortega's part in overthrowing Alfonso XIII and founding the Second Republic and drew attention to Ortega's work as a Europeanizer (p. 33, col. 1). An editorial in the October 20 issue said that he had been a great Europeanizer, a liberal opponent of Fascism, a man whose hopes for Spain had been disappointed, but whose ideas lived on. In the October 25 issue an official of the Franco regime objected to these points, claiming Ortega was a man who had fled in terror from the Republic and who had seen the organic virtues of the Franco state. In the November 4 issue Victoria Kent, who had participated with Ortega in the Constituent Cortes, objected to these claims, stressing Ortega's commitment to democratic liberalism.

v: e. THE TERMS THEMSELVES WERE MEANINGLESS (p. 128). This fact is the basis of a vexing problem in the theory of language; for the terms to be invested effectively with meaning, they must be conventionally dependable and personally significant, a double criterion that is not easily met. With respect to philosophical terms, Ortega put greatest weight on the second criterion. On this importance of a fine sense of understanding in philosophy, see especially the beginning of *Origen y epílogo de la filosofía*, 1944, 1953, 1960, *Obras* XI, pp. 349–351. These very late strictures against knowledge without comprehension are completely consistent with his youthful deprecation of mere erudition in *Meditaciones del Quijote*, 1914, *Obras* I, pp. 316–7. The issue is well put from the opposite perspective by C. K. Ogden and I. A. Richards, in *The Meaning of Meaning*, p. 19, where they stipulate that "we should develop our theory of signs from observations of other people, and only admit evidence drawn from introspection when we know how to appraise it." Although I would not like to argue that we learn how to observe other people *only* by using evidence drawn from introspection, I would contend that Ogden and Richard's formulation, if followed to the letter, would lead to a rather inexpressive realm of discourse. The tension between objective denotation and personal comprehension might be better maintained if we kept in mind (if I may so speak) that denotation is a conventional feature of speech that permits the communication of factual statements stripped of their human import. Comprehension can then be seen as something additional to the mechanism of communication, through which the recipient of a statement converts it into a thought. Since the listener must always invest the statements he hears with comprehension, the conception of the plastic pupil that is the basis of contemporary educational theory is inappropriate, fundamentally false.

v: f.   ORTEGA'S HISTORICISM WAS A MODE OF EXPLANATION, NOT A SET OF ONTOLOGICAL ASSERTIONS (p. 131). Karl Popper has caused great confusion by giving an idiosyncratic definition of historicism in his influential book, *The Poverty of Historicism*. He proclaimed: "I mean by 'historicism' an approach to the social sciences which assumes that *historical prediction* is their principle aim, and which assumes that this aim is attainable by discovering the 'rhythms' or the 'patterns,' the 'laws' or the 'trends' that underlie the evolution of history" (p. 3). The serious difficulty with Popper's position is that his definition excludes those historians who would admit to being historicists and who have generally been considered historicists. The great historicists—Dilthey, Rickert, Croce, Meinecke, Ortega—are among the leading opponents to that approach to the social sciences that Popper called "historicism." Hans Meyerhoff has effectively identified the general features of historicism, and his proper meaning is antithetical to Popper's meaning. "(1) The denial of a systematic approach to history; (2) the repudiation of any single, unified interpretation of history, and (3) the positive assertions (a) that the basic concepts of history are change and particularity, (b) that the historian has a special way of explaining things by telling a story, and (c) that history is all-pervasive, that historical categories permeate all aspects of *human* life, including morality and philosophy." (Meyerhoff, ed., *The Philosophy of History in Our Time*, p. 27.) Ortega was a historicist in Meyerhoff's sense.

For Ortega, freedom was an intrinsic component of the process of historical determination, and human thought was central to freedom as an historical reality, for thought was man's free response to his circumstances. Major works pertinent to this matter are "Historia como sistema," 1936, *Obras* VI, pp. 11–50; "Guillermo Dilthey y la idea de la vida," 1933, *Obras* VI, pp. 165–214; "Prólogo a *Historia de la filosofía* de Karl Vorländer," 1922, *Obras* VI, pp. 292–300; "Prólogo a *Historia de la filosofía* de Emile Bréhier," 1942, *Obras* VI, pp. 377–418; *En torno a Galileo*, 1933, *Obras* V, pp. 13–164; and *Origen y epílogo de la filosofía*, 1944, 1953, 1960, *Obras* IX, pp. 349–434.

v: g. TO COMMUNICATE PRINCIPLES, ONE EXEMPLIFIED THEIR HUMANE USES (p. 131). This procedure was used by Ortega in the many philosophical lectures that are transcribed in his works. His recently published lectures, *Unas lecciones de metafísica*, give an excellent example of this effort. In addition, see "La percepción del prójimo," 1929, *Obras* VI, pp. 153-163; "Por que se vuelve a la filosofía," 1930, *Obras* IV, pp. 89–109; "Sobre el estudiar y el estudiante," 1933, *Obras* IV, pp. 545–554; *En torno a Galileo*, 1933, *Obras* V, pp. 13–166; ¿*Qué es filosofía?*, 1929, 1957, *Obras* VII, pp. 275–438; "Conciencia, objecto y las tres distancias de este," 1915, *Obras* II, pp. 61–6; "Sensación, construcción e intuición," 1913, in Ortega, *Apuntes sobre el pensamiento*, pp. 99–117; and "¿Qué es el conocimiento?", *El Sol*, January 18 and 25, February 1 and 22, and March 1, 1931. Ortega's ability to exemplify the uses of principles is described first-hand by Rodríguez, *Con Ortega*, "Aspectos del magisterio orteguiano," pp. 19–30. See also, Paulino Garagorri, *Relacciones y disputaciones orteguianas*.

v: h. A PERSON'S MISSION WAS AN ACTIVITY THAT HE HAD TO DO (p. 132). The best discussion of this topic is in "No ser hombre de partido," 1930, *Obras* IV, pp. 75–9. See also *Misión de la universidad*, 1930, *Obras* IV, pp. 313–353; and "Misión del bibliotecario," 1935, *Obras* V, pp. 21–234. On the hero see especially *Meditaciones del Quijote*, 1914, *Obras* I, pp. 389–390. On the relation of destiny to the history of a community see especially Lección VI and VII of *En torno a Galileo*, 1933, *Obras* V, pp. 69–92. A corollary of Ortega's idea that a mission had great positive importance in a man's life was his conviction that stereotypes were of great danger to the authentic life. See "Qué pasa en el mundo," *El Sol,* June 1 and 3, 1933, for an excellent example of Ortega's concern that the young resist the influence of stereotypes. In "Sobre las carreras," 1934, *Obras* V, pp. 167–183, Ortega tried to indicate the very limited, proper use that stereotypes might have in the service of authentic life. Later, his distrust of stereotypes came to the fore in his assertion that the social (properly understood as usages, dead conventions) was actually the basis of the "anti-social" in human life, imposing meaningless separations that hindered meaningful, interpersonal exchange; see *El hombre y la gente,* 1949, 1957, *Obras* VII, pp. 268–9.

v: i. THE GREEK DEBATE WHETHER VIRTUE CAN BE TAUGHT (p. 134). Plato's texts are fundamental: first *Protagoras;* then *Euthyphro, Apology, Crito, Phaedo;* then *Gorgias;* then *Republic;* then *Statesman, Sophist,* and the *Laws.* Thucydides' *History of the Peloponnesian War* is also essential for showing how events operate as a powerful pedagogue, slowly destroying the public virtues of a people. Werner Jaeger's *Paideia: The Ideals of Greek Culture,* Gilbert Highet, trans., is a profound contribution to our understanding of the Greek debate. It is too often treated, however, as the last word on the matter, which it is not. There is a useful review of the idea of *areté* in Robert William Hall, *Plato and the Individual,* pp. 34–66. Three general studies that help expand our understanding of the Greek debate are *Merit and Responsibility: A Study in Greek Values* by Arthur W. H. Adkins; *Sophrosyne: Self-Knowledge and Self-Restraint in Greek Literature* by Helen North; and *Ilustración y política en la Grecia clásica* by Francisco Rodríguez Adrados.

v: j. ORTEGA AS A SPOKESMAN FOR THE FACULTY (p. 137). See "Ortega y Gasset, candidato a la senaduría por Universidad de Madrid," *El Sol,* April 10, 1923, p. 4; notices concerning Ortega's public course "¿Qué es filosofía?" given in defiance of Primo de Rivera's order closing the University of Madrid, *El Sol,* March 23 and 27; April 6, 9, 12, 16, 19, 23, 26, and 30; May 3, 7, 10, 14, and 16, 1929; "De la 'Gaceta' de hoy: Se admite la renuncia de sus cátedras," *El Sol,* May 10, 1929; articles by Luis de Zulueta, *El Sol,* May 10, 1929, and by Manuel García Morente, *El Sol,* June 2, 9, 25, and 30, 1929; "Keyserling y Ortega y Gasset, al Ateneo guipuzcoano," *El Sol,* March 15, 1930; a pamphlet by a group of young intellectuals,

Madrid, April 1929, ("Señor Don . . . ," *Obras* XI, pp. 102–6); and so on.

v: k. EDUCATIONAL THEORISTS HAVE PLUNGED INTO PEDAGOGICAL PATERNALISM (p. 141). The central question in the tension between liberal and paternal education concerns whether the student is considered to be a free, responsible agent prior to his education or whether his education is considered to be that which turns the slavish soul into a free autonomous person. The assumption, characteristic of the liberal tradition—that the student seeks to educate himself because he is a free man—has come under severe criticism in the past century. Herbart denied the compatibility of education with the doctrine of transcendental freedom. This incompatibility exists only if education is hypostatized and made into something independent of the student; into something that is done to him, not something that he does to himself. Having denied transcendental freedom, Herbart rightly made the science of education, the science that the teacher preeminently needed, into the major problem of pedagogy. Paternalism pervaded Herbart's pedagogy because of his denial of transcendental freedom. The child was seen to be a plastic being that lacked its own will and was to have a will molded in it. See *The Science of Education: Its General Principles Deduced from Its Aim*, Felkin and Felkin, trans., pp. 57–77, 83–90, 94–5, etc. To be sure, p. 61, Herbart tried to guard against the more extreme consequences of his denial, but to little avail. He said that the teacher was not to create the pupil's power of choice, but merely to act upon the pupil's potential for choice in such a way that "it must infallibly and surely" come to fruition. In either case, Herbart began the fatal practice of thinking out of existence the pupil's right and power to refuse education and instruction. Cf. Herbart, *Letters and Lectures on Education*, Felkin and Felkin, trans., pp. 102–8. Of this passage, the question should be asked: is *inner freedom* the result of education or the condition of education? For Ortega on Herbart, see "Prólogo a *Pedagogía general derivada del fin de la educación*, de J. F. Herbart," *Obras* VI, pp. 265–291.

Even in classical times the rationale for the circle of studies that became known as the liberal arts was not easy to maintain. Plato made it clear in the *Republic* that their purpose was not to teach virtue, but to equip men to search for virtue. See especially VI, 502–VII, 541. Traditionally this has been the basis of the liberal position: rather than assert that the truth will make men free, the liberal recognizes that because a man is free, he must seek the truth. The goal of instruction in the liberal tradition is to make the student independent of his teachers.

Epistle 88 of Seneca's *Epistulae Morales*, Richard M. Gummere, trans., is of great importance for understanding this pedagogy of the liberal arts. The liberal arts are "useful only insofar as they give the mind a preparation and do not engage it permanently. One should linger upon them only so long as the mind can occupy itself with nothing greater; they are our apprenticeship, not our real work." (88:1) "We ought not to be learning such things; we should have done with learning them." (88:2) " 'What then,' you say, 'do the liberal studies contribute nothing to our welfare?' Very much in other respects, but nothing at all as regards virtue. For even these arts of which I have spoken, though admittedly of a low grade—depending as they do upon handiwork—contribute greatly toward the equipment of life, but nevertheless have nothing to do with virtue. And if you inquire, 'Why, then, do we educate our children in the liberal studies?' it is not because they can bestow virtue, but because they prepare the soul for the reception of virtue. Just as that 'primary course,' as the ancients called it, in grammar, which gave boys their elementary training, does not teach them the liberal arts, so the liberal arts do not conduct the soul all the way to virtue, but merely set it going in that direction." (88:20) The importance of being able to follow studies without a teacher was subtly implied in Augustine's description of how, even though he did not need to rely on a teacher, he mastered the liberal arts yet derived little from them; *Confessions*, Bk. IV, Chapter 16. Unless we recognize the virtue of going without a teacher, his statement is absurd. Even more explicit is the Renaissance educator, Battista Guarino, in "Concerning the Order and the Method to be Observed in Teaching." He wrote: "A master who should carry his scholars through the curriculum which I have now laid down may have confidence that he has given them a training which will enable them, not only to carry forward their own reading without assistance, but also to act efficiently as teachers in their turn." W. H. Woodward, trans., in his *Vittorino da Feltre and Other Humanist Educators*, p. 172.

This rationale of the liberal arts gives the basis for a revision of our understanding of the old-time collegiate curriculum and of the significance of its demise. As I have pointed out very briefly with Jean McClintock in our essay

"Architecture and Pedagogy," *The Journal of Aesthetic Education*, October 1968, especially pp. 69–71, 75–6, the purpose of the old-time pedagogy was to equip the student as efficiently as possible for self-education. This rationale is well explained in the much maligned, but little comprehended "Yale Report of 1828" in Hofstadter and Smith, eds., *American Higher Education*, Vol. 1, pp. 275–291. The way this curriculum functions is exemplified in Perry Miller's study of *Jonathan Edwards*, pp. 54–68. As Perry Miller makes obvious, there was very little substantive content in the old college curriculum, despite its ambitious "technologia." Jonathan Edwards was not the only young man who was effectively prepared by a narrow, formal curriculum to be able to get a rich general education by his own devices through the extracurriculum.

In addition to whatever academic value it had, the replacement of this old-time curriculum keyed to the self-education of each student, with an elective system, was a development that clearly served the needs of a growing, paternal, industrial state. The elective system was a system introduced in the name of the students' freedom: each could choose what subjects he would study. At the same time the system was extremely useful in distributing socially beneficial skills. The American educator, Francis Wayland, explained the rationale for this system well in "Thoughts on the Present Collegiate System," 1842, and his "Report to the Corporation of Brown"; see Hofstadter and Smith, eds., *American Higher Education*, Vol. I, p. 341; Vol. II, pp. 478–487. For these tendencies in the European university, see Nietzsche, *Schopenhauer as Educator*, pp. 59–82, but whereas Wayland was enthusiastic, Nietzsche was bitterly critical, for Nietzsche saw that a specialized education not only disseminated useful skills, but it also made the acquirer rather dependent on that skill, increasing the moral inertia of men in high places.

Owing to the paternal idea that an education is to provide a student with a certain set of skills, we have seriously hypostatized and even personified the curriculum. It is a standard assumption in schools of education that a well-designed curriculum has causal power over those who study it, and even friends of the liberal tradition create difficulties for themselves by putting their hope in the curriculum, not the student.

An indication of how contemporary educators attribute purposes to the curriculum rather than to students is to be found in Daniel Bell's excellent critique of general education, *The Reforming of General Education*, p. 152. Purposes that are properly embodied in men are spoken of as embodied in the curriculum. "In the more limited and specific ways that such purposes can be embodied in a curriculum, the content of liberal education . . . can be defined through six purposes: 1) To overcome intellectual provincialism; 2) To appreciate the centrality of method; 3) To gain an awareness of history; 4) To show how ideas relate to social structures; 5) To understand the way values infuse all inquiry; 6) To demonstrate the civilizing role of the humanities." Take the first purpose, to overcome intellectual provincialism. If it is to be embodied in the curriculum, many intellectual provinces will have to be presented sympathetically. If it is embodied in the student, the curriculum will need to give effective instruction in the many languages, the use of which will permit the student to chart his own course through the various provinces. A cosmopolitan curriculum is a kind of intellectual Disneyland, whereas a true cosmopolitan has really made the Grand Tour, learning to use a rich inheritance—monetary or spiritual—with effect. I have discussed the rationale of study and the liberal arts more fully in "On the Liberality of the Liberal Arts," *Teachers College Record*, Vol. 72, No. 3, February 1971, pp. 405–416; and "Towards a Place for Study in a World of Instruction," to be published in *Teachers College Record*, Vol. 73, No. 2, December 1971.

VI: THE PEOPLE'S PEDAGOGUE

VI: a. ORTEGA EARLY BROKE WITH EL IMPARCIAL (p. 153). My account of Ortega's break with his family's paper diverges from the usual accounts. Both Lorenzo Luzuriaga, in his "Las fundaciones de Ortega y Gasset," Instituto de Filosofía, *Homenaje a Ortega y Gasset*, and Evelyne López-Campillo, in her "Ortega: *El Imparcial* y las Juntas," *Revista de Occidente*, June 1969, pp. 311–7, base the chronology of their account almost solely on a remark by Ortega in *La decencia nacional*, 1932. Ortega's remark, a note explaining why he included "Bajo el arco en ruina" in the book, was as follows: "This article was published in *El Imparcial* on June 11, 1917. A few days before, in Barcelona, the Juntas de Defensa del Arma de Infanteria had declared themselves in rebellion. The disputes to which this article gave rise had, as a result, the founding of the newspaper *El Sol* by D. Nicolás M.ª de Urgoiti." (*Obras* XI, p. 265, n. 1). On this basis, both Luzuriaga and López-Campillo contend that Ortega's break with *El Imparcial* came at this time. This contention, however, is unsatisfactory.

The most useful evidence for understanding Ortega's relations with *El Imparcial* is a rather complete listing of his journalistic articles. Such a list shows rather clearly the following chronology: up until April 22, 1913, with "De un estorbo nacional" Ortega was quite content to write for *El Imparcial*; "De un estorbo nacional" provoked a break with *El Imparcial* and Ortega switched to *El País*, for which he wrote through 1914, a year in which he wrote few newspaper articles undoubtedly because of his preoccupation with the League for Spanish Political Education and *Meditaciones del Quijote*. From then until his Argentine tour in late 1916, Ortega was content to publish through *España* and *El Espectador*. During his joint lecture tour with his father, a tour through which he established many contacts with Argentine newspaper publishers and writers, Ortega was probably convinced to give *El Imparcial* another try, for in the Spring of 1917 Ortega wrote two articles for *El Imparcial*, first "Bajo el arco en ruina" and two weeks later "El verano, ¿sera tranquilo?"; and finally, in the Fall of 1917 Ortega wrote briefly for *El Día* and then, starting in December, he devoted himself to the newly-founded *El Sol*. From these facts, it is clear that when *El Imparcial* refused the second part of "De un estorbo nacional" Ortega decided to go it on his own. It takes time to organize an enterprise on the scale of *El Sol*, and it is probable that Ortega's short rapprochement with *El Imparcial* in 1917 came when María de Urgoiti was negotiating for the purchase of *El Imparcial* and that Liberal displeasure over Ortega's articles on the Juntas may have prevented the purchase. This interpretation is as consistent with Ortega's remarks in *La decencia nacional* as is that of Luzuriaga and López-Campillo, more so because Ortega's remarks speak only of disputes that led to *El Sol* (by blocking the purchase of *El Imparcial*) and nothing of disputes causing *El Imparcial* to close its columns to Ortega. As a matter of fact, two weeks after "Bajo el arco en ruina" *El Imparcial* published another essay by Ortega. Fuller evidence on Ortega's relations with *El Imparcial* and *El Sol,* and all his other publishing ventures, for that matter, would help greatly.

VI: b.   AFTER RETURNING FROM GERMANY, ORTEGA HELPED FOUND FARO (p. 153). Ortega mentioned his participation in its founding in "El Señor Dato, responsable de un atropello a la constitución," *El Sol*, June 17, 1920, *Obras* X, p. 654. His articles in *Faro* were "La reforma liberal" in the first issue, February 23,

1908; "La conservación de la cultura," March 8, 1908; "Sobre el proceso Rull," April 12, 1908; and "La moral visigótica," May 10, 1908; *Obras* X, pp. 31–8, 39–46, 47–50, and 56–8.

My account of Ortega's involvement in publishing is based on a survey of the publications in question. The Hemeroteca Municipal of Madrid has an excellent collection of newspapers and magazines from the late nineteenth century on. With the publication of Vols. X and XI of Ortega's works, his contributions to *Faro, Europa, España, El Imparcial, El Sol,* and other papers are now available, but to get a feel for the type of publications that these were it is important to go to the archives. The best available study of Spanish journalism is by Henry F. Schulte, *The Spanish Press, 1470–1966: Print, Power, Politics.* It is not a good study, however; some of my disagreements with it may be found in a review of it in the *Comparative Education Review,* June 1969, pp. 235–8.

In addition to the initiatives discussed in the text, Ortega took part in the mass journalism of *Crisol* and *Luz,* for which he wrote in 1931 and 1932. The papers were backed by the *El Sol* group. Their format was more popular, close to that of a tabloid, although their content was of high quality. Unlike *El Sol,* which in addition to politics devoted much attention to cultural events, these papers concentrated mainly on politics, and they seem to have been intended as popular, partisan papers for the Republicanism of the Group in the Service of the Republic. In addition, Ortega had close relations with the Argentine press, not to my knowledge involving the creation of any publications, but using them to publish numerous articles. Although Ortega had, prior to 1916, published in Argentine papers, he established close connections with them in 1916 when he went on a successful lecture trip to Buenos Aires with his father. The trip was sponsored by the Institución Cultural Española and it is described in detail in its *Anales,* Tomo primero: 1912–1920, pp. 149–208. A careful cataloguing of Ortega's writings that appeared in *La Prensa* and *La Nación* might add significantly to his bibliography.

VI: C. WRITERS HAVE CONFUSED THE CONCEPT OF CULTURE (p. 173). The erroneous belief, unfortunately propagated by T. S. Eliot in *Notes Towards the Definition of Culture,* 1949, that there is a divergence between the so-called "literary" idea of culture and the "anthropological" has freed too many writers who should know better to play fast and loose with the idea of culture. If "culture" is to denote human artifacts, the word itself is meaningless, for it will denote everything. Hence, it will become significant only when qualified: aristocratic, democratic, proletarian, mass, high, middle, low, popular, impopular, primitive, and so on ad infinitum. There are, taking up this procedure, many interesting essays on the problems of popular or mass culture. Many of these are gathered by Bernard Rosenberg and David Manning White in *Mass Culture: The Popular Arts in America*. See also Dwight Macdonald, "Masscult and Midcult," in *Against the American Grain*. Most of this writing seems to have missed the reality of culture, which is not in the artifact, but in the man. Both the literary humanist and the anthropologist seem to be nearing agreement that culture is man's symbolic means for giving a particular character to himself. The important book here is not the overrated compendium by A. L. Kroeber and Clyde Kluckhohn, *Culture: A Critical Review of Concepts and Definitions*, but Eric R. Wolf's *Anthropology*. Wolf shows that anthropologists need to view the culture of any particular people as a *hierarchical* symbolic system by which those people give themselves their unique character. As soon as culture can again be seen as an hierarchical system, the disjunction between different strata of culture can be overcome, and we can make the concept serve as a powerful tool for fashioning a better understanding of education. In this context, John Dewey's *Freedom and Culture* will be found to be a much more effective examination of the function of culture in industrial democracies than the confused talk about mass culture.

There is an immense literature on the idea of culture. Raymond Williams' *Culture and Society* is a useful survey of the development of these two concepts in English intellectual history. Such a study should be made of how ideas of culture and education have developed since 1750, for it may well be that many of the current difficulties with the idea of culture have arisen because educators, in the name of democratic egalitarianism, have avoided dealing with "culture," which can only be defined properly in relation to education. Matthew Arnold's *Culture and Anarchy: An Essay in Political and Social Criticism* is an excellent companion to Ortega's *Revolt of the Masses*. Arnold's conception of culture as the pursuit of perfection (see especially Chapter 1) is still valid; it is consistent with current anthropological findings; and it is crucial to developing an alternative to the continued aggrandisement of the contemporary state, a state very different from the one Arnold so revered.

VII: THE SPAIN THAT IS

VII: a. ROUSSEAU'S PRESENTATION OF THE WILL OF ALL AND THE GENERAL WILL WAS FLAWED (p. 202). From the beginning Rousseau has suffered at the hands of critics who will substitute a *bon mot* for an argument. To me, Rousseau's writings are second only to Plato's in their heuristic value; and being inclined to approach Rousseau's writings as heuristic stimulants, not epitomes of some dogma—romantic, democratic, totalitarian, or anti-intellectual—I find most of the debate about Rousseau incomprehensible. Rousseau's writing reflects a deep sympathy with the thought of Plato and the Stoics; Rousseau had internalized their work, and surely the greatness of the "Discourse on the Arts and Sciences" is that it displays the proper use of civilization in the course of condemning the abuse of civilization. Rousseau should be read, responded to, reflected on; he does not provide doctrines: he may, however, stimulate thought.

Since my sophomore year in college I have found Rousseau to repay careful, recurrent reading. I am closest to the two "Discourses," *Emile*, and *The Social Contract*, and have learned much from having dealt with the last two works in a Colloquium I have given over the past five years. I think, as a brief commentary, Jacques Barzun's discussion of Rousseau in *Classic, Romantic, and Modern*, II, i–ii, pp. 18–28, is without match. It is especially valuable for driving home the point that *The Social Contract* does not concern the mode of conducting practical politics—Rousseau was neither a democrat nor a totalitarian—but the conditions under which any system of conducting practical politics can be considered legitimate. The two books by Ernst Cassirer, *The Question of Jean-Jacques Rousseau*, Peter Gay, trans., and *Rousseau, Kant, and Goethe*, Gutmann, Kristeller, and Randall, trans., are helpful, especially in locating Rousseau in the history of ideas. For those who want a check on the *Confessions*, Jean Guéhenno's *Jean-Jacques Rousseau*, 2 vols., John and Dorean Weightman, trans., is excellent, although it does not try to assess Rousseau's intellectual background in much depth—an assessment that seems to me crucial in deciding how to read Rousseau. The Bibliothèque de la Pléiade edition of Rousseau's *Oeuvres complètes* is excellent, presenting his works in a readable format, with sufficient critical apparatus to inform oneself of the issues but not so extensive or intrusive that it interferes with following Rousseau's argument.

VIII: FAILURE

VIII: a. ORTEGA'S PREROGATIVES AS A CLERC EXISTED NO MORE (p. 213). An indication of the difficulty that Ortega had in acting as a *clerc* after he had participated in politics is found in the reaction of his fellow intellectual-turned-politician, Manuel Azaña. Thus, in the *Memorias intimas de Azaña,* edited by Joaquín Arrarás, 1939, pp. 179–180, Ortega's criticisms of partisanship in the Republic were dismissed as an attempt to appease the Jesuit backers of *El Sol* for the passage of Article 26, which closed the religious orders. *El Sol,* which had long crusaded for better lay education, was anything but a pro-Jesuit paper! Care, however, should prevent one from taking the *Memorias* to be an accurate indication of Azaña's views and character; the book was an extremely fragmentary selection from Azaña's diary, and the selection was made by an enthusiast of Franco and published just after the Civil War. It is a masterpiece of political satire, and the added Falangist caricatures show that not all of the Spanish wits were on the loyalist side.

VIII: b. IN 1928 ORTEGA HAD A SUCCESSFUL TOUR IN LATIN AMERICA (p. 213). For Ortega's activities in Argentina and Chile at this time see articles about him in *La Nación,* September 1, p. 1; September 1, p. 6; September 6, p. 6; September 12, p. 6; November 24, p. 1; and December 6, p. 6. For the excellent reports of his lectures with extensive transcripts, see *La Nación,* September 25, p. 7; October 1, p. 4; October 9, p. 8; October 15, p. 11; October 29, p. 7; November 10, p. 8; November 14, p. 8; December 25, p. 6; and December 28, p. 6. There are good records of his tour and lectures in Institución Cultural Española, *Anales,* Vol. III, pp. 185–248. For the Madrid interest in Ortega's lectures see the news reports in *El Sol,* April 3, May 30, September 1, November 9 and 15, 1928; and January 3, 19, and 22, 1929. In addition, see the commentaries in *El Sol:* "Un discurso: Ortega y Gasset en la Argentina," January 8, 1929; "Impresiones de Hispanoamérica: Hoy llega a Madrid D. José Ortega y Gasset," January 20, 1929; and Luis Echavarri, "Ortega y Gasset y la joven intelectualidad argentina," February 16 and 22, and March 6, 1929. The text of Ortega's "Discurso en el parlamento chileno," 1928, 1955, is in *Obras* VIII, pp. 377–382.

VIII: c. WITH "THE COURSE" AN ELITE SEEMED TO PRESENT ITSELF (p. 215). For press coverage of Ortega's lectures see *El Sol,* April 10,

13, 17, 23, and 27; May 4, 8, 11, 15, and 18, 1929. The lec-
tures were also reported carefully in *Voz*, same dates. In
addition to the commentaries cited in footnotes, see Victoriano
García Martí, "Comentarios del día: Las conferencias de
Ortega y Gasset," *Voz*, April 30, 1929; and Manuel García
Morente, "El curso de D. José Ortega y Gasset," *El Sol*, June
2, 9, 25, and 30, 1929. For transcripts of the lectures see
¿Qué es filosofía?, 1929, 1957, *Obras* VII, pp. 275–438.

VIII: d. THE GROUP AIMED TO PUT INTELLECT IN THE SERVICE OF THE RE-
PUBLIC (p. 217). There are a number of documents of and
about the Group in the Service of the Republic in Ortega's
Obras XI, especially pp. 125–143, 291–300, 425–431, 516–8.
Other important documents on the Group are in Ramón
Pérez de Ayala, *Escritos politícos*, especially pp. 214–236.

VIII: e. THE ACTUAL CONSTITUENT ASSEMBLY DID NOT PROCEED AS ORTEGA
PRESUMED (p. 221). I rely for my knowledge of the Constituent Assembly on Mori, *Crónica*, especially Vols. 1–4, 6, 7,
and 9; and on Rhea Marsh Smith, *The Day of the Liberals in
Spain*, which is the best study of the Assembly in English.
The judgments, however, about how it might have succeeded
are my own. There is a good, concise chapter on the Constituent Assembly by Gabriel Jackson in *The Spanish Republic
and the Civil War, 1931–1936*, pp. 43–55.

VIII: f. "LA VIEJA POLÍTICA" IN THE NEW CONSTITUTION (p. 225). For
Ortega's position on the Catalán Statute, see Mori, *Crónica*,
Vol. 6, especially pp. 112–153, 331–429; and Vol. 9, especially pp. 402–468. This source is much more useful than
the text of Ortega's speeches as they were reproduced in *El
Sol* or in books, for Mori included the whole development of
the issue, other important speeches, comments from the floor,
etc. The transcripts of Ortega's speeches are also in *Obras*
XI, pp. 455–488, but Mori is still a better source. Unamuno's
position may be found in "Discurso sobre la lengua española,"
his *Obras* III, pp. 1350–1361; the transcript of his statement
on the issue shows that he was allied with Ortega's position.

For Ortega's views on the welfare state as they were expressed in the Assembly see "En el debate político," "Sobre
lo de ahora," and "Rectificatión de la República," *Obras* XI,
pp. 348–356, 360–6, 398–417. For Ortega's view of the relation of church and state, see his speech in the Assembly,

"Proyecto de Constitución," September 4, 1931, *Obras* XI, especially pp. 382–3. For his view of anti-clericalism and the Monarchy after its fall, see "Rectificación de la República," December 6, 1931, *Obras* XI, especially pp. 407–9, and "Anti-monarquía y República," *Luz*, January 7, 1932, *Obras* XI, pp. 418–9. As can be seen from Mori, *Crónica*, Vol. 3, pp. 280–6, the Law of the Defense of the Republic went through with surprisingly little discussion. For the feelings raised by the trial see *Ibid.*, Vol. 4, pp. 295–370.

VIII: g. ONLY A NON-PARTISAN PARTY COULD PREVENT POLARIZATION (p. 226). For the publicity campaign leading up to Ortega's speech, see "En vísperas de un discurso: Ortega y Gasset y el futuro de España," *El Sol*, November 17, 1931; "Una cuartilla de Don José Ortega y Gasset," *El Sol*, November 18, 1931; "Notas políticas: El esperado discurso de Don José Ortega y Gasset," *El Sol*, November 27, 1931; and "El discurso de Don José Ortega y Gasset: Un llamamiento para la creación de un partido de amplitud nacional," *El Sol*, December 8, 1931. Cf. "Hablando con el Sr. Ortega y Gasset después de su discurso," *Crisol*, December 7, 1931. The last two articles have very useful information on judging the effect of Ortega's speech. For his desire for a national party prior to the fall of the Monarchy, see "Organización de la decencia nacional," *El Sol*, February 5, 1930, *Obras* XI, pp. 269–273. Ramón Pérez de Ayala's essays "Sobre los partidos políticos," *Escritos políticos*, pp. 237–252, are also pertinent.

VIII: h. ORTEGA TRIED TO CONVERT THE GROUP IN THE SERVICE OF THE RE-PUBLIC INTO A NATIONAL PARTY (p. 228). For speeches made in this effort, see "Nación y Trabajo: he aquí el lema de la Agrupación al Servicio de la República: 'Hoy no es possible un partido conservador': Elocuente brindis de Don José Ortega y Gasset en Granada," *El Sol*, February 5, 1932; and "Don José Ortega y Gasset en Oviedo: 'La política Republicana se ha de cimentar sobre dos principios: Nación y Trabajo'," *El Sol*, April 12, 1932. For articles written about a national party, see "Hacia un partido de la nación," *Luz*, January 7, 15, and 29, 1932; "Estos republicanos no son la República," *Luz*, June 16, 1932; and "Hay que reanimar a la República," *Luz*, June 18, 1932. Ortega's withdrawal from politics was first made public in "Conferencia de Don José Ortega y Gasset en la Universidad de Granada: 'Tras dos años de exorbitancia política—dice—vuelvo plenamente a la conciencia intelectual'." *El Sol*, October 9, 1932. See for all except the first and last mentioned *Obras* XI, pp. 425–450, 489–493.

IX: ON THE CRISIS OF EUROPE

IX: a. ORTEGA CONTRIBUTED TO THE GEISTESWISSENSCHAFTEN (p. 239). There is an immense literature on the human sciences, much of which is egregiously unfamiliar to American scholars. As the exposition unfolds, many works will be cited in more particular contexts. Here mention should be made of the best introduction to the subject so far written in America, *The Decline of the German Mandarins: The German Academic Community, 1890–1933,* by Fritz K. Ringer. Unfortunately, this work does not give a sympathetic treatment to the human sciences; it subjects them instead to a reductive sociological explanation. Nevertheless, until a writer comes forward who is willing to take the subject seriously, contending rigorously with the substance as well as the social source of the human sciences, Ringer's book will stand as the most useful introduction to the literature.

A thorough study of the different modes of applying knowledge to life would help define the mission of various disciplines. For a study of this question with respect to the human sciences, a provocative source is *Briefwechsel zwischen Wilhelm Dilthey und Graf Paul Yorck von Wartenburg.* A lack of subtlety on this matter has impeded the ability of some contemporary philosophers to maintain confidence in the "relevance" of their enterprise. Thus, a good antidote to efforts to make philosophy a propaedeutic to science is *Der pädagogische Beruf der Philosophie* by Günther Böhme, a book which is excellent background reading for understanding the centrality of education to Ortega's reflective effort.

IX: b. "EXEMPLARITY AND APTNESS" (p. 244). The Spanish is *"ejemplaridad y docilidad."* I have translated *docilidad* as "aptness" because the latter lacks the connotations of passivity that "docility" has in English, and the meaning of "aptness," "quick to learn," is very close to Ortega's usage of *docilidad.* The Spanish meaning has remained close to its etymological meaning of "teachable, willing to be taught" (from the Latin, *docilis*). This sense has been lost in current English usage of "docility."

"Exemplarity" has different connotations in English than in Spanish. American scepticism about the "good example" is quintessentially reflected in Sinclair Lewis' *Babbitt*. Harry S. Broudy and John R. Palmer have stressed the idea of exemplarity in their book *Exemplars of Teaching Method*, but their use of exemplar is not the same as Ortega's, for Broudy and Palmer find a quality, teaching method, to be given and they seek exemplars of it, whereas Ortega finds the exemplar given, a person of great spiritual force, and others seek the qualities the exemplar manifests. Those interested in the idea of exemplarity should consult Kant's *Critique of Judgment*, #17–22, in addition to the novels by Cervantes and Unamuno mentioned in the text.

In later paragraphs, I have used "connoisseurs" to translate "*dociles*" since the English neologism "dociles" sounds badly, as does "apts." Since translating the passage, I have encountered Michael Polanyi's remarks on "connoisseurship" in his *Personal Knowledge: Towards a Post-Critical Philosophy*, pp. 54–5. The coincidence of usage is fortunate, and a comprehension of either Polanyi or Ortega adds to an understanding of the other.

IX: C. EXEMPLARITY AND APTNESS REAFFIRMS THE CLASSIC CONCEPTION OF COMMUNITY (p. 247). Two subjects should be distinguished here: the history of Greek political theory and the history of Greek influence on political theory. My remarks on Homer and later Greeks might engender objections if they are taken as part of the former subject; they are unobjectionable, I think, as part of the latter. Homer is usually touched on but lightly in histories of Greek political thought. Compare the treatment he receives in Sir Ernest Barker's great works: in *The Political Thought of Plato and Aristotle* (1906), Homer is allotted a single sentence, "Homer is a believer in the divine right of monarchy . . ."; whereas in *Greek Political Theory* (1917), the same sentence takes on more cautious form, "Homer is sometimes quoted as a believer in the divine right of monarchy . . ." (p. 18), and a few remarks follow suggesting that it might not have been so (p. 47). T. A. Sinclair devotes a brief chapter to Homer in *A History of Greek Political Thought*, pp. 10–8, but his account is, as it must be, tentative.

Much more leeway for imagination arises when one deals with the Greek influence on political theory. One may look on Jaeger's *Paideia* as a treatise on the Homeric influence on later Greek political and educational theory. The potential excess of this influence is pointed out profoundly in *The Tyranny of Greece over Germany* by E. M. Butler. But it is not only "the Germanic mind," if that exists, that can draw fruitfully from the Greek example, as is shown by Herbert J. Muller in *Freedom in the Ancient World* and Eric A. Havelock in *The Liberal Temper in Greek Politics*, two worthy books with which I have learned to have basic disagreements.

My conception of Homer has been influenced primarily by Bruno Snell through *The Discovery of the Mind: The Greek Origins of European Thought* and Cedric H. Whitman through *Homer and the Homeric Tradition*, as well as secondarily by M. I. Finley, *The World of Odysseus*, T. B. L. Webster, *From Mycenae to Homer*, and G. S. Kirk, *Homer and the Epic*. Rhys Carpenter's brief essay *Discontinuity in Greek Civilization* is stimulating if read with caution.

IX: d. SPENGLER'S DECLINE OF THE WEST EPITOMIZED THE LITERATURE OF DECAY (p. 252). For other such writers see Hans Kohn, *The Mind of Germany: The Education of a Nation*, pp. 336–343; and Fritz Stern, *The Politics of Cultural Despair, passim*. The assumption common to arguments of decay, as well as to many about progress, is that society or civilization is an organic creature, something that can grow, develop, become diseased, and die. Recently, the sociologist Robert Nisbet has subjected such assumptions to an extensive critique in *Social Change and History*. He has chosen a target that needs to be severely criticized, but his criticism is sadly unconvincing. Nisbet shows that theories of organic development in history are based on a metaphor; so far so good. But then, he is not content to show that the metaphor is inappropriate, a cause of more confusion than clarity; he argues that metaphor itself has no place in historical theory. To suppress metaphor, however, simply heightens our vulnerability; the solution is not to avoid all metaphor, but to recognize that all works of intellect can at most be metaphorical: none can give us positive knowledge of the social reality, not even the most dogmatically empirical. If Nisbet had looked further in his research, he might have found Tocqueville using such an argument quite subtly against Gobineau: no historical theory can be established conclusively, and when there is a danger that a doctrine will have destructive consequences, exaggerated claims for its truth should be resisted. See Tocqueville, *The European Revolution and Correspondence with Gobineau*, especially, pp. 221–3, 226–9, 231–2, 266–8 (a masterpiece of irony), 268–270, 290–5, and 303–310.

IX: e. THERE IS AN ELEMENT OF TRUTH IN THE GERMANOPHOBE-ANGLO-PHILE CRITIQUE OF EUROPEAN POLITICS (p. 256). Some of the sources of this critique have been discussed in a note to II: k. Many other works might be added to it; for instance, Eric Bentley, *A Century of Hero-Worship*. The Marxian rejection of English liberalism was fundamental. It may be sampled, for instance, in Marx's "The Future Results of British Rule in India" (1853), *Marx-Engels Selected Works*, Vol. 1, pp. 352–8. In some ways, however, Marx's most explicit and influential criticism of the English type of liberalism is not in his writings on England, but in his polemics against more reformist tendencies in the Continental workers' movements; see *The Communist Manifesto, Ibid.,* Vol. 1, pp. 21–65, especially 54–64; and *The German Ideology, passim.* Nietzsche's rejection was more rhetorical. See, for instance, *The Will to Power*, Walter Kaufmann, trans., sections 31: "that gruesome ugliness that characterizes all English inventions"; 382: "the shopkeeper's philosophy of Mr. Spencer; complete absence of an ideal, except that of the mediocre man"; 926: "Against John Stuart Mill—I abhor his vulgarity . . ."; 944: "happiness as peace of soul, virtue, comfort, Anglo-angelic shopkeeperdom *à la* Spencer"; etc.

No adequate study of the political implications of contemporary European philosophy has been made. It is also far from clear what significance these have for judging philosophies *qua* philosophies. Sartre and Merleau-Ponty are usually treated positively for having backed the resistance in World War II, whereas Gentile has been largely dismissed as a Fascist and Heidegger has been severely criticized for originally cooperating with Hitler. On this matter, I have found Merleau-Ponty's *Humanisme et terreur: essai sur le probleme communiste*, H. Stuart Hughes' *The Obstructed Path: French Social Thought, 1930–1960*, and Stanley Rosen's *Nihilism: A Philosophical Essay* to be instructive.

IX: f. IDEOLOGY, BUREAUCRACY, AND MASS COMMUNICATIONS HAVE COMPLICATED THE FUNCTIONING OF LIBERALISM (p. 257). The literature pertinent to these matters is immense, and I can only indicate those small parts of it that have entered into my reflections on Ortega's conception of the European crisis. In particular, Martin S. Dworkin's course "Education, Ideology, and Mass Communications" and ensuing conversations have done much to deepen my reading in these areas.

The first aspect of the matter to raise fundamental questions is that the liberal theory of toleration does not adequately anticipate ideological criticism as it has developed in the past two hundred years. For the basic theory, see Locke, "A Letter Concerning Toleration," and John Stuart Mill, *On*

Liberty, especially Chapter 2. The assumption that free discussion can only strengthen truth is in theory unobjectionable; what theories of ideology do is to raise the question whether discussion can in fact be free, and doubts to this effect lead to very serious consequences. For good introductions to the development of the concept of ideology see Henry D. Aiken, "Philosophy and Ideology in the Nineteenth Century," *The Age of Ideology,* pp. 13–26, and George Lichtheim, *The Concept of Ideology and Other Essays,* pp. 3–46.

Three of the most significant examples of committed ideological criticism are *The German Ideology* by Marx and Engels, *The Theory of the Leisure Class* by Veblen, and *The Illusions of Progress* by Georges Sorel. These critics used their powers to expose the rationalization of interests by the established groups and to advance the interests of those who were exploited. This tradition of ideological criticism has by no means died out, but it has been complemented by another which aspires to be more disinterested. The best known work of this sort is Karl Mannheim's *Ideology and Utopia,* in which a program for the sociology of knowledge is set forth. There is much more work along these lines that deserves to be better known. For instance, Theodor Geiger gives a rather different, more open value to ideology in his *Ideologie und Wahrheit* and other works. For a good introduction to his work see Paolo Farneti, *Theodor Geiger e la coscienza della società industriale.* Whereas Geiger sees ideological differences indicating real differences that should not be destroyed through reductionism, much of contemporary thought on the subject leads in the opposite direction, indicating a hope that ideology will disappear. This is the theme sounded in the conclusions to *The Opium of the Intellectuals* by Raymond Aron and *The End of Ideology* by Daniel Bell. Both writers are learned and humane, yet one should ask whether a purported end of ideology is not itself an ideological rationalization of interests of technicians, bureaucrats, and social scientists: ideological conflicts are the most serious impediments to *their* rational control of society. But is it perfectly rational? This question is put movingly by Alberto Moravia in *Man as an End.*

For the purposes of this study, these and other works that might also be mentioned add up to a serious difficulty for liberal political theory. What is the relation between opinion, interest, and truth? How can men who are convinced that discussion between ordinary persons leads to the imposition of falsehood, not the uncovering of truth, be persuaded to defend political freedoms and liberal procedures? For a clear statement of the direction in which such convictions lead see *A Critique of Pure Tolerance* by Robert Paul Wolff, Barrington Moore, Jr., and Herbert Marcuse.

If the theory of ideology tends to release the opponents of the established system from the restraints of liberalism, the facts of bureaucracy do the same for the members of the established system. The classic presentations of liberal theory on this matter are the discussion of faction and its dangers in *The Federalist Papers* and the analysis of the unchecked power of the majority in chapters 15 and 16 of Tocqueville's *Democracy in America*. Government should be conducted by responsible individuals if the rights of minorities are to be defended. Tocqueville argued that one of the few factors mitigating the natural power of the majority was the lack of a centralized administrative apparatus in the United States; that check has disappeared.

By the development of bureaucracy, I mean something more inclusive than a particular form of administrative organization; in that sense bureaucracy has always existed. What is important is the application in the nineteenth and twentieth centuries of highly formalized, rational group organization to major military, economic, and political institutions. A number of general histories are useful in following the development of these organizations and attempts at alternatives to them. In *Western Civilization Since the Renaissance: Peace, War, Industry, and the Arts*, John U. Nef puts some of the central questions concerning the relation of war, industry, and impersonal organization, raising the suspicion that the so-called civilian benefits from military development may not be worth the cost. Friedrich Meinecke's *Machiavellism: The Doctrine of Raison D'Etat and Its Place in Modern History*, Douglas Scott, trans., is an excellent study laying bare the arguments by which the responsible public servant converts himself into an irresponsible servant of the state. In a less profound work, *European History, 1789–1914: Men, Machines, and Freedom*, John McManners charts the economic and political developments behind the growth of national administrative systems and in pp. 403–6 he indicates some of the dilemmas that arose with the modern state, namely, that it brings mixed blessings. Guido de Ruggiero in *The History of European Liberalism*, R. G. Collingwood, trans., traces the development of the liberal view of the state and shows how it culminates in parallel conflicts between individualism and bureaucracy as well as between Liberalism and Socialism.

One of the central matters that should be considered in reflecting on the impact of bureaucracy upon our political forms is the character of war and the military. An excellent introduction to this subject is *Makers of Modern Strategy: Military Thought from Machiavelli to Hitler,* edited by Edward Mead Earle. A great work for clarifying the impact of war on twentieth-century life is Quincy Wright's *A Study of War,* and a more popular work covering some of the same ground is Raymond Aron's *The Century of Total War.* The background informing a reading of these works should be an involvement as a citizen in the national debates concerning arms expenditure, disarmanent, and foreign commitments. To me, such a combination of concerns quite undercuts the whole system of political theory upon which the nation-state is based; we should go back to fundamentals and seriously consider the question whether sane men can responsibly hold mere nations to be sovereign.

The problem of bureaucracy is not confined to war and international politics. Various aspects of the problem are brought out, with varying personal reactions to the phenomena they uncover, by James Burnham's *The Managerial Revolution: What is Happening in the World;* Joseph A. Schumpeter's *Capitalism, Socialism, and Democracy;* William H. Whyte's *The Organization Man;* Milovan Djilas' *The New Class: An Analysis of the Communist System;* Jacques Ellul's *The Technological Society;* C. Wright Mills' *The Power Elite;* Hannah Arendt's *Eichmann in Jerusalem;* and Sebastian de Grazia's *Of Time, Work, and Leisure.* All these have, in one way or another, influenced my view of the question.

The problems that bureaucracy raises for our inherited political principles are compounded by the closely related problem of mass communications. Liberal political theory has been traditionally cautious about the contagion of opinion. For instance, those who would blame Rousseau for the excesses committed in the French Revolution in the name of the general will overlook the fact that the acts ensued from political deliberations antithetical to those Rousseau commended. Rousseau insisted that each have full information and that each deliberate alone, the authenticity of his opinion protected from contamination by that of others. Whether or not we can preserve the approximate possibility for such deliberations is the great conundrum of mass communications.

One group of studies, which suggests difficulties in preserving autonomous deliberation, is the study of crowds, which actually goes back very far into our tradition as readers of Heraclitus, Thucydides, Plato, and Seneca know. In more recent times, the issue has come back to the fore. Gustave Le Bon's work *The Crowd: A Study of the Popular Mind,* is often connected to Ortega's *Revolt of the Masses* although they are about quite different phenomena: the latter concerns a chronic condition of personal character; the former, the characteristics regularly manifested by crowds, groups in which men lose their individuality. Since Le Bon's book, there have been a number of popularizations, connecting the crowd or mob to American culture, especially popular culture; among these are Gerald Stanley Lee's *Crowds: A Moving-Picture of Democracy* (1913); Frank K. Notch's *King Mob: A Study of the Present-Day Mind* (1930); and Bernard Iddings Bell's *Crowd Culture: An Examination of the American Way of Life* (1952). On a quite different level of ambition is *Crowds and Power* by Elias Canetti, Carol Stewart, trans., a far-reaching, profound study of the nature of crowds and their relation to political power throughout world history.

Studies of propaganda and mass communication are legion. *Propaganda* by Jacques Ellul strikes me as the best introduction to the subject, for Ellul does not shirk the difficult aspects of the matter: he shows that propaganda is an established element of everyone's way of life, that it has definite effects, some good and many bad, and that there is a tremendous, perhaps impossible, problem in reconciling the facts of propaganda with our political heritage and hopes. An earlier work that also excels as an introduction to the matter is Walter Lippmann's *Public Opinion,* which expresses greater optimism about the ability of reason to control and absorb propaganda than does Ellul's work. Both Lippmann and Ellul raise questions ultimately reflecting doubts whether the recipient of propaganda and mass communications can maintain his autonomous powers of judgment, whether the recipient can keep from being drawn into a crowd. Wilbur Schramm in his important book *Responsibility in Mass Communication* looks at the matter from the other end, asking whether open, responsible access to the means of communication can be maintained. Although this is itself a crucial question, on which there is a great deal of discussion that may be found by using Schramm's bibliography, the questions raised by Ellul and Lippmann seem to me more fundamental.

Many other works have contributed to my understanding

not only of the problems raised by mass communications, but also by bureaucracy and ideological criticism. Among them are *The Bias of Communications* by Harold A. Innis; *Le temps hacerlant* by Enrico Castelli; *The Origins of Totalitarianism* by Hannah Arendt; *Man in the Modern Age* by Karl Jaspers; *The House of Intellect* by Jacques Barzun, and many others. In calling attention to these difficulties, one is not foretelling doom or condemning traditional aspirations. One is, however, asking for the reinvigoration of the theoretical imagination. The empirical obsessions of social science seem to me to indicate a deep-seated death wish. The political forces in the midst of which we live have little to do, integrally, organically, with our national institutions; yet our conceptions of what political procedures are proper, which ones will allow the human spirit to flourish humanely, are all keyed to the nation-states. The productive capital of political theory that we have inherited from the Enlightenment is fast wearing out, yet very few people have been trying speculatively to construct replacements. The defense of freedom and reason must find an arena other than national politics, and its absurd extension in inter-national politics, in which to conduct its campaign. Political and pedagogical theorists have before them the task of setting forth such a supranational community.

X: SCARCITY AND ABUNDANCE

X: a. FOR AGES THE WISE HAVE KNOWN THAT LUXURY WEAKENS THE WILL (p. 279). By reading this proposition as a statement about the effects of wealth on individual character, with the only social effects seen being certain invidious aspersions on the *nouveau riche*, one can ignore its most serious import. In such a form, the idea is quite uninteresting; but its more profound exponents have been concerned not with wealth as an individual attribute, but with wealth as a social attribute. Thus Heraclitus wished riches not on his individual enemies, but on Ephesus as a whole. The debilitative effects of wealth may develop even though the wealthiest are very active and far from debauched. What is unhealthy is not the effect of wealth on the particular individuals who hold it, but use of the category "wealth," by both rich and poor, as the basic means of making judgments of human worth. For this practice of making wealth a major standard of value, modern Western civilization has been roundly condemned by a series of critics who have not opposed the existence of material well-being, but who have rejected the common practice of using distinctions between the degree of well-being various persons enjoy as means of judging the relative worth of those persons. Thus the spiritual power of money is decried. Witness Nietzsche: "money now stands for power, glory, pre-eminence, dignity, and influence . . ." (*The Dawn of Day*, #203, J. M. Kennedy, trans.); ". . . what was once done 'for the love of God' is now done for the love of money, i.e. for the love of that which at present affords us the highest feeling of power and a good conscience" (*Ibid.*, #204). Witness also Jacob Burckhardt: "money becomes and remains the greatest measure of things, poverty the greatest vice," in his *On History and Historians*, Harry Zohn, trans., p. 222.

Ortega's criticism of the use of wealth as a criterion for judging our highest values was paralleled by his contemporaries. For instance, in "Mass Civilization and Minority Culture" (1930), F. R. Leavis objected to the practice of denoting the goods that the average man could buy as "*the* standard of living." Leavis, of course, was not arguing, as critics like Lord Snow seem to suggest, that the poor should be made to persist at poor subsistence; Leavis' argument was against the arbitrary elevation of income statistics into the most common arbiter of values. To argue against wealth as a standard of value is not to argue against the value of wealth. Instead, the concern was with the extra-economic significance attached to economic criteria. No economist had demonstrated that, of all possible standards, the measure of purchasing power was the only valid valuation of life, *the* standard of living. See: Leavis, *Education and the University*, pp. 146, 149; cf. p. 119.

x: b.   IBN KHALDÛN PERCEIVED HOW POVERTY BEGAT VIRTUE . . . (p. 290). While Ortega was preparing *The Revolt of the Masses* he wrote about Ibn Khaldûn and his philosophy of history; see "Abenjaldun nos revela el secreto: pensamientos sobre Africa menor," 1928, *Obras* III, pp. 669–687. In *The Muqaddimah: An Introduction to History*, Ibn Khaldûn developed a cyclic theory of history based on the complementary social systems of the nomads and the city dwellers. On the desert a pedagogy of scarcity, a subsistence economy, maintained the elemental, vital virtues of the Bedouin; he remained tough, adaptable, courageous, honest, and religious, as well as brutal, uncouth, and uncivilized. In the city a pedagogy of abundance, a luxury economy, inculcated a hedonistic view of life.

The urbanite became sensitive and civilized, as well as wily, dishonest, base, and profane. The pleasures of the city always attracted the Bedouin; and once the urbanite's moral decline went too far, the city would not be able to defend itself from the desert dwellers. The Bedouins would take the city over in stages; and slowly the city would urbanize its barbarian masters, and convert them from their elemental virtues. Eventually, these new city dynasties would fall before the pressures of another wave of nomadic hordes. See *The Muqaddimah: An Introduction to History*, Franz Rosenthal, trans., especially Vol. 1, pp. 71–86, 249–310, Vol. II, pp. 117–137. Ibn Khaldûn's system was quite similar to Ortega's except that the North African's pedagogy of scarcity and pedagogy of abundance were in effect at the same time but in different places (the desert and the city), whereas Ortega's operated in the same place (Europe) but at different times (nineteenth century and twentieth century). The main difference between the two was that Ibn Khaldûn's cycle was closed, whereas Ortega saw a way to break his.

XI: THE CRITIC'S POWER

XI: a. HISTORIC DEVELOPMENTS OCCUR AS CRITICS ALTER A PEOPLE'S VIEW OF LIFE (p. 296). An example of this critical power has become manifest on a small scale in recent years: the reluctance of many talented college graduates to consider business careers. This reluctance can be traced back to critical assessments of corporate culture such as *The Organization Man* by William H. Whyte, Jr. The antipathy for business may turn out to be simply the leading edge of a much deeper shift in aspirations and expectations, one on a par with the Renaissance and Reformation or the democratic revolution.

There is need for a truly "critical" history of modern Europe, that is, a history that shows the constructive effects of criticism over time. Such a history would be neither an account of political development nor of ideological development; rather it would lay bare the underlying systems of expectation that sustain politics and inform ideology. So far, the closest to such critical history is the *Weltanschauung* analysis initiated by Wilhelm Dilthey. His fullest effort is his *Weltanschauung und Analyse des Menschen seit Renaissance und Reformation*, in *Gesammelte Schriften*, Vol. 2, but this work is hard to differentiate from an intellectual history of the period. What is needed, as Dilthey suggested in his *Päda-*

gogik: Geschichte und Grundlinien des Systems, in *Gesammelte Schriften,* Vol. 9, is a means of showing the effect of a world view on historical development; one place to look for this is in the history of education. A major effort influenced by Dilthey's historiography was Hermann Leser's *Das pädagogische Problem,* which tries to show how, from the Renaissance through Romanticism, changes in world views affected people's conceptions of pedagogical aims and methods. It is a history that has been unduly ignored by American historians of education.

XI: b. THE MORE PEOPLE CONSUME CRITICISM, THE LESS CRITICAL THEY BECOME (p. 297). An interesting subject for historical inquiry would be a study of how criticism has been presented to the public at different times in history, for the current commercialization of criticism may be a unique, portentous phenomenon. What connection is there between the present penchant for socio-political criticism and the taste for sermons in the seventeenth and early eighteenth centuries? Perhaps a zeal to be reproved is the harbinger indicating that the concerns in question will soon be considered irrelevant, for to maintain their waning place, people must remind themselves daily that doom is nigh.

XI: c. THERE HAS BEEN LITTLE AGREEMENT ABOUT THE PLACE OF LIFE IN THE LIFE SCIENCES (p. 298). On the basis of the name, *life* should be the central concern of biology, but life is a difficult substance to work with scientifically. At the edge, with certain viral bodies, it is difficult to distinguish a living system from certain inanimate molecules; hence vitalists have been hard put to give an adequate operational definition of life. At the same time, despite some progress towards the synthesis of living substance, the chemist is still a long way from the creation of complicated living *forms.*

Philosophers such as Ernest Nagel have condemned vitalism for scientific infertility—a fatal flaw according to those who account for truth by its cash value; see Nagel's "Mechanistic Explanation and Organismic Biology," in *Philosophy and Phenomenological Research,* Vol. II, 1951, p. 327. Basically, Nagel's argument is that vitalism is dead because it has given rise to no significant research. It is not clear, however, whether such a conclusion is founded on an observed lack of research or whether the observed lack of research is founded on the conclusion. This alternative should be considered seriously because there have been a number of vitalistically inclined researchers whose work has not been considered in a spirit of "sweetness and light" by members of the dominant schools. In *Modern Science and the Nature of Life*, pp. 291–2, William S. Beck scornfully dismisses vitalistic dissenters from his materialistic interpretation of the nature of life. His method is not scientific. Thus Beck responds to the work of Edmund W. Sinnott: "The author presents 'scientific' evidence for the existence of the soul. . . ." A pair of well-placed quotation marks thus substitutes for an argument, and Beck goes on to exclaim at Sinnott's imbecility for considering a vitalistic position as possibly scientific: "This from within our scientific ranks. This in a discussion of the very subject upon which our ultimate understanding of cancer must depend, the nature of the organism." A soul, indeed!

Despite the hostile response vitalism has received in twentieth-century biology, it has not died out. There is no adequate survey of early twentieth-century vitalism. H. S. Jennings' article "Doctrines Held as Vitalism," *The American Naturalist*, Vol. XLVIII, No. 559, July 1913, pp. 385–417, is a useful survey. During the 1920's the Italian magazine *Scientia* carried over thirty articles about different aspects of vitalistic thought; see Vols. 33–40. Three fairly recent books written from a non-mechanistic point of view are E. S. Russell, *The Directiveness of Organic Activities*, 1945; Raymond Ruyer, *Néo-finalisme*, 1952; and Edmund W. Sinnott, *Cell and Psyche: The Biology of Purpose*, 1950. These synthesize a good deal of twentieth-century vitalism, but they do not agree on what is important in it. The work of Ludwig von Bertalanffy, especially as reflected in *Modern Theories of Development: An Introduction to Theoretical Biology*, carries on Uexküll's tradition of inquiry.

XI: d. THERE IS NOTHING VITAL ABOUT UNPERCEIVED FORCES THAT DETERMINE THE OUTCOME OF CERTAIN ACTIVITIES (p. 299). This distinction between absolute "problems" and perceived or vital problems explains much about the humor of animated cartoons, which usually depends on the audience's perception of the ridiculous irrelevance of the disasters that the protagonists unwittingly encounter. It is significant that these cartoon disasters are never final; after having been squashed by a falling safe or overrun by a speeding steamroller, Puddycat can always peel himself off the pavement and return to the vital drama of chasing Tweety. To go from the ridiculous to the sublime, one should consult Book I, Chapter I, of *Arrian's*

Discourses by Epictetus, "On things which are under our control and not under our control." Both comic humor and stoic sobriety remind us that the important things in *life* are things of which the living being is aware.

XI: e. IN THESE THOUGHTS ORTEGA DREW ON THE BIOLOGY OF UEXKÜLL (p. 301). The most concise statement of Uexküll's work is his *Die Lebenslehre*, 1930. A translation of his major book, *Theoretical Biology*, is the only one available in English. Ortega published an article by Uexküll, "La biología de la ostra jacobea," *Revista de Occidente*, March 1924, pp. 297–331, in which Uexküll's fundamental ideas were presented. Uexküll's major research findings were summarized in his *Umwelt und Innenwelt des Tiers*, 1909.

Commentators who were not familiar with the particular theories that Ortega drew from have misunderstood his use of biological thought. Thus, in his *Ortega y Gasset*, pp. 32–33, José Ferrater Mora was embarrassed by Ortega's predilection for biological theories "of the von Uexküll-Driesch brand." In "Ni vitalismo, ni racionalismo" (1924, *Obras* III, pp. 270–280) Ortega denied that Driesch had influenced him. He said nothing about Uexküll, whose influence he warmly acknowledged elsewhere. We can conclude that Ortega was influenced by Uexküll and that he did not consider Uexküll to be a vitalist of the Driesch brand. Writers such as Ferrater Mora think that Ortega's use of Uexküll's ideas needs to be defended because it seems inconsistent that an anti-positivist philosopher like Ortega would use biological science to support his philosophy. The inconsistency is an appearance that arises with the erroneous assumption that Uexküll's biology was positivistic. It was not. Uexküll was a neo-Kantian transcendental idealist who began his biological theory with a meditation on the *Critique of Pure Reason*. Uexküll's idealistic conception of science, rather than his vitalism, seems to have been the major difficulty that other biologists encountered in his work, for most of them were positivists. Even vitalistic writers, such as Raymond Ruyer (*Néo-finalisme*, p. 217, fn. 1) criticized Uexküll's conception of science. The following quotation from Uexküll's *Theoretical Biology*, (Mackinnon, trans., p. x) gives a sense of his anti-positivism and of his agreement with Ortega's idea of science: "In Nature everything is certain; in science everything is problematical. Science can fulfill its purpose only if it is built up like a scaffolding against the wall of a house. Its purpose is to ensure the workman of a firm support everywhere, so that he may get to any point without losing a general survey of the whole. Accordingly, it is of first importance that the structure of the scaffolding be built in such a way as to afford this comprehensive view, and it must never be forgotten that the scaffolding does not itself pertain to Nature, but is always something extraneous." Surely, there was no inconsistency in an anti-positivist drawing on Uexküll's theories.

Thus far, Uexküll's thought has not had great influence on biology, except perhaps on the speculations of Ludwig von Bertalanffy, who is laconic, however, about his sources. Uexküll did influence a number of twentieth-century humanists besides Ortega, in particular Ernst Cassirer. For the influence of Uexküll on Cassirer see the latter's *The Logic of the Humanities,* Clarence Smith Howe, trans., pp. 71–77, especially pp. 72–3: "This task for modern biology, which is set forth with great originality and carried out with extraordinary fruitfulness in Uexküll's writings, also affords us a path that can lead to a clear and definite delineation of the boundary between 'life' and 'spirit', between the world of organic forms and the world of cultural forms." Besides Cassirer and Ortega, it is altogether probable that Henri Bergson knew of Uexküll's work when he wrote *The Two Sources of Morality and Religion.* But Bergson's reticence about his sources makes it hard to trace influences. Further, Josef Pieper made use of Uexküll's work in "The Philosophical Act," in *Leisure, The Basis of Culture,* pp. 83–7.

XI: f.   THE DUTY OF THE CRITIC WAS TO REMIND MEN TO FORM INTELLI-GIBLE REASONS FOR THEIR VIEWS (p. 314). See *En torno a Galileo,* 1933, *Obras* V, pp. 295–315; *El hombre y la gente,* 1949, 1957, *Obras* VIII, pp. 99–196; and *¿Qué es filosofía?,* 1929, 1957, *Obras* VII, pp. 277–438. Ortega's critique of rationalism and relativism has similarities to positions Immanuel Kant adopted in "Criticism of the Fourth Paralogism of Transcendental Psychology." Both the rationalists and the relativists were transcendental realists who therefore had to treat phenomena with either a dogmatic, or a skeptical, empirical idealism. In contrast, Ortega was a transcendental idealist whose doctrine of perspectivism elaborated the fact that all knowledge was of phenomena. With reference to phenomena Ortega could maintain an empirical realism that was neither dogmatic nor skeptical. Also, in "Considerations on the whole of Pure Psychology" Kant showed that dogmatic and skeptical criticism both claimed to have enough knowledge about an object to assert or deny anything about it. Critical criticism, much like Ortega's canon, claimed no knowledge of the object but examined the adequacy of the claims made by others. Critical objections established no doctrine, they simply indicated where others erred. See *The Critique of Pure Reason*, first edition, Chapter I of Book II of the Second Division, "Transcendental Dialectic." Ortega differed from Kant on the possibility of an ontology; see below.

It is interesting that at about the same time, Walter Lippmann contended that the complications of public policy had become so great that voters should no longer attempt to judge the rightness or wrongness of various policies. Instead, they should try to evaluate whether or not the policy was arrived at by means of proper procedure. See *Public Opinion*, 1922, Part VII, pp. 369–418.

XI: g.   HERE, ORTEGA PUT HIMSELF IN THE RANKS OF TWENTIETH-CENTURY VISIONARIES (p. 321). The literature that might be mentioned with respect to this point is vast. In contemporary public affairs there are a number of visionary strands interwoven in current reform and protest movements; these are not all based on the same values and procedures. The problem for all is to work out a program and locus of action. On this question, many are proving unable to develop any vision; their program of action is negative, self-pitying, and potentially very destructive. At this stage, any program of visionary reform that makes the state and the economy the central locus of action—whether the action be negative or positive— is futile, destructive, and intrinsically insignificant. Our *Kinderland* lies in creating a more inclusive arena of action than the nation-state.

To create such an arena, however, one needs more than a good will. One needs first to define the issues that will be at stake within it, and one needs second to locate the institutions by means of which men can make effective decisions about the issues at stake. To me, it seems increasingly clear: the issues will be those that might be denoted as the problems affecting the humane quality of life in this world; the institutions will be the cultural and educational institutions, with the university developing in the future a place in public affairs somewhat like that which the state now holds, except that the university will not be national. Somewhere in the current academic turmoil, the foundations for such developments may be building up.

Ortega's work was an element in the ongoing effort to define the issues affecting the humane quality of life in this world. This effort, of course, has a rich history. But in the twentieth century, it has become the central concern in a great number of works, some good, some bad, and each with its unique bent. Among those pertinent to reading Ortega, I would include the following: Albert Camus, *L'Homme révolté*, 1957, as well as most of his other writings; M. Merleau-Ponty, *Sens et non-sens*, Cinquième édition, 1965; Jacques Maritain, *Humanisme intégral*, Nouvelle édition, 1936; Karl Jaspers, *Man in the Modern Age*, Eden and Cedar Paul, trans., 1931, *Philosophy and the World*, 1963, and *The Future of Mankind*, E. B. Ashton, trans., 1961; Nicolas Berdyaev, *The Destiny of Man*, Natalie Duddington, trans., 1960; and so on. From such studies—and many more might be listed—agreement about the quality of life is not to be expected; rather what is happening is that the issues are being sharpened, our awareness of the connection between seemingly separate concerns is building up, and out of this awareness new issues for concerted action may emerge.

XII: TOWARDS AN EXUBERANT EUROPE

XII: a. THERE IS AN END OF CERTAIN SORTS OF IDEOLOGY (p. 331). Throughout *The End of Ideology* and especially in the epilogue, "The End of Ideology in the West" (p. 373), Daniel Bell makes points similar to Shklar about the condition of political theory. A difference, however, is that Shklar sought a rebirth of political theory, whereas Bell was content to see it pass, to be replaced by the techniques of administration. Bell's view, which itself can be considered as a widely shared ideology in a rigorous sense of the word, a body of ideas reflecting the interests of a group, in this case the students and practioners of social, economic, and political technique, is not convincing. In the essays that Bell gathered under the heading "The End of Ideology," he did not really come to grips with the important subject that the phrase announced, and it is regrettable that such a weak book carried such an influential title.

Ideological conflict is no closer to ending than is political theory, but the categories of both are going through transformations. To come to grips with these transformations, we need a truly post-Marxian social theory, one that can go beyond the categories that Marx set forth. We do not need more neo-Marxian theories, ones that rely on Marx's categories and that find, as a result, an end of ideology. The means of production have arrived at a point at which class warfare in its Marxian sense is disappearing. The great issue in the resultant situation is the one about which Marx was prophetic and obscure: the withering away of the state. The state will not wither unless it is made to do so—that has become clear in recent decades—and it has become equally clear that certain people have an interest in maintaining the state apparatus and others have an interest in dismantling it. Contemporary ideologies will be found to be arising from conflicts engendered by these divergent interests, not between the rich and the poor, but between the governors and the governed.

XII: b. FROM HIS YOUTH, ORTEGA HAD A DUAL CONCEPTION OF SOCIETY (p. 338). See "Los dos patriotismos," in "La pedagogía social como programa político," 1910, Obras I, pp. 505–6; and "La España official y la España vital," in Vieja y nueva política, 1914, Obras I, pp. 271–5. In El tema de nuestro tiempo, Ortega applied his dual conception to civilization rather than to society, in the three chapters "Cultura y vida," "El doble imperativo," and "Las dos ironías," Obras III, pp. 163–178; in La rebelión de las masas, 1930, the world of the noble man is close to that of the vital society, whereas that of the mass man is like the official society, "Vida noble y vulgar, o esfuerzo e inercia," Obras IV, pp. 180–5; in En torno a Galileo, 1933, the dual conception was used to analyze historical crises, in which the official society collapses and men are forced to live in a vital society or perish, see especially "Cambio y crisis," Obras V, pp. 69–80; the duality is in Ensimismamiento y alteración, 1939, in which the idea of being inside oneself (vital) and being outside oneself (official) is set forth, Obras V, pp. 293–316; finally, this essay developed into El hombre y la gente, 1949, 1957, Obras VII, pp. 71–272, the significance of which for this problem is apparent from its title. The similarity with Henri Bergson's The Two Sources of Morality and Religion is not due to mutual influence, as shown by the fact that Ortega's division between official and vital society goes back to his very earliest writings, which appeared long before Bergson published his essay on morality and religion. Both were drawing on a tradition of thought that suggested such a distinction.

XII: c. THE NATIONALIST SUBTERFUGE IN THEORIES OF INTERNATIONALISM (p. 339). Internationalism has generally been deemed "good" by the liberal spirit, and it has hence not received its due share of constructive criticism. To be meaningful, government must have direct contact with the people it governs; for this reason, existing world institutions are far from satisfactory: they have no basis, no power, no constituency. The question that should be asked is what world-wide institutions have direct involvement with persons in every country and have potentially universal functions. One set of institutions does meet these criteria: the educational institutions. For this reason, a significant world community, one populated by people, not secretaries of state, will be a cultural community with its institutional reality in the educational agencies. Consequently, the truly historic issue of our time concerns the relationship between the state and the school, and the hope for a world community depends largely on our ability to free intellect from state control. For a preliminary, very sketchy adumbration of these matters see Robert Oliver, "Towards the Separation of School and State," *Teachers College Record*, Vol. 70, No. 1, October 1968, pp. 73–6.

XII: d. A THEORY OF SOCIAL CONTRACT WAS MORE PERTINENT THAN A KINSHIP THEORY (p. 347). Variations on the kinship theory of the state have long been the standard historical interpretation of man's social origins. For instance, it was asserted forcefully by Woodrow Wilson: "What is known of the central nations of history clearly reveals the fact that social organization, and consequently government . . . , originated in *kinship*." *The State: Elements of Historical and Practical Politics*, p. 2. The kinship theory of Adam and Eve in the Book of Genesis is notorious. Less well known are Hesiod's descriptions of the beginnings of the human community in the gift of Pandora to Epimetheus *(Works and Days)* and to Prometheus *(Theogony)*. The Hesiodic version of the original family is curiously consistent with Ortega's contention that the family came as a defense against bands of young men, for Hesiod described a time before women existed, when there were roving tribes of mortal men: "For ere this the tribes of men lived on earth remote and free from ills and hard toil and heavy sickness which bring the Fates upon men. . . ." *Hesiod, The Homeric Hymns and Homerica*, Hugh G. Evelyn-White, trans., p. 9; cf. p. 123. Fustel de Coulanges, *The Ancient City*, Book II, "The Family," pp. 40–116, makes good, albeit exaggerated, use of the kinship theory in historical explanation. In *De l'inégalité parmi les hommes*, Rousseau raised some serious questions about the more anachronistic versions of the kinship theory, and anthropological research has borne out his suspicion that the family as it was known in Europe was not necessarily natural to primitive man. Be that as it may, the source of most types of social organization was one or another arrangement for the birth and nurture of infants.

In Plato's *Republic* Glaucon presented a social contract theory in Book II, 358–360; and the just state, especially in its early stages, is described as the result of an "as if" social contract in 368–374. See also: Thomas Hobbes, *Leviathan*, Part One, Chapter XIV; John Locke, *The Second Treatise of Government*, Chapter VIII; and Rousseau, *Du Contrat social*, Livre I. In "Conjectural Beginning of Human History" Kant used both theories and in "Idea for a Universal History from a Cosmopolitan Point of View" and in "Perpetual Peace" he relied mainly on the contract. See Kant, *On History*, pp. 11–26, 53–68, 85–135. Ortega's own conception included several contracts. There was a contract between the virile males, and contract between the less active groups to control the virile males. See "El origen deportivo del estado," 1924, *Obras* II, especially pp. 618–9.

XII: e.   THE STATE ORIGINATED IN AN EXUBERANT OVERFLOW OF ENERGY (p. 351). Evidence for Ortega's theory was considerable. The legendary rape of the Sabine women was an obvious example. Historical examination of Sparta, with its association of male warriors, and anthropological study of primitive societies, in which "houses of the unmarried" and other male associations were important, bore out Ortega's theory. Ortega mentioned Rome and Sparta: "El origen deportivo del estado," 1924, *Obras* II, pp. 619–620, and the houses of the unmarried, p. 617. A German anthropologist, H. Schurtz, had previously used the male associations as the basis for a theory about primitive societies, *Altersklassen und Männerbünde*, 1902. There is no evidence that Ortega was familiar with this work, although in 1937 ("Ictiosauros y editores clandestinos," *Obras* VIII, p. 386) Ortega praised Robert H. Lowie's *Primitive Society*, in which Schurtz's theory was criticized at length, pp. 257–337. But this was well after Ortega composed his essay on the origin of the state.

XII: f.   ORTEGA ON FASCISM (p. 353). Each time Ortega dealt with the problem of Fascism he took it seriously; he assumed that there was some positive significance in it that could be uncovered. This is the true characteristic of the "open minded" person. He does not pliantly accept anything that comes his way; he tries to turn everything that comes his way to the best use he can. Thus Ortega used Fascism and other extreme movements to learn something about the problems that underlay twentieth-century politics. See "Sobre el fascismo," 1925, *Obras* II, pp. 497–505; *La rebelión* . . . , *Obras* IV, pp. 189–192, 205, 211–5; "No ser hombre de partido," 1930, *Obras* IV, pp. 75–83; "¿Instituciones?", 1931, *Obras* IV, pp. 362–5; and "Un rasgo de la vida alemana," 1935, *Obras* V, pp. 184–206.

XII: g. FREE, PRINCIPLED EFFORT ORIGINATED IN EXUBERANT SPORT (p. 353). Huizinga developed this idea at greater length in *Homo Ludens: A Study of the Play Element in Culture.* His chapters III–V are the most relevant to Ortega's conception and Huizinga referred to Ortega's "Sportive Origin of the State." Ortega thought highly of Huizinga's book. He referred to it twice, both times appreciatively: *Idea del teatro*, 1958, *Obras* VII, p. 489, and "Comentario al *Banquete* de Platón," 1946, 1962, *Obras* IX, pp. 753–4. In 1943, *Homo Ludens* was the one book that Ortega, the unsuppressible publisher, put out in a Spanish translation, through Editorial Azar, which he had established in Portugal. Ortega's writings on sport and exuberance preceded Huizinga's by several years, and he claimed (*Obras* VII, p. 490, fn. 1) an important influence on his Dutch friend. But priority matters little, for the work of each makes a significant whole and both were surely familiar with Friedrich Schiller's "play impulse" that he found essential to art (see Gilbert and Kuhn, *A History of Esthetics*, Revised edition, pp. 366–8).

XII: h. WEALTH WAS ACQUIRED THROUGH SPORTING EFFORT (p. 354). In *The Protestant Ethic and the Spirit of Capitalism,* Max Weber showed that it would be difficult to find a "sportive origin" of modern capitalism. The worldly asceticism of the Protestant ethic had extremely serious motives. Rather than disprove Ortega's theory, this difficulty gives a clue to the historical function that his exuberant ethic was to perform. Ortega believed that the spirit of industrialism, along with that of democracy, was in crisis. One of the causes of this crisis was the bankruptcy of the Protestant ethic and of its offspring—rationalistic individualism. To put the matter another way, since the Reformation, Western civilization had been inspired essentially by serious motives, which the Protestant ethic typified. In the twentieth century the faiths that had justified this seriousness—belief in God, confidence in Reason, the lawfulness of Nature—were collapsing. These collapses plunged many Europeans into a deep nihilism. Ortega shared the general skepticism about the old justifications, but he was remarkably free of the despair and anguish that generally accompany contemporary skepticism, for he was deeply engaged in an attempt to transvalue our values. Ortega's position was premised on the belief that Western civilization could draw inspiration from a sense of the superfluous as well as it had from the serious. Whereas the Judeo-Christian fount of Western civilization was predominantly serious, the Greek heritage was essentially sportive. Unlike the Christian, the Greek basis for ethics was not invalidated by contemporary skepticism. Hence, the importance of Weber's analysis was not that it was an invalidation, but that it posed a challenge: will it ever be possible for a future Weber to consider "The Agonistic Ethic and the Spirit of Humanism"?

Ortega's statement that even wealth is a sporting achievement does not necessarily conflict with Weber's reflections about the relation of the Protestant ethic and the spirit of capitalism. Salvation was the truly serious matter for the Protestant because it was so difficult. Weber's analysis of the relation of Calvinism to the spirit of capitalism unwittingly brought the latter very close to a form of sport, however. Calvinists believed in predestination, and therefore there was no earning grace through good works. One gained nothing of personal significance through business activity. "The life of the saint was directed solely toward a transcendent end, salvation. But precisely for that reason it was thoroughly rationalized in this world and dominated entirely by the aim to add to the glory of God on earth" (p. 118). As in sport, honor and glory were the end, only it was the glory of God rather than of the contestant. Also, there was another sportive quality to Calvinistic capitalism. The athlete seeks to prove to himself that he can perform the feat he attempts. Likewise, "in the course of its development Calvinism added something positive to this [confrontation of the ascetic with the world by ending monasticism], the idea of the necessity of proving [to oneself and one's peers, for God knew] one's faith by worldly activity" (p. 121). In general, see Weber, *The Protestant Ethic*, pp. 99–154. The possibility of a sportive interpretation of Weber's thesis does not contradict the observations in the previous paragraph; it is to pursue an answer to the concluding question.

XII: i.   "A DAILY PLEBISCITE," A CONCEPTION ORTEGA BORROWED FROM RENAN (p. 357). Renan used the image in his address "Qu'est-ce qu'une nation?" Ortega used the image at least three times in his writings: *La rebelión de las masas*, 1930, *Obras* IV, p. 265; *España invertebrada*, 1921, *Obras* III, p. 71; and *Vieja y nueva política*, 1914, *Obras* I, p. 291. Each time he used it to point out that a society had to be based on a project that would win the commitment of the participants in it. Hans Kohn's conception of the nation is similar to Ortega's. For Kohn, nationality was not a natural phenomenon; it was formed by means of the decision to create a nation: "Although some of these objective factors [tradition, geography, etc.] are of great importance for the formation of nationalities, the most essential element is a living and active corporate will. Nationality is formed by the decision to form a nationality." *The Idea of Nationalism: A Study of Its Origin and Background*, p. 15. In conjunction with this point, Kohn, like Ortega, cited Renan's statement about the daily plebiscite (see p. 581, n. 13). Further, Kohn contended that some kind of supranationalism was necessary because democracy and industrialism had outgrown the national structures.

XII: j. YOUTH WAS THE CHANTAGE (p. 359). Ortega's polemic was against a caricature of youth, depicting it as a period with no duties—those good old college days, the best ones of your life. Consequently, in "Juventud," 1927, *Obras* III, pp. 463–471, Ortega was more favorable to the youth of his time, but he reminded his readers that youthfulness was an obligation to set one's course for maturity. See also *En torno a Galileo*, 1933, *Obras* V, pp. 46–50, for more on the missions of youth, maturity, and old age. At the end of "Pasado y porvenir para el hombre actual," 1962, *Obras* IX, p. 663, Ortega made a dramatic appeal to youth, but it was an appeal that threw great obligations on the young. According to the stages of life Ortega gave in *En torno a Galileo* the mature man had to contend against those both younger and older than himself in order to realize his aspirations in the world. The old man, having attempted the active fulfillment of his destiny, would instead try to incite the young to define their destinies in view of the problems that the aged had found to be important. Curiously, the difference between somewhat skeptical attitudes toward youth in *The Revolt of the Masses* and the very enthusiastic attitude in "The Past and Future of Present Man" may be accounted for by Ortega's own transition from maturity to old age. In keeping with his own description of the stages of life, at 45 Ortega was skeptical and at 68 he was enthusiastic. Who says that Ortega was not systematic?

XIII: THE REFORM OF TECHNIQUE

XIII: a. ORTEGA SPOKE OF AN INSUFFICIENCY IN EUROPEAN CULTURE (p. 364). European writers have been less moved than American and English writers by the development of anthropology to absorb the traditional, pedagogical conception of culture into a scientific one. Thus, whereas Matthew Arnold's *Culture and Anarchy* is good background for studying Ortega's position, Raymond Williams' *Culture and Society* and T. S. Eliot's *Notes Towards the Definition of Culture* are not particularly useful. The German conception of culture is fundamental to understanding Ortega. In *Force and Freedom* Jacob Burckhardt pointed out some of the public functions of culture in this sense. For the development and use of the idea by some of Ortega's contemporaries, see Georg Simmel, *The Conflict in Modern Culture and Other Essays*, K. Peter Etzkorn, trans.; Max Scheler, *Man's Place in Nature*, Hans Meyerhoff, trans., and *Probleme einer Soziologie des Wissens* in Scheler, *Gesammelte Werke*, Vol. 8; and Eduard Spranger, *Cultura y educación*. Two historical works are particularly useful: Bruno Snell, *The Discovery of the Mind*, and Werner Jaeger, *Paideia: The Ideals of Greek Culture*, Gilbert Highet, trans.

XIII: b. MEN WERE UNABLE TO NOURISH THEIR MORAL SENSE (p. 364). My discussion of the problem of amorality as Ortega saw it owes a great deal to Kant and Nietzsche, as did Ortega. For Kant see particularly the *Critique of Practical Reason* and the *Foundation of the Metaphysics of Morals*, and in general the *Critique of Pure Reason*, the method of which is essential to understanding the other two works. For Nietzsche see in particular *Beyond Good and Evil* and *On the Genealogy of Morals*.

XIII: c. THAT MEPHISTOPHELEAN CREATURE, TECHNOLOGY (p. 377). Numerous books are coming out on the subject of technology; see for instance Victor C. Ferkiss, *Technological Man: The Myth and the Reality*. One of the best is still Lewis Mumford's *Technics and Civilization*, which, along with Ellul's *Technological Society*, provides a solid introduction to the humane issues raised by our technical creativity. For the historical development of technology in its socio-economic setting, see the excellent study by David S. Landes, *The Unbound Prometheus: Technological Change, 1750 to the Present*.

XIII: d. ORTEGA'S CONCEPTION OF TECHNOLOGY DIFFERED FROM THOSE ELLUL DEALT WITH (p. 383). Technology was explicitly the subject of Ortega's "Meditación de la técnica," 1939, *Obras* V, pp. 319–375; "El mito del hombre allende la técnica," 1951, *Obras* IX, pp. 617–624. In the shape of "organization" it was the topic of "Un rasgo de la vida alemana," 1935, *Obras* V, pp. 184–206; "Individuo y organización," 1953, *Obras* IX, pp. 677–690. Technology was a subject that Ortega mentioned frequently in many other writings. One can fall into a semantic morass by trying to compare definitions of technology used by different writers. For a useful attempt see Jacques Ellul, *The Technological Society*, pp. 13–22. For a helpful analysis of the differences between the philosophical and the historical modes of theorizing see Leo Strauss, *What Is Political Philosophy and Other Studies*, especially pp. 17–27, 52–55, 56–77.

XIII: e. ORTEGA WAS NOT A PRAGMATIST, IF ONE THINKS THAT A PRAGMATIST BELIEVES THAT TRUTH DEPENDS ON USEFULNESS (p. 385). In "Para dos revistas argentinas," 1924, *Obras* VIII, pp. 372–6, Ortega discussed the differences he had with pragmatism. It was precisely that utility had nothing to do directly with ideas—actions were useful or harmful depending on whether the ideas that guided the activity were true or false, as well as significant or trivial. Ortega scorned pragmatism as an inferior philosophy. Nevertheless, there are possibilities for comparing Ortega and Dewey and American pragmatism on this question of the instrumentality of knowledge. However, again it would be important to resist the ubiquitous danger of assimilating the whole to one of its parts. "American" pragmatism is not a whole and it would be wrong to draw a direct connection between it and Ortega. Instead, the similarities between them should eventually be explained by showing that both were part of a larger Western intellectual movement. During the nineteenth century faith in a purposive, meaningful universe was undermined by the flood of scientific knowledge. Purpose was expelled from nature, but the human mind rebels at thinking of itself as a meaningless, purposeless interloper in a gratuitous universe. Therefore, during the later nineteenth and early twentieth centuries many philosophers and psychologists tried to salvage the situation by locating purpose in our ways of knowing, which were anterior to our conception of the universe. Ortega and the American pragmatists were both parts of this larger whole.

XIII: f. IN ADDITION TO BEING TRUE, ALL KNOWLEDGE SHOULD BE INSTRU-
MENTAL (p. 386). A short statement of this is in the section
"Acción y contemplación," in *Ideas sobre la novela*, 1925,
Obras III, pp. 403–7. It is so basic in Ortega's outlook that it
will be found wherever he wrote about culture, thought, reason, or intelligence; all these had vital functions. Nietzsche
took this position when he argued that beliefs that were
necessary for life might be false; see *The Will to Power*, 483,
487, 493, and 497 (cf. Walter Kaufmann, *Nietzsche*, pp.
305–6). Hans Vaihinger developed a similar position in *Die
Philosophie des Als Ob*, especially pp. 1–20. Both Nietzsche
and Vaihinger, however, contended merely that the false or
fictional was important nevertheless for its instrumentality,
for the fact that it guides beneficent action. Ortega's instru-
mentalism was more fully akin to Socrates when he renounced
the study of the natural philosophers because they did not
answer the questions that he thought were important; see
Phaedo, 96 100. Ortega frequently criticized positivism for
being obsessed with finding "Truths" even when they were
far too insignificant to be worth the effort.

Ortega should be carefully compared to Dewey on three
points: the present one of their respective views of the instrumentality of knowledge, Ortega's use of perspectivism as
a means of overcoming the difficulties that led Dewey to
criticize all forms of dualism, and their common emphasis on
education as the foundation of public affairs. These problems
were touched on only obliquely by José Arsenio Torres in his
dissertation "Philosophic Reconstruction and Social Reform
in John Dewey and José Ortega y Gasset."

XIII: g. THE TECHNICIAN NEEDED A THEORY OF VALUATION (p. 386). Although popular interpretations of pragmatism do not
acknowledge it, certainly James and Dewey reasoned in a
similar way from the practical to the ethical. For James see
The Will to Believe; and for Dewey, *Theory of Valuation*.
The press of progress is making the scientist come around to
a similar position. Scientists have realized that there are more
possible research problems than there are researchers. To
judge wisely which problems will receive effort one must
resort to nonscientific ethical and political considerations.
See Derek J. de Solla Price, *Science Since Babylon*, pp. 92–
124; and J. Robert Oppenheimer, "On Science and Culture,"
Encounter, October 1962, pp. 3–10. For some of the political
problems that arise from having to guide scientific inquiry by
means of a policy see *Science and the Federal Patron* by
Michael D. Reagan.

XIII: h. PRACTICAL PLANNERS WILL DISLIKE ORTEGA'S CONCEPTION OF TECHNOLOGY (p. 393). Ortega will fall under the heading of the apocalyptic rebels that Daniel Bell sees as one pole of the contemporary academic view of the post-industrial world, for Ortega was willing to see that world fall apart in a rather profound social transformation based on an ineluctable transvaluation of values. See Bell's "The Scholar Cornered: About *The Reforming of General Education,*" *The American Scholar,* Summer 1968, pp. 401–6. For the planners' views of such issues see *Toward the Year 2000, Daedalus,* Summer 1967. The complacency of the practical outlook on technology and related problems is well criticized by John McDermott, "Technology: The Opiate of the Intellectuals," *The New York Review of Books,* July 31, 1969. The complacency McDermott castigates is quintessentially exemplified by Irving Kristol, "American Intellectuals and Foreign Policy," *Foreign Affairs,* July 1967.

XIV: THE REFORM OF REASON

XIV: a. VICO AND THE GEISTESWISSENSCHAFTEN (p. 399). Recently an important contribution to the understanding of Vico's place in the history of thought has been made through the substantial volume *Giambattista Vico: An International Symposium,* edited by Giorgio Tagliacozzo. For Vico's works in English, see *The New Science of Giambattista Vico,* Thomas G. Bergin and Max H. Fisch, trans., and *On the Study Methods of Our Time,* Elio Gianturco, trans. In *Immagine e parola nella formazione dell'uomo,* M. T. Gentile indicates the pattern for a reinterpretation of the history of educational theory that assigns a very important place to Vico.

XIV: b. NIETZSCHE IS STILL CONDEMNED AS AN IRRATIONALIST (p. 402). See for instance, George Lichtheim, *The Concept of Ideology,* pp. 16–7, 26–30. For criticism of Ortega as an irrationalist, see J. Roland Pennock, *Liberal Democracy: Its Merits and Prospects.* In "Ni vitalismo ni racionalismo," 1924, *Obras* III, pp. 270–280, Ortega protested that *El tema de nuestro tiempo* had not been meant as a defense of irrationalism. In the usage of the time, "vitalism" meant the irrational assertion of life against intellect, and not the philosophical-scientific question of whether or not there is a vital principle distinct from physical principles. Ortega contended that instead of irrationally asserting the claims of life against reason, men should reasonably assert the claims of life against rationalism, which he considered to be an unfounded, mystical, *irrational* belief in the power of reason to know objective reality. For Ortega, reason, reasonably conceived, was a function of life, not something in opposition to it.

XIV: c. YET REASON HAS A HISTORY (p. 405). The book that most made me aware of this fact is Bruno Snell's *The Discovery of Mind: The Greek Origins of European Thought.* An important study for the theme, one that does much to outline a history of moral reason, is *Le progrès de la conscience dans la philosophie occidentale* by Léon Brunschvicg. Also very valuable as a prelude to a history of reason is Ernst Cassirer's great work, *The Philosophy of Symbolic Forms.* Enlightening as these studies are, the history of reason as such is still largely to be written. The key step in the undertaking would be, I think, correlating the developing forms of thinking rationally with the crucial problems of life at various historic periods. Thus, the modern tendency to dismiss the intellectual life of the middle ages as one dominated by blind belief, dogma, and superstition, may be due to a failure to grasp the connections between the formulaic, liturgic, symbolic modes of reasoning then common with the human difficulties that men authentically felt.

XIV: d. THE RELATION OF HERACLITUS AND PARMENIDES (p. 409). The pre-Socratics present an interesting historiographical problem, for they make us confront the question whether history refers to the past or to the sources. The sources for the pre-Socratics are in such fragmentary condition that it is probable that any account that adheres strictly to the sources will falsely depict the past actuality to which it purportedly adheres. At the same time, without strict adherence to the sources, there ceases to be any way to evaluate the historical truth of an interpretation. Because of this problem, it seems most sound to distinguish two forms of scholarship with respect to the pre-Socratics, which, although distinct, should inform one another. The first is the well established tradition of the philological study of the sources; the second a speculative, synthetic return from the corpus of post-Socratic philosophy to imagining what might have come before it. With this endeavor, one should treat discussions of the pre-Socratics as *as if* constructions that can be put forward within limits set down by the philological reconstruction of the fragments. Although frankly speculative, such constructions can be very helpful in explicating the possible meaning of Plato and Aristotle, and one can distinguish between the value, if not the truth, of such constructions according to how well they help one explicate post-Socratic philosophy.

Although completely devoid of technical expertise in philology, I have found that meditating on the possible meaning of the pre-Socratics to be a fruitful heuristic. With respect to all periods, the problem for the educational historian is to appreciate the eventual rationality of diverse, very strange modes of thinking. I do not believe that there are any conclusions, in a real sense, to this process; it is, if you will, a continuous entry. Yet, although no conclusions develop, there is real progress; layer after layer of possibility appears and unexpected systems of connections unfold.

My reflections on the pre-Socratics have been based on rather standard sources: Kathleen Freeman's *Ancilla to the Pre-Socratic Philosophers* and her *Companion to the Pre-Socratic Philosophers*; John Burnet's *Early Greek Philosophy*; G. S. Kirk and J. E. Raven's *The Presocratic Philosophers: A Critical History with a Selection of Texts*; Philip Wheelwright's *Heraclitus*; Werner Jaeger's *Theology of the Early Greek Philosophers*; and W. K. C. Guthrie's *History of Greek Philosophy*, Vols. I and II.

XIV: e. TRANSCENDENTAL IDEALS WERE USED AS IF THEY TOLD ABOUT REALITY IN ORDER TO ESTABLISH INTELLECTUAL STANDARDS (p. 415). A great deal of ensuing Continental philosophy turns on this point and the problems for reason that it gives rise to. The transcendental ideal is discussed by Kant in *Critique of Pure Reason*, I, Pt. 2, Div. 2, Ch. 3, Sec. 2; see especially pp. A576, A580 (Norman Kemp Smith, trans.): "But the concept of what thus possesses all reality is just the concept of a *thing in itself* as completely determined. . . . It is therefore a transcendental *ideal* which serves as basis for the complete determination that necessarily belongs to all that exists. This ideal is the supreme and complete material condition of the possibility of all that exists—the condition to which all thought of objects, so far as their content is concerned, has to be traced back. . . .

"If, in following up this idea of ours, we proceed to hypostatize it, we shall be able to determine the primordial being through the mere concept of the highest reality, as a being that is one, simple, all-sufficient, eternal, etc. In short, we shall be able to determine it, in its unconditioned completeness, through all predicaments. The concept of such a being

is the concept of *God,* taken in the transcendental sense. . . .
In any such use of the transcendental idea we should, however, be overstepping the limits of its purpose and validity.
For reason, in employing it as a basis for the complete determination of things, has used it only as the *concept* of all
reality, without requiring that all this reality be objectively
given and be itself a thing. Such a thing is a mere fiction. . . ."

XV: THE DAWN OF HISTORIC REASON

XV: a. WERE THIS A BOOK ON THE REFORM OF REASON, NUMEROUS CON-
TRIBUTORS WOULD HAVE TO BE DISCUSSED IN ADDITION TO ORTEGA
(p. 121). Speculative philosophy faces forward; it is not, as
Alfred North Whitehead would have had us believe, a series
of footnotes to Plato, or it does not at least arise in this retrospective manner. On the contrary, speculative philosophy is
our effort to solve in the future certain problems we perceive
in the present; and only when we are searching for a day
yet to come can we usefully write footnotes to Plato, for in
this way they gain a prospective significance. Present problems and future hopes are the foundation of all historical
valuations: history is the teleological science *par excellence;*
and anachronism is an historical sin, not because it violates
the past, but because it diminishes our sense of the future.
Since history is a teleological study, historians often overturn
the valuations of their predecessors, and historical figures are
usually most comprehensible when they are seen, not as the
genetic product of their past, but as the teleological creation
of their future. The continuity of culture lies, not in the
mysterious power of great works to mold their progeny in
the pattern of the past, but in the magnificent capacity of
great men to appropriate their patrimony in the work of the
future. Since we have by no means finished appropriating
the patrimony of the last hundred years, the intellectual history of this period is still indeterminate.

What is it that a creative thinker appropriates from his
peers? It is not primarily a series of particular points; men
of large mind take in so much from their past and present
that one would lose control of one's work trying to identify
each bit and assign it to its proper source. A creative thinker
primarily appropriates a set of central concerns from his
peers; in communicating with them in fact and fancy, he
comes to see certain problems as the ones that must be

mastered if he is to take a leading part in the thought of his time. The job of the intellectual historian is to make manifest the great systems of concern that give rise over time and space to an intellectual community.

So far, only H. Stuart Hughes has essayed a full assessment of the concerns uniting European social thinkers since the late nineteenth century. *Consciousness and Society: The Reconstruction of European Social Thought, 1890–1930* and *The Obstructed Path: French Social Thought in the Years of Desperation, 1930–1960* are the first two of a three part survey of the situation. These are competent works. Hughes has, unlike many popularizers of particular movements, acquainted himself with the full range of what was written. This is especially true of *Consciousness and Society,* but even in this book there is discernible an obtrusion of American behaviorism onto the controlling definition of social thought, which prompts the author to ignore significant thinkers. In the sequel, the complete omission of Jacques Ellul and Georges Gurvitch from his assessment of French social thought is a serious flaw, which could on the proper occasion lead into a full-scale critique of Hughes' division of the social thought of 1930 to 1960 into "French" and "anti-Fascist emigré" schools.

A less satisfactory general survey is *After Utopia* by Judith N. Shklar. This book was criticized in the text, pp. 327–30. Its weakness is integral, arising it seems to me because the author did not have a thorough acquaintance with any single writer with whom she dealt; as a consequence, she did not really understand her subject. A scholar develops a much surer sense of the issues of a time after he has contended with the complete work of one of its representatives. My own conception of European social philosophy is shaped by my study of Ortega: my knowledge of Ortega has affected the way I read others, and a reading of other writers has informed my understanding of Ortega. I have become convinced that the lines along which the social philosophy of the last hundred years have been described are wrong and arbitrary and that we should ignore these and construct alternatives. This is not the right occasion to develop the theme that I think holds together the divergent lines of inquiry during this period; namely, the desirability of creating a system of normative discourse equal to the scope, range, and intimacy of our actual, normative relations. My sense of this problem is still dominated by Ortega; I see him at the center of a large group that is united by a common concern for the disjunction between our ability to act upon each other and our ability to assume reasonable responsibility for the consequences of these actions. Whether after the full study of this group I will still find Ortega central to it, is for the future to tell.

Men have never been able to anticipate perfectly the consequences of their actions, and thus philosophers have always been concerned to improve our capacity to think through the implications of our deeds. But in recent times, the scale of human action has greatly expanded, which has intensified the age-old problem of understanding our personal and collective responsibilities. This concern has unified the work of many recent thinkers, all of whom have worried intensely about what might best be described by a phrase of Wolfgang Köhler, "the place of value in a world of facts." The literature that developed from this concern is variegated and profound. A full discussion of it here would take us too far afield; I hope in the future to take up such a discussion on the scale it merits in a three volume study of cosmopolitanism and nationalism in modern thought, *Power and Pedagogy*. Here I shall merely note the contributions to the concern that have informed my understanding of Ortega. For the sake of brevity, these writers can be grouped as Ortega's elders, peers, and juniors. I mention those who, although not necessarily an influence on Ortega or influenced by Ortega, have contributed to my understanding of Ortega.

Foremost among Ortega's elders was Wilhelm Dilthey. I do not agree with interpreters who think that Dilthey's form of historicism ends in a relativism; whenever locally circumscribed systems of value come up against evidence of the diversity of human mores, the first step is to recognize the dependence on locality of every particular precept and to find the highest values not in the particular precepts, but in the quality of the relation between different precepts and the situations to which they pertain. The works by Dilthey I have consulted are given in the bibliographical list. Most illuminating of them for displaying the concern animating Dilthey's reflection is *Briefwechsel zwischen Dilthey und Graf Yorck*. Although a biologist, Jacob von Uexküll was deeply concerned with finding a place for value in biological science by uncovering its place in life. For Uexküll see the bibliographical annotation XI:e. Neo-Kantianism, in the version of the Marburg school and in Hans Vaihinger's work, was an effort, among other things, to provide a foundation for rational valuation. Cohen's works cited in annotation II:e and

Natorp's mentioned in II:m have already been discussed. *Die Philosophie des Als Ob* by Hans Vaihinger seems to those of a naturalistic orientation to lead to skeptical consequences; but in its context of replying to a naïve overconfidence in positivistic science, it should be seen as a rather successful and influential effort to put reasoning about fact and reasoning about value on an equal footing, on which the proponents of one cannot denigrate the other as "mere speculation." The important work of Brentano, Meinong, and Ehrenfels in searching for a rigorous conception of value as it is manifest in life is well surveyed by Howard O. Eaton, *The Austrian Philosophy of Values.* Also of great importance in giving a common basis to our reasoning about facts and values is the work of Edmund Husserl, which I am acquainted with through *Phenomenology and the Crisis of Philosophy*, Quentin Lauer, trans.; *Ideas: General Introduction to Pure Phenomenology*, W. R. Boyce Gibson, trans.; and "Phenomenology," in the 14th edition of the *Encyclopedia Britannica*, Vol. XVII, pp. 700–22.

Although German thinkers such as these were most influential on Ortega, others contributed to the clarification of the place of values in a world of fact. I have learned much from the works of Henri Bergson, *Creative Evolution*, Arthur Mitchell, trans.; *The Two Sources of Morality and Religion*, Andrea and Brenton, trans.; *Time and Free Will*, F. L. Pogson, trans.; and *Matter and Memory*, Paul and Palmer, trans. My own introduction to the problem of values has been in large part through American writers. Henry Adams is, I think, more important with respect to this question than is generally recognized. In addition to *The Education of Henry Adams*, a sustained treatise on the dilemmas arising from the disjunction between power and our understanding, see *The Degradation of the Democratic Dogma, Democracy*, and many of his letters, which all have penetrating insights into the problem of values in industrial democracies. For William James, see *The Will to Believe, Varieties of Religious Experience*, and *Pragmatism*. For Dewey, see *Art as Experience, Democracy and Education, Experience and Nature, Freedom and Culture, The Quest for Certainty*, and *Theory of Valuation*. It is important to treat serious pragmatism in its European, neo-Kantian context, rather than in the usual one of "American" pragmatism. James and Dewey both had the problem of value at the center of their concern, a fact inexcusably obscured by Dewey by his cant about scientific method, which opened his ideas to debasement by a horde of hangers-on. Three books by Santayana have been useful to me in forming my ideas about Ortega: *Scepticism and Animal Faith, The Life of Reason,* and *The Sense of Beauty.* Unlike many, Santayana was far less concerned to apply the great tradition to contemporary problems and developments as he was to give a contemporary restatement of the tradition; thus his work lacks a pretension to novelty, a lack that repels some, but it has a grasp of the fundamentals and a literary grace that are an invaluable propaedeutic to a study of Ortega. Another writer of this era whose work is pertinent but not as well known to me is Alfred North Whitehead.

The thought of Ortega's peers has been presented in English in a way that reveals the herd instincts of the scholar. Neither phenomenology nor "existentialism" is a self-contained movement; and the attention that has been lavished on these has been way out of proportion to the relative lack of interest in closely related developments. To right the balance we need a work that will bring out the community of concern between men like Ernst Cassirer, Eduard Spranger, Freidrich Meinecke, Martin Buber, Theodor Litt, Werner Jaeger, Max Scheler, Georg Simmel, Martin Heidegger, Karl Jaspers, Gabriel Marcel, Jacques Maritain, Johan Huizinga, and many others. Unlike his fellow neo-Kantians, Cassirer was not interested in writing and re-writing fundamental critiques of reason; he seems to have agreed tacitly with the Hegelian position that the true phenomenology of mind is to be found in the historical unfolding of reason. Hence, his epistemology owes more to history than to logic. For instance, many of his works at first seem to be dispassionate historical reports, and rather dry reports at that. *The Philosophy of the Enlightenment,* Koelln and Pettegrove, trans., does not preserve the wit characteristic of Enlightenment thinkers; but it performs a much greater service, that of making present-day readers contend with the systematic convictions upon which Enlightenment thinkers based modern politics and philosophy, for these convictions are usually ignored by historians. By laying bare these convictions, as Cassirer said (p. xi), we confront not only our history, but the implicit premises of our living orthodoxies; and when we find these premises to be difficult and obscure, the intellectual history of the Enlightenment becomes the occasion for our critical examination of our present. This integral combination of history and philosophy characterized Cassirer's other major works—*Substance and Function,* Swabey and Swabey, trans.; *The Problem of Knowledge,* Woglom and Hendel, trans.; *The*

Myth of the State; An Essay on Man; and *The Philosophy of Symbolic Forms,* 3 vols., Ralph Manheim, trans. These works have provided important background for my study of Ortega; both the subjects they deal with and the discipline they engender are valuable in understanding Ortega. Eduard Spranger was well known to Ortega and he is of much greater importance than is recognized in the United States. His *Types of Men: the Psychology and Ethics of Personality,* Paul J. W. Pigors, trans., has never found an American audience, partly because the translation, although "authorized," is far from the best one possible, and partly because Spranger's thought, like that of so many Europeans of his time, is too wide ranging to fit neatly into any of America's academic niches. In addition to *Types of Men,* I have found Spranger's *Cultura y educación* useful in my study of Ortega. Of Buber's work, I have studied *I and Thou,* R. G. Smith, trans.; *Daniel: Dialogues on Realization,* Maurice Friedman, trans.; and *Pointing the Way,* Maurice Friedman, trans. In addition, Friedman's biography, *Martin Buber: The Life of Dialogue,* is well worth consulting. Buber's place in neo-Kantianism has not yet been adequately studied, and an inquiry into the relations between Buber and Cassirer, Spranger, Litt, and others would be fruitful. For instance, Theodor Litt, who has been almost completely ignored, advanced ideas about the I-thou relation quite parallel and prior to Buber's, in *Individuum und Gemeinschaft: Grundlage der Kulturphilosophie,* which is, I think, an important book for the problem of value in the twentieth century.

Max Scheler was highly respected by Ortega, who memorialized Scheler's death in 1928 in "Max Scheler," *Obras* IV, pp. 507–511. I am familiar with Scheler's work through his *On the Eternal in Man,* Bernard Noble, trans.; *Man's Place in Nature,* Hans Meyerhoff, trans.; *Philosophical Perspectives,* Oscar A. Haac, trans.; and *Probleme einer Soziologie des Wissens.* John Raphael Staude's *Max Scheler, 1874–1928: An Intellectual Portrait* is an adequate introduction to Scheler's work, although Scheler's complicated and ever-changing relations to the intellectual developments of his time still need further elucidation.

There is no escaping the fact, no matter how much one may dislike his character, style, or politics, that Heidegger's *Being and Time* is a most important book for anyone engaged in the study of systematic philosophy in the twentieth century. For such a person, the discipline of following Heidegger's reasoning leads to a tremendous clarification of certain problems discussed in the text above. However, let us be wary of Heideggerians who find his language a handy means for making a claim to personal profundity by aping their master's obscurity without matching his mission. Heidegger's ideas are not all that difficult, and it is these, not his jargon, that the student needs to master. In addition to *Being and Time*, I have studied *Kant and the Problem of Metaphysics*, James S. Churchill, trans., and *Existence and Being*, Werner Brock, trans. The most helpful secondary source on Heidegger is, I think, Thomas Langan's *The Meaning of Heidegger: A Critical Study of An Existentialist Phenomenology*. The work of Karl Jaspers has been less satisfactorily presented in English. More of Jaspers' writing has been translated than of Heidegger's, but until recently the major works by Heidegger had been translated whereas only the minor and middling works of Jaspers had been published here. Two books by Jaspers are closely related in concern and subject to books by Ortega, Jaspers' *Man in the Modern Age* (1931) to Ortega's *Revolt of the Masses* (1930), and *The Idea of the University* to *The Mission of the University*. In addition, I have found *The Future of Mankind*, E. B. Ashton, trans.; *Philosophy and the World*, E. B. Ashton, trans.; and *The Origin and Goal of History*, Michael Bullock, trans., significant in my work on Ortega. The recent publication of E. B. Ashton's translation of Jaspers' *Philosophy*, Vol. I, is a major addition, which begins to bring the English presentation of Jaspers into balance with that of Heidegger. The important relation of Huizinga's *Homo Ludens* to Ortega's thought is discussed in annotation XII:g.

Among the books by Ortega's juniors that illuminate his thought, I would single out the following. Ortega himself pointed to similarities and differences between his thought and that of French existentialism, which meant to him primarily Sartre and Merleau-Ponty. For Sartre, see *L'être et le néant*, and for Merleau-Ponty see *Phénoménologie de la perception, La structure du comportement, Humanisme et terreur: essai sur le probleme communiste*, and *Sens et Non-sens*. Two secondary works that are competent analyses are Joseph P. Fell, III, *Emotion in the Thought of Sartre*, which goes beyond the strict limits of its title, and Albert Rabil, Jr., *Merleau-Ponty: Existentialist of the Social World*. The two most interesting writers carrying on Ortega's concern for the relation between technique and the humane value of life are Jacques Ellul in *The Technological Society, Propagandes*, and *The Political Illusion*, which are all discussed in the bibliographical annotations, and the Italian, Enrico Castelli, in *Le temps harcelant, Introduction a une phénoménologie de notre époque,* and *L'enquête quotidienne.* Of the two, Ellul is the more substantial and systematic thinker. There is a good review article on Ellul by William Gorman, "Ellul—A Prophetic Voice," in *The Center Magazine,* October-November 1967, pp. 34–7.

Martin S. Dworkin has directed me to many of the writers already discussed, and a number of others whose work needs to be taken into account, some of whose books I deal with in the text or bibliographical annotations. Among these are Gustave Le Bon, Julien Benda, Alain, Léon Brunschwicg, Alexandre Kojève, Alfred Schütz, Maurice Blondel, Jacques Maritain, Gabriel Marcel, Georges Gurvitch, Heinrich Rickert, Georg Simmel, Theodor Geiger, Karl Mannheim, Werner Sombart, Wilhelm Flitner, Friedrich Meinecke, Kurt Riezler, Florian Znaniecki, Alfred Weber, Nicolai Hartmann, Otto F. Bollnow, Benedetto Croce, Giovanni Gentile, Guido de Ruggiero, R. G. Collingwood, and so on.

xv: b. ORTEGA'S ATTEMPT AT A NEW ONTOLOGY (p. 424). Most of the important sources are mentioned in the notes. It may be helpful, however, to list here the major sources for this effort along with their approximate dates of composition: *¿Qué es filosofía* (1929), "*¿Qué es el conocimiento?*" (1931), *Unas lecciones de metafísica* (1932), *En torno a Galileo* (1933), "Guillermo Dilthey y la idea de la vida" (1934), "Historia como sistema" (1936), *Ideas y creencias* (1940), "Apuntes sobre el pensamiento" (1941), "Prólogo a *Veinte años de caza mayor,* del Conde de Yerbes" (1942), *Origen y epílogo de la filosofía* (1943), "Commentario al *Banquete* de Platón" (1946), and *La idea de principio en Leibniz y la evolución de la teoría deductiva* (1947).

XVI: ON THE PAST AND FUTURE OF PRESENT MAN

XVI: a. LITERATURE ON THE REFORM OF THE CULTURAL INSTITUTIONS (p. 472). This literature is immense and can be merely introduced here. In keeping with the analysis below, it can be divided into two kinds: prescriptive and protreptic. Representative examples of the prescriptive are: F. R. Leavis, *Education and the University: A Sketch for an 'English School';* the Committee on the Objectives of a General Education in a Free Society, *General Education in a Free Society;* Howard Mumford Jones, *Education and World Tragedy;* The American Assembly, *The Federal Government and Higher Education;* Charles G. Dobbins, ed., *Higher Education and the Federal Government;* The Commission on the Humanities, *Report of the Commission on the Humanities;* James Bryant Conant, *The Education of American Teachers;* and Daniel Bell, *The Reforming of General Education.* Leading examples of the protreptic group are, besides Ortega's *Misión de la universidad,* Robert Maynard Hutchins, *The Higher Learning in America;* Mark van Doren, *Liberal Education;* Karl Jaspers, *The Idea of the University;* Jacques Barzun, *Teacher in America;* Jacques Barzun, *The House of Intellect;* C. P. Snow, *The Two Cultures;* and James A. Perkins, *The University in Transition.* These groups, of course, reflect similarities of method, not of aim.

XVI: b.   SOURCES FOR ORTEGA'S VIEWS ABOUT THE CULTURAL INSTITUTIONS (p. 473). In 1932, speaking at the centenary of the University of Granada, he suggested that the university was one of the basic European institutions that with a reform of reason might again be of crucial historic importance. "En el centenario de una universidad," 1932, *Obras* V, pp. 463–474.

In 1934, writing "On Careers," he observed that the idea of a career could be a very useful historical concept to the young if they did not hypostatize it, seeking thoughtlessly to fit themselves to the form it suggested; if they used it as a mere idea they could map great new possibilities for their personal programs of life. "Sobre las carreras," 1934, *Obras* V, pp. 167–183.

In 1935, speaking about the "Mission of the Librarian," Ortega contended that, owing to the profusion of books, that venerable instrument of thought was falling into crisis; "from now on it will be necessary to care for the book as a living function; it will be necessary to control books by means of a policy and to become the tamers of the tumultuous tomes." Here was the librarian's mission. "Misión del bibliotecario," 1935, *Obras* V, p. 227, cf. pp. 209–234.

In 1935, speaking in the P.E.N. club of Madrid, Ortega stated that "the mission of the writer, the biped with a pen, is to elevate towards the heights everything inert and dull. When the writer does not succeed or, at least, when he does not manage to do this, ah!, then the writer is not the writer because then the pen is not a pen, but a gun." Fateful words, these! "En el P.E.N. Club de Madrid," 1935, *Obras* VI, p. 233.

In 1937, musing on "A Quarrel in Physics," he contended

that physicists should accept a systematic philosophic discipline in order to settle disagreements that were significant but insoluble by physical experiment; and if the physicists developed such intellectual foundations they would point the way to the rebirth of a European concord. "Bronca en la física," 1937, *Obras* V, pp. 271–287.

In 1937, reflecting on "The Misery and Splendor of Translation," Ortega perceived a great educational mission for the translator: as Goethe had observed, the humane can live fully only among *all* men, and the task before the translator was to enable each of us, everyman, to live among all men, regardless of historic and linguistic barriers. "Miseria y esplendor de la traducción," 1937, *Obras* V, pp. 433–452.

In 1943 and 1946, celebrating *Velázquez,* Ortega suggested to painters that men who had the capacity like Velázquez to reshape fundamentally the office of the painter are basic influences in the evolution of society: "they transcend, thus, the history of art and consign us to history in its entirety, the only one that is truly history." *Velázquez,* 1943, 1946, 1959, *Obras* VIII, p. 501, cf. pp. 484–5.

In 1946, writing on *The Idea of the Theater,* Ortega called it "a visible metaphor" that, like any metaphor, should allow men to go beyond themselves, intuiting things presently outside their powers of apprehension, for a few hours achieving "the supreme aspiration of the human being: managing to be sublime." *Idea del teatro,* 1946, 1958, *Obras* VII, pp. 459, 471, cf. pp. 443–501.

In 1948, in the "Prospectus of the Institute of the Humanities," Ortega proposed that those interested band together to partake in "man's most constitutive sport, that is theorizing," in this case theorizing in an atmosphere of healthy calm about how men can further humanize themselves. "Prospecto del Instituto de Humanidades," 1948, *Obras* VII, pp. 11–23.

In 1951, at a conference at Darmstadt on *Man and Room,* he called on the architect to free himself, like the technician, from reasoning from necessity and to fantasize new forms within which men might live. "El mito del hombre allende la técnica," 1951, *Obras* IX, pp. 617–623.

In 1953, at another Darmstadt conference, this time on *The Individual and Organization,* he contended that organization for its own sake was a threat to human life, that the welfare state, which aims to make life good for the individual, tends by virtue of its paternalism "to asphyxiate the individual," but that contemporary organization, if used as a basis, not a substitute, for individual effort, could be the groundwork of tremendous improvement in the quality of life. "Individuo y organización," 1953, *Obras* IX, pp. 677–680.

In 1954, speaking about "The Liberal Professions," he called on lawyers, doctors, engineers, financiers, and other professionals to resist the "hermeticism," the tendency to close themselves to larger issues, which they had recently manifested, and to "create new forms of individual activity," to invent ever more demanding realms of practice, and thus to preserve the "variety of situations" that characterized Europe. "Las profesiones liberales," 1954, *Obras* IX, pp. 691–706.

In 1954, in his last public speech, "A Look at the Situation of the Director or Manager in Present Society," Ortega reiterated his characteristic concerns: the manager had to resist specialism for he possessed enormous social power; the times were ones in which the limits of the nation-states had been reached and the vitality of public life was declining in sloth, politicians were ineffective, intellectuals could only theorize; the only potentially dynamic, constructive enterprise was a movement towards European unity, a unified Europe was a prerequisite of a stable world, and leadership in the movement towards unity was the managers' mission: "Peace— and not this or that little peace like so many that history has known, but peace as a stable form, almost definitive, of living together among the countries is not a pure desire; it is a thing, and as such it therefore requires being fabricated. For this, it is necessary to find new and radical principles of law. Europe has always been prodigous in inventions. Why not have the hope that it can succeed as well in this?" "Una vista sobre la situación del gerente o 'manager' en la sociedad actual," 1954, *Obras* IX, p. 746, cf. pp. 727–746.

BIBLIOGRAPHY

Ortega's Work

José Ortega y Gasset: *Obras completas,* 11 vols., Madrid: Revista de Occidente, 1946–1969.

Material not yet in the *Obras completas*

BOOKS:

José Ortega y Gasset: *Unas lecciones de metafísica,* Madrid: Alianza Editorial, 1966.

ARTICLES (LISTED CHRONOLOGICALLY):

José Ortega y Gasset: "Al margen del libro," *El Imparcial* (Madrid), January 9, 1911.

——————: "Gratitud de 'España' " and "Propositos," unsigned, *España* (Madrid), February 5, 1915. (Attributed to Ortega by Ricardo Senabre Sempere and reprinted in his study, *Lengua y estilo de Ortega y Gasset,* pp. 283–4.)

——————: "Figuras contemporaneas: Heriberto Jorge Wells," unsigned, *España,* July 9, 1915. (Attributed to Ortega by Ricardo Senabre Sempere and reprinted in his study, *Lengua y estilo de Ortega y Gasset,* pp. 289–290.)

——————: "Cervantes, plenitud española," *España,* May 4, 1916, pp. 10–11.

——————: " 'La primera peseta' de Ortega y Gasset," *El Sol* (Madrid), April 4, 1922, p. 1.

——————: "Sobre el vuelo de las aves anilladas," *El Sol,* August 13 (p. 3) and 18 (p. 3), 1929.

——————: "¿Que es el conocimiento?," I, II, III, IV, V, *El Sol,* January 18 (p. 3) and 25 (p. 3), February 1 (p. 3) and 23 (p. 3), and March 1 (p. 3), 1931. (This is a substantial philosophical essay and an excellent example of Ortega's humanism.)

——————: "Geografía e historia: la mesta, el valle y la costa," *Luz* (Madrid), March 1 (p. 8) and 3 (p. 9), 1932. (The first is an exposition of Hegel's theory of history; the page on which the second was was missing from the copy I saw.)

——————: "Il medioevo y la idèa de la nazione," in *La civiltà Veneziana del trecento,* Sansoni, 1955.

——————: "Sensación, construcción e intuición" (1913), in *Apuntes sobre el pensamiento,* Madrid: Revista de Occidente, 1959, pp. 99–117.

REPORTS OF LECTURES (LISTED CHRONOLOGICALLY):

"Una conferencia en 'El Sitio', La pedagogía social," *El Imparcial,* March 13, 1910, p. 1.

"En la Facultad de Filosofía: Cuarto conferencia pública de Ortega y Gasset," *La Prensa* (Buenos Aires), September 3, 1916, p. 12. (Useful report.)

"En la Facultad de Filosofía: Quinta conferencia de Ortega y Gasset," *La Prensa*, September 10, 1916, p. 6. (Useful report.)

"Centro Estudiantes de Filosofía y Letras: Palabras de Ortega y Gasset sobre las bellezas del alma juvenil," *La Prensa*, September 16, 1916, p. 12. (Good report.)

"En la Facultad de Filosofía: Sexta conferencia de Ortega y Gasset," *La Prensa*, September 17, 1916, p. 11. (Report.)

"Conferencia de Ortega y Gasset: En la Facultad de Filosofía," *La Prensa*, September 24, 1916, p. 10. (Report.)

"Conferencia del Señor Ortega y Gasset," *El Sol*, May 16, 1921, p. 2.

"Conferencia del Señor Ortega y Gasset," *El Sol*, May 25, 1921, p. 3.

"El arte de Marcel Proust," *El Sol*, May 10, 1922, p. 1.

"Un discurso de Ortega y Gasset: Einstein en la Residencia de Estudiantes," *El Sol*, March 10, 1923, p. 1.

"Conferencia de Ortega y Gasset: 'La juventud, el estado y el carnival'," *El Sol*, December 13, 1924, p. 8. (The lecture is in *Obras completas*, II, entitled "Origen deportiva del estado.")

"Conferencias: D. José Ortega y Gasset," *El Sol*, May 1, 1925, p. 4. ("Temas de Antropología filosofía." Substantial report.)

"La clausura de una exposición: Discurso de D. José Ortega y Gasset," *El Sol*, February 2, 1926, p. 4. (On art—partial.)

"Sociedad de Cursos y Conferencias: D. José Ortega y Gasset en la Residencia de Estudiantes," *El Sol*, June 16, 1927, p. 5. ("Estudias sobre el corazon"—full report.)

"En 'La Nación': D. José Ortega y Gasset," *La Nación* (Buenos Aires), September 1, 1928, p. 6. (Talk by Ortega in which he compares Spanish and Argentine newspapers.)

"Ortega y Gasset disertó en la Sociedad de Conferencias," *La Nación*, September 25, 1928, p. 7. ("Preambulo sobre qué es nuestra vida"—full report.)

"D. José Ortega y Gasset disertó sobre 'La edad de nuestra tiempo'," *La Natión*, October 1, 1928, p. 4. ("La edad de nuestra tiempo," full report. Cf. *El Sol*, October 26, 1928, p. 1.)

"D. José Ortega y Gasset disertó sobre 'El sexo de nuestro tiempo'," *La Nación*, October 9, 1928, p. 8. ("El sexo de nuestro tiempo," full report. Cf. *El Sol*, November 1, 1928, p. 3.)

"D. José Ortega y Gasset disertó sobre 'El nivel de nuestro tiempo',"

La Nación, October 16, 1928, p. 11. (Full report. Cf. *El Sol*, November 14, 1928, p. 2.)

"D. José Ortega y Gasset disertó sobre 'El peligro de nuestro tiempo'," *La Nación*, October 29, 1928, p. 7. (Full report. Cf. *El Sol*, November 24, 1928, p. 2.)

"D. José Ortega y Gasset inició ayer su curso en la Facultad de Filosofía y Letras," *La Nación*, November 10, 1928, pp. 8–9. (Full report.)

"D. José Ortega y Gasset dictó su segunda conferencia en la Facultad de Filosofía," *La Nación*, November 14, 1928, pp. 8–9. (Full report.)

"D. José Ortega y Gasset reanudó su curso en la Facultad de Filosofía," *La Nación*, December 25, 1928, pp. 6–7. (Full report.)

"D. José Ortega y Gasset terminió su curso de la Facultad de Filosofía," *La Nación*, December 28, 1928, pp. 6–7. (Full report.)

Reports on lectures "¿Qué es filosofía?," *El Sol*, April 10 (p. 1), 13 (p. 1), 17 (p. 7), 20 (pp. 1, 6), and 27 (pp. 1, 2), and May 4 (p. 1), 8 (pp. 1, 2), 11 (pp. 1, 6), 15 (pp. 1, 2), and 18 (pp. 1, 2), 1929. (Text is in *Obras completas*.)

"Actos de la F.U.E.: Conferencia de Don José Ortega y Gasset," *El Sol*, October 10, 1930, p. 7. (Transcription of the lecture with which *Mislon de la Universidad* was introduced. The text is not in the Spanish version, but is in the English.)

"Don José Ortega y Gasset habla en León," *Crisol*, June 27, 1931, p. 5. (Report.)

"Ortega y Gasset habla en León de la España que hay que hacer," *El Sol*, June 28, 1931, pp. 1, 12. (Text.)

"Habló ayer un gran español: Texto taquigráfico del discurso pronunciado en la Cámara por don José Ortega y Gasset," *El Sol*, July 31, 1931, p. 1. (Text and background—the text is in *Obras completas*.)

"La Camara ratifica los pederes al gobierno provisional: Un gran discurso de don José Ortega y Gasset," *Crisol*, July 31, 1931, pp. 5–6. (Text and background.)

"Una conferencia de Ortega y Gasset en Gijon: 'El hombre y su circumstancia'," *Crisol*, August 24, 1931, pp. 5–6.

"Conferencia de Don José Ortega y Gasset: Meditación sobre 'Nuestra vida' o sobre 'El hombre y su circumstancia'," *El Sol*, August 25, 1931, p. 3. (Text.)

"La sesión de ayer: Don José Ortega y Gasset y el proyecto de constitución," *Crisol*, September 5, 1931, pp. 10–12. (Text and background.)

582 : : BIBLIOGRAPHY

"La sesión de ayer: Discurso de don José Ortega y Gasset," *Crisol*, September 26, 1931, pp. 11–12. (Text and background.)

"Se discute una proposición de don José Ortega y Gasset," *Crisol*, October 30, 1931, p. 12. (Discurso and discussion—text.)

"Discurso en un debate: El Presidente de la República será elegido por el Parlamento," *El Sol*, October 31, 1931, p. 5. (Minor comments in debate.)

"Discurso de don José Ortega y Gasset: Ayer en el cine de la opera," *Crisol*, December 7, 1931, pp. 7–10. (Text and background—text is in *Obras* XI.)

"El discurso de don José Ortega y Gasset: Un llamaniento para la creación de un partido de amplitud nacional," *El Sol,* December 8, 1931, pp. 5–6. (Text and background. The text is in *Obras* XI.)

"En el centenario de un gran filósofo: Hegel y la historia de la filosofía: Conferencia de D. José Ortega y Gasset en la Residencia de señoritas—texto taquigráfico," *El Sol*, December 15, 1931, p. 4. (Text is in *Obras completas.*)

"Conferencia de don Ortega y Gasset: Hegel y la filosofía de la historia," *Crisol*, December 15, 1931, p. 8. (Report.)

" 'Nación y Trabajo': he aquí el lema de la Agrupación al Servicio de la República. . . . Elocuente brindis de don José Ortega y Gasset," *El Sol*, February 5, 1932, p. 1. (Text.)

"El Sr. Ortega y Gasset en Granada," *El Sol*, February 6, 1932, p. 1. (Short report on a talk by Ortega about the provinces.)

"Don José Ortega y Gasset en Granada," *Luz*, February 6, 1932, p. 5. (Report, less complete than in *El Sol*.)

" 'Goethe, liberador': Fragmentos de la conferencia que dió ayer tarde en el paraninfo de la Universidad el ilustre escritor don José Ortega y Gasset," *El Sol*, March 31, 1932, p. 8. (Fragmentary text with background. Text is in *Obras completas*. Cf. *Luz*, March 31, p. 5, and April 20, pp. 8–9.)

"Don José Ortega y Gasset, en Oviedo: 'La política republicana se ha de cimentar sobre dos principios: Nación y Trabajo'," *El Sol*, April 13, 1932, p. 3. (Text and background. Cf. *Luz*, April 11, 1932, p. 5.)

"Discurso de Don José Ortega y Gasset en el banquete celebrado en su honor," *El Sol*, April 12, 1932, p. 4. (Report.)

"Don José Ortega y Gasset pronunció ayer un gran discurso acerca del Estatuo de Cataluña," *El Sol*, May 14, 1932, pp. 4, 5. (Text and background. Text is also in Juan Díaz del Morel and José Ortega y Gasset, *La Reforma Agraria y El Estatuo Catalán*, Madrid: Revista de Occidente, 1932.)

"En torno el statuto de mantuvo ayer un importante debate político: Discurso de D. José Ortega y Gasset," *El Sol*, June 3, 1932, p. 3. (Text. It is also in Díaz de Moral and Ortega, *La Reforma Agraria y El Estatuo Catalán*.)

"Don José Ortega y Gasset se nuestra contrario a la universidad bilingüe," *El Sol*, July 28, 1932, p. 3. (Text.)

"Conferencia de Don José Ortega y Gasset en la Universidad de Granada," *El Sol*, October 9, 1932, p. 3. (Report. Text is in *Obras completas*. The Report included a long quotation of Ortega's opening remarks that is not in the published text. Cf. *Luz*, October 10, 1932, p. 12.)

"En la Fundación del Amo: Conferencia del ilustre professor don José Ortega y Gasset," *El Sol*, November 11, 1932, p. 8. (Short report.)

"Conferencias de D. José Ortega y Gasset: Las crises historicas y la crisis actual," *Luz*, March 24, 1933, p. 6. (Single report on six lectures "En torno a las generaciones decisivas de la evolución del pensamiento europeo." See *En torno a Galileo, Obras completas*.)

"A beneficio del crucero por el Mediterráneo: 'Qué pasa en el mundo', por el profesor Ortega y Gasset," *El Sol*, June 1, 1933, p. 10. (Full report.)

"Don José Ortega y Gasset traza un analisis hondo y sutil de la situación del mundo," *Luz*, June 1, 1933, p. 11. (Report, more forceful, but less complete than in *El Sol*.)

"A beneficio del crucero por el Mediterráneo: 'Qué pasa en el mundo', segunda conferencia del profesor Ortega y Gasset en el teatro Español," *El Sol*, June 3, 1933, p. 10. (Full report.)

"En su segunda conferencia Don José Ortega y Gasset estudia los movimientos políticos del presente: comunismo, fascismo, nacional socialismo," *Luz*, June 3, 1933, p. 11. (This reports Ortega's conclusion more effectively than *El Sol*.)

"Ayer se inauguró el II Congreso Internacional de Bibliotecas y Bibliografía con un discurso de D. José Ortega y Gasset," *El Sol*, May 21, 1935, p. 4. (Report. Text in *Obras completas*.)

"El hombre y la gente: Introducción," *La Nación*, September 20, 1939, p. 6. (Full report.)

"El hombre y la gente: La Concurrencia," *La Nación*, October 5, 1939, p. 6. (Full report.)

"El hombre y la gente: La Persona," *La Nación*, October 12, 1939, p. 6. (Full report.)

"El hombre y la gente: El Auditorio," *La Nación*, October 25, 1939, p. 6. (Full report.)

"El hombre y la gente: La Concurrencia," *La Nación,* November 1, 1939, p. 6. (Full report.)

"El hombre y la gente: El Colectivismo," *La Nación,* November 7, 1939, p. 6. (Full report.)

"Tesis para un sistema de filosofía" (text of a part of a course given 1935/36 at the University of Madrid), *Revista de Occidente,* No. 31, October 1965, pp. 1–8.

Discussion in Baruk, Danielou, Ortega y Gasset, *Hombre y Cultura en el siglo XX,* Madrid: Ediciones Guadarrama, 1957, pp. 349–367.

LETTERS (LISTED CHRONOLOGICALLY BY DATE OF PUBLICATION):

"Dos Cartas a Unamuno" in Miguel de Unamuno, *Almas de jovenes* (1908), tercera edición, Madrid: Colección Austral, Espasa-Calpe, 1958, pp. 12–15, 18–20.

Carta de Ortega a D. Manuel Aznar in "Una conferencia del Sr. Ortega y Gasset," *El Sol,* February 16, 1922, p. 1.

"Sobre el poder de la Prensa: Una carta de Don José Ortega y Gasset," *El Sol,* November 13, 1930, p. 3.

"Don José Ortega y Gasset nos hace unas interesantes manifestaciones sobre su actitud política," *Crisol,* November 17, 1931, p. 1.

"Don José Ortega y Gasset, don Gregorio Marañón y don Ramón Pérez de Ayala resuelven disolver la Agrupación al Servicio de la República," *El Sol,* October 29, 1932, p. 1.

"Una nota de don José Ortega y Gasset," *El Sol,* February 9, 1932, p. 1.

"Don José Ortega y Gasset rectifica en una carta una noticia publicada en la prensa de esta manana," *Luz,* April 1, 1933, p. 13.

"Don José Ortega y Gasset dice a *Luz* en una carta: 'Creo que la República se consolida en estas eleciones'," *Luz,* November 23, 1933, p. 16.

J. Ortega y Gasset y Francisco Navarro Ledesma, "Cartas," *Cuadernos* (Paris), No. 66, November 1962.

J. Ortega y Gasset y E. R. Curtius, "Epistolario," *Revista de Occidente,* Nos. 6 and 7, September and October 1963, pp. 329–341, 3–27.

Juan Maragall y J. Ortega y Gasset, "Epistolario," *Revista de Occidente,* No. 18, September 1964, pp. 261–271.

M. de Unamuno y J. Ortega y Gasset, "Epistolario," *Revista de Occidente,* No. 19, October 1964, pp. 3–28.

Francisco Giner de los Ríos, "Carta a Ortega," *Revista de Occidente,* No. 23, February 1965, pp. 125–133.

W. W. Norton Collection, Special Collections, Butler Library, Columbia University. (Letters between Ortega and his American publishers.)

INTERVIEWS (LISTED CHRONOLOGICALLY):

"Impresiones de Hispano-américa: Hoy llega a Madrid D. José Ortega y Gasset," *El Sol*, January 20, 1929, p. 1.

"Une Heure avec José Ortega y Gasset, philosophe espagnol," Frederic Lefèvre, *Les nouvelles literaires* (Paris), April 13, 1929, pp. 1, 8.

"Una entrevista con D. José Ortega y Gasset," *El Sol*, February 27, 1931, p. 1.

"Una cuartilla de D. José Ortega y Gasset," *El Sol*, November 18, 1931, p. 1.

"Hablando con el Sr. Ortega y Gasset después de su discurso," *Crisol*, December 7, 1931, p. 10.

"D. José Ortega y Gasset y el discurso del Sr. Maura," *El Sol*, January 13, 1932, p. 1.

"Palabras interesantes del Sr. Ortega y Gasset: La juventud, desconectada de la República," *El Sol*, July 23, 1932, p. 4.

"Don José Ortega y Gasset aconseja un gobierno puramente republicano," *Luz*, June 9, 1933, p. 16.

TRANSLATIONS (LISTED IN ORDER OF AMERICAN PUBLICATION):

José Ortega y Gasset: *The Revolt of the Masses* (1932), Authorized translation [J. R. Carey, trans.], New York: W. W. Norton and Co., 1957.

————— : *The Modern Theme* (1933), James Cleugh, trans., New York: Harper Torchbooks, 1961.

————— : *Invertebrate Spain*, Mildred Adams, trans., New York: W. W. Norton and Co., 1937.

————— : *History as a System and other Essays Toward a Philosophy of History* (1941), Helene Weyl, trans., New York: W. W. Norton and Co., 1961.

————— : *Mission of the University* (1944), Howard Lee Nostrand, trans., New York: W. W. Norton and Co., 1966.

————— : *Concord and Liberty* (1946), Helene Weyl, trans., New York: W. W. Norton and Co., 1963.

————— : *The Dehumanization of Art and other Essays on Art, Culture, and Literature* (1948), Princeton: Princeton University Press, 1968.

————— : *On Love: Aspects of a Single Theme* (1957), Toby Talbot, trans., New York: Meridian Books, 1960.

———————: *Man and People*, Willard R. Trask, trans., New York: W. W. Norton and Co., 1957.

———————: *Man and Crisis*, Mildred Adams, trans., New York: W. W. Norton and Co., 1958.

———————: *What Is Philosophy?*, Mildred Adams, trans., New York: W. W. Norton and Co., 1960.

———————: *Meditations on Quixote*, with Introduction and Notes by Julian Marias, Evelyn Rugg and Diego Marin, trans., New York: W. W. Norton and Co., 1961.

———————: *The Origin of Philosophy*, Authorized translation, Toby Talbot, trans., New York: W. W. Norton and Co., 1967.

———————: *Some Lessons in Metaphysics*, Mildred Adams, trans., New York: W. W. Norton and Co., 1969.

Other Books and Articles

Adams, Henry: *The Degradation of the Democratic Dogma*, New York: Capricorn Books, 1958.

———————: *The Education of Henry Adams*, New York: The Modern Library, 1931.

Adkins, Arthur W. H.: *Merit and Responsibility: A Study in Greek Values*, London: Oxford University Press, 1960.

Aiken, Henry David: "Philosophy and Ideology in the Nineteenth Century," Aiken, ed.: *The Age of Ideology*, New York: Mentor Books, 1956.

Alvarez del Vayo, J.: *The Last Optimist*, Charles Duffy, trans., New York: Viking Press, 1950.

American Assembly: *The Federal Government and Higher Education*, Englewood Cliffs, N. J.: Prentice-Hall, 1960.

Anon: "Natorp's Sozialpädagogik," *Educational Review*, Vol. 19, March 1900, pp. 290–5.

Aquinas, Saint Thomas: *Basic Writings*, 2 vols., Anton C. Pegis, ed., New York: Random House, 1945.

Arendt, Hannah: *Eichmann in Jerusalem*, New York: Viking Press, 1963.

———————: *The Origins of Totalitarianism*, 2nd ed., New York: Meridian Books, 1958.

Aristotle: *The Basic Works*, Richard McKeon, ed., New York: Random House, 1941.

———————: *The Metaphysics*, 2 vols., The Loeb Classical Library, Hugh Tredennick, trans., Cambridge: Harvard University Press, 1962.

—————: *Nichomachean Ethics,* The Loeb Classical Library, H. Rackham, trans., Cambridge: Harvard University Press, 1962.

—————: *Politics and Poetics,* Benjamin Jowett and Thomas Twining, trans., New York: Compass Books, 1957.

Arnold, Matthew: *Culture and Anarchy: An Essay in Political and Social Criticism,* New York: The Macmillan Co., 1883.

—————: *The Poems of Matthew Arnold,* London: Humphrey Milford, 1913.

Aron, Raymond: *The Century of Total War,* Boston: Beacon Press, 1955.

—————: *The Opium of the Intellectuals,* Terence Kilmartin, trans., New York: W. W. Norton and Co., 1962.

Arsenio Torres, José: "Philosophic Reconstruction and Social Reform in John Dewey and José Ortega y Gasset," Ph.D. Thesis, Chicago: The University of Chicago, 1954.

Auden, W. H.: "Die Bombe und das menschliche Bewusstsein," *Merkur,* 221, August 1966.

Augustine: *Basic Writings of Saint Augustine,* 2 vols., Whitney J. Oates, ed., New York: Random House, 1948.

Ayer, A. J.: *Language, Truth and Logic,* 2nd ed. (1946), New York: Dover Publications, n.d.

—————: *The Problem of Knowledge,* Baltimore: Penguin Books, 1956.

Azaña, Manuel: *Memorias intimas de Azaña,* Joaquín Arrarás, ed., Madrid: Ediciones Españolas, 1939.

Bacon, Francis: *The Essays, or Counsels, Civil and Moral,* London: A. L. Burt Co., 1883.

—————: *The New Organon and Related Writings,* Fulton H. Anderson, ed., New York: Library of Liberal Arts, 1960.

Bailyn, Bernard: *Education in the Forming of American Society,* New York: Vintage Books, 1960.

Bain, Alexander: *Education as a Science,* New York: D. Appleton and Co., 1879.

Banham, Reyner: *Theory and Design in the First Machine Age,* London: The Architectural Press, 1960.

Bantock, G. H.: *Education and Values,* London: Faber and Faber, 1965.

—————: *Education in an Industrial Society,* London: Faber and Faber, 1963.

—————: *Freedom and Authority in Education,* London: Faber and Faber, 1965.

588 : : BIBLIOGRAPHY

Barker, Ernest: *Greek Political Theory*, London: University Paperbacks, 1960.

_____: *The Political Thought of Plato and Aristotle*, New York: Dover Publications, 1959.

Barrett, William: *Irrational Man: A Study in Existential Philosophy*, Garden City, N. Y.: Doubleday Anchor Books, 1962.

Barzun, Jacques: *Classic, Romantic and Modern*, Garden City, N. Y.: Doubleday Anchor Books, 1961.

_____: *Darwin, Marx, Wagner*, 2nd ed., Garden City, N. Y.: Doubleday Anchor Books, 1958.

_____: *The House of Intellect*, New York: Harper and Brothers, 1959.

_____: *Of Human Freedom*, Boston: Little, Brown and Co., 1939.

_____: *Race: A Study in Superstition*, New York: Harper Torchbooks, 1965.

_____: *Science, The Glorious Entertainment*, New York: Harper and Row, 1964.

_____: *Teacher in America* (1945), Garden City, N. Y.: Doubleday Anchor Books, n.d.

Beck, William S.: *Modern Science and the Nature of Life*, Garden City, N. Y.: The Natural History Library, 1961.

Bell, Bernard Iddings: *Crowd Culture: An Examination of the American Way of Life*, Chicago: Gateway Editions, 1956.

Bell, Daniel: *The End of Ideology*, Glencoe, Ill.: The Free Press, 1960.

_____: *The Reforming of General Education*, New York: Columbia University Press, 1966.

_____: "The Scholar Cornered: About *The Reforming of General Education*," *The American Scholar*, Vol. 37, No. 3, Summer 1968, pp. 401–6.

Benda, Julien: *La trahison des clercs*, Paris: B. Grasset, 1957.

Bentley, Eric: *A Century of Hero-Worship*, 2nd ed., Boston: Beacon Press, 1957.

Berdyaev, Nicolas: *The Destiny of Man*, Natalie Dunndington, trans., New York: Harper Torchbooks, 1960.

Bergson, Henri: *Creative Evolution*, Arthur Mitchell, trans., New York: The Modern Library, 1944.

_____: *Matter and Memory*, N. M. Paul and W. S. Palmer, trans., Garden City, N. Y.: Doubleday Anchor Books, 1959.

_____: *Time and Free Will*, F. L. Pogson, trans., New York: Harper Torchbooks, 1960.

_____: *The Two Sources of Morality and Religion*, R. Ashley Andra and Cloudesley Brereton, trans., Garden City, N. Y.: Doubleday Anchor Books, 1956.

Bernays, Edward L., *et al.*: *The Engineering of Consent*, Norman: University of Oklahoma Press, 1955.

Bertalanffy, Ludwig von: *Modern Theories of Development*, J. H. Woodger, trans., New York: Harper Torchbooks, 1962.

Black, C. E.: *The Dynamics of Modernization*, New York: Harper Torchbooks, 1967.

Boas, George: *The Limits of Reason*, New York: Harper and Brothers, 1961.

Böhme, Günther: *Der pädagogische Beruf der Philosophie*, Munich: Ernst Reinhardt Verlag, 1968.

Bolgar, R. R.: *The Classical Heritage and Its Beneficiaries*, New York: Harper Torchbooks, 1964.

Brenan, Gerald: *The Spanish Labyrinth: An Account of the Social and Political Background of the Spanish Civil War*, paperback edition, London: Cambridge University Press, 1960.

Broudy, Harry S. and John R. Palmer: *Exemplars of Teaching Method*, Chicago: Rand McNally and Co., 1965.

Bruner, Jerome S.: *The Process of Education*, Cambridge: Harvard University Press, 1962.

Brunschvicg, Léon: *Le progrès de la conscience dans la philosophie occidentale*, 2 vols., Paris: Librairie Felix Alcan, 1927.

Buber, Martin: *Daniel: Dialogues on Realization*, Maurice S. Friedman, trans., New York: McGraw-Hill Book Co., 1965.

_____: *I and Thou*, 2nd ed., Ronald Gregor Smith, trans., New York: Charles Scribner's Sons, 1958.

_____: *Pointing the Way*, Maurice S. Friedman, trans., New York: Harper Torchbooks, 1963.

Burckhardt, Jacob: *The Civilization of the Renaissance in Italy*, 2 vols., S. G. C. Middlemore, trans., New York: Harper Torchbooks, 1958.

_____: *Force and Freedom: Reflections on History*, James Hastings Nichols, trans., Boston: Beacon Press, 1964.

_____: *On History and Historians*, Harry Zohn, trans., New York: Harper Torchbooks, 1965.

Burke, Kenneth: *A Grammar of Motives and A Rhetoric of Motives*, Cleveland: Meridian Books, 1962.

Burnet, John: *Early Greek Philosophy*, 4th ed., New York: Meridian Books, 1957.

590 :: BIBLIOGRAPHY

Burnham, James: *The Managerial Revolution*, New York: The John Day Co., 1941.

Butler, E. M.: *The Tyranny of Greece over Germany*, Boston: Beacon Press, 1958.

Campbell, Francis Stuart: *The Menace of the Herd, or Procrustes at Large*, Milwaukee: The Bruce Publishing Co., 1943.

Campo, Mario: "Paul Natorp," *The Encyclopedia of Philosophy*, Vol. 5, pp. 445–8.

Camus, Albert: *L'état de siège*, 3rd ed., Paris: Librairie Gallimard, 1948.

————: *L'homme révolté*, Paris: Librairie Gallimard, 1951.

————: *Resistance, Rebellion, and Death*, Justin O'Brien, trans., New York: Alfred A. Knopf, 1961.

Canetti, Elias: *Crowds and Power*, Carol Stewart, trans., New York: The Viking Press, 1962.

Carnap, Rudolf: *Meaning and Necessity: A Study in Semantics and Modal Logic*, Chicago: Phoenix Books, 1956.

Carpenter, Rhys: *Discontinuity in Greek Civilization*, New York: W. W. Norton and Co., 1968.

Carr, Raymond: *Spain: 1808–1939*, London: Oxford University Press, 1966.

Cascalès, Charles: *L'humanisme d'Ortega y Gasset*, Paris: Presses Universitaires de France, 1957.

Cassirer, Ernst: *An Essay on Man*, New Haven: Yale University Press, 1944.

————: "Hermann Cohen," in Hermann Cohen: *Schriften zur Philosophie und Zeitgeschichte*, Berlin: Akademie-Verlag, 1928, pp. ix–xvi.

————: *The Logic of the Humanities*, Clarence Smith Howe, trans., New Haven: Yale University Press, 1961.

————: *The Myth of the State*, New Haven: Yale University Press, 1946.

————: *The Question of Jean-Jacques Rousseau*, Peter Gay, trans., Bloomington: Indiana University Press, 1963.

————: "Paul Natorp," *Kant-Studien*, Band 30, 1925, pp. 273–298.

————: *The Philosophy of Symbolic Forms*, 3 vols., Ralph Manheim, trans., New Haven: Yale University Press, 1953, 1955, 1957.

————: *The Philosophy of the Enlightenment*, F. C. A. Koelln and J. P. Pettegrove, trans., Boston: Beacon Press, 1955.

_____: *The Problem of Knowledge,* Woglom and Hendel, trans., New Haven: Yale University Press, 1950.

_____: *Rousseau, Kant, and Goethe,* Gutmann, Kristeller, and Randall, trans., New York: Harper Torchbooks, 1963.

_____: *Substance and Function* and *Einstein's Theory of Relativity,* Swabey and Swabey, trans., New York: Dover Publications, 1953.

Castelli, Enrico: *L'enquête quotidienne,* Enrichetta Valenziani, trans., Paris: Presses Universitaires de France, 1959.

_____: *Introduction à une phénoménologie de notre époque,* Paris: Hermann et Companie, 1949.

_____: *Le temps harcelant,* Paris: Presses Universitaires de France, 1952.

Cervantes: *Novelas ejemplares,* texto íntegro, colección hispánica, Garden City, N. Y.: Doubleday and Co., 1962.

Chase, Stuart: *The Tyranny of Words,* New York: Harcourt, Brace and Co., 1938.

Clough, Rosa Trillo: *Futurism,* New York: Philosophical Library, 1961.

Cohen, Hermann: *Aesthetik des reinen Gefühls,* 2 vols., Berlin: Bruno Cassirer, 1912.

_____: *Ethik des reinen Willens,* Berlin: Bruno Cassirer, 1904.

_____: *Kants Begründung der Aesthetik,* Berlin: Ferd. Dümmlers Verlagsbuchhandlung, 1889.

_____: *Kants Begründung der Ethik,* 2nd ed., Berlin: Bruno Cassirer, 1910.

_____: *Kants Theorie der Erfahrung,* Berlin: Ferd. Dümmlers Verlagsbuchhandlung, 1871.

_____: *Logik der reinen Erkenntnis,* 3rd ed., Berlin: Bruno Cassirer, 1922.

_____: *Schriften zur Philosophie und Zeitgeschichte,* Berlin: Adademie-Verlag, 1928.

_____: *Die systematischen Begriff in Kants vorkritischen Schriften nach ihren Verhältnisse zum Kritischen Idealismus,* Weimar: Hofbuchdruckerei, 1873.

Coleridge, Samuel Taylor: *Biographia Literaria,* George Watson, ed., New York: Everyman's Library, 1956.

Commission on the Humanities: *Report of the Commission on the Humanities,* New York: The American Council of Learned Societies, 1964.

592 : : BIBLIOGRAPHY

Committee on the Objectives of General Education: *General Education in a Free Society*, Cambridge: Harvard University Press, 1945.

Conant, James Bryant: *The Education of American Teachers*, New York: McGraw-Hill Book Co., 1963.

Cornford, F. M.: *Principium Sapientiae: A Study of the Origins of Greek Philosophical Thought*, New York: Harper Torchbooks, 1965.

—————: *The Unwritten Philosophy and Other Essays*, Cambridge: Cambridge University Press, 1967.

Costa, Joaquín: *El arbolado y la patria*, Madrid: Biblioteca Costa, 1912.

—————: *Ideario de Costa*, 3rd ed., José García Marcadal, ed., Madrid: Biblioteca Nueva, 1936.

—————: *Maestro, escuela y patria*, Madrid: Biblioteca Costa, 1916.

Cram, Ralph Adams: *The End of Democracy*, Boston: Marshall Jones Co., 1937.

—————: "The Revolt of the Masses," *The Atlantic Monthly Bookshelf*, December 1932.

Cremin, Lawrence A.: *The Genius of American Education*, Pittsburgh: University of Pittsburgh Press, 1965.

—————: *The Transformation of the School*, New York: Alfred A. Knopf, 1961.

—————: *The Wonderful World of Ellwood Patterson Cubberley*, New York: Teachers College Press, 1965.

Crick, Bernard: *In Defense of Politics*, revised ed., Baltimore: Penguin Books, 1964.

Daudet, Léon: *Contre l'esprit allemand: de Kant à Krupp*, Paris: Blond et Gay, 1916.

de Grazia, Sebastian: *Of Time, Work, and Leisure*, Garden City, N. Y.: Doubleday Anchor Books, 1964.

Dewey, John: *Art as Experience*, New York: Capricorn Books, 1958.

—————: *Democracy and Education*, New York: The Macmillan Co., 1916.

—————: *Experience and Nature*, 2nd ed., New York: Dover Publications, 1958.

—————: *Freedom and Culture*, New York: Capricorn Books, 1963.

—————: *German Philosophy and Politics*, New York: Henry Holt and Co., 1915.

—————: *The Quest for Certainty*, New York: Capricorn Books, 1960.

—————: *Theory of Valuation*, International Encyclopedia of Unified

Science, Vol. II, No. 4, Chicago: University of Chicago Press, 1939.

Díaz del Moral, Juan: *Historia de las agitaciones campesinas andaluzas*, Madrid: Alianza Editorial, 1967.

Díaz-Plaja, Guillermo: *Modernismo frente a noventa y ocho*, Madrid: Espasa-Calpe, 1951.

Diccionario de literatura española, 3rd ed., Madrid: Revista de Occidente, 1964.

Díez del Corral, Luis: *El Rapto de Europa*, 2nd ed., Madrid: Revista de Occidente, 1962.

Dilthey, Wilhelm: *Der Aufbau der geschichtlichen Welt in den Geisteswissenschaften*, 4th ed., *Gesammelte Schriften*, Band VII, Stuttgart: B. G. Teubner Verlagsgesellchaft, 1958.

——————: *Briefwechsel zwischen Wilhelm Dilthey und Graf Paul Yorck von Wartenburg*, Halle (Saale): Max Niemeyer Verlag, 1923.

——————: *Einleitung in die Geisteswissenschaften*, 5th ed., *Gesammelte Schriften*, Band I, Stuttgart: B. G. Teubner Verlagsgesellschaft, 1959.

——————: *Die Geistige Welt: Einleitung in die Philosophie des Lebens*, 2 vols., 4th ed., *Gesammelte Schriften*, Bande V und VI, Stuttgart:: B. G. Teubner Verlagsgesellschaft, 1957, 1958.

——————: *Pädagogik: Geschichte und Grundlinien des Systems*, 3rd ed., *Gesammelte Schriften*, Band IX, Stuttgart: B. G. Teubner Verlagsgesellschaft, 1960.

——————: *Weltanschauung und Analyse des Menschen seit Renaissance und Reformation*, 7th ed., *Gesammelte Schriften*, Band II, Stuttgart: B. G. Teubner Verlagsgesellschaft, 1957.

Djilas, Milovan: *The New Class: An Analysis of the Communist System*, New York: Frederick A. Praeger, 1957.

Dobbins, Charles G., ed.: *Higher Education and the Federal Government*, Washington: American Council on Education, 1963.

Dostoevsky, Feodor M.: *Notes from Underground and the Grand Inquisitor*, Ralph E. Matlaw, trans., New York: E. P. Dutton, 1960.

Duffy, Sister Mary Terese Avila: "José Ortega y Gasset: The Creation of a Literary Genre for Philosophy," Ph.D. Thesis, Madison: University of Wisconsin, 1966.

Dussort, Henri: *L'école de Marburg*, Paris: Presses Universitaires de France, 1963.

Dworkin, Martin S.: "A Dedicated Technocrat," *The Dalhousie Review*, Vol. 45, No. 2, 1965, pp. 209–212.

—————: "Disagreement: The Situation of Reason," *The Scientific Monthly*, Vol. LXXV, No. 2, August 1952, pp. 117–9.

—————: "Fiction and Teaching," foreword to Howard Mumford Jones: *Jeffersonianism and the American Novel*, New York: Teachers College Press, 1966.

—————: "John Dewey: A Centennial Review," in Dworkin, ed.: *Dewey on Education, Selections*, New York: Teachers College Press, 1959. Pp. 1–18.

—————: "Seeing for Ourselves: Notes on the Movie Art and Industry, Critics and Audiences," *Journal of Aesthetic Education*, Vol. 3, No. 3, July 1969. pp. 45–55.

—————: "Toward An Image Curriculum: Some Questions and Cautions," *Journal of Aesthetic Education*, Vol. 4, No. 2, April 1970, pp. 129–132.

Earle, Edward Mead, ed.: *Makers of Modern Strategy: Military Thought from Machiavelli to Hitler*, Princeton: Princeton University Press, 1943.

Eaton, Howard O.: *The Austrian Philosophy of Value*, Norman: University of Oklahoma Press, 1930.

Eliot, T. S.: "The Man of Letters and the Future of Europe," *The Sewanee Review*, Vol. LIII, No. 3, Summer 1945, pp. 333–342.

—————: *Notes Towards the Definition of Culture*, New York: Harcourt, Brace and Co., 1949.

—————: *To Criticize the Critic*, New York: Farrar, Straus and Giroux, 1965.

Ellul, Jacques: *The Political Illusion*, Konrad Kallen, trans., New York: Alfred A. Knopf, 1967.

—————: *Propagandes*, Paris: Librairie Armand Colin, 1962.

—————: *The Technological Society*, John Wilkinson, trans., New York: Alfred A. Knopf, 1964.

Emerson, Ralph Waldo: *Selections from Ralph Waldo Emerson*, Stephan E. Whicher, ed., Boston: Houghton Mifflin Co., 1957.

—————: *The Works of Ralph Waldo Emerson*, 5 vols., New York: Hearst's International Library, 1914.

Epictetus: *The Discourses as Reported by Arrian*, 2 vols., The Loeb Classical Library, W. A. Oldfather, trans., Cambridge: Harvard University Press, 1961, 1966.

Farneti, Paolo: *Theodor Geiger e la coscienza della società industriale*, Torino: Edizioni Giappichelli, 1966.

Fell, Joseph P.: *Emotion in the Thought of Sartre*, New York: Columbia University Press, 1965.

Ferkiss, Victor C.: *Technological Man: The Myth and the Reality*, New York: George Braziller, 1969.

Fernández Almago, Melchor: *Historia del reinado de Don Alfonso XIII*, 2nd ed., Barcelona: Montaner y Simon, 1934.

Fernandez de la Mora, Gonzalo: *Ortega y la 98*, Madrid: Ediciones Rialp, 1961.

Ferrater Mora, José: *Obras selectas*, 2 vols., Madrid: Revista de Occidente, 1967.

——————: *Ortega y Gasset: An Outline of His Philosophy*, revised ed., New Haven: Yale University Press, 1963.

Fichte, Johann Gottlieb: *Grundlage der gesamten Wissenschaftslehre*, Hamburg: Verlag von Felix Meiner, 1956.

——————: *The Popular Works of Johann Gottlieb Fichte*, William Smith, trans., 4th ed., 2 vols., London: Trübner and Co., 1889.

——————: *The Vocation of Man*, Roderick M. Chisholm, trans., New York: The Library of Liberal Arts, 1956.

Finley, M. I.: *The World of Odysseus*, revised edition, New York: The Viking Press, 1965.

Frankel, Charles: *The Case for Modern Man*, Boston: Beacon Press, 1959.

Freeman, Kathleen, trans.: *Ancilla to the Pre-Socratic Philosophers*, Cambridge: Harvard University Press, 1956.

——————: *Companion to the Pre-Socratic Philosophers*, 2nd ed., Cambridge: Harvard University Press, 1966.

Friedländer, Paul: *Plato, An Introduction*, Hans Meyerhoff, trans., New York: Harper Torchbooks, 1964.

Friedman, Maurice S.: *Martin Buber: The Life of Dialogue*, New York: Harper Torchbooks, 1960.

Friedrich, Carl J.: *The New Belief in the Common Man*, Boston: Little, Brown and Co., 1943.

Friess, Horace L.: "Paul Natorp," *Encyclopedia of the Social Sciences*, Vol. II, p. 283.

Fustel de Coulanges, Numa: *The Ancient City*, Willard Small, trans., Garden City, N. Y.: Doubleday Anchor Books, n.d.

Galileo: *Dialogues Concerning Two New Sciences*, Henry Crew and Alfonso de Salvo, trans., New York: Dover Publications, n.d.

Garagorri, Paulino: *Ejercicios intelectuales*, Madrid: Revista de Occidente, 1967.

——————: *Ortega, una reforma de la filosofía*, Madrid: Revista de Occidente, 1958.

—————: *Relacciones y disputaciones orteguianas*, Madrid: Taurus Ediciones, 1965.

—————: *Unamuno, Ortega, Zubiri en la filosofía española*, Madrid: Editorial Plenitud, 1968.

García Marti, Victoriano: "Comentarios del día: Las conferencias de Ortega y Gasset," *Voz*, April 30, 1929.

García Morente, Manuel: *Ensayos*, Madrid: Revista de Occidente, 1945.

Gay, Peter: *The Enlightenment: An Interpretation*, Vol. I: "The Rise of Modern Paganism," New York: Alfred A. Knopf, 1967.

Geiger, Theodor: *Ideologie und Wahrheit*, Stuttgart: Humboldt, 1953.

Gentile, Maria Teresa: *Immagine e parola nella formazione dell'uomo*, Rome: Armando Armando Editore, 1965.

Gilbert, Katharine Everett and Helmut Kuhn: *A History of Esthetics*, revised edition, Bloomington: Indiana University Press, 1954.

Goebbels, Paul Joseph: *The Goebbels Diaries*, Louis P. Lochner, trans., New York: The Fireside Press, 1948.

Goethe, Johann Wolfgang von: *Wilhelm Meister's Apprenticeship*, Thomas Carlyle, trans., New York: Collier Books, 1962.

Gorman, William: "Ellul—A Prophetic Voice," *The Center Magazine*, Vol. I, No. 1, October–November 1967, pp. 34–7.

Granell, Manuel: *Ortega y su filosofía*, Madrid: Revista de Occidente, 1960.

Grube, G. M. A.: *Plato's Thought*, Boston: Beacon Press, 1958.

Guéhenno, Jean: *Jean-Jacques Rousseau*, 2 vols., John and Doreen Weightman, trans., New York: Columbia University Press, 1966.

Guthrie, W. K. C.: *A History of Greek Philosophy*, 2 vols., Cambridge: Cambridge University Press, 1965.

Hall, Robert William: *Plato and the Individual*, The Hague: Martinus Nijhoff, 1963.

Hamilton, Alexander, James Madison, and John Jay: *The Federalist or, The New Constitution*, New York: Everyman's Library, Dutton, 1961.

Hamlyn, D. W.: "History of Epistemology," *The Encyclopedia of Philosophy*, Vol. 3, pp. 8–38.

Hansen, N. R.: *Patterns of Discovery*, London: The Scientific Book Guild, 1962.

Harrington, Michael: *The Accidental Century*, New York: The Macmillan Co., 1965.

Harris, William Torrey: *Three Papers on Manual Training*, U.S. Bureau of Education, Washington: Government Printing Office, 1906.

Havelock, Eric A.: *The Liberal Temper in Greek Politics*, New Haven: Yale University Press, 1957.

——————: *Preface to Plato*, Cambridge: Harvard University Press, 1963.

Hegel, G. W. F.: *The Phenomenology of Mind*, J. B. Baillie, trans., New York: Harper Torchbooks, 1967.

——————: *Philosophy of Right*, T. M. Knox, trans., London: Oxford University Press, 1952.

——————: *Political Writings*, T. M. Knox, trans., London:: Oxford University Press, 1964.

——————: *Wissenschaft der Logik*, Hamburg: Verlag von Felix Meiner, 1963.

Heidegger, Martin: *Being and Time*, John Macquarrie and Edward Robinson, trans., New York: Harper and Row, 1962.

——————: *Existence and Being*, Werner Brock, ed., Chicago: Gateway Editions, 1949.

——————: *Kant and the Problem of Metaphysics*, James S. Churchill, trans., Bloomington: Indiana University Press, 1962.

Heine, Heinrich: *Religion and Philosophy in Germany*, John Snodgrass, trans., Boston: Beacon Press, 1959.

Helvétius, Claude Adrien: *A Treatise on Man: His Intellectual Faculties and His Education*, W. Hooper, trans., London: Law and Robinson, 1777.

Henderson, Ernest N.: "Pedagogy," in Paul Monroe, ed.: *A Cyclopedia of Education* (1913), Vol. 4, pp. 621–2.

Heraclitus: "On the Universe," in *Hippocrates—IV, Heracleitus*, W. H. S. Jones, trans., The Loeb Classical Library, Cambridge: Harvard University Press, 1959.

Herbart, Johann Friedrich: *Letters and Lectures on Education*, Felkin and Felkin, trans., London: Swan Sonnenschein and Co., 1895.

——————: *The Science of Education: Its General Principles Deduced from Its Aim*, Felkin and Felkin, trans., Boston: D. C. Heath and Co., n.d.

Hesiod: *Hesiod, The Homeric Hymns, and Homerica*, The Loeb Classical Library, Hugh G. Evelyn-White, trans., Cambridge: Harvard University Press, 1964.

Hobbes: *Leviathan: Parts One and Two*, New York: The Library of Liberal Arts, 1958.

Hofstadter, Richard and Wilson Smith: *American Higher Education: A Documentary History*, 2 vols., Chicago: University of Chicago Press, 1961.

Hoggart, Richard: *The Uses of Literacy*, Boston: Beacon Press, 1961.

Holborn, Hajo: *The Political Collapse of Europe*, New York: Alfred A. Knopf, 1959.

—————: "Wilhelm Dilthey and the Critique of Historical Reason," *The Journal of the History of Ideas*, Vol. XI, No. 1, January 1950, pp. 93–118.

Hook, Sidney: *Political Power and Personal Freedom*, New York: Criterion Books, 1959.

Hughes, H. Stuart: *Consciousness and Society: The Reorientation of European Social Thought, 1890–1930*, New York: Vintage Books, 1961.

—————: *The Obstructed Path: French Social Thought in the Years of Desperation, 1930–1960*, New York: Harper and Row, 1968.

Huizinga, Johan: *Homo Ludens: A Study of the Play Element in Culture*, R. F. C. Hull, trans., Boston: Beacon Press, 1955.

Husserl, Edmund: *Ideas: General Introduction to Pure Phenomenology*, W. R. Boyce Gibson, trans., New York: Collier Books, 1962.

—————: "Phenomenology," *Encyclopedia Britannica*, 14th ed., Vol. XVII, pp. 700–2.

—————: *Phenomenology and the Crisis of Philosophy*, Quentin Lauer, trans., New York: Harper Torchbooks, 1965.

Hutchins, Robert Maynard: *The Higher Learning in America*, New Haven: Yale University Press, 1962.

Innis, Harold A.: *The Bias of Communications*, Toronto: University of Toronto Press, 1951.

Institución Cultural Española: *Anales*, 3 vols., Buenos Aires: Institución Cultural Española, 1953.

Jackson, Gabriel: *The Spanish Republic and the Civil War*, Princeton: Princeton University Press, 1965.

Jaeger, Werner: *Aristotle: Fundamentals of the History of His Development*, Richard Robinson, trans., 2nd ed., London: Oxford University Press, 1962.

—————: *Paideia: The Ideals of Greek Culture*, 3 vols., Gilbert Highet, trans., New York: Oxford University Press, 1939.

—————: *The Theology of the Early Greek Philosophers*, Oxford: Oxford University Press, 1947.

James, William: *Pragmatism*, New York: Meridian Books, 1955.

——————: *The Varieties of Religious Experience: A Study in Human Nature*, New York: The Modern Library, n.d.

——————: *The Will to Believe and Other Essays*, New York: Dover Publications, 1956.

Jaspers, Karl: *The Future of Mankind*, E. B. Ashton, trans., Chicago: The University of Chicago Press, 1961.

——————: *The Idea of the University*, Karl W. Deutsch, trans., Boston: Beacon Press, 1959.

——————: *Man in the Modern Age*, Eden and Cedar Paul, trans., Garden City, N. Y.: Doubleday Anchor Books, n.d.

——————: *Philosophy*, Vol. 1, E. B. Ashton, trans., Chicago: The University of Chicago Press, 1969.

——————: *Philosophy and the World, Selected Essays*, E. B. Ashton, trans., Chicago: Gateway Editions, 1963.

Jato, David: *La rebelión de los estudiantes*, Madrid: CIES, 1953.

Jennings, H. S.: "Doctrines Held as Vitalism," *The American Naturalist*, Vol. XLIII, No. 559, July 1913, pp. 385–417.

Jeschke, Hans: *Die Generation von 1898 in Spanien, Beihefte zur Zeitschrift für Romanische Philologie*, Heft 83, Halle (Saale): Max Niemeyer Verlag, 1934.

Jobit, Pierre: *Les éducateurs de l'Espagne contemporaine*, 2 vols., Paris: E. de Boccard, 1936.

Johnson, Samuel: *A Johnson Reader*, E. L. McAdam, Jr., and George Milne, eds., New York: Pantheon Books, 1964.

Jones, Howard Mumford: *Education and World Tragedy*, Cambridge: Harvard University Press, 1946.

Kant, Immanuel: *Anthropologie in pragmatischer Hinsicht*, in *Werk in sechs Bänden*, Band VI, Frankfurt: Insel-Verlag, 1964.

——————: *Critique of Judgment*, J. H. Bernard, trans., New York: Hafner Publishing Co., 1951.

——————: *Critique of Practical Reason*, Lewis W. Beck, trans., New York: The Library of Liberal Arts, 1956.

——————: *Critique of Pure Reason*, Norman Kemp Smith, trans., New York: St. Martin's Press, 1965.

——————: *Foundations of the Metaphysics of Morals*, Lewis W. Beck, trans., New York: The Library of Liberal Arts, 1959.

——————: *On History*, Lewis W. Beck, trans., New York: The Library of Liberal Arts, 1963.

Kaufmann, Walter: *Critique of Religion and Philosophy*, Garden City, N. Y.: Doubleday Anchor Books, 1961.

—————: *Nietzsche: Philosopher, Psychologist, Antichrist*, New York: Meridian Books, 1956.

Kerr, Clark: *The Uses of the University*, Cambridge: Harvard University Press, 1964.

—————, et al.: *Industrialism and Industrial Man*, Cambridge: Harvard University Press, 1960.

Keyserling, Count Hermann: *Europe*, Maurice Samuel, trans., New York: Harcourt, Brace and Co., 1928.

Khaldûn, Ibn: *The Muqaddimah: An Introduction to History*, 3 vols., Franz Rosenthal, trans., New York: Pantheon Books, 1958.

Kirk, G. S.: *Homer and the Epic*, Cambridge: Cambridge University Press, 1965.

Kirk, G. S. and J. E. Raven: *The Pre-Socratic Philosophers: A Critical History with a Selection of Texts*, Cambridge: Cambridge University Press, 1962.

Köhler, Wolfgang: *The Place of Value in a World of Facts*, New York: Meridian Books, 1959.

Kohn, Hans: *The Idea of Nationalism: A Study of Its Origin and Background*, New York: Collier Books, 1967.

—————: *The Mind of Germany: The Education of a Nation*, New York: Harper Torchbooks, 1965.

Kornhauser, William: *The Politics of Mass Society*, Glencoe, Ill.: The Free Press, 1959.

Kristol, Irving: "American Intellectuals and Foreign Policy," *Foreign Affairs*, Vol. 45, No. 4, July 1967, pp. 594–609.

Kroeber, A. L. and Clyde Kluckhohn: *Culture: A Critical Review of Concepts and Definitions*, New York: Vintage Books, 1963.

Krutch, Joseph Wood: *The Modern Temper*, New York: Harvest Books, 1956.

Kuhn, Thomas: *The Structure of Scientific Revolutions*, Chicago: Phoenix Books, 1964.

Laín Entralgo, Pedro: *España como problema*, 3rd ed., Madrid: Aguilar, 1962.

—————: *La espera y la esperanza: Historia y teoría del esperar humano*, 3rd ed., Madrid: Revista de Occidente, 1962.

—————: *Teoría y realidad del Otro*, 2 vols., Madrid: Revista de Occidente, 1961.

Landes, David S.: *The Unbound Prometheus: Technological Change and*

Industrial Development in Western Europe from 1750 to the Present, Cambridge: Cambridge University Press, 1969.

Langan, Thomas: *The Meaning of Heidegger: A Critical Study of An Existentialist Phenomenology*, New York: Columbia University Press, 1961.

Lasch, Christopher: "The Cold War: Revisited and Re-visioned," *The New York Times Magazine*, January 14, 1968.

Leavis, F. R.: *Education and the University*, new edition, London: Chatto and Windus, 1948.

Leavis, F. R. and Denys Thompson: *Culture and Environment*, London: Chatto and Windus, 1937.

Leavis, F. R.: *Two Cultures? The Significance of C. P. Snow*, and Yudkin, Michael: *Sir Charles Snow's Rede Lectures*, New York: Pantheon Books, 1963.

Leavis, Q. D.: *Fiction and the Reading Public*, New York: Russell and Russell, 1966.

Le Bon, Gustave: *The Crowd: A Study of the Popular Mind*, New York: Compass Books, 1960.

Lee, Gerald Stanley: *Crowds, A Moving-Picture of Democracy*, Garden City, N. Y.: Doubleday, Page and Co., 1913.

Leibniz, Gottfried Wilhelm: *Selections*, Philip P. Wiener, ed., New York: Charles Scribner's Sons, 1951.

Lenin, V. I.: *What Is to Be Done?*, New York: International Library, 1929.

Leser, Hermann: *Das pädagogische Problem*, Munich: Oldenburg, 1925.

Levy, Heinrich: "Paul Natorps praktische Philosophie," *Kant-Studien*, Band 31, 1926, pp. 311–329.

Lewis, Sinclair: *Babbitt*, New York: Signet Classics Editions, 1961.

Lichtheim, George: *The Concept of Ideology and Other Essays*, New York: Vintage Books, 1967.

Lippmann, Walter: *Drift and Mastery: An Attempt to Diagnose the Current Unrest*, Englewood Cliffs, N. J.: Spectrum Books, 1961.

——————: *Public Opinion*, New York: The Macmillan Co., 1922.

Litt, Theodor, *Individuum und Gemeinschaft: Grundlegung der Kulturphilosophie*, 2nd ed., Leipzig: Verlag von B. G. Teubner, 1924.

Locke, John: *Locke on Politics, Religion, and Education*, Maurice Cranston, ed., New York: Collier Books, 1965.

——————: *The Second Treatise of Government*, Thomas P. Peardon, ed., New York: The Library of Liberal Arts, 1952.

López-Campillo, Evelyne: "Ortega: 'El Imparcial' y las Juntas," *Revista de Occidente,* No. 75, June 1969, pp. 311–7.

López-Morillas, Juan: *El Krausismo español: perfil de un aventura intellectual,* Mexico: Fondo de Cultura Económica, 1956.

—————: "Universities and their Mission," *Brown Alumni Monthly,* Vol. 56, No. 5, February 1956, pp. 14–16.

Lowie, Robert H.: *Primitive Society,* New York: Boni and Liveright, 1920.

Luzuriaga, Lorenzo: "Las fundaciones de Ortega y Gasset," in Instituto de Filosofía: *Homenaje a Ortega y Gasset,* Caracas: Universidad Central de Venezuela, 1958.

McClintock, Jean and Robert: "Architecture and Pedagogy," *The Journal of Aesthetic Education,* Vol. 2, No. 4, October 1968, pp. 59–77.

McClintock, Robert: "Machines and Vitalists: Reflections on the Ideology of Cybernetics," *The American Scholar,* Vol. 35, No. 2, Spring 1966, pp. 249–257.

—————: "Ortega y Gasset Rediscovered," *Columbia Forum,* Vol. XIII, No. 2, Summer 1970, pp. 33–6.

—————: "Review of *The Spanish Press* by Henry F. Schulte," *Comparative Education Review,* Vol. XIII, No. 2, June 1969, pp. 235–8.

McDermott, John: "Technology: the Opiate of the Intellectuals," *The New York Review of Books,* Vol. XIII, No. 2, July 31, 1969, pp. 25–35.

Macdonald, Dwight: *Against the American Grain,* New York: Random House, 1962.

MacLeish, Archibald: "The Revolt of the Diminished Man," *Saturday Review,* Vol. LII, No. 23, June 7, 1969, pp. 16–19, 61.

McLuhan, Marshall: *Understanding Media,* New York: McGraw-Hill, 1965.

McManners, John: *European History, 1789–1914: Men, Machines and Freedom,* New York: Harper Torchbooks, 1969.

Machiavelli, Niccolo: *The Prince and the Discourses,* New York: The Modern Library, 1940.

Madariaga, Salvador de: *De Galdós a Lorca,* Buenos Aires: Editorial Sudamericana, 1960.

—————: *Spain: A Modern History,* New York: Frederick A. Praeger, 1958.

Maetzu, María de: *Antología siglo XX: Prosistas españoles,* 3rd ed., Buenos Aires: Espasa Calpe, 1949.

Mallo, Jerónimo:: "La discusión entre católicos sobre la filosofía de Ortega," *Cuadernos Americanos*, 1962, No. 2, pp. 157–166.

Mánnheim, Karl: *Ideology and Utopia: An Introduction to the Sociology of Knowledge*, Louis Wirth and Edward Shils, trans., New York: Harcourt, Brace and Co., 1949.

——————: *Man and Society in an Age of Reconstruction*, New York: Harcourt, Brace and Co., 1954.

Marcuse, Herbert, Barrington Moore, Jr., and Robert Paul Wolff: *A Critique of Pure Tolerance*, Boston: Beacon Press, 1965.

Marek, Kurt W.: *Yestermorrow: Notes on Man's Progress*, Ralph Manheim, trans., New York: Alfred A. Knopf, 1961.

Marías, Julián: *La escuela de Madrid*, in *Obras*, tomo V, Madrid: Revista de Occidente, 1960.

——————: *Ortega, I: Circunstancia y vocación*, Madrid: Revista de Occidente, 1960.

Maritain, Jacques: *Humanisme intégral*, nouvelle édition, Paris: Ferdinand Aubier, 1936.

Markmann, Charles Lam: *The Noblest Cry: A History of the American Civil Liberties Union*, New York: St. Martin's Press, 1965.

Marrero, Domingo: *El Centauro: Persona y pensamiento de Ortega y Gasset*, Santurce, Puerto Rico: Impr. Soltero, 1951.

Martin, Kingsley: *French Liberal Thought in the Eighteenth Century*, New York: Harper Torchbooks, 1962.

Martinetti, Ronald: "I've Been Reading: Wild Bill Buckley," *Columbia Forum*, Fall 1967, p. 45.

Marx, Karl: *Capital: A Critique of Political Economy*, Vol. I, *The Process of Capitalist Production*, edited by Frederick Engels; Moore and Aveling, trans. (1906), New York: The Modern Library, n.d.

Marx, Karl and Frederick Engels: *The German Ideology*, R. Pascal, ed., New York: International Publishers, 1947.

——————: *Selected Works*, 2 vols., Moscow: Foreign Languages Publishing House, 1962.

Mayer, Martin: "The Educational Goals of James B. Conant," *Commentary*, December 1961, pp. 537–40.

Mazzetti, Roberto: *Società e educazione nella Spagna contemporanea*, Florence: La Nuova Italia, 1966.

Meinecke, Friedrich: *Machiavellism: The Doctrine of Raison d'Etat and Its Place in Modern Thought*, Douglas Stark, trans., New Haven: Yale University Press, 1957.

Merleau-Ponty, Maurice: *Humanisme et terreur: essai sur le probleme communiste*, Paris: Editions Gallimard, 1947.

——————: *Phénoménologie de la perception*, Paris: Editions Gallimard, 1945.

——————: *Sens et Non-sens*, 5th ed., Paris: Nagel, 1965.

——————: *La structure du comportement*, 5th ed., Paris: Presses Universitaires de France, 1963.

Merriam, Charles E.: *The New Democracy and the New Despotism*, New York: Whittlesey House, 1939.

Meyerhardt, M. W.: "Paul Natorp's Social Pedagogy," *The Pedagogical Seminary*, Vol. 23, March 1916, pp. 51–62.

Meyerhoff, Hans, ed.: *The Philosophy of History in Our Time*, Garden City, N. Y.: Doubleday Anchor Books, 1959.

Mill, J. S.: *On Liberty*, Alburey Castell, ed., New York: Appleton-Century-Crofts, 1947.

Miller, Perry: *Jonathan Edwards*, New York: Meridian Books, 1959.

Mills, C. Wright: *The Power Elite*, New York: Oxford University Press, 1959.

Montaigne, Michel Eyquem de: *Selected Essays*, Cotton-Hazlitt, trans., New York: The Modern Library, 1949.

——————: *Ouevres complètes*, Paris: Bibliothèque de la Pléiade, 1962.

Moravia, Alberto: *Man as an End: A Defense of Humanism*, Bernard Wall, trans., New York: The Noonday Press, 1966.

Mori, Arturo, ed.: *Crónica de las Cortes Constituyentes de la Segunda República Española*, vols., 1–4, 6, 7, and 9, Madrid: M. Aguilar, 1932.

Morón, Guillermo: *Historia política de José Ortega y Gasset*, Mexico: Ediciones Oasis, 1960.

Mowrer, Richard: "Unrest in Spain," *The New Leader*, Vol. XXXIX, No. 7, February 13, 1956, p. 14.

Muirhead, J. H.: *German Philosophy in Relation to the War*, London: John Murray, 1915.

Muller, Herbert J.: *Freedom in the Ancient World*, New York: Harper and Brothers, 1961.

Mumford, Lewis: *Technics and Civilization*, New York: Harbinger Books, 1963.

Murray, Gilbert, *et al.*: *The Oxford Pamphlets*, London: Oxford University Press, 1914, 1915, 1916.

Nagel, Ernest: "Mechanistic Explanation and Organismic Biology," *Phi-*

losophy and Phenomenological Research, Vol. XI, No. 3, March 1951, pp. 327–338.

Natorp, Paul: *Gesammelte Abhandlungen zur Sozialpädagogik,* 2nd ed., Stuttgart: Fr. Frommanns Verlag, 1922.

—————: *Der Idealismus Pestalozzis,* Leipzig: Felix Meiner, 1919.

—————: *Kant über Krieg und Frieden,* Erlangen: Verlag der Philosophischen Akademie, 1924.

—————: *Philosophie: Ihr Problem und ihre Probleme,* 2nd ed., Göttingen: Dandenhoeck und Ruprecht, 1918.

—————: *Philosophische Systematik,* Hans Natorp, ed., Hamburg: Verlag von Felix Meiner, 1958.

—————: *Platos Ideenlehre: Ein Einführung in den Idealismus,* Leipzig: Verlag von Dürr'schen Buchhandlung, 1903.

—————: *Sozialidealismus: Neue Richtlinien sozialer Erziehung,* 2nd ed., Berlin: Verlag von Julius Springer, 1922.

—————: *Sozialpädagogik: Theorie der Willenserziehung auf der Grundlage der Gemeinschaft,* 3rd ed., Stuttgart: Fr. Frommanns Verlag, 1909.

—————: *Vorlesungen über praktische Philosophie,* Erlangen: Verlag der Philosophischen Akademic, 1925.

Nef, John U.: *Cultural Foundations of Industrial Civilization,* New York: Harper Torchbooks, 1960.

—————: *Western Civilization since the Renaissance: Peace, War, Industry and the Arts,* New York: Harper Torchbooks, 1963.

Neumann, Sigmund: *Permanent Revolution: Totalitarianism in the Age of Civil War,* 2nd ed., New York: Frederick A. Praeger, 1965.

Nietzsche, Friedrich: *Beyond Good and Evil,* Walter Kaufmann, trans., New York: Vintage Books, 1966.

—————: *The Dawn of Day,* J. M. Kennedy, trans., *Works,* Levy, ed., Vol. 9, Edinburgh: T. N. Foulis, 1911.

—————: *The Joyful Wisdom,* Thomas Common, trans., *Works,* Levy, ed., Vol. 10, New York: Russell and Russell, 1964.

—————: *On the Genealogy of Morals,* Walter Kaufmann, trans., New York: Vintage Books, 1967.

—————: *Schopenhauer as Educator,* Hillesheim and Simpson, trans., Chicago: Gateway Editions, 1965.

—————: *Thus Spoke Zarathustra,* Walter Kaufmann, trans., *The Portable Nietzsche,* New York: The Viking Press, 1954.

—————: *The Use and Abuse of History,* Adrian Collins, trans., New York: The Library of Liberal Arts, 1957.

606 : : BIBLIOGRAPHY

——————: *Werke in drei Bänden*, Karl Schlechta, ed., Munich: Carl Hanser Verlag, 1956.

——————: *The Will to Power*, Anthony M. Ludovici, trans., 2 vols., *Works*, Levy, ed., Vols. 14 and 15, Edinburgh: T. N. Foulis, 1909.

——————: *The Will to Power*, Walter Kaufmann and R. J. Hollingsdale, trans., New York: Vintage Books, 1968.

Nisbet, Robert A.: *Social Change and History: Aspects of the Western Theory of Development*, New York: Oxford University Press, 1969.

——————: "The Year 2000 and All That," *Commentary*, June 1968, pp. 60–6.

Nock, Albert J.: *Our Enemy, the State*, Caldwell, Idaho: The Caxton Printers, 1946.

North, Helen: *Sophrosyne: Self-Knowledge and Self-Restraint in Greek Literature*, Ithaca: Cornell University Press, 1966.

Notch, Frank K.: *King Mob: A Study of the Present-Day Mind*, New York: Harcourt, Brace and Co., 1930.

Ogden, C. K. and I. A. Richards: *The Meaning of Meaning*, 8th ed., New York: Harvest Books, n.d.

Oliver, Robert: "Towards the Separation of School and State," *Teachers College Record*, Vol. 70, No. 1, October 1968, pp. 73–6.

Oppenheimer, J. Robert: "On Science and Culture," *Encounter*, October 1962, pp. 3–10.

Ortega y Gasset, Manuel: *"El Imparcial": Biografía de un gran periódico español*, Zaragoza: Librería General, 1956.

——————: *Niñez y mocedad de Ortega y Gasset*, Madrid: C.L.A.V.E., 1964.

Ortega y Gasset, José: See list of his works above.

Pannwitz, Rudolf: *Der Nihilismus und der werdende Welt*, Nürnberg: Verlag Hans Carl, 1951.

Parsons, Talcott, *et al.*, eds.: *Theories of Society: Foundations of Modern Sociological Theory*, 2 vols., Glencoe, Ill.: The Free Press, 1961.

Pascal, Blaise: *Pensées*, W. F. Trotter, trans., New York: E. P. Dutton and Co., 1958.

Pennock, J. Roland: *Liberal Democracy: Its Merits and Prospects*, New York: Holt, Rinehart & Winston, 1950.

Pérez de Ayala, Ramón: *A.M.D.G.: La vida en un colegio de Jesuitas*, *Obras completas*, Vol. IV, Madrid: Editorial Pueyo, 1931.

—————: *Escritos políticos*, Madrid: Editorial Alianza, 1967.

Perkins, James A.: *The University in Transition*, Princeton: Princeton University Press, 1966.

Pieper, Joseph: *Leisure: The Basis of Culture*, Alexander Dru, trans., New York: Mentor-Omega Books, 1963.

Pierce, J. R.: *Symbols, Signals, and Noise*, New York: Harper Torchbooks, 1965.

Plato: *The Collected Dialogues of Plato including the Letters*, Edith Hamilton and Huntington Cairns, eds., Bollingen Series LXXI, New York: Pantheon Books, 1961.

—————: *Euthyphro, Apology, Crito, Phaedo, Phaedrus*, H. N. Fowler, trans., The Loeb Classical Library, Cambridge: Harvard University Press, 1966.

—————: *Laches, Protagoras, Meno, Euthydemus*, W. R. M. Lamb, trans., The Loeb Classical Library, Cambridge: Harvard University Press, 1962.

—————: *Laws*, 2 vols., R. G. Bury, trans., The Loeb Classical Library, Cambridge: Harvard University Press, 1961.

—————: *Lysis, Symposium, Gorgias*, W. R. M. Lamb, trans., The Loeb Classical Library, Cambridge: Harvard University Press, 1961.

—————: *The Republic of Plato*, Allan Bloom, trans., New York: Basic Books, 1968.

—————: *The Republic*, F. M. Cornford, trans., New York: Oxford University Press, 1945.

—————: *The Republic*, 2 vols., Paul Shorey, trans., The Loeb Classical Library, Cambridge: Harvard University Press, 1930.

—————: *Statesman, Philebus, Ion*, H. N. Fowler and W. R. M. Lamb, trans., The Loeb Classical Library, Cambridge: Harvard University Press, 1962.

—————: *Theaetetus, Sophist*, H. N. Fowler, trans., the Loeb Classical Library, Cambridge: Harvard University Press, 1961.

Polanyi, Michael: *Personal Knowledge: Towards a Post-Critical Philosophy*, New York: Harper Torchbooks, 1964.

Popper, Karl R.: *The Logic of Scientific Discovery*, New York: Harper Torchbooks, 1963.

—————: *The Open Society and Its Enemies*, Princeton: Princeton University Press, 1950.

—————: *The Poverty of Historicism*, New York: Harper Torchbooks, 1964.

608 : : BIBLIOGRAPHY

Price, Derek J. de Solla: *Science Since Babylon*, New Haven: Yale University Press, 1961.

Rabil, Albert: *Merleau-Ponty: Existentialist of the Social World*, New York: Columbia University Press, 1967.

Read, Herbert: "Mediodía y noche oscura," *Revista de Occidente*, No. 40, July 1966, pp. 1–18.

Reagan, Michael D.: *Science and the Federal Patron*, New York: Oxford University Press, 1969.

Renan, Joseph Ernest: "Qu'est-ce qu'une nation?," in *Discours et conférences*, Paris: Calmann-Lévy, 1887.

Rickover, H. G.: *Education and Freedom*, New York: E. P. Dutton and Co., 1959.

Riemer, Niel: *The Revival of Democratic Theory*, New York: Appleton-Century-Crofts, 1962.

Ringer, Fritz K.: *The Decline of the German Mandarins: The German Academic Community, 1890–1933*, Cambridge: Harvard University Press, 1969.

Robinson, R. E.: "The Partition of Africa," *The New Cambridge Modern History*, Vol. XI, London: Cambridge University Press, 1962.

Rodríguez Adrados, Francisco: *Ilustración y política en la Grecia clásica*, Madrid: Revista de Occidente, 1966.

Rodríguez Huescar, Antonio: *Con Ortega y otros escritos*, Madrid: Taurus, 1964.

Rosen, Stanley: *Nihilism: A Philosophical Essay*, New Haven: Yale University Press, 1969.

Rosenberg, Bernard and D. M. White, eds.,: *Mass Culture: The Popular Arts in America*, Glencoe, Ill.: The Free Press, 1957.

Rousseau, Jean-Jacques: *Emile*, Barbara Foxley, trans., New York: E. P. Dutton and Co., 1911.

_____: *Oeuvres complètes*, 4 vols., Paris: Bibliothèque de la Pléiade, Editions Gallimard, 1959ff.

Royce, Josiah: *The Spirit of Modern Philosophy*, New York: W. W. Norton and Co., 1967.

Ruggiero, Guido de: *The History of European Liberalism*, R. C. Collingwood, trans., Boston: Beacon Press, 1959.

Rukser, Udo: *Nietzsche in der Hispania*, Bern: Francke Verlag, 1962.

_____: "Ortega y Alemania," *Discursos Academicos*, Santiago: Universidad de Chile, 1967.

Russell, Bertrand: *The Basic Writings of Bertrand Russell*, Robert E.

Egner and Lester E. Dennon, eds., New York: Simon and Schuster, 1961.

——————: *Education and the Good Life,* New York: Boni and Liveright, 1926.

——————: *Power: A New Social Analysis,* Unwin Books Edition, New York: Barnes and Noble, 1962.

——————: *The Problems of Philosophy,* New York: Galaxy Books, 1959.

Russell, Edward S.: *The Directiveness of Organic Activities,* Cambridge: Cambridge University Press, 1945.

Ruyer, Raymond: *Néo-finalisme,* Paris: Presses Universitaires de France, 1952.

Ryle, Gilbert: *The Concept of Mind,* New York: Barnes and Noble, 1949.

S., J. M. M.: "Ortega y Gasset en America," *España,* March 7, 1917, p. 11.

Sánchez Villaseñor, José: *Ortega y Gasset, Existentialist: A Critical Study of His Thought and Its Sources,* Joseph Small, trans., Chicago: Henry Regnery Co., 1949.

Santayana, George: *Egotism in German Philosophy,* New York: Charles Scribner's Sons, 1916.

——————: *The Life of Reason,* 5 vols., New York: Collier Books, 1962.

——————: *Scepticism and Animal Faith,* New York: Dover Publications, 1955.

——————: *The Sense of Beauty,* New York: Dover Publications, 1955.

Sartre, Jean-Paul: *Critique de la raison dialectique,* Paris: Librairie Gallimard, 1960.

——————: *L'être et le néant,* Paris: Librairie Gallimard, 1943.

Scheler, Max: *Man's Place in Nature,* Hans Meyerhoff, trans., New York: Harper and Row, 1962.

——————: *On the Eternal in Man,* Bernard Noble, trans., New York: Harper and Row, 1961.

——————: *Philosophical Perspectives,* Oscar A. Haac, trans., Boston: Beacon Press, 1958.

——————: *Probleme einer Soziologie des Wissens,* in *Gesammelte Werke,* Vol. 8, 2nd ed., Bern: Francke Verlag, 1960.

——————: *Wesen und Formen der Sympathie,* 2nd ed., Bonn: Verlag von Friedrich Cohen, 1923.

Schopenhauer: *On the Basis of Morality,* E. F. J. Payne, trans., New York: The Library of Liberal Arts, 1965.

610 :: BIBLIOGRAPHY

——————: *Über die Universitäts-Philosophie*, in *Sämtliche Werke*, Band V, Wiesbaden: F. A. Brockhaus, 1960.

Schramm, Wilbur: *Responsibility in Mass Communication*, New York: Harper and Brothers, 1957.

Schulte, Henry F.: *The Spanish Press, 1470–1966: Print, Power, and Politics*, Urbana: University of Illinois Press, 1968.

Schumpeter, Joseph A.: *Capitalism, Socialism, and Democracy*, 3rd ed., New York: Harper and Brothers, 1950.

Segura Covarsi, E.: *Indice de la Revista de Occidente*, Madrid: Instituto Miguel de Cervantes, 1952.

Seidenberg, Roderick: *Post-Historic Man: An Inquiry*, Boston: Beacon Press, 1957.

Senabre Sempere, Ricardo: *Lengua y estilo de Ortega y Gasset*, Filosofía y Letras Tomo XVIII, No. 3, Salamanca: Universidad de Salamanca, 1964.

Seneca: *Epistulae Morales*, Richard M. Gummere, trans., 3 vols., The Loeb Classical Library, Cambridge: Harvard University Press, 1962.

Shklar, Judith N.: *After Utopia: The Decline of Political Faith*, Princeton: Princeton University Press, 1957.

Simmel, Georg: *The Conflict in Modern Culture and Other Essays*, K. Peter Etzkorn, trans., New York: Teachers College Press, 1968.

Sinclair, T. A.: *A History of Greek Political Thought*, Cleveland: Meridian Books, 1968.

Sinnott, Edmund W.: *Cell and Psyche: The Biology of Purpose*, New York: Harper Torchbooks, 1961.

Smith, Rhea Marsh: *The Day of the Liberals in Spain*, Philadelphia: University of Pennsylvania Press, 1938.

——————: *Spain: A Modern History*, Ann Arbor: The University of Michigan Press, 1965.

Smith, T. V.: *The Democratic Way of Life*, Chicago: The University of Chicago Press, 1939.

Snell, Bruno: *The Discovery of the Mind: The Greek Origins of European Thought*, New York: Harper Torchbooks, 1960.

Snow, C. P.: *The Two Cultures and a Second Look*, New York: Mentor Books, 1964.

Sorel, Georges: *The Illusions of Progress*, John and Charlotte Stanley, trans., Berkeley: University of California Press, 1969.

——————: *Reflections on Violence*, T. E. Hulme, trans., New York: Collier Books, 1961.

Spengler, Oswald: *The Decline of the West*, abridged edition, C. F. Atkinson, trans., New York: Alfred A. Knopf, 1962.

Spitz, David: *Patterns of Anti-Democratic Thought*, New York: The Macmillan Co., 1949.

Spranger, Eduard: *Cultura y educación*, 2 vols., Buenos Aires: Espasa-Calpe Argentine, 1948.

——————: *Types of Men: The Psychology and Ethics of Personality*, Paul J. W. Pigors, trans., Halle (Saale): Max Niemeyer Verlag, 1928.

Stamps, Norman L.: *Why Democracies Fail; a Critical Evaluation of the Causes for Modern Dictatorship*, Notre Dame, Ind.: University of Notre Dame Press, 1957.

Stankiewicz, W. J.: *Political Thought Since World War II*, Glencoe, Ill.: The Free Press, 1967.

Staude, John Raphael: *Max Scheler, 1874–1928: An Intellectual Portrait*, New York: The Free Press, 1967.

Stenzel, Julius: *Platon der Erzieher*, Leipzig: Felix Meiner Verlag, 1928.

Stern, Fritz: *The Politics of Cultural Despair: A Study in the Rise of the Germanic Ideology*, Garden City, N. Y.: Doubleday Anchor Books, 1965.

Strauss, Leo: *Natural Right and History*, Chicago: The University of Chicago Press, 1953.

——————: *The Political Philosophy of Hobbes*, Elsa M. Sinclair, trans., Chicago: Phoenix Books, 1963.

——————: *What Is Political Philosophy? and Other Studies*, Glencoe, Ill.: The Free Press, 1959.

Tagliacozzo, Giorgio, ed.: *Giambattista Vico: An International Symposium*, Baltimore: The Johns Hopkins Press, 1969.

Taylor, A. J. P.: *The Origins of the Second World War*, New York: Atheneum, 1966.

Teilhard de Chardin, Pierre: *L'Avenir de l'homme*, Paris: Editions du Seuil, 1959.

——————: *The Phenomenon of Man*, Bernard Wall, trans., New York: Harper and Brothers, 1959.

Thomas, Hugh: *The Spanish Civil War*, New York: Harper and Brothers, 1961.

Thucydides: *History of the Peloponnesian War*, 4 vols., Charles Forster Smith, trans., The Loeb Classical Library, Cambridge: Harvard University Press, 1962.

612 : : BIBLIOGRAPHY

Tocqueville, Alexis de: *Democracy in America,* Henry Reeve, *et al.,* trans., 2 vols., New York: Vintage Books, 1954.

————: *The French Revolution and Correspondence with Gobineau,* John Lukas, trans., Garden City, N. Y.: Doubleday Anchor Books, 1959.

————: *The Old Regime and the French Revolution,* Stuart Gilbert, trans., Garden City, N. Y.: Doubleday Anchor Books, 1955.

Toffler, Alvin: *The Culture Consumers: Art and Affluence in America,* Baltimore: Penguin Books, 1965.

Toulmin, Stephen: *Foresight and Understanding: An Enquiry into the Aims of Science,* New York: Harper Torchbooks, 1963.

Trend, J. B.: *The Origins of Modern Spain,* New York: Russell and Russell, 1965.

————: *Picture of Modern Spain,* London: Constable and Co., 1921.

Turin, Yvonne: *L'Education et l'école en Espagne de 1874 à 1902: libéralisme et tradition,* Paris: Presses Universitaires de France, 1959.

————: *Miguel de Unamuno, universitaire,* Paris: S.E.V.P.E.N., 1962.

Uexküll, Jacob von: "La biología de la ostra jacobea," *Revista de Occidente,* March 1924, pp. 297–331.

————: *Die Lebenslehre,* Potsdam: Muller Kiepenheuer Verlag, 1930.

————: *Theoretical Biology,* Mackinnon, trans., London: Kegan Paul, Trench, Tuebner and Co., 1926.

————: *Umwelt und Innewelt des Tiers,* Berlin: Verlag von Julius Springer, 1909.

Unamuno, Miguel de: *Almas de jóvenes,* 3rd ed., Madrid: Espasa-Calpe, 1958.

————: *Obras completas,* 11 vols., Madrid: Afrodisio Aguado, 1958.

————: *Obras completas,* edición definitiva, 8 vols., Madrid: Escelicer, 1966 ff.

————: *Tres novelas ejemplares y un prólogo,* 9th ed., Madrid: Espasa-Calpe, 1958.

Vaihinger, Hans: *Die Philosophie das Als Ob,* 7th and 8th eds., Leipzig: Verlag von Felix Meiner, 1922.

Valéry, Paul: "Letter to Ortega," *Revista de Occidente,* No. 11, 1924, p. 259.

————: *Oeuvres,* Vol. II, Bibliothèque de la Pléiade, Paris: Librairie Gallimard, 1960.

Van Doren, Mark: *Liberal Education*, Boston: Beacon Press, 1959.

Veblen, Thorstein: *The Higher Learning in America*, New York: Saga-more Press, 1957.

————: *The Theory of the Leisure Class: An Economic Study of Institutions*, New York: Mentor Books, 1953.

Vico, Giambattista: *The New Science*, T. G. Bergin, trans., Garden City, N. Y.: Doubleday Anchor Books, 1961.

————: *On the Study Methods of Our Time*, Elio Gianturco, trans., New York: The Library of Liberal Arts, 1965.

Voltaire: *Candide, Or Optimism*, John Butt, trans., Baltimore: Penguin Books, 1956.

Vorländer, Karl: *Kant und Marx*, Tübingen: Verlag von J. C. B. Mohr, 1911.

Vuillemin, Jules: *L'Héritage Kantien et la revolution Copernicienne*, Paris: Presses Universitaires de France, 1954.

Walgrave, J. H.: *La filosofía de Ortega y Gasset*, Luis G. Daal, trans., Madrid: Revista de Occidente, 1965.

Warnock, G. J.: "Reason," *The Encyclopedia of Philosophy*, Vol. 7, pp. 83–5.

Weaver, D. A., ed.: *Builders of American Universities*, Alton, Ill.: Shurt-leff College Press, 1950.

Weber, Alfred: *Farewell to European History, Or the Conquest of Nihil-ism*, R. F. C. Hull, trans., New Haven: Yale University Press, 1948.

Weber, Max: *Basic Concepts in Sociology*, H. P. Secher, trans., New York: Citadel Press, 1962.

————: *The Protestant Ethic and the Spirit of Capitalism*, Talcott Parsons, trans., New York: Charles Scribner's Sons, 1958.

Webster, T. B. L.: *From Mycenae to Homer*, New York: W. W. Norton and Co., 1964.

Wheelwright, Philip: *Heraclitus*, New York: Atheneum, 1959.

Whitaker, Virgil K.: *Shakespeare's Use of Learning: An Inquiry into the Growth of his Mind and Art*, San Marino, Calif.: The Huntington Library, 1964.

Whitman, Cedric H.: *Homer and the Heroic Tradition*, New York: W. W. Norton and Co., 1965.

Whyte, William H., Jr.: *The Organization Man*, Garden City, N. Y.: Doubleday Anchor Books, 1957.

Williams, Raymond: *Culture and Society: 1780–1950*, Garden City, N. Y.: Doubleday Anchor Books, 1960.

614 :: BIBLIOGRAPHY

_____: *The Long Revolution*, New York: Columbia University Press, 1960.

Wilson, Woodrow: *The State: Elements of Historical and Practical Politics*, revised edition, Boston: D. C. Heath and Co., 1899.

Wittgenstein, Ludwig: *Tractatus Logico-Philosophicus*, Pears and McGuinness, trans., London: Routledge and Kegan Paul, 1961.

Wolf, Eric A., *Anthropology*, Englewood Cliffs, N. J.: Prentice Hall, 1964.

Woodward, W. H.: *Vittorino da Feltre and Other Humanist Educators*, New York: Teachers College Press, 1964.

Wordsworth, William: *The Prelude, Selected Poems, and Sonnets*, Carlos Baker, ed., New York: Holt, Rinehart & Winston, 1961.

Wright, Quincy: *A Study of War*, abridged edition, Chicago: The University of Chicago Press, 1964.

Yates, Frances A.: *The Art of Memory*, Chicago: The University of Chicago Press, 1966.

Yeats, W. B.: *The Collected Poems of W. B. Yeats*, New York: The Macmillan Co., 1959.

Zubiri, Xavier: "Ortega, Maestro de filosofía," *El Sol*, March 8, 1936.

_____: *Sobre la esencia*, 3rd ed., Madrid: Sociedad de Estudios y Publicaciones, 1963.

NAME INDEX

talism, 385–87, 563; held that technicians could not avoid the problem of purpose by appealing to necessity, 387–92, 563; necessity of the superfluous, 387–88; spontaneous leadership still possible, 393–94.

A reform of reason could give power to the human sciences, 401–02; a reform of reason was not an irrationalism, 402–05, 564–65; held that reason had a history, 407–08; on the problem created by idealism, 414–15; historic purpose of historic reason, 418–21; influence of Heidegger on, 423–24; his historic reason founded on his ontology of life, 424–39, 574; his elucidation of moral reasoning, 432–36; his elucidation of scientific reasoning, 436–39; his plan for *The Dawn of Historic Reason*, 439–45; his first philosophy, 440–44; his ultimate reliance on man's exuberance, 448–50.

On history as a system, 455–59; on generations and beliefs, 457–59, 466–67; on the social, 459–67; on the effect of historic reason on philosophy, 467–70; his invitation to the men of culture and the intellectual professions, 470–75, 575–77; believed the present order to be illegitimate, 479–82; did not advocate cultural discontinuity, 483–84; his concluding call to the young, 485.

His family, 488; his historicism, 524–25; his views on wealth compared to Weber's, 558–59; the sources for aspects of his thought discussed, 491, 494, 495, 502–09, 513–14, 518, 521, 530–31, 535, 536–37, 551, 552–53, 555, 556–57, 558, 559–60, 563, 564, 574, 575–77.

Ortega y Gasset, Manuel, 488, 489

Ortega Munilla, José, 11, 153, 155, 531

Ozenfant, Amédée, 168

Palmer, John R., 539
Pandora, 348, 556
Pannwitz, Rudolf, 500
Parmenides, 53, 408, 408/*n*13, *409–10*, 410/*n*19, 410/*n*20, 411, 412, 414, 416, *555–56*
Pascal, Blaise, 220
Pavlov, Ivan Petrovich, 394
Pennock, J. Roland, 564
Pérez de Ayala, Ramón, 12, 12/*n*6, 88, 154, 164, 218, 536, 537
Perkins, James A., 575
Pestalozzi, Johann Heinrich, 28, 41, 52, 56–57, 62, 501
Pirandello, Luigi, 167
Plato, x, xii, 5, 21, 22, 26/*n*19, 28, 35/*n*2, 36, 36/*n*4, 37, 38, 40, 45, 51/*n*24, 52, 54, 55, 55/*n*27, 56, 57, 62, 74, 103, 103/*n*15, 107, 108, 126, 133, 134, 136, 162, 169, 180, 180/*n*5, 180/*n*6, 187, 203, 234, 237, 244, 246, 249, 249/*n*17, 250, 266, 267, 267/*n*6, 267/*n*7, 268, 270, 272, 314, 321, 347, 379, 388, 388/*n*20, 389, 390, 401, 404, 411, 412, 443, 449, 472, 490, 492, 501, 510, 526, 527, 534, 545, 557, 566, 567
Polanyi, Michael, 539
Polus, 180/*n*6
Popper, Karl, 254, 499, 510, 524
Posidonius, 111

SUBJECT INDEX

Robert McClintock is Associate Professor of History and Education, and Research Associate of the Institute of Philosophy and Politics of Education, at Teachers College, Columbia University. Teaching in the area of the history of European education, he places a primary emphasis on the history of educational theory and cultural criticism in Western Europe since 1750. Professor McClintock graduated Princeton University *magna cum laude* in 1961, and was awarded the Gale F. Johnson Prize of the Woodrow Wilson School of Public Affairs. An International Fellow at Columbia University, he earned the M.A. degree in 1963, then the Ph.D. at Teachers College in 1968, having taught meanwhile at Newark State College, Finch College, and The Johns Hopkins University. He has published articles in *The American Scholar, Perspectives On Education, Columbia Forum, Revista de Occidente* (Madrid), *The Teachers College Record,* and other magazines; he introduced a new edition of R. L. Nettleship's *The Theory of Education in the Republic of Plato* (1968); and, with his wife, Jean, he edited *Henry Barnard's School Architecture* (1970).